# Luke

## VOLUME 2

# REFORMED EXPOSITORY COMMENTARY

## *A Series*

*Series Editors*

Richard D. Phillips
Philip Graham Ryken

*Testament Editors*

Iain M. Duguid, Old Testament
Daniel M. Doriani, New Testament

# Luke

PHILIP GRAHAM RYKEN

VOLUME 2

LUKE 13-24

P U B L I S H I N G
P.O. BOX 817 • PHILLIPSBURG • NEW JERSEY 08865-0817

*Page design by Lakeside Design Plus*

Printed in the United States of America

**Library of Congress Cataloging-in-Publication Data**

Ryken, Philip Graham, 1966–
Luke / Philip Graham Ryken.
p. cm.
Includes bibliographical references and index.
ISBN 978-1-59638-070-7 (cloth vol. 1) — ISBN 978-1-59638-133-9 (cloth vol. 2)
1. Bible. N.T. Luke—Commentaries. I. Title.
BS2595.53.R95 2009
226.4'077—dc22

2008051651

# CONTENTS

# Contents

# 56

# REPENT OR PERISH

## *Luke 13:1–9*

*And he answered them, "Do you think that these Galileans were worse sinners than all the other Galileans, because they suffered in this way? No, I tell you; but unless you repent, you will all likewise perish." (Luke 13:2–3)*

On the day after a disaster, people always ask the same unanswerable questions. Who is to blame for what happened? Why did God allow it? What did the victims do to deserve such terrible suffering?

People ask these questions in the aftermath of any atrocity. They were asking them after September 11, 2001, when two airplanes slammed into the twin towers of New York's World Trade Center. Thousands of workers were trapped in the fireball and crushed in the collapse. Afterwards, people wanted to know who was to blame for making the attack, or for not preventing it. They wanted to know why God allowed such terrible suffering, and what the victims did to deserve it.

People were asking the same questions after December 26, 2004, when a powerful tsunami slammed into the coast of Indonesia, Sri Lanka, and India. More than a hundred thousand people perished; millions lost their

1

homes. Then people started to ask the questions: Why did God allow this to happen? Why wasn't there any warning? What did the victims do to deserve such a deadly deluge?

The disasters change, but the questions remain the same. Sometimes death and destruction are caused by human beings: military aggression, religious persecution, violence in the city streets. Other times the disaster has a natural cause: tornado, earthquake, tsunami, disease. But whatever the cause, people ask the same questions: Who is to blame, and why didn't God do something to stop it?

## A TERRIBLE ATROCITY

Jesus said there is something else we ought to ask instead—a question we may find surprising. He said that when disaster strikes, we should consider our own inevitable demise and our eternal destiny. We too will die someday, so we need to be ready. Unless we repent, we will perish. So we need to ask this question: Do I have a right relationship with God?

Jesus made this evangelistic appeal in response to two disasters from his own day—shocking events that people were talking about and trying to understand. The first was a terrible atrocity carried out by Roman soldiers against a group of pious Israelites. While Jesus was teaching, some people reported what had happened: "There were some present at that very time who told him about the Galileans whose blood Pilate had mingled with their sacrifices" (Luke 13:1).

We do not know anything else about this incident because this is the only place it is mentioned in the historical records. Apparently a group of Galileans had been offering animal sacrifices. Presumably they had done this at the temple at Jerusalem, and probably during Passover, which is when pilgrims typically made their sacrifices. While they were engaged in this religious act of worship to the one true God, the Galileans were viciously murdered by soldiers under the governance of Pontius Pilate, the Roman ruler of Judea.

The Galileans were fiercely independent in those days, so perhaps Pilate saw these men as a political threat. Certainly such senseless slaughter was in keeping with the governor's bloodthirsty reputation, for "many massacres marked his administration."[1] In this particular massacre, the blood of the victims mingled with the blood of their sacrifices, turning their sacred ritual into a sacrilege. To help explain how enraged people were when they heard about this, Art Lindsley makes the following comparison: "It would be as if terrorists came into a church and shot worshipers as they were partaking of Communion, then mingled their blood with the Communion wine."[2]

It is not clear why people brought this report to Jesus. Maybe they thought he would be interested because Jesus himself was a Galilean. Maybe they were responding to what he had been saying about the coming judgment and interpreting the signs of the times. But whatever their reasons for mentioning this terrible atrocity, they assumed that the victims themselves were to blame. We know this from the way that Jesus answered: "Do you think that these Galileans were worse sinners than all the other Galileans, because they suffered in this way? No, I tell you" (Luke 13:2–3).

Whenever something terrible happens to someone, there are always some people who say that it must be the person's own fault. Bad things only happen to bad people. This theology of sin and suffering was especially common in ancient Israel: "At that time it was a generally accepted notion that whenever calamities visited people this was a proof that they were exceptionally sinful and that for this reason God allowed them to be overtaken by such disasters."[3]

There are some well-known examples of this kind of blame-making in Scripture. When Job suffered his many calamities, his so-called friends came and chided him by saying, "Remember: who that was innocent ever perished? Or where were the upright cut off?" (Job 4:7). In other words, "Only the guilty get punished, so you must be guilty." The disciples followed the same line of reasoning when they met a man who had been blind from birth. They asked Jesus, "Who sinned, this man or his parents, that he was born blind?" (John 9:2). The disciples assumed that he had to be suffering because of somebody's sin. The only question was who the sinner was.

1. John Richardson Major, quoted in Norval Geldenhuys, *The Gospel of Luke*, New International Commentary on the New Testament (Grand Rapids: Eerdmans, 1951), 371.

2. Art Lindsley, *True Truth: Defending Absolute Truth in a Relativistic World* (Downers Grove, IL: InterVarsity, 2004), 37.

3. Geldenhuys, *Luke*, 370.

Some people still think the same way today. They believe that suffering is always and only caused by the sin of those who suffer. Therefore, they say that you are to blame for whatever goes wrong. If something bad happens—if you lose your job, or come down with a serious illness—then you must have done something bad to deserve it. You have brought your troubles on yourself.

Sometimes people do suffer the consequences for their own actions. However, not all suffering is caused by someone's sin. Even when it is, we do not know all of God's reasons for doing what he is doing in someone's life—including our own lives. Therefore, we simply do not have the right to make moral judgments that are based on someone's suffering. Jesus rejected this whole line of reasoning. He said no one should think that the Galilean martyrs were any worse than anyone else. When their blood was shed, God was not singling them out to punish them for their sins.

When something bad happens, rather than leaping to conclusions about how guilty someone is, we have something far more important to think about: our own sin and the punishment that it deserves. "Unless you repent," Jesus warned, "you will all likewise perish" (Luke 13:3).

This statement assumes that we are guilty sinners, and so we are. Our depravity is so self-evident, so noncontroversial, that Jesus does not even assert it; he just assumes it. Some sins are more obvious than others, and some are easier to hide. Some sins are worse than others in their destructive power. But all sin is sin, and even the smallest sin is a violation against the holiness of an infinitely perfect God. We are no different from anyone else. We all fall short of the glory of God.

Furthermore, we are all going to die. This is something people often seem to forget after a disaster. We are horrified at the way people have died, and rightly so. We are shocked and grieved that people have fallen from the sky, or been swept out to sea, or killed in cold blood. In our distress we sometimes fail to see the real tragedy, which is that we are all going to die. In a disaster, death comes all of a sudden. Yet the overall death rate remains unchanged: it is still 100 percent. Since we belong to a lost and fallen race, we are all destined to die, and after that, we will face the final judgment. John Calvin wisely said, "All the calamities that happen in the world are testimonies of the wrath of God."[4] And according to Jesus, this is what we should think about after a disaster: our own imminent demise and our great need for the forgiveness of our sins. Unless we repent, we too will perish.

## A TRAGIC ACCIDENT

Jesus used a second example to make the same spiritual point. This example involved a tragic accident rather than a terrible atrocity, but Jesus used it to give the same warning: "Or those eighteen on whom the tower in Siloam fell and killed them: do you think that they were worse offenders than all the others who lived in Jerusalem? No, I tell you; but unless you repent, you will all likewise perish" (Luke 13:4–5).

Once again, the Bible is the only place where this incident is mentioned. Some have speculated that it was a construction accident. The tower may have fallen while workers were building an aqueduct at the famous pool of Siloam. But in any case, the way Jesus referred to the accident shows that it was common knowledge. Everyone knew about the fallen tower. They knew where it happened, and how many people were killed. As people talked about this tragedy, asking the usual questions, some of them concluded that the people who died were at fault. For something this terrible to happen to them, they must have done something wrong.

Today people would probably blame God for what happened. Why didn't he do anything to stop it? Nevertheless, most people thought that the victims themselves were to blame. They believed in the sovereignty of God, and they concluded (wrongly, as it turned out) that the people who died were being punished for their sins. There are still some people who think this way today. They assume that some are better and some are worse, and people generally get what they deserve in this life. Our misfortune is the result of our misdeeds.

This way of thinking is wrong for a couple of reasons. To begin with, this life is not the life of ultimate reward. In the course of our earthly existence, God sometimes rewards people for obedience and punishes them for disobedience. But the books of his justice are not yet balanced. Evil often

4. John Calvin, *A Harmony of the Gospels*, 3 vols. (Grand Rapids: Eerdmans, 1972), 2:95.

goes unpunished in this life, while virtue goes unrewarded. We must wait until the day of judgment for total justice to be done. In the meantime, we should be very cautious about making our own judgments about what people deserve, based on how much blessing they seem to be getting.

There is another problem with assuming that God treats us better or worse according to what we do, which is that we are all sinful enough to deserve the wrath of God. Notice the precise place where Jesus disagreed with his listeners. He did not say they were wrong to hold God responsible for the fall of the tower. Jesus knew that this too was under God's sovereign control. No, the place he disagreed with them was in their assumption that they were morally superior to the people who died at Siloam. On the contrary, the people who died in that tragic accident were no better and no worse than anyone else.

The word Jesus used to describe the victims is spiritually significant. The word translated "offenders" is the Greek word for debtors *(opheiletai)*, which is the best word to describe people who owe something to God for their sin. "The fact is," writes Michael Wilcock, "that we are all sinners, all in need of repentance, all deserving of punishment, and all preserved from the wrath of God—at least until judgment day—purely by his mercy."[5]

If this is our true spiritual condition—that due to our sin we are debtors to God—then we need to obey the command of Christ and repent! Jesus says it twice in this passage, once after talking about the Galileans, and then again after speaking about Siloam: "Unless you repent, you will all likewise perish" (Luke 13:3, 5).

To repent is to *confess* the sinfulness of our sin against God. It is to make a full and open acknowledgment that we have done what is wrong in God's sight, or that we have failed to do what is right. It is to be honest enough to admit that we are guilty of pride, lust, greed, bitterness, worry, self-pity, self-righteousness, and all the other sins that we have committed.

To repent is also to be *contrite*. It is to be sorry for what we have done. It is to feel sadness and remorse—not just because we got caught, or have to face the consequences, but because we are grieved by our sin itself as an offense against God.

---

5. Michael Wilcock, *The Message of Luke*, The Bible Speaks Today (Downers Grove, IL: InterVarsity, 1979), 138.

Then to repent is to *change* our ways, turning away from our sin. It is not enough to know that sin is sin, or even to shed tears of sorrow. If we are truly penitent, then we will leave our sin behind and follow after God. Kent Hughes thus calls repentance "a change of mind that brings a change of actions."[6]

These are the three elements of true repentance: *confession, contrition,* and *change.* The Westminster Confession of Faith summarizes by saying that in repentance "a sinner, out of the sight and sense not only of the danger, but also of the filthiness and odiousness of his sins, as contrary to the holy nature, and righteous law of God . . . so grieves for, and hates his sins, as to turn from them all unto God, purposing and endeavoring to walk with Him in all the ways of His commandments" (15.2).

Have you repented in the biblical way? Confession is the intellectual aspect of repentance: we know in our minds that we have sinned. Contrition is the emotional aspect of repentance: we feel in our hearts that we have sinned. Change is the volitional aspect of repentance: we resolve in our wills that we will go and sin no more. All three aspects are essential for our repentance to be genuine. It is one thing to know that we have sinned, and another thing to grieve for what we have done. But even that is not enough. We have not truly repented until we have started turning away from sin and towards the righteousness of God.

Unless we so repent, we will perish. Here Jesus is speaking about the final judgment. By "perish" he does not mean that we will lose our lives in some terrible accident, but that we will suffer the eternal wrath of God. Jesus has already said that the Son of Man will come again when he is least expected (Luke 12:40). He has said that when he returns, he will reward his faithful servants and punish his unfaithful servants (Luke 12:37–38, 46–48). He has said that we need to settle our case with God before it is too late; otherwise, we will never get out of prison (Luke 12:57–59). Now he says that we must either repent or perish (Luke 13:3), and then he says it again (Luke 13:5).

No one can make the choice any clearer than Jesus made it. If we truly repent—making a full confession of our sin, with genuine sorrow and a sincere determination to follow Jesus—God will forgive all our sins. On the basis of the death that Jesus died on the cross, he will grant us a full pardon.

6. R. Kent Hughes, *Luke: That You May Know the Truth,* 2 vols., Preaching the Word (Wheaton, IL: Crossway, 1998), 2:82.

But if we do not repent—if we hold on to our sins, not confessing what we have done, not being sorry for it, and not changing our ways—we will never be forgiven.

Be sure to repent of all your sin and trust in Jesus Christ for your salvation. Philip Henry wisely said, "Some people do not like to hear much of repentance. But I think it so necessary, that if I should die in the pulpit, I should desire to die preaching repentance, and if I should die out of the pulpit, I should desire to die practicing it."[7]

## A BARREN TREE

To reinforce what he was saying about the need for repentance and the fruit that repentance brings, Jesus told another famous parable: "A man had a fig tree planted in his vineyard, and he came seeking fruit on it and found none. And he said to the vinedresser, 'Look, for three years now I have come seeking fruit on this fig tree, and I find none. Cut it down. Why should it use up the ground?'" (Luke 13:6–7).

Some trees are more fruitful than others. By virtue of their cultivation, their choice location, or their native strength, they bear a rich harvest of juicy fruit. When a farmer plants a vineyard, he will settle for nothing less. But of course he will give any new tree enough time to get established before expecting it to bear fruit—years in some cases, depending on the type of tree.

The landowner in this parable felt that he had waited long enough. Year after year he had come hoping to find figs on his fruit tree, but it was an annual disappointment. Although it was planted in fertile soil, it was not producing the expected fruit. It was still barren, and by now the owner had seen enough. "Cut it down!" he said to his gardener.

I have had the same frustration in Center City Philadelphia. New trees were planted outside the windows of my second-floor study at the church. I waited impatiently for them to grow tall enough so that birds could nest in their branches and I could watch the leaves change with the seasons. But the trees were stunted by salt in the wintertime, making them the last to bloom and the first to fade. The leaves did not even cover the branches. I

7. Philip Henry, quoted in J. C. Ryle, *Expository Thoughts on the Gospels, Luke* (1858; reprint Cambridge: James Clarke, 1976), 2:112.

waited a couple of years to see if they might recover, but when they failed again the following spring, I said, "It's time to take down those trees and start again."

God was starting to feel the same way about his people Israel. To see this, we need to know the vital background to this parable in the Old Testament, where God often used the image of the vine or the fig tree to refer to his people. "Like grapes in the wilderness, I found Israel," God said. "Like the first fruit on the fig tree in its first season, I saw your fathers" (Hos. 9:10). You are "my vine," he said to his people (Joel 1:7). "The vineyard of the LORD of hosts is the house of Israel" (Isa. 5:7).

God cultivated Israel to be a fruitful tree in his vineyard. Thus he had every right to expect them to bear good fruit. They had every spiritual advantage: the Word of God in Scripture, the promises of the covenant, and the sacrifices of atonement. Now they were in the presence of the Messiah. Therefore, they should bear the abundant fruit of obedience to God.

Surely God expects the same thing from us. We have heard the good news of the gospel—that Jesus died for our sins and rose again. We can read the entire Bible in both of its testaments. We have received the Holy Spirit, who is working in us to produce love, joy, peace, and all the other virtues of his grace (Gal. 5:22–23; cf. Eph. 5:9). We are connected to Jesus Christ, the true and living vine (John 15:5). Therefore, we ought to bear good fruit for God. We should be growing in godliness, gaining spiritual ground in our struggle against sin. We should be active in ministry, doing something for the service of God. We should be effective in evangelism, giving a good testimony of what it means to have a saving relationship with Jesus Christ. We should have a life-giving spiritual influence on other people. We are called "to walk in a manner worthy of the Lord, fully pleasing to him, bearing fruit in every good work and increasing in the knowledge of God" (Col. 1:10; cf. John 15:8).

Otherwise, we are just taking up space, which was the problem with the fig tree in the parable. Because it failed to bear good fruit, it was wasting valuable soil. By using this analogy, Jesus was saying that the Israelites were just as barren. They had no spiritual vitality. God was looking for good fruit in their lives, but he was not finding any, so he was getting ready to cut them down (cf. Matt. 21:43).

9

How fruitful are you? Are you bearing the good fruit of spiritual growth, faithful service, and influential discipleship? Are you as fruitful as you ought to be, or are you spiritually scrawny? Are you producing Golden Delicious, or is it only crabapple?

God is looking for good fruit, and if he cannot find any, we need to repent before we perish. In a poem called "Contrition," Ralph Knevet wrote, "The fig tree yields a fruit that's sweet." Yet deep down the poet knew that he was more barren than fruitful, so he made the following confession:

> But I that wretched tree am, which
> The hunger of my Christ deceives,
> He fruit expects, but I am rich
> In nothing but vain spreading leaves. . . .
>
> Yea, I am that same fig tree vain,
> Which in Christ's vineyard planted was,
> Dressed many years with care, and pain,
> Yet only serve to fill a place:
> I therefore fear the axes wound,
> Because I cumber but the ground.[8]

## STAY OF EXECUTION

The parable of the fig tree is a sober warning for fruitless souls. "I find no fruit," the owner says, rendering his verdict on the barren tree. Then he passes his sentence on people who stand in God's vineyard, but have no spiritual life in them: "Cut it down," he commands. The axe is laid to the root of the tree; the tree is ready to fall.

At this point someone suddenly intercedes on behalf of the tree and wins a stay of execution. The servant who cared for the vineyard says to the owner: "Sir, let it alone this year also, until I dig around it and put on manure. Then if it should bear fruit next year, well and good; but if not, you can cut it down" (Luke 13:8–9).

8. Ralph Knevet, "Contrition," in *Chapters into Verse: Poetry in English Inspired by the Bible, vol. 2: Gospels to Revelation*, ed. Robert Atwan and Laurance Wieder (Oxford: Oxford University Press, 1993), 129.

The servant did not deny that the fig tree had failed to bear good fruit, or that it deserved to be chopped down. Nevertheless, he believed that the tree deserved one last chance. He would give it every opportunity to bear good fruit. He would loosen the soil around its roots; he would be liberal in his application of fertilizer; then he would wait to see what happened the following year. If the tree began to bear good fruit, it would be allowed to stand; if not, it would perish. We decided to follow a similar course of action to save the trees on our street in Philadelphia: we asked an arborist to tell us how to rescue them before it was too late.

This parable is about God's patience with his people Israel. They had every opportunity to come to Christ and bear good fruit. For nearly three years, Jesus had been healing them and teaching them to follow God. Alas, they were bearing so little fruit! Most of the Jews rejected Jesus. Yet in his mercy, God would give them one final opportunity. Jesus would die on the cross; he would be raised from the grave; his gospel would be preached in Israel. Thus there was still time for people to repent and bear good spiritual fruit through faith in Jesus Christ.

Nevertheless, the window of opportunity would not stay open forever. This was the last chance for the people of that generation. If they did not repent, they would perish, as many of them did. Not many years later Jerusalem was besieged, the temple was destroyed, and Israel was scattered. Like the owner in the parable, God would not wait forever: "Although God through His grace postpones for such a long time the punishment of the impenitent, in order to give them the opportunity of repentance, the day will nevertheless finally dawn when the time of grace expires."[9] Eventually the time will come for every fruitless tree to be cut down. As Jesus said on another occasion, "If anyone does not abide in me he is thrown away like a branch and withers; and the branches are gathered, thrown into the fire, and burned" (John 15:6).

Today many people are in a similar situation, including many people in the church. They are not bearing good spiritual fruit. If they remain barren, then eventually they will be chopped down. God will not spare us forever. The day of disaster will not be delayed indefinitely. Judgment will come. But it has not happened yet, and therefore there is still time to repent. There

9. Geldenhuys, *Luke*, 373.

is still time to believe in Jesus Christ and bear good spiritual fruit. The Bible says that the Lord "is patient toward you, not wishing that any should perish, but that all should reach repentance" (2 Peter 3:9).

The reason we still have time to repent is that God is so patient with us. We have not yet perished, not because we are any better than anyone else, but because God is long in showing us mercy. Even now, like the vinedresser in the parable, Jesus is interceding for our salvation. Matthew Henry said, "had it not been for Christ's intercession, the whole world had been cut down."[10] But by the mercy of Christ, we are still standing, and we still have time to believe the gospel and repent of our sin.

In his preaching on this passage, John Bunyan identified Jesus as the vinedresser in the parable, who is cultivating us for repentance, preparing us for salvation. Treating the passage somewhat allegorically, Bunyan imagined him saying to the owner: "I will loosen his roots; I will dig up this earth, I will lay his roots bare. My hand shall be upon him by sickness, by disappointments, by cross providences." These are some of the life experiences that God uses to bring us to repentance: sickness, sadness, and trouble. Jesus does this so that we will bear more spiritual fruit, in keeping with our repentance (see Luke 3:8). Here is how Bunyan explained it:

> Thus, I say, deals the Lord Jesus ofttimes with the barren professor; He diggeth about him, He smiteth one blow at his heart, another blow at his lusts, a third at his pleasures, a fourth at his comforts, another at his self-conceitedness: thus He diggeth about him. This is the way to take bad earth from the roots, and to loosen his roots from the earth. Barren fig-tree! See here the care, the love, the labor, and way, which the Lord Jesus, the Dresser of the vineyard, is fair to take with thee, if haply thou mayest be made fruitful.[11]

What is Jesus doing to cultivate spiritual fruit in your life? Perhaps he is using difficult experiences to bring you to repentance. Certainly he is using his Word to fertilize your soul. How then are you responding to his gracious work for your salvation? The best way to respond is to repent, believe, and bear good fruit.

10. Matthew Henry, quoted in Ryle, *Luke*, 2:118.
11. John Bunyan, "The Barren Fig-Tree," quoted in Hughes, *Luke*, 2:83–84.

But whatever you do, do not presume upon the patience of God. While others have perished in the day of disaster, your life has been spared. Do not let the delay of death mislead you into thinking that you will escape disaster forever. Eventually you too will die. After that, you will face the judgment. Jesus says, "Unless you repent, you too will perish." It is hard to see how he could make it any clearer than that.

Jesus has made the way of escape just as clear. Do you think the Galileans would have gone to the temple if they had known that soldiers were coming to kill them? Or that people would have gone up the tower of Siloam that day if they had known that it was going to fall? Unlike them, we know that a day of disaster is coming. How merciful Jesus is to tell us this! How gracious God is to provide a way of escape! "For God so loved the world, that he gave his only Son, that whoever believes in him should not perish, but have eternal life" (John 3:16).

# 57

# A DAY FOR MERCY

## *Luke 13:10–17*

*Then the Lord answered him, "You hypocrites! Does not each*
*of you on the Sabbath untie his ox or his donkey from the man-*
*ger and lead it away to water it? And ought not this woman, a*
*daughter of Abraham whom Satan bound for eighteen years, be*
*loosed from this bond on the Sabbath day?"* (Luke 13:15–16)

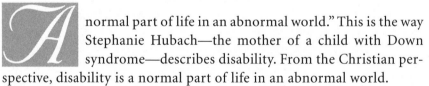 normal part of life in an abnormal world." This is the way
Stephanie Hubach—the mother of a child with Down
syndrome—describes disability. From the Christian perspective, disability is a normal part of life in an abnormal world.

Disabilities are often considered *ab*normal. But if "normal" means
something that many people experience, and that nearly everyone is
familiar with, disability is certainly normal. Tenth Presbyterian Church in
Philadelphia has dozens of people with disabilities. Various church members are blind, deaf, or lame. Some are physically deformed; others are
completely crippled. Some are confined to wheelchairs; others are unable
to leave their homes. Whether these disabilities were there from birth or
came later on in life, it is normal to have them, and normal to have friends
who have them. Disability is a regular part of life.

Nevertheless, a disability is still a *dis*ability, and this is where the abnormality comes in. Disability is normal only in an abnormal world. It was not this way from the beginning, when God created a perfect world for perfect people with perfect bodies. Adam and Eve were not created disabled, and their children never would have been disabled unless sin had entered the world. Hubach explains it like this:

> According to the biblical account in Genesis, tragedy struck with the Fall of mankind—with a devastating impact on every aspect of creation. As Paul states in Romans 8:20, "the creation was subjected to frustration, not by its own choice." Our world became an abnormal world. . . . Disability is simply a more noticeable form of the brokenness that is common to human experience—a *normal* part of life in an *abnormal* world.[1]

## CRIPPLED BY SATAN'S CRUELTY

It was normal for Jesus to meet people with disabilities too, except that he had the power to do something about them. We see his power in the true story that Luke told about Jesus and a woman with a disabling spirit. She was crippled by Satan's cruelty, but cured by Christ's compassion. From what happened afterwards, we see the callous indifference of religious people who oppose the grace of God, and also the wonderful opportunity we have to glorify God by showing mercy on his holy day.

The story begins with someone in desperate need: "Now he was teaching in one of the synagogues on the Sabbath. And there was a woman who had had a disabling spirit for eighteen years. She was bent over and could not fully straighten herself" (Luke 13:10–11).

It was obvious to all who saw her that the woman was suffering from a crippling disability. Some medical experts theorize that she may have suffered from "*spondylitis deformans;* the bones of her spine were fused into a rigid mass."[2] But whatever the proper diagnosis, the woman's suffering was acute. She was stooped over with pain, and her disability affected everything in life. It limited her capacity for work, it disturbed her nighttime

---

1. Stephanie Hubach, "Those with Help to Make Us," *byFaith,* March/April 2005, 33.
2. A. Rendle Short, *Modern Discovery and the Bible* (London: Inter-Varsity, 1947), 91.

rest, hindered her relationships, and prevented her from holding her head up high. The woman's dignity seemed to be diminished.

There must have been times when the woman struggled with deep discouragement and maybe even despondent despair, for she had suffered all this for nearly twenty years. As anyone with a disability can testify, it is hard to be content with chronic pain and permanent physical limitations. In such circumstances, even someone who knows the joy of the Lord may be tempted to self-pity, at least sometimes.

Some people probably wondered what the woman had done to deserve all this. In those days it was common to think that people always suffered because of their own sins. But from everything we know, this woman had done nothing wrong. She was "a daughter of Abraham" (Luke 13:16). Since Abraham is the man of faith (Rom. 4:3), she therefore belonged to the community of faith, which is why she was worshiping at the synagogue. This woman was not to blame for her suffering. On the contrary, her case had a different cause: she was crippled by Satan's cruelty.

Luke hints at the devil's involvement when he says that she had "a disabling spirit" (Luke 13:11). This expression is not simply a figure of speech. Nor does it reflect a primitive, premodern understanding of the human body, in which every disability is attributed to some evil spirit. As a doctor, Luke knew that this woman's disability (or "weakness," to translate the term more literally) had a supernatural cause. This is the only place where he describes someone as having a disabling spirit. He knew that in this unusual case, the victim was under spiritual attack. This diagnosis is confirmed in verse 16, where Jesus says that she was bound by Satan.

We should be careful not to attribute every medical difficulty we have to a direct attack from Satan. Some Christians misinterpret Luke 13:11 to mean that all of our physical (or spiritual) troubles are caused by some demonic "spirit." Yet as mysterious as it may seem, God sometimes allows his people to suffer a spiritual attack that causes a physical disability, and this was a clear example. The woman was bowed low by demonic oppression. Her physical trouble was caused by spiritual torment.

Satan's cruelty in crippling this woman is only one example of the hatred he has for all of us. Her physical disability is a picture of our own spiritual oppression:

The woman's physical condition was not due simply to physical causes. Christ declared it to be a bondage induced by Satan, whose malevolence has always sought from the very beginning to rob man of his dominion and dignity and degrade him into a slave. Few men and women have bent backs physically: but morally and spiritually all men and women find themselves sooner or later bent and bowed by weaknesses of one kind or another from which they have not the strength to free themselves.[3]

Even if God has not allowed him to afflict our bodies, as he does on some occasions, Satan is always trying to break our spiritual backs with the burden of our guilty sin.

## CURED BY CHRIST'S COMPASSION

There is no way for us to free ourselves from this debilitating spiritual bondage, any more than the woman in the Gospel could ever save herself from this disabling spirit. As it says in the Westminster Larger Catechism, without the saving work of God we are "utterly indisposed, disabled, and made opposite to all that is spiritually good" (A. 25). We cannot get rid of our back-bending burden of sin. But Jesus can save us, just as he saved this woman: "When Jesus saw her, he called her over and said to her, 'Woman, you are freed from your disability.' And he laid his hands on her, and immediately she was made straight, and she glorified God" (Luke 13:12–13).

The woman crippled by Satan's cruelty was cured by Christ's compassion. First, Jesus saw her. He noticed her and paid attention to her. When she shuffled into that synagogue, doubled over by her disability, immediately he perceived her need. Everyone else ignored her, but Jesus noticed her right away and understood her case. Jesus Christ is the God who sees, and when he saw this woman, he had compassion on her suffering. So he called her over, not leaving her where she was, struggling under the weight of demonic oppression, but inviting her to come where he was. Jesus summoned her to himself.

Then Jesus saved her. He spoke the words of her deliverance: "Woman, thou art loosed" (Luke 13:12 KJV). At the same time, Jesus gave her his

3. David Gooding, *According to Luke: A New Exposition of the Third Gospel* (Grand Rapids, Eerdmans: 1987), 253.

healing touch. This was an uncommon gesture. In those days some people would not touch the disabled, and religious leaders usually refused to have any direct contact with women. But Jesus reached out and touched this crippled woman, and the moment he touched her, she stood straight up. For eighteen long years she had been disabled, but one touch from Jesus, and the devil's work was undone. The woman was fully cured.

Immediately, she responded by giving praise to God. With a heart full of grateful thanksgiving, she stood up straight and tall and started to worship. Once she had experienced the saving work of Jesus Christ, she wanted to give all the glory to God.

This true account of deliverance shows how Jesus saves us from all our disabilities, including the brokenness of our sin. It is a picture of salvation. First Jesus noticed us in all our need. Looking down from heaven, he saw our lost and fallen race, bowed low by the bondage of Satan. When he saw this, he had mercy on our souls. Gregory of Nyssa defined mercy as "a voluntary sorrow which enjoins itself to the suffering of another,"[4] and this is exactly the kind of mercy that Jesus showed to us. By becoming a man and going to the cross, he joined himself to our suffering, and in dying for our sins, he voluntarily undertook the greatest of all sorrows.

Then, by the power of the Holy Spirit, Jesus called us to himself. He spoke the gospel words of our deliverance. He said, "Man, you are free from the guilt of your sin; woman, you are free from all the disabling cruelty of Satan." He touched us with his grace, healing our souls. In response, we begin to sing his praises, glorifying God for the cure that is ours through the compassion of Christ.

Jesus has the same compassion for us right now. Even if it seems as if no one else cares, he sees our need. Even if we think that no one else knows about our situation, he knows all our troubles: the burden of our guilt, the torment of Satan, the struggle in our soul, the distress of our grief, the breakdown of our close relationships, and whatever physical limitations we have. He sees all this with the mercy and pity of his loving heart, and in his compassion he calls us to himself. He says, "Come and be healed." He touches us with his nail-scarred hands, and heals us to glorify God.

4. Gregory of Nyssa, quoted in Hubach, "Those with Help," 34.

We should never think that our situation is beyond help. Know for sure that with Jesus, no case is incurable. No matter how long we have suffered, Jesus can heal us. No matter how long we have been in bondage, Jesus can save us. We do not need to wait even one day longer. He can deliver us from guilt by forgiving our sins. He can loose us from sin and from Satan by sending the Holy Spirit to take control of our lives. He can heal all the deformities our souls have suffered in this fallen world. One day, by the power of his resurrection life, he will deliver us from all our physical disabilities as well.

Jesus has not promised full deliverance in this life, but in the life to come. Remember that we are living in an abnormal world, in which disability is normal. Sooner or later almost everyone who lives long enough becomes disabled. Even if we are not disabled from birth or by an injury, most of us will be disabled by the breakdown of our bodies as we grow old. We rebel against this, because it is not the way we were created to be. We are dismayed by all the debilitating effects of the fall on our physical bodies. Yet we live in the hope of our perfection at the resurrection.

The miracle Jesus performed for this crippled woman shows what cure he will bring when he comes again. The day is coming when the blind will see, the deaf will hear, and the lame will walk again. Whatever physical weakness we may suffer in this life, whatever diseases and disabilities we endure, some day Jesus will say to us what he said to this woman: "You are freed from your disability." He will give us perfect new bodies that will be young and strong forever.

## A CALLOUS CRITICISM

As strange as it may seem, there was a man at the synagogue who was not altogether happy with the miracle that Jesus performed. In fact, he was rather annoyed. Luke tells us that "the ruler of the synagogue" was "indignant because Jesus had healed on the Sabbath" (Luke 13:14). As the head of his religious community, this man ought to have been nearly the holiest person around. But rather than sharing the compassion of Christ, he had callous indifference for people in need. Rather than glorifying God for what he had done, he could only find fault.

Part of the man's problem was that he had his own set of rules that people had to follow if they wanted God's blessing, and one of those rules was that you could scarcely lift a finger to help anybody on the Sabbath. Thus the man was highly offended when Jesus performed this healing miracle. Like many of the Pharisees, nothing upset him more than seeing Jesus do his saving work on the Sabbath.

The man did not even have the courage to confront Jesus about this directly. Instead, he cowardly leveled his criticism at the congregation and said, "There are six days in which work ought to be done. Come on those days and be healed, and not on the Sabbath day" (Luke 13:14). "You will have to wait," the man said. "You can be healed only on a weekday."

This was ironic, because it presumed that the woman could have been healed if she had come back on Sunday. But what would the man have done to heal her when she returned the following day? Absolutely nothing, because only Jesus had the power to heal, and unlike the ruler of the synagogue, he was ready to do it right away. This poor woman had been suffering for eighteen agonizing years, and he would not let her suffer even one day longer. It was time for her to be healed.

Do you see how hard-hearted the man was? With cold indifference, he ignored the woman's need. As ruler of the synagogue, it was his responsibility to provide spiritual and practical care for the people in his spiritual community—especially the disabled. But he had no compassion on this woman's suffering and no joy in her salvation. Not loving his neighbor, he opposed the mercy of God.

To be fair, the man thought he had a good biblical, theological reason for telling people to come back tomorrow. He thought that healing people on the Sabbath was against the law of God. As far as the ruler was concerned, the Sabbath was a day for worship and a day for rest, but not a day for mercy.

Jesus rebuked the man sharply for this—and not just the man, but everyone who agreed with him. "You hypocrites!" he said. "Does not each of you on the Sabbath untie his ox or his donkey from the manger and lead it away to water it? And ought not this woman, a daughter of Abraham whom Satan bound for eighteen years, be loosed from this bond on the Sabbath day?" (Luke 13:15–16).

Notice what Jesus did not do. He did not deny the significance of the Sabbath. He did not say that the Sabbath was no longer binding, so that he could do whatever he wanted on Saturdays. Instead, he restored the Sabbath to God's intention by saying it was a day for doing mercy. In doing this, Jesus was claiming lordship over his holy day. The title that Luke uses here is significant. When Jesus answered the ruler of the synagogue, he was speaking as "Lord" (Luke 13:15)—the Lord of the Sabbath.

The Lord of the Sabbath accused this man (and his associates) of hypocrisy. He pointed out that they were perfectly willing to care for their animals on the Sabbath by leading them to water. This was true. The rabbis had precise regulations for watering livestock on the Sabbath. According to later rabbinic writings known as the Mishnah, people could lead their animals to water as long as they didn't carry anything (*Shabbath* 5.1). Although they were not allowed to hold a bucket for an animal to drink, they were allowed to draw water and pour it into a trough (*Erubin* 20b, 21a).

These human traditions were intended to keep people from breaking the Sabbath; there was nothing about them in the Bible, however. When God gave his law to Moses, he said that people should not work on the seventh day. The fourth commandment said, "Remember the Sabbath day, to keep it holy. Six days you shall labor, and do all your work, but the seventh day is a Sabbath to the LORD your God. On it you shall not do any work, you, or your son, or your daughter, your male servant, or your female servant, or your livestock, or the sojourner who is within your gates" (Ex. 20:8–10).

Unlike the Pharisees, God did not minutely regulate the details of what it did and did not mean to work. As far as he was concerned, it was perfectly appropriate for people to meet the daily needs of their animals. The Sabbath was not just for people; it was also for animals. As beasts of burden rested from their work in the fields, they needed something to drink, and people could give it to them without breaking the Sabbath. Even the Pharisees—for all their legalism—found a way to be kind to animals.

If only they had cared as much for people! This was their inconsistency— or as Jesus called it, their hypocrisy. Although the ruler of the synagogue would take care of his animals on the Sabbath, he would not let human beings come and receive a healing touch from their Savior. But if the Sabbath was good for animals, shouldn't it be even better for people made in the image of God? What better day for a woman to be delivered from a debilitating disability than the Sabbath?

The rebuke Jesus gave this man condemns our own callous indifference to people in need. The man's real problem was not primarily theological, but spiritual. Admittedly, he misunderstood the true purpose of the Sabbath. But his deeper problem was his hard-hearted resistance to the saving work of Jesus Christ. He thought his own human traditions were more important than helping someone who was suffering. In defending his law, he was keeping people from grace.

We face the same temptation today. We are tempted to discriminate between the people we think deserve our help, and those who do not. We are tempted to ignore people who seem to be struggling, pretending not to notice their need. Even if we do not use the Sabbath to do it, we often come up with excuses for refusing to help people in serious need, including people with disabilities:

"That's not my gift. I don't have the skills I would need to help."

"It's not good stewardship. People like that just take advantage of what you give them."

"That's not my priority. If I take the time to help, then I won't have time to do the other things God is calling me to do."

"They don't deserve it. They're in that situation because of the choices they've made, and now they have to suffer the consequences."

"We have a ministry for that. It's someone else's responsibility."

We may not always have the gifts or the calling to help a particular person, and there are times when it is unwise and unmerciful to help people the way they want to be helped. But is your heart in the place where Jesus wants it to be? How easy it is to come up with a spiritual-sounding excuse for letting someone continue to suffer. Yet how hard it is to offer the sacrificial grace that God might use to save someone in need. How easy it is to be callous, like the ruler of the synagogue; how hard it is to show compassion, like Christ.

Joni Eareckson Tada, who herself has suffered the disability of quadriplegia for most of her adult life, describes what it is like to share in Christ's compassion for broken people. As she visited a residential facility for disabled young people, Joni was

> trying to listen to this mentally handicapped girl, who had approached me, and wanted to tell me all about her Jesus. Although dishes were clattering, others were calling, and wheelchair motors were grinding, this kid had my heart. It seemed that she was the most important person in the world, saying these profound things. She was talking about the Savior. And over by the wall, where a nurse was calling me to talk with someone else, I pictured Jesus. There he was, ahead of me, delighting in the smiles of each one of those residents in that home. And as sure as I was there, He was there, carrying their cares, touching every need, returning every gesture, ministering to every hurt. Jesus was there serving with all His heart. And that meant that I could do that too.[5]

## The New Normal

Jesus calls us to give other people the same kind of grace that he has given to us through his cross and the empty tomb. This is a grace that notices what people need. It is a grace that is not afraid to touch the broken places in someone's life. It is a grace that brings people to Jesus for healing. One of the best ways for us to show this grace is to follow our Lord's example and use the Sabbath as a day for mercy.

When God created the world, he gave his people the gift of one full day in seven for worship and rest. From the beginning of the world until the coming of Christ, that one special day was the seventh day of the week, which the Israelites called "the Sabbath." But from the resurrection of Jesus until the end of the world, that one special day is the first day of the week, which Christians call "the Lord's day."

The Lord's day is for resting from our regular work. It is also for the worship of God, and the disabled woman at the synagogue is a marvelous example. It was only with the greatest difficulty that she was able to leave her home and go to worship. But she knew how important public worship

5. Joni Eareckson Tada, "Sent to Serve," *Wheaton*, Autumn 2005, 59.

was for the state of her soul, so she was there in the synagogue on the Sabbath. What a blessing she received that day!

What a blessing we ourselves receive when we meet Jesus for worship on his holy day. J. C. Ryle said, "The conduct of this suffering Jewess may well put to shame many a strong and healthy professing Christian. How many in the full enjoyment of bodily vigor, allow the most frivolous excuses to keep them away from the house of God! . . . How many find religious services a weariness while they attend them, and feel relieved when they are over!"[6] And yet, as Ryle went on to say,

> Where there is a will there is always a way. Let us never forget that our feelings about Sundays are sure tests of the state of our souls. The man who can find no pleasure in giving God one day in the week, is manifestly unfit for heaven. Heaven itself is nothing but an eternal Sabbath. If we cannot enjoy a few hours in God's service once a week in this world, it is plain that we could not enjoy an eternity in His service in the world to come.[7]

Nevertheless, worship and rest are not the only purposes of this day. Jesus taught that it is also a day for showing compassion to people in need. The commandment against working on the Sabbath was never intended to prohibit works of mercy or necessity, which explains why Jesus said that this woman *ought* to be healed on the Sabbath (see Luke 13:16). What better day for Satan to be defeated, for a soul in bondage to be released, and for her body to be restored to what it was created to be?

There is no better day for us to show the compassion of Christ to people in need than the day God has given us for holy rest. The Lord's day is for releasing people from their bondage to sin by preaching forgiveness through the cross. It is also a day for ministering to people's physical and spiritual needs. The Lord's day is for giving comfort to those who are grieving, showing kindness to children and the elderly, visiting the sick and the infirm, befriending the friendless, and feeding the homeless. It is a day for bringing the disabled to church, or for bringing church to the disabled, as we take the gospel to shut-ins in their homes and nursing homes.

6. J. C. Ryle, *Expository Thoughts on the Gospels, Luke* (1858; reprint Cambridge: James Clarke, 1976), 2:119.
7. Ibid., 2:120.

We do not have the power to cure people the way that Jesus did. But by our love and compassion we can be agents of his saving work. We can give people a healing encounter with his grace. We can also prepare them for his everlasting kingdom, where death is destroyed, the devil is defeated, and every disability of the body and deformity of the soul is cured by Christ.

What marvelous praise is given to God whenever Jesus works his saving cure! Luke reports, "As he said these things, all his adversaries were put to shame, and all the people rejoiced at all the glorious things that were done by him" (Luke 13:17). Earlier the disabled woman glorified God for her deliverance. Now all the people praised him. They reveled in his triumph over his enemies and rejoiced in his power to take the abnormalities of fallen humanity and transform them by his mercy.

When Jesus did this on the Sabbath for the woman with a disabling spirit, it was a sign of things to come. Again and again, Jesus glorified God by putting his adversaries to shame for the glory of God. He did this on the cross when he defeated Satan by the open triumph of his atonement. He did it again on Easter Sunday when he defied the powers of hell and came back from the dead. He is doing it now through the church, as we reach out to broken people with his compassion and the Holy Spirit releases them from bondage.

Jesus will do the same thing for us, if only we will go to him for grace. He will do it again at the end of history, when Satan and all his followers are doomed to destruction, and everyone who has been cured by Christ will rejoice for all the glorious things he has done. We live in the hope of that great day, even when we are bent and bowed by the disabling effects of sin and the spiritual attacks of Satan.

Stephanie Hubach writes about the overwhelming grief she suffered at the death of a friend's severely disabled child. After the funeral she went away to be alone with her tears. When she returned, a man with Down syndrome noticed that she had been crying and confronted her. "Do you love Jesus?" he demanded.

Stephanie was not in the mood for conversation and tried to disengage. But the man was not to be deterred. "Ben loved Jesus," he said, referring to the boy who died. "And Ben is with Jesus! And he grew up!" Stephanie mumbled a polite response, but the man with Down syndrome would not stop until he knew she understood what he was saying. He became very animated. He strutted around the church, gesturing wildly with his arms. "And he can walk!" the man said. Finally he stopped right in front of Stephanie, looked into her face, and said, "And he can *see* Him!"[8]

The man understood that one day there will be a new normal for every broken-down, body-weary, sin-disabled child of God who is tired of suffering in this abnormal world. We will experience that new normal ourselves, if only we will go to Jesus for the healing that only he can give.

8. Hubach, "Those with Help," 35.

# 58

# SEE HOW IT GROWS

## *Luke 13:18–21*

*And again he said, "To what shall I compare the kingdom of God?*
*It is like leaven that a woman took and hid in three measures of*
*flour, until it was all leavened." (Luke 13:20–21)*

*I*n 1945 the eminent German pastor and theologian Helmut Thielicke stood in the ruined choirs of his church in Hamburg to preach on the kingdom of God. Amid the ravages of war, Thielicke criticized the idea—so common in nineteenth-century Christianity—that the world was becoming more and more Christian, until finally the kingdom of God would come on earth. "Such dreams and delusions," he said, "have vanished in the terrors of our man-made misery." Thielicke went on to ask:

> Who can still believe today that we are developing toward a state in which the kingdom of God reigns in the world of nations, in culture, and in the life of the individual? The earth has been plowed too deep by the curse of war, the streams of blood and tears have swollen all too terribly, injustice and bestiality have become all too cruel and obvious for us to consider such dreams to be anything but bubbles and froth.[1]

1. Helmut Thielicke, *Our Heavenly Father* (Grand Rapids: Baker, 1980), 60, 62.

It is easy to understand why Thielicke would say this. The horrors of World War II had destroyed any delusion that humanity was making moral progress, and under such circumstances, it was tempting to wonder whether God's kingdom would ever come.

We face the same temptation. Often we are encouraged by signs of progress in the church, both locally and globally. At times we may see at least some spiritual growth in our own Christian lives. More often, however, things seem to be in spiritual decline. We are troubled by the spread of evil in our society and grieved by the persecution of the church. We are burdened by the problems we are having in ministry. We are brokenhearted by our own struggle with sin and the backsliding we see in other believers. The apparent lack of spiritual progress in those and many other areas of life leads us to wonder sometimes whether the kingdom will ever come.

## TWO PARABLES OF THE KINGDOM

Jesus taught two parables to help us understand the growth of the kingdom of God—the parables of the mustard seed and the leaven. In Luke these two parables are connected to the Sabbath miracle that Jesus performed for the woman with a disabling spirit: "He said therefore, 'What is the kingdom of God like? And to what shall I compare it?'" (Luke 13:18).

The word "therefore" makes a connection. There was something about the miracle Jesus had just performed that prompted him to teach about the kingdom of God. Maybe he was still responding to the ruler of the synagogue, who had criticized him for healing on the Sabbath. In that case, Jesus told his two parables to show that despite all fierce opposition, God's rule would continue to grow.

Or perhaps Jesus wanted to show that this miracle was a sign of things to come. In and of itself, the woman's healing was something small—the personal deliverance of a solitary individual. Yet this was the beginning of something much bigger. The woman's salvation contained the seed of the devil's defeat and the glory of God's kingdom. This one healing miracle "would one day spread to the bounds of the universe, until creation herself would be delivered from the bondage of corruption into the glorious liberty of the sons of God, and all in heaven and earth would find security, satisfaction and delight in the magnificence of his dominion."[2] Therefore, Jesus followed his miracle with two parables about the spread of the kingdom of God.

It is typical for Luke to put things in pairs, and here he records two closely-related parables about the kingdom of God. The kingdom of God is the rule of God, the exercise of his royal authority. One of these two parables shows the *extensive* growth of this kingdom, while the other shows its *intensive* growth.[3]

The first parable came from the farm. What is the kingdom of God like? "It is like a grain of mustard seed that a man took and sowed in his garden, and it grew and became a tree, and the birds of the air made nests in its branches" (Luke 13:19).

Mustard was the tiniest seed that farmers sowed in ancient Israel, with a diameter of barely one millimeter. Luke does not mention how small mustard is, the way that Matthew does in his Gospel (see Matt. 13:32), but then he did not have to. This was something everybody knew. The mustard seed was proverbially small.

The parable thus draws an implied contrast between the small size of the seed and the large size of the plant that it produces. At first the mustard plant of the Middle East looks more or less like a bush, but it grows to a height of anywhere between eight and twelve feet tall. This is hardly what anyone would expect simply from looking at the seed. Nevertheless, mustard has branches big enough for birds to come and make their nests. As small as it is, the seed grows up to become a veritable tree.

The second parable comes from the daily routine of baking bread, such as Jesus undoubtedly had observed in Mary's kitchen. He asked once again, "To what shall I compare the kingdom of God? It is like leaven that a woman took and hid in three measures of flour, until it was all leavened" (Luke 13:20–21).

Like the mustard seed, the parable of the leaven starts with something that seems insignificant. All the woman adds to her dough is a little bit of yeast, or a lump of leaven from an old batch of bread. As it gets mixed in, the leaven quickly becomes totally invisible. Yet it will still have its effect:

---

2. David Gooding, *According to Luke: A New Exposition of the Third Gospel* (Grand Rapids: Eerdmans, 1987), 254.

3. A. B. Bruce, *The Parabolic Teaching of Christ* (New York: A. C. Armstrong, 1908), 91.

overnight, the dough will grow. On this occasion, the woman was making a very large amount of bread; three measures is about fifty pounds of flour—enough to feed one hundred fifty people. But even a small amount of active yeast culture will cause that much dough to rise, leavening many loaves of bread.

## First Principles of Growth

What do these parables mean? There is a danger here of overinterpretation. Some scholars have used these parables to defend the postmillennial position that Christianity will triumph in the world before the second coming of Jesus Christ. Others have used them to defend the nearly opposite view that the church will become completely corrupt before Jesus establishes his millennial kingdom (a view based largely on taking leaven as an entirely negative image).

Rather than making these two parables carry more weight than they can bear, it seems wiser and safer to see what general principles they teach about the progress of God's kingdom work. What they teach may be summarized as follows: From a small and seemingly insignificant beginning, the kingdom of God grows—at times invisibly and almost imperceptibly—until it reaches all nations with its transforming power.

Let us consider each phrase in this summary statement, starting with *from a small and seemingly insignificant beginning*. The mustard plant started to grow with one tiny little seed. The bread began to rise with one small lump of leaven. At the beginning, it was hard to imagine that the seed would become a tree, or that the lump would make very many loaves of bread. Yet that is how the tree and the bread started to grow.

So it is with the kingdom of God: big things grow from small beginnings. In establishing his rule over his people, God started with something small. His work in the world began with one man, Adam. His covenant with the nations began with one man, Abraham. His dynasty over his people Israel began with one man, David. And the new covenant of his salvation began with one man, Jesus Christ.

How insignificant it all seemed at the beginning. A child is conceived out of wedlock in a backwater town not far from Galilee. Can anything good come from Nazareth? The child is born in poverty and relative obscu-

30

rity. Until the age of thirty he lives at home and runs the family business. After rapidly and unexpectedly rising to national prominence as an itinerant teacher and miracle worker, he dies a criminal's death and is buried in another man's tomb. The man's loyal followers are few in number and feeble in their faith. Most of them run away when he gets killed.

Who would ever imagine that this was the seed of God's everlasting kingdom? J. C. Ryle describes Christianity as:

> A religion which seemed at first so feeble, and helpless, and powerless, that it could not live. Its first founder was One who was poor in this world, and ended His life by dying the death of a malefactor on the cross.—Its first adherents were a little company, whose number probably did not exceed a thousand when the Lord Jesus left the world.—Its first preachers were a few fishermen and publicans, who were, most of them, unlearned and ignorant men.—Its first starting point was a despised corner of the earth, called Judea, a petty tributary province in the vast empire of Rome.—Its first doctrine was eminently calculated to call forth the enmity of the natural heart. Christ crucified was to the Jews a stumbling block, and to the Greeks foolishness.—Its first movements brought down on its friends persecutions from all quarters. . . . If ever there was a religion which was a little grain of seed at its beginning, that religion was the Gospel.[4]

Yet from that small and seemingly insignificant beginning, *the kingdom of God grows*. It grows because there are life in its seed and yeast in its leaven. It grows because it has all the power of God within it. It grows by his life-giving grace, and nothing can stop it from growing.

Some scholars suggest that these parables are about the slow growth of the kingdom of God. Others disagree, pointing out that mustard is a relatively fast-growing plant, and that if the yeast is good, bread will rise overnight. However, these parables say nothing specific about how fast the kingdom grows. The point is not whether it grows slowly or rapidly, but that in any event, it grows!

The kingdom of God grows like a tree. It grows because there is life in the seed of the gospel, and in Jesus himself. "Born a man," wrote Maximus of Turin, "he was humbled like a seed and in ascending to heaven was exalted

---

4. J. C. Ryle, *Expository Thoughts on the Gospels, Luke* (1858; reprint Cambridge: James Clarke, 1976), 2:124–25.

31

like a tree. It is clear that Christ is a seed when he suffers and a tree when he rises."[5] Maximus was speaking about our Savior's death and resurrection. Now the good news of his dying and rising again brings salvation: "Whoever believes in the Son has eternal life" (John 3:36).

The kingdom also grows like rising dough. There are several places in the Bible where yeast has a negative connotation. At the time of Passover, the Israelites swept the leaven out of their homes as a symbol of spiritual renewal (see Ex. 12:15). Similarly, the apostle Paul warned the Corinthians that a little of the leaven of sin is all it takes to corrupt the whole loaf of bread. "Cleanse out the old leaven," he said, "that you may be a new lump" (1 Cor. 5:7). Some have tried to give a similar interpretation to the parable of the yeast in the bread. Yet here the image has nearly the opposite meaning. Jesus can hardly be saying that the kingdom of God spreads the corruption of sin! Quite the contrary; he is using the image in a positive way to say that his kingdom will grow, just the way that leaven causes bread to rise, or that it will have a pervasive, transformative influence—like leaven.

There are times when it is hard to see that the kingdom is growing. This brings us to our next growth principle of the kingdom: From a small and seemingly insignificant beginning, the kingdom of God grows—*at times invisibly and almost imperceptibly.*

To some extent, this is true of the mustard seed. The first thing a farmer does with his seed is bury it under ground. Thus the first stages of its growth are entirely hidden from view. Jesus used a similar image to describe his death and resurrection: "Truly, truly, I say to you, unless a grain of wheat falls into the earth and dies, it remains alone; but if it dies, it bears much fruit" (John 12:24).

The secrecy of the kingdom is even more clearly taught in the second parable. Once the old leaven is mixed in with the new dough, it is completely hidden from view. Its permeating power can only be seen by the effect that it has on the rising bread.

The kingdom of God is like that. There are times when its growth is almost imperceptible. This was true at the first coming of Christ, when the glory of his deity was concealed by his humanity. As Charles Wesley wrote in his famous Christmas hymn ("Hark, the Herald Angels Sing"): "veiled

---

5. Maximus of Turin, quoted in *Luke*, ed. Arthur A. Just, Jr., Ancient Christian Commentary on Scripture, NT 3 (Downers Grove, IL: InterVarsity, 2003), 228.

in flesh, the Godhead see." It was all the more true on the cross, when the power and beauty of his sacrifice were obscured by the ugliness of his suffering and his bloody, bloody death. Who could see that Jesus was offering his life as atonement for sin?

So too the life-giving work of the gospel is often unseen, yet little by little the kingdom is growing. It grows behind closed doors when a sinner kneels secretly in prayer to receive Jesus as Savior and Lord. It grows in the heart when a little boy or girl promises to live for Jesus, no matter what. It grows in the home when by faith a husband takes spiritual responsibility for his household, and a wife respects her husband. It grows behind bars when prisoners hear the gospel. It grows on the streets of the city when Christians show quiet mercy to people society has forgotten. It grows in all the lost places of the world where missionaries live out their faith in daily obedience to Christ. The real work of the kingdom of God—and of the church in the world—is not always obvious, but sometimes invisible and almost imperceptible, like the yeast hidden in a loaf of bread.

## Further Principles of Growth

However small it begins, and however secretly it spreads, the kingdom keeps growing and growing. This is a fourth principle of its growth: the kingdom of God continues to grow *until it reaches all nations.*

The universal expansion of the kingdom of God—its *extensive* growth—seems to be the main point of the first parable. The size of a full-grown mustard plant is out of all proportion to the size of its seed. One tiny little seed becomes an entire tree—a tree big enough for birds to come and make their nests.

This image of a tree for nesting birds goes back to the Old Testament. Ezekiel prophesied that God would plant his people like a tree on a high mountain, and that "in the shade of its branches birds of every sort will nest" (Ezek. 17:23; cf. 31:6). There is a similar prophecy in Daniel, where King Nebuchadnezzar dreams of birds coming to nest in a mighty tree. In that case, the tree represented Babylon rather than Israel, but the imagery was the same. When a mighty empire sheltered and protected smaller nations, it was commonly depicted as a large tree giving refuge to little birds.

Furthermore, in some ancient Jewish writings, "the birds of the heavens" referred specifically to Gentiles.[6] So in the parable of the mustard seed Jesus was talking about something more than the size of the kingdom. This was also a prophecy about the global reach of the gospel. The kingdom of God will be a tree for the refuge of all nations. It will be "a vast movement in which members of various nations will find protection and rest (as the birds of heaven build their nests in the mustard tree)."[7]

This prophecy began to find its fulfillment already in the New Testament. At the beginning of Acts, Jesus told his disciples that they would be his witnesses "in Jerusalem and in all Judea and Samaria, and to the end of the earth" (Acts 1:8). Just a few days later, Peter found himself preaching the gospel in Jerusalem to people from all over the world. They repented, they received the gospel by faith, and when they returned to their homelands, they took the gospel back with them. Soon the apostles joined them in going out to the Gentile nations. Within a matter of decades, the apostle Paul was able to testify that he had preached the gospel from Jerusalem to Albania (Rom. 15:19). From there he would go on to Rome and, he hoped, to Spain. Here is how J. C. Ryle summarized the great progress of the gospel in the first centuries of the Christian church:

> In spite of persecution, opposition, and violence, Christianity gradually spread and increased. Year after year its adherents became more numerous. Year after year idolatry withered away before it. City after city, country after country, received the new faith. Church after church was formed in almost every quarter of the earth then known. Preacher after preacher rose up, and missionary after missionary came forward to fill the place of those who died. . . . In a few hundred years, the religion of the despised Nazarene—the religion which began in the upper chamber at Jerusalem—had overrun the civilized world.[8]

By the beginning of the third century there were thriving churches in every province of the vast Roman Empire. Like birds flocking to a mighty tree, the nations were coming to Christ. From Europe Christians carried

---

6. Norval Geldenhuys, *The Gospel of Luke*, New International Commentary on the New Testament (Grand Rapids: Eerdmans, 1951), 378.

7. Ibid., 377.

8. Ryle, *Luke*, 2:125–26.

the gospel to the Americas, and after that, to Asia, Africa, and Australia. This missionary work was advanced with special boldness in the nineteenth century, and then on into the twentieth century. Now the kingdom of God is growing in Africa, China, South America, and among the immigrant peoples of the United States. Christians are going out to the last missionary frontiers, reaching unreached peoples with the gospel and carrying the light of Jesus Christ into the dark places of Communism, Hinduism, Buddhism, and Islam.

This is how the kingdom grows. It grows to all nations, until the kingdoms of this world "become the kingdom of our Lord and of his Christ, and he shall reign forever and ever" (Rev. 11:15). Amazingly, all this growth comes from the one little seed of Christ's death on the cross, and from the kernel of life in his resurrection.

As the kingdom grows, it touches people with its transforming power. This is the last principle of growth taught in these two parables: From a small and seemingly insignificant beginning, the kingdom of God grows—at times invisibly and almost imperceptibly—until it reaches all nations *with its transforming power*.

This transforming work of the kingdom—its *intensive* growth—seems to be the main point of the second parable. Once the leaven gets mixed in with the dough, it grows and spreads until it permeates everything. The basis for comparison is not so much that the bread itself gets bigger and bigger, but that an active culture of yeast works its way all through the dough and makes it rise (even if there are fifty pounds of the stuff).

This is the way the kingdom grows. It penetrates and permeates until its influence is pervasive. This is what happens to an individual when he or she submits to the rule of God. God is not satisfied to have this part of a person's life, or that part; he wants the whole thing. So as the Spirit does his kingdom work in the believer, his influence spreads to every part of life: mind and body, work and play, worship and outreach, family and friends. Becoming a Christian affects everything, as the good leaven of God's grace grows and grows until it fills someone's entire life.

The kingdom rule of Jesus Christ has the same kind of influence on the church. As people submit to God's sovereign control, his grace permeates the Christian community with its transforming power. The gospel transforms our worship, as we celebrate what God has done for us in Christ. The gospel transforms our relationships, as we are reconciled to one another in mutual forgiveness. The gospel transforms our ministry, as we learn to depend on the Holy Spirit to do his life-changing work, instead of trying to make something happen ourselves.

Then, as the gospel transforms the church, the church transforms the world, and this is how the kingdom grows. Like the leaven in the loaf, the church often seems to be hidden in the world. But just because it is in the world, the church has a growing influence on society, advancing the kingdom of Christ. According to Simon Kistemaker, the parable of the leaven is about "Christianizing every sector and segment of life." The Christian who serves Christ as King

> champions the cause of justice in behalf of the oppressed; he demands honesty from those elected or appointed to rule the nation; he elevates the standards of morality and decency; he defends the sanctity of life; he upholds the laws of the land; he requires integrity in business, commerce, industry, labor, and the professions (medical, legal, religious); and in the area of education he meaningfully explains that in Christ "are hidden all the treasures of wisdom and knowledge" (Col. 2:3).[9]

This does not mean that our society will ever become wholly Christian, any more than we ourselves will ever be perfect in this life. We are waiting for the second coming of Jesus Christ. Only then will we see the kingdom in all its glory; only then will God's rule be fully established over the whole of saved humanity. But even now the kingdom is coming, and we see it grow wherever Christ is known as King and wherever the law of God becomes the rule of human society.

## How Are You Growing?

These principles of kingdom growth help to give us the proper perspective on our own spiritual growth, on the progress of our ministry, and on the work of the church around the world.

9. Simon J. Kistemaker, *The Parables: Understanding the Stories Jesus Told* (Grand Rapids: Baker, 2002), 55–56.

How easy it is for us to grow discouraged by our apparent lack of spiritual progress. This happens at the personal level. We start out in the Christian life and there is so much to learn. How will we ever get to the place where we want to be spiritually? Then we get a little farther along in the Christian life, and we find that we cannot seem to break a particular pattern of destructive sin. When will we ever be free? Or we reach a place of spiritual stagnation, and we find ourselves wondering: Is this all that God has for me? How slowly the kingdom sometimes seems to grow as God does his secret work in our lives.

We face the same kind of discouragement in ministry and missions. We have grand ambitions for the ministry God has called us to start, or the place where he has called us to serve, but reality fails to meet our expectations. Our ministry is small and struggling. We wonder what impact we are having, or whether we are having any impact at all. We may well feel the same way about God's work in the world generally. In America the church is in decline. In Europe it has all but disappeared. In Africa and South America it seems to be getting much bigger, but at times it also seems very shallow, and we wonder what will last. In the Arab world we hardly see the kingdom at all. There are times when we are tempted to be discouraged by what seems to be the slow progress of Christianity.

Whenever we get discouraged, we need to remember how the kingdom grows. It grows from a small and seemingly insignificant beginning. Sometimes it grows secretly and almost imperceptibly. But it does grow.

We need to remember this when it comes to our own spiritual progress. Even when we are just starting out in the Christian life, if we have the true seed of faith in Jesus Christ—if we know Jesus for sure—then his gospel work will grow until it fills our entire lives. "I am sure of this," the Scripture says, "that he who began a good work in you will bring it to completion at the day of Jesus Christ" (Phil. 1:6). Even when we are struggling spiritually, or seem to be stagnant, the life-transforming Spirit of God is still at work in our lives, growing the kingdom.

We need to apply the same kind of thinking to our ministry. We may have a similar sense of discouragement about whatever spiritual work we are doing for God. Because of the opposition of Satan, and because of our own weakness and sin, Christian ministry can be very discouraging. Whether we are starting a new church, teaching a class, hosting a Bible study, doing mercy ministry, caring for people's daily needs, or leading an evangelistic outreach—whatever the ministry—sometimes we are so discouraged and disappointed that we are tempted to give up altogether. Ministry usually starts small, and there are times when it is hard to see whether we are accomplishing anything. Even when we cannot see him because his work is almost hidden, the Holy Spirit is still there, bringing people to faith in Christ, growing them by grace, and transforming the world by his life-giving power.

J. C. Ryle said, "Let us learn from this parable never to despair of any work for Christ, because its first beginnings are feeble and small."[10] Think of Luther nailing his 95 Theses to the door of the Wittenberg Church. Who could have imagined that this simple act would change the world? Think of Calvin going to Geneva and transforming an entire city simply by preaching the gospel. Think of the Haystack Revival: a handful of college students finding refuge from a thunderstorm and having the prayer meeting that launched the modern missionary movement. Think of Hudson Taylor: one man going alone to reach China with the gospel. Or think of any church that has ever been planted anywhere in the world.

Kingdom work almost always starts small. But like the mustard seed in the ground and the yeast in the dough, it grows by the life-giving power of God in the gospel. Perhaps God is starting something good in your life—in your family, your church, or your city. Do not be discouraged by present difficulties, but believe in Jesus and his guarantee for the growth of God's kingdom.

10. Ryle, *Luke*, 2:126.

# 59

# ONE NARROW DOOR

## *Luke 13:22–30*

*And someone said to him, "Lord, will those who are saved be
few?" And he said to them, "Strive to enter through the narrow
door. For many, I tell you, will seek to enter and will not be able."*
(Luke 13:23–24)

oday there are more than one thousand organized religions in
America, each with its own system of belief, doctrine of God,
explanation of reality, view of humanity, and sense of destiny.
Imagine for a moment that each of these different religions has its own
doorway, and imagine standing in a hallway that is lined with these door-
ways as far as the eye can see. Door after door, religion after religion—
which one will you choose to enter?

Some people say it does not matter which doorway you enter because
they all lead to the same place. There is no need to worry about your choice
of religion because they all teach the same thing anyway. Open any door
you like and you will still get to heaven. This is the way many people think
about religion—maybe most people. They see it as a personal preference
that makes no ultimate difference.

But is that really true? Is it truly the case that all doors lead to heaven? What if the other doors do not lead anywhere at all, or even worse, if they lead straight to hell? What if there is only one doorway that leads to salvation, one portal to the glory of God? What if it happens to be such a small door that many people miss it? What if that door will not stay open forever, but will soon close firmly shut, leaving people outside in eternal darkness?

In that case, you would want to know for sure which door was the right door. As you stood in the hallway, looking down the corridor of all the religions, you would want to be sure not to make a mistake. You would give anything in the world to know which door was the only door that would lead you to God.

## A KEY QUESTION

Jesus Christ said there is only one narrow door that leads to eternal life, and that we need to make sure we enter that door while we still have time. He said this as he "went on his way through towns and villages, teaching and journeying toward Jerusalem" (Luke 13:22). Jesus had set his face toward Jerusalem in chapter 9, fixing his gaze on the work he was chosen to do for sinners. In chapter 13 he was still on his way, journeying towards Jerusalem, going up to Calvary and the cross.

The closer Jesus came to his own destiny, the more frequently he spoke about the destiny of all humanity. He told people to know the times, to get ready for his coming, and to repent before they perished. In the course of this teaching ministry someone asked him how many people would be saved: "Lord, will those who are saved be few?" (Luke 13:23).

This was a key question in that religious community. The rabbis all agreed that some people would be saved, while others would be damned. They had different opinions about the relative numbers of the redeemed and the reprobate, yet there seemed to be a consensus that all Israelites would be saved, except for a few notorious sinners. According to one ancient writing, "All Israelites have a share in the world to come, for it is written: 'Thy people also shall be all righteous, they shall inherit the land for ever; the branch of my planting, the work of my hands that I may be glorified.' And these are they that have no share in the world to come: he that says that there is no resurrection of the dead . . . and that the Law is not from Heaven" (Sandhedrin 10.1).

Most Jews thought that only a few people would be saved, because they believed that Gentiles were outside the kingdom of God. One man wanted to know what Jesus had to say about this key question. But his question was a key one for other reasons too. It was a key question because Jesus was facing increasing opposition. Some people followed him, but many others rejected him. How many would be saved in the end? It was also a key question because Jesus was on his way to the cross. How many people would he save by dying for sinners—few or many?

The question the man asked is important for us as well. It is important because it has to do with the plan of salvation, with God's intention for lost humanity. It is a question that we ourselves often ask as we see what is happening in the world. We hear the promise in the parable of the mustard seed: God is growing a kingdom for all nations. Yet we also see so many people who do not know Christ. We wonder about the fate of those who have never heard the gospel, and those who have heard it but rejected it. What is God's plan in all of this? How many people will he save?

This is also a key question because it confronts the pervasive pluralism of our times. Today many people think that everyone will get to heaven (or almost everyone). Even people who do not believe in God think they will go to a better place when they die. Over against such relativism, pluralism, and universalism, the claim that there is only one way to God is bound to be viewed as religious bigotry. No one wants to be considered a bigot, and as a result, some Christians downplay or even deny the unique claims of Christ. They want to believe that everyone will be saved in the end, even if God saves some people through other religions. Hence the importance of the man's question: How many people will be saved? Only a few, or might it be many?

## THE WAY IS NARROW

For many reasons, the answer to the man's question is as important now as it was the day it was asked, but especially for this one: because Jesus used it to unlock the secret door of salvation.

41

Most people probably assumed that Jesus would answer by saying that only a few people would be saved. After all, this is what most Jewish people expected in those days: with relatively few exceptions, only the Jews would be saved. That is not the way that Jesus answered, however. In fact, he did not answer the question directly at all.

If he had answered it directly, Jesus probably would have said what he said in his Sermon on the Mount: "Enter by the narrow gate. For the gate is wide and the way is easy that leads to destruction, and those who enter by it are many. For the gate is narrow and the way is hard that leads to life, and those who find it are few" (Matt. 7:13–14). How many people enter the wide gate that leads to death? Many people. How many find the narrow way to life? Only a few. But the Gospel of Luke has a different emphasis from Matthew. Although Jesus certainly implied that only a few people would be saved, his main concern was the salvation of those who were listening.

Instead of speculating about the relative numbers of the lost and the saved, Jesus made the issue personal and practical. Addressing the entire crowd, he said, "Strive to enter through the narrow door" (Luke 13:24). Cyril of Alexandria comments that Jesus is "purposely silent to the useless question," but "proceeds to speak of what was essential."[1] What was and is essential is the destiny of one's own eternal soul. Rather than trying to figure out what God will do with somebody else, the most important question for me to address is my own personal relationship with Jesus Christ: Am I certain that I have walked through the door that leads to eternal life? Do I know for sure that I will be saved? Whether God saves many people or only a few, the important thing for me is to make sure that I have eternal life.

Jesus says the way to be sure is to "strive to enter through the narrow door" (Luke 13:24). The Greek word for "strive" *(agōnizesthe)* is a word for intense exertion, like the effort it takes to train for an athletic competition. As a point of comparison, the English word "agonize" comes from the same Greek root. Jesus said we need to make every possible effort to enter the narrow door that leads to salvation.

This does not mean, of course, that we can ever be saved by our own efforts. The Bible is clear that salvation is by grace, not works, so that God

---

1. Cyril of Alexandria, "Commentary on Luke," in *Luke*, ed. Arthur A. Just, Jr., Ancient Christian Commentary on Scripture, NT 3 (Downers Grove, IL: InterVarsity, 2003), 229.

will receive all of the glory. But until we have entered salvation—until we have received the assurance of eternal life through faith in Jesus Christ—we need to keep striving to understand the gospel. Have you found the narrow way and walked through the narrow door? If not, then keep reading the Bible; keep listening to the gospel; keep praying for the help of God's Spirit; and Jesus will show you the way.

The way is not wide. I once visited a cave in Turkey, near Cappadocia. Its various caverns were large enough to accommodate an entire underground community. Christians sometimes went there to escape persecution. As we made our descent, we came to a narrow tunnel—fifty or sixty feet long—that narrowed as it went deeper into the ground. If I had not been told in advance that it was large enough for me to crawl through, I would have worried about making it out the other side. The way of salvation is like that: it is very narrow. Rather than saying, "You can't miss it," Jesus says that we can miss it very easily, and that if we do not work hard to find it, we will miss it entirely. People sometimes complain that Christianity is a narrow religion. Well, it *is* narrow! According to Jesus himself, there is only one narrow door that leads to eternal life, while every other way leads to destruction. The reason for this is that only Jesus has done what needs to be done for salvation: he alone has offered perfect atonement for sin.

This is not a very popular position to take in these pluralistic times. Today people prefer to say that all doors lead to heaven, and that the only people who ought to be excluded are people who say that some people are excluded. It is the very exclusivity of Christianity that offends people. They say, "I hope you're not one of those Christians who believe that Jesus is the only way to eternal life."

Yet that is exactly what we *do* believe, that there is only one door to salvation—one narrow door. We believe this because Jesus said it. We also believe it because we know what salvation demands. Something has to be done about the great burden of our sin. We need a perfect sacrifice to atone for all the wrong things that we have done, and a perfect holiness to make us righteous before God. The only place to find that sacrifice is at the cross, and the only person who has that perfect holiness is the Lord Jesus Christ. In the words of one of Cecil Frances Alexander's wonderful hymns for children, "There was no other good enough to pay the price of sin; he only could unlock the gate of heav'n, and let us in."[2] Therefore, it is only through Jesus that we can enter salvation. He is the only gateway to eternal life. As Jesus himself said, "I am the door. If anyone enters by me, he will be saved" (John 10:9).

Some people still insist on finding their own way to God. They object to the very idea that there is only one door, yet that is the way doors generally operate. Imagine someone coming to visit your house and complaining that there is only one front door. "I don't want to go through that door," your visitor might say. "Isn't there another entrance?" Imagine how foolish it would be for him to refuse to enter, or even worse, to start making his own doorway. Yet that is exactly what many people do when they stand outside the house of God. Instead of entering, they complain about the number of doors in God's house, or else they walk through the door to some other dwelling and expect that they will still end up in God's house!

The problem is not God, or the door, but the sinner who refuses to use it. It is God's house, and he has every right to make his own door. How gracious he is to open a door for sinners at all, and how gracious Jesus is to invite us to enter! Understand this: the reason he tells us that the door is narrow is not to keep us out, but so that we will find our way through. Have you entered the narrow door?

In his wonderful allegory *The Pilgrim's Progress*, John Bunyan tells how a man named Christian left the City of Destruction to look for eternal life. One of the first people he met was a man named Evangelist, who told him how to begin his pilgrimage. Evangelist pointed to a gate, and told Christian to go and knock on it for further instructions. When Christian reached the gate and started knocking, he suddenly became afraid that his sins would keep him out. "May I now enter here?" he wondered. "Will he within / Open to sorry me, though I have been / An undeserving rebel?" When someone came to answer his knock, Christian said, "Here is a poor burdened sinner. I come from the City of Destruction, but am going to Mount Zion, that I may be delivered from the wrath to come; I would therefore, sir, since I am informed that by this gate is the way thither, know if you are willing to let me in."[3] This is the burdened cry of every sinner: Will God really let someone like me enter the one narrow door to salvation?

2. Cecil Frances Alexander, "There Is a Green Hill Far Away" (1848).
3. John Bunyan, *The Pilgrim's Progress* (New York: New American Library, 1981), 31.

The answer is yes, as Christian discovered. Jesus answers our prayers for mercy and grace. He not only shows us the door, but by faith he lets us in, so that we can live with him forever.

## Shut Out

If the door to salvation is so narrow, it is not surprising that some people never enter. What *is* surprising is that some who never enter have every expectation of getting in. They assume that God will let them into his everlasting house, but eventually they will discover that they are badly mistaken. Jesus said, "Strive to enter through the narrow door. For many, I tell you, will seek to enter and will not be able" (Luke 13:24).

This is a partial answer to the question Jesus was asked about how many people will be saved. However many will be saved, it is certainly true that many will be lost. Many of the people who listened to Jesus that day, as well as many people throughout history—maybe even the majority—will never enter salvation.

Jesus proceeded to describe what it is like to be excluded from the kingdom of God. It almost sounds like a parable, but Jesus was speaking directly to their situation:

> When once the master of the house has risen and shut the door, and you begin to stand outside and to knock at the door, saying, "Lord, open to us," then he will answer you, "I do not know where you come from." Then you will begin to say, "We ate and drank in your presence, and you taught in our streets." But he will say, "I tell you, I do not know where you come from. Depart from me, all you workers of evil!" (Luke 13:25–27)

Jesus is not speaking here about the lost in general, but specifically about people who think that they are saved, especially among the religious people of his own day. They assumed they had a right to enter God's house, so they were shocked to discover that they were locked out. They thought they were in, but they were actually out, and by the time they started looking for the narrow door, it was already locked and bolted. Jesus Christ is the master of God's house—the one who determines who gets in and who stays out—and once he shuts the door, it stays shut.

45

The reason Jesus shuts these people out is that he does not know them—not in a personal and saving way. They are completely surprised by this because they thought they knew Jesus, and they assumed that he knew them. After all, they had direct exposure to his earthly ministry. There were people in the crowd that day who witnessed his miraculous wonders and listened to him preach in their own home towns, hearing the first sermons of the world's greatest teacher. Some of them even shared table fellowship with him. They knew Jesus socially. Perhaps they even liked to tell people that they had met him personally.

Nevertheless, they did not know Jesus as their Savior and their God. Presuming on their outward privileges, they never went through the narrow door to salvation. Assuming that they were already in, they never took the trouble to commit their lives to Christ. So in the end, Jesus says (not once, but twice; see Luke 13:25, 27) that he does not even know where they are coming from. What a tragic situation! Many people who think they know Jesus are not united to him by faith, and when they try to get into God's house, Jesus will refuse to let them enter.

This warning is not just for the Jews who saw Jesus, but for every person who has ever worshiped in a Christian church. Even if we have never seen Jesus in the flesh, we have enjoyed even greater privileges. We have read the miracles of Jesus in the pages of the New Testament. We have heard his preaching of the gospel. We have seen his saving work through the eyewitnesses of his crucifixion and resurrection. We have sat at his table to eat and drink with him in the sacrament of the Lord's Supper. But do we know Jesus? Do we have a real, personal relationship with him? Have we gone to him in repentance, confessing our sins? Have we received him in faith, trusting in his cross? Or do we know him only socially and superficially?

Jesus invites us to enter God's house and receive eternal life. He welcomes us to go in by the narrow door of his salvation, which is the only way that anyone can ever enter. Understand that if you refuse to enter, the day will come when you will be the one doing the pleading, begging Jesus to let you in or else to destroy you altogether (see Rev. 6:15–17). But by then it will be too late! The door will be shut on the day of judgment, and when it shuts, you will be shut out. This is only fair. The master of the house has opened the door and invited you to come in. If you refuse to enter, does he not have every right to bar the door? A refusal to enter the narrow door is an outright denial of the blood of the Son of God.

What terrible suffering there will be for everyone who gets shut out from God's kingdom. To make sure we know what is at stake, Jesus speaks about this with perfect clarity: "In that place there will be weeping and gnashing of teeth, when you see Abraham and Isaac and Jacob and all the prophets in the kingdom of God but you yourselves cast out" (Luke 13:28). Jesus was speaking plainly about the pains of hell.

Hell will be a place of anguish and affliction. It will be a place of remorse, as people cry bitter tears of grief for all that they have lost. It will be a place of rage, as they gnash their teeth in angry defiance of God. It will be a place of regret, as people mourn the folly of their unbelief. Apparently they will have some awareness of what they are missing. Jesus describes them standing outside his kingdom and looking in to see the prophets and the patriarchs. They watch the guests arrive to feast in the house of God.

How galling it will be for them to know that they themselves were once on the guest list, but that they declined the free invitation of Jesus Christ. They had once been close to eternal life, yet now they will end up so far away from God! "To have been so near to Christ on earth," writes David Gooding, "without receiving him and without coming to know him personally, and therefore to be shut out for ever from the glorious company of the saints, while others from distant times and cultures have found the way in—who shall measure the disappointment and frustration of it?"[4]

As much as anything else, hell will be a place of lost opportunity. This conversation started with a question about how many people would be saved. Rather than talking about numbers, Jesus confronted the crowd with their own need to find the one narrow door to salvation. What he especially emphasized was the need to find that door before it is too late. People wanted to know how many (how many people would get in), but Jesus wanted them to think about how soon (how soon the door would close for all eternity).

Time is running out. There is a time limit on the free offer of salvation. Soon the door of God's mercy will be slammed shut, just as God shut the door of Noah's ark before he flooded the world in judgment (Gen. 7:16).

---

4. David Gooding, *According to Luke: A New Exposition of the Third Gospel* (Grand Rapids: Eerdmans, 1987), 262.

This is why Jesus told the parable of the rich fool, and of the servants waiting for their master. This is why Jesus told people to repent or perish. This is why he told them to strive to enter the narrow door. It was because he knew the door would not stay open forever. Salvation in Christ is a limited-time offer. There will be no second chance to repent after death, or to trust in Christ at the final judgment, for that will be a day when God displays his justice against evil. There will be no preaching of the gospel in hell. If the truth about salvation is known there at all, it is known too late: too late to repent, too late to believe, and too late to enter eternal life.

Jesus obviously thought that entering the narrow door to salvation was a matter of real urgency. Does it seem as urgent to you as it did to him? The question is not how many doors there are. God knows there is only one! The question is whether you will make it through that one and only door while you still have time.

## Everyone's Invited

Jesus promises that on the other side of the door there will be everlasting joy for everyone who comes to God through faith in him. So at the end of this encounter, Jesus gives us a glimpse of what it will be like to enter God's house. He describes it as a place for Abraham, Isaac, and Jacob, as well as for Isaiah, Jeremiah, Ezekiel, and all the rest of the Old Testament prophets. God always said he was the God of Abraham, Isaac, and Jacob (e.g., Ex. 3:6)—the big three of covenant faith—and he will prove it when Jesus comes in all his glory.

These great men are not the only ones who will enter the kingdom, however. In addition to the prophets and patriarchs, God will bring in many believers from the nations. Jesus said, "People will come from east and west, and from north and south, and recline at table in the kingdom of God" (Luke 13:29). In other words, God was interested in something more than saving the Jews; he had a plan for the salvation of the whole world. "And behold," Jesus went on to say, "some are last who will be first, and some are first who will be last" (Luke 13:30). In other words, people who had always been outsiders would enter the household of God, and people who always thought they were insiders would find themselves outside, looking in. God was not only for the Jews, but also for the Gentiles.

An international banquet as an image of salvation, fellowship, and blessing comes from the Old Testament. Isaiah prophesied that people would come to God from far away, from north and south and east and west (Isa. 45:6; 49:12). He also prophesied that on the mountain of salvation, "the LORD of hosts will make for all peoples a feast of rich food, a feast of well-aged wine, of rich food full of marrow, of aged wine well refined" (Isa. 25:6).

This prophecy is about being at home with God. It is about enjoying the soul-satisfying pleasures of his triune being. What blessings God has in store for everyone who enters his everlasting house! What fellowship we will share with the ancient men of faith, and with believers from all nations! What feasting we will enjoy as we recline together at the table of God! And what joy we will have in Christ, who is the master of God's house!

This prophecy is also about the inclusion of Gentiles in the kingdom of God. They are the last who will be first. The man who asked Jesus how many people would be saved thought he knew who was on the guest list: only the Israelites. But by the invitation of God, salvation is not just for the Jews; it is also for everyone who enters the narrow door of salvation through faith in Jesus Christ. We see this at Pentecost, when people from all over the world heard Peter preach the gospel in their own languages and came to faith in Jesus Christ (Acts 2:7–11, 36–41).

This shows how inclusive Christianity is. In one sense, Christianity is the most *exclusive* of all religions. According to Jesus himself, there is only one narrow way of salvation. Those who find it are included; everyone else is excluded. But in another sense, Christianity is the most *inclusive* of all religions. It is not just for people from a particular ethnic background. It is not just for people who are able to obey God better than other people, or who have reached a certain level of enlightenment. You do not have to be any smarter, any more religious, or any holier than anyone else. You just have to be a sinner who is praying for God to give you grace in Jesus Christ.

How much hope this gives to every spiritual outsider! The last will be first. You may say that you do not come from a very good background. You may think you have done something so terrible that no one can ever accept you, least of all God. You may feel that you do not even belong in church. But Jesus has a place for you. He says the last will be first, the outsiders will become insiders, and he invites you to enter. Will you come in and sit down to feast with God?

One Saturday night I went into Philadelphia's Tenth Presbyterian Church to pray. The sanctuary was darkening in the twilight, but I saw a light glimmering behind the pulpit. It was coming from the back door that leads to the platform where I preach Sunday by Sunday. The door was open just far enough for a golden ray of light to escape in the space between the door and the frame. The light was warm in its glow, inviting me to enter. It reminded me of the invitation to go in by the narrow door. Jesus has told us that there is only one door to salvation. He has also given us a glimpse of the light beyond the door—the joy of his Father's house. Now he invites us to open the door and come in.

Be sure to enter, because the same Lord Jesus who said the last will be first also warned that the first will be last. This familiar expression is almost always quoted out of context. It is the kind of thing people say at church when someone is served last for dinner and then gets first in line for dessert. But when Jesus said this he was talking with deadly seriousness about our eternal destiny. It is true that some who started out last in this life will be as first as anyone in the kingdom of God. But this is also true: some people who always thought they were number one with God will end up last for salvation. In fact, they will be shut out of the kingdom of God. What a complete surprise! What a total disaster! And what a terrible tragedy.

With this warning we close, just as Jesus did. The first will be last. So strive to enter through the narrow door—the one and only door that leads to salvation, through faith in Jesus Christ.

# 60

# A Lament for the City

## Luke 13:31–35

*"O Jerusalem, Jerusalem, the city that kills the prophets and stones those who are sent to it! How often would I have gathered your children together as a hen gathers her brood under her wings, and you would not!"* (Luke 13:34)

He seems so serene, so unaffected by the intense emotions that grip a more passionate soul. This is the Jesus we usually see in paintings, especially the famous portrait by Warner Sallman. Since it first appeared in 1940, Sallman's "Head of Christ" has been reproduced more than half a billion times.

The Christ in Sallman's portrait is perfectly calm. He looks to one side with a steady and upward gaze. His silken hair flows to his shoulders; his smooth, radiant face is tanned to bronze. He looks alert and athletic, yet he does not betray any obvious emotion. His lips are closed, keeping what he feels deep in the recesses of his heart.

This is the Jesus we often see in the portraits, but it is not the Jesus we meet in the Gospels, where a very passionate Savior experiences with full intensity every holy emotion of the human spirit. When Jesus rejoiced, as he did when the seventy-two came back from their first mission trip (Luke 10:17–22), he rejoiced in the full exultation of his Father's joy. When Jesus laughed, his voice danced with the mirth of redemption. When Jesus was angry, as he was with the salesmen who filled his Father's house with their unholy merchandise (Luke 19:45–46), he trembled with righteous indignation. When Jesus grieved, as he did outside the tomb of Lazarus (John 11:35), he grieved with all the pathos of a broken heart. According to Hebrews, "Jesus offered up prayers and supplications, with loud cries and tears" (Heb. 5:7). When he suffered, as he did in the Garden of Gethsemane and on the cross of Calvary, he endured the absolute torment of being forsaken by God for our sin (Matt. 27:46).

No one has ever had a more dynamic emotional life than the Lord Jesus Christ. He did not go though life with unmoved serenity, but passionate intensity.[1]

## OUTFOXING HEROD AND THE PHARISEES

We get a window into our Savior's soul in his tragic lament for the city of Jerusalem. Matthew tells us that Jesus offered a similar lament the week he died on the cross (see Matt. 23:37–39). Luke will also show Jesus weeping over Jerusalem at the end of chapter 19. But here he records an earlier incident, of equal intensity, which took place while Jesus was still on his journey to Jerusalem. In these verses we see our Savior working to finish his calling with a heart full of compassion.

First we need to know the context. Jesus had been speaking about the narrow door to eternal life, which many spiritual outsiders would find, but many religious insiders would never enter. The last will be first, Jesus said, and the first will be last. "At that very hour some Pharisees came" to offer him some friendly advice. They said to Jesus, "Get away from here, for Herod wants to kill you" (Luke 13:31).

This was a plausible threat. King Herod had already murdered John the Baptist (Matt. 14:1–12), and presumably would not think twice about killing another prophet. Undoubtedly by now the king had heard about the large crowds that were following Jesus. As insecure as he was,

---

1. See B. B. Warfield's masterful essay, "On the Emotional Life of Our Lord," in *The Person and Work of Christ*, ed. Samuel G. Craig (Philadelphia, PA: Presbyterian & Reformed, 1950), 93–145.

Herod probably feared the influence that Jesus was gaining. So if Herod was starting to make death threats, it would not be at all surprising.

We may be excused, however, for viewing the Pharisees with some suspicion. What had they ever done for Jesus? These were the very men who for months had been trying "to catch him in something he might say" (Luke 11:54). Jesus had just warned them about getting shut out of the kingdom of God, and now they were trying to save his life? Their concern would be almost touching, were it not contradicted by almost everything else we read about the Pharisees and their attitude towards Jesus.

What were their real motives? Maybe their concern for Jesus was genuine, but maybe they were conspiring with Herod. One wonders, for example, where the Pharisees received their intelligence about these terroristic threats. Had they been talking to Herod? Maybe so, because when Jesus gives his answer, he tells the Pharisees to take it back to Herod, as if they were in close communication. Perhaps Herod was using the Pharisees to intimidate Jesus. Or maybe they were using Herod to get Jesus out of Galilee, where Herod ruled, and into Jerusalem, where they had more control. In any case, it seems ironic that the Pharisees were the ones who were trying to keep Jesus safe. It also seems more than a little suspicious.

Whatever motives may have been behind it, Herod's threat presented Jesus with the temptation to save his own life rather than to finish the work of saving sinners. Jesus did not hesitate for a moment, but said to the Pharisees: "Go and tell that fox, 'Behold, I cast out demons and perform cures today and tomorrow, and the third day I finish my course. Nevertheless, I must go on my way today and tomorrow and the day following, for it cannot be that a prophet should perish away from Jerusalem'" (Luke 13:32–33).

Jesus could always tell what was in a man, and his description of Herod was right on the mark. A fox is cunning, and predatory, but relatively weak. T. W. Manson explained that in Jewish usage, the term fox "typifies low cunning as opposed to straightforward dealing, and it is used in contrast to 'lion' to describe an insignificant third-rate person as opposed to a person of real power and greatness."[2] Needless to say, Jesus had no intention of taking orders from a second-rate ruler like Herod. His response to the Pharisees put that sly old fox back in his place. Rather than running away

---

2. T. W. Manson, quoted in Norval Geldenhuys, *The Gospel of Luke*, New International Commentary on the New Testament (Grand Rapids: Eerdmans, 1951), 384.

from danger, Jesus would keep working away at his calling until he finished what he had come to do, even unto death.

## WORKING TO FINISH HIS CALLING

The message Jesus sent back to Herod deserves careful consideration because of the deep insight it gives into his saving work. As Jesus tells us how he approached his calling as the Savior of sinners, he opens a window to his soul. Consider at least four things we learn about the way Jesus worked to finish his calling.

First, we learn what kind of work Jesus came to do. He said, "Behold, I cast out demons and perform cures" (Luke 13:32). Jesus came to do the kingdom work of delivering people from the devil. We see this over and over again in the Gospels: Jesus casting out demons as a sign of his ultimate triumph over all the powers of hell. He also cured people's diseases, reversing one of the effects of the fall by meeting their physical needs. In his ministry of healing, Jesus came to save people's bodies as well as their souls. The miracles he performed in his earthly ministry point us to heavenly glory, when our bodies will rise again in immortal and incorruptible splendor.

Second, we learn how long Jesus would continue to do this work: until the work was finished. He said, "Behold, I cast out demons and perform cures today and tomorrow, and the third day I finish my course" (Luke 13:32). Most people find it easier to start things than they do to finish them. Our lives are full of academic degrees that never quite get completed, home improvements that are only half finished, and dozens of smaller projects that pile up on our desks and work benches. But Jesus never started something he was not totally committed to finish. He did his work one day at a time, day after day. He had work to do today. He would do the same work tomorrow, and he would keep working away at a steady pace until his work finally was done. "My food is to do the will of him who sent me," Jesus said on another occasion, "and to accomplish his work" (John 4:34).

The expression "today and tomorrow and the third day" does not seem to refer to the resurrection, at least not explicitly. It is certainly true that Jesus rose from the dead on the third day, and in many ways that was the culmination of his ministry. But "today and tomorrow and the third day" was a common poetic expression that people used to refer to a short, definite period of time. How long would Jesus continue to carry out his earthly ministry? He had work to do today and also tomorrow. There would be more work to do after that, but it would not go on forever. Eventually, his work would get finished, and the third day was symbolic of its completion.

As Jesus did this work, nothing would stop him. No obstacle could ever delay him, no enemy deter him, no threat defeat him. Completing his mission was more important to him than life itself. With unwavering courage, he was determined to do the work he was called to do. Like an athlete running his race, or a champion completing his course, he would keep going to the very end.

One man who knows what it takes to make it to the end of a course is Dick Hoyt, who has completed more than eighty marathons and more than two hundred triathlons. That in itself is an accomplishment that few people can match. But Dick Hoyt has done it all while carrying his son with him: pushing him down the street as he runs, pulling him through the water in a dinghy while he swims, hauling him on a bicycle as he pedals. Dick Hoyt's son was born disabled, unable to control his limbs. But ever since he said, "Dad, when we were running it felt like I wasn't disabled anymore," Dick Hoyt has worked hard to finish every race.[3]

This story reminds us of the commitment Jesus had to finish his course, and to carry us all the way to salvation. Jesus was telling Herod that he would keep healing, keep preaching, keep casting out demons, and keep bearing the burden of our sins until his saving work was done.

## Doing What He Had to Do, Unto Death

A third truth we learn from this episode is why Jesus did this saving work. He did it because he had to do it. Jesus said, "I must go on my way today and tomorrow and the day following" (Luke 13:33). When he said "must," Jesus was saying that he was under a holy obligation. It was divinely necessary for him to finish this healing, saving work.

Jesus had to do it because it was the desire of his own loving heart. He had come into the world for the very purpose of saving poor sinners from the diseases of their bodies, the demons of their souls, and the depravity

---

3. The story of Dick and Rick Hoyt is told in Rick Reilly, "Strongest Dad in the World," *Sports Illustrated* (June 20, 2005): 88.

of their sinful hearts. Jesus had to do this because the mercy of his divine character compelled him to do it.

But he also had to do it because this work was his Father's will. Jesus said, "Behold, I have come to do your will, O God" (Heb. 10:7). The will of God was for the Son to do everything that the Father said needed to be done for our salvation—the full work of redemption. This was something the Father and the Son had agreed in eternity past, when they established an everlasting covenant, in which the Father would forgive the sinners that the Son would come to save. Under the terms of that eternal arrangement, the Son was bound to finish his saving work. By his own consent, he was required to keep the whole law for his people, to preach to them the gospel of peace, and to suffer the penalty they deserved for their sins. So when Jesus said "I must go on my way," he was reaffirming the sacred obligation he had undertaken in the courts of heaven. The Son of God must do what he eternally promised that he would do.

We can summarize what we have said so far by answering a series of questions: What kind of work did Jesus come to do? The kingdom work of saving sinners. How long would he do this work? Until he was totally finished. Why did he do it? Because he had to. Now what would it take to bring his great task to completion? Jesus would have to suffer to the very death. He was not afraid of Herod's murderous threats because dying was the very reason that he came. Jesus said, "I must go on my way today and tomorrow and the day following, for it cannot be that a prophet should perish away from Jerusalem" (Luke 13:33).

Once again, Jesus was speaking about his death. He saw it coming. He knew that his work would end in death, so he was preparing to die. Luke began to show us this in chapter 9, when Jesus said, "The Son of Man must suffer many things and be rejected by the elders and chief priests and scribes, and be killed, and on the third day be raised" (Luke 9:22). These things would happen in the city of Jerusalem. This is why Jesus set his face to go to Jerusalem (see Luke 9:51): he was going up to die. It is also why he said his work would not be finished until he went back to that great city, for Jerusalem is where prophets went to die. Jesus was emphatic about this: he *must* go on his way and it *could not be* that he would die outside Jerusalem.

Nevertheless, what Jesus said about prophets perishing there was full of irony. Jerusalem was the city where God placed his name and established his temple. It was the center of worship for the people of God. Surely it was the last place that one of God's holy prophets would ever be killed! Yet Jesus knew that Jerusalem was exactly where he would be killed.

He also knew that this is how he would finish his work: by dying on the cross for the sinners he had come to save. What Jesus literally says at the end of verse 32 is "I will be finished." This statement anticipates the climactic declaration he later made on the cross: "It is finished" (John 19:30). By the time he died on the cross, Jesus was finished with his earthly ministry of healing diseases and casting out demons. He was finished with his holy obligation to keep the law of God. He was finished with life itself, at least for his three days in the grave. Most of all, he was finished suffering the penalty that we deserve: the wrath of God against our sin. Praise God, Jesus finished all the work that he was called to do!

The finished work of Jesus Christ gives us the assurance of our salvation. There is nothing more that we need to do to get rid of the guilt of our sin if we are trusting in Christ. By his perfect obedience and by the bleeding death he died on our behalf, Jesus has done all the work that needs to be done to make us right with God.

The finished work of Jesus Christ also gives us an example to follow. Our own work often makes us weary. We get tired of doing what God has called us to do. We find it easier to start things than to finish them, and even when we do finish them, it is hard for us to finish them well. But Jesus set the example for us to follow. His extraordinary work in salvation shows us how to do our own ordinary work of Christian service. Keep working away at whatever work God has given you to do; work until it is finished. Keep teaching, helping, serving, and loving until your work is done. Do not be intimidated by any opposition you face, even if you are threatened with death. With all obedient faith and steadfast courage, keep working for Christ until your work for him is done. As the Scripture says, "Let us run with endurance the race that is set before us, looking to Jesus, the founder and perfecter of our faith, who for the joy that was set before him endured the cross, despising the shame, and is seated at the right hand of the throne of God" (Heb. 12:1–2).

## WITH A HEART FULL OF COMPASSION

As Jesus worked to finish his calling, he did it with a heart full of compassion. It is one thing to work away at something, but it is another thing to do it with love for the people you serve. Every parent knows the difference between the work children do with joy and the work they do with grudging obedience. Every worker knows the difference, too. There are times when every second of our daily occupation is sheer drudgery, but there are also times when our work is so engaging that we do it with all our strength. This is the way Jesus did the work of our salvation. He did not simply finish the work; he did it with all his heart.

The compassion of Christ comes through clearly in his lament for the city. "O Jerusalem, Jerusalem," he said, "the city that kills the prophets and stones those who are sent to it!" (Luke 13:34). Once again we are reminded of Jerusalem's proverbial rejection of the prophets. As the city of God, Jerusalem represented the people of God. Yet how often that city had rejected God's prophets! Think of Zechariah, who was stoned at the very temple (2 Chron. 24:21). Think of the abuse that Jeremiah suffered in the days before Jerusalem fell to the Babylonians. What Nehemiah said to God about the citizens of Jerusalem was true: "They were disobedient and rebelled against you and cast your law behind their back and killed your prophets" (Neh. 9:26).

The city's murderous rebellion broke Jesus' heart. "O Jerusalem, Jerusalem," he said, addressing the city with a woeful lament. Then he uttered the longing ache of his broken heart: "How often would I have gathered your children together as a hen gathers her brood under her wings, and you would not!" (Luke 13:34).

The word "often" reminds us how many times Jesus went to Jerusalem for Israel's religious festivals, starting when he was a young boy. He loved the holy city, its people and its worship. He loved its temple, which he called his Father's house. Whenever he went up to that great city, he cried out to be its Savior. With tender compassion, Jesus yearned to gather all its lost and broken people into his loving arms.

Here he describes that yearning with an almost motherly compassion. Like a mother hen gathering her little chicks, Jesus wanted to bring Jerusalem under the wings of his protection. What is so amazing about this is that the people of that city were in rebellion against God. Soon they would put Jesus to death, as Jesus well knew. Nevertheless, he was longing for their salvation. He was also working for their salvation, ready to endure the suffering and the cross. What great compassion Jesus has for sinners! In the words of J. C. Ryle, "He knew well the wickedness of that city. He knew what crimes had been committed there in times past. He knew what was coming on Himself, at the time of His crucifixion. Yet even to Jerusalem He says, 'How often would I have gathered thy children together as a hen doth gather her brood under her wings.'"[4]

If Jesus had compassion for the lost sinners of Jerusalem, then he has compassion for us. The invitation to come under his sheltering wing is offered to everyone, without exception, in all of life's troubles. When you are afraid of your enemies, pray the way David prayed when he was hiding from wicked King Saul: "Be merciful to me, O God, be merciful to me, for in you my soul takes refuge; in the shadow of your wings I will take refuge, till the storms of destruction pass by" (Ps. 57:1). When you are in danger, believe what God has said in his Word: "He will cover you with his pinions, and under his wings you will find refuge" (Ps. 91:4). If you feel unwanted and unloved, then claim this biblical promise: "How precious is your steadfast love, O God! The children of mankind take refuge in the shadow of your wings" (Ps. 36:7). If you want the free gift of eternal life, then go to God and make this prayer: "Let me dwell in your tent forever! Let me take refuge under the shelter of your wings!" (Ps. 61:4). Jesus is ready and willing to take you under his wing, if only you will come to him in faith. Then you will be able to say, "O God, you are my God . . . for you have been my help, and in the shadow of your wings I will sing for joy" (Ps. 63:1, 7).

In offering us this shelter, Jesus is not only our Savior, but also our example. The love that Jesus had for Jerusalem is the model for our own compassion for lost sinners, especially in the city. When we see people living in rebellion against God—the drug traffickers, the drag queens, the gang members, the crooked businessmen, the corrupt politicians, and all the people like us who live for themselves—we usually want to push them as far away as possible. But Jesus was dying to draw them in by his grace, so that they could come and find salvation.

4. J. C. Ryle, *Expository Thoughts on the Gospels, Luke* (1858; reprint Cambridge: James Clarke, 1976), 2:140.

Today Jesus extends his gracious invitation through the church—through our message of forgiveness and our ministry of mercy. Pray for the people you are longing for Jesus to save. Show mercy to people who are lost in the city. Spread the wings of Christ's compassion to bring them to safety.

## But They Would Not

If only the people who need Christ would come under his wing! Some of them will, of course. It happens every day: people hear the good news of the cross and the empty tomb; they are invited to receive Jesus as Savior and Lord; they repent of their sins, they believe in Christ, and they are saved forever. But sadly, many people refuse to come to Jesus at all.

This was the reason for our Lord's heartfelt lament. "O Jerusalem, Jerusalem," he said, "How often would I have gathered your children together as a hen gathers her brood under her wings, and you would not!" (Luke 13:34). Jesus had been busy doing the work of his kingdom. Time and again, he had told people to repent of their sins and warned them to find safety from the judgment to come. Time and again, he had invited them to receive him by faith. Yet time and again, they had refused his gracious invitation. They would not repent; they would not believe; they would not be saved. In the end, they would have no one to blame but themselves.

Jesus Christ is willing to save. With tender compassion, he "desires all people to be saved and to come to the knowledge of the truth" (1 Tim. 2:4). He does not wish "that any should perish, but that all should reach repentance" (2 Peter 3:9). It is true that God is sovereign in salvation—no one can come to Christ without the saving work of God's Spirit. But it is also true that Jesus Christ is freely and genuinely offered to everyone, and that people who have the will to reject him are choosing their own destruction. We can never blame God for our own unbelief. God leaves us free to follow the defiant rebellion of our own sinful hearts. If we do not come to Christ, it is not because God has not invited us, but because we will not come.

What a heartbreak it is when the people we love refuse to come to Christ. Jesus knows what a heartbreak it is, because he himself was brokenhearted for Jerusalem. He knew that judgment was coming. He knew that the door of salvation would not stay open forever, but soon would close to shut people out. He knew that many people in Jerusalem would remain in their rebellion. His compassionate response shows how we should respond when people turn away from God: with deep sadness for those who will not come to Christ, and a firm commitment to do God's work until it is done.

Jerusalem's rebellion was a special grief to our Savior's soul because he knew what suffering was about to fall on that proud city. He said to the people of Jerusalem, "Behold, your house is forsaken" (Luke 13:35). Some scholars say that here Jesus was referring to the city as a whole as a house for God's people. Others say he was speaking more specifically about the temple, which was the house of God. But either way, this prophecy came true. God withdrew his protection from Jerusalem. His holy presence no longer rested on the temple. Within a matter of years the city was overthrown and its temple was utterly destroyed.

What happened to Jerusalem will happen to any nation, city, church, or individual who refuses to find safety in Christ. If we will not come to him, we will be forsaken by God, and eventually we will be destroyed.

Yet there is still time for us to come to him in faith. There is still time for us to come under the safety of his wings. There is still time for us to be saved, as there was for Jerusalem. Jesus ended by saying "I tell you, you will not see me until you say, 'Blessed is he who comes in the name of the Lord!'" (Luke 13:35).

The statement "Blessed is he who comes in the name of the Lord!" (Ps. 118:26) was a benediction from the Old Testament. It was also a promise of salvation that people shouted on Palm Sunday, when Jesus rode into Jerusalem the week before he died (see Luke 19:28–38). So perhaps Jesus was making a prophecy about his triumphal entry. Jerusalem was rejecting him, yet he was still busy doing his saving work, and the day was rapidly approaching when the city would see him again. Sadly, even after that great day they still rejected him, because many of the same people who shouted his blessing on Palm Sunday called for his crucifixion on Good Friday.

Alternatively, Jesus may have been speaking about his second coming at the end of history. This is also a common interpretation. On that great day everyone will know that Jesus is the Savior, including many people who rejected him in Jerusalem. Every eye will see him, every knee will bow before him, and every tongue will confess his name as Lord. His second coming will mean salvation for many, but damnation for those who never received Jesus by faith. He invited them to come under his sheltering wing, but they would not, and by the time they finally see Jesus as he truly is, it will be too late. Just as Jerusalem's walls were torn down, its buildings burned, and its people led away in chains, so too everyone who rejects Jesus and his salvation will suffer eternal death under the righteous wrath of God.

However we interpret the end of Luke 13:35, the most important application to make is personal. When will *you* see Jesus? That is to say, when will you know him as he truly is—not the Jesus you might see in some sentimental portrait, but the real Jesus you meet in the Gospels? When will you know the Savior who faithfully did the work of salvation until he finished it to the very death, and who with a heart full of compassion lamented the city he loved? When will you acknowledge him as your Savior and your God?

I pray that Jesus will not have to make the same lament for you that he made for Jerusalem—that he longed to gather you in, but you would not come. Rather, I pray that you will say "Blessed is he who comes in the name of the Lord!" and then find safety in Christ by faith.

61

# The Best Seat in the House

## Luke 14:1–11

*"But when you are invited, go and sit in the lowest place, so that when your host comes he may say to you, 'Friend, move up higher.' Then you will be honored in the presence of all who sit at table with you." (Luke 14:10)*

*I*n order to go higher up, sometimes you first have to go lower down. Ronald Pinkerton experienced this paradoxical phenomenon while hang gliding. Caught up on a powerful air current, Pinkerton rose effortlessly to four thousand feet. Then disaster struck: a sudden downdraft sent his hang glider plummeting down toward the ground. Here is how Pinkerton described his near-death experience:

> I was falling at an alarming rate. Trapped in an airborne riptide, I was going to crash! Then I saw him—a red-tailed hawk. He was six feet off my right wingtip, fighting the same gust I was. . . .
> I looked down: 300 feet from the ground and still falling. The trees below seemed like menacing pikes.

I looked at the hawk again. Suddenly he banked and flew straight downwind. Downwind! If the right air is anywhere, it's upwind! The hawk was committing suicide.

Two hundred feet. From nowhere the thought entered my mind: *Follow the hawk.* It went against everything I knew about flying. But now all my knowledge was useless. I was at the mercy of the wind. I followed the hawk.

One hundred feet. Suddenly the hawk gained altitude. For a split second I seemed to be suspended motionless in space. Then a warm surge of air started pushing the glider upward. I was stunned. Nothing I knew as a pilot could explain this phenomenon. But it was true: I was rising.[1]

This true story provides a physical illustration of a basic spiritual principle of the gospel and the Christian life: in order to rise up to glory, we first have to fall down in humility. In doing this we are following the example of Jesus Christ, who was humiliated before he was exalted.

## It Happened One Sabbath

Jesus taught this gospel paradox while he was sitting down to eat dinner at the house of a Pharisee. But first, as a sort of hors d'oeuvre, he had a miracle to perform: "One Sabbath, when he went to dine at the house of a ruler of the Pharisees, they were watching him carefully. And behold, there was a man before him who had dropsy" (Luke 14:1–2).

It was typical for pious Jews to sit down to the biggest and best meal of the week after worshiping in the synagogue on the Sabbath. It was typical as well for a local leader to invite a visiting teacher like Jesus to come over for dinner. Then too it was typical for Jesus to accept the invitation. He was willing to eat with anybody—even Pharisees—and some of his most important encounters took place over a meal.

It was also typical for the Pharisees to try to catch Jesus saying or doing something wrong. This is what legalists love to do: to trap people in a transgression so they can feel superior about their own spirituality. Here we see Pharisees up to their old tricks. Luke tells us that they were watching Jesus carefully.

1. Ronald Pinkerton, *Guideposts*, quoted in Craig Brian Larson, *750 Engaging Illustrations for Preachers, Teachers, and Writers* (Grand Rapids: Baker, 2002), 337.

Luke also tells us that there was a man there with dropsy. It was not unusual for Jesus to meet someone with a medical condition, and this man's condition was serious. Dropsy, or edema, is characterized by the buildup of excess fluid in the cavities or tissues of the body. The man was swollen by the retention of water, possibly indicating that his organs were failing. This was the first thing Jesus noticed when he went into the Pharisee's house: a man in serious need. It is the first thing Jesus notices about all of us: the needs we have that only he can supply.

In this case, however, the whole situation seems like a setup. Luke has already told us that the Pharisees were lying in wait for Jesus, trying to trap him (see Luke 11:54). Here we are told that they were watching him closely, and—surprise, surprise—as soon as he walked in the door there was a man with dropsy. In all likelihood, the Pharisees were tempting Jesus to break their rules by healing this man on the Sabbath. Apparently the man was not even on the guest list for dinner, because after he was healed, Jesus sent him away (see Luke 14:4). Instead, the man seems to have been planted there because the Pharisees knew that, given half a chance, Jesus would break their man-made regulations for the Sabbath. Then maybe they would be able to report him to the authorities in Jerusalem.

Jesus knew exactly what they were thinking, of course. Luke tells us that he "*responded* to the lawyers and Pharisees" (Luke 14:3). What is striking about this expression is that the Pharisees had not actually *said* anything. Nevertheless, Jesus knew the objection they were raising in their hearts, and by way of response, he put the question back to them: "Is it lawful to heal on the Sabbath, or not?" (Luke 14:3).

Now the tables were turned. The Pharisees had been trying to trap Jesus, but when he asked this question, they were the ones who were trapped. Was it lawful to heal on the Sabbath? They could not say yes, because according to their own religious principles, it was *not* lawful to heal anyone on the Sabbath, except perhaps if it was a matter of life or death. This had been the whole point of trying to get Jesus to heal the man with dropsy. If they now gave him the go-ahead to heal on the Sabbath, they would be contradicting everything they stood for. But the Pharisees could not say no either, because if they told Jesus that he could not heal on the Sabbath, everyone would know how heartless they were.

Trapped by the contradictions of their godless, merciless legalism, there was nothing the Pharisees could say. "They remained silent," Luke says. However, Jesus knew exactly what to do. His mercy demanded deliverance without delay, so he took the man with dropsy "and healed him and sent him away" (Luke 14:4).

Then Jesus made his triumph complete by asking the Pharisees a further question: "And he said to them, 'Which of you, having a son or an ox that has fallen into a well on a Sabbath day, will not immediately pull him out?'" (Luke 14:5). Some translations say "a donkey or an ox," but many scholars believe that "son" is the more accurate reading. Either way, the Pharisees had to admit that Jesus was right. If one of their own children—or even one of their animals—happened to fall into an open cistern, they would never let him drown. Of course not! In that kind of emergency, they would find some way to justify doing whatever they had to do to pull him out. But if they would do all that for one of their animals, then why shouldn't Jesus have mercy on a man with dropsy and heal his disease?

The Pharisees knew that Jesus was right, so they responded with stony silence. "They could not reply to these things" (Luke 14:6), because really there was nothing they could say. Once again, they were ensnared by the inconsistencies in their faulty interpretation of the law of God. Their legalism was preventing them from showing the mercy that God requires.

Unlike the Pharisees, Jesus understood the real purpose of the Sabbath. It was *not* a day for trying to catch people making a moral mistake, or to gain spiritual merit by keeping laws that were even stricter than the law of God. But it *was* a day for worship and rest, and also for showing mercy to people in need. As J. C. Ryle explained it, "The Sabbath was made for man—for his benefit, not for his injury—for his advantage, not for his hurt. The interpretation of God's law respecting the Sabbath was never intended to be strained so far as to interfere with charity, kindness, and the real wants of human nature."[2]

Praise God for the healing mercy of Jesus Christ! Praise him for the complete cure he brings the diseases of the body and the troubles of the soul. Praise him also for the sanity he restored to the Sabbath! In his heal-

---

2. J. C. Ryle, *Expository Thoughts on the Gospels, Luke* (1858; reprint Cambridge: James Clarke, 1976), 2:149.

ing ministry, Jesus did as much good on the Sabbath as any other day of the week, which was fully in keeping with the purposes of the day.

Today Christians celebrate a day of worship and rest on the first day of the week—the day Jesus was raised from the dead. But do we use the Lord's day the way that Jesus used it, as a day for doing mercy? In a column for *Time* magazine, Nancy Gibbs commented, "Over time, Sunday has gone from a day we could do only a very few things to the only day we can do just about anything we want. The U.S. is too diverse, our lives too busy, our economy too global and our appetites too vast to lose a whole day that could be spent working or playing or power shopping."[3] In other words, Sunday has become a day for doing whatever we want, not a day for doing what God wants, or what other people need.

Jesus calls us away from the selfishness and the legalism of our sinful hearts to follow him in loving mercy and doing justice. The Lord's day is for the healthy to show mercy to the sick by visiting them on their beds. It is for fathers to show mercy to their children by putting them at the top of their agenda, for families to show mercy to singles by welcoming them into their homes, and for the wealthy to show mercy to the poor by feeding them bread. It is a day for people who have found Christ to show mercy to people who are still lost by giving them the gospel. The Lord's day is for showing every compassion of Christ to every person in need, just like Jesus.

## Don't Take the Highest Place

The miracle that Jesus performed for the man with dropsy was merely an appetizer for the next thing he did at the dinner party, which was to comment on the seating arrangements. Jesus taught the dinner guests not to take the highest place, but to take the lowest place, and to let God raise them up.

Up until this point, Jesus had been speaking primarily to the Pharisees. But now, as the guests were taking their places, he addressed himself to the dinner party in general: "He told a parable to those who were invited, when he noticed how they chose the places of honor" (Luke 14:7). Jesus was deeply attentive to the spiritual dynamics of any social situation. He

3. Nancy Gibbs, "And on the Seventh Day We Rested?" *Time* (August 2, 2004): 90.

noticed what people did, and why they did it. Earlier he had observed how the Pharisees loved to get the best seat in the synagogues (see Luke 11:43). On this occasion he noticed the way people tried to get the best seat in the house.

This was a major social event: a dinner party hosted by the wealthiest man in town, with a well-known public figure in attendance. In all likelihood, the table was arranged in a U-shaped formation, with the host sitting at the center and the guests sitting on cushions or low couches on either side. The best places were the ones right next to the host, on his right and his left. After that, the best place to sit was as close to the host as one could get.

As Jesus watched the guests gather for dinner, he noticed the subtle and not-so-subtle ways they inched their way closer to the best seats in the house. It is easy to imagine the scene: one man engaging the host in close conversation so as to be right next to him when the call came for dinner; another man sauntering to the head of the table, or casually placing his hand on the low sofa where the host would sit with his most honored guests. They all wanted the best seat in the house. They did it so smoothly that some people might not even notice. But as Jesus watched them make their moves, he could see what they were really doing. He knew that behind their seeming indifference lurked a selfish intention. The close conversation with the host was a social maneuver. The casual hand on the low sofa was a calculated grasp for public recognition.

How proud these men were of their perceived position, and how hard they worked to protect it! Their spiritual problem went much deeper than simply having bad manners. They were enslaved to their selfish ambitions. What mattered most to them was their public reputation, not their private godliness. This is why they were so legalistic. They were all about external obedience, and the sense of pride that goes with it. Kent Hughes comments: "The Pharisees and scribes, despite all their god-talk and religious posturing, were a selfish, self-seeking, ambitious lot. Selfishness always reduces the importance of others and enlarges the importance of one's own life."[4]

People who are full of their own self-importance always insist on having the best seat in the house, and they feel slighted when they do not get it. It

4. R. Kent Hughes, *Luke: That You May Know the Truth*, 2 vols., Preaching the Word (Wheaton, IL: Crossway, 1998), 2:110–11.

happens in the home, where brothers and sisters complain any time they think their siblings are getting a special advantage. It happens in politics, where insiders work their connections to get preferential treatment, and it also happens in business, where workers angle for the next promotion and read books like *How to Get Your Competition Fired.*[5] It happens in the church, where people want their service to receive the full recognition they think it deserves. The same thing happens any time and any place there is a chance to get something better than somebody else, like in the chow line, or at the rummage sale, or on the freeway.

We ourselves are guilty of this sinful pride whenever we step in front of someone who wants the same thing that we want, or secretly rejoice in the downfall of a rival. It is pride when we reflect on our own reputation, or exaggerate our accomplishments, or encourage someone to speak our praise. We are equally guilty of the same sin whenever we fail to get the place we think we deserve, and then resent it.

The scene at the Pharisee's house reminds me of the seating arrangements at the memorial service for the late Dr. James Montgomery Boice, who served for more than thirty years as senior minister of Philadelphia's Tenth Presbyterian Church. The church was full beyond capacity. Anticipating this, we had set up television monitors in other parts of the building, so that people who could not sit in the sanctuary could still be part of the service. We also decided not to give priority seating to special guests, but simply to seat people on a first-come, first-served basis. Afterwards I received an angry letter from a family that came too late to sit in the sanctuary and had to go downstairs. They told me in no uncertain terms that they deserved better treatment and would never worship at our church again!

Jesus teaches us not to seek a place of high position, but to sit somewhere lower down. He said this in the form of a parable: "When you are invited by someone to a wedding feast, do not sit down in a place of honor, lest someone more distinguished than you be invited by him, and he who invited you both will come and say to you, 'Give your place to this person,' and then you will begin with shame to take the lowest place" (Luke 14:8–9).

Do not have too high an opinion of yourself. Do not claim your own honor or take the best seat in the house. Do not work your way into a

---

5. Randy Schwantz, *How to Get Your Competition Fired (without Saying Anything Bad about Them): Using the Wedge to Increase Your Sales* (Hoboken, NJ: John Wiley & Sons, 2005).

more prominent position while pretending not to try, or even to care, because if you take a higher place than you truly deserve, you will end up getting completely humiliated. What Jesus said is similar to something King Solomon said in one of his famous proverbs: "Do not put yourself forward in the king's presence or stand in the place of the great, for it is better to be told, 'Come up here,' than to be put lower in the presence of a noble" (Prov. 25:6–7).

People who demand more recognition than they deserve will never get the honor they crave, but to their shame, they will get put right back into their place. This is an especially good rule to follow in ministry: never push yourself forward for a more prominent position, but let the Lord pull you into the place where he wants you to serve. As Francis Schaeffer argues in his marvelous sermon "No Little People, No Little Places," the Christian "should choose the lesser place until God extrudes him into a position of more responsibility and authority."[6]

## Take the Lowest Place

Instead of taking the highest place, Jesus tells us to sit lower down: "But when you are invited, go and sit in the lowest place, so that when your host comes he may say to you, 'Friend, move up higher.' Then you will be honored in the presence of all who sit at table with you" (Luke 14:10).

I had a similar experience when I attended the installation service for Dr. Jae Sung Kim as senior minister of Philadelphia's historic Korean United Church. The church was packed with well-wishers, and I slipped into the back just as the service was beginning. However, some of the deacons recognized me as the pastor of a sister church and welcomed me as a friend. Before I knew what was happening, someone had pinned a boutonniere to my lapel and ushered me to the front of the church. During the service I was called on to give a short message, and afterwards I was invited to sit down with the church leaders for a banquet. Although I had come to sit in the lowest place, I received unexpected and undeserved honor in front of the entire congregation. They gave me one of the best seats in the house.

6. Francis Schaeffer, "No Little People, No Little Places," *A Christian View of Spirituality*, vol. 3, 2nd ed. (Westchester, IL: Crossway, 1982), 12.

This kind of reversal is one of the deep working principles of God's justice and mercy. Jesus did not teach the parable of the wedding places to improve our etiquette, but to show us the way God works in salvation. To make sure we did not miss the point, he explained what the parable meant: "For everyone who exalts himself will be humbled, and he who humbles himself will be exalted" (Luke 14:11; cf. 1:52; 18:14).

This kingdom principle is not just for wedding receptions and other dinner parties, but for all of life. The world tells us to elevate ourselves, but Jesus says that if we do, God will bring us down. He will humble our pride. We see this in many stories of the Bible, from the fall of Adam to the fall of Jerusalem. We see the same thing throughout human history, as God tears down proud nations and destroys the vain powers of darkness. We see it in society whenever entertainers, or politicians, or businessmen come to public disgrace.

But we will see it most clearly at the end of all days. When Jesus gave this parable about humiliation and exaltation, he was preparing us for the final judgment.

> There is more here than social wisdom. Our Lord was not concerned that his hearers merely learn to take the lower seat so they would avoid embarrassment and then achieve high human honor when they were ostentatiously ushered from the lowest seat to the highest. Neither was he teaching the Pharisees and scribes to put on a staged humility, so they would be greatly honored above their peers. Jesus hated the pride that pretends to be humble. Rather, he was imparting an eternal spiritual principle that will be evident in the end when everything is made right.[7]

For people who exalt themselves—who think they are good enough to stand before God on their own merits—the final judgment will be a total humiliation. People like the Pharisees, who believe in "salvation by recognition,"[8] will not get what *they* think they deserve; they will get what *God* thinks they deserve. Norval Geldenhuys comments: "Just as at a wedding-feast the occupying of seats of honour does not depend on a person's self-assertive attitude but on the discretion of the host, so also a place of honour in the

7. Hughes, *Luke*, 2:112.
8. I am borrowing this evocative phrase from Hughes, *Luke*, 2:111.

kingdom of heaven does not depend on self-assertiveness or on a man's opinion of himself but on the righteous judgment of God."[9]

What righteous judgment will God render upon those who think they deserve his glory? He will disgrace them for their ungodly pride. As Michael Wilcock explains, "To claim God's approval as a right, on the grounds of one's position in the church, or one's reputation in the community, or even one's good opinion of oneself, is a positive disqualification. There is no entry through the narrow door for the one who is laden with status symbols and a sense of his own importance."[10] Augustine had a simpler way of saying it: "There are humble religious, and there are proud religious. The proud ones should not promise themselves the kingdom of God."[11]

No, if there is any place at all for us at the eternal banquet, it is only by the grace of God. The only people who will be exalted at the final judgment are people who humble themselves before God, who know for sure that they are unworthy sinners, and who therefore put their total trust in the mercy of Jesus Christ, on the basis of his death on the cross. To go up to glory, we first have to go down in humility. Peter said, "God opposes the proud but gives grace to the humble. Humble yourselves, therefore, under the mighty hand of God so that at the proper time he may exalt you" (1 Peter 5:5–6). What better time to be exalted than at the final judgment, when Christ comes into his kingdom? There may be times when God exalts the humble in this life, but he is certain to exalt them in the life to come, lifting them up to the glory of God. If you refuse to claim that you deserve something from God, but recognize that you do not deserve anything at all without Christ, God will raise you up to eternal life.

In the meantime, make humility your way of life, the governing principle of your ministry or your mission work. Give yourself to others in humble service, honoring them above yourself. For the Christian, this kind of humility ought to be our ambition. J. C. Ryle said, "The man who really knows himself and his own heart—who knows God and His infinite majesty and holiness—who knows Christ, and the price at which he

9. Norval Geldenhuys, *The Gospel of Luke*, New International Commentary on the New Testament (Grand Rapids: Eerdmans, 1951), 389–90.

10. Michael Wilcock, *The Message of Luke*, The Bible Speaks Today (Downers Grove, IL: InterVarsity, 1979), 145.

11. Augustine, "Sermon 354.8," in *Luke*, ed. Arthur A. Just, Jr., Ancient Christian Commentary on Scripture, NT 3 (Downers Grove, IL: InterVarsity, 2003), 236.

was redeemed—that man will never be a proud man."[12] If we truly know the grace that God has for us in Christ—the death he died on the cross to save us from our sins—then we know we have nothing to be proud of. This makes us content to take the lowest place, not out of false humility, or as a subtle strategy for self-advancement, but out of true love and honor for Christ. As far as Jesus is concerned, the lowest place *is* the best seat in the house.

Years ago I saw this kind of humility in action at a family wedding in New York City. There had been a mix-up with the caterer, or perhaps there were a bunch of gate-crashers, but in any case, there were not enough places for the dinner guests. One of my wife's cousins knew just what to do. Quickly she organized members of the family to set up makeshift tables in an out-of-the-way corner. As close members of the bride's own family, they deserved a better place. But because they considered others better than themselves, they cheerfully sat down to make the best of things, sharing as much joy as anyone has ever had at a wedding.

## LOWER DOWN, HIGHER UP

Where do we learn to live and to love with this kind of humility? We learn it from the Son of God, who took the very lowest place that anyone has ever taken, and as a result, is now exalted to the highest place in the universe. This is the great parabola of redemption that the apostle Paul traces in Philippians 2. Jesus Christ is very God of very God. Nevertheless, he did not "count equality with God a thing to be grasped, but made himself nothing, taking the form of a servant, being born in the likeness of men" (Phil. 2:6–7). This in itself was an extreme humiliation, when God the Son set aside the prerogatives of his deity to share in our humanity. But Jesus went lower still, "and being found in human form, he humbled himself by becoming obedient to the point of death, even death on a cross" (Phil. 2:7–8). So complete was his humility that he was willing to die the most ignominious of all deaths: the painful and shameful death of the cross.

As a direct result of his dying humility, we receive the forgiveness of our sins. But that is not all. Jesus himself receives something: he receives glory

12. Ryle, *Luke*, 2:153.

for his humility. Having followed his downward descent to the humiliation of the cross, we must also trace the ascending arc of his exaltation. Jesus humbled himself unto death. "Therefore," the Scripture goes on to say, "God has highly exalted him and bestowed on him the name that is above every name, so that at the name of Jesus every knee should bow, in heaven and on earth and under the earth, and every tongue confess that Jesus Christ is Lord, to the glory of God the Father" (Phil. 2:9–11). Jesus went from the lowest place on earth to the highest place in heaven. Humiliated in his death, he was exalted in his resurrection. Therefore, his saving work is the ultimate proof of his own claim that "he who humbles himself will be exalted" (Luke 14:11).

To go higher up, first you have to go lower down. One day everyone who believes in Jesus Christ—everyone who humbly trusts in his crucifixion and resurrection—will be lifted up to his glory. What joy will be ours when God elevates us to a place infinitely higher than we deserve, and infinitely more glorious than we can even imagine!

I experienced a small measure of that joy when I took my own seat at Dr. Boice's memorial service. Seven men were on the platform to lead worship that day—all of them my elders and superiors, including great Christian leaders like the Reverend Eric Alexander, Dr. C. Everett Koop, and Dr. R. C. Sproul. There were seven men, but only three chairs, as well as some less prominent and less comfortable seating at the back of the platform. Since I was opening the service, I was in charge of handing out the seating assignments. Needless to say, I took a back seat to the others. Yet to the credit of their humility, those worthy men insisted that I should sit up front. As they invited me to take the best seat in the house, they said essentially what the host said in the parable of the wedding places: "Friend, move up higher."

What joy it was to be elevated by men I love and honor. But how much greater my joy will be when I am elevated by the worthiest of all men—the God-man who humbled himself for my exaltation—the Lord Jesus Christ. And how great your joy will be, as a believer in Christ, when Jesus invites you to sit down with him in glory and says, "Friend, move up higher."

# 62

# AN OPEN INVITATION

## *Luke 14:12–24*

*"And the master said to the servant, 'Go out to the highways
and hedges and compel people to come in, that my house may
be filled. For I tell you, none of those men who were invited shall
taste my banquet.'"* (Luke 14:23–24)

Near the end of *The Last Battle*, which is the last of C. S. Lewis's seven Chronicles of Narnia, the great lion king Aslan spreads a sumptuous feast before a group of grumpy old dwarfs. But the dwarfs do not believe in Aslan, and therefore they are suspicious of anything he tries to do for them—so suspicious that they neither see nor taste his royal food. Here is how Lewis describes the scene:

> Aslan raised his head and shook his mane. Instantly a glorious feast appeared on the Dwarfs' knees: pies and pigeons and trifles and ices, and each Dwarf had a goblet of good wine in his right hand. But it wasn't much use. They began eating and drinking greedily enough, but it was clear that they couldn't taste it properly. They thought they were eating and drinking only the sort of things you might find in a Stable. One said he was trying to eat hay and another said he had got a bit of an old turnip and a third said he'd found a

raw cabbage leaf. And they raised golden goblets of rich red wine to their lips and said "Ugh! Fancy drinking dirty water out of a trough that a donkey's been at! Never thought we'd come to this."[1]

When the dwarfs had finished their miserable meal, they congratulated themselves for refusing the king's royal banquet. This episode has strong biblical overtones, because in his Word God has promised to give his people a feast. This feast is only for those who receive it by faith, however, and like those foolish dwarfs, many people refuse to enjoy God's invitation to dinner.

## God's Guest List

Jesus taught about God's banquet while he was at a Pharisee's house one Sabbath for dinner. The dinner party began when Jesus walked in the door and healed a man's disease. Then, as the guests scrambled to claim the best seats in the house, Jesus told them a parable about taking the lowest place instead of the highest place. According to the saving principles of God's justice and mercy, people who exalt themselves will be humbled, while people who humble themselves for Christ will be exalted.

The parable was mainly for the invited guests, but Jesus also had something important to say to their host: "When you give a dinner or a banquet, do not invite your friends or your brothers or your relatives or rich neighbors, lest they also invite you in return and you be repaid. But when you give a feast, invite the poor, the crippled, the lame, the blind, and you will be blessed, because they cannot repay you. You will be repaid at the resurrection of the just" (Luke 14:12–14).

Earlier Jesus had told people where to sit and where not to sit. Now he was telling them whom to invite, or not to invite, and he was putting it in the strongest possible terms. When you are having a dinner party, he said, do not invite your friends only, or your family members, or the richest family in town, because those people will probably return the invitation. The only selfless way to serve is to invite a guest who has nothing to offer except his need.

Obviously Jesus was exaggerating to make a point. He loved his family and often ate with his friends. Such relationships need to be nurtured. Thus

---

1. C. S. Lewis, *The Last Battle* (London: Bodley Head, 1956), 149–50.

there is a place in the Christian community for reciprocal hospitality, which the command of Christ does not rule out (e.g., Job 1:13; Acts 2:44–45). But for many people this is as far as hospitality ever goes. So Jesus put all of his emphasis on inviting people who are in no position to invite us back. Do not invite your friends only, he was saying, but also invite people who are down and out.

Jesus was distinguishing here between charity, which is a selfless act of love, and mere civility, which is a lesser virtue because it is more in our self-interest. Civility has its place in life, but we should not make the mistake of thinking that we are being charitable when in fact we are only being civil. We should also be careful not to let our civility get in the way of true Christian charity.

How easy it is to help people who will help us in return, and how hard it is to help people who will be nothing but trouble. If we are honest, we have to admit that many of our relationships are based on quid pro quo, which is a fancy way of saying, "If you scratch my back, I'll scratch yours." If you invite me over for dinner, then I will invite you; if you watch my kids for a while, then I will watch yours; and so forth. There is nothing wrong with this kind of mutual assistance, but there is too much self-interest involved for it to be a full demonstration of the mercy of God.

Often we look less like Jesus and more like the character Templeton in the movie *Charlotte's Web*. Templeton was a clever rat, and the other animals in the barnyard sometimes required his services, but he never did anything for anyone else unless it was also in his own self-interest. "What's in it for me, Charlotte?" he would say whenever he was asked to do something.

In order for our lives to show the love of Christ, we need to go beyond doing good to people who do good to us, which may simply be another way of loving ourselves. Instead, we need to give without any thought for what we might get in return. One good way to do this is to expand the guest list for our ministry and hospitality. Jesus tells us to serve people who are living in poverty or suffering from a disability. This means recognizing their dignity as people made in the image of God and caring for their practical needs. It means enabling them to participate in public life. It means developing meaningful relationships with people outside our community and welcoming awkward or difficult people into our fellowship. It also means doing all of this for people who do not seem to have anything to give us in return.

This is a serious issue for self-examination. When was the last time you did something for someone who was not in any position to do something for you? What are you doing to help the people who are disabled? How much are you giving to the poor? J. C. Ryle said, "The Lord Jesus would have us care for our poorer brethren, and help them according to our power. He would have us know that it is a solemn duty never to neglect the poor, but to aid them, and relieve them in their time of need."[2]

Jesus would have us do this because he wants us to have his heart for people in need—the same heart he had for us when he gave his life for our sins. The guest list he gives us—the poor, the crippled, the blind, and the lame—is the guest list of his own grace. These are the very people Jesus came to save.

If we receive them as our guests in Jesus' name, then we will have God's blessing. These people may not be able to repay us for what we give them, but God can repay us. He will repay us at the resurrection, which Jesus calls "the resurrection of the just" because only the just will receive any happy reward.

What an encouragement this promise is to Christians who give their lives in sacrificial service—who work in the world's ghettoes, or welcome street children into their homes, or do relief work in places where people are hostile to the gospel. Even if their service does not receive any recognition from the people they serve, God will not let their work go unrewarded. They will receive full recompense at the resurrection.

## THE GREAT BANQUET

By this point in the meal, Jesus had offended just about everyone at the table: the Pharisees by healing a man on the Sabbath, the invited guests by telling them not to take the best seats in the house, and the host by criticizing his guest list. Who else was left for him to offend?

Socially, this must have been a very awkward situation. Yet one man tried to salvage the dinner party by taking what Jesus had just said about the resurrection and making a spiritual comment that everyone should agree

2. J. C. Ryle, *Expository Thoughts on the Gospels, Luke* (1858; reprint Cambridge: James Clarke, 1976), 2:154.

with (or so he thought): "When one of those who reclined at table with him heard these things, he said to him, 'Blessed is everyone who will eat bread in the kingdom of God!'" (Luke 14:15).

This statement was true, as far as it went. According to one of the great salvation promises of the Old Testament, the King of kings is preparing an eternal banquet for his people (see Isa. 25:6–9). What a blessing it will be to sit down at that great feast! However, the man who uttered this pious sentiment was making a potentially dangerous assumption. In his self-satisfaction, he assumed that he would be there for that great feast, along with all the other respectable religious people who deserve a place at God's table. The man also assumed that Jesus would agree with what he had said, confirming God's blessing.

Many people make the same assumption today. They like to talk about heaven; they are confident that they deserve to go to that better place; and they assume that Jesus agrees with their assessment of their spiritual condition. Yet not everyone who talks about heaven is going there. On the contrary, as Jesus went on to explain in his parable of the great banquet, the only people who will ever sit down at God's table are those who respond to his invitation by faith.

There are five main parts to this parable: a gracious invitation (Luke 14:16–17), a rude rejection (Luke 14:18–20), a wider invitation (Luke 14:21), a compelling exhortation (Luke 14:22–23), and a final caution (Luke 14:24). The parable begins with a *gracious invitation*: "A man once gave a great banquet and invited many. And at the time for the banquet he sent his servant to say to those who had been invited, 'Come, for everything is now ready'" (Luke 14:16–17).

According to custom, a wealthy man hosting a banquet would have issued two invitations. The first invitation is the one mentioned in verse 16; it came a day or two before the great event. To say yes to this invitation was to make a firm commitment to attend, because once the host knew how many people were coming, he would start killing as many animals as he needed to feed meat to his hungry guests. Then, when everything was finally ready, a servant was sent to tell everyone that the time had come. Hosts and hostesses sometimes do the same thing today, mailing an invitation in advance, and then sending an e-mail or making a phone call as a reminder. But in a culture that was somewhat less concerned with clocks and calendars, there was always a second invitation, which guests were duty-bound to obey.

This parable was really about God's plan of salvation and the coming of Christ. As we have seen, the banquet was an ancient symbol of salvation. God wants to have fellowship with his people and to satisfy them with good things. So in the parable, the man hosting the banquet represents God, and the banquet represents his kingdom—the greatest feast that any king has ever set before any guest.

God first gave a free and gracious invitation to come to his banquet in the promises of the Old Testament. The "many" whom God invited (see Luke 14:16) were primarily the people of Israel. Now it was time for them to receive their second invitation. Therefore, Jesus was announcing that the kingdom had come. He himself was the servant sent to tell Israel that God's banquet was ready. He was the Messiah, the Son of God, the Savior. Soon he would finish the work of salvation by dying on the cross for sinners and rising again from the dead. The time for the banquet had finally arrived, so in his teaching ministry Jesus offered this gracious invitation: "Come, for everything is ready!"

Anyone who has ever attended a feast—like a wedding reception, perhaps, or an anniversary dinner, or an honors banquet—knows how wonderful it is to be invited. It is even more wonderful to hear the happy news that dinner is served! This is what Jesus was announcing to the people of God. Everything we need for salvation is ready because God has prepared it all for us in Christ: forgiveness through the cross, and life through the empty tomb. We have been invited to God's invitation-only banquet, so all we need to do now is come. The complete readiness of the feast is a strong inducement for us to come without delay. J. C. Ryle comments: "There is nothing wanting on God's part for the salvation of man. If man is not saved, the fault is not on God's side. The Father is ready to receive all who come to Him by Christ. The Son is ready to cleanse all from their sins who apply to Him by faith. The Spirit is ready to come to all who ask for Him. There is an infinite willingness in God to save man, if man is only willing to be saved."[3]

Are *you* willing to be saved? God has given you a gracious invitation. He wants you to come. Everything is ready for you in Christ. But you need

3. Ryle, *Luke*, 2:160–61.

to do something more than just talk about how nice it would be to go to heaven; you need to respond to God in faith. To be saved is to say yes to God's gracious invitation in Jesus Christ.

## EXCUSES, EXCUSES

Tragically, many people who get invited never come, including some who said that they would come. This is the second part of the parable: a *rude rejection*. When the servant came with a second invitation to dinner, the guests were obligated to come without delay: "But they all alike began to make excuses. The first said to him, 'I have bought a field, and I must go out and see it. Please have me excused.' And another said, 'I have bought five yoke of oxen, and I go to examine them. Please have me excused.' And another said, 'I have married a wife, and therefore I cannot come'" (Luke 14:18–20).

These people had all made their RSVP, but then they were no-shows. Each of them offered some kind of excuse. In fact, Leon Morris calls this "The Parable of Excuses."[4] The first excuse was horticultural, the second was agricultural, and the third was matrimonial—but they were all equally absurd. Who would ever wait to inspect his new property until *after* he had purchased it? Certainly no one in the Middle East, where land transactions could take years, and where every foot of land was carefully described in the agreement of sale.[5] The same thing could be said about the oxen. No one who had any idea how to farm would even think of buying five pairs of oxen without seeing if they could pull together as a team. Kenneth Bailey compares this to buying five used cars sight unseen, without knowing the make or the model, and without knowing whether they would even start.[6] Besides, if the man wanted to test the oxen they would still be there when the banquet was over. As for this newlywed—who did not even have the decency to ask to be excused—why not bring his bride to the banquet and dance the night away?

4. Leon Morris, *The Gospel According to St. Luke: An Introduction and Commentary*, Tyndale New Testament Commentaries (Grand Rapids: Eerdmans, 1974), 233.

5. Kenneth E. Bailey, *Through Peasant Eyes* (Grand Rapids: Eerdmans, 1980), 95–96.

6. Ibid., 98.

These bad excuses (from people, it should be remembered, who had already accepted the master's invitation) remind me of a song my sixth-grade class in grammar school used to sing—a simple chorus based on this parable:

> I cannot come to the banquet, don't trouble me now;
> I have married a wife; I have bought me a cow.
> I have fields and dominions that cost a tidy sum;
> Don't trouble me now—I cannot come.

To our music teacher's consternation, some of the boys in the back row sang a slightly different version, in which the second line went like this: "I have bought me a wife; I have married a cow." But really, this was only slightly more absurd than the original parable, with its own outrageous excuses.

These people simply did not want to come to the banquet. There is no other explanation for what they did. They were busy pursuing their own interests and thought they had something better to do. The first two men were wealthy enough to buy entire fields or teams of oxen, and thus it was their wealth that kept them from coming. The last man was so inwardly focused on his family that he refused to go out and celebrate with the wider community. In the words of Cyril of Alexandria, these men "scorned a surpassing invitation, because they had turned aside to earthly things and focused their mind on the vain distractions of this world."[7]

Each invited guest had a different excuse, but on this they were all agreed: they would not come to the banquet (cf. Luke 13:34). In the culture of Jesus' day, such a deliberate refusal was unthinkably rude. No one ever rejected a second invitation. To accept a first invitation and then fail to come to a party was an unconscionable and probably intentional insult. It could only mean that the invited guests had the utmost disdain for their would-be host. In fact, in some parts of the Middle East such a rude refusal virtually amounted to a declaration of war.[8]

---

7. Cyril of Alexandria, "Commentary on Luke," in *Luke*, ed. Arthur A. Just, Jr., Ancient Christian Commentary on Scripture, NT 3 (Downers Grove, IL: InterVarsity, 2003), 239.

8. Simon J. Kistemaker, *The Parables: Understanding the Stories Jesus Told*, 2nd ed. (Grand Rapids: Baker, 2002), 164.

Jesus was saying that this was exactly what Israel's religious leaders were doing to him. They had received God's first invitation in the promises of the Old Testament, so they were committed to come. But when God's servant summoned them to the great banquet, they deliberately insulted him by refusing to come by faith.

Many people treat Jesus the same way today. They have been invited to receive the free gift of eternal life by trusting in his cross and the empty tomb, yet they will not come. Some of them say that they will, but they never do. They offer the same lame excuses that people made in the parable. God is not as important to them as their own interests. They are too busy pursuing their earthly entertainments. They are tied up with their commitments at work. They have family and friends that pull them away from church. They say they do not have time for God, at least not right now. But whatever excuses they come up with, the real reason for their rude rejection is that they simply will not come to Christ.

Have you come to the banquet by putting your faith in Jesus Christ? Perhaps you are in the church already. Maybe you grew up in the church as a covenant child. But have you come to Jesus for salvation? If not, then what is your excuse? People always have some reason or another for staying away from Jesus. But what business could possibly be more important than making sure that you have eternal life? What property could be more valuable to have than a title to heaven? And what relationship could ever be more important than the one you can have with the God who made you and sent his Son to die for your sins? If all you have to offer God are excuses, they will sound all too flimsy at the final judgment, when the only people who sit down at God's great banquet are the people who actually came to Christ.

## THE OUTCASTS INVITED IN

When none of his guests showed up for dinner, the host was extremely angry, and rightly so. Yet in the righteousness of his wrath he also remembered to show mercy: "The servant came and reported these things to his master. Then the master of the house became angry and said to his servant, 'Go out quickly to the streets and lanes of the city, and bring in the poor and crippled and blind and lame'" (Luke 14:21–22).

83

Here was a *wider invitation*. The master's hospitality had been spurned, but he still had a feast to give away, so he opened his doors to the outcasts in his community. If all his wealthy guests refused to come, well then, he would scour the city streets for anyone who wanted a free meal—anyone who was willing to accept his hospitality. He expanded his guest list to include the poor, the crippled, the blind, and the lame. In other words, he invited exactly the kinds of people that Jesus had been talking about earlier: people who would never have the resources to return his invitation.

This wider invitation was a rebuke to the Pharisees and Israel's other religious leaders. They were the invited guests, the men who had received God's initial invitation in the Old Testament. But when Jesus came and summoned them to salvation, they refused to come. So now Jesus was taking the gospel out to all the lost sinners of Israel, including the homeless unbelievers that the Pharisees were too proud to have over for dinner. God's invitation to salvation was not just for religious insiders; it was also for poor, broken-down sinners who had never been religious at all. Unless the religious people came to Christ, they would never be saved. Here is how Kenneth Bailey summarizes the meaning of the parable of the great supper:

> God's Messiah is here. He is inviting you to the messianic banquet of the day of salvation. The banquet is now ready. Do not refuse! For if you do (with your ridiculous excuses) others will fill your places from among the outcasts of Israel, and (in the future) an invitation will go out to the gentiles. The banquet will proceed without you. It will not be cancelled or postponed. The eschatological age has dawned. Respond to the invitation or opt out of participation in God's salvation.[9]

At the same time that the Pharisees were in danger of being excluded, many others would be invited into God's kingdom: poor, blind, and crippled sinners. Who would invite such outcasts in for dinner? Only a God of mercy and grace. Under Old Testament law the physically disabled were barred from participating as priests in the temple worship of Israel (Lev. 21:17–23), and people like the Pharisees used this law to justify their prejudice against people with disabilities. But according to Jesus, disability is no disbarment from the kingdom of God. The lame, the crippled, the deaf, the dumb, and the blind

9. Bailey, *Through Peasant Eyes*, 111.

84

are all invited to sit at his table. How glad they are to come! Charles Spurgeon imagined one of the unlikely guests to God's banquet saying, "I can hardly believe that I am really in a palace dining with a king. . . . Long live the king, say I, and blessings on the prince and his bride!"[10]

The extravagant love that Jesus has for people with disabilities can be illustrated from a documentary film about quadriplegics who play full-contact wheelchair rugby. *Murderball* tells the story of players who overcome extreme personal obstacles to compete in the 2004 Paralympic Games in Athens, Greece. One of the most dramatic moments in the film comes when one of the teams loses its chance to win a gold medal. As they come off the court, the disappointment shows on their faces. They have struggled so hard and come so close, only to go down to bitter defeat. Then one man's father comes over to comfort one of the players, and with tears streaming down his face, he says, "You're the best son a dad could ever have!"

This is the love that our Father has for all his children in Christ. Impoverished by sin, broken by pain, and disabled by all our troubles in a fallen world, we are called to come to the banquet of God, where Jesus welcomes us by his grace and satisfies us with his love.

## Going Out and Coming In

But that is not all. The invitation goes wider, because there is still more room at God's table, and even more people that Jesus is calling to save. First the master invited his friends to dinner. When they rudely refused to come, he sent his servant out to invite people in off the streets. Even after that, he still had plenty of empty seats at his table. So his servant came and said, "Sir, what you commanded has been done, and still there is room" (Luke 14:22). To which the master replied with this *compelling exhortation*: "Go out to the highways and hedges and compel people to come in, that my house may be filled" (Luke 14:23).

This time the servant would go outside the city to the surrounding roadsides. There he would give his master's gracious invitation to anyone he could find, including whatever dubious characters might be lurking in the highways and byways. It would take some doing to get them to come to dinner. Presumably these people did not know the master. According to the

10. Charles H. Spurgeon, quoted in Richard D. Phillips, *Turning Your World Upside Down: Kingdom Priorities in the Parables of Jesus* (Phillipsburg, NJ: P&R, 2003), 106.

social conventions of the Middle East, strangers like this were expected to refuse the master's invitation, especially if they belonged to a lower social class. Here is how Kenneth Bailey describes the situation:

> A stranger from outside the city is suddenly invited to a great banquet. He is not a relative or even a citizen of the host's city. The offer is generous and delightful but (thinks the stranger) *he cannot possibly mean it.* After some discussion the servant will finally have to take the startled guest by the arm and gently pull him along. There is no other way to convince him that he is really invited to the great banquet, irrespective of his being a foreigner. Grace is *unbelievable!* How could it be true?[11]

If the servant was going to get these people to the banquet, he was going to have to persuade them by any means possible. Hence the urgency of his master's command: "Go out and compel people to come in."

This parable proves that God wants his house to be full for dinner. It also shows that his invitation is not just for the Jewish leaders, or for the Jewish people in general, but also for the Gentile nations of the world (cf. Rom. 1:16). The banquet of his salvation has been set for all peoples. It would be hard for many people to believe, but it was true: God was welcoming everyone, even people who had never had any connection with him before at all.

Notice that this command does not actually get carried out in the parable. The master tells his servant to go out, but we do not know for certain whether he obeys. We assume that he does, but Jesus does not say this, perhaps for an important reason: because it was not yet time for the gospel to go out into the wider world.[12] That job was for the apostles, and for us. Jesus came to preach in Israel, and it was only later that he sent his people out to preach the gospel to the nations. This is our Great Commission: to go into all the world and preach the gospel—or, as Jesus put it in the parable of the great supper, to go out to the highways and byways and compel people to come in.

Are you going out into the world with the gospel? People are dying outside of Christ, and we must go and invite them to come in. Answer God's call to missions and evangelism. Share the gospel on whatever highways

11. Bailey, *Through Peasant Eyes*, 108.
12. Ibid., 101.

you travel. Take advantage of the spiritual opportunities you have in the byways of your own community. By your words and witness, compel people to come in. Deal earnestly with people about their spiritual situation until they come to Christ. People need to be persuaded; otherwise, they will not come to Christ. There is no question here of coercion, but only the sweet compulsion of a heart that is persuaded of gospel truth and therefore is persuasive in the way it shares the truth of the gospel.

Our Lord has such a heart for lost outcasts that he will not stop issuing his wide and gracious invitation until his banqueting house is full. He knows that sinners are still outside and will not come in unless they are invited by one of the master's servants. Therefore, he has sent his ministers to preach the gospel and his people to live the gospel by faith. "We are ambassadors for Christ," wrote the apostle Paul, "God making his appeal through us. We implore you on behalf of Christ, be reconciled to God" (2 Cor. 5:20).

What an encouragement this invitation is for people who have not yet received the free gift of eternal life! There is still room for you at God's table, if only you will come to Christ. When the Scottish theologian Thomas Boston preached on this parable he said, "This is a comfortable word for those who have not yet complied with the invitations of the gospel; the doors are not yet shut, and such sinners may yet have access to Christ."[13]

Yet we cannot give this comforting word without also giving the same *final word of caution* that Jesus gave at the end of his parable: "I tell you, none of those men who were invited shall taste my banquet" (Luke 14:24). This verse makes a significant grammatical shift to bring the parable to a dramatic conclusion. Right at the end Jesus speaks in the first person, making it clear that the banquet is *his* banquet. Jesus is the host of the great supper and the master of all its invitations. Here he says very plainly that people like the Pharisees, who refuse to come to him by faith, will never taste his salvation.

Heed his warning! The Savior is here. His banquet is ready. There is still room at his table. But if we are so foolish as to refuse his open invitation—no matter what excuse we make—it is not just dinner that we will miss, but our very salvation. Do not miss out on what Jesus wants to give you, but come when you are called!

13. Thomas Boston, *The Complete Works of the Late Rev. Thomas Boston, Ettrick*, ed. Samuel M'Millan, 12 vols. (London, 1853; reprint Wheaton, IL: Richard Owen Roberts, 1980), 3:260.

# 63

# THE CRUCIFORM LIFE

## *Luke 14:25—35*

*"If anyone comes to me and does not hate his own father and
mother and wife and children and brothers and sisters, yes, and
even his own life, he cannot be my disciple. Whoever does not
bear his own cross and come after me cannot be my disciple."*
(Luke 14:26–27)

ollowing the success of the 1997 Mars Pathfinder Lander,
the National Aeronautics and Space Administration (NASA)
planned a series of scientific missions to the planet Mars.
Intending to launch at least one new mission every two years, their motto
was "Faster. Better. Cheaper." Things did not go quite the way that NASA
planned, however. In December of 1999 the Mars Polar Lander failed to
slow its descent and slammed into the surface of the Red Planet, smash-
ing into thousands of pieces.

Later it was determined that a design flaw in the 165 million dollar
spacecraft had caused the braking system to shut off too soon. According to
the engineers, this was a flaw that could have been detected and prevented if
only they had run the right simulation on their computers. Why, then, did
they fail to run the right simulation? Because NASA was trying to cut costs

and decided not to purchase the necessary software.[1] They may have done it cheaper, but they did not do it better. The Mars Lander crashed because the administration failed to count the cost for completing the mission.

This is a mistake Jesus wants to be sure that all of his disciples are careful to avoid. Therefore, he tells us in advance how much it will cost us to follow him to the very end. Even before we come to faith in Christ, he calls us to count the true cost of Christian discipleship, which demands us to love him more than anything else in the world and to carry the cross of our own sacrificial love.

## "HATING" YOUR FAMILY

Never was this accounting more important than when Jesus was rising to the height of his popularity. Luke tells us that "great crowds accompanied him" (Luke 14:25). Some of these multitudes wanted to see more of his miracles or hear more of his teaching, but many of them were just following the crowd. The atmosphere was electric, and people wanted to get in on the excitement. Jesus was there to do something more than make people curious, however: he was calling them to make a commitment.[2] So Jesus turned around and told his followers—three times—that unless they met his strict criteria, they could never be his disciples. If people wanted to follow him, they had to hate their families (Luke 14:26), carry their crosses (Luke 14:27), and count the cost (Luke 14:28–33).

Jesus had given many generous invitations to come into his kingdom, but now he was making sure people knew how much it would cost them to enter: "If anyone comes to me and does not hate his own father and mother and wife and children and brothers and sisters, yes, and even his own life, he cannot be my disciple" (Luke 14:26). Telling people to hate what they love is hardly the way to become more popular, and Jesus knew this demand would have exactly the opposite effect. Rather than increasing the number of his followers, such a confrontational statement would cause many of them to walk away. But Jesus was not looking for spectators; he was

1. The story of the Mars Polar Lander is adapted from Blake Shipp, "Counting the Cost," in *Perfect Illustrations for Every Topic and Occasion* (Wheaton, IL: Tyndale, 2002), 52.

2. Michael Wilcock, *The Message of Luke*, The Bible Speaks Today (Downers Grove, IL: InterVarsity, 1979), 147.

calling for recruits,[3] and he knew that the only disciples who would go the distance with him were the ones who had counted the cost.

What Jesus said about hating our families is hard to accept and often has been misunderstood. In his infamous diatribe against biblical Christianity, Joseph-Ernest Renan complained that here Jesus was "trampling under foot everything that is human—blood and love and country . . . despising the healthy limits of man's nature . . . abolishing all natural ties."[4] Is that really what Jesus was doing?

We should not understand what Jesus said about hating our families and even our very own lives in any way that contradicts the rest of the teaching of Scripture. It cannot contradict the fifth commandment, which tells us to honor our fathers and mothers (Ex. 20:12)—a commandment that Jesus himself defended against the impieties of the Pharisees (Mark 7:9–13). Nor can it contradict Christ's own command to love as he loved us (John 13:34), to love our neighbor as ourselves (Matt. 22:39), and even to love our enemies (Luke 6:27). More than anyone else, Jesus taught us to love.

So what *does* Jesus mean when he tells us to hate our families? According to Scottish theologian Thomas Boston, he means that "no man can be a true disciple of Christ, to whom Christ is not dearer than what is dearest to him in the world."[5] Here it is important to understand that the Bible sometimes uses the absolute language of hatred to express a comparative degree of affection. A notable example comes from the book of Genesis, where Jacob is said to have "loved Rachel more than Leah" (Gen. 29:30). Yet in the very next verse the Scripture says that "Leah was hated" (Gen. 29:31). To "hate" in this sense is to have a preferential affection. It is to love one thing more than another, so that if it comes down to a choice, there is no doubt as to which affection we will choose (cf. Matt. 6:24). To hate is "to give second place to, and if need be to let go, all else."[6]

Love for Christ is the true disciple's only ultimate loyalty. Here Jesus takes our dearest affections and says that he must mean more to us than

3. G. B. Caird, *Saint Luke*, Pelican Gospel Commentaries (London: Pelican, 1963), 178.

4. Joseph-Ernest Renan, *The Life of Jesus*, quoted in R. Kent Hughes, *Luke: That You May Know the Truth*, 2 vols., Preaching the Word (Wheaton, IL: Crossway, 1998), 2:125.

5. Thomas Boston, *The Complete Works of the Late Rev. Thomas Boston, Ettrick*, ed. Samuel M'Millan, 12 vols. (London, 1853; reprint Wheaton, IL: Richard Owen Roberts, 1980), 9:370.

6. David Gooding, *According to Luke: A New Exposition of the Third Gospel* (Grand Rapids: Eerdmans, 1987), 268.

anything else in the world. He must mean more to us than our daily work, however much time we give to it; more than our pleasures, however much we enjoy them; and more than life itself, however dearly we hold it.

Jesus must also mean more to us than our own families, however much we love them. There are times when our love for our families can get in the way of our love for Jesus Christ. It does this when we let our parents discourage us from making a more complete commitment to Christ. It does this when a marriage turns inward instead of outward to serve others out of the strength of a godly partnership, or when we have an idolatrous attachment to our children and their activities, with little time left over to show mercy or share the gospel.

Jesus is not telling us to neglect the responsibility we have to care for our families (any more than he is telling us to loathe our own existence). Even when we "hate" our families in the biblical sense, we still have to love them. But Jesus *is* telling us not to let the claims that our families make on us interfere with the claims that he makes on us. Many temptations come with focusing on our family, and our love for Jesus must take precedence over everything else—even life itself.

For some Christians this will mean going against the family religion to be baptized as a believer in Jesus Christ, even if they are disowned. This is a trial new Christians face in many hard places of the world. For some it will merely mean resisting the subtle pressure to pursue worldly success. But whenever we face a choice between doing what our families want (or what we want) and what Jesus wants, our supreme affection must be for Christ alone. It is really only then that we are able to love our families in the right and best way—not for ourselves and our own benefit, but for God and his glory.

A true disciple "hates" his family, loving Jesus more than anything else he loves in this world. Unless Jesus is our highest affection, we cannot be his disciples.

## CARRYING OUR CROSS

To show how serious he was about hating our very lives, Jesus gave a second criterion for true Christian discipleship: "Whoever does not bear his own cross and come after me cannot be my disciple" (Luke 14:27). To follow Jesus is to carry our cross.

What did cross-bearing mean to the first disciples? Even before Jesus was crucified, they would have recognized the cross as a symbol of rejection, humiliation, and excruciating pain. Crucifixion was the most gruesome form of execution in the Roman world, a death penalty reserved for traitors, criminals, and slaves. To see a man carrying his cross was to see a man going to die the worst of all possible deaths.

The disciples knew this, but they did not yet understand that Jesus was going to die this kind of death. He had been trying to tell them, of course. He had told them that he would suffer many things, and that he would be rejected and killed (Luke 9:22; cf. 9:44). He had also told them that if they wanted to follow him, they would have to carry their crosses every day, laying their lives down for him (Luke 9:23–24). Jesus himself was walking in the way of the cross, and anyone who wanted to follow him would have to walk that way too, suffering for him. This was especially true for the first disciples, who suffered when Jesus died, and in most cases later died a suffering death for his sake.

Yet cross-bearing is for any and every disciple. This is the way we live and die for Jesus because it is the way that he lived and died for us. The very image of cross-bearing reminds us that we have given up any claim to our own lives, and are now prepared to face any kind of suffering, up to and including martyrdom. In the words of David Gooding, "A man carrying his own cross along the street of some ancient city was normally a condemned criminal or a defeated rebel sentenced to death, deprived of all rights and possessions, and on his way to execution. Everyone who claims forgiveness because Christ died as his substitute, thereby confesses himself as a sinner who has forfeited all his rights and everything except what the grace of Christ gives him."[7]

Today it is not uncommon to hear people say, "Well, I guess that is just my cross to bear." Usually people who say this are talking about some ongoing medical, financial, or relational burden they have to carry through life. But not all of our burdens are crosses in the biblical sense, and to talk this way may have the unintended effect of minimizing the Christian's true cross. The New Testament scholar Norval Geldenhuys is emphatic on this point:

7. Gooding, *Luke*, 268.

The general idea that these words of Jesus about "bearing the cross" refer to passive submission to all kinds of afflictions, like disappointments, pain, sickness and grief that come upon man in this life, is totally wrong. The people to whom Jesus spoke those words fully realized that He meant thereby that whosoever desires to follow Him must be willing to hate his own life and even to be crucified by the Roman authorities for the sake of his fidelity to Him.[8]

In other words, cross-bearing is a particular kind of suffering: it is the suffering we endure for the very reason that we are followers of Jesus Christ. Geldenhuys goes on to explain that taking up our cross "means the acceptance of all sacrifice, suffering, persecution *experienced in the whole-hearted following of Jesus*, and not just ordinary suffering."[9] Cross-bearing therefore includes any form of persecution. Whenever we are disrespected at school, or disadvantaged at work, or disowned by our families because we take a strong stand for Christ, we are bearing his cross. Whenever we face the spiritual and other hardships that come with whatever ministry we are doing in the name of Christ, we are bearing his cross. We are also bearing his cross whenever we share the sufferings of others because we love them for Jesus' sake.

Jesus says that unless we bear these kinds of crosses, we *cannot* be his disciples. The exclusion he makes is absolute because a cross-bearing disciple is the only kind of disciple there is. If we claim to follow Jesus Christ as Lord, then our lives must be patterned after the cross where he died for our sins. Therefore, the first question any would-be disciple needs to ask is, Am I willing to die with Jesus and for Jesus, just as he was willing to die on the cross for me? Because if I am not willing to die for Jesus, then I am not ready to live for him either—not in the way he calls me to live.

By way of analogy, consider the basic form of church architecture. At least until modern times, nearly all Christian churches were built in the shape of a cross, with a long central nave crossed by a transept. This cruciform pattern of architecture made an important theological and practical point: the church lives and worships within the cross. The Christian

8. Norval Geldenhuys, *The Gospel of Luke*, New International Commentary on the New Testament (Grand Rapids: Eerdmans, 1951), 398.
9. Ibid., 400.

93

community is cruciform; it is cross-shaped. Because of our connection to Christ, our lives will be marked by the sufferings of the cross.

This is the same pattern we follow in our own Christian experience. The life of discipleship is also cruciform. As we follow Christ, our lives are conformed to the pattern of Jesus and his sacrifice. Rather than living for ourselves, we lay down our lives for others, giving them our time, our help, our service, our sympathy, and our charity. Jesus has given his life for us; now we give our lives to him by serving in sacrificial love.

In their heart-pounding account of one of the battles that changed the course of the Vietnam War, retired Lieutenant General Harold Moore and journalist Joseph Galloway describe the death of a medic named Calvin Bouknight. Bouknight was running from one wounded soldier to another, administering first aid, when he was shot between the shoulder blades. His fellow soldiers carried him off the field of battle in a bloody poncho and laid him at the feet of his commanding officer. "I didn't make it," Bouknight said, knowing his wound was fatal. Then the authors add this comment: "The Scriptures say that there is no greater love than to lay down your life for your friends. This is what Calvin Bouknight did in that fire-filled jungle. He sheltered the wounded he was treating with his own body, his back to the enemy guns, completely vulnerable."[10]

In the loving service and selfless death of Calvin Bouknight we catch a glimpse of the true form of Christian discipleship. Christianity is a Christ-like, cruciform way of life in which we die to ourselves and live for others.

## Renouncing Everything You Have

It is very costly to follow Jesus in the true way of discipleship. It means releasing our claim on the things we love the most and carrying a cross of suffering and pain. We must count this cost very carefully. Jesus gives many warm and gracious invitations to come to him for salvation. Indeed, what Jesus says here about costly, cross-bearing discipleship follows immediately after his parable of the great banquet with its emphasis on the free and gracious offer of the gospel (see Luke 14:21–23). But before we decide to follow Jesus, we need to know exactly what we are getting into. Salvation

10. Harold G. Moore and Joseph L. Galloway, *We Were Soldiers Once . . . and Young* (New York: HarperCollins, 1992), 153.

by grace is free, but following him will cost us everything we have. Unless we count this cost before we begin to pay it, we will never reach the goal of our salvation.

In order to help his disciples calculate the cost of following him, Jesus gave them two examples from daily life. His first example came from the building trade: "For which of you, desiring to build a tower, does not first sit down and count the cost, whether he has enough to complete it? Otherwise, when he has laid a foundation and is not able to finish, all who see it begin to mock him, saying, 'This man began to build and was not able to finish'" (Luke 14:28–30).

There is no sense starting a project—especially a big project that requires a strong foundation, like a tower—unless one has the resources to finish it. I think of a half-finished house on Delancey Street in Philadelphia, just down the street from Tenth Presbyterian Church. The house was half-finished when I came to the church in 1995, and it was still only half-finished more than a decade later. Presumably the owner failed to count the cost. This often happens with construction projects: building costs are higher than expected, and unless the owner has made the necessary contingencies, the project may never get finished. Jesus wanted to make sure that we do not make the same mistake in the Christian life. It will cost us everything to follow him, so before we begin, we need to sit down and decide whether we can pay that price.

Jesus then took a second example from the ancient and expensive art of war: "Or what king, going out to encounter another king in war, will not sit down first and deliberate whether he is able with ten thousand to meet him who comes against him with twenty thousand? And if not, while the other is yet a great way off, he sends a delegation and asks for terms of peace" (Luke 14:31–32).

According to the famous military advice of Sun Tzu, a foolish general begins a battle hoping for a victory, whereas a wise general begins a battle already having secured it. This was the advice that Hannibal followed when he defeated superior Roman forces at Cannae in 216 B.C., and that Napoleon followed in his triumph over the Russians and the Austrians at Austerlitz in 1805. Those generals won their famous victories because they counted the cost *before* they went into battle. When the enemy forces are overwhelming, however, a wise general will not fight at all but instead negotiate the terms of peace. This is what Robert E. Lee did when he finally surrendered to Ulysses S. Grant at Appomattox. As General Lee counted the cost, he knew that his only wise course was to surrender.

Like the parable of the unfinished tower, the parable of the two kings warns us to count the cost. Only this time what Jesus calls us to consider is not the cost of discipleship, but the cost of *non*-discipleship.[11] Verse 31 encourages us to see things from the perspective of the weaker king, who is about to be invaded, and perhaps also to connect the stronger king with the person of God himself. Faced with the threat of a superior army, the weaker party should consider his resources carefully before deciding to defend himself. According to verse 32, he should also consider the consequences of inaction, and choose instead to sue for peace and settle terms with his opponent. Can we afford to follow Jesus? the first parable asks. To which the second parable offers a rejoinder: Can we afford not to?

Jesus calls us to do some careful reckoning before we decide to follow him. What he requires is nothing less than the total surrender of all that we are and have. "So therefore," he said, "any one of you who does not renounce all that he has cannot be my disciple" (Luke 14:33). Here is a third statement of complete exclusion. Unless we "hate" our families, carry our crosses, and count the cost to renounce our right to everything we have, we *cannot* be his disciples. Here is how Joseph Fitzmyer translates verse 33: "Everyone one of you who does not say goodbye to all he has cannot be a disciple of mine."[12] A disciple who has renounced everything to follow Jesus is the only kind of disciple there is.

It may well be that Jesus will want us to keep some of what we have in order to use it for his glory. But if Jesus calls us to do it, we must be ready to give up anything and everything for him. This is what it means to count the cost. Every disciple

> must relinquish *all* his possessions—not merely money and material things, but also his dear ones and everything that his heart clings to, yea, even his own life, his own desires, plans, ideals and interests. This does not mean that he must sell all his possessions or give away all his money or desert his dear ones and become a hermit or beggar or wanderer, but it means that he must

11. I am indebted to Dan Doriani for this interpretation.
12. Joseph A. Fitzmyer, *The Gospel According to Luke* (Garden City, NY: Doubleday, 1981), 33.

give Christ full control over his whole life with everything that he is and all that he possesses, and that under His guidance and in His service he should deal with his possessions in the manner that is best.[13]

Have you counted the cost to follow Jesus? Many Christians give up precious little for Jesus, especially those of us who enjoy abundant material prosperity in the United States of America. How tempting it is to treat Christianity as a religious justification for doing what we already do, and how tempting it is to hold on to what we want in life and refuse to let God have it—our money, time, possessions, relationships, and ambitions, even the wounds we lick to nourish our self-pity. What are you clutching that is keeping you from following Jesus the way he demands to be followed? Jesus calls us to renounce everything for him, and then to receive back from him whatever he wants us to have. Once I have given Jesus my family, my life, and my all, what else is left? Only the life that Jesus wants me to have, the way he wants me to have it.

Know this: the Savior who calls us to do this is the very Savior who counted the cost of his own obedience. Jesus knew that he would be betrayed. He knew that he would suffer and die a God-forsaken death. Long before he ever went to the cross, Jesus had counted the cost and determined that he would pay it for our salvation. Jesus set his face toward Jerusalem (see Luke 9:51). He determined to continue on his way until he finished his work (see Luke 13:33)—which he did, to the agony of his body and soul. Now Jesus rightly calls us to imitate him in our discipleship, giving up everything to follow him. As the missionary Elizabeth Freeman wrote in the last letter she sent to her sister before being martyred by Muslims in 1857, "Should I be called to lay down my life, do not grieve, dear sister, that I came here, for most joyfully will I die for him who laid down His life for me."[14]

One man who counted the cost of coming after Jesus was the great American theologian Jonathan Edwards. When Edwards was only nineteen years old, he made the following entry in his personal diary: "I have this day . . . been before God, and have given myself, all that I am and have to God; so that I am not, in any respect, my own. . . . I have given myself clear away, and have not retained any thing, as my own. . . . I have given every power to him, so that

13. Geldenhuys, *Luke*, 399.
14. Elizabeth Freeman, quoted in *The Voice of the Martyrs* (Sept. 2007): 11.

for the future, I'll challenge no right to myself. . . . This, I have done; and I pray God, for the sake of Christ, . . . to receive me now, as entirely his own."[15]

## Being Worth Our Salt

The personal dedication that Jonathan Edwards made to God is not extraordinary, but fits the normal, cruciform pattern of Christian discipleship. This is what it means to be a disciple of the Lord Jesus Christ: it means "hating" our family, carrying our cross, and renouncing everything for his dear sake. Since this is the only kind of disciple there is, if we do not do these things, we simply cannot be his disciples.

If we are not disciples of Jesus Christ, then we are of no spiritual use. This is the point of the miniparable that Jesus gave to close this discourse: "Salt is good, but if salt has lost its taste, how shall its saltiness be restored? It is of no use either for the soil or for the manure pile. It is thrown away. He who has ears to hear, let him hear" (Luke 14:34–35; cf. Matt. 5:13). Jesus used this expression when he wanted people to pay attention to something important. What is important here is that unless we follow Jesus in the true way of Christian discipleship, we are worthless to the kingdom of God—as worthless as salt that isn't even salty.

Salt has many useful purposes. Unless it is salty, however, it is not good for anything at all. This is a surprising image because the very essence of salt is to be salty. How can salt possibly lose its taste, and still be salt? This could never happen to pure sodium chloride, of course, but it could happen to the kind of salt that Jesus used. When people "passed the salt" in those days, it was an impure chemical compound produced by the evaporation of saltwater from the Dead Sea—sodium chloride mixed with other crystals. Thus it was possible for the salt to leach out of the compound, and when this happened, what was left was completely useless.[16] There was nothing that anyone could do with it; it was not even good enough to use for fertilizer.

What Jesus said about salt that isn't salty can also be said of a disciple who is not really a disciple. In the same way that salt has to be salty in order

---

15. Jonathan Edwards, diary entry for January 12, 1723, quoted in Sam Storms, "Jonathan Edwards' Personal Narrative (7)," posted on the Enjoying God Ministries Web site on July 7, 2005.

16. I. Howard Marshall, *The Gospel of Luke*, New International Greek Testament Commentary (Grand Rapids: Eerdmans, 1978), 596.

to be salt, so also a disciple has to be a disciple in order to be a disciple! This means being a disciple in the biblical sense: a hating-your-family, carrying-your-cross, renouncing-everything-for-Jesus disciple. A disciple who does not love Jesus more than anything else he loves is not his disciple. A disciple who does not carry his cross in daily death to self is not his disciple. A disciple who does not give everything over to Jesus is not his disciple. However extreme this may sound, it is Jesus himself who says that unless we do these things, we *cannot* be his disciples.

Be worth your salt in the kingdom of God. Live a life of useful Christian discipleship. Let your love for Jesus grow stronger, surpassing all other affections. Make self-renouncing sacrifices for the glory of God. Conform your life to the cruciform pattern of Christian discipleship.

If the cross is the only pattern for our discipleship, then every Christian has a cross-shaped life. Jesus tells us to count the cost of living this kind of life at the very beginning. Then he calls us to keep living it to the very end, so that when the time finally comes for us to die, we will be ready, because we have been laying down our lives for Jesus all life long.

A powerful witness to the cruciform life comes from the death of the Scottish Covenanter Hugh Mackail, who lived and died during the bloody 1660s, when many Presbyterians were put to death for their faith in Jesus Christ. Because Mackail steadfastly refused to reveal the names of his brothers and sisters in Christ, his captors subjected him to excruciating torture. They put his leg in an iron case; they set a wedge of iron against his knee; and when he refused to answer their demands, they repeatedly struck his leg with a heavy mallet until finally his leg shattered. Mackail said, "I protest solemnly in the sight of God; I can say no more, though all the joints in my body were in as great anguish as my leg."[17]

Mackail's leg would not be of use to him much longer, because soon he was sentenced to die. When he was executed, his dying words became the cry of many a martyr:

> Now I leave off to speak any more to creatures, and turn my speech to Thee, O Lord. Now I begin my intercourse with God, which shall never be broken off. Farewell, father and mother, friends and relations! Farewell, the world

17. Hugh Mackail, quoted in Alexander Smellie, *Men of the Covenant* (London: Banner of Truth, 1960), 177.

99

and all delights! Farewell meat and drink! Farewell, sun, moon, and stars! Welcome, God and Father! Welcome, sweet Lord Jesus, the Mediator of the new covenant! Welcome, blessed Spirit of grace, God of all consolation! Welcome, glory! Welcome, eternal life! Welcome, death![18]

When the time came for Mackail to die, he was ready to give up everything he loved for the love of Jesus. He was ready because he had counted the cost of Christian discipleship when he first came to Christ.

If you could see Hugh Mackail now, in all his glory, you would know that it was well worth whatever price he paid. Lord willing, you will not have to die the way Mackail died. But if you want to have eternal life in Christ, you must live the way that he lived, because Jesus says, "Whoever does not hate his own life, whoever does not bear his own cross, and whoever does not renounce all that he has cannot be my disciple."

18. Ibid., 181.

# 64

# THE LOST SHEEP

## *Luke 15:1–7*

*"What man of you, having a hundred sheep, if he has lost one of them, does not leave the ninety-nine in the open country, and go after the one that is lost, until he finds it?"* (Luke 15:4)

*I*t was a marvelous moment of spiritual insight. As the shepherd went about his daily work of tending sheep, and as he reflected on his relationship with God, he suddenly realized that there was a vital connection. The loving care that he gave his sheep was like the loving care he received from his God. So David began his most famous psalm: "The LORD is *my* shepherd" (Ps. 23:1). From there David proceeded to list all the things his shepherd did for him: laying him down in green pastures, leading him beside still waters, restoring his soul, walking with him through death's valley, anointing his head with soothing oil, and filling his cup with overflowing joy.

The shepherd from David's psalm became part of Israel's working definition of God. Whenever people needed help, they looked to their shepherd for salvation. This is how they prayed in times of trouble: "Give ear, O Shepherd of Israel, you who lead Joseph like a flock! . . . . Restore us, O God; . . . that we may be saved!" (Ps. 80:1, 3).

This great truth—that God is a good shepherd—was further developed by the prophets. Isaiah emphasized God's loving care for his littlest sheep: "He will tend his flock like a shepherd; he will gather the lambs in his arms; he will carry them in his bosom" (Isa. 40:11). But some of the prophets also pointed out a problem. God had entrusted the work of his shepherding care to the spiritual leaders of his people, but they were not always good shepherds. Jeremiah accused them of scattering God's flock (Jer. 23:2). Ezekiel's condemnation was even harsher: "The weak you have not strengthened, the sick you have not healed, the injured you have not bound up, the strayed you have not brought back. . . . My sheep were scattered over all the face of the earth, with none to search or seek for them" (Ezek. 34:4, 6).

According to the prophets, God's sheep were lost. But the prophets also saw the solution to this problem: the Good Shepherd himself would come to seek and to save his people. So Ezekiel gave people this message from God: "I myself will search for my sheep and will seek them out. As a shepherd seeks out his flock when he is among his sheep that have been scattered, so will I seek out my sheep, and I will rescue them from all places where they have been scattered" (Ezek. 34:11–12). Jeremiah made a similar promise, and said that Israel's saving shepherd would be the son of David (see Jer. 23:3, 5).

## THREE PARABLES IN ONE

What the Scripture said about shepherds was familiar to anyone who knew the Old Testament. It certainly would have been familiar to the scribes and Pharisees who made trouble for Jesus in his earthly ministry. These men claimed that the Lord was their shepherd and considered themselves to be the spiritual shepherds of Israel, yet they failed to recognize Jesus as the answer to God's promise to come and save his people. Nor did they see themselves as part of the problem.

Rather than searching for the lost sheep of Israel, the scribes and Pharisees misled them. Thus they were deeply offended when they saw Jesus associating with people who did not keep God's law the way they did, including people who were not even religious at all. This was typical of Jesus: he always seemed to attract religious outsiders, which is one of the main reasons that religious insiders complained about his ministry. Luke tells us,

"Now the tax collectors and sinners were all drawing near to hear him. And the Pharisees and the scribes grumbled, saying, 'This man receives sinners and eats with them'" (Luke 15:1–2).

In those days tax collectors were social and spiritual outcasts. Because they were part of the Roman bureaucracy, and because they collected money from fellow Israelites, they were considered traitors to the people of God. The word "sinners" was a catchall for people who had a notorious reputation for bad behavior—thieves, drunkards, prostitutes, and anyone else who refused to conform to the holy habits of the religious community. Sinners and the tax collectors were people who almost never went to worship and never seemed to have any interest in following God.

Members of the religious establishment stayed as far away from such people as they could, believing that any contact would contaminate them. As far as the scribes and Pharisees were concerned, sinners and tax collectors were outside of Israel, outside of the faith, and outside of God. People in the church sometimes have the same attitude today, despising people who do not meet their standards for holy living.

As far as Jesus was concerned, however, their sorry condition was exactly the point! These outcasts were the lost sheep of Israel—the very people that Israel's shepherds were supposed to rescue, and the very people that he himself had come to save. Therefore, sinners and tax collectors were just the people that Jesus *ought* to be eating with. Here is how Kenneth Bailey summarizes the response that Jesus gave his critics:

> You wonder why I receive sinners and eat with them? I do so because in my person God is fulfilling his great promise hinted at in David's shepherd psalm and spelled out clearly in Jeremiah and Ezekiel. Through those prophets he pledged himself to come in person and round up the lost sheep. He also pledged himself to rescue the flock from the shepherds who destroy them. This is who I am, and this is why I do what I do.[1]

Jesus did not say this directly, of course; he said it by telling a story. But in telling this story Jesus identified himself as the Good Shepherd who saves the lost sheep.

1. Kenneth E. Bailey, *Jacob and the Prodigal: How Jesus Retold Israel's Story* (Downers Grove, IL: InterVarsity, 2003), 69.

The story of the lost sheep is the first part of a longer parable that is really three stories in one. When the scribes and the Pharisees started to grumble, Jesus "told them *this parable*" (Luke 15:3). What follows is a discourse that runs all the way to the end of chapter 15 and includes not only the story of the lost sheep, but also the story of the lost coin and the story of the lost son. So we might have expected Luke to use the plural: "these parables." Instead, he says that Jesus told them "this parable."

All three stories have the same theme and make the same basic point. In each story something lost is found, and then people celebrate. According to Michael Wilcock, "the plain meaning of the chapter is that just as there is joy when any shepherd or any housewife or any father recovers a loss, so there is joy in heaven when a sinner is reunited with God."[2] This three-in-one parable is about the joy of God in finding what is lost—a joy that we will share only if we have the heart that Jesus has for lost and dying sinners.

The first story in the parable is about finding a lost sheep. It is told in three episodes: First, there is the shepherd's *quest* (Luke 15:4); this shows the patient endurance of the shepherd as he seeks until he finds. Second, there is the shepherd's *burden* (Luke 15:5), which shows his gentle strength in shouldering a heavy load. Third, there is the shepherd's *celebration* (Luke 15:6); this shows the shepherd's exuberant joy as he rejoices in the salvation of his sheep. This is followed by a practical conclusion, in which Jesus invites us to share in his joy—both for our own repentance and for the repentance of other lost sinners who are coming to Christ.

## THE SHEPHERD'S QUEST

The shepherd's quest began when he discovered that one of his sheep was missing: "What man of you, having a hundred sheep, if he has lost one of them, does not leave the ninety-nine in the open country, and go after the one that is lost, until he finds it?" (Luke 15:4).

A man with a hundred sheep was doing rather well financially. He could probably afford to lose a sheep or two: losing one out of a hundred is no great loss. But letting sheep stray is bad business practice, so he did what any good shepherd would do. He left the rest of his flock behind—

---

2. Michael Wilcock, *The Message of Luke,* The Bible Speaks Today (Downers Grove, IL: InterVarsity, 1979), 149–50.

presumably under the care of some helper or friend—and went out to look for his lost sheep.

By the time the shepherd began his quest, the sheep was already in a dangerous situation. Sheep are too disoriented to find their way home, and as soon as they stray, they are defenseless against almost any danger. Sooner or later a lost sheep will fall from a precipice, or die of starvation, or get torn apart by a wild beast. Sheep do not adapt to the wild. When they wander, they can only wait to be rescued.

What a picture this is of our own spiritual condition! Apart from Christ, we are lost in the rocky wilderness. Wandering in the wasteland, we fall into sin and starve for lack of spiritual food. To our terror, Satan is roaring like a wild beast to devour us. We *cannot* find our way back to God on our own; all we can do is to wait for Jesus to come and find us. If he does not save us, we will surely be destroyed.

How different this was from what most of the old Jewish rabbis taught about sin and grace.[3] According to their understanding of salvation, a sinner had to turn back to God first. It was his act of repentance that would restore God's favor. In other words, if a sheep wanted to come under the care of the shepherd, it had to find its way back to the fold. Many people think the same way today. They know they are lost and hope that God will still accept them, but they imagine that they have to find their way back on their own. God will not come to them; they must go to him.

The Bible does tell us to seek after God, of course. But here Jesus bears witness to God's saving initiative in grace. Like the shepherd in the story, God "goes after" his sheep (Luke 15:4). When we are lost, when we have wandered on the far hills of disobedience, when we are alone and afraid, when we are wounded and weak, when we are defenseless against our enemies, when we are unable to save ourselves—it is just then that Jesus comes to rescue us.

I say "Jesus" because this is really his story. One of the central themes of Luke's Gospel is that Jesus came "to seek and to save the lost" (Luke 19:10). Here Jesus compares that seeking and saving work to a shepherd's quest for his lost sheep. Jesus is the Good Shepherd who travels the wild terrain, climbs the steep hill, goes down into the rocky ravine, and braves

---

3. See Bailey, *Jacob and the Prodigal*, 81, for some examples.

105

every danger to find his lost sheep. Rest assured, he will keep looking until he finds what he is looking for. As we see from the end of verse 4, the good shepherd will not stop searching until he has achieved the goal of his quest. With patient endurance, he seeks until he finds.

As much as we admire the shepherd in this story, what Jesus has done for us is even more remarkable. The sheep that he seeks were lost through no fault of his own. Nevertheless, he takes the responsibility to find them. This is an extraordinary condescension. Ordinarily a man wealthy enough to have a hundred sheep would send someone else to find them. According to Kenneth Bailey, "Shepherds in the Middle East are poor men, clothed in simple dress, who wander in privation over the countryside. No educated man would spend his days tramping over the wilderness for any purpose."[4] But Jesus humbly came to seek the lost, taking on the poor dress of our humanity so that he could bring us back to the fold of God.

Nor was it only one sheep out of a hundred that Jesus came to find. He must track down every last sheep, because the whole flock is lost. As the Scripture says, "All we like sheep have gone astray; we have turned every one to his own way" (Isa. 53:6). There is not one single sheep that started out in God's fold and stayed there. We are all lost! Therefore, Jesus has a quest that is a hundred, a million, or even a billion times harder to fulfill. But he will do it. He will fulfill God's ancient promise: "I myself will search for my sheep and will seek them out" (Ezek. 34:11).

What hope this gives to anyone who is lost in the spiritual wilderness, has wandered away from God, or has been wounded by this fallen world. Jesus is seeking to come and rescue you. What security this gives to all the sheep he has already found. People sometimes think that the shepherd's quest is mainly important for the sheep that is lost. After all, he is the one who is in the most danger. But unless the Good Shepherd is willing to go out and find that one little sheep, the rest of the flock will live in mortal fear. They are only sheep, after all, so there is always the danger that they might stray, and what will become of them then? To quote again from Kenneth Bailey, "It is the shepherd's willingness to go after the one that gives the ninety-nine their real security. If the one is sacrificed in the name of the larger good of

---

4. Kenneth E. Bailey, *The Cross and the Prodigal: Luke 15 Through the Eyes of Middle Eastern Peasants* (Downers Grove, IL: InterVarsity, 2005), 30.

the group, then each individual in the group is insecure. He knows that he too is of little value. If lost, he will be left to die. When the shepherd pays a high price to find the one, he thereby offers the profoundest security to the many."[5]

In his preaching on this parable, Charles Spurgeon imagined the Good Shepherd going out and finding his sheep in a dark glen on the mountainside. But before Jesus can bring them home, Satan tries to stop him. First the devil tries to say that because the sheep are in the wilderness they belong to him and not to Jesus. But Jesus shows Satan that the sheep have been marked with his blood and therefore they belong to him. Then the devil tries to wrestle with Jesus in open spiritual combat, but he is defeated. Next Satan gives up most of the sheep while keeping some of them for himself, but of course Jesus refuses to fall for this trick. Finally, when Jesus insists that all the sheep must come with him, Satan tries to keep one little lamb for himself. "This is such a little one," he says. "This is so weak. Thou wouldst not have such a shriveled, scabby one as this in thy bright flock, thou fair Shepherd of God." But Jesus says, "Sooner than lose one of them I will die again, and shed my blood once more to buy it back. All that my Father gave me I will have."[6]

All God's sheep will be rescued; none will be left behind; every last suffering, straying believer will be carried home to God. "Shriveled and scabby" we may be, but once we are in God's flock we belong to him forever. One of the major questions many people have is whether or not anyone will be there for them in the end. The answer Jesus gives is that he will never give up on us or let us go.

## THE SHEPHERD'S BURDEN

It is one thing to find a lost sheep, but another thing entirely to bring it back home. No sooner has the shepherd fulfilled his quest than he must begin to shoulder his burden: "And when he has found it, he lays it on his shoulders" (Luke 15:5). Here we see the shepherd's heavy burden, and his gentle strength to carry it.

5. Bailey, *Cross and the Prodigal*, 31.
6. Charles Spurgeon, "Full Redemption," *The New Park Street Pulpit*, vol. 6 (London, 1861; reprint Pasadena, TX: Pilgrim, 1974), 185.

It is not hard to picture the scene. Once he found his lost sheep, the shepherd draped it around his neck, firmly grasped its four legs together in front of him, and started his long trek home. Here is a relationship of astonishing intimacy. The shepherd can feel the weight and the warmth of his sheep—the rise and fall of its breathing, the beating of its heart. The sheep is close enough to nuzzle the shepherd's face. Exhausted by its struggle in the wilderness and too weak to walk back home, the sheep has found safety and security in its shepherd's arms.

This glad image captured the heart of the early church. The earliest Christian statue still in existence—a statue which may have come from the catacombs and is still in Rome at the Lateran Museum—depicts a shepherd carrying a sheep on his shoulders.[7] It must have been a comforting image for the persecuted church: although they were wounded and weak, their Good Shepherd would lift them up and carry them home.

This was no easy burden. A full-grown sheep weighs more than a hundred pounds. It took a good measure of physical strength to carry a sheep back to the fold, especially if it had wandered far into the wilderness, but the shepherd was able and willing to bear that burden. What comfort this gives to all his sheep! Weary and worn, we do not have the strength to go home. Nevertheless, we are lifted up by mighty arms and gently carried back to the fold. The ancient hymn writer Prudentius put this comforting truth into verse:

When one ailing sheep lags behind the others
And loses itself in the sylvan mazes,
Tearing its white fleece on the thorns and briers,
　　Sharp in the brambles,

Unwearied the Shepherd, that lost one seeking,
Drives away the wolves and on his strong shoulders
Brings it home again to the fold's safekeeping,
　　Healed and unsullied.[8]

Here we see the answer to a prayer of David: "Oh, save your people and bless your heritage! Be their shepherd and carry them forever" (Ps. 28:9).

7. R. Kent Hughes, *Luke: That You May Know the Truth*, 2 vols., Preaching the Word (Wheaton, IL: Crossway, 1998), 2:136–37.

8. Prudentius, "Hymn for Every Day" (8.33–45), quoted in *Luke*, ed. Arthur A. Just, Jr., Ancient Christian Commentary on Scripture, NT 3 (Downers Grove, IL: InterVarsity, 2003), 244.

We also see the fulfillment of Ezekiel's ancient promise: "I will seek the lost, and I will bring back the strayed, and I will bind up the injured, and I will strengthen the weak" (Ezek. 34:16). This prayer is answered—this promise is fulfilled—in the shepherding ministry of Jesus Christ. With gentle strength, he carries the shepherd's burden.

Consider how heavy a burden Jesus has shouldered for our salvation. Even as he taught this parable, Jesus was getting ready to do the heavy lifting of redemption. It was not just one little lamb he needed to carry, but every last sheep in God's flock. The place he needed to carry us was to the cross. When the German Reformer Philipp Melanchthon taught this parable, he said that interwoven into the text "is a sweet signification of the passion of Christ: He places upon his shoulders the sheep He has found, that is, He transfers to himself the burden of us."[9]

What a killing burden this was! When Jesus lifted us up, the burden he had to bear was the dead weight of our sin—the sin that killed him on the cross. Earlier we noted Isaiah's prophecy: "All we like sheep have gone astray; we have turned every one to his own way." The verse ends by telling what it would take for our Savior to rescue us and redeem us: "the LORD has laid on him the iniquity of us all" (Isa. 53:6). In other words, the Savior had to do something more than simply bring the sheep home; he also had to suffer the punishment for their sin. Then Isaiah proceeds to describe the agonies of the crucifixion, when our Savior "poured out his soul to death . . . and bore the sin of many" (Isa. 53:12).

Jesus did not come simply to lift us up in the troubles of life (although we can praise God that he does lift us up), but mainly to bear the weight of our sin, and to do so by dying in our place on the cross. He is the Good Shepherd who laid down his life for his sheep (see John 10:11). In the words of the apostle Peter, "He himself bore our sins in his body on the tree, that we might die to sin and live to righteousness. By his wounds you have been healed. For you were straying like sheep, but have now returned to the Shepherd and Overseer of your souls" (1 Peter 2:24–25).

Return to the Shepherd of your soul. Know Jesus as your Savior. Ask him to bear the deadly weight of your sin. "Let us rejoice," wrote the venerable Ambrose, "that the sheep that had strayed in Adam is lifted on Christ. The

9. Philipp Melanchthon, quoted in Hughes, *Luke*, 2:136.

shoulders of Christ are the arms of the cross. There, I laid down my sins. I rested on the neck of that noble yoke."[10] Every lost sinner who rests on the crucified Christ will be carried home safe to God.

## THE SHEPHERD'S CELEBRATION

A shepherd has great joy in finding lost sheep and bringing them back home. Having completed his quest and carried his burden, he starts to celebrate, although in fact the celebration may begin while he is still in the wilderness. Jesus said that when the good shepherd finds his sheep, he "lays it on his shoulders, *rejoicing*" (Luke 15:5). He is so overjoyed to find the lost sheep that he goes singing all the way home.

Here we catch a glimpse of the joy that Jesus has in bringing us to God. Even our great joy in being saved does not surpass the joy that he has in saving us. The Bible says that "for the joy that was set before him" Jesus "endured the cross, despising the shame" (Heb. 12:2). Having suffered the agony of crucifixion, his joy is to come and find lost sinners who are still wandering in the spiritual wilderness. His joy is to save us by the preaching of his gospel, to send us the Holy Spirit, and to welcome us home to his Father. No one enjoys the salvation of a sinner any more than Jesus does! So when we tell him how grateful we are that he saved us, he can truly say, "It was my pleasure."

The joy of Jesus is infectious, as we see from the parable. When the shepherd "comes home, he calls together his friends and his neighbors, saying to them, 'Rejoice with me, for I have found my sheep that was lost'" (Luke 15:6). So great is the shepherd's joy that he cannot help but share it. As he comes home in triumph, with the spoils of victory draped around his neck, he shouts to the first person he sees. Then the whole community gathers for a spontaneous celebration.

This exuberant joy is well illustrated by Mick Inkpen in a children's book called *The Lost Sheep*,[11] a contemporary retelling of the biblical parable. When at last the shepherd returns home with his lost sheep, the

---

10. Ambrose, "Exposition of the Gospel of Luke" (7.209), quoted in *Luke*, ed. Arthur A. Just, Jr., Ancient Christian Commentary on Scripture, NT 3 (Downers Grove, IL: InterVarsity, 2003), 244.

11. Nick Butterworth and Mick Inkpen, *The Lost Sheep* (London: Marshall Pickering, 1986).

other members of the flock are euphoric. Indeed, they are absolutely the happiest sheep that anyone has ever seen. They smile big toothy grins, raise their hooves in triumph, and then celebrate with balloons, streamers, and noisemakers. Needless to say, the illustrator has taken a few liberties with the biblical text! Nevertheless, he has captured the right mood. The keynote of this biblical story is joy—the joy of God in finding what is lost.

What a joy it is when Jesus finds a lost sinner! For someone to repent of sin and trust in Christ is the greatest joy in life. In the week this chapter was written, I heard about a little boy who prayed to receive Jesus as his Savior and Lord, a young couple who came to Christ as they were preparing for marriage, and an Indian man who was saved out of a Muslim family and wants to reach street children with the love of Christ. How happy they are! They have the great joy of knowing for sure that all their sins are forgiven, that God accepts them as beloved children, and that Jesus will keep them safe for all eternity.

## SHARING THE SHEPHERD'S JOY

Jesus brings the first part of his triple parable to a practical conclusion by inviting everyone to share his joy: "Just so," Jesus tells us, "there will be more joy in heaven over one sinner who repents than over ninety-nine righteous persons who need no repentance" (Luke 15:7).

It is just possible that Jesus was making a serious comparison here. Perhaps it could be said that there are some people who do not need to repent—at least not for the first time—because they have already asked God to forgive all their sins. In that case, Jesus was saying that although heaven always rejoices in the righteous, it rings with even greater joy any time a sinner comes to Christ.

What seems more likely, however, is that Jesus was speaking ironically. Think about it: Who is ever so righteous that he has no need to repent? No one is! The Scripture says that we have all gone astray, that no one is righteous, "not even one" (Rom. 3:12). So when Jesus talked about "righteous persons who need no repentance," he was taking a sharp jab at the Pharisees, who were so sure of their own righteousness that they did not even think they needed to repent. Sadly, their spiritual pride kept them from finding any joy in repentance, which is precisely why Jesus told them this parable—a parable that must have made them furious.

The scribes and Pharisees were grumbling when they should have been rejoicing. Jesus wanted them to celebrate the work he was doing to save the lost sheep of Israel, but all they wanted to do was criticize. Instead of complaining about Jesus, they actually should have been helping him. After all, if they had been doing the kind of shepherding work they were supposed to be doing, the lost sheep of Israel probably would not be lost in the first place. In fact, by beginning his parable with the words "what man of you" (Luke 15:4), Jesus was practically inviting them to share in his shepherding work. Yet these men were so far out of sympathy with Jesus that they had no joy in finding what was lost. They did not think anyone else was worthy to be saved. Although they did not realize it, they themselves were like the sheep in verse 4 that the shepherd left behind in the open country! They were still in the wilderness; they had not yet come home to God.

Jesus wants us to share the joy that he has in finding the lost. We share our shepherd's joy when we admit that we have gone astray and need him to come and find us. We share his joy when we accept being found and ask him to carry us back home, and even more when we celebrate our salvation.

Then, once we are saved, we share the shepherd's joy by having his heart for lost sheep (especially if God has called us to serve as shepherds in the work of pastoral ministry). We share his joy by joining his quest to seek and to save people who are lost spiritually. This means having compassion on their condition—not blaming them for their problems, but seeing their spiritual need. It means loving them and praying for them until they trust in Christ—not leaving them to find their way into the fold (which lost sheep can never do), but going after them with the gospel. It also means shouldering the heavy burden of servant ministry—not complaining about all the trouble we have with people who need to know Christ, but asking Jesus for the strength to keep on caring.

How easy it is to be as cynical as the scribes, thinking that some people are beyond redemption, and not wanting to get involved with their problems. How hard it is to be as compassionate as Christ, searching and searching for sinners until they get saved. But if we are friends with the Good Shepherd, we will learn his patience in the looking and share his joy in the finding.

# 65

# THE LOST COIN

## *Luke 15:8—10*

*"Or what woman, having ten silver coins, if she loses one coin,
does not light a lamp and sweep the house and seek diligently
until she finds it?"* (Luke 15:8)

*T*he Pharisees we meet in the Gospels were wrong about many
things, including God's requirements for salvation and their
own righteousness, and wrong about the true identity of Jesus
Christ. But at least they were right about this: Jesus was a man who welcomed sinners. We know this because they said, "This man receives sinners
and eats with them" (Luke 15:2).

This is one of the best summaries of Jesus' ministry anywhere in the Gospels. How ironic that it comes from the scribes and the Pharisees, who were
speaking more truly than they even knew! To "receive" people in the biblical
sense of the word (Gk. *prosdechomai*) was to welcome them into fellowship,
to accept them and associate with them. In that culture, one of the most tan-
gible ways to establish this kind of friendship was to share a meal. "To invite
a man to a meal," writes one scholar, "was an offer of peace, trust, brother-
hood, and forgiveness; in short, sharing a table meant sharing life."[1]

1. Joachim Jeremias, *Theology of the New Testament*, quoted in Richard D. Phillips, *Turning Your World Upside Down: Kingdom Priorities in the Parables of Jesus* (Phillipsburg, NJ: P&R, 2003), 110.

This is the very essence of salvation: God the Son sharing his life with us. Remarkably, he shares his life with *sinners*. Some Bible translations put the word "sinners" in quotes, as if to indicate that somehow this was the wrong word for the Pharisees to use. But these people *were* sinners; this was just the word for them. They were reprobates. They were liars and cheats, lechers and lawbreakers, swindlers and thieves. In the words of John Chrysostom, "The tax-gatherer is the personification of licensed violence, of legal sin, of specious greed."[2] Yet Jesus welcomed these people into his fellowship. He even ate with them—not as a duty of philanthropy, but because he had mercy on people who were lost in their sins.

## AT THE TABLE WITH JESUS

Jesus Christ is the friend of sinners. If you know that you are a sinner, then this is the best of all possible news, because it means that there is still hope. Despite the fact that we have fallen into sin—doing things we should never do, as well as not doing things that we really should do, and therefore deserving the wrath and curse of God—Jesus is ready to receive us. He wants to welcome us. If we come to him—even after everything we have done wrong—he will take us to himself. This ought to make what the Pharisees said one of the most joyful statements in Scripture: "This man receives sinners and eats with them" (Luke 15:2). Praise God!

The Pharisees did not say this with joyful praise, however. This is one of those times when you have to know how somebody said something to know what they really meant. Here Luke uses the little word "grumbled" to indicate what tone of voice the Pharisees used. The Greek version of the Old Testament used the same word to describe the way the children of Israel grumbled in the wilderness (e.g., Ex. 15:24). It expresses a strong undercurrent of discontent. When the Pharisees saw that Jesus was eating with sinners, they complained about it bitterly. Rather than making their remark with admiration, they made it with condemnation.

Jesus hardly could have done anything to give these men greater offense than to eat with sinners. A man is known by the company he keeps, and thus the Pharisees were shocked to see that Jesus preferred "the society of

2. John Chrysostom, quoted in R. Kent Hughes, *Luke: That You May Know the Truth*, 2 vols., Preaching the Word (Wheaton, IL: Crossway, 1998), 2:131.

notorious sinners to their own irreproachable manners and decorous conversation. . . . They could not understand why a teacher of holy life, instead of frowning upon the notoriously profligate, should show a preference for their society."[3] As far as they were concerned, this could only mean that Jesus was guilty of moral laxity. He was not taking sin seriously enough, but going soft on depravity. The Pharisees believed that to eat with people who were known for loose living was to condone their immoral behavior. "Let not a man associate with the wicked," the rabbis said, "not even to bring him to the law."[4] Jesus broke this tradition every time he sat down to eat dinner with sinners (which he did, of course, any time he ate with anyone at all, including the Pharisees!). To associate with people of low moral character was to give them public recognition. Thus the Pharisees accused Jesus of sharing in unrighteousness.

What the Pharisees saw as a problem was actually the solution! The very thing they criticized was the very thing Jesus had come to do. He had come to make sinners holy for God, and sharing table fellowship was part of his plan. It is only in being received by Jesus that anyone can ever be saved. How can Jesus help us unless he has a relationship with us? In that culture—and perhaps in any culture—having a relationship meant sharing a meal. So Jesus ate with sinners.

Rather than getting grumpy about this, the Pharisees should have been rejoicing. If they had, then the rest of what Jesus said in this chapter would not even be necessary. Replace the word "grumbled" with "rejoiced" in verse 2 and you get rid of everything that follows. But the Pharisees *were* grumbling, and therefore Jesus taught them a three-part parable about sharing God's joy in finding what is lost.

## WHAT WOMAN . . . ?

In the first part of this triple parable, a shepherd finds a lost sheep and brings it back home, rejoicing. In the third part of the parable, a father runs to embrace his long-lost son. In between those two famous parables Jesus told a story about a housewife who found her missing money: "Or what

3. Marcus Dods, quoted in Phillips, *Turning Your World*, 110.
4. Quoted in I. Howard Marshall, *The Gospel of Luke*, New International Greek Testament Commentary (Grand Rapids: Eerdmans, 1978), 599.

woman, having ten silver coins, if she loses one coin, does not light a lamp and sweep the house and seek diligently until she finds it? And when she has found it, she calls together her friends and neighbors, saying, 'Rejoice with me, for I have found the coin that I had lost.' Just so, I tell you, there is joy before the angels of God over one sinner who repents" (Luke 15:8–10).

The first lesson this story teaches is that Jesus cares as much about women as he cares about men. Although at first this may seem like an insignificant detail, Jesus begins by talking about a woman. He could just as well have told this story about a man, of course. In fact, one of the old Jewish rabbis told a somewhat similar story about a man who lost a little coin and then looked for it until he found it. The rabbi then compared the man's careful search process to the way faithful Jews should look for hidden treasure in the Torah.[5]

Jesus could have told his story about a man, too, but instead he chose to tell it about a woman. He did this despite the fact that he was speaking most directly to a group of men—the scribes and the Pharisees. There must have been women in the audience too, as there almost always were. In chapter 8 Luke told us that as Jesus went from place to place a large group of women went with him (Luke 8:1–3). These women were devoted to Jesus' teaching. They wanted to hear everything he said, and on this occasion he told a story that touched the world of their experience—the story of a poor woman at home who lost one of her only coins.

As far as we know, this is something the rabbis never did: set the story of a woman side by side with the story of a man.[6] First Jesus told a story about a man who went out into the wilderness to look for his sheep; then he told a story about a woman who swept her floor to look for her coin. By putting the story of a woman next to the story of a man, Jesus was reaching his whole audience.

This may still seem insignificant, but consider how many times something like this happens in the Gospel of Luke. Two miracles are performed, two stories are told, or two examples are given, and one of them relates specifically to women. First Jesus healed a centurion's servant (Luke 7:1–10); then he raised a widow's son (Luke 7:11–17). Jesus told two parables about

5. Kenneth E. Bailey, *Jacob and the Prodigal: How Jesus Retold Israel's Story* (Downers Grove, IL: InterVarsity, 2003), 88.
6. Ibid., 90.

how God answers prayer: one is the friend at midnight—a story about the man of the house (Luke 11:5–13), but the other is the story of the persistent widow (Luke 18:1–8). In teaching about the sign of Jonah, Jesus used two examples from the Old Testament: the men of Nineveh and the Queen of the South (Luke 11:29–32). Jesus performed two miracles on the Sabbath: one was the woman with the disabling spirit (Luke 13:10–17), while the other was the man with dropsy (Luke 14:1–6). In describing the people that he saved, Jesus called one of them "a daughter of Abraham" (Luke 13:16) and the other "a son of Abraham" (Luke 19:9). Jesus told two parables about the kingdom of God. The first story was about a man working in his garden to sow a mustard seed (Luke 13:18–19); the second was about a woman working in the kitchen to mix leaven in with her dough (Luke 13:20–21). Similarly, in his teaching about the coming of the Son of Man, Jesus used examples of men working in the fields and women grinding out their grain (Luke 17:34–36).

Can you see what Jesus was doing? In contrast to the other preachers of his day, he wanted to teach women as much as men. To do that effectively, he made a point of using examples that related to their life experience. According to Luke, Jesus Christ is not a male chauvinist: his ministry, his gospel, his teaching, and his theology are explicitly for women.

There is more, because the woman in this parable represents the character of God himself. As she looks for her lost coin, and as she rejoices in finding it, she shows us the joy that God has in finding lost sinners. This is a connection people sometimes miss. It is easy to see that the shepherd who finds his lost sheep must be God the Son, who said, "I am the good shepherd" (John 10:14). It is also easy to see that the father who finds his lost son must be God the Father. But if these three stories are parallel, then in some way the woman who finds her lost coin must also represent God.

Going back to the early church fathers, many Christians have thought that this woman represents the Holy Spirit—an interpretation that seems to fit with the other stories in the parable. If the first story is about Jesus the Good Shepherd and the third story is about God the loving Father, then it would make good sense for the middle story to show us the Holy Spirit. There may even be a specific point of connection in the story, because in order to find her coin, the woman had to light her lamp. Perhaps this refers to the work of the Spirit in lighting our way to God.

Admittedly, this interpretation seems somewhat speculative. But whether the woman in the parable stands for the Spirit or not, she certainly shows us something about God. This is not to say that God is a woman. (He is not a man, either; God does not have a gender, although most commonly he uses masculine terms to reveal himself to us as the Father and the Son.) But from time to time—on rare occasions—God compares his attitudes and actions to the love of a woman. For example, speaking through the prophet Isaiah, God said, "As one whom his mother comforts, so I will comfort you" (Isa. 66:13). To help us understand the comfort of his compassion, God says that his love is like a mother's affection for her only son. Here in Luke, Jesus tells us that the love of God pursues us the way a poor woman pursues a lost coin.

God is not embarrassed to make this kind of comparison. The women he made in his image are able to reflect his grace, as Jesus showed throughout his earthly ministry. Jesus cared for the women in his life in a way that elevated their sense of dignity. Therefore anyone who treats women with disrespect, or fails to prize their gifts, or dismisses their capacity to learn sound theology, or puts them down in any way does not have the love of Christ, who cares about women as much as he cares about men.

## As Precious as Silver

The story of the lost coin also teaches how precious we are to God. Notice that there is a progression in the larger parable. The lost sheep was only one out of a hundred. The lost coin is one of out ten. The lost son will be one out of two (although really both sons were lost, as we shall see). Needless to say, a coin cannot possibly compare with the precious life of a son, but since it is one out of ten, it would seem to be more precious than the sheep—at least as far as the ratio is concerned.

The coin was certainly precious to the woman, who we may infer was very poor. The coin she lost was a drachma, which in those days was roughly equivalent to a full day's wage for a common laborer. It is hard to work out an exact equivalent, and it depends on what kind of work a person does, of course, but it would amount to perhaps a hundred dollars in today's economy.

Needless to say, anyone who dropped a hundred dollar bill would take the trouble to look for it, especially someone living below the poverty line. Although the parable does not give us any other details about the woman's financial situation, ten coins may well have represented her life savings, and therefore she would have guarded them with her life. According to custom, in those days a housewife would have kept her money in a chain around her neck, or else tied them up in a little rag. When she discovered that one of her coins was missing, she would have done anything to get it back. Her coin was too precious to lose; it had to be found.

The value this woman placed on her lost coin shows the great love that God has for lost sinners. We are as precious to him as silver—an analogy that works at several levels. To begin with, the relationship between the woman and her coin was that of ownership. Even when it was lost, the coin still belonged to her. In the same way, each of us belongs to God. Even if we have fallen away, and even if we never acknowledge him, we still belong to him by virtue of the fact that he made us. So when we finally come to God in repentance, through faith in Jesus Christ, God is getting back his own.

Another point of comparison—not mentioned explicitly in the parable, but illustrated by its central image—is that like the coin, we bear a royal likeness. At the time of Christ, coins generally bore the imprint of the Caesar in Rome. Since we are made in the image of our King, we too have been stamped with his likeness. Furthermore, silver is a metal that remains precious even after it tarnishes. Unless it is kept polished, silver will darken with time; nevertheless, it retains its value. This is our situation exactly. We were made precious when God fashioned us in his own image, giving us a dignity that surpasses all the other creatures. Sadly, our race has fallen into sin and is now darkened by all the sins of our depravity. Nevertheless, we are still valuable to God. Even in our lost and fallen condition, he considers us his prized possession.

Know for sure that we are precious to God. Now that Jesus has paid the price for our redemption by bleeding and dying for our sins on the cross, we are more precious to God than ever. Do not wonder whether or not your life is even worth living. Do not feel forgotten. Do not doubt that God loves you. The story of the lost coin shows that God loves each one of us as if there were only one of us to love. Even when we are lost, we are still precious to God and will be useful to him when he finds us.

Lost!

This story also teaches that until God does find us, we are helplessly lost. A lost coin is certain to stay lost until it is found. We are in the same situation spiritually, for we cannot find ourselves. Once we are lost, we will stay lost until we are found by God.

Each of the stories in this triple parable has to do with something that is lost: a lost sheep, a lost coin, a lost son. But notice that each of these things gets lost in a different way, so that together these stories give us a full picture of what it means to be lost. The sheep simply wandered away from its shepherd. Heedless of danger, it followed its own instincts and appetites. The same thing happens to us when we go off and pursue our own pleasures: we end up far away from God, and whether we realize it or not, our souls are in mortal danger. As we shall see, the son got lost by his own deliberate will. He chose to walk down the path of rebellion, and when he discovered that he was lost, he knew that he had no one to blame but himself. Yet the coin was lost through no apparent fault of its own. It slipped between the woman's fingers, or fell out of her purse, or got knocked off the table, and then it was truly lost.

When we use this parable as an illustration of our own spiritual experience, we have to admit that what happened to the coin is never the whole story for us. We can never say that we got lost through no fault of our own. We are like the sheep that wandered away, or like the son who turned his back on his father and went to live in a far country. Yet, we may well be able to say that what happened to the coin is *part* of our story. The hard circumstances of our lives conspired to keep us away from God. Maybe no one took us to church when we were children, or taught us what the Bible says about salvation. Or maybe people sinned against us, and this only drove us further into sin. But however it happened, the reality is that we are as helplessly lost as a silver coin that has fallen from a woman's purse and rolled into a forgotten corner of her home.

Now, despite our intrinsic value, we are useless to God. We do not have a faith relationship with Jesus Christ, and therefore we do not praise him, have not loved him, and will not serve him. This is what it means to be lost. "Like a coin that is lost," writes Richard Phillips, "sinners lie unused and unseen, no longer contributing the value for which they were fashioned, while God's image with which they were stamped is increasingly tarnished and covered with the dust of sinful living."[7]

Are you able to identify with that coin? Do you know what it means to be lost spiritually? What makes the situation so completely helpless is that coins cannot find themselves. A lost coin is hardly able to leap off the floor, land on the table, and roll back into its owner's money bag! This is why the woman made such a diligent search: a coin will stay lost until it is found.

This illustrates our own spiritual situation until we are found by Christ: we will stay helplessly lost until Jesus comes to find us. Michael Wilcock describes this part of the parable as a story about "the finding of that which cannot help itself." He explains:

> The coin is lifeless, it cannot move, it can certainly not find its own way back like the son, it cannot even bleat for help like the sheep. Of course in some senses lost mankind is not, like the silver coin, inanimate. But spiritually—from the point of view of the Spirit—it is lifeless; and the coin is an apt symbol of those who see the requirements of God and know themselves incapable of rising to them. Only the all-powerful Spirit can rescue men who in that sense are lost.[8]

## A Thorough Search

We may be helplessly lost, but we are not *hopelessly* lost, because Jesus is able to come and save us. This is a fourth lesson from the story of the lost coin. Jesus does not simply leave us in our lost condition, but is looking to find us.

When the woman in the parable discovered that one of her precious coins was missing, she started to search for it. Although her coin was lost, it was not forgotten, and she was determined to get it back. In those days most homes were only about the size of a one-car garage, but they were very dark, with only a few small slits to let in the light. Typically floors were made of dirt, sometimes covered with straw. In Galilee, where Jesus came from, they were usually made of flagstones. How easy it was, therefore, for the woman's coin to get covered with straw, or to be concealed by the dust,

7. Phillips, *Turning Your World*, 111.
8. Michael Wilcock, *The Message of Luke*, The Bible Speaks Today (Downers Grove, IL: Inter-Varsity, 1979), 154.

or to fall into a crack between two stones. In order to find it, she would have to light a lamp, get out her broom, and make a clean sweep.

In the first part of this parable, Jesus emphasized the persistence of the good shepherd, who looked for his lost sheep until he found it. The woman who lost her coin was equally persistent. She knew that the missing money had to be in her house somewhere, and she would not stop looking until she found it. But what Jesus especially emphasized was the meticulous thoroughness of her search. With extreme care the woman lit her lamp, swept her house, and searched diligently to find her lost coin. We can imagine her getting down on her hands and knees to examine every square inch of her home. Subjecting her floor to the most careful scrutiny, she looked in such a way as to find. This is the way people look for anything they really want to find. First they look in the most obvious places, but if the missing item is still nowhere to be found, they go back and conduct a more thorough investigation.

This is also the way that Jesus looks for lost sinners: in such a way as to find. The reason Jesus came to earth in the first place was to seek and to save what was lost. This is why he became a man, why he performed miracles, why he preached the kingdom of God, and why he died and rose again. Jesus was looking to find.

Even now he is still conducting his search, looking in every corner of the world for the sinners he died to save. Jesus has sent his gospel out into the world—the gospel that says everyone who trusts in his cross and believes in his empty tomb will be saved. He has sent his Spirit out into the world—the Spirit who convinces people they are lost in sin and invites them to come to Christ. He has sent his church out into the world—the church that proclaims the gospel, by the power of the Spirit, to all the unreached peoples on all the lost continents of the globe. Jesus is looking to find and seeking to save. With painstaking thoroughness, he will keep searching and searching until he finds every last one of the precious coins that belongs in his pocket.

If you are lost and waiting to be found, Jesus is looking to find you. He is searching and seeking to save you. Here is how Anne Lamott described her experience of being lost and getting found:

[Jesus] was relentless. I didn't experience Him so much as the hound of heaven, as the old description has it, as the alley cat of heaven, who seemed to believe that if it just keeps showing up, mewling outside your door, you'd eventually open up and give him a bowl of milk. . . . I resisted as long as I could, like Sam-I-Am in *Green Eggs and Ham*. . . . He wore me out. He won. I was tired and vulnerable and He won. . . . Then, when I was dozing, tiny kitten that I was, He picked me up like a mother cat, by the scruff of my neck, and deposited me in a little church. . . . That's where I was when I came to. And then I came to believe.[9]

## THE JOY OF BEING FOUND

Every lost sinner has a different story to tell, because we all get found in different ways. But whenever and wherever and however Jesus finds us, we all share the same joy. This is the fifth and final lesson from the story of the lost coin: it is a joy to be found by Jesus Christ—a joy that lasts forever.

When the woman found her lost coin, she gathered her girlfriends to celebrate (the Greek words that Luke uses for "friends and neighbors" are feminine). Because her search was so rewarding, it led to great rejoicing, which is really the main point of this story. Thus Jesus ended this part of his parable by saying: "Just so, I tell you, there is joy before the angels of God over one sinner who repents" (Luke 15:10).

This statement is virtually repeated from verse 7, where Jesus said there is "more joy in heaven over one sinner who repents than over ninety-nine righteous persons who need no repentance" (Luke 15:7). Here in verse 10 he makes no comparison, but when he mentions "the angels of God," once again he is pulling back the curtain so that we can see what joy there is in heaven whenever Jesus finds a lost sinner. Jesus ought to know, because he has been there!

It is always a joy to find something that is missing, as we know from everyday experience. Even if what we find is only something small, we invariably tell someone else about it. "Hey! Look what I found!" we say. "You'll never guess what I just discovered!" Yet the simple joy of finding something lost cannot compare with the surpassing joy of being found by Jesus Christ. What a joy it is when Jesus finds you in your lost and helpless situation, when you respond by repenting of your sins and receiving the

9. Anne Lamott, quoted by Susan Olasky in "Like a Puppy in a Christmas Stocking," *World* (Sept. 20, 2003): 25.

123

free gift of eternal life. What a joy it is to see someone else come to Christ. What a joy it is to the angels, who love to celebrate the grace of God for the poor lost sinners of our fallen race. What a joy it also is to God himself. When Jesus spoke about "joy before the angels," he was not referring only or even primarily to the joy that the angels have, but also to the joy which they witness every time a sinner gets saved. The angels see the joy of God.

If you want to bring joy to the heart of God—and to your own heart—then turn away from your sin and trust in Jesus Christ for your salvation. If you are not yet a believer, the angels are waiting to celebrate. What joy there will be in heaven when you finally come to Christ! Then, once you have come to Christ, do everything you can to welcome other people with the love of God, just as Jesus welcomed the tax collectors and the sinners. Jesus is looking to receive sinners, and he is calling you to be part of the search party.

A beautiful example of the way Jesus looks for lost sinners—and of the joy he brings when they are found—comes from the Bayview Glen Church in Toronto, Ontario, where Pastor Sam Nasser was preaching in Persian to an Iranian congregation during the summer of 2004. Pastor Nasser was troubled by the fact that one of the women in the church was talking on her cell phone during the worship service. At first he thought it must be some kind of emergency, but when it happened again the following week he was even more disturbed.

Nasser invited the woman to his office to confront her about this ongoing distraction. "Pastor," she said, "I already told you! My husband in Iran is very interested in how I became a Christian because of listening to you." This still did not explain the cell phone, but when the pastor asked for a further explanation, the woman said,

> I bought a calling card, and I call my husband in Tehran so he can hear you preaching. He puts the call on the speakerphone so my mother and sister can hear too. They have been inviting other friends and family over, and for the past three months, they have been listening to you preach. More people come every week. I am not talking on the phone. I'm just holding it up so they can hear your message about Jesus!

Needless to say, Pastor Nasser invited the woman to sit right at the front of the church. The following week he preached on the love of Jesus for his precious children. At the end of the service he asked if anyone wanted to pray to receive Christ. Suddenly the woman with the cell phone started to shout: "My husband! My husband! My husband got saved! My mother and sister want to come to the Lord too!"[10]

Even if he does it over the cell phone halfway around the world, Jesus is looking for lost sinners. He is looking for them every time somebody preaches the gospel. He is looking for them right now. I pray that he will find you, because I know that when he does, you will rejoice. So will the hosts of heaven. And so will Jesus.

10. This account was first published in *Lifeline*, the Bayview Glen Church newsletter, in September of 2004.

# 66

# THE LOST SON

## *Luke 15:11—24*

*"Not many days later, the younger son gathered all he had and took a journey into a far country, and there he squandered his property in reckless living."* (Luke 15:13)

*I*f ever there was a boy who broke his father's heart, it was the prodigal son. Sick of his father, sick of his family, and sick of living on the family farm, he went off to make his way in the world. First he demanded his share of his father's inheritance—even before the old man died. Then he ran away from home, taking everything with him and leaving nothing behind. The young man wanted to do whatever he wanted to do, wherever and with whomever he wanted to do it. Soon the prodigal son had squandered everything his father gave him, and almost before he realized what was happening, he was living like a filthy animal. The boy was as lost as lost can be.

LOST AND FOUND

The story of this lost son is one of the most famous stories ever told. It is famous because it was told by Jesus Christ, the only Son of the Father.

It is famous because it is told so perfectly; not one single detail is wasted. And it is famous because when we hear it we sense that it is really our own story, that we are all lost children who desperately need to know the Father's love.

The parable of the prodigal son comes as the climax to a series of three stories in a triple parable about the joy of God in finding lost sinners: the lost sheep (Luke 15:1–7), the lost coin (Luke 15:8–10), and now the lost son (Luke 15:11–32). Really, though, the parable is about lost *sons*, because even though he never left home, the elder brother was just as lost as the prodigal son (see Luke 15:25–32). Jesus has both brothers clearly in view: "There was a man who had two sons" (Luke 15:11).

These three stories go together. Hearing them is like hearing the same melody played on three different musical instruments: it is all the same music, but each story has its own unique sound.[1] The third story brings the parable to its unmistakable climax. We pity the lost sheep and prize a lost coin, but identify most closely with the lost son. The son gets lost by his own deliberate will—not haphazardly like the sheep, or helplessly like the coin, but willfully and defiantly. He is lost because he wants to be lost, but just because he is a son, there is even greater joy when he is found.

The prodigal son is usually regarded as among the most familiar of all the parables that Jesus told. Most people know its general outline, which may be summarized as follows: sick of home, sick, homesick, home. The lost son was sick of home (Luke 15:11–12), then he was just plain sick (Luke 15:13–16), until he became homesick (Luke 15:17–19), and finally went back home (Luke 15:20–24). It all sounds so familiar. But do we really know this story as well as we think we know it?

One way to find out is to study each of the three main characters: the lost son, the prodigal father, and the lost brother. We begin with the lost son. When we study his actions and attitudes carefully, we discover that he was even more lost than we ever realized. If we are honest, we may also discover that we ourselves are more lost than we like to admit. The prodigal son is partly who we are, not just who we were, because in our hearts we want to leave home again and again.

1. Michael Wilcock makes this analogy in *The Message of Luke*, The Bible Speaks Today (Downers Grove, IL: InterVarsity, 1979), 153.

127

## Lost at Home

Consider all the ways that the prodigal son was lost before he was found. He was lost at home, even before he left his father's house. Jesus said, "There was a man who had two sons. And the younger of them said to his father, 'Father, give me the share of property that is coming to me.' And he divided his property between them" (Luke 15:11–12).

At first it may seem that the son was simply asking his father for money, as sons will do. Yet this request was far more sinister because it really meant that he could not wait for his father to die.[2] The son knew that when his old man died, he stood to inherit one-third of everything he owned (his older brother would get two-thirds). But he did not want to wait that long. As the years passed, he spent more and more time thinking about what he wanted to do with his father's wealth. The old man was getting older, but he still wouldn't die. Finally, the son decided he could not wait any longer, so he went in and demanded what he had coming to him.

Here it is important to know some of the basics about ancient property law. In those days a man did not have to wait until he died to bequeath his legacy. In fact, it was not uncommon for a father to grant his son the legal right to his inheritance while he was still living. If a father did this, however, the income from that property still belonged to him. Although his son now had a legal right to the capital, he did not have the right to sell it. The father's property belonged to the son, but he could not use it for himself until his father died.[3]

Something similar happens today when a mother says to one of her daughters, "After I die, I want you to have this antique table." One day it will belong to the daughter, but not until her mother dies. In the meantime, her mother is still using the table, and it would be the height of insolence to take it away from her. Something similar also happens today when someone buys an annuity. Say, for example, that Mr. Smith puts the money for his annuity into a trust, with the capital to go to his son when he dies. While Mr. Smith is still living, he cannot touch the capital, but continues to draw

2. Kenneth E. Bailey, *Jacob and the Prodigal: How Jesus Retold Israel's Story* (Downers Grove, IL: InterVarsity, 2003), 38.

3. Leon Morris, *The Gospel According to St. Luke: An Introduction and Commentary*, Tyndale New Testament Commentaries (Grand Rapids: Eerdmans, 1974), 240.

interest from the annuity. His son now has a legal right to the capital, but he cannot claim that right until his father dies.

In effect, what the prodigal son did was to go in and tell his father to hand over his capital. It was not just the property he wanted, but also the right to sell it. To put this in legal terms, he wanted the right of disposition as well as possession.[4] He wanted full control of his inheritance, and he wanted it now. For a son to make such a demand was utterly unthinkable. It could only mean that he regarded his father with complete contempt. When he said, "Give me my inheritance," he was saying, in effect, "I wish you would just go ahead and die!"

No doubt the young man had despised his father for a good long time, maybe all his life. His outrageous demand does not sound like the kind of speech that someone makes on the spur of the moment, but the kind that comes after years of disdain. With customary wit, here is how Rudyard Kipling summarizes the son's attitude toward his family in the years leading up to the day he finally rejected them:

My father glooms and advises me,
My brother sulks and despises me,
My mother catechises me,
Till I want to go out and swear![5]

The prodigal son wanted to do a lot more than swear, however. He was tired of always having his father tell him what to do. He wanted to go wherever he wanted to go and do whatever he wanted to do. But in order to do that, he had to be able to spend whatever he wanted to spend, which meant getting as much money from his father as he could. Like the tax collectors who were among the sinners listening to this parable (see Luke 15:1), the young man was greedy for money.

Do you see how lost the son was? He was lost when he was still at home, even before he left the family farm. He was lost in selfishness, ingratitude, rebellion, and greed. He was lost in his rejection of authority. But mainly

---

4. Kenneth E. Bailey, *The Cross and the Prodigal: Luke 15 Through the Eyes of Middle Eastern Peasants* (Downers Grove, IL: InterVarsity, 2005), 41.

5. Rudyard Kipling, "The Prodigal Son (Western Version)," in R. Kent Hughes, *Luke: That You May Know the Truth*, 2 vols., Preaching the Word (Wheaton, IL: Crossway, 1998), 2:140.

he was lost because he did not love his father. Not that it was against the law for him to demand his inheritance. According to the law of Moses, he was entitled to one-third of his father's estate (Deut. 21:17). But even if he did not break the law, he did break a relationship, and in doing so he broke his father's heart.[6]

Can you also see how lost you sometimes are, or may be altogether? Here was a young man who wanted what his father could give him but did not want his father himself. This is what it means for us to be lost. It means not loving the Father. It means putting demands on God without desiring God himself. It means wanting his gifts without loving him as the Giver.

When we take this attitude, what we are really expressing is hatred to God. And of course there are times when all of us *do* take this attitude. We object to God's fatherly discipline, wanting to have life on our own terms. We complain about God's fatherly care, demanding something better than what he is providing for us. We presume upon God's fatherly affection, expecting his blessing without depending upon him in prayer. Even when we are at home with God, our prodigal hearts sometimes long to run away. This is what sin is: running from God.

## In a Far Country

As lost as the prodigal son was at home, he was even more lost when he eventually ran away: "Not many days later, the younger son gathered all he had and took a journey into a far country, and there he squandered his property in reckless living" (Luke 15:13).

In case there had been any doubt, now it is perfectly clear why the lost son demanded the capital from his father's estate: he was leaving home as fast as he could, and he was not coming back. The Greek expression for "gathered all he had" *(synagagōn)* comes from the world of finance. It means to take one's property and turn it into cash. Within a matter of days, the prodigal son had liquidated all his new assets, and by the time he was finished, he had a lot of money. We know from the end of the story that his father was a wealthy man, with herds of livestock, hired servants, and a banqueting hall he could afford to fill with

---

6. Bailey, *The Cross and the Prodigal*, 42.

music. Now the prodigal son had a big chunk of all that change in his pocket, and he was off to see the world.

What he really wanted, of course, was the freedom to sin, and in order to have that freedom he had to get away from his father, away from his family, and away from the community of faith. As long as he stayed home, he would be unable to use his money the way he wanted; so he had to run away. And once he took everything with him, there was nothing left to tie him to his father's house.

Douglas Milne sees this parable as a paradigm for postmodern times. The attitude of the lost son, he says, is "reminiscent of the relativist temper that inspires the postmodern spirit." According to Milne, the prodigal son was a kind of relativist, choosing his own values without showing very much concern for others. His journey to a far country was a "quest of personal freedom and fulfillment." But the full enjoyment of that freedom "could only be attained in fleeing from the father's house with all that it stood for in terms of tradition, authority, objective values and social-moral responsibilities to his father and his brother."[7]

These attitudes may be part of the postmodern spirit, but they are as old as the prodigal son, because they come from the fallen condition of our sinful hearts. Left to ourselves, we would not choose to stay under God's authority, but instead to wander in the far country of sin. How often the prodigal sons and daughters of the church have made the same journey. Sometimes they are lost even before they leave home, but usually they have to leave home to be as lost as they want to be. So they run off to the big city or go away for college and start to party.

The result is all too predictable. Today people call it "getting wasted." Jesus said it like this: "he squandered his property in reckless living" (Luke 15:13). Jesus did not say exactly how the young man spent his money, but it is not hard to guess. The Greek term for "reckless living" *(zōn asōtōs)* has the connotation of luxury. Here was a young man with expensive tastes, who tended to confuse the high cost of living with the cost of high living. He wore the finest clothes, went to the fanciest dinners, and enjoyed the wildest entertainments. As J. B. Phillips put it in his paraphrase of this passage, "he squandered his wealth in the wildest extravagance." In a word, he

7. Douglas J. W. Milne, "The Father with Two Sons: A Modern Reading of Luke 15," *Themelios* 27. 1 (2001), 13.

was "prodigal," which means "recklessly wasteful." As Aristotle said, a prodigal is "a man who has a single evil quality, that of wasting his substance."[8]

Soon, and not surprisingly, all of his money was gone—every last denarius. The lost son had lived without any thought for tomorrow, so when tomorrow came, there was nothing left. His father's legacy was supposed to set him up for life, but he practically gave it away. How irresponsible he was! What a spendthrift! What a wastrel! What a slacker!

As lost as the young man was, it is more important to see the temptations of our own prodigal hearts. Like the lost son, we want to run away from God and live the way that we want to live. We squander our time pursuing our pleasures. We squander our money, spending so much on ourselves that there is little or nothing left for God. We squander our talents by not using them for our Father's joy. Jesus calls this "reckless living." How recklessly are you living? Do not waste your life feeding your addictions, indulging your passions, and giving away your Father's inheritance. Do not squander your time, your money, and your talents on yourself when you could and should be investing them in the kingdom of God.

## THE LOWEST OF THE LOW

It was bad enough for the lost son to waste all his money, but then something happened that turned his situation into a total catastrophe. There was a famine in the land—an unspeakable horror that brought him to the very brink of starvation: "And when he had spent everything, a severe famine arose in that country, and he began to be in need. So he went and hired himself out to one of the citizens of that country, who sent him into his fields to feed pigs. And he was longing to be fed with the pods that the pigs ate, and no one gave him anything" (Luke 15:14–16).

Here was one humiliation after another. Although he had always planned on spending a lot of money, the lost son had never planned on running out of it, and he certainly had never planned on running out of food. But his situation became so critical that in a desperate attempt to stave off starvation, he took the only job he could find. Usually parents are glad to see their children go out and get a job, but this job was completely degrading. Rather

---

8. Aristotle, *Nicomachean Ethics*, quoted in Bailey, *The Cross and the Prodigal*, 53.

than going home to get help, or serving some devout member of the Jewish community, the lost son attached himself to a citizen of the far country.

Even worse, this godless Gentile was a hog farmer, which was utterly detestable to the Jews. According to the law of Moses, pigs were ceremonially unclean (see Lev. 11:7). "Cursed be the man who would breed swine," the rabbis said.[9] When Jesus told this story, the Pharisees must have murmured with dismay at the thought of a nice Jewish boy herding Gentile pigs, which to them was "the most humiliating and repulsive form of servile labor."[10] What could be more disgusting than farming hogs?

Only this: the young man was so hungry that he wanted to eat what they were eating. Under ordinary circumstances, pig slop would not even be considered fit for human consumption. Yet the prodigal son was absolutely desperate. No matter how much he begged, no one was able or willing to help him—not even his employer, who may well have been trying to get rid of him. The lost son grew so desperately hungry that he began to envy the pigs, of all creatures, craving their food. Now he was as low as anyone could possibly go—lower even than the filthiest animal. He was helpless, homeless, hungry, and humiliated. He was as lost as lost can be.

What a picture this is of our own spiritual condition outside of Christ. This is what it means to be lost. It is like being without money, without food, and without friends—a complete failure in life. In the words of Peter Chrysologus,

> This is the experience that comes to one who refuses to trust himself to his father but delivers himself to a stranger. . . . A deserter from affection, a refugee from fatherly love, he is assigned to the swine, sentenced to them, and given over to their service. He wallows in their muddy fodder. The rush of the restless herd bruises and soils him so he perceives how wretched and bitter it is to have lost the happiness of peaceful life in his father's house.[11]

This is where reckless living always leads. To run away from God and decide to go our own way in life is to end up living in spiritual squalor.

9. *Baba Kamma* 82b, quoted in Morris, *Luke*, 241.
10. Norval Geldenhuys, *The Gospel of Luke*, New International Commentary on the New Testament (Grand Rapids: Eerdmans, 1951), 407.
11. Peter Chrysologus, "Sermon 1," in *Luke*, ed. Arthur A. Just, Jr., Ancient Christian Commentary on Scripture, NT 3 (Downers Grove, IL: InterVarsity, 2003), 249.

When we gratify ourselves with sinful pleasures, when we live for more possessions, and when we rush from one entertainment to the next, we are starving our souls. Soon we will end up as disillusioned as the lost soul in a Morris West novel who said:

> I was lost a long time, without knowing it. Without the Faith, one is free, and that is a pleasant feeling at first. There are no questions of conscience, no constraints, except the constraints of custom, convention, and the law, and these are flexible enough for most purposes. It is only later that the terror comes. One is free—but free in chaos, in an unexplained and unexplainable world. One is free in a desert, from which there is no retreat but inward, towards the hollow core of oneself. There is nothing to build on the small rock of one's own price, and this is nothing, based on nothing.[12]

## THOUGHTS OF HOME

This is what the lost son was left with: absolutely nothing. He did not even have the bare necessities, but was dying of starvation. Then he had the thought that saved his life. Up until this point, the lost son had been willing to endure anything, as long as he did not have to swallow his pride and go back to his father: "But when he came to himself, he said, 'How many of my father's hired servants have more than enough bread, but I perish here with hunger! I will arise and go to my father, and I will say to him, "Father, I have sinned against heaven and before you. I am no longer worthy to be called your son. Treat me as one of your hired servants"'" (Luke 15:17–19).

Now that he had hit hog bottom, the lost son was finally coming to his senses. He was seeing how lost he really was, which is always the first step to recovery. He realized that he had nowhere to go but home. "He was truly lost," writes Henri Nouwen, "and it was this complete lostness that brought him to his senses. He was shocked into the awareness of his utter alienation and suddenly understood that he had embarked on the road to death. . . . He knew that one more step in the direction he was going would take him to self-destruction."[13]

12. Morris West, *The Devil's Advocate* (London: Fontana, 1977), 262.
13. Henri J. M. Nouwen, *The Return of the Prodigal Son: A Story of Homecoming* (New York: Doubleday, 1994), 48.

The ensuing monologue gives many encouraging indications of the young man's spiritual progress. He has decided to get up and go back home, to the place where he was before he took his wrong turn in life. He is starting to think about repenting of his sin and to prepare the speech he hopes will touch his father's heart. In that speech he identifies himself as a sinner, knowing that this is the moral category in which he truly belongs. He does not make any excuses for himself. He does not blame his desperate situation on the famine, or on God, or on the people who will not give him anything, but on his own deliberate rebellion.

Furthermore, the prodigal son recognized that his sin was multidimensional. In other words, he had sinned against both his father and his God. This sin was so serious that he no longer deserved to be called his father's son. Thus he expressed a deep sense of personal unworthiness, which was only appropriate for someone who had rejected his father, disgraced his family, and wasted everything they ever gave him.

These are all marks of true repentance—the joyful repentance Jesus has been talking about in this triple parable (see Luke 15:7, 10). When we are lost, the thing to do is to go back and see where we made our mistake. This means admitting that we are sinners, not making excuses, but confessing our sin. It means confessing our sin both to God and to the people we have wronged. It means acknowledging that we are no longer worthy to be considered God's son or daughter.

Yet even as we confess our utter unworthiness, we also need to remember that God is still our Father. This was the lost son's only hope. He did not feel worthy to be called a son. Nevertheless, when he spoke about his father, he was still able to call him his father. "I will arise and go to *my* father," he said (Luke 15:18). Although he was a sinner, he was still a son, and just because the father was *his* father, he could hope that he would not be completely rejected, but accepted enough to be saved. So he got back on his feet and headed for home—the place where every lost sinner needs to return. Repentance is a rising up and a coming back to God.

## A FLAWED REPENTANCE

From his proposed repentance, we can see that the prodigal son was moving in the right spiritual direction. There were some problems, however, with

135

the little speech that he kept rehearsing. Although his repentance seemed to be sincere, it was not sufficient. We get our first hint of a problem when Jesus says that the lost son "came to himself" (Luke 15:17), or more literally, "returned to himself." But this was the *last* place he should turn. With apologies to Benjamin Franklin, God does *not* help those who help themselves. After all, it was by turning to himself that the lost son first got himself into trouble.

There also seems to be a problem with his motivation. His main concern is getting something to eat. But the real issue is not just the lost son's survival; it is the relationship that he has broken with his father. Even though he is getting ready to go back home, it is not at all clear that he is ready to return his father's love. He is still thinking of his father as a means of getting what he wants.

There may be a subtle clue about this in the wording of his proposed confession: "I have sinned against heaven and before you" (Luke 15:18). There is only one other person in the Bible who made this same confession. Do you know who it was? It was Pharaoh, who made his confession only because he wanted Moses to get rid of all the locusts that were plaguing Egypt (see Ex. 10:16).

The prodigal son was nearly as manipulative. He intended to go to his father and say, "Treat me as one of your hired servants" (Luke 15:19). These are the words of someone who is trying to work the system. He is still telling his father what to do, just as he did when he first left home. He is also trying to solve his own problem by working off his debt. He knows that his father's servants have "more than enough bread" (Luke 15:17). More literally, they have "bread and to spare," meaning that they are paid decently enough to save a little money. If he works long enough and hard enough, maybe he can gather enough money to pay off his debts.

In short, his approach to his deliverance is Pelagian: he will be saved by his own efforts. The prodigal is thinking like a servant, not like a son. As Kenneth Bailey explains, "the prodigal plans to offer *his* solution to the problem of their estrangement: job training. He will acquire a skill, work as a paid craftsman and be able to save money. For the present the prodigal will not live at home. Only after the lost money is recovered will he presume to suggest reconciliation. Having failed to find a paying job in the far country, he will try to obtain his father's backing to become gainfully employed in his home community. *He will yet save himself by keeping the law.*"[14] Bailey

14. Bailey, *Jacob and the Prodigal*, 106.

concludes by saying, "The prodigal thinks the problem is lost money. His anticipated solution trivializes the problem, which is not merely a matter of a broken law but is about a broken relationship."[15]

So often we treat God the same way, even after we come to Christ. We know that we are in his debt, and to a certain extent we are sorry for what we have done. But we still imagine that there must be some way for us to balance the books, and thus to earn back God's favor. Even after we have come to God through faith in Christ, we are tempted to treat him more as a master than as a Father. Henri Nouwen writes, "Although claiming my true identity as a child of God, I still live as though the God to whom I am returning demands an explanation. I still think about his love as conditional and about home as a place I am not yet fully sure of. While walking home, I keep entertaining doubts about whether I will be truly welcome when I get there. . . . Belief in total, absolute forgiveness does not come readily."[16]

Like the lost son, we too may be lost in our rebellion against the Father, lost in our headlong pursuit of sin, lost in the humiliation of life's failure, and lost in our last desperate attempt to work our way back to God. Not even our repentance is worthy of his grace. To quote from Nouwen again, "There is repentance, but not a repentance in the light of the immense love of a forgiving God. It is a self-serving repentance that offers the possibility of survival."[17]

## HOMECOMING

As lost as we have been, all is not lost, because we are found in the Father's love. Soon we will see the full extent of this father's love, but understand that he was loving and loving his son the whole time that he was lost. The father loved his son when his son hated him and ran away from home, when he squandered his inheritance, when he was a total failure. We know this because of what happened the day he finally came back home.

By the time the lost son reached the edge of town he was almost home, but he was still lost because he did not know his father's love. "He was still a long way off," Jesus said, and this was true spiritually as well as

15. Ibid., 107.
16. Nouwen, *Return of the Prodigal*, 52.
17. Ibid.

geographically. Yet his father was always looking for him in love, scanning the horizon for a silhouette that he could never forget. So "while he was still a long way off, his father saw him and felt compassion, and ran and embraced him and kissed him" (Luke 15:20). This is the love that God has for lost sinners. It is a love that is running to receive you even before you have a full chance to repent, a love that wraps its arms around you even when you have been wallowing in the pig-sty of sin.

It was at this point that the son finally offered the kind of repentance that Jesus was talking about all the way through this parable—a repentance that responds to the Father's love. No more labor demands; no more strategies for having this relationship on his own terms; no more telling his father what to do—just a free confession of his guilty sin. Placing himself entirely under his father's mercy, the prodigal son said, "Father, I have sinned against heaven and before you. I am no longer worthy to be called your son" (Luke 15:21).

That is all the farther he got, because before he could say anything more, his father was calling for fancy clothes, a fattened calf, and the biggest party anyone could ever remember (Luke 15:22–24). According to the ancient Arab commentator Ibn al-Tayyib, the lost son "did not complete what he was planning to say . . . because he saw from the running of his father to him and the grace-filled way his father met him and embraced him that there was no longer any place for this request to be made into a craftsman. For if after such acts he had made such a request, it would have appeared that he doubted the genuineness of his father's offered forgiveness."[18] The lost son was found in his father's love. However imperfect it may have been, his repentance was accepted, and thus his sins were fully forgiven. Here we see a "persistent man received readily, pardoned freely, and completely accepted with God."[19]

Do you know how much the Father loves you? He loves you so much that he sent Jesus to be your Savior, so much that he is calling you back from the far country of your sin, so much that he is looking for you and longing to receive you. Will you come home to the Father's love? Will you confess that you are more lost than you have ever wanted to admit?

18. Ibn al-Tayyib, quoted in Bailey, *Jacob and the Prodigal*, 109.
19. J. C. Ryle, *Expository Thoughts on the Gospels, Luke* (1858; reprint Cambridge: James Clarke, 1976), 2:184.

And will you ask him to forgive you through the crucifixion and resurrection of Jesus Christ?

In her book *The Hurting Parent*, Margie Lewis tells the story of a lost son who reached the end of his prodigal road, before he was found in the Father's love:

> After years of degenerate living and sampling a catalog of sinful lifestyles, he tried to take his life. One night, half a continent from home and his Christian parents, he stumbled into an all night laundry, picked up the only piece of paper he could find, and scribbled out a suicide note. He tucked it in his pocket and went out to the parking lot. There he took a length of rubber hose he used for a tourniquet when he shot heroin, tied it around his neck, and hanged himself from the luggage rack of a parked car.
>
> He woke up in a hospital emergency room, recovered and eventually went home. A little over a year later, he came to a real and profound experience with the Lord. Shortly after that, he was sorting through some of his things when he happened upon that suicide note. He turned it over and found to his amazement he had written it on a Christian tract about the prodigal son.
>
> "That spoke to me," he said, "It told me that even at the lowest point in my life, I hadn't been able to escape God."[20]

Every lost son and daughter who comes home to God can offer the same testimony. The Father found us when we were lost, loved us when we were unworthy, forgave us before we really knew how to ask for his forgiveness, and sent Jesus to bring us home.

---

20. Margie M. Lewis, *The Hurting Parent* (Grand Rapids: Zondervan, 1980), 132–33.

67

# THE PRODIGAL FATHER

## *Luke 15:11—24*

*"And he arose and came to his father. But while he was still a long way off, his father saw him and felt compassion, and ran and embraced him and kissed him." (Luke 15:20)*

*I*f ever there was a father who loved a son, it was the prodigal father. Usually the son is the one they call the prodigal, and with good reason. In the dictionary, the first definition for the word "prodigal" is "recklessly wasteful." That was the prodigal son—so recklessly wasteful that he squandered everything he had: his money, his reputation, his dignity, his family, and his community. But there is another definition for the word "prodigal." It also means "lavish," and since the story is really about the love a father lavishes on his undeserving son, we can also call it the parable of the prodigal father.

Joe Farrone was a prodigal father. As he spent Labor Day with his family one year, Mr. Farrone's thoughts inevitably turned to Tony, his prodigal son. Joe did not even know whether Tony was alive or dead, but he still hoped that maybe his son would call home. Late that night Tony did call home, and immediately it was evident that he was in bad condition, probably because he was on drugs. "I'm so sick," he said, "and so hungry. I'm really hurting. Tell me what to do."

Tony had placed his call from the lobby of a Holiday Inn more than a hundred miles away. Immediately the family jumped in the car and went to find him. When the Farrones saw their lost son they could hardly recognize him. He seemed more dead than alive. His greasy hair was hanging across his face; his ragged clothes were covered with filthy vomit; his shoes were worn all the way through. Their prodigal son was so weak and confused he had to be carried out to the car. As they drove home, the stench was all but unbearable. Joe said to himself, "I've heard so many sermons about the prodigal son in a stinking pigpen. Now here I am holding my nose and living out that very scene." Then he said this: "My son. I love him because he is my son. He has come back home and that's all that matters now."[1]

Tony Farrone was saved by his father's extravagant love. How costly it was for Joe Farrone to keep loving and loving his son, even when he was wasting away, but this is what a good father does: he lavishes his wayward children with love, no matter what the cost. We see this in the parable of the prodigal father, whose affection came at a much higher price than most people even realize. In this story Jesus shows us what Kenneth Bailey calls "the costly demonstration of unexpected love"[2]—the undeserved affection of a Father who loves us even more than we ever dared to hope.

## THE COST OF LETTING GO

This father loved his son when they were both still living at home. How costly it was for him to be a father to this lost son then! Jesus said, "There was a man who had two sons. And the younger of them said to his father, 'Father, give me the share of property that is coming to me.' And he divided his property between them" (Luke 15:11–12).

Obviously this cost the prodigal father a large amount of money. Imagine how expensive it would be to give up, on demand, one full third of everything you have worked so hard to gain. In those days, the most that

1. The Farrones' story is told by Margie M. Lewis in *The Hurting Parent* (Grand Rapids: Zondervan, 1980), 77–80.

2. Kenneth E. Bailey, *Jacob and the Prodigal: How Jesus Retold Israel's Story* (Downers Grove, IL: InterVarsity, 2003), 111.

a father ever gave his son was the right to have his inheritance, never the right to sell it. Even if he began handing on his property before he died, as some fathers did, he still needed to live off the proceeds. So his legacy was like an annuity held in trust, which could be reinvested only after he died. In this case, however, the son demanded both the right to own and the right to sell.

Speaking purely in financial terms, this was a costly demand. When the Scripture says that the father "divided his property" (Luke 15:12), it uses the word for property that also means "life" *(bion)*, as if to say that the father was giving his very life to his son. Yet this is what the prodigal father did. He responded to his son's unreasonable request with unimaginable generosity. Rather than disowning his son and driving him out of the house, as many fathers would have done, he gave him what he asked.

Then the lost son actually sold the property, and this cost his father even more. Jesus said, "Not many days later, the younger son gathered all he had and took a journey into a far country" (Luke 15:13). The phrase "gathered all he had" indicates that he sold his third of his father's estate, turning it into cash. Kenneth Bailey explains that this would have been "a staggering loss to the entire family clan. The parable specifically states that the prodigal settled his affairs in a few days. This means that he liquidated his assets in a hurry which in turn indicates a 'sale at any price.' The accumulated economic gains of generations would be lost in a few days."[3]

The whole family suffered for this selfishness, but no one suffered more than the father. The real loss to him in all of this was not financial, but relational. When his son started to sell his property, the man was exposed to the insult of public humiliation. There were no secrets in a town like this. People would talk, and soon everyone would hear what his son was doing. This would reflect very badly on the family name. The prodigal son was putting them all to shame.

Even that is not the worst of it, however. No, what cost the father most was the heartless rebellion of his own beloved son. When the boy demanded his share of the inheritance, he was really saying that he wished his father would go ahead and die.[4] It was a total rejection. The son was saying "no"

3. Kenneth E. Bailey, *The Cross and the Prodigal: Luke 15 Through the Eyes of Middle Eastern Peasants* (Downers Grove, IL: InterVarsity, 2005), 42.

4. See Bailey, *The Cross and the Prodigal*, 41.

to the family, "no" to their community, and "no" to his father's heart. All he wanted was the money and nothing else, with complete control to live the way that he wanted to live. It must have cut his father to the very heart. How humiliated he was to be despised by his own son, and how heartbroken to know that despite all the advantages he had in life, his son would never reach his potential to take a place of leadership in society.

As costly it was for this father to let go of his son, it was just as costly to go on loving his son the whole time that he was lost! The prodigal father thought about the boy *every* day that he was gone, as any parent who has ever lost a child can testify. His son may have been lost, but he was never forgotten. Every day his father wondered where he was and what he was doing. He was always hoping for the best, but fearing the worst, because anyone could see that the boy would end up losing everything he had.

Knowing there was nothing he could do to stop him, the father virtually gave his son up for dead. But this did not mean he ever stopped loving his son, or longing that he might return. Although the son was far away from his father's house, he was never away from his father's heart.[5] So the old man watched and waited for his return in suffering silence. As Kenneth Bailey describes it, the father "does not sever his relationship with his son . . . but . . . holds out his broken end of the rope of relationship hoping that the other end can yet be joined. In so doing he suffers. If the father had disowned the son, there would then be no possibility of reconciliation. The father's suffering provides the foundation of the possibility of his son's return."[6]

## THE COST OF WELCOMING HOME

As much as it cost the father to wait for his son, it was even more costly to welcome him home. The boy did not return in triumph, but in disgrace. It would have been customary for someone in his situation to return bearing gifts, especially if he wanted to be reconciled with his family. But to his shame, the lost son was coming back empty-handed. He

5. Alistair Begg uses a similar turn of phrase on page 30 of a Truth for Life booklet called "Parable Portraits."

6. Bailey, *The Cross and the Prodigal*, 47.

returned "with nothing: his money, his health, his honor, his self-respect, his reputation . . . everything has been squandered."[7]

Having lost everything, he looked more like a slave than a son. This is brilliantly portrayed in Rembrandt's painting *The Return of the Prodigal Son*. Rembrandt shows the prodigal son kneeling at his father's feet in penitent surrender, while his father leans over him in an aspect of grace. As the father reaches to embrace his son's shoulders and hold him close to his heart, the contrast between the two figures is unmistakable. The father is covered in scarlet, but his son is dingy and disheveled from his long prodigal road. His head is shaven like a slave's and he is wearing the plain undergarments of servitude. Since he kneels with his back to the viewer, one can see that the soles of his scarred feet have worn all the way through his sandals. This detail is faithful to the biblical text, because as Rembrandt knew, one of the first things the father did for his lost son was to give him a new pair of shoes (Luke 15:22). The prodigal son was the very picture of the degradation that comes when we give ourselves over to the power of sin.

The real humiliation was not the way the young man looked, however, but the way people would treat him when he returned. In those days Jewish people had a deep revulsion for anyone who squandered his inheritance among the Gentiles. By way of example, consider this fatherly warning from one of the Dead Sea Scrolls: "And now, my sons, be watchful of your inheritance that has been bequeathed to you, which your fathers gave you. Do not give your inheritance to Gentiles, . . . lest you be humiliated in their eyes, and foolish, and they trample upon you . . . and become your masters."[8] This is exactly what the prodigal son had done: rather than guarding his father's inheritance, he had given it away to the Gentiles. Now he would have to face the withering scorn of his old friends and neighbors.

The people in his hometown would certainly despise him, but they might well do something even worse. They might cut him off from their community entirely, much the way that the Old Order Amish shun people who violate the code of their community. According to Kenneth Bailey, who has devoted a lifetime to studying the customs of the Middle East, the Jewish community had

7. Henri J. M. Nouwen, *The Return of the Prodigal Son: A Story of Homecoming* (New York: Doubleday, 1994), 46.

8. *The Testament of Kohath*, quoted in Bailey, *Jacob and the Prodigal*, 102.

developed what was called the *kezazah* ceremony (the cutting-off ceremony). Any Jewish boy who lost his inheritance among Gentiles faced the ceremony if he dared return to his home village. The ceremony itself was simple. Fellow villagers would fill a large earthenware pot with burned nuts and burned corn and break it in front of the guilty individual. While doing this, they would shout, "So-and-so is cut off from his people." From that point on, the village would have nothing to do with the hapless lad.[9]

If the lost son received this punishment, it would be no more than he deserved. By disgracing his family, he had earned the condemnation of his community. But the prodigal father did not wait for the village to reject his son. Instead, "while he was still a long way off, his father saw him and felt compassion, and ran and embraced him and kissed him" (Luke 15:20).

What is perhaps most surprising about this costly demonstration of unexpected love is the way the father ran. Even today it is uncommon to see an old man run, but this was especially true in the ancient Near East, where it was considered very undignified for a man of age and position to run. The Greek word used here for "run" *(dramōn)* was usually reserved for competitive footraces. But men who wear long robes do not sprint; they stroll. If an older man *did* want to run, he would have to gather up his robes like a youngster, and his undergarments would probably show. So in all likelihood, a traditional man like the prodigal father had not run anywhere to meet anyone for decades. It simply wasn't done, as anyone who heard this parable would have understood, even without being told.

So why did the old man run? Why did he make such a spectacle of himself? He did it because he could not wait to see his son, of course. But he may also have done it so that he could be reconciled to his son before anyone in the community could even think about cutting him off. Here is how Kenneth Bailey explains the father's strategy:

> [The father] waits day after day, staring down the crowded village street to the road in the distance along which his son disappeared with arrogance and high hopes. The father also remembers the *kezazah* ceremony. He knows only too well how the village will treat his son when he returns in rags. Thus, the father also prepares a plan for their meeting. His plan is to reach the boy

9. Bailey, *Jacob and the Prodigal*, 102.

before the boy reaches the village and thereby protect him from the wrath of the community.

The father realizes that if he is able to achieve reconciliation with his son, *in public*, no one in the village will treat the prodigal badly. If the community witnesses the reconciliation, there will be no suggestion from any quarter that the *kezazah* ceremony should be enacted. But to achieve that goal, self-emptying humiliation will be required of the father.[10]

Understand that when the father ran to meet his son, he was deliberately exposing himself to public humiliation. Rather than looking at the lost son and seeing what a mess he had made of his life, people would look instead at the extraordinary spectacle of a distinguished, landed gentleman hitching up his robes and racing down the street, bare legs and all. By the time anyone realized what was happening, the father and son would already be reconciled. The prodigal father was so lavishly compassionate in his love that he was willing to suffer any humiliation to restore his long-lost son.

So many parents do exactly the opposite—even Christian parents. When their children start going off in the wrong direction, they speak to them with scorn and treat them with shame. Instead of humbling themselves, they humiliate their children, even to their own destruction. But here Jesus gives fathers and mothers a better model to follow, redefining what it means to be a godly parent. The prodigal father does not wait to see what his son has to say for himself. He does not demand an account of what he has done and where he has been. His welcome is not contingent on his son's prior repentance, or on his promise to do better.

Instead, the father takes the initiative to go out and gather his unworthy son into the embrace of his self-humiliating love. His kiss is not so much a response to repentance as it is the cause of reconciliation. The costly expression of the father's love comes first. It is a preemptive reconciliation, offered without any reproach, and before any words of repentance are uttered. "Let it be noted," writes J. C. Ryle, "that the father does not say a single word to his son about his profligacy and wickedness. There is neither rebuke nor reproof for the past, nor galling admonitions for the present, nor irritating

---

10. Ibid., 107.

advice for the future. The one idea that is represented as filling his mind is joy that his son has come home."[11]

What great hope this gives to lost sinners! Even after we have wandered in the far country of sin, even after we have wasted everything we have, and even after we have wallowed in the foul pigpen of our rebellion against God, we have a good and loving Father who is running to welcome us home.

## ONCE A SON, ALWAYS A SON

What a homecoming this was for the long-lost son of the prodigal father. When he left home he gave his father an unqualified rejection, but when he came back he received unqualified acceptance. Almost before the prodigal son knew what was happening, he found himself in his father's arms. He must have been as surprised as anyone to see his father running toward him on the open road—surprised, and maybe a little scared. But there could be no doubt about the old man's intentions when he took his son in his arms and started to kiss him.

I say "started" to kiss him because the form of the Greek verb is intensive. The father was kissing and kissing his son. He was as prodigal with his kisses as he was with the rest of his affections, and this spoke volumes about his feelings for his son. Charles Spurgeon once preached an entire sermon on the father kissing the prodigal son—a seven-point sermon (!) about what it means to be restored to God the Father. Spurgeon said the father's kiss revealed much love, much forgiveness, a full restoration, exceeding joy, overflowing comfort, strong assurance of salvation, and intimate communion with his beloved son.[12]

The son must have been overwhelmed by his father's welcome, but not so overwhelmed that he forgot to make his apologies. "Father," he said, "I have sinned against heaven and before you. I am no longer worthy to be called your son" (Luke 15:21). The boy was right: his sins were so great that he was no longer worthy to be called his father's son. But worthy or not, his father was there to receive him *as a son*. With eager impatience, he said to

---

11. J. C. Ryle, *Expository Thoughts on the Gospels, Luke* (1858; reprint Cambridge: James Clarke, 1976), 2:187–88.

12. Charles Spurgeon, as summarized by Richard D. Phillips in *Turning Your World Upside Down: Kingdom Priorities in the Parables of Jesus* (Phillipsburg, NJ: P&R, 2003), 120.

his servants, "'Bring quickly the best robe, and put it on him, and put a ring on his hand, and shoes on his feet. And bring the fattened calf and kill it, and let us eat and celebrate. For this my son was dead, and is alive again; he was lost, and is found.' And they began to celebrate" (Luke 15:22–24).

There seems to be an ironic twist here, because as we have seen, the son is really the one who ought to be bearing all the gifts. He is the one who owes the great debt; however, he has nothing to give. Empty-handed, he returns with nothing for anyone. He has nothing to give his father except his need—his need for food, his need for clothing, and his need to be forgiven.

What a picture this is of our own spiritual need! What do we have to offer to God? Nothing—absolutely nothing. We owe God an infinite debt for all our sin against his perfect holiness, but we have nothing to pay him, nothing to offer him, nothing to give him. All we can bring is our spiritual need. Augustus Toplady said it well in his famous hymn "Rock of Ages, Cleft for Me." In fact, the hymn sounds like something the prodigal son might say: "Nothing in my hand I bring, simply to thy cross I cling; / naked, come to thee for dress; helpless, look to thee for grace." This is the only way that any prodigal child can come to God: bringing nothing but our need for his grace.

This is exactly what this father gave his long-lost son: the unmerited favor of his grace. No one has ever been more completely saved by grace than the prodigal son. His father gave him free forgiveness and unconditional acceptance, with the full right to be his son. He gave him back everything that he had lost.

Notice the significance of the gifts that the father lavished on his son, each of which signified sonship. When the father called for the best robe in the house, he was placing his mantle on his son. As long as the boy continued to wear the ragged garments of servitude, people would think that he was still a slave. But when he put on the finest robe from his father's house, they would recognize his position as a son. If anything, the ring was even more significant. In all likelihood, it was a signet ring: whoever wore it controlled the estate. Thus the ring was an emblem of authority and the restoration of his inheritance. Even his shoes were a sign of sonship. Servants did not wear shoes in those days, but sons *did* wear shoes, as free men who belonged to a wealthy house. The boy was not received as a servant, but as a son.

His last gift was a fatted calf—specifically, *the* fatted calf—which the family had been saving for a special occasion. With the celebration of this rare feast, the prodigal son was welcomed back into table fellowship at his father's house, and their relationship was fully restored. This was another costly demonstration of unexpected love. The prodigal father spared no expense in welcoming home his long-lost son. He gave him the best of everything, expecting nothing in return: the robe of honor, the ring of inheritance, the footwear of freedom, and the feast of fellowship. He did all this because he wanted everyone to know that his son was still his son.

In fact, this is exactly the language that the father uses in verse 24, when he says, "this my son." Surely this was the greatest gift of all. Twice his son had renounced his sonship: once when he sold his father's estate, and once again when he said "I am no longer worthy to be called your son" (Luke 15:21). But the father has never regarded his son as anything but his son. No matter how much it cost him, his heart would never let him go. So when the prodigal son finally came home, the prodigal father said, "this my son," and the boy was found in his father's love.

## THE LOVE OF GOD

Jesus told this story so we would know for sure of our own acceptance in the extravagant love and exuberant joy of our prodigal God. We too have been welcomed as sons and daughters in the Father's house. We too have been blessed with a costly and "freely offered love that seeks and suffers in order to save."[13] To put this another way, "The same God who suffers because of his immense love for his children is the God who is rich in goodness and mercy and who desires to reveal to his children the richness of his glory."[14]

In this parable we see the compassion of God the Father, who loves us even more than we ever dared to hope. Some people have questioned whether the father in this parable stands for God or not. Yet we know from Scripture that all fatherhood comes from God (see Eph. 3:14–15), so wherever we see a good and godly father, we catch a glimpse of our Father God. We can see from the parable itself how clearly his character is displayed

13. Bailey, *The Cross and the Prodigal*, 88.
14. Nouwen, *Return of the Prodigal*, 111.

in the actions of the prodigal father, who is a human expression of divine compassion. Even when his son was lost in rebellion, he went out to save him from being cut off. So also God the Father has come to save us, not waiting until we get our lives back together, but running to meet us at the end of our prodigal road.

This is good news for every prodigal sinner, as well as every prodigal son or daughter that we love with a wounded heart. God is running to save us with his arms wide to receive us and his heart ready to forgive us. If we come home to God in repentance and faith, we will be found in the Father's love.

This parable also shows us the love of God the Son. Again, some people have questioned this. In fact, many Muslims say this parable proves that we do not need Jesus to be our Savior. All we need to do is turn away from sin by coming to our senses and going back to God. We do not need Jesus to come and save us; we can go back and find God on our own. Even some Christian theologians have said that this is a parable without a Christ because it has no incarnation and no atonement.[15]

Admittedly, no single parable is capable of presenting the whole gospel. For that we need the gospel story itself, with the incarnation, crucifixion, and resurrection of Jesus Christ. What this parable mainly shows us is the joy of God in finding lost sinners. But can we not say that Jesus is in this parable too, that it reveals the love that he has for sinners? J. C. Ryle said, "I believe that the father's kind reception of his son was meant to represent the Lord Jesus Christ's kindness and love toward sinners who come to Him, and the free and full pardon which He bestows on them."[16] Using the imagery of the parable as a reference point, perhaps we can put it like this: God the Father runs to us on the legs of Jesus Christ, for as the Scripture says, "in Christ God was reconciling the world to himself" (2 Cor. 5:19).

Furthermore, when we see such a costly demonstration of unexpected love—especially when it comes at the expense of suffering and humiliation—are we not drawn to the cross where Jesus died? Like the father in the parable he told, in his crucifixion Jesus endured the agony of

15. Most notably B. B. Warfield, "The Prodigal Son," in *Biblical and Theological Studies* (Philadelphia: Presbyterian and Reformed, 1968), 523–42.

16. Ryle, *Luke*, 2:185.

rejected love. Now what the prodigal father said about his prodigal son is true for us by the cross and the empty tomb: once we were dead, but now we are alive.

Here is how Norval Geldenhuys summarizes what the parable of the prodigal father teaches us about the extravagant love of the triune God:

> So inexplicably wonderful is the love of God that He not merely forgives the repentant sinner, but actually goes to meet him and embraces him in His love and grace. Indeed, as the two preceding parables taught, He seeks and attracts the sinner through the redeeming work of Jesus and through the silent influence of the Holy Ghost, even long before the sinner shows remorse for his sins. He does all this without abandoning His holy righteousness, for Christ Jesus sacrificed Himself as an everlasting ransom, and whosoever comes to God in His name as a repentant sinner is welcomed by Him in perfect love, without reproaches, into the Fatherly home. The sinner may forget God, but He remains unalterably faithful in His seeking love and grace.[17]

In showing us the love of the Father and the Son, this parable also shows our own privileged position as sons and daughters of the Most High God. The gifts that the prodigal father lavished on his long-lost son are emblems of our own salvation, with a rich background in the imagery of the Bible. We are robed in the righteousness of Jesus Christ—the garment of our salvation—and now we are reckoned as holy before God as his own perfect Son (see Isa. 61:10; Rom. 3:21–22). We have been sealed by the Holy Spirit, who serves as the signet ring of God (see Eph. 1:13–14). Peter Chrysologus called it "the ring of honor, the title of liberty, the outstanding pledge of the spirit, the seal of the faith, and the dowry of the heavenly marriage."[18] Our feet are shod with the gospel of peace (see Eph. 6:15)—the shoes of salvation. We have been invited to sit down and share table fellowship with God in the banquet of heaven. Best of all, through faith in Christ and by the adopting grace of the Holy Spirit, God the Father now says to us the words that our hearts are longing to hear: "This my son; this my daughter."

17. Norval Geldenhuys, *The Gospel of Luke*, New International Commentary on the New Testament (Grand Rapids: Eerdmans, 1951), 408.

18. Peter Chrysologus, "Sermon 5," in *Luke*, ed. Arthur A. Just, Jr., Ancient Christian Commentary on Scripture, NT 3 (Downers Grove, IL: InterVarsity, 2003), 251.

## THE JOY OF GOD

What great joy the Father has in welcoming his children home, forgiving all their sins, and granting them all the gifts of salvation! What great joy the Son has in suffering the humiliation they deserve, and then seeking to find them! What great joy God has in declaring that the dead are alive, that the lost are found, and that his children *are* his children! And what great joy there is in heaven whenever a long-lost sinner returns to God. In our Father's house there are music and dancing every time a prodigal son or daughter comes back home.

Is there any joy as full as a father's joy in welcoming home his long-lost son? Alexander McCall Smith has written a series of touching stories about everyday life in Botswana. In *The No. 1 Ladies' Detective Agency* he describes a terrible tragedy that befalls the headmaster of a local school. The man's young son has been kidnapped by evil strangers who practice the magic arts. Fearing the worst, the schoolmaster all but gives his son up for dead. Yet a lady detective is on the case, and many days later she unexpectedly arrives at the master's house:

> The schoolmaster looked out of the window of his house and saw a small white van draw up outside. He saw the woman get out and look at his door, and the child—what about the child—was she a parent who was bringing her child to him for some reason?
>
> He went outside and found her at the low wall of his yard.
>
> "You are the teacher, Rra?"
>
> "I am the teacher, Mma. Can I do anything for you?"
>
> She turned to the van and signaled to the child within. The door opened and his son came out. And the teacher cried out, and ran forward, and stopped and looked at Mma Ramotswe as if for confirmation. She nodded, and he ran forward again, almost stumbling, an unlaced shoe coming off, to seize his son, and hold him, while he shouted wildly, incoherently, for the village and the world to hear his joy.[19]

When the child returns, the father rejoices. Through faith in Christ, this is the way your own story will end: with your Father running to meet you, taking you into his arms, and shouting to the world that you have finally come home.

19. Alexander McCall Smith, *The No. 1 Ladies' Detective Agency* (New York: Anchor, 2002), 230.

# 68

# THE LOST BROTHER

*Luke 15:25–32*

*"But he answered his father, 'Look, these many years I have*
*served you, and I never disobeyed your command, yet you never*
*gave me a young goat, that I might celebrate with my friends. But*
*when this son of yours came, who has devoured your property*
*with prostitutes, you killed the fattened calf for him!' "*
(Luke 15:29–30)

*I*f ever there was a son who hated his brother, it was the elder
brother in the parable of the prodigal son. But if ever there
was a father who loved a son, it was that elder brother's
prodigal father.

Many people know the parable of the prodigal son, but what people
sometimes forget is how the story ends: with his jealous, judgmental older
brother apparently refusing to share his father's welcome. This is unfortunate, because the ending is really the most important part of the story.

Remember the context: Jesus was speaking to the Pharisees and the
scribes who had criticized him for receiving sinners and eating with them
(Luke 15:1–2). In response, Jesus told them a three-part story about three

things that were lost: a lost sheep (Luke 15:3–7), a lost coin (Luke 15:8–10), and a lost son (Luke 15:11–24). In each case, the seeker rejoiced in finding what was lost, and then celebrated that joy by sharing it with friends.

Jesus told this triple parable to show what joy God has in seeking and saving lost sinners. Yet the scribes and the Pharisees refused to welcome that joy into their own hearts. Rather than receiving people who were lost, they rejected them, and therefore they were unwilling and unable to rejoice. To show them what was wrong with their attitude, and why, Jesus put them into his story. If the prodigal father is God himself, and if the prodigal son represents ordinary Jewish people who turn back to God in repentance (like the tax collectors and other sinners that were flocking to Jesus), then the elder brother must represent the proud Pharisees who refused to share the joy of Jesus in the salvation of sinners. These religious leaders were a lot like the elder brother, and so are we at times, if only we will admit it.

## THE ELDER BROTHER'S REFUSAL

It is easy to see how lost the prodigal son was, but do you see how lost the elder brother was? He was as lost as his little brother—maybe even more lost, because he was lost on the inside, not the outside, so nobody could tell how lost he really was. Even though he had never left the family farm, he had abandoned his father's heart, and thus he was lost in his own home.

At first the elder brother was lost because he refused to reconcile his family's broken relationships. We see this right in the opening lines of the story, which Jesus began by saying, "There was a man who had two sons" (Luke 15:11). From the outset we know that this is a story about two brothers, yet the elder brother is strangely silent, not saying a word until after his prodigal brother returns. This is strange because we would expect a man in his position to serve as a mediator. By demanding his inheritance and leaving home, the younger brother was breaking all his sacred bonds to the family, not to mention breaking his father's heart. Yet the elder brother stands by in silence. "We know the younger son by what he asks," writes Kenneth Bailey, "the father by what he does, and the other son by what he does not do."[1]

---

1. Kenneth E. Bailey, *The Cross and the Prodigal: Luke 15 Through the Eyes of Middle Eastern Peasants* (Downers Grove, IL: InterVarsity, 2005), 47.

What the elder brother does not do is fulfill his sacred responsibility to reconcile his family. He loves his brother and his father too little to help them before it is too late. The elder brother seems to be lost right from the beginning of the story.

By the time his brother returned he was more lost than ever. Once again he failed to do what he ought to do: he refused to share his father's joy. After showing what joy the prodigal father had in welcoming home his long-lost son, Jesus said, "Now his older son was in the field, and as he came and drew near to the house, he heard music and dancing. And he called one of the servants and asked what these things meant" (Luke 15:25–26). The elder brother had been working out in the fields (not slaving away, in all likelihood, but supervising). On his way back home he was amazed to hear the sound of music and dancing floating across the fields. It sounded like a party, but if it *was* a party, then why had he not been invited? He could not imagine what was going on. Then again, maybe he could, because his questions sound suspicious. Before he entered the house, he wanted to know what there was to celebrate.

The servant's response is important because it helps us to interpret what is happening in the story—almost like the chorus in a Greek drama.[2] Here is what the servant said: "Your brother has come, and your father has killed the fattened calf, because he has received him back safe and sound" (Luke 15:27). These words reminded the elder brother of his place in the family as both the brother of the prodigal son ("your brother") and the son of the prodigal father ("your father"). They also correctly identified the reason for rejoicing. It was not simply because the lost son had come back home, but also because his loving father had received him as a son. To "receive" in this sense is to offer reconciliation. People were celebrating the father's unlimited welcome, not simply the son's unexpected return.

Now the elder brother was expected to join the party. This was the obvious thing for him to do, especially in the context of the larger parable. When the sheep and the coin were found, everyone shared in the celebration. This time a *son* had been found, so the party would be even bigger. "But," the Scripture says, against all expectation, "he was angry and

---

2. Kenneth E. Bailey, *Jacob and the Prodigal: How Jesus Retold Israel's Story* (Downers Grove, IL: InterVarsity, 2003), 112.

refused to go in" (Luke 15:28). The elder brother was more than annoyed; he was *angry*. The Greek word here *(ōrgisthē)* denotes an explosive rage. The elder brother was infuriated by his father's freely offered forgiveness. He wanted his brother to pay for his sins. Thus he refused to share his father's joy in his brother's salvation.

It is a good thing the father saw the prodigal son before his brother did, because if the elder brother had met him first, he probably would have told him to go out and get a job. In all likelihood, he would have said that his brother had a lot of nerve showing up back at home after the way he had broken his father's heart. The last thing in the world the elder brother wanted to do was celebrate his brother's return. He could hear the music, but there was no song in his joyless heart, and thus he refused to join the dance of reconciliation.

## THE ELDER BROTHER'S RESENTMENT

This was something more than the usual sibling rivalry. Children naturally resent any show of favoritism, and older children get touchy any time their younger siblings are granted special privileges that they themselves were denied. But the elder brother's complaint was especially bitter: "Look, these many years I have served you, and I never disobeyed your command, yet you never gave me a young goat, that I might celebrate with my friends. But when this son of yours came, who has devoured your property with prostitutes, you killed the fattened calf for him!" (Luke 15:29–30).

With these bitter words, all the years of secret resentment came pouring out. "I mean, what do you have to do to get a party around here?" This is what the elder brother wanted to know. "How come he got a cow, Dad, but I never even got a goat?" Once again, we see how lost the son was. He was lost because he resented the grace that his father lavished on that unworthy sinner, his second-born son.

What made this especially galling was that when the prodigal father threw a party for this prodigal son, he was spending the elder brother's money. The father had already granted the elder son the legal right to everything that was left of his inheritance (see Luke 15:12), and therefore this banquet came at his own expense. This was more than the elder brother could bear. His motto was "No reconciliation without compensation."[3] Here is how David Gooding describes his attitude: "Generosity to a bankrupt but repentant prodigal was to him not an expression of his undeserved wealth as the heir of all the father had, but the squandering of hard-won earnings which he could not afford to give away."[4]

Honestly, the elder brother had a good point. Look how faithful he had been in working on the family farm, and look how irresponsible his brother was. What kind of world would this be if people were rewarded for squandering their inheritance, while hardworking people got nothing in return for doing the right thing? Oh, the injustice of it all!

> If his brother could go off, live a dissolute life, bring disgrace on the family, waste all his money and opportunities, and then come home, make some kind of a profession of repentance and immediately be received, made a fuss of, treated as if nothing had happened, indeed treated better than he had ever been in his life before, then that put a premium on sin and evil living. It made a mockery of all the long years of hard work that he himself had put in on the farm serving his father like a slave. If that was his father's idea of forgiveness, of "saving the lost," he wanted nothing to do with it.[5]

The elder brother's recitation of his service record showed what high regard he had for his own obedience. In his own humble opinion, the elder brother thought he had done everything right. Certainly he had never disobeyed his father, or done anything that required repentance. If anyone needed to be forgiven, it certainly wasn't he. All he wanted now was credit where credit was due (not to mention penance where penance was due). His self-righteous attitude reminds one of Mark Twain's famous put-down, "He was a 'good man' in the worst sense of the word."[6]

Was he really as righteous, however, as he thought he was (or said he was)? The elder brother accused his brother of squandering his inheritance on prostitutes. But how did he know this? It was nothing more than

---

3. Bailey, *Jacob and the Prodigal*, 179.
4. David Gooding, *According to Luke: A New Exposition of the Third Gospel* (Grand Rapids: Eerdmans, 1987), 272.
5. Ibid., 270–71.
6. Mark Twain, quoted in R. Kent Hughes, *Luke: That You May Know the Truth*, 2 vols., Preaching the Word (Wheaton, IL: Crossway, 1998), 2:144.

a scandalous assumption; the elder brother had no idea how his brother had wasted his money.

In truth, his reckless accusation tells us more about his own wicked heart than it tells us about the prodigal son. Why was he talking about prostitutes? Probably because that is what *he* would have done with the money. Here was a man who prided himself on keeping the law, while at the same time cherishing adultery in his heart. The sin that he censured most vociferously may well have been the one that he most wanted to commit. If so, this was worse than what his little brother did, because at least that prodigal son was honest about how much he loved his sins.

The elder brother was completely lost: lost in his refusal to reconcile, lost in his rejection of his father's joy, lost in his striving for self-salvation, lost in resentment for his brother's reward, and lost in the unrighteous desires of his own sinful heart. But he was lost mostly because he rejected his sonship, seeing himself as a slave instead of a son.

This is clear already from his refusal to join the festivities. As the firstborn son, his presence would have been demanded on any festive occasion. In fact, it would have been customary for him to honor his father's guests by serving them at the table, functioning almost like a head waiter.[7] By refusing to take his place at the table, the elder brother was renouncing one of the responsibilities of his sonship. But what he said to his father was even worse. He did not even address him as his father, but rudely made his angry complaint. "Look, these many years I have served you, and I never disobeyed your command, yet you never gave me a young goat, that I might celebrate with my friends. But when this son of yours came, who has devoured your property with prostitutes, you killed the fattened calf for him!" (Luke 15:29–30).

The word "look" is a direct challenge, virtually to the point of insolence. When the elder brother called the prodigal son "this son of yours," rather than "this brother of mine," he was denying the claims of brotherly love. This is hardly surprising; he had disowned his brother long ago. But when he called himself a servant, he was also denying the privileges of his own sonship. Now he was even more lost than his brother, and farther away from home, because he had no idea what it meant to be his father's son.

7. Bailey, *The Cross and the Prodigal*, 81–82.

Indeed, it is clear from what he says that he regarded his loving father as a stingy slavedriver.

The word that the elder brother used for service *(douleuō)* was commonly used for slave labor. He used this word because he had always been such a hard worker. He was the model son: staying at home, working in the family business, doing as he was told, succeeding in life where his brother had failed. The elder brother was the paragon of traditional morality, but in this moment of unguarded anger, he inadvertently revealed the true attitude of his heart. His relationship with his father had always been performance-based. His service had become a kind of slavery to him; he had never served in love, but only out of obligation. Now he demanded what he thought his duty deserved: he wanted his goat, and he wanted it now! According to his calculations, if he did not get the reward that he had earned, then everything he ever did for his father was wasted. Notice further that even if he did get his goat, he would not share it with his father at all; he only wanted to eat it with his friends! In this respect, he was no better than his younger brother: both sons wanted their father's wealth, but not their father's fellowship.

See how lost the elder brother was, and how far away he was from his father's heart. Strangely enough, it was not the obviously evil son who refused to join the father's feast, but the one who thought of himself as the "good" son. Even though he had kept the letter of the law (at least to his own satisfaction), he was still estranged from his father's love. As Tim Keller explains, "it is not his badness keeping him out, but his goodness. It is not his sins that are keeping him from sharing in the feast of the Father so much as his righteousness. The elder brother in the end is lost not despite his good record, but because of it."[8] He did not understand that his father loved him because he loved him, not because of anything that he had done or ever could do.

## THE PHARISEE WITHIN

The prodigal son's elder brother is one of the most spiritually unattractive people in the entire Bible. He is stingy, self-pitying, resentful, proud, bitter, unrepentant, unforgiving, and unwilling to show grace to other sinners.

8. Timothy J. Keller, "The Two Prodigal Sons" (unpublished sermon), n.p., n.d. See also Keller's book *The Prodigal God: Recovering the Heart of the Christian Faith* (New York: Dutton, 2008).

The only thing he knew how to celebrate was his own accomplishments. In other words, he was a lot like the Pharisees, and probably a lot more like us than we usually dare to admit.

The scribes and the Pharisees thought of themselves as model children who did as they were told. Certainly they never disobeyed their Father in heaven, or did anything that demanded costly repentance. Yet for that very reason their joyless hearts were estranged from the love of God. Because they did not see their own need for grace, they had no grace to give to anyone else.

Like the elder brother in the parable, the elders of Israel refused to reconcile their brothers and sisters to God. Rather than pursuing other sinners with the grace of God, they had retreated within the proud walls of their own spiritual community. David Gooding comments: "The Pharisees derived great personal satisfaction out of successfully keeping their own religious rules, but they had little interest in the joy of retrieving for God those who had broken God's laws."[9]

This suggests an excellent standard for evaluating our own heart for the lost. Are we running to meet the wandering sinners? When we find them, are they drawn to us the way sinners and tax collectors were drawn to Jesus? This is one of the noteworthy features of the ministry of our Lord: whereas moral people were sometimes put off by the company he kept, outcasts and reprobates were almost always drawn to him. When we live with the love of Christ, they will be drawn to us the same way. Here is how Tim Keller explains this principle:

> The way to know that you are communicating and living the same gospel message of Jesus is that "younger brothers" are more attracted to you than elder brothers. This is a very searching test, because almost always, our churches are not like that. The kind of people attracted to Jesus are not attracted to us. We only attract conservative, buttoned-down, moral people. The licentious, the "liberated," the broken, the people out of the mainstream very much despise us. That can only mean one thing. We may think we understand the gospel of Jesus, but we don't. If we don't see the same effect Jesus saw, then we lack the same message Jesus had. If our churches aren't filled with younger brothers, then we must be more like the elder brother than we like to think.[10]

9. Gooding, *Luke*, 270.
10. Keller, "Two Prodigal Sons," n.p.

Like the elder brother in the parable, the elders of Israel resented the welcome that Jesus gave to the people they called "sinners." When Jesus sat down to share table fellowship with tax collectors and other infamous individuals, the Pharisees thought it was practically immoral. If there was one thing they never did, it was to eat with sinners. So they refused to join the celebration of Jesus in welcoming lost sinners.

Notice the connection that Jesus was making. The objection that the Pharisees raised back in verse 2—"This man receives sinners and eats with them"—is *exactly* the same objection that the elder brother raised against his father the day his brother came home: the old man was receiving a sinner. Even worse, he was eating with his pig-farmer of a son.

The reason the Pharisees sounded so much like the elder brother was that they had made the same underlying spiritual mistake. By telling this parable, Jesus was doing something more than telling the Pharisees that they had the wrong attitude. He was also analyzing why—why they did not have any love for the lost or very much joy in their worship, even though they prided themselves on all the things they were doing for God. It was because they had never embraced the Father's grace for them as sinners and love for them as sons. They thought they could be justified by the merits of their own legalistic obedience. Thus they claimed that they had never broken the law and boasted of their long hard years of slaving away for God. Here is how Norval Geldenhuys explains what Jesus was saying about the Pharisees in his parable of the two lost sons:

> The Savior effectively depicts the whole attitude of the Pharisees—for they also are inwardly estranged from God and have allowed their religion to degenerate into slavish bondage and self-righteousness. While they themselves remain spiritually cold and far removed from God, they despise and avoid persons like the "publicans" and sinners who in their eyes are no longer worthy to be members of the real people of Israel. . . . Jesus reveals the root of the error of the Pharisees and scribes by making them feel that God's attitude towards men is not paid for through so-called meritorious works like slavish observance of the Law and faithful compliance with outward forms, but through His love and grace towards everyone who truly turns to God and thus comes into real inward communion with Him.[11]

11. Norval Geldenhuys, *The Gospel of Luke*, New International Commentary on the New Testament (Grand Rapids: Eerdmans, 1951), 410–11.

What the Pharisees failed to understand is that people who try to be law-keepers are just as guilty as people who know that they are law-breakers. It is not just the prodigal sons who need to be forgiven, but also the elder brothers. It is not just sin that keeps us from being found in the love of God, but also self-righteousness. As B. B. Warfield once wrote, "the Father in heaven has no righteous children on earth; His grace is needed for all, and most of all for those who dream they have no need of it."[12] Tim Keller said it like this: there are "two kinds of people, and thus two kinds of running from God and fathers, but still just one way home."[13]

How often we find ourselves thinking like the elder brother! We ignore the desperate situation of people who are spiritually lost, not pursuing relationships that might reconcile them to God. We look down on people who are outside the church, and thus we are unable to attract them with Christ-like love. We have an outward reputation for doing the right thing, but inside our hearts are cold to God. We cherish secret sins, including some we have never committed, but certainly would if we could get away with it. We want more recognition for what we are doing, and resent it when we do not get the praise we think we deserve. We get angry when others are elevated and we get overlooked. Even if we believe that we are saved by grace, our inner Pharisee drags us back into making a performance-based assessment of the Christian life, in which our standing with God rises or falls based on the fulfillment of our religious duties.

Rather than seeing ourselves as desperately needy sinners, we see ourselves as people who basically do what God wants us to do. We think that we are good people who deserve a greater reward, not bad people who can be saved only by grace. Even if we first came to God like the prodigal son, we have gradually turned into the elder brother. This is evident from our lack of joy in the worship of God, from our judgmental remarks about people who do not meet our moral standards, from the self-righteous assumptions we make about our own spiritual accomplishments, and from the way we misrepresent the gospel. Rather than telling people to "come and clean up" the way Jesus did, we give them the impression that they have to "clean up

12. B. B. Warfield, "The Prodigal Son," in *Biblical and Theological Studies* (Philadelphia: Presbyterian and Reformed, 1968), 535.

13. Keller, "Two Prodigal Sons," n. p.

and come," as if anyone could ever come to God on the basis of their own self-improvement.[14]

If only we could see how lost we are, even if we think we are living with the Father. If only we understood how much damage our self-righteousness does to our relationship with God. If only we learned how to repent of our supposed righteousness as well as our sinful depravity. If only we knew that we need as much grace as anyone does. J. C. Ryle said, "The man who really feels that we all stand by grace and are all debtors, and that the best of us has nothing to boast of, and has nothing which he has not received—such a man will not be found talking like the 'elder brother.'"[15]

## THE FATHER'S JOY

There were two lost sons in this family, and the father loved them both—not just the one who went off to a far country, but also the one who stayed home. As lost as the elder brother was, he could not escape his father's love. For when in his anger he refused to enter the house and celebrate his brother's return, "his father came out and entreated him" (Luke 15:28).

Here was another costly demonstration of the father's unexpected love. Once again, a beloved son is lost in sin—not a sin of self-indulgence, like his younger brother, but of self-righteousness. Yet once again the prodigal father goes out to find his lost son—not waiting for him to come home, but going out with more of the grace he kept giving and giving away.

The father does this at the cost of his own humiliation, because when the elder brother failed to join the party, he brought shame to his entire family. His refusal was a personal and public insult to his father, to his long-lost brother, and to all of their invited guests. Kenneth Bailey compares it to a son starting a shouting match with his father at his sister's wedding reception—it simply wasn't done![16] Ordinarily a father who received such an insult would ignore his son entirely, or else have him restrained so that

14. This insight comes from page 28 of a Truth for Life booklet by Alistair Begg called "Parable Portraits."
15. J. C. Ryle, *Expository Thoughts on the Gospels, Luke* (1858; reprint Cambridge: James Clarke, 1976), 2:191.
16. Bailey, *Jacob and the Prodigal*, 114.

he could deal with him later. But here is how Bailey describes the father's loving response:

> Once again he demonstrates a willingness to endure shame and self-emptying love in order to reconcile. . . . It is almost impossible to convey the shock that must have reverberated through the banquet hall when the father deliberately left his guests, humiliated himself before all, and went out in the courtyard to try to reconcile his older son. . . . The same self-emptying sacrificial love is demonstrated visibly and dramatically on the same day in similar ways for two different sons with different kinds of needs. . . . Earlier in the day, the father paid the price of self-emptying love in order to reconcile the prodigal to himself. Now he must pay the same price to try to win the older son.[17]

The father's approach was ever so gentle. Rather than reproaching the elder brother, he "entreated" him, tenderly trying to reconcile him to his family. When he addressed his firstborn and called him "Son," he used the term of endearment *(teknon)* that a father would use with a young boy, as if to say, "my dear child." Not only did this remind the elder brother of his proper place in the family, but it also spoke to him of his father's love. The welcoming father appealed to his boy with all his affection, pleading with him to come back home to his fatherly heart.

Then the prodigal father opened wide the storehouse of his grace. He reminded the elder brother of all the blessings he enjoyed in his father's house. He said, "Son, you are always with me, and all that is mine is yours" (Luke 15:31). What more could any son want? Everything that belonged to his father belonged to him. He had it all, every day: the best robe in the house, the ring of inheritance, the shoes of sonship. Even the fatted calf was his to enjoy, if only he would come and sit down for dinner. But more than any of that, he had a son's greatest blessing, which was his father's love. He was always with his father. So rather than thinking about how much this would cost him, the elder brother should have been thinking about how much he already had: the father-son relationship that was his to enjoy every day of his life.

Now his father was calling him to share more fully in his fatherly joy by rejoicing in his brother's return. He said, "It was fitting to celebrate

17. Bailey, *The Cross and the Prodigal*, 82–84.

and be glad, for this your brother was dead, and is alive; he was lost, and is found" (Luke 15:32). Indeed, it was more than fitting to celebrate: it was necessary, as the original Greek term *(edei)* indicates. This simply had to be done—not because the prodigal son deserved it, but because the father's love demanded it. Now his love demanded both of his sons to share in his joy. "This your brother" (Luke 15:32), the father said, drawing the elder brother back into the family.

In this joyous invitation we see how much love Jesus still had for the Pharisees. They too were invited to share in the joy of salvation, if only they would embrace the Father's heart for lost sinners and come to Jesus in repentance and faith. Praise God! It is not just the prodigal sons that Jesus loves, but also the elder brothers.

What good news this is for both kinds of sinners. Like the prodigal son, some of us are law-breakers; we like to wander in the far country of sin. Others are more like the elder brother; we pride ourselves on keeping the law, even though our hearts may be just as far from the Father's love. I am both of those kinds of sinners, and maybe you are too. I am the selfish son who wants to go off and sin; I am also the stingy brother who prides myself on doing my duty. But there is grace for me in the Father's love. Everything that belongs to him now belongs to me through the death and resurrection of Jesus Christ. He is always with me, by the presence of his Spirit. There is boundless joy for me, if only I will have it: joy in the forgiveness God has for me as a prodigal son, joy in the grace he has for me as an elder brother, and joy in the mercy he has for other lost sinners.

## WRITING YOUR OWN ENDING

We will never know how the elder brother responded to his father's entreaty. Did he come inside and join the celebration? Or did he stay outside, sullenly insisting on his own superior righteousness? Jesus deliberately left this part of the story untold. The parable has no ending, happy or otherwise.

In effect, Jesus was telling the Pharisees an unfinished parable and giving them the opportunity to write the ending into the story of their own lives. The real question was not what the elder brother would do, but what *they* would do. Would they continue to think that they were so much better than everyone else that they were not even sinners? Would they continue to criticize Jesus for welcoming people they thought were unworthy of his grace? Or would they come back to their Father God in repentance, admitting their own need for grace? Would they share in the joy of the Father's welcome by receiving other sinners with as much grace as Jesus was willing to offer them?

For us the most important question is how the parable will end in our own lives. How will I respond to the Father's welcome? Will I share my Father's joy by repenting of my sin and acknowledging that I am both the prodigal son and the elder brother? Will I share his joy by confessing my need for the grace that he offers through the death and resurrection of Jesus Christ? Will I share his joy by pleading with people to be reconciled to God through faith in Jesus Christ? Will I rejoice every time I hear a testimony of someone coming to faith in Christ? Will I offer the Father's welcome to prodigal children, both inside and outside the church? Henri Nouwen writes:

> As long as I keep looking at God as a landowner, as a father who wants to get the most out of me for the least cost, I cannot but become jealous, bitter, and resentful toward my fellow workers or my brothers and sisters. But if I am able to look at the world with the eyes of God's love and discover that God's vision is not that of a stereotypical landowner or patriarch but rather that of an all-giving and forgiving father who does not measure out his love to his children according to how well they behave, then I quickly see that my only true response can be deep gratitude.[18]

One Sunday after I had preached on the prodigal son our family walked home for lunch. It was a simple meal, but somewhat more festive than usual because it was my son Jack's fifth birthday. During lunch Jack's older brother Josh asked what he could have to drink. "Anything in the refrigerator," I said magnanimously, without stopping to consider all of the implications.

Josh is the kind of person who likes to know what all his options are, and after rummaging around in the refrigerator for several minutes, he returned in triumph, brandishing a large bottle of sparkling apple cider. "Can I have this?" he demanded.

---

18. Henri J. M. Nouwen, *The Return of the Prodigal Son: A Story of Homecoming* (New York: Doubleday, 1994), 105.

When everyone was finished laughing, I said, "I guess I didn't stop to think about what was in the fridge. I'm not sure you can have that," I continued cautiously—"we were saving it for a special occasion."

"But, Dad," Josh said, "this *is* a special occasion. It's Jack's birthday!" When he could see that I was starting to waver, he came through with the clincher, called to mind by that morning's sermon: "Come on, Dad, kill him the fatted calf!"

Realizing that I was on the losing end of this argument, I called for the bottle opener, poured the sparkling cider into paper birthday cups, and proposed a family toast: "To James Maxwell Ryken, a favored son in his father's house."

After we had touched our cups and downed our drinks, I proposed another toast. This one was for Josh, who had done exactly what an elder brother should do: he had celebrated his brother's sonship and reveled in his father's joy. Admittedly, this was in his own self-interest, because Josh wanted a taste of the bubbly himself. But that is exactly the point of the parable: a party for one is a party for all. The elder brother has nothing to lose in welcoming home the prodigal son, and only joy to gain.

We see this most clearly when we consider the saving work of Jesus Christ as our elder brother. The Scripture says that by virtue of both his humanity and his charity, Jesus rejoices to call himself our brother (Heb. 2:11). As our brother, he has offered full and perfect obedience to the Father—not self-righteousness, but righteousness itself. Rather than clutching to his Father's riches, he gave them all up to come looking for lost sinners. At the expense of his own life, he has given us the robe of his righteousness, the ring to his kingdom, and the feast of his grace.

Now the prodigal God is welcoming us into the embrace of his fatherly love. He is calling us back from the far country of our sin. He is pleading with us to set aside our self-righteousness and join him in receiving other sinners. Will you taste the banquet of his joy?

# 69

# YOUR MONEY OR YOUR LIFE

## *Luke 16:1—13*

*"No servant can serve two masters, for either he will hate the one and love the other, or he will be devoted to the one and despise the other. You cannot serve God and money."* (Luke 16:13)

You can use your money to win friends or to make enemies. Basketball star Latrell Sprewell put himself in the latter category one season by demanding a bigger contract from the Minnesota Timberwolves. Sprewell told the media he was disgusted with his one-year, $14.6 million contract. When a reporter asked why he didn't try to help his team win an NBA championship first and then worry about getting a better contract, Mr. Sprewell said, "Why would I want to help them win a title? They're not doing anything for me. I'm at risk. I have a lot of risk here. I got my family to feed."

Needless to say, $14.6 million was more than enough money to feed Mr. Sprewell and his family. But when your money becomes your life, you never think you have enough. Rather than using it to do some spiritual good, and to make some everlasting friends in the process, you end up wasting it all on yourself.

What, then, will you do with your money? This is the very practical issue that Jesus raises at the beginning of Luke 16. If chapter 15 dealt with wrong attitudes towards people, chapter 16 is about wrong attitudes toward possessions. If we do not master our money by using it for the glory of God, then it will master us, and we will end up bankrupt for eternity.

## THE DISHONEST MANAGER

Jesus taught this simple lesson by telling a parable and then applying it to daily life. But the parable itself is not so simple. Indeed, few other parables have caused as much perplexity or received as many interpretations as this one. There are a number of difficulties with "the parable of the unjust steward," as it is often called, but perhaps the biggest problem is that on a first reading Jesus seems to be encouraging the greedy pursuit of selfish gain and the unethical practice of business. Obviously, this cannot be right. So we need to go back and study the parable carefully to see what it says (and what it does not say).

In chapter 15 Jesus had been speaking to the Pharisees about the joy of God in finding what is lost. Now he turns his attention back to his disciples: "He also said to the disciples" (Luke 16:1). Very likely this group included the tax collectors who had been coming to hear Jesus teach (see Luke 15:1). These wealthy men would have had a natural interest in a story about someone's finances, as well as a genuine need for good spiritual instruction about what to do with all their money. So Jesus told them a story about a business relationship gone bad: "There was a rich man who had a manager, and charges were brought to him that this man was wasting his possessions. And he called him and said to him, 'What is this that I hear about you? Turn in the account of your management, for you can no longer be manager'" (Luke 16:1–2).

This kind of situation is familiar to anyone in business. An executive is accused of mismanagement. He is guilty of the misappropriation of funds, or embezzlement, or he has mishandled his business in some other way. In this case, the manager was "wasting" his master's possessions—the same word (*diaskorpizō*) that Jesus used to describe how the prodigal son squandered his father's inheritance. But whatever he has done, or failed to do, the manager is charged with wrongdoing. His superior rightly demands an

169

immediate explanation, and if he finds out that the allegation is true, then the man will have to leave the organization. He will be given notice and told to return company property. In a word, he will be fired.

This time the accusations were all true. The manager was guilty. We know this because of the way he reacted, and also because later Jesus describes him as "the dishonest manager" (Luke 16:8). He knew full well that when he handed over the books, his master would discover that they didn't balance. So rather than trying to defend himself, he started looking to land another position as soon as he could.

Needless to say, someone who was out of a job in those days was not about to get any kind of severance package or collect unemployment benefits. So "the manager said to himself, 'What shall I do, since my master is taking the management away from me? I am not strong enough to dig, and I am ashamed to beg'" (Luke 16:3). The man was in a bad situation. He had been working at a desk job in finance, and he knew that he did not have the physical stamina to do hard manual labor. The man was a white collar worker all the way, and he thought that a blue collar job would just about kill him. Nor did he have any interest in becoming a beggar. He had lost his job, but he was not about to lose his dignity. Still, he had to do something to maintain his standard of living. What could he do?

Suddenly the man had an idea: "I have decided what to do, so that when I am removed from management, people may receive me into their houses" (Luke 16:4). There was not a moment to lose: in order to carry out his plan, he needed to act before his termination became public knowledge. "So summoning his master's debtors one by one, he said to the first, 'How much do you owe my master?' He said, 'A hundred measures of oil.' He said to him, 'Take your bill, and sit down quickly and write fifty.' Then he said to another, 'And how much do you owe?' He said, 'A hundred measures of wheat.' He said to him, 'Take your bill, and write eighty'" (Luke 16:5–7).

This plan may not have been very honest, but it certainly was shrewd. While the estate manager still had control of the books, he would call in the people who owed his master money and write off some of their debts. He could not write them off entirely, but he would reduce them enough to save people a lot of money. The amounts involved here were substantial: nearly a thousand gallons of oil and more than a thousand bushels of wheat— more than a full year's wages for the average earner.

It was a brilliant scheme. The master's debtors had no reason to suspect that the manager was acting dishonestly. Everything seemed perfectly aboveboard. After all, the manager was their creditor's personal representative, and if he wanted to reduce their debt, that was his business. They were just grateful to have the books fixed in their favor—so grateful that they would feel personally indebted to the manager. He had made friends with his master's money. Later, when he was out of a job and needed a place to stay, he could ask them to return the favor.

Today the Securities and Exchange Commission would convict this manager for financial fraud. Admittedly, some commentators have tried to defend his actions. They have speculated that he was simply giving up his own commission in these transactions, or that he had been overcharging people and had decided to stop pocketing the difference. However, that kind of money would have been "under the table," not written into any contract.[1] Others have said that he was canceling the interest part of a loan, which he had been charging in goods rather than money so as to avoid breaking the old laws against usury (see Deut. 23:19–20).[2] Yet, this too was unlawful. The man's actions speak for themselves: he was stealing money from his master, and this was morally wrong. Besides, Jesus plainly identifies him as "the dishonest manager" (Luke 16:8).

The manager's deception makes his master's response all the more surprising: "The master commended the dishonest manager for his shrewdness" (Luke 16:8). We would expect the master to be angry, and maybe he was. Now that new notes had been legally executed, there was no way for him to recover his losses. But as he thought about what his former manager had done, he could not help but admire how resourceful he had been in planning for his unemployment. Though he could hardly credit the man for his honesty or integrity, when it came to shrewdness, he had to give the man his due.

There is a legitimate moral difference between saying, "I applaud the clever steward because he acted dishonestly," and saying, "I applaud the dishonest steward because he acted cleverly."[3] The master was saying the latter, not the

1. Kenneth E. Bailey, *Poet and Peasant* (Grand Rapids: Eerdmans, 1976), 89–90.
2. Leon Morris, *The Gospel According to St. Luke: An Introduction and Commentary*, Tyndale New Testament Commentaries (Grand Rapids: Eerdmans, 1974), 246.
3. T. W. Manson, *The Sayings of Jesus* (London: SCM, 1949), 292.

former, and this is the key to understanding the parable. Jesus was not coming out in favor of fraud, or telling us that it is right to cheat people. He was not saying that dishonesty is the best policy. Instead, he was giving an example of how clever worldly people can be when they act in their own best interest.

Jesus used this story to set up some very practical advice about how to use our money for spiritual gain. There are three principles in this parable: first, use your worldly wealth to make everlasting friends (Luke 16:9); second, be faithful with what you have so you can receive something even better (Luke 16:10–12); and third, do not make money your master (Luke 16:13).

### Friends Forever

We have already seen how shrewd the manager was. According to Jesus, this is typical of the way unbelievers operate: "For the sons of this world are more shrewd in dealing with their own generation than the sons of light" (Luke 16:8). The "sons of this world" are people who belong to this world, who have not yet received the free gift of eternal life through faith in Jesus Christ. Such people are usually very skillful at doing things for their own advantage. Unburdened by the high claims of a godly conscience, they pour all their energy into getting ahead in life. They know how unbelievers operate and can use this to their earthly advantage.

Christians tend to be far less shrewd when it comes to worldly matters. In fact, sometimes we are so naïve that people can easily take advantage of us. But worldly matters are not the matters that really matter! The most important thing is getting ready for eternity. If only people would give as much attention to their eternal souls as they give to their earthly business! Jesus said, "I tell you, make friends for yourselves by means of unrighteous wealth, so that when it fails they may receive you into the eternal dwellings" (Luke 16:9). In other words, *use your worldly wealth to make everlasting friends.*

It is possible that Jesus was speaking ironically here. If so, then he was saying something like this: "Go ahead and do what the dishonest manager did: use your money to make as many friends as you can for as long as you can. But just see if they can save you when the time comes." The implication, of course, is that they will not be able to save you at all; they have no eternal lodgings where they can receive you. It seems better, however, to take what Jesus says as a straightforward affirmation of the way to get ready for the life to come. Jesus was speaking to his disciples at this point, not to "the sons of this world," and he was drawing an analogy between the way the manager prepared for his unemployment and the way we ought to prepare for eternity.

Time is running out for us, as it was running out for the manager; only what we will lose is not just a job: we will lose life itself. Jesus did not say "when *it* fails" in verse 9, referring to the "unrighteous wealth," but literally "when *you* fail," referring to our own inevitable demise. Everyone must be prepared to leave it all behind, and in the meantime, we are called to use our money in a way that shows we have the right eternal priorities. Are you willing to act decisively in your spiritual interest, the way the manager acted in his financial interest? Augustine asked, "Why did the Lord Jesus Christ present this parable to us? He surely did not approve of that cheat of a servant who cheated his master, stole from him and did not make it up from his own pocket. . . . Why did the Lord set this before us? It is not because that servant cheated but because he exercised foresight for the future. . . . He was insuring himself for a life that was going to end." Then Augustine pressed his point home with a practical question: "Would you not insure yourself for eternal life?"[4]

The point is not that we can buy our way to heaven. Heaven's only entrance requirement is faith in Jesus Christ, who has paid the price by dying on the cross for our sins. Jesus has opened the door by rising from the dead and going ahead of us into glory. But the Bible also speaks of the blessedness that is the right and proper reward for the obedience of our faith. We are called to obey God in the godly use of our wealth. J. C. Ryle said, "a right use of our money in this world, from right motives, will be for our benefit in the world to come. It will not justify us. It will not bear the severity of God's judgment, any more than other good works. But it shall be an evidence of our grace, which shall befriend our souls."[5] What happens to us then will depend in some way on what we do with what we have now.

4. Augustine, Sermon 359A.10, in *Luke*, ed. Arthur A. Just, Jr., Ancient Christian Commentary on Scripture, NT 3 (Downers Grove, IL: InterVarsity, 2003), 255.
5. J. C. Ryle, *Expository Thoughts on the Gospels, Luke* (1858; reprint Cambridge: James Clarke, 1976), 2:204.

Jesus describes our money as "unrighteous wealth" (Luke 16:9). His word for "wealth" is the old word "mammon" (Aramaic, *mamon*), which refers to someone's material possessions. Mammon is everything we have that we cannot take with us. Here Jesus called it "unrighteous" mammon, which is surprising because money itself is value-neutral: it can be used for either good or evil purposes. Maybe Jesus said this "because injustice is so often involved in the accumulation and use of earthly possessions."[6] But whatever reasons he had for saying it, he advises us to use our worldly wealth for spiritual gain, spending it wisely before we have to leave it all behind.

This advice is contrary to every impulse of a consumer culture. When people know they are running out of time, they usually spend *more* on themselves, not less. They are like the precocious child in a well-known comic strip. As Calvin and his friend Hobbes contemplate a snowman they have made, Hobbes comments, "This snowman doesn't look very happy." "He's not," Calvin says. "He knows it's just a matter of time before he melts. The sun ignores his existence. He feels his existence is meaningless." Hobbes responds by asking if existence is really as meaningless as the snowman thinks it is. "Nope," Calvin replies. "He's about to buy a big-screen TV."[7] This is the way many people operate. They are living for the moment, not for eternity, and when from time to time they sense the meaninglessness of their existence, they just go out and buy something to make themselves feel better.

Jesus advises us to make a better investment. He tells us to use our money to make friends that will last forever. The dishonest manager hoped he would be welcomed into the homes of people he had helped in his line of business. We are hoping to be welcomed into everlasting glory, and if we have used our money wisely, friends will be waiting there to receive us.

Maybe the "friends" Jesus has in mind are the Father, the Son, and the Holy Spirit. More likely they are fellow human beings we have befriended by giving help in time of need. We will see them when we get to heaven: the victims of a natural disaster whom we helped by sending emergency relief; members of distant tribes who heard the gospel through a missionary we

6. Norval Geldenhuys, *The Gospel of Luke*, New International Commentary on the New Testament (Grand Rapids: Eerdmans, 1951), 416.

7. This *Calvin and Hobbes* comic strip is described by Steven Garber in *The Fabric of Faithfulness* (Downers Grove, IL: InterVarsity, 1994), 88–89.

supported or a Bible translation we funded; sex addicts and drug addicts who were saved through a ministry that we helped to start; people across the country who came to Christ through a radio broadcast we financed; people who were converted in the church where we tithed, giving at least a full 10 percent of our gross income to the preaching of the gospel.

These are the kinds of friends Jesus advises us to make with our worldly wealth: people who will call us friends on the day of Jesus Christ. Norval Geldenhuys asks: "Do we use our worldly possessions in such a manner that there will be persons in Eternity who will be glad to receive us? Or will there be numbers who will point accusing fingers at us because we neglected or injured them through our unfaithful conduct in connection with the earthly goods entrusted to us?"[8] The only investment we can make that will give us the joy of everlasting friendship is an investment in the kingdom of God.

## FAITHFUL IS AS FAITHFUL DOES

Sometimes Christians say they would give more to help the poor and spread the gospel if only they had more to give. "I don't have that much money right now," people say, "but if I had a million dollars, I would give so much to the church and so much to my favorite ministry." Such talk can be cheap, but there is an easy way to find out whether it is really true. The way to see what we would do with more is to see what we do with what we already have. Jesus said, "One who is faithful in a very little is also faithful in much, and one who is dishonest in a very little is also dishonest in much" (Luke 16:10). This is a second principle for life and money: *be faithful with what you have so that you can receive something even better.*

This principle has many real-life applications. Generally speaking, people who are trustworthy in carrying out some small responsibility can also be trusted to do something bigger, as long as it is something they are gifted to do. People who are faithful with a little can be trusted with a lot.

This is true in any human enterprise, but especially true in ministry. I remember a time when I became aware of an acute pastoral need in my congregation—a church member who was having real trouble in life. As I

8. Geldenhuys, *Luke*, 417.

began to think about what the elders and deacons could do to help, I discovered that one of our pastoral interns was already giving most of the care that was needed, and had been giving it on a regular basis for quite some time. This told me virtually everything I needed to know about the intern's readiness for pastoral ministry. He had been faithful with a little, even when no one was watching, and when the time was right, God would trust him with much more.

On the other hand, people who fail to follow through on small commitments do not somehow rise to the occasion when they have something more important to do. On the contrary, they are just as irresponsible as always, only the consequences will be much worse, because more people are counting on them. I remember the time a friend tried to get me to cover up an accident that threatened to cost our student organization a substantial amount of money. "Now, Phil," he said, "before you tell them what happened, let's think about what to say." I knew right then that he was the kind of man who could not fully be trusted.

Character is built by the little choices we make to keep our commitments, or else to cut corners in life, compromising our integrity. Jesus calls us to be faithful in the little things. By way of example, consider how Coach John Wooden started basketball practice every year at UCLA. He always began by showing his players the right way to put on their socks: two pairs, not just one, with the creases aligned with the toes so as to prevent any blisters. Mr. Wooden won ten NCAA championships—not because he was an expert on socks, but because he was faithful in the little things, and therefore also the big things.

The same principle applies to the spiritual life. Be faithful in doing whatever God has called you to do. Even if what you are doing for the Lord seems insignificant, do it in an excellent way. Work as hard when people are not watching as when they are. Pray for God's help. Take good spiritual care of the people right next to you. Be grateful for any sign of God's blessing, however small. Do not give in to little temptations that erode the purity of holiness. Keep your promises. Fulfill your commitments. Finish what you start.

Nowhere is faithfulness more important than in the use we make of our material possessions, because what we do with our money always reveals what is really in our hearts. Jesus said: "If then you have not been faithful in the unrighteous wealth, who will entrust to you the true riches? And if you have not been faithful in that which is another's, who will give you that which is your own?" (Luke 16:11–12).

Jesus makes several comparisons here, and we should consider each one carefully. He is still talking about what we do with the little and the much. Somewhat surprisingly, the little thing here is what we do with our "unrighteous wealth." Most of us think of our worldly wealth as a big thing, not a little thing, but as far as God is concerned, it is one of the little areas of everyday faithfulness. Yet what we do with our wealth turns out to be a big thing because it is tied to our eternal destiny. When Jesus speaks here about "true riches," he is referring to the treasures of the kingdom. The point is that if we are unfaithful with something as small as our earthly income, then God cannot trust us to be faithful with what he has in heaven, where his people will rule over angels and kingdoms (see 2 Tim. 2:12). Be faithful with what you have, here and now, so you can receive something even better when the time comes.

In verse 12 Jesus makes a slightly different comparison: he compares what belongs to someone else with what belongs to us. We might have expected Jesus to say this the other way around: "If you have not been faithful with what is your own, how can you be trusted with what belongs to someone else?" However, Jesus is still talking about money here, and the point is that we are only stewards, not owners. What we have does not belong to us; it belongs to God. Like the manager in the parable, we are looking after something for our master. We need to be faithful in this stewardship. If we are not faithful, how could we ever be trusted with something of our own, namely, the riches that God has for us in heaven? J. C. Ryle said, "He who is dishonest and unfaithful in the discharge of his duties on earth, must not expect to have heavenly treasure, or to be saved."[9] Even more dramatically, he said: "unfaithfulness in money transactions is a sure evidence of a rotten state of soul."[10]

Whether we have a little or a lot, the money we have is a sacred trust, and our destiny depends on what we do with it. We are using borrowed goods, living on borrowed time. Therefore, said Martin Luther:

We must use all these things upon earth in no other way than as a guest who travels through the land and comes to a hotel where he must lodge

9. Ryle, *Luke*, 2:204.
10. Ibid. 2:199.

overnight. He takes only food and lodging from the host, and he says not that the property of the host belongs to him. Just so should we also treat our temporal possessions, as if they were not ours, and enjoy only so much of them as we need to nourish the body and then help our neighbors with the balance.[11]

## Only One Master

We will never be able to exercise good stewardship unless we have mastered our money, instead of being mastered by it. So Jesus took everything he had been saying about the faithful use of possessions and summarized it in these famous words: "No servant can serve two masters, for either he will hate the one and love the other, or he will be devoted to the one and despise the other. You cannot serve God and money" (Luke 16:13). This is a third principle for your money and your life: *do not make money your master, but bring yourself and everything you have under the mastery of Jesus Christ.*

Jesus knows the spiritual power of possessions. When he speaks about "money" in this verse he is once again using the word "mammon" (Greek, *mamōnas*), which refers to everything we own. We can use what we have for the glory of God, but we can also use it to serve almost any idol we choose. Therefore, money has the power to dominate our hearts. Are we enslaved to material things—to buying and selling them, to holding on to them and taking the trouble to look after them—or are we using them in the service of God? This is one of the ways to evaluate our true spiritual condition. Every time we reach into our pocketbooks we are pulling something out of our hearts.

There is no middle ground here. We would prefer to do the very thing Jesus tells us we cannot do: serve God *and* money. If only we could serve God with some of our money and then serve ourselves with the rest of it. Better yet, if only we could use most of it for ourselves and then give God whatever is left! But Jesus says we have to choose. Our hearts have the capacity for only one dominating love. This affection, and this affection alone, is what we will serve. The word Jesus uses for serving (Greek, *douleuein*)

11. Martin Luther, quoted in R. Kent Hughes, *Luke: That You May Know the Truth*, 2 vols., Preaching the Word (Wheaton, IL: Crossway, 1998), 2:151.

denotes the servitude a slave is obligated to give his master. Money wants to enslave us. The best way to destroy its spiritual power is to give it over to God and use it only for his glory.

This does not mean that we can never spend anything on ourselves, or on the people we love. Our own needs and the needs of the people in our care are part of what God is doing in the world. Nor does it mean that Christians can never be wealthy. Money can be used to accomplish spiritual good, and in certain instances God gives people the capacity to generate wealth so they can finance kingdom work. But Jesus does mean that we must first surrender everything we have to God, so that he can use what we have the way he wants to use it.

A good place to begin is by tithing to Christian work. Imagine how much spiritual good the church could do—both locally and nationally—if Christians gave a full 10 percent instead of the barely 2 percent that average evangelicals give in America.[12] But do not stop there! Give a higher and higher percentage as you grow in the grace of sacrificial giving to the Savior who gave his own life for your sins.

The rest of what we own also belongs to God. If we are using it wisely, then our expenditures will be able to pass some simple tests: Does this purchase reflect my ultimate spiritual priorities? Does it take adequate account of the world's great need for the gospel? Is it the best use of my money, or is there someone somewhere in the world who needs it more than I do? Is this the way I would spend my money if Jesus were right here with me right now (as in fact he is)? Is this an expense that will seem like a good investment in the light of eternity? When our spending meets these standards, we are in a good position to honor God with our money.

Do not let money master you, but bring yourself and everything you have under the mastery of Jesus Christ. Remember how many riches he left behind to be your Savior. Remember his own great expense in giving his blood for your sins on the cross. Believe that Jesus has your best interests at heart when he tells you not to waste your money or your life. He is not trying to rob you of any joy, but to give you more joy by giving you more of himself.

12. John R. Throop mentions these widely cited statistics in "New Approaches to Stewardship," *The Church Report* (Oct. 2004): 34.

It is wise to follow the good spiritual and financial advice engraved on the tombstone of Thomas Lowes in the ruins of Edinburgh's Holyrood Abbey:

> One instance among thousands
> Of the uncertainty of human life
> And the instability of earthly possessions
> And enjoyments.
> Born to ample property
> He for several years experienced
> A distressing reverse of fortune
> And no sooner was he restored to
> His former affluence
> Than it pleased Divine Providence
> To withdraw this together with his life.
> READER
> Be thou taught by this
> To seek those riches which never can fail
> And those pleasures
> Which are at God's right hand
> For evermore
> The gracious gift of God
> And to be enjoyed through faith
> In JESUS CHRIST our Savior.[13]

---

13. The inscription is quoted by Ligon Duncan in "Pastor's Perspective," *The First Epistle* 32.28 (July 26, 2001): n.p.

# 70

# THE LAW, THE GOSPEL, AND THE KINGDOM

## *Luke 16:14–18*

*"The Law and the Prophets were until John; since then the good news of the kingdom of God is preached, and everyone forces his way into it. But it is easier for heaven and earth to pass away than for one dot of the Law to become void."* (Luke 16:16–17)

The human heart was made to love God, who is infinite in all his perfections, and thus we have within us the capacity for a vast affection. We are designed to love the Supreme Being supremely. However, there is room in our hearts for one and only one predominating affection. There may be many things we love, but one of them must have the controlling influence, because our hearts were made to serve under the mastery of only one governing desire. Jesus said, "No servant can serve two masters, for either he will hate the one and love the other, or he will be devoted to the one and despise the other. You cannot serve God and money" (Luke 16:13).

Anyone who has ever tried to work for two bosses knows how impossible it is to satisfy two different sets of demands. So it is with God and money. God demands that we worship him alone and live to serve others, but money demands that we work for what the world has to offer and live for ourselves. How could anyone serve both demands at the same time? Yet this is precisely what many people try to do:

> Thousands on every side are continually trying to do the thing which Christ pronounces impossible. They are endeavouring to be friends of the world and friends of God at the same time. Their consciences are so far enlightened, that they feel they must have *some* religion. But their affections are so chained down to earthly things, that they never come up to the mark of being true Christians. And hence they live in a state of constant discomfort. They have too much religion to be happy in the world, and they have too much of the world in their hearts to be happy in their religion.[1]

Maybe these haunting words explain why sometimes life is so disappointing for us. We love God too much to be satisfied with the world, but we love our money too much to find our true joy in God.

## THE RIDICULE OF THE PHARISEES

The Pharisees were like that. They were busy doing many things for God, but in their heart of hearts they loved money more than they ever loved God. As a result, they disagreed with most of the things Jesus said about money.

Jesus had just finished teaching and then applying the parable of the unjust steward (Luke 16:1–13). He was giving his disciples an eternal perspective on their earthly possessions. He had warned them to plan for the future, using their worldly wealth to gain everlasting friends. He had also encouraged them to be faithful with what they had so that one day they would be ready to manage the true riches of God. Then he had spoken with them about the mutually exclusive mastery of God and money.

The Pharisees heard what Jesus said about all this, but rather than letting it rule their hearts, they only sneered at him. This set the stage for another

1. J. C. Ryle, *Expository Thoughts on the Gospels, Luke* (1858; reprint Cambridge: James Clarke, 1976), 2:205.

important exchange between Jesus and his leading opponents within the religious community—an exchange in which we hear the ridicule of the Pharisees (Luke 16:14), the rebuke of Jesus (Luke 16:15), and the only way to get right with God (Luke 16:16–18).

Earlier the Pharisees had scoffed at Jesus for being soft on sin. Back at the beginning of chapter 15 they grumbled about the way he was receiving tax collectors and eating with sinners. Obviously Jesus was much too lenient with people who were not even religious. Now the Pharisees had nearly the opposite complaint. By speaking against the love of money, he was being so strict that it was almost laughable. "The Pharisees, who were lovers of money, heard all these things, and they ridiculed him" (Luke 16:14). Here Luke shows us the real motivation of these religious leaders: they were in love with money, and this explains why they had so much scorn for what Jesus said about serving only one master.

If we are not in love with Jesus, then we must be more in love with someone or something else. It is what we love that keeps us away from Jesus, and what the Pharisees loved was money, as well as all the things they wanted to do with it.

Maybe these men ridiculed Jesus because he was poor. The Pharisees generally believed that material prosperity was a status sign of spiritual success. As far as they were concerned, one of the best ways to tell if God was pleased was to look at one's annual income. They wanted to listen only to teachers who were rich, like today's health and wealth preachers with their fancy clothes and fine automobiles. By this standard Jesus was an obvious failure. How could such a poor man prove that he had God's blessing, and what could he possibly teach them about God and money? Of course Jesus was criticizing the wealthy: poor people always do!

Or maybe the Pharisees ridiculed Jesus because they had an uneasy conscience about their money and how they had obtained it. People typically scoff at things they find threatening, and the fact that the Pharisees were scoffing at Jesus suggests that they felt threatened by what he was saying about the love of money. These men made a sharp division between the sacred and the secular. They said they were serious about following God, but this was only in a narrow range of religious duties. When it came to their secular business, they were trying to get ahead in life just like everyone else. They were trying to serve *both* God *and* money, and they thought it was absurd for Jesus to say they had to make a choice.

Which master are you serving? Is Jesus Christ the master of your heart, or are you still slaving away for money? Here are some warning signs that we are more in love with money than we are with God:

> when we are anxious about our finances, not trusting God to provide for our needs today and tomorrow, we are in love with money and its power to make us feel more secure;

> when our lives are so full of work that we have to say "no" to Christian service, we are in love with money and have given it mastery over our schedule;

> when we find our thoughts returning again and again to something we are hoping to buy, we are in love with money and its power to get us what we think we want;

> when we make employment decisions that are spiritually unwise for ourselves and our families, we are in love with money and our plans for getting more of it;

> when we find ourselves wishing we had some material possession that God has given to someone else, we are in love with money and the status or convenience or pleasure it seems to bring;

> when we spend more time complaining about what we do not have than rejoicing in what we do have, we are in love with money and depend on our possessions rather than on God to give us contentment and joy;

> when it seems difficult or even impossible to give up something we want in order to give a full biblical tithe or to make a sacrificial gift to Christian work, we are more in love with money than we are with the gospel and what it can do to change the world.

The presence or absence of these warning signs will indicate whether God is our strongest affection, or whether we need to confess that we have the kind of love affair with money that can destroy our souls.

## THE REBUKE OF JESUS

We are generally inclined to think that the love of money is only a small moral failing, that it is much farther down the list of evil deeds than something like cursing against God or committing sexual sin. But according to Jesus, the love of money is an appalling betrayal of our love for God that sets us squarely against the gospel of salvation and the kingdom of God. So Jesus rebuked the Pharisees for their ridicule: "You are those who justify yourselves before men, but God knows your hearts. For what is exalted among men is an abomination in the sight of God" (Luke 16:15).

When the Pharisees ridiculed Jesus, they were really rejecting God's whole way of salvation. So Jesus peeled back the layers of self-deception to show us the heart of their sin, and maybe our own. The Pharisees' love of money was connected to an even deeper spiritual problem, namely, their inclination to justify themselves rather than trusting God to justify them through Jesus Christ. They ridiculed Jesus because they loved their money, and in loving their money they were seeking to secure their own standing before God and men.

Jesus identified the Pharisees as people who tried to justify themselves. But this is the way people always are until they learn the grace of God. Our sinful human impulse for self-justification goes all the way back to the Garden of Eden, when Adam and Eve tried to cover themselves up from one another and hide away from God. This is what we are always trying to do: conceal our sin by making ourselves look better than we really are.

As we have seen, one way the Pharisees tried to justify themselves was by treating their financial prosperity as a confirmation of their spiritual success. Their money was a sign of God's favor that proved their godliness. We may try to justify ourselves in other ways. We may justify ourselves by measuring our amount of spiritual activity, by letting people know how much we are doing for God and how much it is costing us to do it. We may do it by refusing to confess our sins, secretly struggling and often failing in our fight with temptation because we are too proud to admit that we are sinners too. We may do it by being proud of our church or our denomination, as if we could be saved simply by our ecclesiastical affiliation. We may do it by pretending to be something on the outside that is nearly the opposite of what we are on the inside.

How different this all is from the true way of being justified before God. What Jesus said to the Pharisees is equally true for us: God knows what is really in our hearts. He knows what acts of spiritual rebellion we have committed this very week. He knows what sins we are longing to commit, if only we could get the chance. He knows what quiet cursing we do about our little discouragements in life, what private animosity we have towards a brother or sister in Christ, and what secret feelings of self-pity we are nursing in our hearts. He knows how superior we think we are to other people, and how deceptively we give them a better impression of ourselves than we really deserve.

The important question is not what other people think of us, but what God thinks of us. The reality is that he has a completely different way of looking at things than we do, with a much higher standard for godliness. In fact, what God thinks is commendable is exactly the opposite of the things that sinners love to celebrate. As Jesus said, "What is exalted among men is an abomination in the sight of God" (Luke 16:15). What a shocking thing to say: that what sinful people praise actually deserves divine damnation!

An abomination is anything that is disgusting to God. Many Christians think of an abomination as an evil deed committed by unrepentant sinners, like an act of terrorist violence, for example, or abortion, or homosexual sin. But what Jesus calls an abomination in Luke 16 is the love of money, especially when it has a corrupting influence on people who belong to the community of faith. Is anything more disgusting to God than people who claim to follow Jesus, but serve themselves with what they have instead of serving him?

By its very nature, this kind of abomination will only be found inside the church, never outside of it. But if all it takes to be guilty of abominable sin is to love a little money, then what hope do we have of salvation?

## Getting Right with God

Our only hope is the good news of the grace of God. What we need is not a human way of gaining the approval of other people, like what the Pharisees wanted, but God's way of getting right with God, which comes only through faith in Christ.

The singer and songwriter known around the world simply as Bono tried to explain this good news to one of his interviewers. He said, "The thing that keeps me on my knees is the difference between Grace and Karma." When he was asked to explain the difference, Bono said,

> At the center of all religions is the idea of Karma. You know, what you put out comes back to you. . . . Yet along comes this idea called Grace to upend all that. . . . Love interrupts . . . the consequences of your actions, which in my case is very good news indeed, because I've done a lot of stupid stuff. . . . It doesn't excuse my mistakes, but I'm holding out for Grace. I'm holding out that Jesus took my sins onto the Cross, because I know who I am, and I hope I don't have to depend on my own religiosity.[2]

Bono is right: we could never be saved by our own religiosity, or by anything else that we could do to gain God's favor. The good news is that we do not have to, because Jesus has come to save us. This is the world-changing, life-transforming truth that Jesus announced to the Pharisees, and to everyone else who will receive it by faith: "The Law and the Prophets were until John; since then the good news of the kingdom of God is preached" (Luke 16:16).

The coming of Christ marked a major shift in human history. Before Christ was the time of the Law and the Prophets—the Scriptures of the Old Testament. Even in those days God offered people his grace, but always in anticipation of the Savior who was still to come. Everyone from Adam all the way up through John the Baptist was waiting for the Christ. They were looking forward to the day when the Savior would come in all the power of God's saving grace.

Then Jesus came preaching the gospel. Right from the beginning of his earthly ministry, he announced that he had been sent by God to proclaim "the good news of the kingdom of God" (Luke 4:43; cf. 16:16). It was good news because it meant that grace had come. Soon Jesus would die on the cross for the abomination of our sins, and then rise from the dead with the power of eternal life. This is the good news that God has for us in the gospel: by faith in the crucifixion and resurrection of Jesus

---

2. Bono, from an interview with Michka Assayas in *Bono in Conversation*, as quoted by Gene Edward Veith, "Salty Dogma," *World* (Aug. 6, 2005): 24.

Christ we have the forgiveness of our sins and the promise that we will live forever with God.

Many of the people who heard this good news really did not understand it. Some of them would understand it better after Jesus died and rose again. But even to this day, many people are like the Pharisees. They continue to misuse the law of God, treating it as a way of salvation. They imagine that there is something they can do to justify themselves before God and men. This is even true in the evangelical church, where nearly 90 percent of people in one opinion poll agreed that in salvation God helps those who help themselves.[3]

But this is the time of the gospel. From the day that Jesus began his earthly ministry right up until today, the kingdom of God has been preached. This means that there is good news for all the money-loving sinners whose transgressions are an abomination to God: we do not have to be saved by fulfilling a law that we cannot keep, but simply by trusting the grace that Jesus has for us in the gospel. This is how we are justified: by true faith in Jesus Christ. "A man will be justified by faith," said Calvin, when he "lays hold of the righteousness of Christ . . . and appears in the sight of God not as a sinner, but as righteous."[4]

## THE LAW IS STILL THE LAW

Before we see what it takes to get into the gracious kingdom of God, we need to make one very important clarification—a clarification that Jesus himself made: "But it is easier for heaven and earth to pass away than for one dot of the Law to become void" (Luke 16:17). Jesus needed to say this because when he distinguished the Law and the Prophets from the gospel, some people might think that God's law was no longer in effect. The kingdom of grace had come—what need did anyone have for the law?

Yet Jesus said that the law of God would last at least until the end of the world. He said basically the same thing in his famous Sermon on the Mount: "Do not think that I have come to abolish the Law or the Prophets;

---

3. This statistic is cited by R. C. Sproul in *Faith Alone: The Evangelical Doctrine of Justification* (Grand Rapids: Baker, 1995), 12.

4. John Calvin, *Institutes of the Christian Religion*, ed. John T. McNeill, trans. Ford Lewis Battles, 2 vols., Library of Christian Classics 20–21 (Philadelphia: Westminster, 1960), 3.11.2.

I have not come to abolish them but to fulfill them. For truly, I say to you, until heaven and earth pass away, not an iota, not a dot, will pass from the Law until all is accomplished" (Matt. 5:17–18). When Jesus spoke about a dot or an iota, he was referring to the littlest parts of Hebrew letters, which would compare in English to dotting our "i's" and crossing our "t's." Jesus fully accepted every last Scripture in the Old Testament as the enduring Word of God.

Jesus also accepted the validity of the law as an abiding expression of God's will for his people. God's character does not change, and therefore his demand for holiness, purity, honesty, and integrity does not change. God still wants from us what he has always wanted: a life that is totally dedicated to his glory. To make this point, Jesus proceeded to give an example of a biblical law that is still in force today: "Everyone who divorces his wife and marries another commits adultery, and he who marries a woman divorced from her husband commits adultery" (Luke 16:18).

In other words, divorce is still divorce, and adultery is still adultery. We cannot set aside God's laws for marriage any more than we can set aside his laws for anything else. God's intention is for men and women to remain single-hearted in their devotion to Christ, or else for one man to marry one woman in a love covenant for life. Of course, there are certain circumstances in which divorce is biblically permissible—most notably in the case of adultery (see Matt. 5:32; 19:9) or the abandonment of a believer by an unbelieving spouse (see 1 Cor. 7:15).[5] But divorce is never God's desire for any marriage, and these exceptions were only granted because of the hardness of the human heart (Matt. 19:7–8). Jesus wants to promote the purity of our sexuality and protect the sanctity of marriage, and to that end, he says that if we follow an unlawful divorce with a second marriage we are adding a sin to a sin.

This statute reminds us that marriage is a sacred covenant. The high rate of divorce in our culture—even in the church—is a grief to anyone who loves the law of God, as it must be to Jesus himself. But why did Jesus talk about divorce here? Of all the regulations he could have chosen to show the ongoing validity of the law, why did he use this particular example?

---

5. For a fuller statement of the Bible's teaching on divorce, including pastoral guidance for real-life situations, contact Tenth Presbyterian Church in Philadelphia and request the church's statement on "Marriage, Divorce, and Remarriage."

Probably because this was one of the very laws that the Pharisees were failing to keep. Norval Geldenhuys says, "These words are especially directed against those Pharisees who allowed divorce to the husbands on various kinds of trifling matters, but violated the right of the wife in such a manner that no right of divorce was granted her if she was unjustly or cruelly treated by her husband."[6] Leon Morris explains that some Pharisees "were very permissive, allowing men divorce on the most trivial grounds. Thus Hillel thought it enough if a wife spoiled her husband's dinner and Akiba went so far as to permit divorce if the man found someone prettier than his wife."[7]

The Pharisees thought they would be justified by keeping the law. But in order to have any hope of actually keeping it, they had to make it easier to keep! So Jesus was saying something like this:

> You Pharisees claim for yourselves righteousness according to the law of Moses. But the more value you attach to outward righteousness, the less real inward value does it have in God's sight. Your attitude to the law is wrong. . . . You have . . . tried to limit the law. But in fact its scope is unlimited, and is of the widest application; and you yourselves, for example in the matter of divorce, regularly break it.[8]

This is what legalism always does. It makes a great show of keeping the law, but in fact it ends up destroying the law, because when the law is preserved in all its perfection it is too demanding for sinners to keep! The only way we can possibly keep it is by finding a way to lower God's standard. This is what the Pharisees were doing with regard to marriage and divorce and many other commandments. As Jesus said to them on another occasion, "You have a fine way of rejecting the commandment of God . . . thus making void the word of God by your tradition that you have handed down. And many such things you do" (Mark 7:9, 13).

We are tempted to do the same thing. We would like to think of ourselves as people who do what God says, but in order to think of ourselves that way,

6. Norval Geldenhuys, *The Gospel of Luke*, New International Commentary on the New Testament (Grand Rapids: Eerdmans, 1951), 423.

7. Leon Morris, *The Gospel According to St. Luke: An Introduction and Commentary*, Tyndale New Testament Commentaries (Grand Rapids: Eerdmans, 1974), 251.

8. Michael Wilcock, *The Message of Luke*, The Bible Speaks Today (Downers Grove, IL: InterVarsity, 1979), 161.

we inevitably end up lowering God's standards. Some Christians do this in the area of marriage and divorce, thinking that somehow their own difficult marriage situation is an exception to God's law. But the principle applies more widely to any area of Christian obedience. We generally have a lower standard than God for what does and what does not count as gossip, for example, or how much of a right we have to be angry with our children or our parents, or what it truly means to show compassion to the poor, or the extent to which our buying and selling are honest and fair.

How could people like us ever justify ourselves? And if we cannot justify ourselves, how is it possible for us to get into the kingdom of God?

## GETTING INTO THE KINGDOM

This is why the gospel is such good news, because the gospel is for sinners, and it tells us there is a way for sinners to be saved. As important as it is for us to understand that the law is still God's standard for our behavior, it is even more important for us to know the grace God has for us in the gospel. Bono said it well: "The point of the death of Christ is that Christ took on the sins of the world, so that what we put out did not come back to us, and that our sinful nature does not reap the obvious death. It's not our own good works that get us through the gates of Heaven."[9]

No, what gets us through the gates of heaven is not our own good works, but the work that Jesus did on the cross, which counts for us when we trust in him. Entrance to the kingdom of God is through faith in Jesus Christ.

Jesus said that in his day people were forcing their way into his kingdom (Luke 16:16). This strange expression reminds some people of something similar that Jesus said in the Gospel of Matthew: "From the days of John the Baptist until now the kingdom of heaven has suffered violence, and the violent take it by force" (Matt. 11:12). What does it mean to say that people are forcing their way into the kingdom of God? It is almost as if they are getting in by their own strenuous effort, maybe even against God's will. It means, rather, that when people finally understand the good news of salvation, they will do whatever it takes to come to Jesus. In the words of Norval Geldenhuys, "Everyone who listens to Him in faith presses with the greatest

9. Bono, quoted in Veith, "Salty Dogma," 24.

earnestness, self-denial and determination, as though with spiritual violence, into the kingdom."[10]

This is what happened when Jesus preached the gospel: people flocked to hear what he had to say. We saw this at the beginning of chapter 15, when tax collectors and sinners were coming to meet with him and eat with him. There are other examples of this in Luke's Gospel. Think of the men who broke through a roof to bring their paralyzed friend to Jesus for healing (Luke 5:18–19). Or think of the woman who pressed through the crowd to touch the hem of Jesus' robe (Luke 8:42–44). These people were "forcing" their way into the kingdom of God.

Everyone was drawn to Jesus, and when they heard what he had to say about the kingdom of God, they wanted to enter, almost as if they were storming the gates of heaven. Like a crowd of football fans trying to get into the stadium in time for the kickoff, or a crush of shoppers pressing through the doors at the beginning of a storewide sale, they were pushing to get inside. The people of God had been waiting for the Messiah for centuries, and now that he was here, they were practically breaking down the doors to get into the kingdom of God. Not that God's kingdom could ever actually be taken by force, of course. But this is how eager people were to get in, and how eager we ourselves ought to be to find salvation in Christ.

People will go to extraordinary lengths to get into a place they really want to go. I had this experience when I traveled to Istanbul one winter with friends. On our only free morning we traveled up icy hills to the Kariya Church, which contains the finest Byzantine mosaics and frescoes anywhere in the world. To enter the church and see the beautiful scenes from the life of Christ is to travel back a millennium and walk in the footsteps of ancient pilgrims. Unfortunately, the church was closed that morning, and we were bitterly disappointed. We had traveled almost halfway around the world to get to Istanbul; when would we ever have another chance to see the treasures on the other side of those ancient doors?

We were determined to get inside, and willing to do whatever it took to enter, so we decided to knock. An anxious custodian met us briefly at the door, and after hurried negotiations sent us around to the side entrance. He did not have the authority to let us in, but where there's a will, there's

10. Geldenhuys, *Luke*, 420–21.

a way, and after we handed over an unreasonable amount of money, he let us inside. We had forced our way in, and it was well worth the effort and the expense, as anyone who has ever seen the splendor of Kariya Church can tell.

What would you be willing to do to pass through the ancient gates of heaven? It would be worth any effort and every expense to see the Lord Jesus Christ in all the majesty of his everlasting kingdom. If necessary, would you not force your way inside? But of course it is not necessary. All that is required is faith in Jesus Christ. So do what it takes to get into the kingdom of God. Receive the gospel. Believe the good news. Trust in Jesus. And you will enter the kingdom that never ends.

# 71

# THE GREAT DIVORCE

## *Luke 16:19–31*

*"But Abraham said, 'Child, remember that you in your lifetime*
*received your good things, and Lazarus in like manner bad things;*
*but now he is comforted here, and you are in anguish. And besides*
*all this, between us and you a great chasm has been fixed, in order*
*that those who would pass from here to you may not be able, and*
*none may cross from there to us.'"* (Luke 16:25–26)

Some people say that God is so completely a God of love that he would never send anyone to hell. They are like the priest whom Robert Benson tells about in *Between the Dreaming and the Coming True*, who was asked what his faith in the all-inclusive love of God did to his doctrine of heaven and hell: "'Oh, I believe there is a hell all right,' he said, flashing his grin again, as though he had heard this question before, and from some folks who were more theologically imposing than we were. 'I just do not believe there is anyone in it.'"[1]

Benson's priest may not have believed there is anyone in hell, but Jesus certainly did. According to Jesus, there is a heaven and there is a hell, and

1. Robert Benson, *Between the Dreaming and the Coming True* (San Francisco: HarperSanFrancisco, 1996), 60–61.

everyone goes to either one place or the other, but never to both. Further-more, the time for choosing where we will go is now, and the way we choose is by believing or not believing in Jesus Christ.

C. S. Lewis wrote about this choice in his preface to *The Great Divorce*, a fictional work in which a busload of people from hell take a trip to heaven. Lewis pointed out that some people try to bring heaven and hell together, as if there is no real difference between them. This attempt, he wrote,

> is based on the belief that reality never presents us with an absolutely unavoidable "either-or"; that . . . some way of embracing both alternatives can always be found . . . without our being called on for a final and total rejection of anything we should like to retain. This belief I take to be a disastrous error. You cannot take all luggage with you on all journeys; on one journey even your right hand and your right eye may be among the things you have to leave behind.[2]

Lewis went on to say that the choices we are making right now deter-mine our eternal destiny. For people who choose the world instead of God, earth itself will turn out to be a suburb of hell, while for those who follow after God, earth will prove "to have been from the begin-ning a part of Heaven itself."[3] Which choice are you making, and where will it lead in the end?

## TWO MEN

Jesus showed what is at stake by telling about a rich man and a poor man named Lazarus (Luke 16:19–31). Some people refer to what he said as "The Parable of the Rich Man and Lazarus." Yet Luke does not refer to this teaching as a parable. So perhaps this is not a parable at all, but simply a straightforward record of something that really happened.

Still, the narrative feels more like a story told to make a spiritual point than a factual account. But even if it is simply a story—as most scholars think—and even if it may not give us a literal description of the geography

2. C. S. Lewis, *The Great Divorce* (New York: Macmillan, 1946), 5.
3. Ibid., 7.

of heaven and hell, it still tells us the truth about time and eternity. As John Calvin explained:

> The Lord is painting a picture which represents the condition of the future life in a way that we can understand. The sum of it is that believing souls when they leave the body lead a joyful and blessed life outside the world, but that for the reprobate are prepared terrifying torments which can no more be conceived by our minds than can the infinite glory of God.[4]

Jesus paints this picture by telling us about two men (Luke 16:19–21), two destinations (Luke 16:22–23), and two desperate prayers that never get answered in hell (Luke 16:24–31). He began by saying: "There was a rich man who was clothed in purple and fine linen and who feasted sumptuously every day. And at his gate was laid a poor man named Lazarus, covered with sores, who desired to be fed with what fell from the rich man's table. Moreover, even the dogs came and licked his sores" (Luke 16:19–21).

The contrast between these two men could hardly have been greater. One was a "have," while the other, most definitely, was a "have not." Like most Americans, the first man was very wealthy. This in itself is not a criticism, because there are at least some rich people who know how to glorify God with what they have (like Abraham, Joseph, and David, to name three notable examples). But this particular man was self-indulgent to extreme excess. He went around clothed in royal purple, as if he fancied himself to be some kind of king, and wearing linen underwear imported from Egypt. He ate the finest foods, feasting gluttonously on gourmet cuisine. In short, the rich man was a lover of money, just like the Pharisees. Even more than the money, it was the way that he used it to gratify his worldly pleasures. He was not just rich: he was filthy rich.

If the rich man seemed as if he had everything going for him, the poor man seemed to have everything against him. He was sick, with painful sores all over his miserable body. He was disabled; the only way he could get from place to place was for someone to carry him. He was hungry—so desperately hungry that he longed for the leftovers from another man's table. This poor man was not able to help himself; he could only beg someone else to give him what he needed. Day after day he hoped against hope that he

---

4. John Calvin, *A Harmony of the Gospels* (Grand Rapids: Eerdmans, 1972), 119.

could get something—anything—from the rich man's table. But the only comfort he ever received came from the pack of dogs that satisfied their own hunger by licking at his open sores.

Ironically enough, people called the poor man "Lazarus." To be clear, this was not the same Lazarus who lived with Mary and Martha and who was famous for coming back to life from the dead. This was a different Lazarus— a man who had the same common Hebrew name meaning "God has helped." How ironic! If Lazarus believed in the help of God, it was only by faith and not because of his outward circumstances. Where was God in his poverty? Where was God in his illness? Where was God in his disability?

We do not know how this poor man Lazarus learned to trust God for the answers to these questions. What we do know is that the one human being in the whole world who was in the best position to help him refused to do it. Lazarus was lying at his very doorstep! It was not just any doorstep, either; the Greek term used here *(pylōna)* refers to the kind of ornamental gate that one would ordinarily find at the entrance to a palace. There was more than enough wealth behind those gates to provide anything and everything the poor man needed, but only if the rich man would open wide the door of his heart.

Now we see how selfish the rich man really was. Every time he went in or out of his house he saw Lazarus and was confronted with his need for care, yet he refused to show any compassion. Every day he had a chance to feed the hungry, dress the naked, and heal the sick. But he never invited the poor man in for dinner, or even told his servants to take him some of the leftovers. He did not arrange for Lazarus to receive medical care, or help him in any way. In other words, he did not use his earthly wealth to make an eternal friend the way Jesus said that people should (see Luke 16:9). It was not simply his riches that were the problem; it was his greedy, money-loving heart.

This sin is common in contemporary culture. Students in the MBA program at Harvard University were asked to create a strategic plan for their lives under the title "What Do I Hope to Achieve in Life after Graduation?" The top three answers were wealth, notoriety, and status. No one said anything at all about service.[5] But the Bible asks, "If anyone has the world's goods and sees his brother in need, yet closes his heart against him,

5. The Harvard study is cited by Joni Eareckson Tada in "Sent to Serve," *Wheaton* (Autumn 2005): 58.

how does God's love abide in him?" (1 John 3:17; cf. James 2:15–16). This is an excellent test of our own godliness. Do we use what we have only for ourselves, or do we use it for people who are in greater need than we are? Feed the hungry, clothe the naked, and heal the sick. Help people who are right on your doorstep, whatever their needs may be.

## Two Destinations

There were two men, one on each side of the gate. One was rich and the other was poor, but both men died, and that changed everything, because they ended up on two different sides of eternity: "The poor man died and was carried by the angels to Abraham's side. The rich man also died and was buried, and in Hades, being in torment, he lifted up his eyes and saw Abraham far off and Lazarus at his side" (Luke 16:22–23).

Death is the great equalizer. As wealthy as he was, the rich man was just as likely to die as Lazarus was, because whether we are rich or poor, none of us can escape the cold hand of the grave. No matter how much money we have, it will never completely save our lives. Worldly wealth cannot prevent our own inevitable demise, and when it finally happens, the only thing that will matter is our relationship to God.

From an earthly perspective, the death of Lazarus must have seemed rather pathetic, especially in comparison to the other man in this story. The rich man received a proper burial (see Luke 16:22), and it must have been an elaborate affair. Yet nothing is said about the poor man's burial at all. He simply died of starvation; his body was cast aside, with his blood on the rich man's hands.

That is only from the earthly perspective, however, because at the very moment Lazarus died, he was gathered into the arms of God's angels. Then his name came fully, finally, and forever true: "God has helped." When there was no one else to help him, Lazarus was helped by almighty God, who rescued him from all his troubles and healed every wound of his broken body. Everyone else may have forgotten Lazarus, but he was remembered by God. In his preaching on this passage, Augustine observed:

> Jesus kept quiet about the rich man's name and mentioned the name of the
> poor man. The rich man's name was thrown around, but God kept quiet about

it. The other's name was lost in silence, and God spoke it. . . . You see, God who lives in heaven kept quiet about the rich man's name, because he did not find it written in heaven. He spoke the poor man's name, because he found it written there, indeed he gave instructions for it to be written there.[6]

Since the name of Lazarus was written in heaven, the angels came for him when he died. What a touching picture this is of the love that God has for his people at the time of death. The Scripture says, "Precious in the sight of the LORD is the death of his saints" (Ps. 116:15), and here in Luke we see proof that this is true. By nature we are afraid of death and all the unknowns of eternity. But in his kindness and compassion God will send the fairest creatures in heaven to receive us.

In this case, the angels carried Lazarus "to Abraham's side" (Luke 16:22), sometimes referred to as "the bosom of Abraham." This is the place where believers go when they die, or at least it was until the resurrection of Jesus Christ. Since Abraham is "the father of all who believe" (Rom. 4:11), it makes sense for believers to be with him when they die. I say "believers" because it is clear that Lazarus must have been a believer. It was not the fact of his poverty that saved him, as if his earthly suffering merited an eternal reward. No, Lazarus was saved by his trust in God. Although this is not stated explicitly anywhere in the passage, it is an obvious and necessary inference from his destination when he died (not to mention the plain teaching of the entire Bible). If Abraham is the father of all who believe, then to say that Lazarus went to Abraham's side clearly indicates that he was a believer. The true children of Abraham—and the true children of God—are saved by grace through faith.

Although being poor does not save people any more than being rich does, it is still a great encouragement to see what riches the poor may receive by faith. When Lazarus died, the torment of his earthly troubles was over. Immediately he went to be with all the saints, the place Jesus described as resting on the bosom of Abraham. This symbolizes the blessed joy every believer has after death, giving us a vivid picture of the intimate fellowship we will have with God's people in glory. But if anything our joy will be even greater, because when we die we will rest on the very bosom of Jesus Christ.

6. Augustine, "Sermon 33A.4", in *Luke*, ed. Arthur A. Just, Jr., Ancient Christian Commentary on Scripture, NT 3 (Downers Grove, IL: InterVarsity, 2003), 261.

For to be "away from the body," the Scripture says, is to be "at home with the Lord" (2 Cor. 5:8).

When we die, the angels will carry us to Christ. There we will wait in perfect blessedness until the day when, by the power of his resurrection, Jesus will give us everlasting bodies. In other words, we will not be fully glorified immediately when we die, but only at the final resurrection. In the meantime, our souls will rejoice in Christ as we live in what theologians sometimes call "the intermediate state." As the Westminster Shorter Catechism explains it, "The souls of believers are at their death made perfect in holiness, and do immediately pass into glory; and their bodies, being still united to Christ, do rest in their graves till the resurrection" (A. 37).

How different it was for the rich man! He had always assumed that he would go to heaven, but when he died he found himself in Hades, of all places! He had always scoffed at the very idea of hell. He certainly never expected to end up there. But after death he found himself in utter torment. Admittedly, Hades is not the biblical term for hell, but simply the place where people go after they die and before they face God at the final judgment. Hades is the realm of the dead and departed. In the New Testament, however, the term is never used for the saved.[7] It is only used with reference to the souls of unbelievers, and here Jesus tells us that when such people go to Hades, they are already afflicted with the flames of divine judgment that will fully and eternally torment them in hell.

Jesus described the rich man's distress in graphic physical terms. As we see from verse 24, he was burning in agony and desperate for a little water to cool his tongue. At this point the rich man did not have a physical body, so we need to allow for metaphor here. Jesus is giving us a physical description of a spiritual torment. However, he is describing that torment in the way that gives us the clearest picture of what it is like to be under the judgment of God. In the words of Klaus Schilder, "Let no one say: it is *merely* symbolic *and therefore* not so terrible. By mere inversion one should rather say: if the symbol, the mere picture, is already awe-inspiring, how terrible the original must be!"[8]

---

7. Leon Morris, *The Gospel According to St. Luke: An Introduction and Commentary*, Tyndale New Testament Commentaries (Grand Rapids: Eerdmans, 1974), 253.

8. Klaus Schilder, *Wat is de hel?* 2nd ed. (Kampen: Kok, 1932), 40.

Now the contrast between the two men was complete. On earth one man lived in a palace of luxury, while the other man died in the dust at his very doorstep. But when they reached their destination after death, the situation was utterly and eternally reversed: one man rested on the bosom of Abraham, while the other man burned in the agonies of Hades. Here we see the truth of what Jesus said back in verse 15: "What is exalted among men is an abomination in the sight of God." However much praise the rich man may have received for his riches, the way he treated the poor was a damnable sin, and he would suffer for it when he died.

The point here is not that salvation depends on one's tax bracket. No, the real issue is our faith response to God—a response that is plainly revealed by what we do with our circumstances in life. Lazarus trusted in God and waited for his salvation. His silence here is impressive: "He does not speak at all. He neither complains of his hard lot on earth, nor gloats over the rich man after death, nor expresses resentment at the latter's endeavours to have him sent on errands. Throughout he accepts what God sends him."[9] By contrast, the rich man was full of selfish greed and wicked neglect, and as a result he was condemned to fiery judgment.

Our response to God is revealed in the way we handle our circumstances. Where we will go in the end is presaged by what we are doing right now with what we have: "Everything depends on the attitude which a person reveals towards his wealth or towards his poverty—whether he believes in God with a repentant heart and serves Him, whatever his external circumstances may be, or whether he rejects Him—a thing which may be done in poverty as well as in wealth."[10]

## THE FIRST PLEA: MERCY FOR THE MAN HIMSELF

The contrast between these two men was made all the more intense by the way they could communicate. Perhaps this is the way things really are in the afterlife, or perhaps Jesus was simply using his imagination to make a spiritual point. But in any case, the rich man could look across the vast abyss between his torment and Abraham's bliss. Out of

9. Morris, *Luke*, 254.

10. Norval Geldenhuys, *The Gospel of Luke*, New International Commentary on the New Testament (Grand Rapids: Eerdmans, 1951), 427.

his excruciating suffering the rich man made the first of two desperate cries for help: "Father Abraham, have mercy on me, and send Lazarus to dip the end of his finger in water and cool my tongue, for I am in anguish in this flame" (Luke 16:24).

This request, in all its irony, summarizes the whole situation. The rich man knows who Abraham is, and even calls him "Father" the way the Pharisees did (see Luke 3:8). Yet he never followed Abraham's example in using his wealth for the glory of God, or planning ahead for eternity. He also knows who Lazarus is! On earth he had tried to ignore Lazarus, stepping past him every day on his way out of the house and pretending not to notice his needs. Nevertheless, he knew exactly who the man was and thus was able to call him by name. Most ironically of all, *he* is now the person in need, begging for the kind of help that he himself never gave anyone:

> The rich man who, while on earth, had regarded himself as totally independent and had, on account of his wealth, never needed to ask for anything from anybody else, now experiences such misery that he begs for help, even if it is only a single drop of water for his thirsty tongue, at the hand of the formerly despised beggar. Now he, in his turn, is the beggar who yearns for relief from the inexpressible tortures endured by him in the flame of remorse and eternal despair.[11]

How desperate the damned must be for mercy, and how reasonable their request for relief must seem! The rich man was not asking for much. He was not even praying for his salvation; he just wanted one little drop of water to soothe his burning tongue. Yet even that request was firmly denied, because God has no mercy for people who die without Christ. Here is how Abraham explained it to the rich man who had now become the beggar: "Child, remember that you in your lifetime received your good things, and Lazarus in like manner bad things; but now he is comforted here, and you are in anguish" (Luke 16:25).

In other words, according to God's perfect justice, the rich man's request could not and would not be answered. He had failed to follow Jesus' advice and make friends for himself in eternity (see Luke 16:9). Therefore, he had already received what was rightfully his—all the good things he had

11. Geldenhuys, *Luke*, 425.

enjoyed in his lifetime—and he had nothing more coming to him, not even one single drop of water.

The point here is not that all poor people will go to heaven (although it is certainly true that many rich people will go to hell—maybe even most of them—while many others will be saved by the gospel Jesus preached to the poor). The point is rather that people who live only for the things of this world will get nothing from heaven. As Jesus said back in his Sermon on the Plain, "Woe to you who are rich, for you have received your consolation" (Luke 6:24). If we live for this life, it is all we will get, which is fair enough. People in hell will never be able to claim that they have been treated unfairly. No, God will treat them with perfect justice, and if they are unhappy with where they end up, they will have only themselves to blame.

But there is more. Abraham said, "And besides all this, between us and you a great chasm has been fixed, in order that those who would pass from here to you may not be able, and none may cross from there to us" (Luke 16:26). These two men had lived practically right next door to one another, but now they were separated forever. Here, in the bridgeless chasm between Hades and the bosom of Abraham, we see the great divorce between heaven and hell. An eternal divide has been set in place, put there by almighty God. Hell has been eternally separated from heaven by divine decree.

God has done this for a very explicit purpose. According to Jesus, he has done it "in order that" no one from hell can escape to heaven and no one from heaven can go to help anyone in hell. People sometimes imagine that there must be some way for the saints in glory to go and rescue people who are trapped in hell. But Jesus says that God has made a chasm between heaven and hell for the very purpose of preventing this from happening. Other people hope that even if they do end up in hell they will be able to find their way out. But even if a man has all the wealth in the world, "this will not in eternity be able to effect the slightest change in his condition if he has departed this life without the salvation of God."[12] It is now or never! Once we die, the decision we have made about Jesus Christ becomes irrevocable and irreversible.

Hell has no exit. So by the time an unbeliever gets there it will be too late to be saved, too late to hear the gospel, too late to believe in Jesus

12. Geldenhuys, *Luke*, 427.

Christ, too late to beg for mercy, and too late to avoid the everlasting agony of eternity without God.

What urgency this should give to our preaching of the gospel! Now is the time when people have the opportunity to be saved. Therefore, we must give them the good news about Jesus Christ while they still have time to receive it. And how urgently we all need to believe the gospel! Jesus Christ is the only bridge from wrath to righteousness. It is only by faith in him that we will ever find forgiveness for our sins, or the joy of God, or the hope of eternal life. Put your faith in Jesus now, while you still have time, or else very soon you will find yourself in a place where no one can come and rescue you at all. No one will be allowed to come there and preach you the gospel, and once you are there you will not be able to come to Christ, because after death there is no passage that leads to heaven from hell.

## THE SECOND PLEA: MERCY FOR HIS BROTHERS

The awful fixity of hell must have terrified the rich man with many despairing thoughts of eternal doom. But when he discovered that he was beyond any hope of rescue, he did give a thought to someone else. Even if God did not have any mercy for him, perhaps he could still show mercy to his family. So he made his second desperate plea: "Then I beg you, father, to send him to my father's house—for I have five brothers—so that he may warn them, lest they also come into this place of torment" (Luke 16:27–28).

The horrors of Hades were so awful that suddenly the rich man was interested in the missionary work of the gospel. He did not want his brothers to have to experience the pain that he had to endure. He was desperate for some evangelist to go and warn them to turn away from their sins before it was too late. Once again, his request seems perfectly reasonable (although from the way he orders Lazarus around it is evident how superior he still thinks he is). What could be more reasonable than a dead man's prayer for his family's salvation?

Yet this plea was also denied. Or rather, it is not much so denied as it is said to be unnecessary: "But Abraham said, 'They have Moses and the Prophets; let them hear them'" (Luke 16:29). In other words, the rich man's brothers already had the means of salvation. They had in their possession everything they needed to get to heaven. They had Moses and the Prophets—the very Word of God.

This indicates that the rich man came from a religious family. His people lived in a community where they could go to the local synagogue and hear the Scriptures of the Old Testament. If only they had believed what the Bible said, it would be enough to save them. They would know the promises of God about the coming of salvation, they would know that they needed blood to atone for their sins, and they would know that Jesus was the Christ. It was all there in the Scriptures: all they needed to do was believe it.

This is all that anyone ever needs. The Word of God is enough to show us our sin, enough to guide us into the way of salvation, and enough to teach us how to give glory to God. The Bible has the power to bring us to full salvation, all by itself, if only we will believe what it says about Jesus Christ.

But notice the rich man's objection. He thought that the Word of God was *not* enough without some kind of supernatural sign, so he said, "No, father Abraham, but if someone goes to them from the dead, they will repent" (Luke 16:30). Once again, we may be inclined to think that this is a reasonable request. In a way, it even points us back to the gospel, because when we hear about someone coming back from the dead to preach repentance, we immediately think of Jesus himself and his own resurrection.

That is not at all what the rich man had in mind, however. He was remembering what things were like before he died and went to Hades. Frankly, he knew how little attention he had ever paid to God's Word. He was the kind of man who never really understood the point of going to a worship service and listening to someone teach the Bible. In fact, this is what kept him out of glory: he did not believe the Word of God. His sinful lack of compassion for the poor was simply the outward evidence of his inner unbelief—the unbelief that sent him to Hades.

The rich man knew his brothers well enough to know that they did not believe the Bible any more than he did. But what if God showed them some kind of sign? What if a ghost came and preached them the gospel? Surely then they would have to sit up and take notice, wouldn't they?

No, they would not. On the contrary, Abraham said, "If they do not hear Moses and the Prophets, neither will they be convinced if someone should rise from the dead" (Luke 16:31; cf. John 5:46–47). Here we are given a deep insight into the heart of unbelief—an insight so powerful and profound that it could save a person's soul: *If you do not believe what God has said in his Word, then you will never believe anything else God does either, and you will never truly believe in Jesus.*

See the logic of what Abraham is saying. If people are not willing to listen to the Scriptures, then even the most spectacular miracle will not persuade them of the truth about Jesus Christ. There is ample proof of this in the Gospels. Consider what happened when Jesus raised that other Lazarus from the dead: rather then believing in Jesus, the religious leaders began plotting to kill him (John 11:43–53). The same thing happened when Jesus himself rose from the dead: instead of believing in his resurrection, the men who killed him tried to cover the whole thing up (Matt. 28:11–15). Not even the resurrection is enough to convince people to trust in Jesus Christ if they will not believe what God has said in his Word.

This is the real problem with unbelievers who are on their way to hell. It is not that God has failed to give them what they need to get to heaven; it is that they refuse to receive what he has given. The Bible is enough to save you, if only you will believe what it says about the cross and the empty tomb. But if you do not believe what God says in his Word, you will never believe in Jesus, you will never get to heaven, and you will have only yourself to blame.

In the end there are really only two kinds of people, who will reach two very different destinations. Do not end up in the terrible place where even prayers for mercy will not be answered, but cross into glory now, while you still have the opportunity. Jesus said, "Whoever hears my word and believes him who sent me has eternal life. He does not come into judgment, but has passed from death to life" (John 5:24).

# 72

# THE FAITH TO FORGIVE

## *Luke 17:1—6*

*The apostles said to the Lord, "Increase our faith!" And the Lord*
*said, "If you had faith like a grain of mustard seed, you could*
*say to this mulberry tree, 'Be uprooted and planted in the sea,'*
*and it would obey you." (Luke 17:5–6)*

Historians tell us that King Louis XII was cast into prison and kept in chains before eventually rising to the throne of France. The story is also told that upon his ascension to power, his close advisors urged him to seek deadly revenge by every means of violence. In response to their entreaties, Louis XII prepared a scroll listing the names of all the enemies who had committed crimes against his royal person. Opposite every name he inscribed a cross in red ink. Surely the men who committed these misdeeds would have to die!

Word of the king's blood-red list soon reached his enemies, who assumed the crosses meant that they were dead men and fled for their lives. But then Louis XII clarified his true and surprising intention. He said, "The cross which I drew beside each name was not a sign of punishment but a pledge of forgiveness extended for the sake of the crucified Savior, who upon His cross forgave His enemies and prayed for them."[1]

The flight of the king's enemies reminds us how unexpected it is to find forgiveness. When people are wronged, they do not want to offer forgiveness; they want to exact revenge. So it is always surprising when someone offers full and free forgiveness. When people do this, it is almost always because they themselves know what it means to be forgiven. What Louis XII offered his enemies was the same kind of grace that he himself had received from the crucified Christ. He had the faith to forgive.

## Don't Tempt Me!

Jesus taught his disciples to exercise this faith at the beginning of Luke 17. After speaking with the Pharisees about heaven and hell, he told his disciples not to give offense (Luke 17:1–2), or take offense (Luke 17:3–4), but to forgive by faith (Luke 17:5–6).

Jesus began this discourse by warning his disciples not to become a stumbling block for other believers by causing them to sin. He said: "Temptations to sin are sure to come, but woe to the one through whom they come! It would be better for him if a millstone were hung around his neck and he were cast into the sea than that he should cause one of these little ones to sin" (Luke 17:1–2).

When it came to sin, Jesus was enough of a realist to know that in a fallen world people will always be tempted. He knew this from his own experience, for he himself was tempted as we are. Temptation happens. Even if we are not tempted by anything in the world outside us, we are still tempted by the twisted desires of our own fallen hearts. But woe to us if we are the ones who do the tempting—especially if we tempt the children of God!

The word Jesus used for temptation *(skandala)* refers generally to anything that is a stumbling block for people, anything that causes them to fall. The same word appears in the first letter of John, where it is used in a similar way: "Whoever loves his brother abides in the light, and in him there is no cause for stumbling" (1 John 2:10; cf. Rom. 11:9; 14:13). Here in Luke it

1. Eric E. Wright, *Revolutionary Forgiveness* (Auburn, MA: Evangelical Press, 2002), 256.

seems clear that Jesus is talking about something that causes people to fall down spiritually, something that leads them sinfully astray.

What are some ways we lead people astray? We do it any time our actions or attitudes set a bad spiritual example. We do it when our complaining spirit causes other people to be discontent. We do it by speaking evil words that unfairly influence someone else's opinion. We do it by carrying on an argument to the point where we provoke an angry response. We do it by enticing someone to commit sexual sin or join us for some juicy gossip. We do it by boasting of our accomplishments or acquisitions in a way that makes other people envious or boastful. These are only some of the many ways that we can become a spiritual hindrance to other people. Of course they have to take responsibility for their own actions. But woe to us if we make it easier for them to sin, or harder for them to be godly!

Tempting people is a very great sin, especially if the people we tempt happen to be less spiritually mature. The phrase "little ones" can refer literally to children (e.g., Matt. 8:10) or else metaphorically to anyone who is a follower of Jesus Christ, including the original disciples themselves (see Mark 10:24; Luke 10:21). We are all "little ones" who need special protection and spiritual care. But here Jesus may be referring more specifically to people who are just beginning to follow him, like the tax collectors and other sinners mentioned at the beginning of chapter 15. New believers are at the most vulnerable stage of their Christian experience, and more experienced disciples need to be very careful not to lead them astray.

This is a strong warning about "the great sinfulness of putting stumbling-blocks in the way of other men's souls."[2] Along with all the other sins we need to confess, we need to confess the spread of our sin through the negative influence it has on others. We need to pray the way John Donne prayed in his "Hymn to God the Father": "Wilt Thou forgive that sin which I have won // Others to sin, and made my sin their door?"[3] The answer is yes. If we come to God in true repentance, he will forgive us even for the sins that have caused other people to sin.

---

2. J. C. Ryle, *Expository Thoughts on the Gospels, Luke* (1858; reprint Cambridge: James Clarke, 1976), 2:220.

3. John Donne, "A Hymn to God the Father," in *Poems of John Donne*, ed. E. K. Chambers (London: Lawrence & Bullen, 1896), 1:213.

But we must repent. Jesus did not explain exactly what woe will befall us if we fail to heed his warning, but the comparison he makes is frightening. It would be better for us to die a violent death by drowning than to lead one of God's little children into sin. The large round millstones people used in those days for grinding their grain were much too heavy for a single person to lift. Needless to say, someone with a millstone around his neck would fall straight to the bottom of the sea.

Better that, though, than to lead God's people astray—better for the children of God, and better for the person who causes them to stumble. Bruce McDowell, who is minister of global outreach at Philadelphia's Tenth Presbyterian Church, tells the story of two grade-school children who were led into grievous sin by someone who ought to have known better—an older boy from a Christian family. When the sin was discovered, the younger boys were sorry for what they had done, but the older boy never seemed to show any sign of repentance. Several years later the older boy drowned while scuba diving in an undersea cave, and people were reminded of what Jesus said: better for him to be cast into the sea than to lead little ones astray.

Leading God's children astray is a very great sin. Consider all the moral, financial, and sexual scandals that have corrupted the church and dishonored the name of Christ. Would it not have been better for everyone if these things had never happened—indeed, if the perpetrators had died before their downfall? We should pray for ourselves and for our own spiritual leaders, that God will protect us from falling into such grievous sins ourselves.

## SEVENFOLD FORGIVENESS

As important as it is not to give offense by causing other people to sin, it is also important not to take offense when other people sin against us. By the grace of God, when temptation happens there is an opportunity for repentance and reconciliation through the forgiveness of sins. Jesus said: "Pay attention to yourselves! If your brother sins, rebuke him, and if he repents, forgive him, and if he sins against you seven times in the day, and turns to you seven times, saying, 'I repent,' you must forgive him" (Luke 17:3–4).

The sequence here is important. First comes the rebuke—specifically, the rebuke of a brother or sister in Christ. If a fellow believer has committed an offense, then we have a spiritual responsibility to show him his fault. Presumably the sin that Jesus mainly has in mind is the kind he was talking about in verses 1 and 2: a sin that leads other people astray. But the same principle applies to any scandalous sin: for the glory of God and for the real spiritual good of our spiritual brothers and sisters, Jesus commands us to rebuke unrighteousness in the family of God, especially if God has put us in a position of spiritual leadership.

There is a right way and a wrong way to confront sin. We need to go to one another courageously, not timidly, willing to say what needs to be said, no matter what the cost. We need to go to one another gently, not judgmentally, demonstrating the tender mercy of Christ (see Gal. 6:1). We need to go to one another humbly, not proudly, having already confessed our own great sin. We need to go to one another affectionately, not harshly, showing how much we love our brother or sister in Christ. We need to go to one another prayerfully, not impulsively, asking God to glorify himself through our ministry of reconciliation. But we do need to go to one another. A sin needs to be called a sin in a way that leads to repentance. Do we care enough to confront, and are we godly enough to do it with Christ-like compassion? It takes grace to do this, and to do it well.

The rebuke is only the first step. Next comes the repentance, or at least that is what we pray for. Jesus said, "if he repents." Unfortunately, some have taken the word "if" here as an absolute qualification on our forgiveness. Thus they have understood Jesus to mean that we have the right to withhold forgiveness in our hearts until someone actually comes to us with satisfactory repentance. But this is contrary to the example of Jesus himself, who forgave his enemies even before they asked (Luke 23:34). It is also contrary to the whole direction of his teaching in this passage, where the emphasis falls on freely offered forgiveness.

Surely Jesus wants us to have a forgiving heart toward someone who has done us wrong, even before we have the opportunity to offer formal forgiveness. Surely he does not want us to hold on to a grudge, even when we have been greatly harmed. So why does he say "if"? J. C. Ryle answers by saying: "This expression is remarkable. It doubtless cannot mean that we are not to forgive men unless they do repent. At this rate there would

211

be much bitterness constantly kept alive. But it does mean that when there is no repentance or regret for an injury done, there can be no renewal of cordial friendship, or complete reconciliation between man and man."[4]

What Jesus has in view is a situation in which everything has gone the way we hope and now it is up to us to complete the process of reconciliation. Although a sin has been committed, a rebuke has been rightly given and graciously received. True repentance has been offered. Now it is time to forgive and forgive again. How many times do we have to forgive someone? Every day, if necessary—even seven times a day, the number of perfection. The point is that we never reach the point where we can say we will no longer forgive. Jesus puts this in the imperative: "you must forgive him" (Luke 17:4). There is no limit to the forgiveness a believer in Christ is obligated to offer a penitent sinner.

Immediately we think of all kinds of objections. What about accountability and church discipline? How can someone really be repentant if he has to keep repenting again and again? And so on. These are legitimate questions, and the Bible speaks to them in other places. But here Jesus is telling us to forgive and forgive and forgive. This is not to deny that people need to be held accountable for their actions by people in spiritual authority so that they do not keep committing the same sins over and over again. Nor is it to deny that there is a proper place for justice, or that when someone else has sinned against us, it may take time to rebuild trust. But Jesus wants us to have a heart of forgiveness, and when we have the heart of Jesus, we are able to forgive again and again. Leon Morris puts it like this: "From the world's point of view a sevenfold repetition of an offence in one day must cast doubt on the genuineness of the sinner's repentance. But that is not the believer's concern. His business is forgiveness."[5]

Cyril of Alexandria compared forgiveness to the work of a medical doctor. We should "imitate those whose business it is to heal our bodily diseases," Cyril said, "and who do not care for a sick person once only or twice, but just as often as he happens to become ill."[6] When a patient

---

4. Ryle, *Luke*, 2:225.

5. Leon Morris, *The Gospel According to St. Luke: An Introduction and Commentary*, Tyndale New Testament Commentaries (Grand Rapids: Eerdmans, 1974), 256.

6. Cyril of Alexandria, "Commentary on Luke," in *Luke*, ed. Arthur A. Just, Jr., Ancient Christian Commentary on Scripture, NT 3 (Downers Grove, IL: InterVarsity, 2003), 266.

has some sort of illness, the doctor will provide the necessary cure. If the patient later suffers a relapse, or comes down with another disease, the doctor will not claim that he has treated the patient already, but will prescribe another cure. So it is with the soul-healing work of forgiveness: however many times someone comes to tell us they are sorry, we are to say, "I forgive you."

## MORE FAITH!

At this point the disciples simply had to interrupt. What Jesus was telling them to do went so far beyond their capabilities that they needed to ask for help. We can understand how they felt because none of these things is easy for us to do either. It is hard to set a good example for people, not leading them astray. It is hard to rebuke a brother's sin in a way that leads to real repentance. It is hard to forgive people who have done us some kind of wrong. But forgiving someone seven times a day? Impossible! How could anyone do *that?!?* With customary hyperbole, Jesus is telling us to take forgiveness to the ultimate extreme. He is telling us to forgive the unforgivable.

But what if we had to offer such forgiveness repeatedly? How could we even do it? The Croatian theologian Miroslav Volf wrestled with this question after giving a public lecture on Christian forgiveness. As soon as the lecture ended, the German theologian Jürgen Moltmann stood up and asked, "But can you embrace a *cetnik?*" Here is how Volf explains what Moltmann was really asking, and the answer he gave:

> It was the winter of 1993. For months now the notorious Serbian fighters called "*cetnik*" had been sowing desolation in my native country, herding people into concentration camps, raping women, burning down churches, and destroying cities. I had just argued that we ought to embrace our enemies as God has embraced us in Christ. Can I embrace a *cetnik*—the ultimate other, so to speak, the evil other? What would justify the embrace? Where would I draw the strength for it?

Sooner or later this is a question we all have to face: Can I embrace the *cetnik* in my life—the person who has done me the most harm? Can I forgive the abuser and the betrayer? Miroslav Volf waited a long time before giving his answer. But finally, he said, "No, I cannot—but as a follower of Christ I think I should be able to."[7]

This is what the disciples thought, too. They did not know how they could possibly forgive anyone seven times in a single day, even though they knew that this is what the grace of God demanded. So they asked Jesus for help: "The apostles said to the Lord, 'Increase our faith!'" (Luke 17:5).

This may be one of the smartest things the disciples ever did.[8] They did not ask for more obedience to live the way Jesus wanted them to live. They did not ask for more courage and compassion to confront people's sin. They did not ask for more patience with people it was hard for them to love. All of those things were needed, of course, but what the disciples demanded was more faith, especially the faith to forgive. This is what we need any time Jesus tells us to do something that seems impossible: more faith. We need more faith in the promises of God the Father, more faith in the grace of God the Son, and more faith in the power of God the Holy Spirit. Since we cannot increase this faith by our own strength, we must ask God for it.

Whenever we put our faith in God, we are trusting him to do something for us that we cannot do for ourselves. Radical forgiveness is a perfect example. We will not find the strength to forgive somewhere in our own good will. We need a supernatural work of divine grace. Only God can give us a forgiving heart, and since forgiveness is a gift, we can receive it only by faith.

To be more specific, we need to put our faith in Jesus Christ, who died for our sins on the cross. As soon as we start talking about forgiveness, we are talking about something very close to the heart of the gospel, something that draws us immediately to the cross where Jesus died. It is only in the cross that we can find any satisfactory answer for the problem of unforgivable sin. The cross fully acknowledges the sinfulness of sin by placing it under the wrath and curse of God. But it also atones for sin, providing a way for sinners like us to be forgiven.

The way we learn to forgive, therefore, is by looking to Jesus and his cross. What people did to him there was unforgivable. It was the wickedest

---

7. Miroslav Volf, *Exclusion and Embrace: A Theological Exploration of Identity, Otherness, and Reconciliation* (Nashville: Abingdon, 1996), 9.

8. Some scholars disagree with this interpretation, arguing instead that the disciples are using their supposed need for more faith as an excuse for disobeying the command to forgive. On this reading verses 7–10 are a rebuke for their reluctance to do their duty and forgive.

thing that anyone has ever done, from the kiss of Judas right on through to our Savior's last cry of desolation. It was wicked for the priests to conspire against Jesus and convict him on an unjust charge. It was wicked for the people to ask for his crucifixion, and just as wicked for Pilate to give in to their demands. It was wicked for the soldiers to mock him, beat him, and put him to death. It was also wicked for his disciples to abandon him. These things were wicked because Jesus was completely innocent. He was the sinless Son of God, and because of his divine majesty, it was an infinitely evil offense against the holiness of God. In a word, it was unforgivable.

But how did Jesus respond? With forgiveness. We see this at the cross itself, when Jesus said, "Father, forgive them" (Luke 23:34). We see it again on the day of Pentecost, when some of the very people who put Jesus to death received forgiveness for their sins in the name of the same Jesus whom they had crucified (Acts 2:38).

As we wrestle with God's call to forgive, we need to keep going back to the cross of Christ. That is where we find our own forgiveness, and also where we find the courage, the freedom, and the grace to forgive others for their unforgivable sins. This is where I must go every time I feel that I cannot forgive: to the cross where Jesus forgave me. If I have faith that Jesus has forgiven me, then I can have faith that he will enable me to forgive others. The forgiveness I offer flows from the forgiveness I myself have received from God in Christ.

The British army officer Ernest Gordon writes about this forgiveness in his book *To End All Wars*, which tells the story of the infamous Japanese prison camp on the River Kwai. Conditions there were horrific, and early in his time there Gordon was given up for dead. Yet by the grace of God he survived, and together with many of the other prisoners he came to saving faith in Jesus Christ.

After these men came to Christ, they began to meet for public worship and to pray the Lord's Prayer. But there was one petition where they always faltered: "Forgive us our debts, as we forgive our debtors." Why did they falter? As Gordon explained it:

> It was because it meant asking forgiveness for the Japanese. We had learned from the gospels that Jesus had his enemies just as we had ours. But there was this difference: he loved his enemies. He prayed for them. Even as the

nails were being hammered through his hands and feet, he cried out, "Father, forgive them, for they know not what they do." We hated our enemies. We could see how wonderful it was that Jesus forgave in this way. Yet for us to do the same seemed beyond our attainment.[9]

For Gordon the breakthrough came by going back to the cross of Christ and finding there both his own forgiveness *and* the grace he needed to forgive the people he found it impossible to love. It happened on Good Friday, and here is how Gordon described the experience:

> I recognized that it was no easy thing to call that figure on the Cross "Lord." I heard again His words, "Father, forgive them, for they know not what they do." This He had said for His enemies; but what was I to say for mine? I could not say what He had said, for He was innocent, whereas I was not. Humbly, I had to ask, "Forgive me and my enemies, for we know not what we do."[10]

Where do we find the faith to forgive? We find it at the cross where we ourselves have been forgiven. If we believe that God has forgiven us for all the wrong things that we have done against him, and against others, then we can forgive our fellow sinners for all the wrong things they have done against us. By faith, we are able to forgive.

## Mustard-Seed Faith

When the disciples asked Jesus for more faith, they were basically asking for the right thing, because it takes faith to forgive. They were also asking the right person, because faith is a gift from God. Rather than giving them more faith, however, Jesus said, "If you had faith like a grain of mustard seed, you could say to this mulberry tree, 'Be uprooted and planted in the sea,' and it would obey you" (Luke 17:6).

At least this time Jesus did not tell us to move any mountains! In Mark 11 he told his disciples, "Have faith in God. Truly, I say to you, whoever says to this mountain, 'Be taken up and thrown into the sea,' and does not doubt in his heart, but believes that what he says will come to pass, it will be done

---

9. Ernest Gordon, *To End All Wars* (1963; reprint Grand Rapids: Eerdmans, 2002), 156.
10. Ibid., 189.

for him" (Mark 11:22–23). At first, what Jesus says in Luke 17 may seem a lot less intimidating. We know we do not have the faith to move mountains, but maybe—just maybe—we could manage a mulberry tree.

Then we realize that even one little tree is well beyond our capabilities. In those days the mulberry was considered the most firmly rooted of trees. In fact, some rabbis said that once a mulberry tree was established it would stay rooted for six hundred years.[11] It was hard enough to uproot a mulberry tree, let alone plant one in the sea. Who has the power to do such a thing simply by saying the word?

Jesus used this illustration to show that we need to trust God to do what only God can do. This is what it means to have faith: it means believing that God is able to do what is impossible for us. Jesus is not saying that faith will give us magic powers, like some kind of supernatural force. Nor is he saying that we should use our faith to do something trivial, like transplant a tree. Moving the tree is simply an illustration of something we cannot do, but God can. The point is that if God calls us to do something impossible (like forgiving someone seven times a day), we need to trust in his enabling power.

All it takes is the tiniest little bit of genuine faith. Mustard was the smallest of seeds, but even that small an amount of true faith has the power to move mulberry trees. In other words, it is not really a matter of having more or less faith; what matters is having true faith in the power of God. Leon Morris writes, "It is not so much great faith in God that is required as faith in a great God."[12]

Even the smallest amount of faith will enable us to do the impossible things that God is calling us to do. Faith enables us to trust God for all the uncertainties of the future, because we trust in an all-knowing God. Faith enables us to trust God to provide what we need, even if we do not have any idea how he will do it, because we trust in a faithful God. Faith enables us to get past the hurt of broken dreams and shattered promises, because we trust in a comforting God. Faith enables us to resist the temptation that is destroying us, because we trust in a powerful God. As Jesus said on another occasion, "All things are possible for one who believes" (Mark 9:23).

11. Morris, *Luke*, 256.
12. Ibid.

In Luke 17, however, the emphasis falls on having the faith to forgive, because we trust in a forgiving God. The story is told of a Zulu chieftain whose wife was converted to faith in Jesus Christ. When he heard what had happened, the chieftain was enraged. He told his wife he would never let her go to an evangelistic meeting ever again. But she was drawn by the beauty of Christ and the grace of his cross, so she went back the very next day to hear the gospel.

When the chieftain discovered where his wife had gone, he went to find her. In his rage he dragged her out of the village, beat her savagely, and left her for dead. But later, when he wondered if she had survived, he went back out into the bush to look for her. He found her lying on the ground—bleeding, gasping, and not far from death. "And what can your Jesus Christ do for you now?" he scoffed. The woman's eyes fluttered open, and she said, very gently, very quietly, "He helps me to forgive you!"[13]

Who is the person that *you* need to forgive? Jesus will help you to do it. By his cross and by his Spirit, he will give you the faith to forgive.

13. This story is recounted in Wright, *Revolutionary Forgiveness*, 24–25.

# 73

# RETURNING THANKS

## *Luke 17:7–19*

*Then one of them, when he saw that he was healed, turned back,
praising God with a loud voice; and he fell on his face at Jesus'
feet, giving him thanks. Now he was a Samaritan.*
(Luke 17:15–16)

hat does God owe to you, and what do you owe to God? The answer we give shows what kind of relationship we have with Jesus Christ. Some people go through life thinking that God owes them something, and then spend a lot of time grumbling about it when he fails to deliver. Even when they get what they wanted, they always find something to complain about. They are rather like the mother in a whimsical parable whose son was swept away by a tornado. The woman cried for help: "Please, Lord, bring back my boy! He's all I have. I'd do anything to get him back." Suddenly her son fell from the sky, right at her feet, a little shaken, but safe and sound. But as the mother joyfully embraced her son, she noticed that something was still missing, so she glared up at the heavens and said, "He had a hat, Lord!"[1]

1. This story is recounted by David P. Barrett, in *Perfect Illustrations for Every Topic and Occasion* (Wheaton, IL: Tyndale, 2002), 48–49.

Other people have an attitude of gratitude. They understand that God does not owe them anything, that even the smallest blessings are a gift of his grace, and that everything he does for them deserves the most thankful praise. They offer the kind of prayer that the English country pastor George Herbert once prayed:

> Thou that has given so much to me,
> Give one thing more—a grateful heart;
> Not thankful when it pleaseth me,
> As if thy blessings had spare days;
> But such a heart, whose pulse may be
> Thy praise.[2]

Whether our hearts pulse with praise largely depends on what we think God owes us, and what we owe to God.

## DOING OUR DUTY

If we say that we are Christians, then we are called to do our spiritual duty, never claiming that we deserve anything from God, but holding on to Jesus by faith, and giving him all the praise for our salvation. Jesus started to explain who owes what to whom by giving his disciples an illustration from daily life:

> Will any one of you who has a servant plowing or keeping sheep say to him when he has come in from the field, "Come at once and recline at table"? Will he not rather say to him, "Prepare supper for me, and dress properly, and serve me while I eat and drink, and afterward you will eat and drink"? Does he thank the servant because he did what was commanded? (Luke 17:7–9)

The situation Jesus described would have been unthinkable in the ancient world, where people knew their place in life, and where an invitation to sit at a wealthy man's table was a high social privilege. To recline at table was virtually to be treated like a member of the family. Masters, therefore, did not fix dinner for their servants. Even after a full day's work out in the fields, a servant still had to do his duty at dinnertime, which meant cleaning up and then waiting on his master hand and foot. The master was not

2. George Herbert, "Gratefulness."

there to serve the servant, but the other way around. It was not the master's responsibility to make life easy for his servant, but the servant's responsibility to work hard for his master.

Perhaps some contemporary examples will help us understand what Jesus was saying.[3] Imagine going out for dinner and hearing the waitress say, "You know, I've been working hard all night, and I'm a terrific waitress, and I'm really hungry right now, and I think I'll just sit down with you folks and eat some of your shrimp Alfredo." Or imagine buying a new house and finding out when you arrive that the realtor is already there with his own truck, busy moving his family in. Why not? After all, he helped to find the place, didn't he?

Obviously, such behavior would be completely outrageous! A waiter and a realtor who tried this would quickly find themselves unemployed. The reason is very simple: it is their *job* to bring the food and find the house, and that they do their job well does not mean that they have a right to be treated like a member of the family. A servant who excels at serving is still only a servant and does not thereby earn the right to become the master.

According to Jesus, the same thing is true in our relationship with God. Here is the spiritual application he gives for his story: "So you also, when you have done all that you were commanded, say, 'We are unworthy servants; we have only done what was our duty'" (Luke 17:10).

Many people take the opposite approach. They think that all the things they do for God amount to something. Now they want God to do *his* duty and welcome them to the banquet of his blessing. This is what the Pharisees thought. They were like the elder brother in the story of the prodigal son: when they came in from the fields, so to speak, they wanted their father to celebrate their obedience. Often we come to God the same way, claiming that we deserve more from him than we are getting. We hear this teaching today from preachers who present Jesus as a better way to get what you want out of life, which of course only makes God the servant of our own desires.

The truth is that God does not *owe* us anything. If this sounds harsh, it is because in our self-righteous pride we think that we have really done something for God. In fact, we may secretly hope that the good things we do will

---

3. These examples are adapted from Bryan Chapell, *Holiness by Grace: Delighting in the Joy That Is Our Strength* (Wheaton, IL: Crossway, 2001), 19–20.

gain us some kind of leverage with the Almighty. But even if we did every-thing he ever wanted us to do—even then we would only have done our duty. We should not think, therefore, that we have merited any favor with God. God is not moved by our obedience. Not one of our best works—or all of our good works put together—give us a right to the household of heaven.

This is what Jesus means when he says that we are "unworthy servants": he means that we do not have any merit of our own. To translate the word another way, we are "unprofitable." In other words, when it comes to our service, God never gets a positive return on his investment. He is our Cre-ator and Redeemer in Christ; therefore he already has a right to all our allegiance. Even if we gave God perfect service, we would only be giving him what he demands and deserves; it would profit God nothing. But in fact we often fail to serve him well, so he actually gets a negative return on his investment.

If even the good things we do are done only by the grace of God, how could we even begin to think of ourselves as the master, and God as our ser-vant? J. C. Ryle said, "He that desires to be saved must confess that there is no good thing in him, and that he has no merit, no goodness, no worthiness of his own. He must be willing to renounce his own righteousness, and to trust in the righteousness of another, even Christ the Lord."[4] Yet how hard it is for us to renounce our own righteousness! How hard it is to admit that we deserve nothing from God, and that whatever good we do is only our duty, done by the grace of God. In the words of Martin Luther:

> Even though we are in faith . . . the heart is always ready to boast of itself before God and say: "After all, I have preached so long and lived so well and done so much, surely he will take this into account.". . . But when you come before God, leave all that boasting at home and remember to appeal from justice to grace. . . . I myself have been preaching [grace] for almost twenty years and still I feel the old clinging dirt of wanting to deal so with God that I may contribute something, so that he will have to give his grace in exchange for my holiness. Still I cannot get it into my head that I should surrender myself completely to sheer grace; yet this is what I should and must do.[5]

---

4. J. C. Ryle, *Expository Thoughts on the Gospels, Luke* (1858; reprint Cambridge: James Clarke, 1976), 2:228.

5. Martin Luther, from "The Sum of the Christian Life," a sermon preached at Worlitz, Nov. 24, 1534.

When we finally do surrender to the grace of God, we make the most amazing discovery: even though we do not deserve it, Jesus did exactly what a master never does and made himself the servant of our salvation. Jesus hinted at this back in chapter 12, when he told a parable about a master who dressed for service, invited his servants to recline at his table, and began to serve them dinner (Luke 12:37). He was beginning to teach his disciples about his own saving grace. Later he would ask them, "Who is the greater, one who reclines at table or one who serves? Is it not the one who reclines at table? But I am among you as the one who serves" (Luke 22:27). Jesus Christ is the worthy servant. He proved it by going to the cross and suffering for our sins, serving us to the very death. Now he welcomes us into the family of God and invites us to sit down and taste the banquet of his joy.

We should never imagine that this is something we deserve. If a master decides to serve his servants, it is not because they have earned the right to be served, but only because of his amazing grace. When we ourselves have received this grace, it becomes our joy to say what Jesus taught us to say: "We are unworthy servants; we have only done what was our duty" (Luke 17:10). This is not false modesty; it is a plain statement of the truth. It is a joy for us to say it because it means that none of the credit goes to us; it all goes to God in Christ. How little we have done for Jesus—infinitely less than he deserves. But how much he has done for us on the cross, through the empty tomb, and every day that we live under his loving care.

## TEN MEN CRY FOR HELP

How shall we respond to God for the gift of all this grace? By continuing to do our duty, demanding nothing in exchange, and also by returning to him our thanks and praise. This may seem perfectly obvious, but it is something that many people never do—maybe most people—which shows that they do not yet understand what God owes them and what they owe to God.

It is sad to say, but as many as nine people out of ten never thank God for what he has done for them. We know this from what happened next: "On the way to Jerusalem he was passing along between Samaria and Galilee. And as he entered a village, he was met by ten lepers, who stood at a distance and lifted up their voices, saying, 'Jesus, Master, have mercy on us'" (Luke 17:11–13).

Jesus was still on his journey to Jerusalem, making his way to Calvary and the cross. He was out in the wilderness between Samaria and Galilee, in the no man's land where one would expect to find the outcasts of society. There he met ten lepers. In those days lepers were social outcasts who lived at the very edge of destruction. According to the law of God, lepers were ceremonially unclean: "The leprous person who has the disease shall wear torn clothes and let the hair of his head hang loose, and he shall cover his upper lip and cry out, 'Unclean, unclean.' He shall remain unclean as long as he has the disease. He is unclean. He shall live alone. His dwelling shall be outside the camp" (Lev. 13:45–46). Lepers led a miserable existence, their lives dominated by their disabling disease. In addition to the physical pains of their illness, they suffered total rejection. They were cut off from the physical affection of their families and the worship of their spiritual community. To be a leper was to be separated from society and alienated from the people of God.

Luke reinforces the sense of separation by saying that the ten lepers "stood at a distance" (Luke 17:12). They were not allowed to come too close. Thus in order to get Jesus' attention, they had to shout at the top of their lungs. What they usually shouted was "Unclean, unclean!" But this time they cried for mercy, begging for relief.

The lepers' cry for help is a good example of the way needy sinners ought to pray. How do we ask for God's help in a time of physical or spiritual need? We cry out to Jesus, the loving and saving Son of God, who alone is able to help us in our time of need. We call him our Master, acknowledging his lordship and remembering that we are only his servants. Then we pray for mercy, not claiming that we deserve anything, or waiting until we think we are good enough for God, but coming right out and asking for the grace that only God can give.

This is the kind of prayer that God loves to answer: a desperate cry for help offered in the name of his Son. He will answer our own deep cry for mercy, just as he answered the prayer of all ten lepers: "When he saw them he said to them, 'Go and show yourselves to the priests.' And as they went they were cleansed" (Luke 17:14). It was a miracle! Jesus just said the word and all ten lepers were totally clean—healed by the word of Christ's power.

When Jesus told these men to go and show themselves to the priests, he was following an Old Testament ritual. According to the law of Moses (see Lev. 14:1–32), the priests were the ones who decided whether someone was clean or unclean. They were something like public health inspectors: they would examine people's skin to determine when their disease was healed and they could return to their community, which they did only after an eight-day ceremony for cleansing. So when Jesus told these men to go to the priests, he was announcing that they would be clean. Even if he did not say this in so many words, what he told them to do entailed their miraculous cure. Jesus was commanding them to do something that only a cured leper could do, and in doing so he was answering their cry for mercy.

## THE TENTH LEPER

All ten lepers did what Jesus told them to do. Even before their skin was healed, they were on their way to their priests, and as they went on their way, they looked down and discovered that their skin was totally clean. As J. C. Ryle put it, "help meets them in the path of obedience."[6] Their prayers were answered, their lives rescued, their bodies cleansed.

Yet the main emphasis here is not so much on the miraculous cure these men received as it is on the way they responded to God's mercy. Luke reports, "Then one of them, when he saw that he was healed, turned back, praising God with a loud voice; and he fell on his face at Jesus' feet, giving him thanks" (Luke 17:15–16).

The man who went back to Jesus had an appreciation that was born out of desperation. What is shocking about this, though, is that he was the only man to do it. Only one man out of ten went back to say "thank you." This was surprising to Jesus himself, as we can tell from his amazement in verse 17: "Were not ten cleansed? Where are the nine?" (Luke 17:17). Where *are* the nine? Why have they not returned to give Jesus thanks?

As far as we know, Jesus never saw these men again; they never came to Christ. The Bible does not tell us exactly why the nine former lepers never returned, but the reason is not hard to perceive. Apparently, although these men were religious enough to know where to find a priest and perform

6. Ryle, *Luke*, 2:233.

the eight-day ritual of cleansing, their hearts were not melted by the grace that God had shown to them in Jesus Christ. They were happy enough to be clean, but they did not see themselves as the recipients of undeserved mercy, because if they had, they surely would have gone back to thank Jesus.

In other words, the nine lepers were a lot like the servant Jesus had been talking about in verses 7 to 10: they called Jesus "Master," but then apparently they expected him to wait on them hand and foot, as if performing miracles for them were simply his duty. They took Jesus for granted, treating him like a Cosmic Butler instead of a Suffering Servant. They did not think they owed him anything, not even their thanksgiving.

Sadly, this is what most people seem to think. When we watch nine people out of ten forget to thank Jesus, we are witnessing a microcosm of humanity. Is any sin more characteristic of our fallen race than ingratitude? "Although they knew God," Paul writes of depraved humanity, "they did not honor him as God or give thanks to him" (Rom. 1:21). Elsewhere he goes so far as to identify ingratitude as one of the prevailing sins of godlessness in the last days (see 2 Tim. 3:1–2). We are inclined to think of ingratitude as a relatively minor sin, but in fact it is one of the worst sins in the Bible.

Ingratitude is a way of saying that God owes us whatever he gives us, and that we owe him nothing in return. Thus it is a complete reversal of our real position before God, namely, that he owes us nothing and we owe him everything. Ingratitude is also a direct assault on God's glory. When we do not thank God for his blessings, we are refusing to give him the praise that he rightly deserves.

These sins are all too common in the church, where we are nearly as likely to hear people complaining about their circumstances as praising God for them. Do you count your blessings and thank God for them? Are you remembering to thank God for your present trials, trusting that he will use them to grow you in godliness? Or do you take God for granted, forgetting to praise him for everything he does and grumbling about every little thing that goes wrong? These are important questions to ask, because if the response to this miracle is at all representative of the human race, 90 percent of people never thank God at all.

Fortunately, there was one man who got it right and found his joy in Jesus. As soon as he saw that his skin was clean, this man started returning thanks. He did it immediately, not waiting until he met with the priests, but going straight to Jesus—first things first. He did it joyously and spontaneously, while he was still on his way to the Savior. He did it loudly and exuberantly, shouting his praises to God. This is what we should do any time God heals us, or rescues us, or blesses us: we should gratefully give glory to God. We should do this right away, before we forget. John Calvin rightly said, "We have short memories in magnifying God's grace. Every blessing that God confers upon us perishes through our carelessness, if we are not prompt and active in giving thanks."[7]

The way to guard against this ungrateful sin is to follow the tenth leper's example and return thanks to God on every occasion of his blessing. Whenever the sun dawns on a bright new day, whenever we sit down to a meal that God has provided, whenever we see God at work in a broken relationship, whenever we sense God's presence in our daily work, whenever we are confronted with a problem that forces us to depend on God—whenever we experience any blessing at all—we should give heartfelt expression to our gratitude by giving praise to God.

We will do this, however, only if we know that we do not deserve anything from God, and that therefore everything he gives us is grace. The Heidelberg Catechism asks how many things we need to know in order to live and die in the comfort of Christ. The answer is three: "First, the greatness of my sin and misery. Second, how I am redeemed from all my sins and misery. Third, how I am to be thankful to God for such redemption" (A. 2). The tenth leper must have known these three things, for he had the kind of gratitude that only grace compels.

Maybe this was partly because the man was a spiritual outsider. Luke calls special attention to this fact: "Now he was a Samaritan" (Luke 17:16). In other words, the first (and only) man to give thanks was the last person any Jew would have expected to do anything exemplary.

The Samaritans were cousins of the Jews who followed only the law of Moses, not the rest of the Old Testament, and who established their own form of worship on Mount Gerizim. Because the Samaritans did not belong to the covenant community, the Jews of Jesus' day generally

---

7. John Calvin, quoted in *The New Encyclopedia of Christian Quotations* (Grand Rapids: Baker, 2000), 1055–56.

did not associate with them (see John 4:9). In fact, even Jesus seemed surprised that this man came back to say thanks. "Was no one found to return and give praise to God except this foreigner?" he asked (Luke 17:18). The answer was no; only the outsider returned. Here was a man who knew that he did not deserve anything from God, and therefore whatever healing he experienced was only by grace.

## SAVED BY FAITH

There was something else that distinguished this man from all the others and put him in the top 10 percent: he had faith in Jesus—*saving* faith. We know this because Jesus said so: "And he said to him, 'Rise and go your way; your faith has made you well'" (Luke 17:19).

The word that Jesus uses here for wellness (Greek *sesōken*) is a form of the New Testament word for salvation. Back in verse 14 the man was cleansed; now he is *saved*. This partly refers to his physical healing, of course, but not only to that. It also reminds us of the total personal transformation that comes from having a faith relationship with Jesus Christ. Here was a man who was isolated and alienated from society, cut off from the community of faith. But now he is at the feet of Jesus. He is no longer separated from human relationships—medically, ethnically, or spiritually—but reconciled to God and man. The man is saved in every sense of the word. He has received "not just physical healing such as the other nine received, but forgiveness and reconciliation and eternal life, and the removal of all alienation and distance between himself and God caused by his sin and moral uncleanness."[8]

What saved the man—what made him well, body and soul—was faith in Jesus Christ. He first exercised that faith when he cried out to Jesus for salvation. "Jesus, Master, have mercy on us"—this was his simple prayer of faith. He exercised his faith again when he obeyed Jesus and went to show himself to the priests. According to verse 14, it was only as he went that his skin was healed; when he started off he was still a leper! Therefore, it took faith for him to follow the command of Christ, and if he did not have that faith, he would not be healed.

---

8. David Gooding, *According to Luke: A New Exposition of the Third Gospel* (Grand Rapids: Eerdmans, 1987), 288.

It was also by faith that he went back to Jesus and worshiped.[9] This is what distinguished the man from the other nine lepers. They too were healed by faith, at least to a certain extent. But their healing only went skin deep. Only one man recognized what his healing revealed about Jesus, and therefore what implications it had for his eternal salvation. So the man returned to Jesus, and when he did, he was doing something more than simply returning thanks: he was coming to trust in Jesus. He wanted something more than physical healing: he wanted to know Jesus in a personal way. It was not simply what Jesus could *do* for him that he wanted, but Jesus himself, in all his grace—not just his work, but also his person. Therefore, the man joined himself to Jesus by faith: "Of the ten men who are touched by the healing power of Jesus, only one realizes that what has happened deserves a personal, heartfelt response to the Savior from whom that power has flowed."[10]

The other nine men did what Jesus said, and they wanted what Jesus could give, but they did not want to be with Jesus in a relationship of loving trust. As far as we know, they never came to him in saving faith. That is what this episode is really about: not just being grateful to God, but coming to Jesus by faith. David Gooding writes:

> Ingratitude for the general gifts of the Creator is bad enough; and many have been the people who in dire trouble have called on God for special deliverance and being granted it, have ungratefully gone further from God than they were before. But our story is dealing with something even more sad and serious. The healing of the lepers was not an ordinary common gift of the Creator to his creatures, nor simply some special gift of providence. It was a miraculous sign intended to point them to Christ so that through faith in Christ they might receive salvation and eternal life.[11]

It is not enough for us to do what God says, as the other nine lepers did (assuming that we could even do it). It is not even enough for us to be

9. By accepting this worship, Jesus tacitly affirmed his own deity, for God alone is worthy of praise. Indeed, in asking why the other (former) lepers have failed to bow down at his feet (see Luke 17:17), Jesus makes a strong claim that his divinity should receive universal acknowledgment.

10. Michael Wilcock, *The Message of Luke*, The Bible Speaks Today (Downers Grove, IL: InterVarsity, 1979), 166.

11. Gooding, *Luke*, 289.

grateful when God restores our health or grants us some other blessing (which some people are, but many people are not). We will be saved forever only if we come to Jesus in faith, trusting him the way the tenth leper did and then worshiping at his feet.

What is your response to what God has done for you? Come to Jesus in faith. Trust in his death and resurrection for the forgiveness of sins and the hope of eternal life. Then return thanks to him for all the blessings of his grace. Show full gratitude by living for the glory of God. Understand that God owes us nothing, and that we owe him everything, starting with the grateful worship of a thankful heart.

Charles Spurgeon once shared the gospel with a woman who was so talkative that even that loquacious preacher could hardly get a word in edgewise. Yet eventually she listened to him long enough to hear the good news, and as she began to understand the mercy God had for her in Christ, she bubbled with excitement and said, "Oh, Mr. Spurgeon, if Christ saves me he will never hear the end of it!"[12]

No, Jesus never will hear the end of it, because his salvation lasts forever, and therefore his grace demands eternal gratitude. We will be returning thanks to him forever.

12. This story from the life of Charles Spurgeon is recounted in R. Kent Hughes, *Luke: That You May Know the Truth*, 2 vols., Preaching the Word (Wheaton, IL: Crossway, 1998), 2:173–74.

# 74

# KINGDOM COME

## *Luke 17:20–37*

*Being asked by the Pharisees when the kingdom of God would
come, he answered them, "The kingdom of God is not coming
with signs to be observed, nor will they say, 'Look, here it is!' or
'There!' for behold, the kingdom of God is in the midst of you."*
(Luke 17:20–21)

Sometimes we cannot help but wonder when the kingdom will
ever come. As we wander through this weary old world, with all
its disappointment and decay, we wonder when God will make
everything right. Deep down we know we were made to live somewhere free
from pain and sorrow and death. We long for a better place—a place where
justice is done, where God reigns supreme, and where his people have peace
and joy. At times when we feel God-forsaken, therefore, when our dreams
are dashed, when we are afraid of the future, when evil seems to triumph and
righteousness seems irrelevant, we ask when the kingdom will ever come.

### THE QUESTION OF THE KINGDOM

The Pharisees asked this question too, not to catch Jesus saying something wrong, but because they wanted to know when God would establish

his righteous rule. The coming of the kingdom was a burning issue in those days, and it is not surprising that people asked Jesus for his opinion. Israel was then under Roman occupation and people were longing for deliverance from their oppression. They wanted to know when God would restore the fortunes of his people and when his righteousness would prevail. Some people thought the kingdom would be a new Jewish government. Others thought more in spiritual terms, but everyone was looking for God to make everything right with their world. When would the kingdom come?

Here is the answer Jesus gave: "Being asked by the Pharisees when the kingdom of God would come, he answered them, 'The kingdom of God is not coming with signs to be observed, nor will they say, "Look, here it is!" or "There!" for behold, the kingdom of God is in the midst of you'" (Luke 17:20–21).

Like many of the things God does—maybe most of them—the kingdom will not come the way people expect. The Pharisees thought the kingdom would come with special signs. They were looking for the kind of fanfare that usually accompanies earthly kingdoms—the pomp and the circumstance. Or they were looking for supernatural signs they could read in the sky—a way of predicting God's future. They expected someone with secret knowledge to tell them where the kingdom was, pointing it out by prophecy.

Many people in the church expect the same things today. They see a culture in spiritual chaos and seek a political solution—the kingdom of God established through human government. Or they speculate about the end-times prophecies in the Bible and develop a timetable for the second coming. Or they claim to have secret and specific knowledge about the end of the world.

Be careful! This is what the Pharisees were looking for, too, but it is not what Jesus promised. How foolish people always look when they have their own ideas about the kingdom of God—like the radio Bible teacher who predicted (wrongly, as it turned out) that the world would end in 1994 and then later told people to leave the church because it was no longer part of God's plan. Jesus said the kingdom would not come with any signs—at least, not the kind that people were looking for. He said people would not be able to predict when it would come, or point to it by their own wisdom.

No one sees the kingdom of God by outward observation; the only way to enter is by faith.

In fact, the kingdom was right in front of the Pharisees, if only they would believe in Jesus as the Son of God and the Savior of the world. Scholars have long puzzled over the precise meaning of the end of verse 21. The kingdom of God is simply the rule of God, his sovereign authority. As Graeme Goldsworthy explains, it is God's people, in God's place, under God's rule.[1] But what did Jesus mean when he said, "the kingdom of God is within you," as the Scripture literally says?

Some people think Jesus means that the kingdom of God is something inside us—an inward spiritual reality. This is certainly true: the first place God needs to rule is in the kingdom of the heart, as the Pharisees so badly needed to learn. However, the kingdom of God is also something more than an inward spiritual reality; it comes to a powerful, public manifestation in the world. The expression "within you" can sometimes be translated "among you," or "in the midst of you," and this seems to be the most likely interpretation here. It could hardly be said that the Pharisees had the kingdom of God within them. Yet they were in the very presence of the kingdom of God. Since Jesus is the King, wherever he is, the kingdom is.

The kingdom of God was present in the preaching of Jesus Christ. Wherever Jesus went, he always proclaimed the good news of the kingdom of God (e.g., Luke 4:43; 8:1). The kingdom was also present in his miracles. Whenever Jesus cast out demons or healed the sick, he was demonstrating the power of God's kingdom. In fact, after one miracle he said to the Pharisees, "the kingdom of God has come upon you" (Luke 11:20). These men did not need any more signs. They did not need anyone to come and tell them where the kingdom was. They simply needed to listen to Jesus.

How ironic this was, and how tragic! The Pharisees were looking for the kingdom, but it was already there. Jesus may have looked as if he was wearing peasant clothing, but he was really the King, and unless people acknowledged his royal person, they would miss out on the kingdom of God. Even the clearest sign cannot help us if we refuse to see Jesus and trust him by faith.

1. Graeme Goldsworthy, *Gospel and Kingdom* (Homebush West, N.S.W., Australia: Anzea, 1992), 47.

If we are wise, we will be careful to avoid making the same mistake the Pharisees made. The only hope of the kingdom is Jesus Christ. Only he can make everything right with the world. J. C. Ryle said, "The vast majority of men are utterly deceived in their expectations with respect to the kingdom of God. They are waiting for signs which will never appear. They are looking for indications which they will never discover."[2] All we really need to do is trust in Jesus, giving him the honor he deserves as our God and our King.

## When Lightning Strikes

Having warned the Pharisees what to look for—and what *not* to look for—Jesus turned his attention to his disciples. They needed to know about the kingdom too, not because they did not know who the King was, but because they were not yet ready for his kingdom to come.

It is important to understand that the kingdom of God does not come all at once, but little by little, until finally the King is seen in all his glory. Earlier Jesus had compared his kingdom to a little seed that develops into a tree or a pinch of leaven that rises into a loaf of bread (Luke 13:18–21). This is how the kingdom grows.

The process had already started. Since Jesus was the King, his first coming to earth was the advent of his kingdom. Truly the kingdom of God was in their midst. But the day was coming when Jesus would reign in the full supremacy of his risen majesty. He was already the King, but his kingdom had not yet come—not the way it would come when he returned in all his glory. The kingdom that came in Christ will come again at his second coming. Therefore, we are living between the "already" and the "not yet," which explains why we are still praying for God's kingdom to come, and why sometimes we wonder when our prayers will ever be answered.

Unlike the Pharisees, the disciples were ready to learn more about this. To prepare them for kingdom come, Jesus said to them: "The days are coming when you will desire to see one of the days of the Son of Man, and you will not see it. And they will say to you, 'Look, there!' or 'Look, here!' Do not go out or follow them. For as the lightning flashes and lights up

2. J. C. Ryle, *Expository Thoughts on the Gospels, Luke* (1858; reprint Cambridge: James Clarke, 1976), 2:238.

the sky from one side to the other, so will the Son of Man be in his day" (Luke 17:22–24).

When Jesus said "the days are coming," he was looking ahead to his future kingdom. He knew the time would come when the disciples would look for his appearance and wonder why he was so long in coming. Some people think "the days of the Son of Man" refers to his earthly ministry. In that case, the disciples would be looking back with fond remembrance on all the happy times they shared with Jesus during his good old days on earth. However, this passage is looking forward, not backwards; what Jesus says is oriented towards the future. Furthermore, when the Bible talks about the day or days of the Son of Man (Luke 17:22, 24, 26, 30; cf. Dan. 7:13–14), generally it is talking about the last day on earth, when Jesus will come again to judge the world. The term "Son of Man," as used in Daniel's prophecy and also by Jesus as a common self-designation, refers to the God-Man who ascends to the throne of God's eternal kingdom. His "day" is the day of final judgment.

Everyone needs to get ready for that awesome eventuality. However, people have so many crazy ideas about the end times that it is easy to go astray, which is why we need to know what Jesus said about the end of the world. He said the time would come when we would start to wonder when his kingdom would ever come. He said that people claiming to have inside information would tell us that the Messiah was here or there, tempting us to believe that we have it all wrong, or that we are missing out on a secret we need to know for salvation. But Jesus knew that all the rumors and speculation would only lead us away from the truth. To protect us from getting taken in, he said, very firmly, "Do not go out or follow them" (Luke 17:23).

When the Son of Man does return, it will be so totally and universally obvious that we will not need anyone to tell us where he is. Any sign would be superfluous. Jesus said the second coming will strike like a bolt of lightning that flashes across the sky: sudden in its appearance, obvious in its shining brightness, and powerful in its mighty display of the glory of God.

I witnessed the power of lightning firsthand while canoeing down the Wisconsin River with a group of junior high students. We saw flashes of lightning in the distance, followed sometime afterwards by rumbles of thunder. Prudently, we headed for the riverbank, where one of the other youth leaders seized the opportunity for a basic lesson in the relative speeds of light and sound. Stopwatch in hand, my friend made a few observations, performed some calculations, and knowingly pronounced: "Well, the storm is about ten miles away. It seems to be heading our direction, but it's not moving very quickly." Only seconds later a bolt of lightning ripped right over the clearing and a simultaneous clap of thunder knocked us all flat on the ground. When I had recovered from the shock sufficiently to know that we were still alive, I wryly said to my coleader, "So, tell us: How far away was *that*?"

So it will be at the end of the world. Jesus Christ, God the Son and Son of Man, will come like lightning from the sky. "At the end time of the world," said Cyril of Alexandria, "he will not descend from heaven obscurely or secretly, but with godlike glory."[3] On that great day, no one will need any signs to tell them what is happening. Jesus Christ will be unmistakably, instantaneously, and universally revealed in all of his majesty. This is how the kingdom will come: with the triumphant and glorious return of the Son of Man.

Something else had to happen first, however, and Jesus made sure to mention it: "But first he must suffer many things and be rejected by this generation" (Luke 17:25). Once again, Jesus was foreshadowing the crucifixion by predicting his sufferings and death. He had already told his disciples that he would die and rise again (Luke 9:22), that he would be put to death by wicked men (Luke 9:44). Jesus could not speak about the coming of the kingdom without making this prediction again. He always viewed the kingdom through the lens of the crucifixion and the resurrection. In order to establish the kingdom of his grace, he first had to die for sinners, taking upon himself the judgment that our sins deserved. His kingdom could not come without the sufferings that would lead him to the cross. Therefore, if people were looking for the kingdom of God, the first thing they would see was Christ crucified.

It is the same for us. The kingdom only comes at the cost of his blood, and we can only enter the kingdom of God by trusting that Jesus died on the cross for our sins. The kingdom will come to us when we believe in Jesus for our salvation.

---

3. Cyril of Alexandria, "Commentary on Luke," in *Luke*, ed. Arthur A. Just, Jr., Ancient Christian Commentary on Scripture, NT 3 (Downers Grove, IL: InterVarsity, 2003), 271.

## THE EXAMPLE OF NOAH

If the kingdom is coming, then we need to be ready. This is the basic exhortation Jesus gives at the end of this discourse. He told the Pharisees that in one sense the kingdom had already come. He told the disciples that in another sense his kingdom is still coming. There are two comings of the kingdom. Jesus came once in the humiliation of his earthly suffering; he will come again in the exaltation of his royal glory. Someday in the future—after his sufferings—the Son of Man will come with sudden and inescapable force. Therefore, we need to be prepared for his coming.

In order to make this practical point, Jesus gave two examples from the Old Testament. These examples show how unexpected the second coming will be, and also how terrible it will be for anyone who falls under the righteous judgment of God. The first example comes from the story of the great flood: "Just as it was in the days of Noah, so will it be in the days of the Son of Man. They were eating and drinking and marrying and being given in marriage, until the day when Noah entered the ark, and the flood came and destroyed them all" (Luke 17:26–27; cf. Gen. 6–7).

It must have taken Noah years to build his enormous ark. How ridiculous it must have seemed for him to build such a large craft so far from any body of water. No one paid any attention to what Noah was doing, or if they did, it was only for the purpose of ridicule. People simply went about their business as usual: eating and drinking and getting married and doing all the other things that people do, but never repenting of their sin or putting their faith in God unto salvation.

Then came the day when Noah went into his ark, together with all God's animals. This was also the day it started to rain. It kept raining and raining until the floods came and everyone was washed away. The people who died never saw it coming. They just went about their lives, never stopping to think that judgment was coming.

The same thing happened on 9/11, when Muslim terrorists destroyed the World Trade Center in New York City. It was just an ordinary September morning, with people doing all the things that people usually do: dropping off their children at school, riding the subway to work, carrying their coffee up the elevator, checking their e-mail, and getting ready for business meetings. None of them knew what terror was about to strike, or that many of them were about to lose their lives.

Jesus said that exactly the same thing will happen at the second coming. People will be going about their business as usual. They will be sitting down for dinner, or walking the dog, or watching television, or putting their children down for the night. They will be loving, or fighting, or serving, or sinning, or doing any of the other things that people do. They will be so caught up in doing these ordinary things that they will be taken completely by surprise—"overtaken in the destruction that they might have avoided."[4]

Are you ready for the day of judgment? Most people are so preoccupied with what is happening today that they hardly ever think about kingdom come. Tell them that the end is near and they laugh at you the way people laughed at Noah. But instead of laughing they ought to be listening. Do not make the same mistake! Listen to the warning of the Son of Man and get ready for his great day by trusting in him for salvation. This is the only way to be safe when the kingdom comes. Just ask Noah and his family!

## The Example of Lot and His Wife

Or consider a second example, also taken from the book of Genesis: "Likewise, just as it was in the days of Lot—they were eating and drinking, buying and selling, planting and building, but on the day when Lot went out from Sodom, fire and sulfur rained from heaven and destroyed them all" (Luke 17:28–29).

This was another terrible disaster, justly inflicted on a corrupt community. Even to this day, the sins of Sodom are infamous: injustice, inhospitality, and immorality—especially flagrant homosexual and heterosexual sin. Day after day the citizens of Sodom went on sinning, never imagining that God would destroy them. On the very day when fire and brimstone fell from heaven, the Sodomites were wining and dining, striking business deals, and breaking ground on new construction. Suddenly they all perished, to their everlasting surprise—every last one of them.

"So will it be," Jesus said, "on the day when the Son of Man is revealed" (Luke 17:30). The thunder and lightning of divine judgment will strike

---

4. Leon Morris, *The Gospel According to St. Luke: An Introduction and Commentary*, Tyndale New Testament Commentaries (Grand Rapids: Eerdmans, 1974), 260.

without warning, right in the middle of daily life. People will be shopping at the mall, or stuck in traffic, or taking out the trash, or reading their financial reports, and they will be overtaken by the wrath of God. Like the rumble of distant thunder, there are signs of the coming judgment in every disaster; but like lightning, the end will come without any last warning.

Will you be ready when the time comes? Many people are not ready, because no matter how many warnings they are given, most people never listen. We see this any time there is a natural or terrorist disaster. People wonder what went wrong and why they were not better prepared. It always turns out that there were plenty of warning signs; only no one paid any attention to them.

In this case, the consequences for not being prepared will be eternally fatal, because although some people will be saved at the second coming, many others will be lost forever. At that point there will be nothing they can do to escape disaster, because they never came to safety in Jesus Christ.

To show how hopeless their situation will be, Jesus said, "On that day, let the one who is on the housetop, with his goods in the house, not come down to take them away, and likewise let the one who is in the field not turn back" (Luke 17:31; cf. Matt. 24:17–18). In other words, when judgment comes, no one will have time to run back inside and get their belongings. In Matthew and Mark this warning almost certainly refers to the judgment that fell on Jerusalem in A.D. 70, when the city was sacked by the Romans. But here Jesus is looking to a farther horizon. He is speaking about the day of the Son of Man and saying that by then it will be too late! The only thing that can be saved on the day of judgment is someone's soul, and the only souls that will be saved are ones that have been joined to Jesus by faith.

Then comes one of the shortest verses in the Bible, and also one of the saddest: "Remember Lot's wife" (Luke 17:32). Lot's wife and her husband had compromised their godliness by living in the sin city of Sodom. They wanted to get as close to the world as they could get away with, little expecting that Sodom was a city God had purposed to destroy. Yet in his mercy God sent angels to deliver Lot and his wife from judgment. These angels gave them some very specific instructions for their escape: "Do not look back or stop anywhere in the valley. Escape to the hills, lest you be swept away" (Gen. 19:17). But Lot's wife *did* look back, and in his justice God suddenly turned her into a pillar of salt (Gen. 19:26).

Why was this woman destroyed? It was not so much because of where she looked, but because of what she loved. When Lot's wife gave a backwards glance at the burning wreckage of Sodom, she was looking back longingly on everything the world had to offer: the security of her family, the pleasures of sin, and the approval of neighbors who knew how to have what they called "a good time." This was her fatal attraction. God had shown her the way of salvation, and she was well on her way to safety. Yet because her heart was still back in Sodom, she perished along the way.

Jesus tells us to remember Lot's wife. Her story is one of the saddest in the whole Bible. She was "almost saved," said Charles Spurgeon, "but not quite."[5] This calls for serious self-examination. How tragic it would be to end up like Lot's wife: almost saved . . . but not quite. We should consider, therefore, what belongings we are still trying to salvage from this fallen world, and what sins our heart still longs to commit. Jesus is warning us against having a "sinful, selfish attachment to worldly things,"[6] including all the things we know we should leave behind, but still hold on to. The nice house, the bigger paycheck, the job or the spouse we always wanted—none of these things will save us on the day of the Son of Man.

## Left Behind

Don't look back, but flee from the wrath to come! For as Jesus went on to say, "Whoever seeks to preserve his life will lose it, but whoever loses his life will keep it" (Luke 17:33). This is one of the strange paradoxes of the gospel. If we try to save our lives—in other words, if we hold on to our position in the world, with all the possessions it has to offer—we will end up losing life itself, as well as everything we have worked so hard to gain.

On the other hand, if we give ourselves away—if we commit our whole lives to Jesus Christ, offering our time and our talents in service and sacrifice to others—then we will get to keep our lives forever. People may think we are crazy for doing it, but when we let go of what earth has to offer, we

5. Charles H. Spurgeon, "Remember Lot's Wife," in *The Metropolitan Tabernacle Pulpit* (Pasadena, TX: Pilgrim, 1972), 25:488.
6. Norval Geldenhuys, *The Gospel of Luke*, New International Commentary on the New Testament (Grand Rapids: Eerdmans, 1951), 441.

gain what only heaven has to give. As Jim Elliot so famously said, "He is no fool who gives what he cannot keep to gain what he cannot lose."[7]

Will we live for ourselves, or will we live for Christ and his kingdom? What a difference our choice makes! When the Son of Man returns, he will make an eternal separation. Some will be saved, while others are lost forever. Jesus wanted to make sure that we knew this, so he said, "I tell you, in that night there will be two in one bed. One will be taken and the other left. There will be two women grinding together. One will be taken and the other left" (Luke 17:34–35). According to some manuscripts, he also said, "Two men will be in the field; one will be taken and the other left" (Luke 17:36).

Possibly Jesus meant that one person would be taken to glory—the "rapture," as some Christians call it—while the other is left behind. What seems more likely is that one person will be taken away to judgment, while the other is spared. This is also the language that the apostle uses in 1 Thessalonians 4:17, where it is clearly believers who are "left behind." Either way, God will cut right down the center of the human race and make a final division between the redeemed and the damned. This eternal separation—this great divorce—will divide even the closest relationships: the husband and wife who share the same bed, the colaborers who work side by side at the office. People who share almost the exact same situation in life will find themselves on opposite sides of eternity. A wife will roll over in the middle of the night to find that her husband is gone forever. One business partner will end up in heaven, while the other goes to hell.

The end of the world could come at any time. How suddenly and unexpectedly Jesus will come again, and how disastrous his coming will be for anyone who is not prepared! If we trust in Jesus Christ and believe that he died on the cross for our sins, there is no need to be afraid. But if we do not trust in Christ, we are not ready for the day of the Son of Man.

Once we understand this, we will never live the same way again. We cannot just go about our business as usual. First we have to make sure that our soul is secure by asking Jesus to be our Savior and our God. Be wise like Noah, who found safety in the ark, not foolish like Lot's wife, who looked back at what she loved and was lost forever.

Then once we put our trust in the Son of Man, we start praying for the people we know who need to know Christ. This means loving them for

---

7. Jim Elliot, journal entry for October 28, 1949, Collection 277, Billy Graham Center, Wheaton College, Wheaton, IL.

Jesus and talking straight with them about the gospel. Consider what will happen on the day of judgment to your husband or wife, to the people who work at your office, to the kid who sits next to you in class, or to the neighbor who lives on your street. Will they be lost when the time comes, or will they find safety in Jesus Christ?

The disciples were deeply troubled when Jesus said all this, and rightly so. They were terrified by the thought of being taken away for judgment. Hoping to find some way of escape, they said, "Where, Lord?" (Luke 17:37). Perhaps they knew better than to ask "when" because Jesus had already told them he would come unexpectedly. But maybe he would at least tell them "where" so they could stay away from danger.

Jesus answered by saying, "Where the corpse is, there the vultures will gather" (Luke 17:37). This statement must have troubled the disciples, because it seems to raise more questions than it answers. What kind of corpse was Jesus talking about, and what kind of vultures?

Many interpretations have been offered,[8] but what Jesus said is perhaps best understood as a proverb about spiritual life and death. The place where people are spiritually dead is the place where the forces of judgment will gather, much the way that vultures circle around a carcass. When Jesus said this, he may have been referring to the Pharisees and their dead hypocrisy. Or perhaps this is simply an image of the terrible finality of the coming judgment. Vultures only feed off the dead, and by the time they have gathered, there is nothing anyone can do for the deceased.

Jesus used this grim and rather grotesque image as a warning. He forces us to ask: Am I still dead in my sins, or have I found new life in Jesus Christ? In one of his famous evangelistic sermons from the book of Romans, Donald Grey Barnhouse told the story of a man he went to visit in a Philadelphia hospital. Dr. Barnhouse heard that the man was dying, and since he knew that the man was not a Christian, he wanted one last chance to give him the gospel.

Even on his deathbed, the man showed so little concern for his eternal destiny that Dr. Barnhouse decided the situation called for drastic measures. He asked the man if he could stay in his room through the

---

8. For a complete list of the interpretive options, see Darrell L. Bock, *Luke 9:51–24:53*, Baker Exegetical Commentary on the New Testament, 3B (Grand Rapids: Baker, 1994), 1439–40.

night. When the man asked why, the pastor pulled up a chair and said, "Because I've never seen a man die without Christ." Suddenly the man realized that he was not nearly as ready to die as he thought he was, and by the time their conversation was over, he prayed to receive Christ as his Savior.

Whoever is wise will do the same thing and acknowledge Christ as King. But do not wait until you are on your deathbed to do it. Do it now, so that you are ready for kingdom come.

# 75

# PERSISTING IN PRAYER

## *Luke 18:1–8*

> *"For a while he refused, but afterward he said to himself, 'Though I neither fear God nor respect man, yet because this widow keeps bothering me, I will give her justice, so that she will not beat me down by her continual coming.'"* (Luke 18:4–5)

*I*t is hard enough to pray at all, let alone to keep on praying until we get God's answer. There are many reasons for this sinful negligence—none of them good ones. There is our physical weakness; sometimes we fall asleep while we pray. There is our lazy lack of discipline; we simply do not make the time to spend time alone with God in prayer. There is our callous indifference to a world in need, which ought to be driving us to our knees. There is our false sense of independence; even if we never come right out and say it, we think we are managing so well on our own that we hardly need to pray. There is our lack of faith in the promises of God. Then there is our outright rebellion: the Spirit calls us to pray, but we refuse. The list goes on and on.

Then sometimes we stop praying because we lose heart. God does not answer our prayers the way we think he ought to. We pray for the sick, but they are not healed. We pray for God to provide, but we are still out of work.

We pray for someone to get saved, and he or she keeps running away from God. We pray for a partner in life, but we are still alone. Soon we start to wonder whether God is listening, and eventually we may get so discouraged that we stop asking God for help at all.

Jesus knew us well enough to know that we would struggle with persisting in prayer. So he told his disciples "a parable to the effect that they ought always to pray and not lose heart" (Luke 18:1). Ordinarily we do not get the key to unlock a parable until the end of the story, but this time the key is already in the lock, and all we need to do is open the door. The Son of God—who always prayed to his Father, and who even now prays for us all the time—is telling us not to give up, but to persist in prayer.

## The Persistent Widow and the Unjust Judge

Jesus had been speaking about the second coming of the Son of Man. Jesus came into the world once for the salvation of sinners: born at Christmas, he died on Good Friday and was raised again on Easter Sunday. He will come again at the end of the world, very suddenly, and very disastrously for anyone who is not ready for his return.

Right now, therefore, we are living between the two comings of Christ, in the long interval between the "already" and the "not yet." We are watching and waiting for Jesus, longing for the day when he will come again to make everything right with our world. But the Son of Man seems to be so long in coming that sometimes we are tempted to wonder whether his promise will really come true.

Nevertheless, Jesus told us to keep praying. He said that "when His coming is apparently slow in taking place believers are not to become discouraged, but should persist in prayer, knowing that He will indeed come at the right time and will answer their supplication by destroying the powers of evil and by causing His chosen ones to triumph."[1] Jesus said all this by telling his disciples the following parable:

In a certain city there was a judge who neither feared God nor respected man. And there was a widow in that city who kept coming to him and saying,

1. Norval Geldenhuys, *The Gospel of Luke*, New International Commentary on the New Testament (Grand Rapids: Eerdmans, 1951), 446.

245

"Give me justice against my adversary." For a while he refused, but afterward
he said to himself, "Though I neither fear God nor respect man, yet because
this woman keeps bothering me, I will give her justice, so that she will not
beat me down by her continual coming." (Luke 18:2–5)

A good story has strong characters, and in this story two clearly drawn
characters stand sharply in contrast. One is a man, while the other is a
woman. One is in a position of power, while the other is almost helpless.
One is wrong, and the other is in the right.

The first character we meet is a crooked judge. In fact, sometimes this
story is called "The Parable of the Unjust Judge," which is what Jesus calls
the man in verse 6. It almost sounds like an oxymoron, but only because
the man's character was in contradiction to his calling. The judge neither
feared God nor respected man (Luke 18:2). In other words, he lacked the
very two qualities which are most necessary for true justice. The best standard for any judge to follow is the one King Jehoshaphat established when
he appointed judges for Judah. "Consider what you do," the king said, "for
you judge not for man but for the LORD. He is with you in giving judgment.
Now then, let the fear of the LORD be upon you. Be careful what you do, for
there is no injustice with the LORD our God, or partiality or taking bribes"
(2 Chron. 19:6–7).

In those days someone who wanted a legal remedy often had to offer
a substantial bribe. Thus a penniless victim basically had no chance with
a man like this. The judge was ungracious, unloving, unmerciful, and
ungodly. Strangely enough, the man knew how unjust he was. "I do not
fear God," he said at the end of verse 4, "and I do not love my neighbor."
The unjust judge did not pretend to be good because he knew that he
wasn't. He was the kind of man who did the right thing only when it was
in his own self-interest.

The other leading character in the story was the woman who wanted
justice, and who would not stop fighting for it until she got it. In fact, sometimes this story is called "The Parable of the Persistent Widow." Her situation was desperate. As a widow, she was one of the most vulnerable members of society. Therefore, she was entitled to special protection under the
law of God, who is the defender of widows. Yet when she was attacked by
an enemy, no one came to her defense, and since she was too poor to hire a

lawyer, she had no one to protect her. Though her cause was righteous, she found herself at the mercy of injustice.

Lacking any power or protection, the woman had only one thing going for her: her persistence (and she wasn't afraid to use it, either). According to Jesus, she "kept coming" to the judge and saying "Give me justice!" (Luke 18:3). This was no less than she deserved, because according to Old Testament law, anyone who oppressed a widow was cursed by God (see Deut. 27:19).

At first the judge ignored her, hoping that she would go away; but the woman was relentless. She would not take "no" for an answer, but kept pestering the judge to give her justice, until finally he said, "because this widow keeps bothering me, I will give her justice, so that she will not beat me down by her continual coming" (Luke 18:5). The woman was such a constant annoyance that in the end she simply wore the man down.

If we keep asking for something long enough, sometimes we can get what we want, even if people do not really want to give it to us. Eventually they realize it will cost them less to give in than it will to put up with our persistent pleading. Children master this strategy at an early age, because often their stubbornness is the only resource they have. Or consider the strange case of the rancher from Powder Bluff, Colorado, who was asked if he wanted to resubscribe to *National Geographic*. The computer handling the magazine's mailing list malfunctioned and generated 9,734 separate renewal notices! The rancher couldn't resist: he traveled ten miles to the nearest post office and sent in a check to renew his subscription, along with a note that read, "I give up! Send me your magazine!"[2]

This is what the crooked judge did as well: he gave up. Finally acquiescing to the widow's incessant cry for help, he belatedly gave her the justice she had always deserved—not because it was the right thing to do, but only to get rid of her once and for all.

## THE GOD WHO HEARS OUR PRAYERS

Jesus told this parable to make one simple and very practical point. Rather obviously, his point is not that God is like the unjust judge. Although some

2. This story first appeared in *Stand Firm* (Sept.1999): and was later reprinted by *Leadership* (Winter 2000): 75.

of the parables make a similar comparison, this particular parable works by way of contrast. The ungodly judge is against everything God stands for. He is unjust, uncaring, and unresponsive to the rights of the oppressed. Jesus did not put him in this story to represent God, therefore, but to make good use of a bad example. His argument thus takes the form of "how much more" as he reasons from the lesser (the unjust judge) to the greater (God the Father). Notice how Jesus explained and applied his parable: "Hear what the unrighteous judge says. And will not God give justice to his elect, who cry to him day and night? Will he delay long over them? I tell you, he will give justice to them speedily" (Luke 18:6–8).

The questions that Jesus asks are rhetorical. Will God give justice to his chosen people? Yes, because in his justice God has promised to save his own. Will he wait too long to save them? No, his deliverance will come at just the right time. The parable proves it. If even the worst judge will do what people demand, as long as they keep demanding it, then how much more will the most righteous judge of all show justice to the people he loves. Cyril of Alexandria said it like this: "How will not he who loves mercy and hates iniquity, and who always gives his helping hand to those that love him, accept those who draw near to him day and night and avenge them as his elect?"[3]

The contrast between God and the unjust judge is meant to encourage us in our prayers. God is everything that the judge is not, and every one of his perfections gives us confidence when we pray. Consider, by way of contrast, three things the parable tells us about the character of God, and consider further how they help us when we pray.

First, God is a *just God*, who is fair in all his decisions and righteous in all his ways. God defends the widow and delivers the oppressed. He is always on the side of what is right, and always against injustice. He is a God who "gives justice" (Luke 18:7).

This means that we always have a final court of appeal. One of the great frustrations of life is that justice is not always done, at least as far as we can see. Ungodliness sometimes triumphs, and the guilty often go free. We see this in the persecution of the church by hostile governments. We see it in the corruption of our legal system. We see it in the systems of society that

---

3. Cyril of Alexandria, "Commentary on Luke," in *Luke*, ed. Arthur A. Just, Jr., Ancient Christian Commentary on Scripture, NT 3 (Downers Grove, IL: InterVarsity, 2003), 276.

work to the disadvantage of people with poor connections. We see it in all the messy interpersonal situations where it is hard to know what really happened and who should be held responsible. We see this most clearly of all when we ourselves have been treated wrongly or unfairly. Sometimes we have no recourse but to accept injustice, no matter how much we rage against it.

There is always something else we can do, however, and that is to pray. We have a mighty Judge who has promised to do what is right. In the end he will render perfect justice in the total universe. He will straighten out every distressing situation that no one else could ever make right, and he will do it on the side of justice. In our own struggle with injustice, therefore, we can pray in faith, the way Abraham prayed when he said, "Shall not the Judge of all the earth do what is just?" (Gen. 18:25).

Second, God is a *loving God*, who knows his people by name and has promised to save us. The widow in the parable was anonymous; Jesus never tells us her name. As far as the judge was concerned, she was a total nobody (otherwise, he would have helped her). But when Jesus speaks about God's justice, he says that God will take care of "his elect" (Luke 18:7). In other words, when we pray, we are praying to a God who knows who we are and has chosen us to belong to him. God has loved us in Christ before the foundation of the world.

The biblical doctrine of election means that God knew us before we ever came to know him. More than that, it means that God has a plan for our salvation, in which he has promised to save us to the very end. According to the Church of England's Thirty-Nine Articles, election is "the everlasting purpose of God, whereby, before the foundations of the world were laid, He hath decreed by His counsel, secret to us, to deliver from the curse and damnation those whom He hath chosen in Christ out of mankind, and to bring them by Christ to everlasting salvation" (Article 17).

What a help this is to us when we pray! On the basis of our election, we have a claim on God that the widow never had on the unjust judge. When we bring our helpless case before our great Judge, we are coming to a God who knows us and cares about us and has already promised to save us. Far from hindering our prayers, the doctrine of election gives us a more confident basis on which to pray. We have been chosen by God, and this assures us that he will hear us when we pray. Now, whenever I am tempted to doubt whether God is concerned about the things that concern me, I can say, "Listen to my prayer, Father, because you have chosen me to be your own beloved child." Even before I pray, I know that God loves me, and cares about me, and is ready to act on my behalf in the best possible way.

This brings us to a third aspect of God's character that helps us when we pray: he is a *wise God*, especially with regard to his timing. Admittedly, God is often criticized for his timing. In fact, when Jesus asks whether God will delay, it may be tempting to say "yes," because sometimes God's justice seems to be so long in coming. Many wrongs will not be righted until the coming of the Son of Man, and as we have seen, there is a long interval between the first and second comings of Christ—long, at least, as it seems to us.

We need to remember "that with the Lord one day is as a thousand years, and a thousand years as one day" (2 Peter 3:8). We also need to recognize that Jesus is not saying justice will come immediately. Sometimes justice is delayed, as everyone knows. In fact, that is the very reason why Jesus told this parable: to teach us always to pray, and never to lose heart, even when our prayers seem to go unanswered. God is not ignoring us, like the unjust judge, or putting things off because he does not wish to be bothered with what we need. His delay is not a denial; he will do things right when they need to be done. As the Scripture says, "If it seems slow, wait for it; it will surely come; it will not delay" (Hab. 2:3; cf. 2 Peter 3:9). God's justice may seem a long time in coming, but it will come swiftly when it comes— like a thief in the night (2 Peter 3:10), in "the twinkling of an eye" (1 Cor. 15:51–52).

This is what Jesus means by speedy justice. There will not be any unnecessary delay, but God will answer our prayers at exactly the time he knows they ought to be answered, in the wisest way, according to what brings him the most glory.

### Praying for Justice

Everything we know about the character of God encourages us to be persistent in our prayers. Jesus told this parable so that we would always pray, and never lose heart. Not that we would spend all our time in prayer, of course, because there are many other things that we are also called to do. But prayer is the holy habit of a sanctified heart. As often as we feel the burden of injustice in a fallen world, or see the need to repent of our sin, or know there is something that someone needs, or try to offer ourselves in Christian service, just that often we are called to pray for the coming of the kingdom of God.

Here Jesus describes his chosen people as crying out to him day and night. We do not need to beg God the way the persistent widow had to beg the unjust judge. This parable is not telling us that we need to keep bugging God until he finally listens. Prayer is not a way of talking God into doing something he does not want to do! On the contrary, we persist in prayer because God is a just, wise, and loving God who listens carefully when we pray and will answer our prayers in his best way, at his best time. Or to put it another way, we do not persist in prayer because God does *not* listen, but just because he *does*.

Persisting in prayer means coming to God with our own personal requests, spending time each day alone with God in prayer. We need God's provision for our daily needs. We need God's protection from Satan and his deadly assaults. We need God's peace for all the stresses we face in our daily work and all the broken relationships that can only be reconciled by grace. We need God's power to triumph in our own desperate struggle with remaining sin. So every day and every night we call upon God in private prayer. Indeed, persistence itself is one the things we need to pray for, asking God to help us keep praying until he provides.

Persisting in prayer also means praying regularly with our families, or else with the people who live in our household or other close Christian friends. It means saving time for prayer in small group Bible studies, and participating in the corporate prayer life of the local church. It means persevering in prayer, even when we do not feel very much like praying at all, and are tempted to wonder whether it makes any difference if we do or not.

The most direct application of this parable, however, is to pray for God's kingdom to come, and for the people of God to get the justice they are waiting so long to receive. Of all the cries that go up to God day and night, and that call for speedy justice, the most urgent are the ones that are offered on behalf of the persecuted church.

Sometimes we ourselves are in need of God's speedy justice. We are suffering because of our commitment to Christ, perhaps, or we are being treated unfairly in some other way—in which case we need to keep appealing to God for the justice that only he can bring. But we have other brothers and sisters who are suffering much more severely than we are, and we need to keep them in our prayers. According to some estimates, more than two hundred million Christians face intimidation, discrimination, and imprisonment every year. House churches in China are under government observation. Christians in Sudan face genocidal violence from militant Muslims. Citizens in Saudi Arabia are not allowed to convert to faith in Jesus Christ. Pastors in Vietnam meet in secret to receive their theological training. Militant Buddhists in Sri Lanka close down churches and threaten believers with physical violence. Christians in Eritrea are jailed in record numbers. Hindus in India deny low-caste Christians (the Dalits and other "untouchables") basic human rights. These are only some of the ways and some of the places that Christians suffer injustice.

In countries that are hostile to the gospel, thousands of Christians are even put to death. In fact, on the day I am writing this, news has come from Iran that the pastor of a house church and father of four has been killed in cold blood. The man was kidnapped by local police and then stabbed to death, with his bleeding body thrown on the street in front of his family's home. There was also a chilling warning for other Christian leaders: "The government knows what you are doing, and we will come for you soon." When we hear such horrific news, our cry goes up to God with the prayer of the martyrs: "O Sovereign Lord, holy and true, how long before you will judge and avenge our blood on those who dwell on the earth?" (Rev. 6:10).

We are waiting and watching for the day when justice finally will be done. While we wait, Jesus tells us always to pray and never to lose heart. He tells us this because he knows that one day justice will be done. Jesus will see to it himself, on the great day of the Son of Man, when he will return like lightning to judge the world.

When Jesus tells us to persist in prayer, he is also speaking on the basis of his own experience of prayer when he suffered and died for our sins. Again and again the Gospels show Jesus at prayer. He did exactly what he later told his disciples to do: he always prayed and never lost heart. Or did he?

There was a time when Jesus almost did seem to lose heart. In his dying hour he was close to despair. As he hung on the cross, Jesus endured the full weight of God's wrath against our sin. For a time the happy fellowship he had always enjoyed with his Father was ruptured. Jesus took the guilt of our sin upon himself, and when he did, the shadow of our sin passed between the Father and the Son. Jesus cried out, "My God, my God, why have you forsaken me?" (Matt. 27:46).

When Jesus said this, he was suffering the greatest injustice in the universe. The sinless Son of God was dying a cruel death for crimes he had never committed and wrongs he had never done. Nevertheless, Jesus persisted in prayer. He did not lose heart, and in his dying moments he said, "Father, into your hands I commit my spirit" (Luke 23:46). Jesus was really praying that justice would be done. He was entrusting the justice of his cause to God, asking the Father to vindicate him by raising him from the dead. Only then would justice be done: justice for Jesus as the sinless Son of God and suffering Savior of sinners.

## ONE FINAL QUESTION

Just as Jesus prayed for justice through the cross and the empty tomb, so now he calls us to entrust our cause to God by persisting in prayer. But he also has one final question for us: "Nevertheless, when the Son of Man comes, will he find faith on earth?" (Luke 18:8).

Most people think that God is the one who has questions to answer—questions like "Is Jesus really coming again?" and "Why is everything going wrong in the world?" and "Will justice ever be done?" Yet those are not the real questions. Of course Jesus is coming again, and of course justice will be done: God has promised this in his Word (e.g., Matt. 24:44–46). The real question is the one God has for us—not whether Jesus will come again, but whether we will be ready for his coming. Or to put it another way, the real question is not whether God will do what he has promised to do, but whether we will trust him to do it. When the Son of Man comes the way he promised in Luke 17, will he find people praying the way he commanded in Luke 18?

We must answer this question at the personal level. In one sense the answer to the question Jesus asks in verse 8 is perfectly obvious: Jesus will indeed find faith on the earth because he has promised that his church will endure. But will he find *you* in the faith? That is the question. Remember Lot's wife: when judgment came, she looked back at all the things she loved and she was lost forever. So what will happen to you when Jesus comes again? Will he find you in the faith?

One of the ways we prove that we really do trust in God is by never losing heart, but always praying for the kingdom to come. It takes faith to persevere in prayer—faith in God and all the promises he has made to us in Christ. Augustine said, "When faith fails, prayer dies. In order to pray, then, we must have faith."[4] We must have faith in the saving work of Jesus Christ, and also faith in the love, justice, and wisdom of God—all the attributes the parable shows us by contrast. It is because we believe that God cares about us and will do what is right in the end that we continue to pray. If we give up on prayer, we are really saying that we think God is more unrighteous than the unjust judge.[5] As unrighteous as he was, at least that judge was willing to listen to the widow's repeated requests. But if we stop praying, we are practically saying that we do not believe God will listen to us at all.

Will Jesus find us in the faith when he comes to earth again? One way to tell is by examining our faithfulness in prayer. So to ask the same question a different way: Am I persisting in prayer? If the honest answer is "No," then it is good to follow the godly counsel of J. C. Ryle, whose words form a practical summary of the lesson we should learn from the parable of the persistent widow:

> Do we ever feel a secret inclination to hurry our prayers, or shorten our prayers, or become careless about our prayers, or omit our prayers altogether? Let us be sure, when we do, that it is a direct temptation from the devil. He is trying to sap and undermine the very citadel of our souls, and to cast us down to hell. Let us resist the temptation, and cast it behind our backs. Let us resolve to pray on steadily, patiently, perseveringly, and let us never doubt that it does us good. However long the answer may be in coming, still let us pray on. Whatever sacrifice and self-denial it may cost us, still let us pray on.[6]

---

4. Augustine, quoted in J. C. Ryle, *Expository Thoughts on the Gospels, Luke* (1858; reprint Cambridge: James Clarke, 1976), 2:258.

5. David Gooding makes this point in *According to Luke: A New Exposition of the Third Gospel* (Grand Rapids: Eerdmans, 1987), 293.

6. Ryle, *Luke*, 2:253.

# 76

# THE SINNER'S PRAYER

## *Luke 18:9–14*

*"But the tax collector, standing far off, would not even lift his
eyes to heaven, but beat his breast, saying, 'God, be merciful to
me, a sinner!'"* (Luke 18:13)

*Two went up into the Temple to pray.*

Two went to pray? O rather say,
One went to brag, th'other to pray:

One stands up close, and treads on high,
Where th'other dares not send his eye.

One nearer to God's altar trod,
The other to the altar's God.[1]

This old poem by Richard Crashaw illustrates the difference between
two kinds of sinners, only one of whom will ever be saved. Crashaw's
poem is based on a story Jesus once told about the justifying mercy that

---

1. Richard Crashaw, *The Complete Works of Richard Crashaw*, ed. William B. Turnbull (London:
J.R. Smith, 1858), 20.

comes only to penitent sinners through the blood sacrifice that God offers for their sin.

## Two Sinners at Prayer

Jesus told this story to some people who were quite sure that they did not need any mercy at all, people "who trusted in themselves that they were righteous, and treated others with contempt" (Luke 18:9). This story, which is often called "The Parable of the Pharisee and the Publican," concerned two men, two prayers, and two destinies. Jesus had been teaching his disciples to persist in prayer, but not all prayers are created equal, and the efficacy of our prayers partly depends on how we pray.

"Two men went up into the temple to pray," Jesus said, "one a Pharisee and the other a tax collector" (Luke 18:10). Already the story contains a surprise, because everyone knows that tax collectors generally do not go to the temple, and that if they do, they certainly do not go there to pray. A praying publican, therefore, is an oxymoron—a contradiction in terms. In the time of Christ, tax collectors were considered the scum of Jewish society, and with good reason. Such men were in the employ of the oppressive Roman government, and thus they were considered traitors to the Jewish people. They were greedy and dishonest, usually relying on extortion for their profit margin. Kent Hughes comments, "In today's culture, the closest social equivalent would be drug pushers and pimps, those who prey on society, who make money off others' bodies and make a living of stealing from others."[2] Make no mistake about it: the tax collector in Jesus' parable was a crook.

The Pharisee, by contrast, represented everything that was right and good. The historian Josephus described the Pharisees as "a certain sect of the Jews that appear more religious than others, and seem to interpret the laws more accurately."[3] Such men had virtually the best reputation in Israel. It was only natural, therefore, for this Pharisee to go up to the temple to pray. He was the good guy, after all, and good guys pray.

---

2. R. Kent Hughes, *Luke: That You May Know the Truth*, 2 vols. (Wheaton, IL: Crossway, 1998), 2:192.

3. Flavius Josephus, *The Wars of the Jews*, in *The Works of Josephus*, trans. William Whiston (Peabody, MA: Hendrickson, 1987), 1.5.2 (p. 551).

In some ways, our respect for the man is increased when we overhear his prayer: "God, I thank you that I am not like other men, extortioners, unjust, adulterers, or even like this tax collector. I fast twice a week; I give tithes of all that I get" (Luke 18:11–12). If we take the Pharisee at his word, he was a man with few obvious vices and many commendable virtues. He was thankful to God. He did not steal (which, as everyone well knew, tax collectors often did). He did not run with a bad crowd. He was faithful to his wife. In short, the Pharisee kept the whole law of God (or thought he did, at any rate). Today he would be a renowned theologian, perhaps, or a respected elder in the church, or a beloved pastor.

Furthermore, the Pharisee went well beyond the law in his devotional practice. Not only was he devoted to prayer, but he also fasted twice a week. The law stipulated only one fast a year, on the day of atonement (Lev. 16:29–31), so this man was fasting a hundred times more often than the law required. He also made a point of tithing all his income, setting aside one tenth of everything he received. This, too, was more than the law required, for the biblical tithe applied only to certain produce (Deut. 14:22–23), but not to other forms of income. By tithing everything, the Pharisee proved himself to be an exceptionally devout man.

Yet for all his devotion, the Pharisee was unrighteous in the sight of God. None of his pious acts improved his standing with God, because God is never impressed with merely external religion. He does not base his judgment on outward acts of religious devotion, but on the inward disposition of the heart. So when the Pharisee was finished with his prayers, he went home unjustified (see Luke 18:14), for God knew his heart and rightly declared that he was not righteous.

What was wrong with the Pharisee and his prayer? His most obvious problem was his pride. Although he began well enough, by addressing God, he spent the rest of his prayer talking about himself. In two short sentences he managed to mention himself five times: I—I—I—I—I! As one commentator explains, "the Pharisee's prayer is so laden with self-congratulation that it can hardly get off the ground, let alone wing its way to the listening ear of God."[4] This is because, as another commentator says, "He glances at

4. Michael Wilcock, *The Message of Luke*, The Bible Speaks Today (Downers Grove, IL: Inter-Varsity, 1979), 165.

God, but contemplates himself."[5] In fact, the Pharisee does something even worse than contemplate himself. Jesus said: "The Pharisee, standing by himself, prayed thus" (Luke 18:11). At best, the Pharisee thought he was so superior to others that he would not even pray with them. But to translate this sentence more literally, "The Pharisee, standing, prayed about himself," or even "to himself," in which case he was not talking to God at all! Prayer reveals our true relationship to God, and for the Pharisee, prayer was just another way of reminding himself what a great guy he was. He did not actually ask God for anything or offer God any praise, but simply reveled in his own sense of superiority.

Whether the Pharisee prayed by himself, about himself, or to himself—or all three—he was much too conceited to admit that he was a sinner. Rather than confessing that he was as depraved as everyone else, he contemptuously thanked God that he was *not* like other men (Luke 18:11). Augustine showed what was wrong with the man's thinking by comparing him to a medical patient:

> The Pharisee was not rejoicing so much in his own clean bill of health as in comparing it with the diseases of others. He came to the doctor. It would have been more worthwhile to inform him by confession of the things that were wrong with himself instead of keeping his wounds secret and having the nerve to crow over the scars of others. It is not surprising that the tax collector went away cured, since he had not been ashamed of showing where he felt pain.[6]

By refusing to acknowledge the painful guilt of his sin, or to ask for atonement, the Pharisee showed how little he knew about salvation. He did not understand that a sinner like him could be saved only by grace. Instead, he expected to be saved by his good works. He thought God would accept him on his own merits. After all, he was a good person—better than most, in fact—so he must be good enough for God. In other words, the Pharisee was exactly like the people listening to Jesus' story: confident of his own righ-

5. A. Plummer, *The Gospel According to Saint Luke*, 5th ed., International Critical Commentary (Edinburgh: T. & T. Clark, 1922), quoted in Norval Geldenhuys, *The Gospel of Luke*, New International Commentary on the New Testament (Grand Rapids: Eerdmans, 1951), 452.

6. Augustine, "Sermon 351.1," in *Luke*, ed. Arthur A. Just, Jr., Ancient Christian Commentary on Scripture, NT 3 (Downers Grove, IL: InterVarsity, 2003), 279.

258

teousness. He had so much faith in his own ability that he had no need to trust in God. As Charles Spurgeon put it in the title of one of his sermons, the man thought he was "Too Good to Be Saved!"[7]

It is easy to see how self-righteous the Pharisee was, but what we really need to see is the same attitude in ourselves. When am I like the Pharisee? When I compare myself to others and congratulate myself for being more spiritual than they are. When I am impressed with how much I am giving to God, especially in comparison to others. When I can go all week (or all month) without confessing any particular sin. And when other people's sins seem more egregious to me than my own.

## THE SINNER BEFORE GOD

There is an entirely different way to pray—the way that will save our souls. Remember that two men went up to the temple—two men who prayed two prayers and reached two destinies. Unlike the Pharisee, the tax collector received atonement for his sins. Whereas the Pharisee was counting on his own merits, the publican was begging for mercy: "But the tax collector, standing far off, would not even lift up his eyes to heaven, but beat his breast, saying, 'God, be merciful to me, a sinner!'" (Luke 18:13).

There were three parts to the tax collector's prayer: God, the sinner, and the mercy between them. The man's prayer started with God, which is where all prayer should begin. The first act of prayer is to approach the majestic throne of almighty God. The Pharisee's prayer also began with God; however, he did not really know God at all. The tax collector began his prayer with the same word, but the difference was that he knew who it was that he was addressing. When the tax collector said "God," he knew that he was approaching the one true and supreme deity, who is awesome in his holiness. This is apparent from his posture as he prayed. The tax collector kept his distance from God, refusing even to look up to heaven, because he had a right and proper fear of God's bright, burning holiness.

The man was afraid because he knew that he was a sinner, which is where his prayer ended. The tax collector began with God, but ended with himself, a sinner. To put it more accurately, he ended with himself, *the* sinner, as

7. Charles H. Spurgeon, "Too Good to Be Saved!" *The Metropolitan Tabernacle Pulpit* (Pasadena, TX: Pilgrim, 1977), 46:373.

if he were the only sinner in the world. The Greek original uses the definite article here because, as far as the tax collector was concerned, he was the only sinner that mattered. Like the apostle Paul, he regarded himself as "the chief of sinners" (1 Tim. 1:15 KJV). Rather than comparing himself to others, the way the Pharisee always did, the publican measured himself against the perfect holiness of God. By that standard, he saw himself for what he was: nothing more and nothing less than a guilty sinner before a holy God.

When it came to confessing his sins, the tax collector's actions spoke as loudly as his words. He stood at a distance. Whereas the Pharisee stood in the temple's inner courts, the publican seems to have stayed in the outer courts, not daring to approach the Most Holy Place. He kept his distance because he sensed that he was separated from God, alienated by his sin. Nor did he dare to look up to heaven. Whereas the Pharisee looked down on everyone else, the publican could only look down to the ground. Ordinarily, people in those days prayed with their eyes raised, but the tax collector could not bring himself to do this because he felt unworthy to seek God's face. He was so weighed down by his guilt that he felt compelled to lower his shameful eyes. All the while, he was beating his breast. This was another sign of his contrition. By standing at a distance, dropping his gaze, and beating his breast, the publican showed that he was a self-confessed sinner.

When the tax collector called himself a sinner, we should take him at his word. This parable is so familiar that Christians generally think of the publican as the sympathetic figure. After all, there is something heartwarming about a man bowing down to confess his sins. But the publican was hardly a role model! On the contrary, he was every bit as bad as he said he was. In his commentary on these verses, T. W. Manson wrote, "The publican is overwhelmed by the sense of his own unworthiness, and rightly so. It is a great mistake to regard the publican as a decent sort of fellow, who knew his own limitations and did not pretend to be better than he was. . . . This publican was a rotter; and he knew it. He asked for God's mercy because mercy was the only thing he dared ask for."[8]

What are you asking for? Do you know how bad you are, and how much mercy you really need? The tax collector knew that he was a sinner who deserved nothing except divine wrath. This was good to know, because it

---

8. T. W. Manson, *The Gospel of Luke*, Moffatt New Testament Commentary (New York: Harper, 1930), 604.

compelled him to seek for a salvation that only God could give, and only by his grace. The fact of our sin should never cause us to despair, for it is only when we know the depth of our own depravity that we are ready to receive the atonement that God offers for our sin. As Basil the Great wisely observed, "Humility often saves a sinner who has committed many terrible transgressions."[9]

## AT THE MERCY SEAT

This brings us to the most striking feature of the tax collector's prayer: in between God's holiness and his own sinfulness he inserted a prayer for mercy. The Greek verb which is translated "be merciful" is an unusual one. It is the verb *hilaskomai*, which means to propitiate or to expiate; in other words, to atone for sin by means of a blood sacrifice. But before explaining what this means, it is necessary to understand how atoning sacrifices were offered at the temple during the time of Christ.

A good place to begin is with the procedure described in Leviticus 16. The chapter begins with a warning intended to give the most serious impression of God's holiness: "The LORD spoke to Moses after the death of the two sons of Aaron, when they drew near before the LORD and died, and the LORD said to Moses, 'Tell Aaron your brother not to come at any time into the Holy Place inside the veil, before the mercy seat that is on the ark, so that he may not die. For I will appear in the cloud over the mercy seat'" (Lev. 16:1–2). What had happened was this: The sons of Israel's first high priest had sauntered into the tabernacle and offered unholy fire, contrary to God's command. Immediately they perished, consumed by the wrath of God (Lev. 10:1–2). God did this to show that he is too holy to be trifled with. Sin leads to death and brings sinners under judgment. Anyone who comes into God's presence must come in the suitable way, or else be destroyed by fire.

Mercifully, God provided a way for sinners to be saved from his wrath. After warning Aaron not to worship any way he pleased, God explained the proper way to come into his holy presence. Once a year, Aaron was to make atonement for the sins of God's people. He was to begin by offering

---

9. Basil the Great, "On Humility," in *Luke*, ed. Arthur A. Just, Jr., Ancient Christian Commentary on Scripture, NT 3 (Downers Grove, IL: InterVarsity, 2003), 280.

a bull to atone for his own sins, as well as the sins of his household (Lev. 16:6, 11–14). Then he was to take a perfect male goat and sacrifice it as a sin offering (Lev. 16:9). God said, "Then he shall kill the goat of the sin offering that is for the people and bring its blood inside the veil and do with its blood as he did with the blood of the bull, sprinkling it over the mercy seat and in front of the mercy seat. Thus he shall make atonement for the Holy Place, because of the uncleannesses of the people of Israel and because of their transgressions, all their sins" (Lev. 16:15–16). In this manner, the high priest "made atonement for himself and for his house and for all the assembly of Israel" (Lev. 16:17).

What did all this signify? The goat represented God's sinful people. In a symbolical way, the sins of God's people were transferred to the goat. Ordinarily, before an animal was sacrificed, the sinner would place his hand on the animal's head while he confessed his sins (see Lev. 4:3–4). This was to show that the sinner's guilt was being charged or *imputed* to the animal. Then the animal—in this case a goat—was sacrificed on the altar. This was necessary because once the sins of the people were imputed to the goat, the goat had to die. The goat was a substitute dying in the place of sinners. Thus the sacrifice offered on the day of atonement was a reminder that the life of every sinner is forfeit to God, that the proper penalty for sin is death.

Once the sacrifice had been offered, the sacrificial blood of the animal was the proof that atonement had been made for sin. This is explained in Leviticus 17:11, where God says, "it is the blood that makes atonement by the life." The reason the blood takes away guilt is that it shows that God has already carried out his death penalty against sin. The priest sprinkled the blood on the mercy seat, which was the golden lid on the ark of the covenant. This was located in the Most Holy Place of the temple (or the tabernacle), which was the earthly location of the divine presence. The mercy seat itself was a place of divine judgment, because the ark contained the law of God, which the people had broken. Sprinkling blood on the mercy seat, therefore, was a way to show that the atoning sacrifice had come between God and his sinful people.

When it was placed between God and sinners, there were two things that the sacrificial blood accomplished. They are expressed in two technical theological terms: expiation and propitiation. *Expiation* refers to the covering of sin. It explains what the sacrifice accomplished with respect to sinners and their guilt. Their sin was covered; their guilt was removed; their iniquity was pardoned. Expiation is what David had in mind when he wrote, "Blessed is the one whose transgression is forgiven, whose sin is covered" (Ps. 32:1). Once the blood of the sacrifice had been sprinkled on the mercy seat, the sinner had made amends. The penalty for sin had been paid and no further guilt remained. In a word, the sins of God's people were expiated.

The second thing the blood accomplished was *propitiation*. This refers to the turning away of wrath. It explains what the atoning sacrifice accomplished with respect to God. Wrath is one of the most frequently mentioned divine attributes in the Bible. It is not a violent emotion or an uncontrollable passion; it is righteous indignation. Wrath is God's holy opposition to sin and personal determination to punish it. John Stott has defined it as God's "steady, unrelenting, unremitting, uncompromising antagonism to evil in all its forms and manifestations."[10] Since it is right and good for God to hate every evil and sinful thing, wrath is one of his divine perfections.

God's wrath against sin explains why the high priest never came into God's presence without the blood of a sacrifice (see Heb. 9:7). If he came without the blood, he would be destroyed, like Aaron's sons. Once the sacrifice had died in place of the sinner, however, no further punishment remained. The priest sprinkled the blood on the mercy seat to show that God's justice was satisfied, his wrath propitiated. To put it another way, the sacrifice made God propitious, or well disposed; it enabled him to look upon the sinner with favor.

By coming between God and the sinner, the atoning blood sprinkled on the mercy seat was both an expiation and a propitiation. With respect to the sinner, the blood was an expiation; it covered the guilt of his sin. With respect to God, the blood was a propitiation; it turned away the wrath of his justice. To bring both ideas together, when the blood of the sacrifice was sprinkled on the mercy seat, the sinner was protected from the wrath of God because his sins were covered.

This is what the tax collector was praying for when he said, "God, be merciful to me, the sinner." He was asking God to make atonement for his sin. There the man was, praying in the temple, where the sacrificial blood

10. John R. W. Stott, *The Cross of Christ* (Downers Grove, IL: InterVarsity, 1986), 173.

was sprinkled on the mercy seat. In fact, when Jesus says "two men went up into the temple to pray," this is generally taken to mean that they were going there around three o'clock in the afternoon with the crowds that attended the daily afternoon sacrifice. Knowing that he was under God's judgment because of his sin, the only thing the tax collector could do was to ask for mercy to come between his guilt and God's wrath. To put it more precisely, he begged for God to be "mercy-seated" to him. This is what the Greek verb *hilaskomai* refers to. The tax collector was asking God to atone for his sins, covering his guilt and protecting him from eternal judgment.

The order of the publican's prayer is significant because it matches the Old Testament pattern for sacrifice. "God, be merciful to me, the sinner." Or more literally, "God, be propitiated to me, the sinner." First comes God, who is perfect in his holiness. Last comes the sinner, who deserves to die for his sins. But in between them comes the blood of the expiating, propitiating sacrifice that takes away the sinner's guilt and turns away the wrath of God.

## Saved by the Blood of the Lamb

Where can we find such mercy? Like the tax collector, we are sinners in need of a Savior. Since God hates sin, we are under his wrath and curse. The only thing that can save us is a perfect sacrifice, for "without the shedding of blood there is no forgiveness of sins" (Heb. 9:22). But where is the blood, where is the sacrifice, and where is the mercy? We do not keep herds of sheep and goats to offer atonement for our sins. Nor could we, for there is no longer any temple where we could make a sacrifice, or any mercy seat where we could sprinkle the blood.

The answer, of course, is that by the offering of his blood, Jesus Christ has become the atoning sacrifice for our sins. The great preacher and hymn-writer John Newton once wrote about this in his diary. At the time, Newton was weighed down by guilt. As he lamented his lost and sinful condition he wrote, "But now I may, I must, I do mention the Atonement. I have sinned, but Christ has died."[11] Newton understood that God is mercy-seated to the sinner through the crucifixion of Jesus

---

11. John Newton, entry for 18 September 1779, quoted in D. Bruce Hindmarsh, *John Newton and the English Evangelical Tradition* (Oxford: Oxford University Press, 1996), 232.

Christ. His death is our substitute; his cross is our mercy seat; and the blood that he sprinkled there is our salvation.

When we say that Jesus died for our sins, we mean that his sacrifice accomplished what the blood on the mercy seat accomplished. His death on the cross was an *expiation*, a removal of our sins. Like the sacrificial lambs of the Old Testament, Jesus died in our place. Our sins were transferred or imputed to him: "For our sake he made him to be sin who knew no sin" (2 Cor. 5:21); "He himself bore our sins in his body on the tree" (1 Peter 2:24). Now our sins are covered. They were punished on the cross, and no further penalty remains. Christ "has appeared once for all at the end of the ages to put away sin by the sacrifice of himself" (Heb. 9:26; cf. 1 Peter 3:18).

Christ's death on the cross was also a *propitiation*. Remember, propitiation is the act of performing a sacrifice by which God's wrath against sin is averted, which is precisely the kind of sacrifice Jesus offered: a sacrifice to turn away God's wrath. On four separate occasions the New Testament describes the death of Christ as a propitiation (using the noun form of the verb for mercy found in Luke 18:13): God presented Jesus "as a propitiation by his blood" (Rom. 3:25); Jesus was made like us in every way so that he could "make propitiation for the sins of the people" (Heb. 2:17); "He is the propitiation for our sins," John wrote in his first epistle (1 John 2:2); and again: "God . . . loved us and sent his Son to be the propitiation for our sins" (1 John 4:10). Not only has the blood of Jesus covered our sins, taking away our guilt, but it has also turned away God's wrath against them. Christ's death on the cross has these two great saving effects: it expiates our sin and propitiates the wrath of God.

## GOING HOME JUSTIFIED

This brings us to a very personal question: Have you received atonement for your sins? To put it in terms of the story Jesus told, Has God been mercy-seated to you? Has your guilt been covered, or are you still under the wrath of God? The urgency of these questions is made clear by the parable's conclusion. Two men went to the temple, a Pharisee and a tax collector. There they offered two very different prayers, and as a result, they went home to meet two entirely different destinies. In Spurgeon's words, "the outwardly worse of the two was accepted rather than the one who was apparently better."[12]

In the end, the tax collector got what he asked for. His prayers were answered. God was mercy-seated to him. His sins were covered and God's wrath was turned aside. Jesus thus closed his story with these words: "I tell you, this man went down to his house justified, rather than the other. For everyone who exalts himself will be humbled, but the one who humbles himself will be exalted" (Luke 18:14).

To be justified is to be counted righteous. Justification is the legal declaration that an unrighteous sinner has been made right with God. By this legal declaration, a sinner is acquitted of all charges, spared from all punishment, and considered acceptable to God. Such justification is what the tax collector received. God declared him righteous, vindicating him before the bar of his perfect justice. The tax collector was not justified as the result of anything he had done, because all he had done was to sin. He was justified rather by God's mercy, on the basis of the atoning blood of a perfect sacrifice.

God did not justify the Pharisee, however. This would have been a total shock to anyone who was listening, so Jesus was very specific on this point. Although the Pharisee declared his own righteousness, he was never declared righteous by God, and therefore he went home *un*justified. Even after all his righteous acts, God still considered him unrighteous. In a way, his righteous acts were part of the problem. He was too busy being self-righteous to receive God's righteousness, which comes only as a gift (see Rom. 5:17; 10:3). As long as the Pharisee counted on his own works to save him, he could never be declared righteous; he would remain under God's wrath.

Sinners cannot be saved by what sinners do; sinners can be saved only by what God has done in Jesus Christ. In other words, sinners can be saved only by grace. The Pharisee's prayer was all about what he could do for God, which is why all his active verbs were first person singular: "I thank . . . I am . . . I fast . . . I give." What made the tax collector's prayer different was that he was asking God to do something for him. The only verb in his prayer is passive: "God, be mercy-seated to me." The tax col-

12. Spurgeon, "Too Good to Be Saved!" 46:373.

lector understood that although there is nothing a sinner can do to get right with God, God makes sinners right with himself through the perfect sacrifice of his own blessed Son.

Some Christians are uncomfortable talking about the doctrine of propitiation, as if somehow this subject is unworthy of God. But the blood atonement of Jesus Christ is God's plan for mercy-seating himself to sinners. John Stott writes:

> It is God himself who in holy wrath needs to be propitiated, God himself who in holy love undertook to do the propitiating, and God himself who in the person of his Son died for the propitiation of our sins. Thus God took his own loving initiative to appease his own righteous anger by bearing it his own self in his own Son when he took our place and died for us. There is no crudity here to evoke our ridicule, only the profundity of holy love to evoke our worship.[13]

Out of his great love for lost humanity, God has made atonement, covering our sin and propitiating his own wrath against it in order that we might be saved. The doctrine of propitiation shows us how much God hates sin and at the same time how much he loves the sinners who come to him through repentance and faith in Jesus Christ.

We will never be saved by thinking how righteous we are—as if we were better than anyone else—but only by acknowledging how unrighteous we are. If we want to be saved from sin, we must go to the mercy seat, and there we will receive God's grace, which is available to us today simply for the asking.

Earlier I quoted from Romans 3:25, which says that God presented Jesus "as a propitiation by his blood." The Scripture goes on to say this: "to be received by faith." In other words, the death of Jesus Christ serves as a propitiation only for those who trust in his saving work. Atonement always requires faith. This was true in the Old Testament. When the sinner placed his hand on the head of a lamb to confess his sins, he was exercising his faith, trusting that God would transfer his sins to the sacrifice. The same thing was true at the temple, when the publican prayed for God to be mercy-seated to him, the sinner. He was putting his trust in the sacrificial blood.

13. Stott, *Cross of Christ*, 175.

Now we do the same thing at the cross of Christ. We lay the hands of our faith on Jesus, the perfect sacrifice. We confess our sins, asking God to transfer them to Jesus as our substitute. We believe that God is mercy-seated to us through the blood that Jesus sprinkled on the cross for our sins. Anyone who offers the sinner's prayer that the publican prayed will be saved. And once we are saved, his prayer becomes our daily petition for grace: "God, be merciful to me, the sinner."

77

# How to Enter God's Kingdom

## *Luke 18:15–27*

*"Truly, I say to you, whoever does not receive the kingdom of God
like a child shall not enter it. . . . For it is easier for a camel to go
through the eye of a needle than for a rich person to enter the
kingdom of God." (Luke 18:17, 25)*

My mother was out running errands when she heard a little
voice from the back seat of the old Pontiac Catalina, singing a little song. "When will he take the sins away?" the
song began. Then came a response, for apparently the song was antiphonal:
" 'God already took the sins away,' he said to the other guy. 'He will take
your sins away. He will stop your naughtiness. So please come to the safe
God. Come to the safe, safe God.'" The vocalist and songwriter was my little
sister Nancy. She was only three years old.

What a wealth of sound doctrine springs from the soul of a little child
who is nourished on the grace of God! Consider how many important
truths were contained in Nancy's little song. The song showed the need for
personal evangelism, for telling "the other guy" about Jesus. It offered the
promise of forgiveness for anyone who comes to Jesus. It testified to God's
protective care, his preservation of the saints. "Out of the mouth of babes"

our God has ordained his praise (Ps. 8:2). And if only we will come to him like little children, then we too will enter the kingdom of God.

## Come to Jesus, Children

Some people underestimate children, or else think that children are less important than adults. Sadly, this was even true of the first disciples. The Gospel of Luke tells us that people "were bringing even infants to him [Jesus] that he might touch them. And when the disciples saw it, they rebuked them" (Luke 18:15).

Since everyone knew that Jesus was a holy man, some people wanted him to bless their children. If only he would put his hand on them (and pray for them, as we read in Matthew 19:13), surely it would make some sort of difference in their lives. First one person brought a little child to Jesus, and then everyone wanted to do it. This is the way parents are: they always want the best for their children. But children tend to be noisy— especially babies, which Luke says that people were bringing (the Greek *brephē* generally refers to the smallest children)—so there must have been a good deal of commotion.

The disciples didn't like it. Maybe they were not all that fond of children to begin with. Maybe they were jealous of the attention the babes were getting. Maybe they thought that Jesus was wasting his time. At best, they were trying to rescue him from the crush of people crowding around him. But whatever their reasons, the disciples told people, in no uncertain terms, to stop bringing their children to Jesus.

The disciples really should have known better, because Jesus had already told them that if they received a child in his name, they were receiving himself (Luke 9:48). But apparently they needed another reminder. So "Jesus called them to him, saying, 'Let the children come to me, and do not hinder them, for to such belongs the kingdom of God'" (Luke 18:16). With these words, Jesus rebuked the rebuking disciples and opened his arms to the littlest people in the kingdom of God.

This precious incident is recorded in three out of the four Gospels. It shows the great love that Jesus has for children. It shows how gentle he was; otherwise, parents would never have put their babies in his arms. Rather than being severe with children, like the disciples, Jesus invited them to climb right up onto his lap. Jesus loves the little children; they are precious in his sight. If we love Jesus, then we will love children too, and children will love us, because they will see in us the same love that attracted children to Jesus.

Jesus loves children right now as much as he loved them the day he gave his gracious invitation to let them come. We are encouraged, therefore, to bring our children to Jesus. We bring them to Jesus by reading them Bible stories. We bring them to Jesus by calling them to faith and repentance. We bring them to Jesus by praying for God to bless them. So bring the baby who is yet unborn; bring the little girl with the disability; bring the boy who loves to disobey—bring them all to the Savior, who loves them, who wants to bless them, and who says, "Let the children come to me."

We are also called to bring our children to Jesus for baptism. People have sometimes used this passage as a proof for infant baptism. Since there is no sacrament here, this interpretation goes too far. However, what happens in this passage certainly is in keeping with the biblical practice of welcoming children as members of the family of God (especially since the little children were brought to Jesus by the faith of their parents). Jesus wants to bless our children, and in the new covenant, the sign of his blessing is the sacrament of Christian baptism. When Jesus welcomed the little children, he said, "To such belongs the kingdom of God" (Luke 18:16). Shall they not then receive the outward sign of belonging to that kingdom?

Those who deny that the children of believers properly are to be baptized should consider the words of Jesus carefully: "Let the children come to me, and do not hinder them" (Luke 18:16). One of the best ways to heed our Savior's warning is to bring our children in faith to receive the sign of the gospel in Christian baptism.

Then we are called to raise our children—all the children of the church— to love and serve the Lord. Some people still think that children's ministry is secondary to the real work of the church. Yet Jesus shows us that nothing is more worthwhile than the time we take to bless little children with the gospel. This is why parents and teachers should teach their children how to worship and pray, why they should read them the Bible, and why they should call them to faith in Jesus Christ.

If we fail to do these things, then we are hindering our children from coming to Christ. But if we do them, we are building up the kingdom of

God. A child who is won to Christ has a whole lifetime to worship Jesus and work for the kingdom of God. Most believers make their decision to receive Christ when they are young. Similarly, most career missionaries make their commitment to follow Christ when they are still in elementary school. As the Scripture says, "Train up a child in the way he should go: and when he is old, he will not depart from it" (Prov. 22:6 KJV).

## THE FAITH OF A CHILD

There are many good reasons for bringing our children to Jesus, including the rightful claim they have on God's blessing. As Jesus said, "To such belongs the kingdom of God" (Luke 18:16). But Jesus went beyond this and said that we need to be like little children ourselves if ever we want to gain eternal life: "Truly, I say to you, whoever does not receive the kingdom of God like a child shall not enter it" (Luke 18:17).

The kingdom of God is not a political principality, but simply the rule of God—everything that comes under the reign of his sovereign power. Here Jesus uses the expression as a kind of shorthand for salvation and all its blessings. To enter the kingdom of God is to have an everlasting saving relationship with the God who rules the universe. The only way to have that relationship is to come to Jesus like a little child. But what does it mean to receive the kingdom of God like a child?

Jesus is not saying that we need to return to some kind of childlike innocence, as if children were any less sinful than adults. No, Jesus knew that when it comes to having a sinful nature, children are no better and no worse than anyone else. We should not idealize childhood. Nor is Jesus saying that we should be childish, as if it were a virtue to be immature.

Nevertheless, small children typically do have some wonderful qualities that show us what it means to know God. They have wide-eyed wonder—the kind that Lucy Pevensie had the first time she went through the wardrobe and saw Narnia in the snow. God wants us to wonder at his grace and worship his majesty with awe.

Children have the full-minded faith to believe whatever you tell them, at least when they are very little. As they get older, of course, they start to question everything; but it is not that way at the beginning, when they take what people give them on total trust. God wants us to have the same kind of confidence in him. "It is those who are childlike in trustfulness," said Jerome, "who are best fitted for the kingdom."[1]

Little children also have a wholehearted love. Once I spent four hours with my daughter Karoline at Chicago's O'Hare International Airport when she had just learned how to walk and was proud to show off. She toddled up to every stranger with a broad smile and open arms, ready to love and be loved. God wants us to open our arms to him with the same kind of affection, for to know him is really to love him.

We cannot know God in any other way except with the wide-eyed wonder, full-minded faith, and wholehearted love of a little child. Yet when Jesus talks about little children coming into the kingdom, the most important word is "receive." It is specifically in our reception of the kingdom that we need to be like little children.

If anything is characteristic of children—especially babies like the ones people were bringing to Jesus—it is their total dependence on other people for what they need. Children come into the world utterly helpless. It takes *years* before a child is able to look after his or her own daily needs. Parents have to dress their children, feed their children, change their children, hold their children, and help their children in all kinds of ways—then they have to do it all over again, day after day after day.

And what do the children do? They simply accept the care that they are given. Babies are so needy in their dependency that all they can do is to receive whatever food or clothing or protection anyone offers. Graze the cheek of a nursing infant and immediately the child will open her mouth, rooting around and sucking for the milk that gives her life. So great is their need that they simply receive the gift of loving care, without ever saying, "Oh, you shouldn't have!" or "Let me do it myself!"

This is how we must come to God, if ever we would come into his kingdom. To enter, we need to receive. We must make a declaration of our dependence, offering God nothing except our need and hungrily receiving the grace he gives to helpless sinners.

---

1. Jerome, quoted in Norval Geldenhuys, *The Gospel of Luke*, New International Commentary on the New Testament (Grand Rapids: Eerdmans, 1951), 455.

## WHAT MUST I DO?

We need to receive God with all the needy dependency of a little child, or else we will not receive him at all. The trouble, of course, is that over time most of us have learned to depend on ourselves in life. "Once upon a time," writes Cornelius Plantinga, Jr., "we knew how to receive something uncritically and then live off it."[2] But now we are so reliant upon ourselves and so critical of others that it is hard for us to receive anything from anyone. Is there a better example than the rich young ruler who asked Jesus how he could enter the kingdom of God?

Once again, Luke is presenting us with a striking contrast. Earlier he presented the parable of the Pharisee and the publican—two men with two prayers that showed the difference between proud self-congratulation and a penitent plea for mercy. The only sinner who ever gets saved is the one who asks for mercy. That parable is followed by another contrast, this time between little children who received Jesus just the way that he is offered and a wealthy adult who wanted to take Jesus only on his own terms.

Luke calls the man "a ruler," which means that whether or not he had any formal position in the government, he was a leader in his local community. Later in the passage we learn that he was "extremely rich" (Luke 18:23). What this wealthy man wanted was to enter the kingdom of God. So he asked, "Good Teacher, what must I do to inherit eternal life?" (Luke 18:18).

Already the ruler was off on the wrong track. For starters, he was thinking of salvation as something he could gain by what he did. Notice his question: "What must I *do* to inherit eternal life?"—as if the grace of God would come as the reward he deserved for his own obedience. Here was a man who worked hard for everything he had, and who thus expected to pay full price for eternal life. To quote him more literally, the man said, "Having done what will I inherit eternal life?" The implication was that he could do one great deed that would merit salvation.

Jesus also rebuked the man for the manner of his address. By calling Jesus "Good Teacher," the ruler was trying to flatter him. But Jesus said to him: "Why do you call me good? No one is good except God alone" (Luke 18:19). In saying this, Jesus was not denying that what the man said was true as far

2. Cornelius Plantinga, Jr., "On the Receiving End," *Christianity Today* (Jan. 10, 2000): 73.

274

as it went. Jesus *was* a good teacher—the very best! But he wanted the man to see that he was something more than just another good teacher; he was also the Son of God.

Far from denying his own deity, Jesus was affirming it by pressing the ruler to follow his statement to its logical conclusion. The first premise was the one he had already granted: Jesus is good. The second premise—namely, that God alone is perfectly good—is the plain teaching of Scripture: "Oh give thanks to the LORD, for he is good" (Ps. 107:1). On the basis of these two premises, the conclusion therefore follows: Jesus is not just good; he is God. Already Jesus was placing his claim on the ruler's life—the same claim he makes on our own lives. Because he is the Son of God incarnate, Jesus Christ is to be served and worshiped as the living God.

Having said that, Jesus still had a question to answer: What did the man have to do to be saved? Well, if anyone wants to be saved by doing, he must keep every last one of the laws of God (see Gal. 3:12). So Jesus said, "You know the commandments: 'Do not commit adultery, Do not murder, Do not steal, Do not bear false witness, Honor your father and mother'" (Luke 18:20). In other words, anyone who wants to be saved by *doing* has to keep the Ten Commandments. Jesus mentioned only five of them here, but he was really saying that they all have to be kept. If we do not come to God ready to receive grace like a little child, then we can be saved only by keeping the law, which demands total perfection.

In his own humble opinion, the ruler was confident that he had met that standard. So he said, "All these I have kept from my youth" (Luke 18:21). The man seems to be more than a little miffed that Jesus gave him such an obvious answer. "The Ten Commandments?" he said. "Is that all there is to it? Everyone knows that you have to keep *those*. In fact, I've been keeping them all my life. But isn't there something else I can do to guarantee my salvation?"

The man's response was as common then as it is today, when many people think of the Ten Commandments as a short list of bad sins they almost never commit. Thus, they also think that they are able to keep God's law, or at least keep it well enough to impress God enough to get into heaven. Is that what you think?

Anyone who thinks this way has the wrong understanding of what God requires. In commenting on what the ruler said ("All these I have kept

275

from my youth"), J. C. Ryle made this disparaging remark: "An answer more full of darkness and self-ignorance it is impossible to conceive! He who made it could have known nothing rightly, either about himself, or God, or God's law."[3]

The truth about God is that he demands perfect holiness. The truth about God's law is that it requires exact obedience. Although the Ten Commandments are stated very simply, what they require is not so simple. Each commandment stands for a whole category of behavior. For example, the seventh commandment forbids any and every kind of sexual misconduct; it is broken, for instance, every time a person looks at pornography. Each commandment has a positive side and a negative side. For example, when God tells us not to steal, he is also telling us to be generous with what we have. Each commandment rules our hearts as well as our words and actions. For example, Jesus said that when we hate someone we are really breaking the sixth commandment by thinking murderous thoughts.

If that is what the commandments require, then does anyone really think the rich young ruler had kept all ten of them? Had he *never* said *anything* that wasn't completely true, or cherished an idol in his heart, or failed to respect his parents? More importantly, what about us? Have we really done the law of God, or not? Rather than saying "All these I have kept from my youth," we had better pray the publican's prayer: "God, be merciful to me, the sinner!" (Luke 18:13).

## Sell Everything

The way Jesus responded to the ruler's outlandish claim to saving obedience was not by disputing his claim to sinless perfection, but by giving him one very simple test. If the man was keeping God's law, then obviously he was keeping the commandment which says, "You shall have no other gods before me" (Ex. 20:3). So, was God first in the man's life, or was something else getting in the way? Jesus took him back to the very first commandment by saying, "One thing you still lack. Sell all that you have and distribute to the poor, and you will have treasure in heaven; and come, follow me" (Luke 18:22).

These specific instructions were only for the ruler, and not necessarily for everyone who wants to follow Christ. Jesus was not saying that we can win

---

3. J. C. Ryle, *Expository Thoughts on the Gospels, Luke* (1858; reprint Cambridge: James Clarke, 1976), 2:271.

our way to heaven simply by giving away all our wealth. If he had, then we would be saved by works rather than by grace through faith—works of generosity. No, the true requirement for salvation is not selling our possessions, but putting our faith in Jesus Christ. In this case, Jesus was identifying the one area of the ruler's life where he refused to let God be God. The man was willing to keep some of the commandments, but he was unwilling to give up his standard of living for the glory of God. He wanted the good life more than he wanted eternal life, and this was keeping him from following after Jesus.

The ruler was like the rich plantation owner that John Wesley is said to have met once in America. Wesley toured the man's vast estate, riding on horseback for hours, yet seeing only a fraction of the man's property. At the end of the day the two men sat down to dinner. The plantation owner eagerly asked, "Well, Mr. Wesley, what do you think?" Wesley replied, "I think you're going to have a hard time leaving all this."[4]

The rich young ruler had the same difficulty, so Jesus told the man to give it all away. Rather than telling him to do something, he told him to get rid of something. To sell his possessions was not to add one more act of pious religion, but to subtract all the things that were standing in the way of his entrance to heaven. It was not simply this asset or that asset that he needed to divest. The man needed to eliminate everything in his life that was keeping him from giving his life to Jesus. In his particular case, this meant giving away everything he had.

It is true that Jesus was speaking most specifically to the ruler himself, and not to anyone else. But why is it that we are so quick to put all kinds of qualifiers on this verse, and to insist that Jesus does not command all Christians everywhere to sell all their possessions? Why do we secretly hope that Jesus won't tell *us* to sell what we have and give it to the poor, but will tell us to do something else instead? Very likely it is because we would be unable to pass the same simple test. If we had to sell everything we had to inherit eternal life, would we be able to do it? If not, then are we not in the same spiritual trouble the ruler was in?

Many people are mastered by the love of money—not so much for the money itself, but for all the friendship, pleasure, and security they think it can buy. People who have many possessions (like most Americans) tend to be self-reliant. Therefore, people who love money usually have exactly the

---

4. This story is recounted by Randy C. Alcorn in *Money, Posessions, and Eternity* (Wheaton: Tyndale house, 2003), 159.

opposite attitude of the little children who Jesus said would enter the kingdom of God. Rather than receiving God in all his grace, they take what they can for themselves. They have too much treasure on earth to lay up treasure in heaven, and thus they are in danger of ending up in hell.

Money is not the only thing that keeps people out of the kingdom of God, however. Sometimes—like the monkey caught in the trap because he will not let go of the coconut—there is something else that we refuse to let go. "Many are ready to give up everything for Christ's sake," wrote J. C. Ryle, "excepting one darling sin, and for the sake of that sin are lost for evermore."[5] For some people it is a self-destructive romance. For others it is a body-wasting addiction. Still others refuse to give up the right to rule their own lives.

For a long time, this is what kept C. S. Lewis from coming to Christ. He did not want to give up his sovereignty over his own life. Most people don't. We would prefer to be the god of our own lives. This was Lewis's main objection to Christianity, as it has been for many other unbelievers. He wanted to be his own Ultimate Authority, but Christianity would not allow this. "There was," Lewis wrote, "no region even in the innermost depth of one's soul . . . which one could surround with a barbed wire fence and guard with a notice 'No Admittance.' And that was what I wanted; some area, however small, of which I could say to all other beings, 'This is my business and mine only.'"[6]

As long as we say this to God, we will never follow Jesus, and we will never enter the kingdom of God. Sadly, that is what the ruler did when Jesus told him to sell his possessions: "But when he heard these things, he became very sad, for he was extremely rich" (Luke 18:23). The man left with such a heavy heart that we can hardly be hopeful about his salvation. For the love of his money, he walked away from the kingdom of God. Rather than coming to Jesus in helpless, childlike dependence, he insisted on going his own way in life.

## THE GOD OF THE POSSIBLE

Is there anything you love that is keeping you away from God? Is there any sin you will not renounce, any relationship you will not release, any treasure you will not relinquish to follow after Jesus?

5. Ryle, *Luke*, 2:272.
6. C. S. Lewis, quoted in Armand M. Nicholi, *The Question of God* (New York: Free Press, 2002), 81.

If there is anything in life that we refuse to let go, then it is very sad for us, because we will not enter God's kingdom. It will be sad to Jesus, too, because it gives him grief whenever a needy sinner turns away from his grace. How grieved Jesus was when the ruler refused to sell what he had and give to the poor. As the man walked away, "Jesus, looking at him with sadness, said, 'How difficult it is for those who have wealth to enter the kingdom of God! For it is easier for a camel to go through the eye of a needle than for a rich person to enter the kingdom of God'" (Luke 18:24–25).

Some commentators have tried to diminish the force of this statement by saying that when Jesus said "camel" he did not really mean camel. They have said, for example, that people used a type of cable that was called a camel. Or they have said that there was a gate in Jerusalem—called the Needle Gate—that was too small for camels, and that therefore a trader using the gate had to unload his animal before entering. These are interesting suggestions; the trouble is that there is no evidence to support them. Besides, they are really missing the point. Jesus wanted to show how hard it is for rich people to get saved. Humanly speaking, it is impossible! So Jesus took the biggest animal that anyone had ever seen in those parts and imagined trying to stuff it through the eye of a needle.

The people listening to Jesus understood his point right away, and they could not believe what he was saying: "Those who heard it said, 'Then who can be saved?'" (Luke 18:26). In other words, if it is impossible for rich people to enter the kingdom of God, then how can anyone be saved at all? The assumption people made in those days was that the wealthy people were the ones who had God's blessing. They believed in a kind of prosperity gospel: the richer you were, the more likely you were to go to heaven. But if Jesus was right, and it was virtually impossible for rich people to enter the kingdom of God, then what hope was there for anyone?

In a way, they were right, not because salvation is based on how much money we make, but because it is impossible for *anyone* to be saved—impossible, that is, without the powerful saving grace of God. So rather than denying the difficulty, Jesus simply agreed with them that it was humanly impossible, but then went on to promise that it was possible with God: "What is impossible with men is possible with God" (Luke 18:27).

It is practically a miracle when rich people come to Christ because it requires them to divest themselves of their dependence on their own wealth

279

and start trusting in God for their salvation.[7] If we want the proof that God ever does this miracle of grace, all we need to do is look at some of the wealthy men in the Bible who believed in the Savior, men like Abraham and David, Boaz and Job, Barnabas and Joseph of Arimathea. Jesus was right: "What is impossible with men *is* possible with God." On the basis of the atoning death that Jesus died on the cross, and by the powerful inward work of the Holy Spirit, God is able to save the richest sinners, granting them the gifts of faith and repentance.

God is the God of the possible, especially when it comes to salvation, which is what Jesus was mainly talking about here. Do you sometimes doubt whether God would ever save a person like you? Do not despair of getting to heaven, because with God, all things are possible. Do not despair of anyone else's salvation either. God can change the hardest heart of even the wealthiest sinner.

The way to pray for this saving grace is the same way that one very wealthy man prayed with the little children in his Bible classes. The man's name was John Wanamaker—the famous Philadelphia businessman who invented the department store, who gave millions of dollars to Christian work, and who established an independent urban Sunday school where five thousand children heard the gospel every Sunday. Mr. Wanamaker would lead little children in the following prayer—an entrance-prayer to the kingdom for every little child of God and every wealthy sinner with childlike faith:

> We will make heart-room for Jesus, Thy Son—the name to sinners most dear. We live in the grace of His redeeming love and our only hope is the finished salvation of Calvary. Empty-handed, full of sin, and sad of heart, we cast ourselves at thy feet, O Christ. God be merciful to me, a sinner.[8]

This is the way that all God's children should pray. I say "children" because there are no adults in the kingdom of God, only children. The Bible never talks about "the adults of God." Instead, it always calls us "the children of God." And that is what we are, if only we will come to Jesus in needy dependence to receive his grace by faith.

---

7. R. Kent Hughes makes a similar point in *Luke: That You May Know the Truth*, 2 vols., Preaching the Word (Wheaton, IL: Crossway, 1998), 2:208.

8. William Allen Zulker, *John Wanamaker: King of Merchants* (Wayne, PA: Eaglecrest, 1993), 79.

# 78

# IS JESUS WORTH IT?

## *Luke 18:28–34*

*And Peter said, "See, we have left our homes and followed you."
And he said to them, "Truly, I say to you, there is no one who has
left house or wife or brothers or parents or children, for the sake of
the kingdom of God, who will not receive many times more in this
time, and in the age to come eternal life." (Luke 18:28–30)*

*T*here are times in life when even the strongest Christian wonders whether it is really worth it to follow Jesus. Once you make a total life commitment to Christ, there are certain commands you are committed to obey, certain pleasures you choose to forgo, and certain sacrifices you are compelled to make. Sometimes it is so hard to follow Jesus that it is tempting to wonder whether it is really worth all the trouble. Maybe life is better with Jesus, but it doesn't always seem that way.

Is it worth it to follow Jesus when doing the right thing makes you unpopular at school, or when people who do not have the same moral scruples are getting ahead of you in business? Is it worth it to follow Jesus when serving God takes you away from your family, or when you have to say no to a romantic relationship that is hindering your growth in godliness? Is it worth it to follow Jesus when sinners seem to have all the fun, or when what

God wants for you is not the same thing that you want for you? This is the question posed by every hard obedience: Is Jesus worth it, or not?

People have been asking this question ever since the days of the first disciples. Early on, the Gospel of Luke tells us that Peter, James, and John "left everything" to follow Jesus (Luke 5:11). But later these men could not help wondering whether they had made the right decision. Was it worth it to follow Jesus or not?

## An Honest Question

Peter raised this question after overhearing what Jesus said to a man who wanted to know what he had to do to inherit eternal life. The man was very rich, and Jesus knew that his money was holding him back from the kingdom of God. So Jesus told him to sell everything he had and give his money away to the poor. But the man refused to do this, because to him, it wasn't worth it. He prized what he owned too much to give it all away, even for Jesus.

Jesus was sad about this, but he was not surprised, because he knew how hard it is for rich people to enter the kingdom of God. Humanly speaking it is impossible—as impossible as threading a camel through the eye of a needle. But the people who heard Jesus say this were surprised. They assumed that as a matter of course, rich people would get into heaven. If God was blessing them in this life, surely he would bless them even more in the life to come. Instead, Jesus told them it was practically impossible for rich people to enter the kingdom of God. They were so amazed to hear this that they asked, "Then who can be saved?" (Luke 18:26). Jesus answered by saying, "What is impossible with men is possible with God" (Luke 18:27). With God, all things are possible—even the salvation of the rich.

This led the disciples to think hard about their own salvation. They were still in the process of learning who Jesus was and what it meant to follow him. They had just heard Jesus tell a man that if he gave everything he had to the poor, he would get treasure in heaven. This sounded like a wise investment: giving on earth to gain in heaven. Although the disciples may not have given their money to the poor, they *had* left all their possessions behind to follow Jesus. So what kind of reward would Jesus have for them? Was it worth it for them to follow Jesus or not?

Speaking for himself and probably also for the other disciples, Peter wistfully said, "See, we have left our homes and followed you" (Luke 18:28). Maybe Peter said this because suddenly he was worried about getting into God's kingdom. Here was a man who did not yet have the full assurance of his salvation, and what Jesus said about the camel and the needle made it seem almost impossible to inherit eternal life. Peter thought he was saved, but what if he was still lost?

In order to find out, Peter put his discipleship forward as the qualification for his salvation. He and the other disciples had done the very thing Jesus said the other man lacked: they had given up everything to follow Jesus. Admittedly, most of them did not have quite as much to give away as the rich man did. But whether it was a little or a lot, it was all the disciples had to give, and Peter wanted to make sure that Jesus knew what they had done.

David Gooding thinks Peter's remark "carried the unfortunate suggestion that their sacrifice was, compared with the rich young man's attitude, wonderfully meritorious."[1] If that is what Peter and the other disciples thought, then they still needed to learn that salvation is by grace and not by works. But whatever they were thinking, these men still had an honest question—a question that every Christian asks eventually: Is it worth it to follow Jesus? In Luke that question is only implied, but in Matthew's parallel account Peter says: "See, we have left everything and followed you. What then will we have?" (Matt. 19:27). If we are going to make the grand divestment and give up everything else in life for Jesus, we want to know what we are getting in return.

## LEAVING IT ALL BEHIND

Jesus did not always answer people's questions directly, especially if they were asking with wrong motives, or if they should have been asking something else instead. In this case, we might have expected Jesus to tell his disciples not to think that they deserved anything in return for what they had done. Instead, Jesus gave them a wonderful promise of vast reward: "Truly, I say to you, there is no one who has left house or wife or

1. David Gooding, *According to Luke: A New Exposition of the Third Gospel* (Grand Rapids: Eerdmans, 1987), 296.

brothers or parents or children, for the sake of the kingdom of God, who will not receive many times more in this time, and in the age to come eternal life" (Luke 18:29–30).

This sweeping promise of present and future blessing is for anyone who leaves everything behind to follow Jesus. There is a general sense in which every believer must do this. A Christian is someone who has decided to have Jesus instead of anything and everything else the world has to offer. The way the Bible tells us to come to Jesus is by repentance and faith. But to repent is to turn away from sin, so in repentance we are leaving our sinful ways behind. And to have faith is to trust in Christ alone for salvation, leaving behind any other way of saving ourselves. So the only way to come to Jesus at all is to leave everything else behind.

The great Scottish theologian Thomas Boston did this when he renewed his personal covenant with God near the end of his life and ministry. Boston went to his secret place for prayer and said:

> O Lord, the God and Father of our Lord Jesus Christ, I confess from my heart, that I am by nature a lost sinner. I am fully convinced that I am utterly unable to help myself. But as there is a covenant of grace, I do now again take hold of that covenant, for life and salvation to me; believing on the name of Christ crucified, who made atonement, paid the ransom, and brought everlasting righteousness for poor sinners. I resign myself, soul and body, to him, to be saved by his blood alone. I give up myself wholly unto him, to serve him for ever.

Then, as Boston came to the end of his personal covenant, he called on the very walls of his house to witness the promise he was making to Jesus Christ:

> Let it be recorded in heaven, O Lord, and let the bed on which I lean, the timber, and the stones, and all other things here in my closet, bear witness that I, though most unworthy, have this second day of December, here taken hold of, and come into thy covenant of grace, offered and exhibited to me in thy gospel, for time and eternity; and that thou art my God in the covenant, and I am one of thy people, from henceforth and for ever.[2]

2. Abridged from the "Copy of His Personal Covenant" printed with Thomas Boston, *Memoirs*, in *The Complete Works of Thomas Boston, Ettrick*, 12 vols. (London, 1853; reprint Wheaton, IL: Richard Owen Roberts, 1980), 12:453–54.

This is essentially what we all need to say to God, even if we use simpler words to say it. If we want to have a saving relationship with Jesus Christ, we need to say to him, "I am yours and you are mine forever." This is the prayer of every believer.

Some Christians are called to go beyond this, however, and to make some more specific sacrifices. This is what Jesus is talking about in Luke 18. For the sake of the kingdom of God, Jesus calls some of his servants to leave their homes and their families behind. In some parts of the world this is what Christians have to do when they are baptized. In many Muslim communities, for example, someone who becomes a Christian will be disowned by his family, and possibly even put to death. Other Christians leave their homes and their families when they go overseas to serve as missionaries. In order to fulfill God's special calling, they must give up some of the things that they love most in the entire world.

This brings us back to the question that Peter had: Is it worth it? Is it worth it to follow Jesus if that means going to some far country and being separated from your family? Is it worth being a missionary if it means taking your children far away from their grandparents? And what about all the other sacrifices that Jesus might demand? Is it worth giving up your dream house to give sacrificially to kingdom work? Is it worth letting go of your plan for a husband in order to pursue the plan that God has for your life and ministry? Is it worth risking your reputation to be known as a follower of Christ? Is it worth it, or not?

## NOW AND LATER

People who make the decision to follow Jesus may sometimes have their doubts, or even their regrets, but they will never end up on the losing end of God's bargain, because Jesus has given this guarantee: anyone who leaves everything behind for the kingdom of God will "receive many times more in this time, and in the age to come eternal life" (Luke 18:30).

The promise is absolute: *no one* who gives something up for the kingdom of God will fail to receive God's blessing. *Everyone* who follows Jesus will gain what he has to offer. What Jesus offers is a double blessing—a blessing for now and a blessing for later. Making sacrifices for the kingdom of God is like making a long-term investment that constantly pays out rich dividends, without ever diminishing the capital.[3] Many people think of Christianity as a good long-term investment that may not do all that much for a person in the meantime. "Maybe Jesus will save you when you die," they say, "but right now being a Christian takes all the fun out of life." Then they doubt whether Jesus is really worth it. But Jesus says that the kingdom of God is *both* the best short-term *and* the best long-term investment that anyone can ever make.

In the short term, Jesus promises to give more to us than we give up for him. If we are called to leave home or family for the kingdom of God, he will give us "many times more" (Luke 18:30). This promise is true in a literal sense, because when we put our faith in Jesus Christ, we become part of the family of God. God is our Father, Christ is our Husband, and all the children of God are our brothers and sisters. In the church, therefore, we have all the family that we could ever need—spiritual sons and daughters and fathers and mothers.

The church is our first and everlasting family, and we should treat it that way all through life. When we first come to Christ, and are learning what it means to follow him, there are spiritual siblings who can show us the way. When we are alone in our singleness, needing companionship, we are called to be a brother or sister to a friend who can be a brother or sister to us. When we are struggling in marriage, there are spiritual fathers and mothers who can teach us to love. When we are without children, we are called to welcome the littlest followers of God, just as Jesus did. When we are far away from our families, we can find a home away from home in the church. And when we come to the end of our days, even if we do not have any living relatives, we have a spiritual family to mourn our passing and bury us in the hope of our resurrection. Whatever home or family we give up to follow Jesus, it is more than made up in the church, if only we will learn to regard it as the true family of God.

Yet when Jesus promised to give us "many times more," he was talking about something more than simply our spiritual relationships in the family of God. He was also talking about giving us himself, which more than makes up for anything we think we are missing in life. J. C. Ryle said that "many times more" means

3. Gooding, *Luke*, 296.

the believer shall find in Christ a full equivalent for anything that he is obliged to give up for Christ's sake. He shall find such peace, and hope, and joy, and comfort, and rest, in communion with the Father and the Son, that his losses shall be more than counterbalanced by his gains. In short, the Lord Jesus Christ shall be more to him than property, or relatives, or friends.[4]

Even if we lose everything else in life—or give it up because God has called us to make radical sacrifices for the gospel—we still have Jesus. We always have Jesus, and what we have in him can never be taken away. When we do not have a home, Jesus is our refuge and our fortress, our shelter in the time of storm. When we cannot seem to find any love, Jesus is the proverbial "friend who sticks closer than a brother" (Prov. 18:24). When we are out of money, Jesus is still the treasure in our soul.

Have you learned to trust in Jesus for everything you need—not just to trust that he will give you what you need, but that he *is* what you need? Jesus really is worth it, because when we have Jesus, we have "many times more" than whatever we give up to follow him. J. Wilbur Chapman said it well in the closing verse of his triumphant hymn:

Jesus! I do now receive him,
More than all in him I find;
He hath granted me forgiveness,
I am his, and he is mine.
Hallelujah! What a Savior!
Hallelujah! What a Friend!
Saving, helping, keeping, loving,
He is with me to the end.[5]

Yes, Jesus is with us to the end, and after that, he will receive us into glory. This is the second part of the double promise that Jesus made: eternal life. In the age to come, anyone who makes a sacrifice for the kingdom of God will receive eternal life. This is not because our sacrifices merit anything. But when, by the grace of God, we leave everything else behind to follow Jesus, we get Jesus now *and* Jesus later—Jesus forever.

4. J. C. Ryle, *Expository Thoughts on the Gospels, Luke* (1858; reprint Cambridge: James Clarke, 1976), 2:277–78.

5. J. Wilbur Chapman, "Jesus! What a Friend for Sinners!" (1910).

Eternal life means, of course, life that is endless in its duration. God has promised that everyone who believes in Jesus Christ will live with him forever. This is essential to the perfection of heaven. Even the best experiences in life are somewhat diminished by the knowledge that soon they must come to an end. With a sudden pang of regret, we realize that the party is ending, the vacation is almost over, the children are about to leave home. But we will never have that feeling in heaven, because eternal life lasts forever.

What a life it will be! It is not just the length of eternal life that makes it so precious, but also the kind of life that it is. Eternal life is a free life. It is a life free from sin, both our own sin and the sins of others. It is free from pain, whether physical or emotional. It is free from sadness: every tear will be wiped from our eyes. Eternal life is also a full life. It is full of worship, with music more glorious than we can imagine. It is full of glory, with beautiful new bodies that are raised with Christ. Best of all, it is a life full of God, lived in the very presence of the Father, the Son, and the Holy Spirit (see John 17:23–24). What blessings are waiting for us in the kingdom of God! Jesus is worth it now, but he will be even more worth it later, when we pass beyond the darkening sky of this fallen world and see the dawn of God's eternal day.

This was the testimony of Elizabeth Freeman, who served as a pioneer missionary to India in the nineteenth century. Living and serving under conditions of extreme hardship, Freeman wrote to her niece back home: "I hope you will be a missionary wherever your lot is cast, and as long as God spares your life; for it makes but little difference after all where we spend these few fleeting years, if they are only spent for the glory of God. Be assured there is nothing else worth living for!"[6] Nor is there anything else worth dying for, as Freeman's tragic death at the hands of Muslim attackers would soon prove. Eternity will prove that nothing is more worth living for, or dying for, than the gospel of Jesus Christ.

## ARE *WE* WORTH IT?

So far we have been looking at things from our perspective, asking whether Jesus is worth it for us. But what Jesus says at the end of this pas-

6. Elizabeth Freeman, quoted in J. Johnston Walsh, *A Memorial of the Futtehgurh Mission and Her Martyred Missionaries* (Philadelphia: Joseph M. Wilson, 1859), 181.

sage compels us to ask a more fundamental question: Are we worth it to Jesus? The question arises because the blessings that Jesus has for us can come only at the cost of his blood: "And taking the twelve, he said to them, 'See, we are going up to Jerusalem, and everything that is written about the Son of Man by the prophets will be accomplished. For he will be delivered over to the Gentiles and will be mocked and shamefully treated and spit upon. And after flogging him, they will kill him, and on the third day he will rise'" (Luke 18:31–33).

This is now at least the fourth time that Jesus has prophesied his sufferings and death. Back in chapter 9, when Jesus "set his face to go to Jerusalem" (Luke 9:51), he said that the Son of Man would suffer many things at the hands of the Jewish leaders, and then be killed (Luke 9:22), and that he would be delivered into the hands of sinful men (Luke 9:44). Later Jesus would say that as a prophet he had to perish in Jerusalem (Luke 13:33). His impending death was never far from his mind, and here in chapter 18, when he says, "we are going up to Jerusalem," his use of the present tense conveys a sense of urgency and immediacy. The crucifixion is now at hand, and the closer Jesus draws to the cross, the more clearly he prophesies about his passion.

In this prophecy Jesus gives new and explicit information about what he will suffer for sinners. For the first time he says that he will be handed over to the Gentiles, so that the entire human race will be complicit in his death—not just the Jews, but also the Gentiles. He speaks of being mocked and beaten and abused—things he has not mentioned before, at least in so many words. When we read this in the context of the Gospel as a whole, we get the impression that Jesus is coming to a clearer awareness of the sufferings he must endure. Perhaps this was directly revealed to him by the Father and the Spirit, or perhaps he could discern it from the way people were plotting against him, but it was also something Jesus had studied in the Scriptures.

Notice the way Jesus introduced the subject of his sufferings, and notice his absolute confidence that the Bible must come true. Jesus said, "Everything that is written about the Son of Man by the prophets will be accomplished" (Luke 18:31). What, exactly, did the prophets say about the Son of Man? As Jesus studied the Scriptures—as he read the words of men like David and Isaiah—he saw that the Son of Man would be forsaken by God

(Ps. 22:1), mocked by his enemies (Ps. 22:7), tormented by thirst (Ps. 22:15), pierced through his hands and feet (Ps. 22:18), despised and rejected by men (Isa. 53:3), wounded for transgressions (Isa. 53:5), and crushed for iniquities (Isa. 53:5), until finally he was poured out unto death (Isa. 53:12).

It was not just that Jesus had to die, but that he had to die *this way:* with the cruel sufferings of a body that was abused before it was crucified and a soul that was forsaken by God. Jesus knew in advance that this is what waited for him at the end of his Calvary road. So he added his own prophecy to the words of the ancient prophets, and said: "See, we are going up to Jerusalem, and everything that is written about the Son of Man by the prophets will be accomplished. For he will be delivered over to the Gentiles and will be mocked and shamefully treated and spit upon. And after flogging him, they will kill him, and on the third day he will rise" (Luke 18:31–33).

The mention of rising on "the third day" shows that Jesus also knew the promise of his resurrection. Even before he died on the cross, he knew the whole gospel, which always includes the resurrection as well as the crucifixion (see 1 Cor. 15:3–4). Jesus knew that his death would not be the end, but that the Spirit of the Father would bring him back to life. But even so, on his journey to Jerusalem, Jesus had to ask if it was worth it. Was it worth it to be the suffering Savior to put up with all the hardships of living as a man among fallen men? Was it worth it to endure the agony of Gethsemane, where he sweated his tears in blood, and then to die the painful and shameful death of the cross? Was it worth it to be so separated from the Father that he would cry out in anguish, "My God, my God, why have you forsaken me?" (Mark 15:34).

And was it worth it to suffer all these things for sinners? Was it worth it to die for people like us, whose sins nailed him to the cross, and who sometimes wonder whether Jesus is worth it for us (as if that were really the question)?

With every step he took toward Jerusalem, Jesus was saying, "Yes, it is worth it! It is worth it to keep the whole law for my people and to die for their sins, even if that will require the most excruciating suffering." It was worth it for Jesus when he was alone in the garden, when he was betrayed, when he was accused, when he was beaten, when he was nailed to the cross, and when he gave his soul up unto death. We know it was worth it because Jesus did it, and because the Scripture tells us why: "For the joy that was set before him [he] endured the cross, despising the shame" (Heb. 12:2)—which is another way of saying that Jesus thought we were worth it. In his great love and amazing grace, Jesus wanted the joy of giving us himself and then bringing us with him into eternal life. We were worth it to him because he wanted to be worth it for us.

The disciples did not understand any of this at the time. When Jesus spoke to them about his sufferings, death, and resurrection, "they understood none of these things. This saying was hidden from them, and they did not grasp what was said" (Luke 18:34). What Jesus said was perfectly clear, but the disciples did not understand a word of it, perhaps because they thought that Jesus could not be taken literally. He said he was going to die and rise again, but the disciples were not yet ready to understand a suffering, bleeding Savior. How could they, until they saw Jesus betrayed with a kiss and nailed to the cross? Or how could they understand his ultimate triumph until they looked into the empty tomb or saw Jesus in the glory of his resurrection body?

The disciples did not understand what Jesus was saying, but Jesus said it anyway, so that they would understand it when the time came. He also said it so that *we* would understand. Do you understand what Jesus did in dying on the cross and rising again on the third day? Do you understand as well that he is offering you eternal life in himself?

If you do understand this, then you know that Jesus is worth it. Absolutely he is worth it—right now and forever. Whatever God is calling you to give up for his kingdom, do not hesitate, even for a moment; Jesus will more than make it up to you. But never forget that Jesus is worth it to us only because we were worth it to him, on the cross where he gave his blood for our sins.

# 79

# SEEING JESUS

## *Luke 18:35–43*

*And Jesus said to him, "Recover your sight; your faith has made you well." And immediately he recovered his sight and followed him, glorifying God. And all the people, when they saw it, gave praise to God.* (Luke 18:42–43)

My brother-in-law is blind. He was not born that way; he used to have almost perfect eyesight. In fact, as an officer in the United States Air Force, Alan used to fly bombers for the Strategic Air Command, before becoming a commercial pilot for American Airlines. But in December of 2000 he came down with a life-threatening case of bacterial meningitis. As his condition worsened, he was airlifted to the University of Texas Medical Center in Dallas. At one critical point Alan was legally dead and had to be resuscitated. He underwent emergency life-saving surgery to relieve the pressure on his brain and spinal cord. He was in a coma for six weeks, before finally coming back to consciousness. By the mercy of God his life was spared, but the damage to his optic nerve is irreparable, and barring a miracle, he will remain blind for the rest of his life.

We are all saddened by my brother-in-law's disability, but we do not treat him with patronizing pity. He has many reasons to be thankful. His body is strong, his trust in God is secure, and his family is growing in godliness. He travels widely, and has many opportunities to testify to his faith in Jesus Christ. But if Alan could wish for one thing in life, it would be to regain his sight.

## WHAT THE BLIND MAN SAW

Jesus met a man with the same desire on his way to Jerusalem: "As he drew near to Jericho, a blind man was sitting by the roadside begging. And hearing a crowd going by, he inquired what this meant. They told him, 'Jesus of Nazareth is passing by'" (Luke 18:35–37).

The beggar heard the commotion as Jesus came down the road with his entourage. Since the man was blind, he could not see Jesus, but there were several things that he could see.

To begin with, he could see his need. Since his eyes were covered with darkness, the man needed sight. So when Jesus gave him the opportunity to say what he needed, his answer was simple and direct: "Lord, let me recover my sight" (Luke 18:41). He also needed money. As a direct result of his blindness, the man was in abject poverty. Day after day he sat by the side of the road, begging. What else could he do? He had no way to earn a steady income. As a blind man living in a culture that made no special provision for the disabled, he was destitute.

The blind man could see his need, and out of his desperate misery he cried for salvation. Mercy was his only plea, so "he cried out, 'Jesus, Son of David, have mercy on me!'" (Luke 18:38). The word "mercy" suggests that he may have perceived his spiritual need as clearly as his physical need. At a minimum, the man was asking for physical healing. But as Darrell Bock indicates, our "need for mercy is often associated with sin, and sometimes mercy is needed because the plight is particularly desperate."[1] In its fullest sense, mercy is the love of God for sinners, the grace by which he rescues us from our lost and sorry condition. Mercy is what David asked for when he prayed: "Have mercy on me, O God, according to your steadfast

---

1. Darrell L. Bock, *Luke 9:51–24:53*, Baker Exegetical Commentary on the New Testament 3B (Grand Rapids: Baker, 1994), 2:1508.

love; according to your abundant mercy blot out my transgressions" (Ps. 51:1). Whether he realized it or not, when the blind man asked for mercy he was asking Jesus for something more than his sight; he was begging for his salvation.

The first step is always to admit that we have a problem, and the blind man who sat by the side of the road saw his need for a Savior. In fact, he saw it much more clearly than did the rich ruler who came to Jesus just a few verses before (Luke 18:18–25). That man's material prosperity prevented him from seeing his spiritual poverty, and he went away unsaved. He would have been much better off if he had been a blind man—even a beggar man—yet able to see his spiritual poverty.

This is what we all need to see: our need for Jesus—specifically, our need for him to save us from the blindness of our sin. In his book on the miracles of Jesus, Richard Phillips points out that the various miracles in Luke show us the deadly and disabling effects of sin: "Leprosy shows sin's corrupting power and condemning presence. The lame show sin's debilitating power. The dead proclaim the wages of sin; the demon-possessed show the destructive domination that is always the result of our bondage to sin and to Satan."[2] For each miracle, there is an analogy between the physical needs of the body and the spiritual needs of the sinful soul. What the beggar of Jericho shows us—by his disability and by his plea for mercy—is the blinding effect of sin. Without the work of the Holy Spirit, we fail to even see how sinful we are, or how much need we have for the grace of God.

Do you see your need for a Savior? If not, the Bible says it is because "the god of this world has blinded the minds of the unbelievers, to keep them from seeing the light of the gospel of the glory of Christ" (2 Cor. 4:4). Ask the Holy Spirit to open your eyes, and you will see how much you need Jesus.

## What Else the Blind Man Saw

The second thing the blind man saw was who Jesus was. Other people may have called him "Jesus of Nazareth," but the blind man called him

2. Richard D. Phillips, *Mighty to Save: Discovering God's Grace in the Miracles of Jesus* (Phillipsburg, NJ: P&R, 2001), 207.

"Jesus, Son of David" (Luke 18:38–39). This title does not appear often in the Gospels, but it would have been familiar to any Jew who knew the Old Testament. It meant that Jesus was the Messiah—the Savior whom God had always promised to send. In those days the traditional Jewish synagogue prayers included a petition asking God to have mercy "on the kingdom of the house of David, of the Messiah of thy righteousness."[3] By calling Jesus the "Son of David," the blind man was acknowledging him as the Savior whom God had promised to send. Perhaps he had heard about the miracles Jesus performed, or maybe the word was out that he was descended from the line of David (see Luke 2:4). In any case, when the blind man called out for the Son of David, he was declaring Jesus as Israel's royal king, David's rightful heir, and God's righteous Messiah. Other people saw Jesus as a preacher and miracle worker; the blind man also saw him as the Savior!

Anyone who calls on the name of Jesus will be saved, as the blind man was. A powerful example of this saving principle at work in today's world comes from the life of a student at Kenya's Scott Theological College. Here is how a teacher at the school describes the man's testimony:

> Francis Ayul comes from the upper Nile River in Southern Sudan. He shared his testimony during the graduation ceremony and we held back our tears: alternating between joy, grief, and then back to joy. He is the only child of 13 siblings still alive. As a young man, he enlisted in the SPLA to fight the Islamic army from the north; he did so for 13 years, earning prestige for his fighting prowess, until he was shot twice in the stomach one hot afternoon. For three days, he lived (barely) among the dead, wondering at times if he was still alive, while hyenas and vultures hovered around his still body. It was during the third day, when—as he held an AK47 to his head to take his own life—he remembered the name of Jesus from his youth and called out, "Jesus, save me." As he was praying, his comrades returned and found his eyes still blinking and carried him to where he could receive medical help. He promised Jesus, out of gratitude, that he would serve him the rest of his life. Francis returns to southern Sudan to train pastors and serve as a missionary in outreach areas.[4]

3. *Theological Dictionary of the New Testament*, ed. Gerhard Kittel and Gerhard Friedrich, trans. Geoffrey W. Bromiley, 10 vols. (Grand Rapids: Eerdmans, 1964–1976), 8:481.

4. Ministry update from Gregg and Kim Okesson, Aug. 15, 2007.

The blind man not only saw Jesus as the Savior, but also received him as his Lord. When Jesus asked him what he wanted, he addressed Jesus as the Lord (Luke 18:41). This was more than a sign of respect; it also amounted to a confession of faith. Whether he fully realized it or not, by calling Jesus "Lord," the blind man was expressing a right relationship with God. There is no way to separate salvation in Christ from the lordship of Christ. Jesus is both Savior and Lord; to receive him as one is to receive him as the other, for the only Savior is the Lord Jesus Christ. Therefore, when the blind man called Jesus "Lord," he was submitting himself to worship and obey the Savior.

So you see, the blind man could see better than most people, including many people in the crowds that followed Jesus around Jericho! His spiritual acuity was nearly 20–20. Someone once asked Helen Keller, "Isn't it terrible to be blind?" She responded by saying, "Better to be blind and see with your heart, than to have two good eyes and see nothing."[5] Keller's words are an apt description of the beggar man by the side of the road who, for all his physical blindness, had penetrating spiritual insight. Do you see your sin and need for a Savior as well as he did?

The third thing the blind man saw was Jesus himself. Or maybe we should say that Jesus was the *first* thing he saw, for by his miraculous divine power, Jesus made the blind man to see. The Scripture says, "Everyone who calls on the name of the Lord will be saved" (Rom. 10:13). The blind man experienced this for himself. King Jesus heard his cry and opened his eyes, delivering him from blindness and beggary by his royal command. As soon as the blind man's eyes were opened, the first person he saw was his Lord and Savior, Jesus Christ. By performing this miracle, Jesus fulfilled the ancient promise that he had come to recover sight for the blind (Luke 4:18).

This promise is fulfilled in a spiritual way any time a sinner comes to faith in Jesus Christ. A believer is someone who has been delivered from the blindness of sin; the eyes of his heart have been enlightened by the grace of God (see Eph. 1:17–18). Yet there is also a physical dimension to God's promise. The restoration of the blind man's sight is a reminder that salvation is for the body as well as the soul. His physical healing fell within the gospel category of salvation. When Jesus described what he had done for the man, he said "your faith has made you well" (Luke 18:42); or, more lit-

---

5. Helen Keller, quoted in R. Kent Hughes, *Luke: That You May Know the Truth*, Preaching the Word (Wheaton, IL: Crossway, 1998), 2:215.

erally, "your faith has saved you." The New Testament verb "to save" *(sōzō)* can encompass physical as well as spiritual health. Depending on the context, salvation may refer to "healing, delivering, rescuing, keeping safe, [or] preserving someone."[6]

Thus, while the blind man's salvation included much more than the recovery of his sight, his sight was not to be overlooked! Jesus saved the man from his physical distress with a view to his eternal destiny. God has promised that in the end he will provide physical as well as spiritual well-being. What hope this gives to the blind, the deaf, the crippled, and anyone else who suffers in the body! One day God will save us from every last consequence of sin, including sickness, disability, and disease.

The healing miracles of Jesus should not mislead us into expecting full salvation right away, however. This is the error of the faith-healers, who expect physical healing to be the immediate result of saving faith. But Jesus did not heal everyone, and God has never promised to save us from suffering in this fallen world. Rather, he promises to save us *through* suffering into glory. Thus the healing miracles of Christ hold the promise of a glorious salvation that is yet to come. We will have perfect health in heaven, where "death shall be no more, neither shall there be mourning nor crying nor pain" (Rev. 21:4).

Even the man that Jesus met on the Jericho road was still waiting for that perfect salvation, but he caught his first glimpse of it when Jesus made his blind eyes to see. As we suffer in the body and struggle with our own physical limitations, his story gives us the hope that Jesus has the power to heal us and make us whole again.

## BELIEVING IS SEEING

Even before Jesus performed his miraculous cure, the blind man could see more than most people. The way he received his sight—both his spiritual sight and his physical sight—was by grace through faith. Jesus said to him, "Recover your sight; your faith has made you well" (Luke 18:42). The blind man was seeing by believing. It was his *faith* that made him well.

6. Ben Witherington, III, "Salvation and Health in Christian Antiquity: The Soteriology of Luke-Acts in Its First Century Setting," in *Witness to the Gospel: The Theology of Acts*, ed. I. Howard Marshall and David Peterson (Grand Rapids: Eerdmans, 1998), 145–66 (p. 164).

Properly speaking, of course, it was Jesus who healed him. But the man received Jesus by faith, and thus faith was the channel by which he received his salvation. B. B. Warfield was right when he said that it is not even faith, strictly speaking, that saves, "but Christ that saves through faith. The saving power resides exclusively, not in the act of faith or the attitude of faith or the nature of faith, but in the object of faith . . . Christ himself."[7] This is what saved the man by the Jericho road: faith in Jesus. Therefore, his example shows us what it means to put our own trust in Christ.

We have considered what the blind man saw, but what did he believe? And what can his example teach us about what it means to have faith in Jesus as the Son of David—our Lord for life and Savior from sin?

First, his example shows that faith is *persistent*. The blind man did something more than simply call out to Jesus; he kept crying for mercy until Jesus stopped and healed him. To put it another way, he kept *praying* until Jesus saved him. Since he could not see his way to Jesus, how else could he get the salvation he so desperately needed? He continued to shout for mercy over the noise of the crowd, even after everyone told him to shut up: "And those who were in front rebuked him, telling him to be silent. But he cried out all the more" (Luke 18:39). The man may have been blind, but he was not dumb, in the sense of being unable to speak. People were trying to stop him from making a scene. But the more they tried to get him to quiet down, the louder he shouted, begging for Jesus to save him. He would not give up on his desire to see.

The blind man was rewarded for the persistence of his faith, because "Jesus stopped and commanded him to be brought to him. And when he came near, he asked him, 'What do you want me to do for you?'" (Luke 18:40–41). The answer, of course, was that the blind man wanted to see. He believed that Jesus had the power to save him, and he would not stop crying out to Jesus until he was saved.

The lesson is easy to apply: do not keep quiet, but cry out for deliverance until Jesus brings you to salvation. There will always be some friends and family members who try to discourage you from calling on Jesus by faith. But be persistent. Keep crying out for salvation, the way the blind man did, until by the word of God you receive your spiritual sight. Then keep crying

---

7. Benjamin B. Warfield, "Faith," in *Biblical and Theological Studies*, ed. Samuel Craig (Philadelphia: Presbyterian and Reformed, 1952), 425.

out for anything and everything that you need. Jesus is listening by the Holy Spirit, and he loves to hear the prayers of the needy. Jesus Christ has mercy for sinners. If you pray in persistent faith, he will not pass you by. Jesus is not too busy helping others to help you; he will stop in the middle of the road to save you.

## Knowing, Believing, Trusting

Unless the blind man's faith had been persistent, he never would have caught Jesus' attention and had the chance to ask for what he needed. Unless his faith had been personal, he never would have asked the way that he did: "Lord, let me recover my sight" (Luke 18:41). This was a second aspect of the man's faith: it was a *personal* faith in Jesus Christ. He called directly on Jesus for his salvation, and he did this with his whole person. Ole Hallesby has written: "The essence of faith is to come to Christ. . . . Faith manifests itself clearly and plainly when sinners . . . come into the presence of Christ with all their sin and all their distress. The sinner who does this believes."[8]

We might add that the sinner who does this is saved, for personal faith in Christ is saving faith. God calls everyone to trust personally in his Son Jesus. If you call out to Christ in faith, he will be your Savior. Protestant theologians have long taught that there are three essential elements to personal saving faith: knowledge *(notitia)*, belief *(assensus)*, and trust *(fiducia)*. The blind man—the beggar man—seems to have had all three.

First he had *knowledge*, the intellectual dimension of faith, which comes from the regenerated mind. It is impossible to have faith in Jesus Christ without knowing who he is and what he has done. Faith is not simply a subjective feeling of ultimate dependence, but has objective, propositional content. In the case of the blind man, faith meant knowing that Jesus was the Son of David, with the power to save. For the Christian, faith means knowing that Jesus is who the Bible says he is and that he has done what the Bible says he has done. Jesus Christ is God the Son—God incarnate—who lived a perfect life, died an atoning death, and was raised to victorious life. Faith means knowing that Jesus Christ is the crucified and risen Savior who offers redemption from sin and reconciliation to God. Since faith requires knowledge, often the first

8. Ole Hallesby, *Prayer* (Minneapolis: Augsburg Publishing House, 1931): 30.

step to becoming a Christian is simply to have someone explain what Christianity teaches.

Faith begins in the mind, but that is not where it ends. John Calvin said that "the Word of God is not received by faith if it flits about in the top of the brain, but when it takes root in the depth of the heart."[9] This brings us to the second essential element of personal saving faith, which is *belief*, or assent, which comes from the regenerated heart. This means accepting the message of salvation—not just knowing what the Bible says about Jesus, but believing from the heart that it is really true. After all, even the demons believe there is a God (James 2:19); the trouble is that they will not accept him. But the blind man *did* accept Jesus. He cried out to the Savior and called him Lord. He had personal saving faith, in which the mind becomes convinced of the truth of Jesus Christ and the heart embraces him as the Savior.

The third element in personal saving faith is *trust*, and the blind man had this as well. Trust is the volitional dimension of faith, in which the regenerated will offers unconditional surrender to Jesus Christ. As Martin Luther explained, there is a difference between "faith which believes what is said of God is true" and "faith which throws itself on God."[10] The trusting aspect of faith was graphically illustrated in the ministry of John Paton, for when Paton

> first went out as a pioneer missionary to the New Hebrides islands, he found that the natives among whom he began to work had no way of writing their language. He began to learn it and in time began to work on a translation of the Bible for them. Soon he discovered that they had no word for "faith." This was serious, of course, for a person can hardly translate the Bible without it. One day he went on a hunt with one of the natives. They shot a large deer in the course of the hunt, and tying its legs together and supporting it on a pole, laboriously trekked back down the mountain path to Paton's home near the seashore. As they reached the veranda both men threw the deer down, and the native immediately flopped into one of the deck chairs that stood on the porch exclaiming, "My, it is good to stretch yourself out here and rest." Paton immediately jumped to his feet and recorded the phrase. In his final transla-

9. John Calvin, *Institutes of the Christian Religion*, ed. John T. McNeill, trans. Ford Lewis Battles, 2 vols., Library of Christian Classics 20–21 (Philadelphia: Westminster, 1960), 3.2.36.

10. Martin Luther, quoted in Donald G. Bloesch, *Essentials of Evangelical Theology, vol.1: God, Authority, and Salvation* (San Francisco: Harper & Row, 1978), 224.

tion of the New Testament this was the word used to convey the idea of trust, faith, and belief.[11]

Faith is resting on Jesus for salvation. Or, to use the most famous definition of all, "faith is the assurance of things hoped for, the conviction of things not seen" (Heb. 11:1). There is no better example than the blind man by the Jericho road, who was certain of what he did not see! Genuine biblical faith always includes a measure of assurance. As Calvin said, faith is "a firm and certain knowledge of God's benevolence towards us, founded upon the truth of the freely given promise in Christ, both revealed to our minds and sealed upon our hearts through the Holy Spirit."[12] This does not mean that Christians never have their doubts. As we learn from the Gospel of Luke, there are times when disciples have little faith (Luke 12:28), and need to ask God for more (Luke 17:5). What the assurance of faith does mean, however, is that true believers never completely lose their trust in the saving work of Christ.

Thankfully, salvation does not depend on the strength of our faith. It depends rather on God's faithfulness, and he has promised that by the abiding presence of his Spirit, we will never abandon our confidence in Jesus to save. True faith, says the Heidelberg Catechism, is "not only a certain knowledge, whereby I hold for truth all that God has revealed to us in his word, but also an assured confidence, which the Holy Ghost works by the gospel in my heart; that not only to others, but to me also, remission of sin, everlasting righteousness, and salvation, are freely given by God, merely of grace, only for the sake of Christ's merits" (A. 21).

Notice that this faith is not something that comes from us, but from the Holy Spirit, who works it into our hearts. Even our faith is a gift from God. Do you have this personal saving faith in Jesus Christ? Do you know him for sure? Believe in him with your whole person—mind, heart, and will.

## Following Jesus

The last thing to be said about the blind man's faith is that it was *productive:* "And immediately he recovered his sight and followed him, glorifying

11. The story is recounted in James Montgomery Boice, *The Gospel of John* (Grand Rapids: Zondervan, 1985), 195.
12. Calvin, *Institutes*, 3.2.7.

God" (Luke 18:43). He was not the only one either: "And all the people, when they saw it, gave praise to God" (Luke 18:43).

This is what happens when someone comes to saving faith in Jesus Christ: it leads to a whole life of worship and obedience. As soon as the blind man could see Jesus, he became one of his followers. Having been saved by faith, he started to live by faith, for saving faith always leads to a life of obedience—"the obedience of faith" (Rom. 1:5). Once the blind man was saved, he started to fulfill the purpose for which he was made, which was to glorify God and enjoy him forever. Then the joy of his salvation was infectious: when other people saw what God had done in the man's life, they started praising God too.

True faith produces joy in God and a commitment to follow Jesus forever. This is a good way to test our relationship to God. Do I experience joy in the worship of God? Am I keeping the commandments of Christ? Does my life point other people to Jesus in a way that makes them want to follow Jesus too? If I say that I am trusting in Jesus, my faith should be evident in the way I worship, the way I witness, and the way I live. Faith, writes Anthony Hoekema, is "a response to God's call by the acceptance of Christ with the total person—that is, with assured conviction of the truth of the gospel, and with trustful reliance on God in Christ for salvation, together with genuine commitment to Christ and to his service."[13]

The story of the blind man by the side of the road is a call to persistent, personal, productive faith in Jesus Christ. One day soon everyone who has this faith will see Jesus. The Son of David has gone ahead of us into glory, where he has promised that we will see him face to face. This is what my brother-in-law Alan is waiting for: not just the recovery of his physical sight, but the glorious appearing of the Lord Jesus Christ. That is what I am waiting for too. I am waiting to see Jesus, and by faith, I *will* see him.

Will you see Jesus? Do not let him pass you by! Imagine how tragic it would have been if the blind man in Jericho had heard Jesus walking by but never cried out to him in faith. Unless the man had raised his voice at that very moment, he would have missed his chance to see Jesus, and he would have been lost forever. Now Jesus has come your way. Will you call out to him in faith? Jesus has to be believed to be seen; if you believe in him, you will see him, and by his mercy you will be saved.

---

13. Anthony A. Hoekema, *Saved by Grace* (Grand Rapids: Eerdmans, 1989), 140.

# 80

# LITTLE MAN, BIG APOLOGY

## *Luke 19:1—10*

*And there was a man named Zacchaeus. He was a chief tax collector and was rich. . . . And Jesus said to him, "Today salvation has come to this house, since he also is a son of Abraham. For the Son of Man came to seek and to save the lost."*
(Luke 19:2, 9–10)

The kids at my elementary school would have called him a "shrimp." These days people are more politically correct, so they would probably just say that he was "vertically challenged." Luke said he was "small of stature" (Luke 19:3). But regardless of how anyone says it, the fact is that in comparison with most other people, Zacchaeus was short.

Height is not the only standard of measurement, however, and there are more important comparisons for us to make. Once again, Luke has placed two characters side by side in his Gospel in order to show them both in their full spiritual significance. Jesus met two men on the Jericho road, one at the end of chapter 18 and one at the beginning of chapter 19. Consider the connections: One man was blind, while the other had his sight, but they both wanted to see Jesus. One man was beggarly poor, while the other man was filthy rich, but they both needed something that money can't buy. One man showed his faith, while the other man demonstrated his repentance, but they both had a saving relationship with Jesus Christ.

By telling these two stories together, Luke is inviting us to come to Jesus in faith *and* repentance, just like the blind man who started to see and the little man who made the big apology. Theologians sometimes wonder which comes first: faith or repentance, repenting or believing, but Luke is showing us that they both go together. It is impossible to repent without believing, or to believe without repenting. Repentance means turning away from sin, but how can you truly repent without trusting that God will forgive you in Christ? And when you put your faith in Jesus, what are you trusting him to do, if not to save you from your sin? Therefore, as John Murray wrote, "The faith that is unto salvation is a penitent faith, and the repentance that is unto life is a believing repentance."[1]

## THE WEE LITTLE MAN

The man who had this believing repentance was Zacchaeus. In his account Luke tells us whom this "wee little man" wanted to see, who wanted to see him, and how his life was changed. Luke begins by telling us that Jesus "entered Jericho and was passing through. And there was a man named Zacchaeus. He was a chief tax collector and was rich. And he was seeking to see who Jesus was, but on account of the crowd he could not, because he was small of stature. So he ran on ahead and climbed up into a sycamore tree to see him, for he was about to pass that way" (Luke 19:1–4).

Zacchaeus may not have been tall in stature, but his biggest problem was that he was short on godliness. Most tax collectors were sinners in those days, but Zacchaeus was more of a sinner than most. As a wealthy city on a major trade route, Jericho was one of three major centers for collecting Israel's taxes. Not surprisingly, collecting taxes there had made Zacchaeus fabulously wealthy. By this point in his career he did not even have to do the collecting himself. As "chief tax collector" he was the ultimate middleman, skimming the proceeds off the customs revenue on its

---

1. John Murray, *Redemption—Accomplished and Applied* (Grand Rapids: Eerdmans, 1955), 113.

way to Rome. No wonder Zacchaeus was so rich—he was the kingpin of the Jericho tax cartel![2]

As a general rule, tax collectors were swindlers and cheats, and thus they were regarded as traitors to their own people. This explains why Zacchaeus was so unpopular, and why perhaps no one gave him enough room to see Jesus. It also explains why they objected later in the story when Jesus invited himself over to the man's house for dinner. According to Norval Geldenhuys, "Among the Jews it was an unheard-of thing for a rabbi or any other religious leader to lower himself by staying at the house of a 'publican.' So they were greatly offended at His allowing Himself to be entertained in the house of Zacchaeus, a prominent member of this despised class."[3] The chief tax collector was Public Enemy Number One—a collaborator with the Romans. How could Jesus associate with him at all, let alone share table fellowship with him? According to the standards of their own self-righteousness, it was beneath his dignity, especially since many people thought that to eat with a known criminal was to be implicated in his crimes.[4] Hence their grumbling disapproval: "He has gone in to be the guest of a man who is a sinner" (Luke 19:7).

What people failed to understand is that salvation is *for* sinners. It is for outsiders and outcasts, swindlers and cheats. In fact, by the end of this passage it turns out that Zacchaeus was exactly the kind of lowlife sinner that Jesus was looking for: "For the Son of Man came to seek and to save the lost" (Luke 19:10). If the Savior had come to save sinners, then who better to save than a man like Zacchaeus, who was as lost as lost can be? Jesus did not meet with Zacchaeus to share in his sin, as some of his critics seemed to think, but to offer the fellowship of his forgiveness.

If Jesus came seeking to save Zacchaeus, then he is willing and able to save any lost sinner whatsoever. He is willing to save you, even after everything you have done to turn away from God. You are not a hopeless case, any more than Zacchaeus was. No one is a hopeless case! Jesus Christ has come to save even the most desperate sinners.

2. R. Kent Hughes, *Luke: That You May Know the Truth*, 2 vols., Preaching the Word (Wheaton, IL: Crossway, 1998), 2:222.

3. Norval Geldenhuys, *The Gospel of Luke*, New International Commentary on the New Testament (Grand Rapids: Eerdmans, 1951), 470.

4. Darrell L. Bock, *Luke*, 2 vols., Baker Exegetical Commentary on the New Testament (Grand Rapids: Baker, 1996), 2:1521.

## Zacchaeus, You Come Down!

As desperate as he was, Zacchaeus was looking for Jesus. The man was curious—a seeker. He had heard people talking about Jesus, and he heard the huge commotion as Jesus went through the city. Maybe he had even heard how sympathetic Jesus was to tax collectors and other religious outsiders. But whatever his reasons, Zacchaeus was drawn to Jesus and wanted to see him. The little man's curiosity is a reminder that some of the people who are secretly interested in Jesus are people we would never expect to be interested in Jesus at all. No one thought Zacchaeus had much interest in spiritual things, but in fact he wanted to know more about Jesus. Some of the people we know have the same interest, whether we suspect it or not. If we talked to them about Jesus, they would engage in the conversation. If we invited them to church, they would visit. They are looking for Jesus already—sitting in their sycamore trees, so to speak. When will we help them see Jesus?

Zacchaeus did what anyone should do who is curious about Jesus: he got into position to get a better look. The way he did this was rather undignified, as everyone knows. First he "ran on ahead" (Luke 19:4), something that a gentleman in those days would rarely do, if ever. Then he climbed a tree, which was even more undignified. But it was worth it, because Zacchaeus wanted to see Jesus. His example encourages us to do whatever it takes to see Jesus. If you do not know Jesus, are you curious to know more about him? Take a look: he is the Son of God and the Savior of the world. Then once we do know Jesus, we should do anything in our power to see him even more clearly. We do not have to climb up a tree to do this; we simply need to spend time with Jesus by speaking to him in prayer and listening to him in the Bible.

Zacchaeus wanted to see Jesus, but as it turned out, Jesus also wanted to see him. Luke tells us that "when Jesus came to the place, he looked up and said to him, 'Zacchaeus, hurry and come down, for I must stay at your house today'" (Luke 19:5). The old children's Sunday school song says it like this:

> And as the Savior passed that way,
> He looked up in the tree.
> And he said, "Zacchaeus, you come down!
> For I'm going to your house today."

Here we see God's sovereignty in salvation. It was the ultimate divine appointment. Zacchaeus did not stop for Jesus; Jesus stopped for Zacchaeus. He even called him by name, as if he had known him from all eternity (which of course he had!). Jesus was on a divine mission; he had come to seek and to save. To that end, he invited himself over for dinner, except that what he said to Zacchaeus was not so much an invitation as it was an imperative. Speaking with divine authority, Jesus commanded the little man to *hurry* down, because he *must* visit his house *today*.

This is the way Jesus saves lost sinners: he does it by walking right into our lives, even uninvited. J. C. Ryle said, "If ever there was a soul sought and saved, without having done anything to deserve it, that soul was the soul of Zacchaeus. . . . Unasked, our Lord stops and speaks to Zacchaeus. Unasked, He offers Himself to be a guest in the house of a sinner. Unasked, He sends into the heart of a publican the renewing grace of the Spirit, and puts him that very day among the children of God."[5] Here is how the Puritan Matthew Henry explained the saving work of God in the sinner's soul: Jesus "brings his own welcome; he opens the heart and inclines it to receive him."[6]

Jesus was calling Zacchaeus to faith and repentance, and with his call came the grace for Zacchaeus to respond. The theological term for this is "effectual calling," which the Westminster Shorter Catechism defines as "the work of God's Spirit, whereby, convincing us of our sin and misery, enlightening our minds in the knowledge of Christ, and renewing our wills, he doth persuade and enable us to embrace Jesus Christ, freely offered to us in the gospel" (A. 31). In other words, when God calls a sinner by the Holy Spirit, he does everything inside us that needs to be done for us to be saved. He convinces us that we are sinners. He teaches us who Jesus is. He changes our minds and hearts so that we are ready to receive Jesus as Savior and Lord. Sooner or later, every true child of God receives this effective call. Through the preaching of the message of salvation, Jesus stops us in the middle of life's busy road and calls us to faith and repentance. He enters our homes to change our hearts.

5. J. C. Ryle, *Expository Thoughts on the Gospels, Luke* (1858; reprint Cambridge: James Clarke, 1976), 2:292.
6. Quoted in Richard D. Phillips, *Encounters with Jesus* (Phillipsburg, NJ: P&R, 2002), 159.

## FAITH AND REPENTANCE

The conversion of Zacchaeus is a story of repentance, but it is also a story of faith. As we saw in the previous chapter, the story of the blind man was mainly about faith, but it was a penitent faith. Likewise, although the story of Zacchaeus is primarily about repentance, it was a believing repentance.

The faith of Zacchaeus is evident from the way he received Jesus. When Jesus stopped and called him by name, he practically fell out of the tree. But then he gave Jesus the glad welcome of faith, embracing him with joyous trust: "he hurried and came down and received him joyfully" (Luke 19:6). To receive Jesus is to come to him by faith, trusting him for eternal life and everything else.

The welcome Zacchaeus gave to Jesus is a reminder that faith is a matter of personal trust, and not merely a matter of propositional belief. The wee little man had heard about Jesus before. In all likelihood, the word was out that the man from Nazareth was a friend of tax collectors and sinners (see Matt. 11:19). Zacchaeus wanted to see for himself, to investigate the claims of Christ. But he did not have to look long before he decided to welcome Jesus into his home, and then into his heart.

Do not delay! There is a time and a place for curiosity, for sitting up in the tree and looking at Jesus. But there is also a time and a place for getting down from the tree and welcoming him with open arms, the way Zacchaeus did. He believed in Jesus almost as soon as Jesus called him. His faith is confirmed by the way he addressed Jesus: "Behold, Lord!" (Luke 19:8). Like the blind man, he called Jesus his Lord. This was more than a title of respect; it was his first confession of faith, a sign that he was coming under the lordship of Jesus Christ.

But the real proof of the man's faith was his repentance: "Zacchaeus stood and said to the Lord, 'Behold, Lord, the half of my goods I give to the poor. And if I have defrauded anyone of anything, I restore it fourfold.' And Jesus said to him, 'Today salvation has come to this house, since he also is a son of Abraham'" (Luke 19:8–9).

By calling Zacchaeus a son of Abraham, Jesus was welcoming him into God's family, together with everyone else in the man's household. This is a notable example of the deep biblical principle of the covenant, that salvation is not just for individuals, but also for families. When grace comes to the head of a house, God is laying his claim on the entire household.

The Pharisees claimed that they were the only true children of Abraham (see Luke 3:8), but Jesus said that tax collectors could be part of the family, too. No one needs to stay outside; there is always more room in God's house. Even though Zacchaeus was a notorious sinner, he was still a Jew, and now he was restored to God's true Israel by faith in Jesus Christ. David Gooding says, "In that moment Zacchaeus not only saw who Jesus was, he discovered his own long-lost identity. He was a man loved by God with an eternal love, and longed for so much that God had sent his Son on purpose to find him and to rescue him from his lostness by coming personally to his home and bringing the sense of acceptance with God into his very heart."[7]

This is what the love of Jesus does in the heart of a sinner. The way he accepts us leads us to accept him. With that acceptance comes a true sense of identity, the assurance that we are children of God and that God loves us in Jesus Christ. There is no longer any need to run away from God, or to hide from other people, or to pretend to be anything except who we really are.

This does not mean, however, that we can go on living the way that we have always lived. When Jesus comes into someone's life, there are some changes that come with him. It is true that Jesus accepted Zacchaeus as he was, but it is equally true that Jesus did not leave Zacchaeus where he was. The love of Jesus called him to repentance.

The story of Zacchaeus shows us two essential elements in what the Bible calls "repentance that leads to life" (Acts 11:18). First there must be confession, a full acknowledgment of sin. But if repentance is genuine, there must also be a change in someone's life, and both aspects of repentance were present in this instance.

When Zacchaeus heard everyone muttering that he was a sinner, he realized that they were right. So he stood up in front of Jesus and everyone else to confess his sins against God. There were sins of omission: he had not shared his riches with the poor. There were sins of commission: he had cheated people out of their hard-earned income. Zacchaeus took

---

7. David Gooding, *According to Luke: A New Exposition of the Third Gospel* (Grand Rapids: Eerdmans, 1987), 299.

his stand to confess it all—all the covetousness, selfishness, greed, extortion, theft, and fraud.

True repentance requires genuine conviction of the sinfulness of one's very own sins. A notable example comes from the life of a nineteenth-century black minister named J. W. C. Pennington. After escaping from slavery in Maryland, Pennington lived with the family of a Presbyterian elder in New York—a family that showed him the love of Jesus. Pennington had been deeply scarred by his awful experiences as a slave, and he vowed that he would never forgive his captors. But the more Pennington heard about the gospel of Jesus Christ, the more he realized that he was not just sinned against, but also a sinner. Here is how Pennington described his repentance: "Day after day, I found myself more deeply convicted of personal guilt before God. . . . Burning with a recollection of the wrongs men had done me—mourning for the injuries my brethren were still enduring, [I also became] deeply convinced of the guilt of my own sins against God."[8]

Anyone who wants to be saved must make the same confession, acknowledging the guilt of our own sin against God. It may well be that we have been sinned against, or even that we are more sinned against than sinning. But the only sin we can confess is our own—the sin that makes us guilty before God.

## Payback Time

A second element of true repentance is change, real spiritual change. If someone recognizes his sin, and is sorry for it, yet there is no lasting change in his life, it may be doubted whether true repentance has ever taken place. Repentance is not repentance unto life unless it includes turning away from sin. Thus Anthony Hoekema defines repentance as "the conscious turning of the regenerate person away from sin and toward God in a complete change of living."[9] It is by repentance, writes the Westminster Confession of Faith, that "a sinner, out of the sight and sense . . . of the filthiness and odiousness of his sins . . . so grieves for, and hates his sins, as to turn from them all unto God" (15.2).

8. James W. C. Pennington, *The Fugitive Blacksmith*, 2nd ed. (London: C. Gilpin, 1849), 53.
9. Anthony A. Hoekema, *Saved by Grace* (Grand Rapids: Eerdmans, 1989), 127.

The biblical terms for repentance all refer to a turning away from sin. The most common word in the Old Testament is *shub*, which means "to turn around," or "to go back in the opposite direction" (e.g., 1 Kings 8:35; Ezek. 33:11). At the same time that a sinner turns away from his sins, he also turns towards God (e.g., Ps. 51:13; Hos. 14:1). The key New Testament terms for repentance—*metanoia* and *epistrephō*—both emphasize a spiritual change. *Metanoia* usually refers more specifically to the inward change that takes place in the mind and heart of the sinner (e.g., Rom. 2:4; 2 Peter 3:9), whereas *epistrephō* typically stresses the outward change in the sinner's actions (e.g., 1 Thess. 1:9).

It was in this outward change that Zacchaeus excelled. It was obvious from what he both said and did that a genuine transformation had taken place in his life, that by the grace of God he had been saved from his sins. It is not certain where he made his speech about giving away his money. He may have spoken these words back at his house, in response to what Jesus said over dinner. But it seems that he repented on the spot, right there under the sycamore tree: "Behold, Lord, the half of my goods I give to the poor. And if I have defrauded anyone of anything, I restore it fourfold" (Luke 19:8).

The word "if" does not express uncertainty, as if there were any doubt about what the man had done. Zacchaeus had often defrauded the poor, and the word "if" simply indicates that he may not have done so in each and every case. But now he had decided to do something about it, and the word "Behold" gives the impression that he was starting right away. Rather than saying "I will give," he said "I give," as if emptying his pockets then and there, handing his money out to the needy. More likely his use of the present tense describes the immediate future, what the man intended to do as soon as he could. In any case, Zacchaeus did not delay. Immediately he started divesting himself of the wealth it had taken him years to accumulate. From that moment forward, he resolved to turn away from sin.

In making amends to people he had defrauded, Zacchaeus intended to go well beyond what the law required. For starters, he would give away half of his possessions. At most, God's people were required to give one-fifth of their property to the poor, but Zacchaeus was willing to go up to 50 percent. The way a man uses his money is one of the best indicators of his spiritual condition, and although Zacchaeus may have been a small man, he had deep pockets. Once he came to Christ in faith and repentance, he revalued his priorities and reached out to help the poor. This is how God does mercy: by the love of Jesus, he changes hearts that start to change the world.

Furthermore, Zacchaeus offered to pay back four times the amount that he had stolen through excess taxation. Double restitution was the norm, and the law required fourfold restitution only for the theft of an animal (see Ex. 22:1). But Zacchaeus had discovered that it is more blessed to give than it is to receive. Now that he was accepted in Christ, he did not have to hoard everything for himself; he was able and willing to give back what he had taken.

By making full restitution, while at the same time giving generously to meet the needs of the poor, Zacchaeus was starting to perform what the Bible calls "deeds in keeping with [his] repentance" (Acts 26:20). He was obeying God in exactly the areas of life where he had most often sinned. This is what repentance requires from all of us: a continual turning away from sin and back to God. When Martin Luther posted his famous Ninety-Five Theses in Wittenberg, his first thesis stated, "Our Lord and Master Jesus Christ . . . willed that the whole life of believers should be repentance."[10]

What are the prevailing sins in your life, and what changes does God want to bring? True repentance means turning away from sin and towards godliness in every area of life. Where you have been taking what does not belong to you, pay it back, with extra. Where you have been lazy, get back to work, and serve in the strength of the Lord. Where you have been neglecting your family, reorganize your schedule and spend time doing the things your wife (or your husband) and your children most need you to do. Where you have been giving in to sexual sin, protect your purity by making a commitment to chastity. Where you have been living selfishly, learn to serve. Where you have been tearing people down, build them up. Where you have been angry with people, or bitter against God, offer forgiveness and praise. These are the kinds of changes that Jesus always wants to bring.

## POWER THROUGH THE CROSS

Does it seem impossible to make all the changes that repentance requires? The changes that Zacchaeus made must have cost him a fortune, but then

10. Martin Luther, *The Works of Martin Luther*, Philadelphia edition (Philadelphia: Muhlenberg, 1943), 1:29.

that is what it takes to pass through the eye of a needle (see Luke 18:22, 25). What makes his repentance so remarkable is that he was so rich. In the previous chapter Luke had recounted the story of a rich man who refused to repent, a man who was not willing to use his fortune to feed the poor. As that man walked sadly away, Jesus said, "It is easier for a camel to go through the eye of a needle than for a rich person to enter the kingdom of God" (Luke 18:24–25). Humanly speaking, it is impossible. But as Jesus went on to say, "What is impossible with men is possible with God" (Luke 18:27).

The truth of those words was confirmed by the repentance of Zacchaeus, who never could have found salvation on his own. Only God could do such an impossible thing as bring a rich little thief to repentance. He needed Jesus to come seeking to save him.

That same grace is now available to us through the cross. At the end of this passage Jesus announced to Zacchaeus and to the world that "the Son of Man came to seek and to save the lost" (Luke 19:10). Jesus had been seeking the lost all the way through the Gospel of Luke, up to and including Zacchaeus. Very soon—in just a matter of days—he would be saving the lost by dying for their sins, before rising again with the victory. Jesus is still doing this saving work today, seeking the lost by the work of the Holy Spirit, and saving the lost by the merits of his crucifixion and resurrection.

Do you have faith in the saving work of Jesus Christ? Are you turning away from your sin and back to God? We are called to be penitent believers who never stop trusting in the saving power of the crucified Christ. The power and the grace to repent only come through his cross—the cross where he died between two thieves for Zacchaeus and all the other thieving sinners who trust in him for their salvation.

One of those sinners was saved through the work of Wycliffe Bible Translators in Brazil, where a team of linguists had finished translating the Book of Luke into the Mamiande language and started recording the soundtrack for the Jesus Film:

> When it came time to record the section where Jesus called Zacchaeus, the only man available to read the part of Zacchaeus was someone who was known as a scoundrel, a man who was always looking for ways to profit at the expense of others. When this man recorded the part of the story where

Zacchaeus repented for his sins, he could not bring himself to say the words "I stole," but instead said "He stole." When this was pointed out to him, he denied that he had made a mistake and refused to record his part again.[11]

This is the difficulty we all have: it is so hard for us to admit our sin. But eventually, after much discussion, the man relented and agreed to record his part properly. When the recording was finished, "the entire village crowded into the school to see the film. Every eye was glued to the screen for the entire two hours. Toward the end, when the film shows Jesus struggling under the heavy cross, showing the price He paid for our sins, the man who had read the part of Zacchaeus could be seen in the middle of the crowd—with tears streaming down his face."[12] The man's thieving heart was touched and his life was transformed by the Savior who died for his very own sins.

This is where we find the power and the grace to repent: by seeing the sacrifice Jesus made on the cross, and believing he did it for us as much as for anyone.

11. This story is recounted in *Select Words* 7 (May 2000).
12. Ibid.

# 81

# WHAT YOU DO WITH
# WHAT YOU HAVE

## *Luke 19:11–27*

*"I tell you that to everyone who has, more will be given, but from
the one who has not, even what he has will be taken away."*
(Luke 19:26)

hen Herod the Great died in 4 B.C., it was obvious to almost
everyone that his son Archelaus would take his throne in
Judea. However, there was only one man in the entire world
who had the power and authority to crown Archelaus as king: the emperor
Caesar in Rome. Although Archelaus began to rule immediately upon the
death of his father, his royal title could be ratified only by Caesar Augustus
himself. So Archelaus made the long journey to Rome, where he expected
to be crowned as king in the temple of the Palatine Apollo.

Unfortunately for Archelaus, there was active opposition to his monar-
chy, and when he arrived in Rome, he discovered that some of his own family members were rival claimants to the throne. Even worse, a delegation of
fifty Jewish leaders came from Jerusalem seeking an audience with Caesar
and claiming that Archelaus was unfit to govern. During Passover there

had been a disturbance at the temple, and soldiers of Archelaus had rashly slaughtered some three thousand worshipers. The delegation from Jerusalem, backed by thousands of Jews who were then living in Rome, petitioned Caesar to liberate them from the authority of Archelaus.

The whole business took much longer than anyone expected, but eventually Caesar decided to give Archelaus the opportunity to prove that he was worthy to be the king. Not surprisingly, when Archelaus returned to Judea he executed swift punishment against the men who had rebelled against his rule.[1] He went away as a contender, but he returned as king, ready to exercise his royal authority.

## THE KING'S DEPARTURE

This famous episode from Israel's history happened not long after the birth of Jesus Christ. It was still in living memory thirty years later, and it seems to form the backdrop for a parable Jesus told about investing with the gospel. Jesus was on his way from Jericho up to Jerusalem. Since it was nearly Passover, and since the king's old winter palace was near that road, it was only natural for Jesus to think about Archelaus. So he began to tell this parable: "A nobleman went into a far country to receive for himself a kingdom and then return. Calling ten of his servants, he gave them ten minas, and said to them, 'Engage in business until I come.' But his citizens hated him and sent a delegation after him, saying, 'We do not want this man to reign over us'" (Luke 19:12–14).

It sounds almost exactly like what happened to Archelaus. The nobleman traveled to a far country hoping to receive a kingdom and then return, but his citizens hated him so much that they sent a delegation to prevent his coronation. Jesus was really talking about himself, however. He was not drawing a comparison to the character of wicked Archelaus, of course, but only to the familiar circumstances of his kingship. Jesus was the nobleman—the Son of the High King—who was about to receive a kingdom all his own. He would travel to a far country to get it, passing through death and the empty grave before being crowned in the courts of heaven and eventually returning to his people. Sadly, many citizens would reject his royal author-

1. Simon J. Kistemaker, *The Parables: Understanding the Stories Jesus Told* (Grand Rapids: Baker, 2002), 215–16.

ity. Some of them would put him to death; others would refuse to believe in his resurrection, or acknowledge his ascension to the royal throne. Lodging their protest in the courts of heaven, they would say of Jesus, "We do not want this man to reign over us."

There are many parallels here with the kingship of Christ, but the most important is the delay in his return. Notice how the parable is introduced: "As they heard these things, he proceeded to tell a parable, because he was near to Jerusalem, and because they supposed that the kingdom of God was to appear immediately" (Luke 19:11).

It is easy to see why people would make this mistake. The more they heard what Jesus said and saw what Jesus could do, the more certain some people became that he was the promised King. Jesus was healing the blind; he was saving sinners, including the kind of rich people who almost never repent; he was preaching the kingdom of God. Soon the gathering masses would sweep him right up to Jerusalem in a frenzy of messianic expectancy. It was almost Palm Sunday, when people would shout, "Blessed is the King who comes in the name of the Lord!" (Luke 19:38). Is it any wonder that they thought the kingdom of God was coming right away?

At the same time, it is easy to see why Jesus was careful to correct their false expectations. The kingdom had come, but it had not yet come in the fullness of its final glory. Jesus still needed to suffer and die on the cross. He still needed to rise from the dead and ascend to heaven. Perhaps most importantly, he still needed to do his gospel work among the nations through the church. The kingdom had come, in one sense, but in another sense it would not come until Jesus came again.

Some Bible scholars seem troubled by the fact that although the New Testament says that Jesus is coming soon, he still hasn't come. Thus they treat the delay of the kingdom as some sort of biblical problem. But this certainly wasn't a problem for Jesus, who knew there would be a gap between the present and future reality of the kingdom of God. This was an important aspect of his teaching about the kingdom. Even before he died and rose again, Jesus prepared his disciples for his long absence by telling them that there would be a delay between his departure and his return. Therefore, we find ourselves living in the interim between the already and the not yet, between what is now and what is yet to come.

317

## The Servants' Test

How should we live in the meantime? This is the great question of our lives, and the question that Jesus answers in this parable. As we wait for the second coming, are we living as faithful servants of God's once and future King? The long delay between his departure and his return reveals our true relationship to Jesus Christ.

In the parable, two groups of people were waiting for the return of the king: his former servants and his future subjects. Here is how Michael Wilcock summarizes the story: "The King would return only after an unspecified, but far from negligible, period of time; and during that time, though his enemies might be plotting against him, he would expect his servants to be laboring to establish his kingdom."[2]

Among the citizens who waited for the nobleman's return were some enemies to his cause—out-and-out rebels. Like the people who opposed Archelaus, they rejected the kingship of the king. Many Israelites had the same attitude about Jesus as he made his way to the cross. They refused to acknowledge him as their rightful king. Very soon they would be calling for his crucifixion and saying to Pilate, "We have no king but Caesar" (John 19:15).

We will see what happened to these rebels shortly, but the parable has much more to say about the king's servants. There were ten servants in all, and each of them was given a mina to manage in the king's absence. A mina was worth about three months' wages—not a huge sum of money, but enough to find out if these servants could be trusted to serve their master. As he gave them their minas, the nobleman said, "Engage in business until I come" (Luke 19:13). The servants were called to get busy with their master's business, putting his money to work in order to turn a good profit.

These ten money managers represent the servants of Christ, the King. As we wait for his royal return, we are called to carry out the spiritual business of his kingdom. But what, exactly, does the money represent?

Here it is important to recognize an important difference between this parable in Luke and a similar parable in the Gospel of Matthew. The parable in Matthew—which is usually called "The Parable of the Talents"—

2. Michael Wilcock, *The Message of Luke*, The Bible Speaks Today (Downers Grove, IL: InterVarsity, 1979), 174.

says nothing about a king, but it does tell the story of a man who went on a long journey and gave his servants money to manage in his absence (Matt. 25:14). Each servant received a different amount of money, depending on his ability (Matt. 25:15). Therefore, the parable in Matthew teaches that we all have different amounts of talent to use in serving the Lord.

The parable in Luke is traditionally called "The Parable of the Pounds." Here each servant receives the *same* amount of money: one mina per servant (Luke 19:13). It is true that we all have different gifts (see 1 Cor. 12)— some more than others (see Matt. 25:14–30)—but that is not the point of this parable. This parable is more about faithfulness than giftedness: every believer has the same responsibility to work hard for the kingdom until Jesus comes again. We have all received the same gospel, and Jesus wants us to put it to work in the world.

The gospel is the good news of God's grace. It is the message of salvation through the death and resurrection of Jesus Christ. It is the royal offer of life and forgiveness through the cross and the empty tomb. God has entrusted this good news to us (see 1 Thess. 2:4), and now he wants us to use it so that he can make it grow. "Each believer receives the same investment capital for his Christian life," writes Kent Hughes. "We all have the good news of Jesus Christ and its marvelous effect in our lives. And we all have the same command, to 'Put this money to work until I come back.' We must invest the investment Christ has made in us! We are to multiply our spiritual capital—invest the gospel—increase the yield of the good news of salvation through Christ!"[3]

This investment opportunity raises some important questions: How am I putting the gospel to work? What return am I making on God's investment? What profit will I have to show when Jesus comes again?

Here are some of the ways we can put the gospel to work: We do it by growing in our own Christian lives through repentance, prayer, and daily dependence on the Holy Spirit. We do it by trusting God to meet our needs and guide our decisions. We also put the gospel to work by serving people in need, showing the love and mercy of Christ to people who are lonely, sick, homeless, grieving, and afraid. Then we put the gospel to work by loving our families with the love of Jesus and sharing our faith with our

---

3. R. Kent Hughes, *Luke: That You May Know the Truth*, 2 vols., Preaching the Word (Wheaton, IL: Crossway, 1998), 2:231–32.

friends. And we put the gospel to work by making a personal investment in missionary work: praying, giving, sending, and going to the nations with the good news about Jesus Christ.

Furthermore, we put the gospel to work by carrying out our regular calling in a way that shows the supremacy of Christ. The worker can do this with his labor, the professor with his scholarship, the educator with her teaching, the lawyer with his justice, the doctor with his medicine, and the artist with her craft. As long as it is done with the intention of bringing glory to God, anything and everything we do is an investment in the kingdom of God. Jesus is coming soon. Get busy for him with the gospel!

## The King's Return

One day the king will return, with the full authority of his royal kingdom. When he returns, one of the first things he will want to know is which servants he can trust to serve him well, based on what they did in his absence. Jesus said, "When he returned, having received the kingdom, he ordered these servants to whom he had given the money to be called to him, that he might know what they had gained by doing business" (Luke 19:15). The day of return was a day of reckoning, on which the king rightly demanded the fruit of faithful service.

Two of the servants made good on the king's investment, at varying rates of return: "The first came before him, saying, 'Lord, your mina has made ten minas more.' And he said to him, 'Well done, good servant! Because you have been faithful in a very little, you shall have authority over ten cities.' And the second came, saying, 'Lord, your mina has made five minas.' And he said to him, 'And you are to be over five cities'" (Luke 19:16–19). It hardly takes a business degree to recognize that this was an excellent rate of return. Anyone who can turn a profit of almost 1000 percent—or even 500 percent, in the case of the second servant—knows how to manage other people's money!

Once again, we need to ask what all this means in spiritual terms, because Jesus told this parable to help us understand God's spiritual economy—the business of the kingdom and the second coming of Jesus Christ.

To begin with, the parable teaches that the gospel grows by its own inherent power. When the servants were asked what they had done with what they had, they almost made it sound as if the money had grown all by itself. "Lord, your mina has made ten minas more," the first servant said (Luke 19:16). Similarly, the second servant said, "Lord, your mina has made five minas" (Luke 19:18). These men did not boast about what they had done, but credited their profit to what the master had given them. It was the mina that made the increase.

So it is with the gospel. God tells us to put the gospel to work, and because that gospel is the power of God unto salvation, it makes the kingdom grow. It is amazing what the gospel can do! It delivers people from their sins, turning God's enemies into friends. It brings people from death to life and makes them the sons and the daughters of God. It builds up the church, so that not even the forces of hell can withstand the onslaught of the kingdom of God. It sends people out into the world with the love of Jesus Christ, to serve and to sacrifice. When we see what the gospel has done, both in our own lives and in the lives of people who have been touched by our ministry, we know that none of the credit goes to us. All the credit goes to God, because his gospel is what makes things grow.

The parable teaches us further that our King is coming again, and that when he comes, he will hold us all accountable for what we have done with what we have. As the Scripture says, "We must all appear before the judgment seat of Christ, so that each one may receive what is due for what he has done" (2 Cor. 5:10). "Behold," Jesus says, "I am coming soon, bringing my recompense with me, to repay everyone for what he has done" (Rev. 22:12).

The parable teaches that when the King returns, he will praise his faithful servants and reward us in a way that is proportional to our service. The man who made ten received ten times the reward; the man who made five received five times the reward; and so on. From this we infer that some believers will receive greater honor than others, according to what they have done with what they had. Of course, we will all gain the same entrance into glory. As the Scripture says to every believer in Christ, "there will be richly provided for you an entrance into the eternal kingdom of our Lord and Savior Jesus Christ" (2 Peter 1:11). But in that kingdom there will be reward upon reward for the faithful servants of God, depending on the fruitfulness of their service. J. C. Ryle said it well: "Our title to heaven is all of grace. Our degree of glory in heaven will be proportioned to our works."[4]

These kingdom rewards are presented as further opportunities for service. The man who made ten minas gets to manage ten cities. What he receives is not so much a reward as a responsibility. Since he was faithful in doing something small, God will trust him to do something much larger. This is the way things work in the kingdom of God. We do not begin with big things, but with little things, and if we are faithful with them, God will give us bigger things to do. Do not complain about a smaller sphere of ministry, but be patient with obscure obedience, believing that a wider ministry will come if and when the time is right—even if it does not come until after the second coming. Eventually the reward for faithful service will be a greater opportunity to serve, which is what a servant wants more than anything else in the world. Our great reward will be a greater opportunity to glorify God by serving Jesus Christ. There will be work for us to do when his kingdom comes—vast enterprises of spiritual employment that will last for all eternity.

At the same time, this parable also teaches that the rewards of the kingdom are completely out of proportion to the work that we do. A man who managed a single mina ended up ruling ten cities! What he received was far more than he could ever imagine. In the same way, whatever rewards God may have for us when Jesus returns to rule his forever kingdom will be infinitely beyond our deserving. The Bible promises that when the King returns, everyone who trusts in him will reign with him in glory (2 Tim. 2:12; cf. Rev. 3:21), ruling over nations and kingdoms. Imagine that: someday, by the grace of God, you will sit with Jesus on the throne of the universe!

So let me ask again, in the expectation of eternity: What are you doing with what you have? King Jesus is watching to see whether we can be trusted to serve him. What we do with our time and our money—what we do with the gospel—has eternal significance. Why waste time thinking about earthly ambitions when God has greater glories in store? Hudson Taylor was right when he said, "A little thing is just a little thing, but faith-

---

4. J. C. Ryle, *Expository Thoughts on the Gospels, Luke* (1858; reprint Cambridge: James Clarke, 1976), 2:305.

fulness in a little thing is a great thing."[5] The truth of that statement will be confirmed in glory, when the little things that people do with the gospel will receive their great reward.

## THE WICKED SERVANT'S LOSS

There was one servant who failed to serve the king, and the parable is about him as much as anyone else: "Then another came, saying, 'Lord, here is your mina, which I kept laid away in a handkerchief; for I was afraid of you'" (Luke 19:20).

What this servant did—or failed to do—was shocking. In complete defiance of the instructions he was given, the man wrapped his mina in a handkerchief, hid it under his mattress, and waited for his master to return. Rather than putting his money to good use, this unprofitable servant refused to use the gift that he was given. The other servants were more enterprising; if they had some money, they tried to get a little more. But this man was so afraid of what he might lose that he failed to work for what he could gain.

Many people do the same thing with the gifts that come from God. Rather than putting the gospel to good use, they are afraid to talk about their faith, afraid to give God more of their money than they think they can spare, afraid to do anything for Jesus that goes beyond their own abilities and therefore forces them to trust in the enabling power of the Holy Spirit. Holding back from the clear call of God like this is not humility; it is pride and rebellion and fear.

Notice that rather than owning up to his failure, the third servant tried to blame his master. "I was afraid of you," he said, "because you are a severe man. You take what you did not deposit, and reap what you did not sow" (Luke 19:21). It wasn't *his* fault for being afraid, in other words; it was the king's fault for frightening him. Even if he made some money, the king would just take it away, so why bother? How could he be expected to work for someone who demanded something for nothing?

Once again, this is the same attitude that many people have towards God. They see him as a harsh taskmaster, who never gives but only takes, never

---

5. A. J. Broomhall, *Hudson Taylor and China's Open Century, Book Four: Survivor's Pact* (London: Hodder and Stoughton, 1984) 154.

donates but only demands. This is slander and blasphemy! The truth is that God has given us everything we have, including the very air that we breathe. Furthermore, through Jesus, God has offered himself for our sins. How can we ever say that God has done nothing for us? When we go to the cross, we see that he has done *everything* for us. Therefore, anything God demands is only a small return on what we have already received.

The servant's misrepresentation of his master—like our own unworthy thoughts about God—is contradicted by the rest of the parable. The master was not stingy; he was generous. But just for the sake of argument, the man momentarily granted his servant's premise: "He said to him, 'I will condemn you with your own words, you wicked servant! You knew that I was a severe man, taking what I did not deposit and reaping what I did not sow? Why then did you not put my money in the bank, and at my coming I might have collected it with interest?'" (Luke 19:22–23).

Even on his own terms, the servant should have done better. "If the thought of reward failed to motivate him," writes Richard Phillips, "the fear of retribution should have!"[6] Besides, if what he said about his master was true, then at the very least he should have deposited his mina in the bank. Even if he was too afraid to put the money to good use himself, he should have given it to someone who knew what to do with it.

Do you see how wicked the man was? The word "wicked" may sound severe, but that is how Jesus described him. Really, what else would you call a servant who refused to obey his master's command, slandered his master's good name, and was so scared of making a mistake that he failed to do what he was supposed to do? According to Jesus, it is wickedness not to use what we have to serve our God.

## USE IT OR LOSE IT

Knowing how Jesus thinks about this may help us understand what happened to the third servant at the end of the parable. The newly crowned king "said to those who stood by, 'Take the mina from him, and give it to the one who has the ten minas'" (Luke 19:24). All the man wanted to do was

---

6. Richard D. Phillips, *Turning Your World Upside Down: Kingdom Priorities in the Parables of Jesus* (Phillipsburg, NJ: P&R, 2003), 184.

protect what he had, but because of his disobedience, even that was taken away from him. The rich get richer, while the poor get poorer. Or, to put it even more bluntly, "use it or lose it."

Immediately, the other servants raised the obvious objection: "And they said to him, 'Lord, he has ten minas!'" (Luke 19:25). In other words, that's not fair! Why should someone who has so much get even more, while someone who has next to nothing loses what little he has? The king responded by saying, "I tell you that to everyone who has, more will be given, but from the one who has not, even what he has will be taken away" (Luke 19:26).

This is a hard saying. Yet simply from the standpoint of good business, this was the obvious thing to do; anyone who had the king's money would have done exactly the same thing. Which servant would make the best use of the mina in the handkerchief? Even to ask the question is to answer it. Money should be invested with someone who has proven that he knows how to make it grow, rather than risking it all on someone who by his own negligence is teetering on the verge of bankruptcy.

As a shrewd investor, Jesus takes the same approach to the work we do in ministry. He has entrusted us with the gospel, and now he wants us to be venture capitalists, spiritually speaking. If we handle his investment well, he will give us even more good work to do for the kingdom of God. The person who has, and uses it well, will get even more. But if we refuse to do anything for Jesus at all—well, what should he do with us and with what he has given to us? With Jesus, it is all or nothing.

Scholars have long wondered whether the third servant was saved, or whether he was lost forever. The story does not say. Maybe the wicked servant stands for someone who is in the church but does not actually have a saving relationship with Jesus Christ. J. C. Ryle thus describes him as a "professing Christian who is content with the idle possession of Christianity, and makes no effort to use it for his soul's good, or the glory of God."[7] The man *is* "wicked," after all, and he does lose the gospel, or at least the opportunity to use it for the King. He has no love for his master, and his service is so unfaithful that he has failed to bear any fruit. Is this man really a Christian, or is he merely someone who goes to church? David Gooding asks: "Could anyone who truly believes that Christ gave his life for him, ever turn round

7. Ryle, *Luke*, 2:306.

and tell the Lord that in asking him to work for him, the Lord was asking for something for nothing? And would any one who believes that Christ's death has secured him forgiveness for all his sins, ever tell Christ that he was afraid to work for him in case he made a mistake?"[8]

So perhaps the third servant is not a believer after all. However, Luke's parable is different from the one in Matthew, where the worthless servant is thrown into "the outer darkness," where there is "weeping and gnashing of teeth" (Matt. 25:30). Furthermore, there may be a distinction between the wicked servant in Luke and the citizens (traitors!) who rejected the king outright and met an even more terrible fate. "But as for these enemies of mine," said the king, "who did not want me to reign over them, bring them here and slaughter them before me" (Luke 19:27). This clearly refers to the final judgment and the damnation of God's enemies. On the day of his royal return, Jesus the King will destroy every traitor to his cause and every rebel against his kingdom. The Bible says that Jesus will be "revealed from heaven with his mighty angels in flaming fire, inflicting vengeance on those who do not know God and on those who do not obey the gospel of our Lord Jesus. They will suffer the punishment of eternal destruction, away from the presence of the Lord and from the glory of his might" (2 Thess. 1:7–9).

Since the wicked servant is not explicitly included with the king's enemies, maybe he managed to escape their horrible fate. Maybe he represents instead a fearful believer who does almost nothing for God, but still has some faith in Jesus Christ and thus barely gets saved. Maybe he is like the person who "will suffer loss, though he himself will be saved, but only as through fire" (1 Cor. 3:15). Yet his case seems far from hopeful, his salvation far from secure. Paralyzed by fear, and motivated only by his own self-preservation, he never did anything courageous for the kingdom of God. In the end, he lost his reward, and perhaps with it his very salvation.

The question for us, of course, is what we are doing with what we have. The Master has been gone a long time, but one day soon he will come again, in royal triumph. Are you working hard for his kingdom? Are you making wise investments with your time and money that will strengthen your spiritual portfolio? What are you doing with the gospel?

---

8. David Gooding, *According to Luke: A New Exposition of the Third Gospel* (Grand Rapids: Eerdmans, 1987), 301.

As I ask myself these questions, I have to confess that I have done far too little for Jesus, especially when compared to how much he has done for me. People who are familiar with my preaching and writing sometimes say they are amazed at how much I have done, but it is very little, really. Maybe you have done more than I have; maybe you have done even less—or at least it seems like less to you. But whatever you have done with what you have, how could it ever be enough for Jesus? Even William Carey—the famous pioneer missionary to India—wrote his son a letter that said, "I am this day 58, but how little I have done for God."[9]

As I feel the guilt of my own failures and lost opportunities, I remember the gospel—the gospel that Jesus wants me to use. What that gospel tells me is that my acceptance before God is not based on who I am or what I have done, but on who Jesus is and what he has done. The Westminster Confession of Faith says it well: "The persons of believers being accepted through Christ, their good works also are accepted in Him." It is not just my person that God accepts in Christ, but also my work, with all its failures. The Confession goes on to say that because God looks upon me in his Son, he is "pleased to accept and reward that which is sincere, although accompanied with many weaknesses and imperfections" (16.6).

Praise God! Because of the gospel, what we do with what we have is accepted in Jesus. He is not a harsh taskmaster, but a generous King, who loves to reward the servants who love him and seek to serve him, however small their service. That makes me want to do more for Jesus than ever. What about you?

9. William Carey, quoted in *Christianity Today* (March 2006): 27.

# 82

# HAIL TO THE KING!

## *Luke 19:28–40*

*As he was drawing near—already on the way down the Mount of Olives—the whole multitude of his disciples began to rejoice and praise God with a loud voice for all the mighty works that they had seen, saying, "Blessed is the King who comes in the name of the Lord! Peace in heaven and glory in the highest!"*
(Luke 19:37–38)

We were made to worship the King. Perhaps this explains the fascination that people have with the pageantry of royalty. When kings and queens go on parade, the world stops to watch their regal procession as it grandly passes by.

One summer I took a bus tour of Edinburgh on the very day that Queen Elizabeth II was scheduled to take up residence in the palace at Holyrood House. As the tour guide was outlining the day's events, she suddenly said, "And there's the Queen!" Immediately everyone ran to one side of the bus to see the royal motorcade and hopefully to catch a glimpse of the queen herself. Unfortunately, I never saw her, but it was still a great day to be in Scotland's capital city: royalty was on parade.

Oh, to have been in Jerusalem on the day when the King of all kings rode into the holy city of God, with everyone shouting his praises! Luke tells us that when Jesus "had said these things, he went on ahead, going up to Jerusalem" (Luke 19:28). Ever since he had set his face towards Jerusalem at the end of chapter 9, Jesus had been moving in this direction. From what he had just taught in the parable of the ten minas, it was clear that there would be some sort of delay in the coming of the kingdom of God. Jesus was not in Jerusalem for his coronation; he was going up to the city to die.

Yet even before that cross, God gave a glimpse of the crown by showing what kingly honor Jesus deserved. His royal entrance into Jerusalem was a momentary triumph before an impending tragedy—a triumph that disclosed his true identity and invited people to acknowledge him as their King. Soon Jesus would suffer the humiliation of his crucifixion, but first God wanted people to see who he really was, and for a few moments at least to give him something like the majesty that he deserved.

As we watch the regal procession that Christians usually call Palm Sunday, we see the King claiming his property, displaying his humility, and receiving some of his glory. As we watch, we should ask ourselves this question: Am I ready to give King Jesus the wealth and the worship that he royally deserves?

## THE KING CLAIMS HIS PROPERTY

Luke begins his account of the triumphal approach (not his entry, quite yet) by relating a little incident that turns out to be essential to the unfolding drama. Jesus was only a couple of miles from Jerusalem, and there was something he needed to get before he entered the city:

When he drew near to Bethphage and Bethany, at the mount that is called Olivet, he sent two of the disciples, saying, "Go into the village in front of you, where on entering you will find a colt tied, on which no one has ever yet sat. Untie it and bring it here. If anyone asks you, 'Why are you untying it?' you shall say this: 'The Lord has need of it.'" So those who were sent went away and found it just as he had told them. And as they were untying the colt, its owners said to them, "Why are you untying the colt?" And they said, "The Lord has need of it" (Luke 19:29–34).

329

Luke simply calls the animal a "colt," but Matthew specifies that it was the colt of a donkey, tied up with its mother (Matt. 21:2). What readers often wonder is why the owners agreed to let someone take it away, as Jesus knew they would, with perfect foreknowledge.

At first it almost seems as if the disciples were guilty of rustling live-stock. When the owners saw them untying the donkey, sure enough, they wanted to know what was going on. So they asked the obvious question: "What are you doing?" The answer they were given almost sounds like a password:[1] "The Lord has need of it." So perhaps Jesus had previously arranged to borrow the donkey. Or perhaps the owners recognized the disciples as followers of Jesus, for Jesus often visited this vicinity. At any rate, they certainly seemed to know who the Lord was, and they were ready to serve him.

What is perhaps more remarkable is that Jesus was asking for anything at all. Jesus hardly had any possessions to call his own—just the robe on his back and the sandals on his feet. Apparently he did not have any money either, because later when he wanted to make a point about God and Caesar, he had to borrow someone else's coin to do it (see Luke 20:24). Jesus was also homeless, for as he once said, "the Son of Man has nowhere to lay his head" (Matt. 8:20).

Not only did Jesus have nothing, but he also asked for nothing. In the Gospels we hardly ever see him claiming any property for himself. The whole purpose of his ministry was to let go of his divine privileges so that he could become our servant in salvation (see Phil. 2:1–8). Jesus was always giving things to others, never getting things for himself. Yet just this once, as he makes his final preparations to enter Jerusalem, orchestrating the events of Palm Sunday, Jesus says that he needs the donkey's colt.

Understand that the donkey was rightfully his, simply by virtue of the fact that he made it in the first place. Jesus Christ is the Creator God. The Scripture says, "By him all things were created, in heaven and on earth . . . all things were created through him and for him" (Col. 1:16). So when the disciples untied the donkey and brought it to their Lord, they were bringing a creature that was made *by* Jesus and *for* Jesus. It was his donkey to begin with, to be used for his glory.

---

1. Leon Morris makes this suggestion in *The Gospel According to St. Luke: An Introduction and Commentary*, Tyndale New Testament Commentaries (Grand Rapids: Eerdmans, 1974), 278.

Therefore, from the very beginning of this famous day, we see what it means for Jesus to be the King of all kings. It means that he has the right to claim personal ownership of everything he has made. The psalmist praised God for owning "the cattle on a thousand hills" (Ps. 50:10). The same principle applies to everything else in the entire universe, from the donkeys tied to a thousand fence posts to the stars in a thousand galaxies. It is all the personal property of God the Son.

At the same time, we see how we ought to respond to his claim of ownership. When the owners of the donkey heard that Jesus needed their donkey, they let him have it immediately. They did not claim it as their own, but offered it for the service of their King. Knowing that their Lord had need of it was all they needed to know.

We should take the same attitude toward everything in life that we like to call our own—our money, our time, and all our possessions. If the Lord needs them, then they are his to use as he pleases. The words of Luke 19 can help us evaluate our stewardship. As we think about how we are going to spend our money, we should ask ourselves: "Does the Lord have need of this?" "Does he need it more for the kingdom of God than I do for my own well-being?" When we consider the vast needs of a world that is lost without the gospel, the answer will almost always be yes. The question is whether we are willing to let the King stake his claim to what we own, which is really his royal property to begin with.

## THE KING DISPLAYS HIS HUMILITY

The reason Jesus needed the donkey was to display his humility, in fulfillment of one of the ancient prophecies about his kingship. By riding into Jerusalem on a borrowed beast of burden, the King was making a public statement. Ordinarily, one would expect a king to come with pomp and circumstance—riding a stallion of war at the head of a mighty army, bringing wealth for his royal treasury. That is not the way King Jesus came, however. He came gentle, riding on a donkey, for he knew the words of the prophecy in Zechariah: "Rejoice greatly, O daughter of Zion! Shout aloud, O daughter of Jerusalem! Behold, your king is coming to you; righteous and having salvation is he, humble and mounted on a donkey, on a colt, the foal of a donkey" (Zech. 9:9; cf. Gen. 49:10–11).

This prophecy explains why Jesus sent his disciples to get a purebred donkey—specifically a colt that had never been ridden. He knew the ancient prophecy, which foretold that the king would come bringing salvation and riding on a donkey's foal. Jesus needed the animal to serve as a prop in the drama of redemption.

As Jesus rode down the Mount of Olives, directly opposite the city of Jerusalem, he was presenting himself as the King. Earlier Luke had prophesied that Jesus would be the King (e.g., Luke 1:32), but now his royalty was in full view. He was riding the donkey of Israel's kingship. The people of Jerusalem immediately recognized this royal symbol, as is clear from their shouts of acclamation: "Blessed is the King who comes in the name of the Lord!" (Luke 19:38). When the people saw Jesus riding towards Jerusalem, they knew he was coming as their King.

What they did not understand was what kind of king he had come to be, although maybe the donkey should have given them a clue. This was not a political statement, as most of them thought; it was a spiritual statement. Jesus had not come to take control of the government. He had not come to overthrow the Romans through military might. No, Jesus was a new kind of king. He had come in meekness and gentleness to be the Messiah–King of peace. If people accepted him, he would receive their praise. But if they rejected him, he would do nothing to defend himself, even to the very point of death.

Jesus rides into our lives the same way today: with all gentleness and humility. He does not crush us with his superior might, but says, "Come to me, all who labor and are heavy laden, and I will give you rest. Take my yoke upon you, and learn from me, for I am gentle and lowly in heart, and you will find rest for your souls" (Matt. 11:28–29).

If Jesus is the King of gentleness, then everyone who loves him should serve him with the same kind of humility. One scholar comments that Jesus could just as well have ridden into the city on a high horse. But the donkey "stands out as a deliberate rejection of this symbol of arrogant trust in human might, expressing subservience to the sovereignty of God. Jerusalem's king is of humble mien, yet victorious, and so it has always been that the church does not effectively spread the gospel by sword or by arrogance, but by mirroring the humble spirit of its king and savior."[2] Rather than

---

2. Thomas E. McComiskey, "Zechariah," in *The Minor Prophets: An Exegetical and Expository Commentary*, 3 vols. (Grand Rapids: Baker, 1998), 3:1166.

riding in to set everyone straight, we are more like Jesus when we come to people with our Savior's gentleness and peace.

## THE KING RECEIVES HIS GLORY

After claiming his property and displaying his humility, the King received his glory (or at least some of it). This is where Luke's emphasis falls: on the royal reception Jesus was given as he rode towards Jerusalem.

The first people to give him the glory were his own closest disciples. This detail is sometimes overlooked, but it sets the stage for everything that follows. After they untied the donkey, "they brought it to Jesus, and throwing their cloaks on the colt, they set Jesus on it" (Luke 19:35). Here was the first acknowledgment that Jesus was the King. Kings do not ride bareback; they sit in a royal saddle, riding a mount decorated with royal purple. If Jesus was the King, then he was too exalted to sit directly on the donkey. The dignity of his royal person demanded special honor; he needed a saddle fit for a king. In the absence of anything else they could find, the disciples stripped off their cloaks and covered the donkey's back.

Then, in a touching display of intimate affection and private homage, they lifted Jesus up and set him on the donkey (Luke 19:35). Here was another exaltation—another demonstration of his kingly glory. The disciples wanted Jesus to receive the honor that he alone deserves. Like athletes who lift their coach up on their shoulders after winning a championship, they took Jesus and put him in the place of a king, setting him on the back of his royal mount.

The disciples were the first to give the King his glory, but soon others started to follow their example: "And as he rode along, they spread their cloaks on the road" (Luke 19:36). This illustrates what happens when we lift Jesus up and worship him as our King: other people start to join us in acknowledging his royal majesty. In this case, they paid their homage by throwing their outer garments (also palm branches—a detail mentioned in the other Gospels, but not in Luke) down on the road in front of him. This was the ancient way to welcome a king. It was a way of saying that Jesus was too worthy to ride on an ordinary road; he deserved a royal carpet. When people threw down their cloaks, they were saying, "King Jesus, you are so much greater than I am—so much more worthy of honor—that when your donkey walks all over my clothes it is not an insult to me, but my privilege."

333

Suddenly and spontaneously, the crowds began to swell. First one person cast his coat before Jesus, then another person, and then another. The closer Jesus came to Jerusalem, the more people joined his parade. Luke tells us, "As he was drawing near—already on the way down the Mount of Olives— the whole multitude of his disciples began to rejoice and praise God with a loud voice for all the mighty works that they had seen" (Luke 19:37).

It was the start of the Passover feast, and the pilgrims were streaming into the holy city. As Jesus rode down the Mount of Olives into the Kidron Valley, and then up to Jerusalem, great throngs of worshipers were pressing towards the city gates. Expectations were running high, so they were excited already; but when they heard that the King was coming, the news supercharged the crowd like lightning. The atmosphere instantly became electric, the mood euphoric.

People love royal pageantry anyway, but this was the culmination of everything the disciples had been hoping for—the proof that Jesus was the Christ. They had seen him heal the sick, cure the blind, and raise the dead. They had heard him preach the good news of the kingdom of God, offering forgiveness through repentance. They had come to know him as the Messiah—the Christ—who had all the power of God.

Now, as Jesus rode his royal mile into the holy city, they could see even more clearly that he was the King, and they wanted everyone to make way for his royal procession. The shouts of praise that came to their lips were ancient songs reserved for the coming king: "Blessed is the King who comes in the name of the Lord! Peace in heaven and glory in the highest!" (Luke 19:38).

The disciples were echoing the words of the psalmist, who said, "Blessed is he who comes in the name of the LORD! We bless you from the house of the LORD" (Ps. 118:26). These words come from one of the "Psalms of Ascent" that the pilgrims sang every year on their way up to Jerusalem. Except on this occasion the disciples took those ancient words and made them more specific. They knew that Psalm 118 was a promise of the Messiah and that the Messiah was royalty. So they took what was implicit in the psalm and made it explicit. Rather than saying, "Blessed is *he* who comes," they said, "Blessed is *the King* who comes." Jesus was Christ the King!

Then the disciples lifted their "Hail to the king!" all the way to the courts of heaven. "Peace in heaven," they said, "and glory in the highest!" (Luke 19:38). These familiar words echoed the birth narratives at the beginning of Luke's Gospel, when the angels said, "Glory to God in the highest, and on earth peace among those with whom he is pleased!" (Luke 2:14). The King had come, and at his coming people gave glory to God. This is the very reason that we were made: to give glory to the Most High God in the name of Jesus Christ, our King.

What would you have done if you were there that day? Would you have joined the parade? Would you have said, "Hail to the King!" and thrown your clothes down in front of his royal donkey? Worship Jesus now, for he is just as worthy now—worthy to receive all praise.

## JOIN THE PARADE

Strangely enough, some of the people in Jerusalem refused to join the celebration. Those grumpy old Pharisees—who always manage to sound like the party poopers of the Gospels—did not believe that Jesus was the Christ, or that he deserved to be worshiped as the King. Therefore, they thought that what the people were doing was blasphemy: "And some of the Pharisees in the crowd said to him, 'Teacher, rebuke your disciples'" (Luke 19:39). These men never did appreciate Jesus. Because of their jealousy, his popularity always aroused their hostility. Here they even tried to rain on his Palm Sunday parade by silencing his praise. This is the way some people are. Not only do they refuse to worship Jesus, but they wish that no one else would worship him either. If only Christians would curb their enthusiasm!

But the King will have his worship. When the Pharisees told him to turn down the volume, Jesus answered, "I tell you, if these were silent, the very stones would cry out" (Luke 19:40). By saying this, Jesus was claiming that he deserved the worship of the whole creation. Even if human beings stop singing his praises, he will still have the glory that he deserves. Jesus was riding down the Mount of Olives when he said this, and if necessary, every stone on that mountainside would join his choir. The very stones of the ground would open their mouths to declare their Maker's praise. The Bible says that the creation "waits with eager longing" for the day of salvation, when it will be "set free from its bondage to decay and obtain the freedom of the glory of the children of God" (Rom. 8:19, 21). Here Jesus gives us the sense that in that painful longing, the creation is almost bursting to sing its song. The rocks are ready at any moment to break their stony silence and shout for joy that Jesus is the King.

There are still some critical scholars who say that Jesus was just a man, that he never claimed to be divine. But what sense can they make of this passage? Here people were praising Jesus as their King. What happened when the Pharisees tried to stop them? Jesus did not say, "You know, you're right: people really shouldn't worship me." On the contrary, Jesus refused to be acknowledged as anything except the King! In fact, he said that if people stopped worshiping him, then the whole universe would fill the silence with praise. Jesus could not and would not deny that this is what he truly deserved. Therefore, Palm Sunday is one of the clearest proofs that Jesus really claimed to be the Christ; it shows us for sure that he is our God and our King.

Will you give King Jesus the honor that he royally deserves? As amazing as it must have been to see his triumphant ride into Jerusalem, Jesus has even more glory now. After he was crucified for our sins, he was raised from the dead and then exalted to the right hand of God, where he sits on his royal throne. The King may not be on parade today, but even now he is receiving the homage he deserves from people all over the world—men and women and children who have been saved by his grace. We have as much opportunity to praise him as anyone. So give Jesus the honor he deserves: acknowledge his sovereign kingship by throwing your life down before him, asking him to govern everything you think and say and do.

One day Jesus will ride again in triumph. On the last of all days, he will come with the angels to gather his people into his royal train. What joy it will be to see the King enter his glory! I never did see the queen of England, but I live in the hope that one day I will see the King of all kings.

This is the theme of some of my favorite hymns—the ones that fill me with the greatest awe and give me the most goosebumps. They are hymns of exaltation in which Jesus is on parade and the veil of heaven is parted long enough for us to see his regal glory. For example, we catch a fleeting glimpse in the last stanza of "At the Name of Jesus" by Caroline Noel:

Brothers, this Lord Jesus shall return again,
With his Father's glory, with his angel train;
For all wreaths of empire meet upon his brow,
And our hearts confess him King of glory now.

As we sing these words, we can almost see Jesus with all his angels, wearing the crowns of all nations.

Or consider the triumphant words of William Walsham How's famous hymn "For All the Saints":

But lo! there breaks a yet more glorious day;
The saints triumphant rise in bright array;
The King of glory passes on his way.
Alleluia! Alleluia!

We see Jesus again in a hymn by Thomas Kelly:

Look, ye saints, the sight is glorious:
See the Man of Sorrows now;
From the fight returned victorious,
Ev'ry knee to him shall bow.
Crown him! Crown him!
Crowns become the Victor's brow.

Hark! those bursts of acclamation!
Hark! those loud triumphant chords!
Jesus takes the highest station;
O what joy the sight affords!
Crown him! Crown him!
King of kings and Lord of lords.

As glorious as it was to see Jesus on the first Palm Sunday, it will be infinitely more glorious to see him go up to take his eternal throne in the city of the new Jerusalem—the heavenly procession of God's once and forever King. Everyone who trusts in Jesus for salvation will be part of the cheering crowd on that great day, straining to see the King. When you get your first glimpse of Jesus in that parade, your heart will leap to the praise that you were born to give, and you will shout, "Oh, the King, the King! It is Jesus, my King! Hallelujah! Hosanna! Hail to the King!"

# 83

# JESUS IN JERUSALEM

## *Luke 19:41—20:8*

*And he was teaching daily in the temple. The chief priests and the*
*scribes and the principal men of the people were seeking to destroy*
*him, but they did not find anything they could do, for all the*
*people were hanging on his words.* (Luke 19:47–48)

or many decades a growing movement of Chinese Christians
has had a burning passion to carry the gospel "back to Jerusalem." These faithful men and women believe they have a
calling from God to evangelize more than five thousand unreached people
groups that live along the old Silk Road between China and Jerusalem—the
ancient city where Christianity began with the crucifixion and resurrection
of Jesus Christ.

One of the first men to have this vision was Uncle Simon Zhao, an evangelist who was imprisoned by the Communists for more than three decades.
As Uncle Simon languished in jail, his dream of going back to Jerusalem
almost died, but when he was finally released, his testimony inspired a new
generation of Chinese Christians to complete the work that others had
begun. Uncle Simon taught them to sing this missionary song:

Jerusalem is in my dreams;
Jerusalem is in my tears.
I looked for you and found you in the fire of the altar;
I looked for you and found you in Jesus' nail-scarred hands.

Jesus came to destroy the chains of death;
He came to open the path to glory!
Let's hurry to fulfill the promise of God![1]

Few Christians anywhere have anything like the life-or-death passion that our Chinese brothers and sisters have for reaching the lost and building the city of God. Their passion flows from the heart of Jesus himself—the Savior of love, who first went to Jerusalem to suffer and die, before rising again with life for the world.

## O JERUSALEM, JERUSALEM

With the triumphal entrance that Jesus made to Jerusalem on the first Palm Sunday, we have begun what many Christians call Passion Week—the passion of the Christ. The term "passion" comes from the Latin word for suffering *(pati)*. So the expression "Passion Week" refers to the suffering that Jesus endured on his way to Calvary, culminating with the cross. The passion of the Christ is his death by crucifixion.

We also use the word "passion" to refer to any "ardent affection," or to an "intense, driving, or overmastering feeling or conviction."[2] The week that Jesus died was a "passion week" in this sense as well, for if ever there was an ardent affection, it was the love that Jesus had for lost people in the city. And if ever there was an intense conviction, it was the zeal that Jesus had for the worship of God.

Jesus Christ was a man of perfect passion. He was not weepy or sentimental, but he did cry about the things that broke his loving heart. He was not moody or bad-tempered, but he was angry about hypocrisy and injustice. In the intensity of his emotions, we see the true and perfect humanity

---

1. Paul Hattaway et al., *Back to Jerusalem: Three Chinese House Leaders Share Their Vision to Complete the Great Commission* (Waynesboro, GA: Authentic Media, 2003), 56.
2. See *Webster's Ninth New Collegiate Dictionary* (Springfield, MA: Merriam-Webster, 1984).

of Jesus Christ. Here, as Jesus enters Jerusalem, we see his love for God's city and his zeal for God's house. We also see how people responded to this passionate man, either by seeking to destroy him or by hanging on his every word. "Jesus went to Jerusalem," writes Henri Nouwen, "to announce the Good News to the people of that city. And Jesus knew that he was going to put a choice before them: Will you be my disciple, or will you be my executioner? There is no middle ground here. Jesus went to Jerusalem to put people in a situation where they had to say yes or no."[3]

We first saw the love that Jesus had for the city back in chapter 13, when he said, "O Jerusalem, Jerusalem, the city that kills the prophets. . . . You will not see me until you say, 'Blessed is he who comes in the name of the Lord'" (Luke 13:34–35). Now Jesus had come in the name of the Lord, to the praise of all the people: "And when he drew near and saw the city, he wept over it" (Luke 19:41). It seemed like a day of triumph for Jesus, but as he made his ascent to Jerusalem and the holy city came into view, he lifted a loud lament. His soul was grieving, even wailing for the rejection of his people and the judgment they would suffer for their sins.

Notice the dramatic contrast between what the people were saying and what Jesus was feeling. It was Palm Sunday, and Jesus was riding into Jerusalem on a donkey—a symbol of royal peace. People were singing his praises and calling him their king. Yet Jesus rightly perceived that they did not know who he really was, and so he wept. The people were cheering, but the King of Sorrows was crying: "Would that you, even you, had known on this day the things that make for peace! But now they are hidden from your eyes" (Luke 19:42). What some people still regard as a triumphal entry was, for Jesus, a tearful entry.

Not that Jesus was weeping for himself, of course, as if he were prone to self-pity. No, he was sobbing with compassion for lost sinners who could not or would not see who he was. He was coming to them with the peace of salvation, but they refused to have it. The "things that make for peace," as Jesus called them, are faith and repentance—faith in Jesus such as the blind man had on the Jericho road, and repentance for sin such as Zacchaeus made when he climbed out of his sycamore tree. The things that make for peace are surrender and submission to the royal lordship of Jesus Christ.

---

3. Henri J. M. Nouwen, "A Spirituality of Waiting," as quoted in Richard A. Kauffman, "Holy Week," *Christianity Today* (April 2006): 94.

But the people could not see it. They were so close to Jesus that they could practically touch him, but they did not recognize his true identity as the suffering Savior. So Jesus wept.

Is anything sadder than someone who comes close to touching Jesus but never grabs hold of him by faith? It broke the Savior's heart, especially because he knew how much they would suffer for rejecting his grace. This added to his sorrow. Jesus did not grieve for their rejection only, but also for the suffering it would bring. "For the days will come upon you," he said, "when your enemies will set up a barricade around you and surround you and hem you in on every side and tear you down to the ground, you and your children within you. And they will not leave one stone upon another in you, because you did not know the time of your visitation" (Luke 19:43–44).

All of these words came true. With perfect foreknowledge, the Son of God was prophesying what would happen when Jerusalem was conquered by the Romans in A.D. 70. The city was surrounded as the general Titus set up giant siege works around its walls. The stones of the city were torn down, the temple was destroyed, and the streets ran red with the blood of women and children. Caesar wanted to make it impossible for anyone to believe that Jerusalem had ever been inhabited. To that end, Titus tore everything down except for three large towers. These he left standing to show how great the city had been and thus to prove the superior power of Rome. According to Josephus, the devastation was so complete that when the general saw it, he "threw his arms heavenward, uttered a groan, and called God to witness that this was not his doing."[4]

This all happened just the way that Jesus said it would, according to the justice of God. Since God is perfectly righteous and supremely worthy of our worship, we are always culpable for our failure to give him the full honor that he deserves. This is especially true when it comes to our relationship with Jesus Christ. Do we acknowledge him as the King of our world? Is this evident in the choices we are making about what we do with our bodies, how we spend our money, the way we treat our families, and what we do in our daily work? If we do not honor Christ as King, then we will be lost when the judgment comes, just like the people of Jerusalem.

4. The story of Jerusalem's fall is retold in R. Kent Hughes, *Luke: That You May Know the Truth*, 2 vols., Preaching the Word (Wheaton, IL: Crossway, 1998), 2:243.

How sad it is to know that some people get close enough to see Jesus but never trust him as their Savior, never receive him as their King, and never reach the joys of heaven. It is so sad that it made Jesus weep. Never imagine that God is unmoved by the sufferings of lost sinners; he has shown us his compassion in Christ. Indeed, Jesus still weeps for us, if we are still lost in our sins. He weeps for us as he wept for Jerusalem. Jesus knew that judgment was coming. As the Second Person of the Trinity, he had divinely ordained the destruction of Jerusalem as an act of his holy justice. Nevertheless, he wept to see the day, and his tears teach us to mourn for a world that is lost in sin. As we weep for the lost people we love, we may know that Jesus knows our sorrow.

When was the last time that you cried tears of concern for people who do not know Jesus—especially people who are lost in the city? J. C. Ryle said, "We know but little of true Christianity, if we do not feel a deep concern about the souls of unconverted people. A lazy indifference about the spiritual state of others, may doubtless save us much trouble. To care nothing whether our neighbors are going to heaven or hell, is no doubt the way of the world." But this attitude, says Ryle, is "very unlike Christ."[5] To have the passion that Jesus had for people who are lost in their sins is to weep for their sorry condition and cry out for their salvation.

## HOUSE OF PRAYER

If Jesus Christ had a crying passion for the lost, he also had a consuming zeal for the worship of God. We see this as "he entered the temple and began to drive out those who sold, saying to them, 'It is written, "My house shall be a house of prayer," but you have made it a den of robbers'" (Luke 19:45–46).

This dramatic confrontation brings the story full circle. The Gospel of Luke began at the temple, with the angel appearing to Zechariah in the Holy Place and heralding the first good news of salvation. Jesus has been to the temple several times since: once in infancy for purification (Luke 2:22–38); once in adolescence to dialogue with the scribes (Luke 2:41–49);

5. J. C. Ryle, *Expository Thoughts on the Gospels, Luke* (1858; reprint Cambridge: James Clarke, 1976), 2:314.

and once as a man to withstand the temptations of Satan (Luke 4:9–12).[6] Now, at the end of his earthly ministry, Jesus has come to the temple in Jerusalem for the last time. His coming is the fulfillment of Malachi's ancient prophecy: "And the Lord whom you seek will suddenly come to his temple" (Mal. 3:1).

In coming to the temple, Jesus was coming to a building of magnificent splendor—the crowning jewel of Jerusalem. King Herod had spent vast sums of money to renovate the temple complex. With its massive stones of dazzling white marble, it was one of the most beautiful buildings in the world. It was also a building of profound spiritual significance. The temple was the place of Israel's pilgrimage, the center of Jewish religion, the dwelling place of God on earth. It was the place where God had promised to meet his people—the very house of God.

Yet the temple had also become a place of religious corruption. In going to the temple, therefore, Jesus was going to the source of Israel's spiritual problems. What he found there made him extremely angry. Matthew tells us that Jesus threw chairs and overturned tables (Matt. 21:12). Mark adds that he "would not allow anyone to carry anything through the temple" (Mark 11:16). Luke's account is somewhat more restrained. He simply says that Jesus "began to drive out those who sold" (Luke 19:45), but this too was an act of spiritual violence. The verb Luke uses for driving out (*ekballō*) is used elsewhere in the Gospels for casting out demons (e.g., Mark 1:34). Jesus was there to clean house.

What made Jesus so mad? Obviously, his outrage had something to do with buying and selling. It was almost Passover, and tens of thousands of pilgrims were thronging into the city. All of them needed unblemished animals to offer as sacrifices, and all of the men needed half-shekels to pay the temple tax in local currency. This required a good deal of buying and selling and money-changing. The exchange rates were high, and travelers were at the mercy of big city prices at a major tourist event. It was very big business, and it was all under the financial control of the high priest, whom the historian Josephus rather cynically called "the great procurer of money."[7]

6. The Gospel of John records additional visits that Jesus made to Jerusalem, especially for the major religious festivals.

7. Josephus, *The Antiquities of the Jews* (20.205), quoted in Hughes, *Luke*, 2:246.

Seeing all this buying and selling made Jesus angry. He hated to see his Father's house turned into a marketplace—the commercialization of religion. Here is how David Gooding describes what had gone wrong at the temple:

> Somebody, of course, had to sell the required sheep and birds to would-be worshippers; but these sales should have been left to secular trade, unassociated with the sacred precincts and activities of the temple. For the temple authorities not only to allow this trading to go on in the temple courts, but to profit unduly from the sales themselves was not only inappropriate, it was scandalous. Instead of being priestly intermediaries to help men find worship and be blessed by God, they had become middlemen, turning their priesthood into a commercial monopoly in order to make financial profit out of men's quest for God. Thus they robbed men, for it is difficult to experience the grace of God and the free gift of his salvation through the services of men bent on making money out of one's spiritual need. They also robbed God, treating his Word and sacraments as though they were the stock-in-trade of their business, and treating God's people not as God's possession, to be developed for God's enjoyment, but as a market to which they as the professionals had exclusive rights.[8]

The same thing happens today whenever ministry is done for the money. It takes money to do certain kinds of ministry, of course, and there are godly ways to encourage the support of Christian work through financial giving. But Christ is not a commodity, and his gospel is not for sale. When we see Jesus on a T-shirt, therefore, or watch health and wealth teaching on television, or hear about churches turning into virtual shopping malls, we are witnessing an affront to the holiness of Christ.

Buying and selling are symptoms of a deeper problem in the heart. To see what that problem is, we need to consider carefully the two quotations that Jesus made from the Old Testament. He said, "It is written, 'My house shall be a house of prayer,' but you have made it a den of robbers" (Luke 19:46).

The first part of this quotation comes from the prophet Isaiah, who said, "my house shall be called a house of prayer for all peoples" (Isa. 56:7). The phrase "for all peoples" is important because this was the prophet's main

---

8. David Gooding, *According to Luke: A New Exposition of the Third Gospel* (Grand Rapids: Eerdmans, 1987), 314.

concern. Listen to Isaiah's fuller prophecy: "And the foreigners who join themselves to the LORD, to minister to him, to love the name of the LORD, and to be his servants . . . these I will bring to my holy mountain, and make them joyful in my house of prayer. . . . The Lord GOD, who gathers the outcasts of Israel, declares, 'I will gather yet others to him besides those already gathered'" (Isa. 56:6–8).

This prophecy is about nothing less than the worldwide mission of the gospel. From the time that the temple was first built in Jerusalem, God had always intended that his house would be a house of prayer for the nations (see 1 Kings 8:41–43). This is why its outermost court was called "the Court of the Gentiles." But who can pray in a supermarket? By buying and selling in the outer court, the money changers were effectively excluding Gentiles from the worship of God, and thus they were failing to fulfill their mission to the world. This is what made Jesus so angry. It was not simply what the people were doing—all the buying and selling; it was also what they were *not* doing: praying to God or reaching the lost.

The second part of the quotation is equally condemning. When Jesus said that God's house had become "a den of robbers," he was quoting from a famous sermon that Jeremiah preached at the very gates of the temple. Jeremiah said, "Has this house, which is called by my name, become a den of robbers?" (Jer. 7:11). That is exactly what the temple had become: a den of robbers. The people of Jeremiah's day were robbing God by neglecting the poor, forsaking widows, and abandoning orphans. Yet in their hypocrisy they still came to worship as if they had done nothing wrong. In effect, the temple had become a safe house—a place for criminals to gather.

When Jesus saw people doing the same thing in his day, it made him angry, and rightly so. In all their buying and selling they were neglecting the poor and forgetting the true worship of God. The house of God was no longer a house of prayer; it had become a haunt for hypocrites who worshiped God neither in spirit nor in truth.

The angry entrance that Jesus made to the temple shows where his passion lies, and therefore where our own passions ought to lie. Jesus has a passion for the lost, for reaching people who are outside the community of faith. He has a passion for the poor, for remembering to show mercy to people that society has forgotten. He has a passion for justice, for standing against persons and systems who perpetrate evil. He has a passion for prayer, for worshiping God with the sincerity of a true heart. He has a passion for making the life of faith the main business of life.

What is your passion? Invite the lost into your life; do not let other activities (including your religious activities) crowd them out. Remember to do deeds of mercy; do not forget the poor. Engage actively in the life of private and corporate prayer; do not wander through life like a person without a God. Do not spend your energy buying and selling, but make the worship of the church the marketplace for your soul. The Bible says that your body is a temple for the Holy Spirit, where Jesus dwells by faith (see 1 Cor. 3:16). Be sure to make that inner temple a house for prayer, lest it should become a den of robbers that steals money from the poor and worship from God.

## By Whose Authority?

We can only lament that some of the same sins which made Jesus so angry in Jerusalem are so common in the contemporary church. Rather than having a burden for the lost, a heart for the poor, and a soul for prayer, we are lazy in our evangelism, greedy in our materialism, and stingy with our prayers. But Jesus came to clean things up, and it is important to notice how he did it: by teaching the Word of God. Jesus did not simply drive people out of the temple, but claimed it for his pulpit and started preaching the kingdom of God. This was the last week of his life, and Luke tells us that Jesus "was teaching daily in the temple" (Luke 19:47). There in the house of God he was giving lost people the gospel, teaching them to show mercy and calling them to prayer—all things that were at the heart of his passion.

Sadly, some people refused to hear a word of it. Luke tells us, "The chief priests and the scribes and the principal men of the people were seeking to destroy him" (Luke 19:47). Of course they were! They were against everything that Jesus stood for. They were for making money, but he was for helping the poor. They were for the saved, but he was for the lost. They were for going to the house of God, but he was for worship and prayer. Even worse, from their perspective, Jesus was preaching his passions in the very temple which they had worked so hard to control. He was a threat to their entire livelihood, so they were determined to destroy him.

Luke tells us how they tried to do it: "One day, as Jesus was teaching the people in the temple and preaching the gospel, the chief priests and the scribes with the elders came up and said to him, 'Tell us by what authority you do these things, or who it is that gave you this authority'" (Luke 20:1–2). When most teachers taught theology, they referred to other authorities—the rabbis of the past. But Jesus taught on the basis of his own authority, and the religious establishment resented this bitterly. What gave him the right to take over the temple like this and teach without their permission? What gave him the right to demand the gospel for the lost and the temple for prayer?

At its heart, this is a question that many people have about Jesus: What gives him the right? What gives him the right to tell me what to do with my money, or to demand my worship, or to tell me that he is the only way to eternal life? Tell us, Jesus, by what authority do you do these things?

When the religious leaders asked Jesus this question, they were trying to trap him on a charge of blasphemy. His entire ministry had been conducted on the basis of his own divine authority. Jesus never asked anyone's permission to perform miracles or to preach the kingdom of God. He just did it! He was acting like God incarnate (which, of course, he was). Yet this is where the religious leaders thought that they could trap Jesus, because if Jesus was not truly God then he was guilty of blasphemy—a capital offense. If he acted as if he had the authority, but really didn't, they could put him to death.

Jesus countered their envious, devious question with a question all his own: "He answered them, 'I also will ask you a question. Now tell me, Was the baptism of John from heaven or from man?'" (Luke 20:3–4). This should have been a no-brainer. We met John the Baptist at the beginning of Luke's Gospel. He was the forerunner to the Messiah (Luke 1:17)—a man sent from God (John 1:6) to prepare the way of the Lord. Therefore, John's baptism was from heaven, as most people knew.

Most people, that is, except for the scribes and priests. They had rejected John's ministry, refusing to be baptized (see Luke 7:30). So for them the question that Jesus raised was a real stumper—something they had to think about for a while: "And they discussed it with one another, saying, 'If we say, "From heaven," he will say, "Why did you not believe him?" But if we say, "From man," all the people will stone us to death, for they are convinced that John was a prophet'" (Luke 20:5–6).

These poor men were caught on the horns of an awkward dilemma. They had been trying to trap Jesus, but now they themselves were trapped in a lose/lose situation. They did not believe that John's baptism was heaven-sent, and if they said that they did, it would only make people wonder why they themselves were never baptized. Furthermore, John was the one who said that Jesus was the Christ. If his ministry was heavenly, then why didn't they believe in Jesus? Saying that John's baptism came from heaven was contrary to their whole position on Jesus.

On the other hand, they could not deny John's baptism either, because if they did, the people would tear them apart. John was gone, but not forgotten, and the people who were thronging to Jesus were many of the same people who loved John the Baptist. The religious leaders had tried to discredit Jesus by questioning his authority, but now they were in danger of publicly discrediting themselves!

Too proud to admit that they had made a mistake, and too people-pleasing to take a stand for what they believed, there was nothing these men could say: "So they answered that they did not know where [John's baptism] came from" (Luke 20:7). Then, having won a complete triumph over his accusers, Jesus said to them, "Neither will I tell you by what authority I do these things" (Luke 20:8).

Jesus was under absolutely no obligation whatsoever to answer a question that was designed to destroy him. But there was no doubt as to where his authority came from: He spoke with the invincible authority of almighty God. We may question Jesus as long as we like, asking him all the questions that trouble us in a fallen world—the questions we sometimes think that even God is hard pressed to answer—but we will never catch him at a disadvantage. The questions that really cannot be answered are the ones that Jesus has for us, if we refuse to believe that he is the Son of God, the King of heaven, and the Savior of the world.

Rather than questioning Jesus the way the religious leaders did, we should trust him with our very lives, now and forever. We should respond to him the way the rest of the people at the temple did. Luke tells us that "all the people were hanging on his words" (Luke 19:48). At first glance, this translation sounds as if it is taking liberties with the Greek text. Did Luke really say that people were "hanging on his words"? Yes, that *is* what Luke said. Literally, he said, "all the people hearing hung on him." They were captivated by his passion for the lost, his passion for the nations, and his passion for God. Whatever Jesus had to say, they wanted to hear it. In colloquial English we say it like this: "They were hanging on his every word." Or, if we take Luke even more literally, maybe he was saying that they were hanging on Jesus himself, holding on to him by faith, trusting him for their salvation.

What is your response to this passionate man? Let your heart be touched by the tender compassion he had for lost people in the city. Let your soul be moved by his zeal for the worship of God's house. Let your spirit be captivated by his vision for reaching the whole world with the message of his grace. Surrender your mind to his supreme authority. Hang on to the words of Jesus Christ! Hang on to Jesus himself, especially in his death on the cross and resurrection from the grave. Then his passions will become your passions: a love for the lost that stretches from Jerusalem to the ends of the earth, a heart for prayer, and holy zeal for the glory of God.

# 84

# THE MURDER OF
# THE OWNER'S SON

## *Luke 20:9–18*

*"Then the owner of the vineyard said, 'What shall I do? I will
send my beloved son; perhaps they will respect him.' But when the
tenants saw him, they said to themselves, 'This is the heir. Let us
kill him, so that the inheritance may be ours.'"* (Luke 20:13–14)

esus of Nazareth is the greatest storyteller who ever lived—the
prince of parables. None of his stories is longer than a page,
and yet every last one of them is a perfect masterpiece. Jesus
told stories about rocks and trees, sinners and saints, farmers and businessmen, fathers and sons. Every time he tells us a story, he inspires our imagi-
nations and gives us a deeper understanding of the kingdom of God.

With every story he told, our Savior also took one step closer to the cross.
Jesus was in Jerusalem now, the city where he came to die. Everything in
the Gospel of Luke has been preparing us for this, from the prophecy that
a sword would pierce his mother's soul (Luke 2:35), right up to the tears of
sorrow that Jesus shed on his way into the holy city (Luke 19:41–44). Ever
since he said that he must be rejected and killed (Luke 9:22) and ever since

he "set his face to go to Jerusalem" (Luke 9:51), we have known that this man was destined to die.

The Storyteller and the Suffering Servant are one. It seems only natural, therefore, for his last full parable in the Gospel of Luke to be about the death of a father's only son. It was the last week of his life on earth, and Jesus told a gospel parable about the cross and the judgment to come.

## THE ALLEGORY OF THE VINE

The parable Jesus told is sometimes called "The Wicked Tenants," but it is more accurate to call it "The Murder of the Owner's Son." Here is how Jesus told it:

> A man planted a vineyard and let it out to tenants and went into another country for a long while. When the time came, he sent a servant to the tenants, so that they would give him some of the fruit of the vineyard. But the tenants beat him and sent him away empty-handed. And he sent another servant. But they also beat and treated him shamefully, and sent him away empty-handed. And he sent yet a third. This one also they wounded and cast out. (Luke 20:9–12)

Usually we need to be careful not to overinterpret the parables by finding spiritual meaning in every detail. This is the most allegorical of all the parables, however, and in it each of the main characters stands for someone. Rather obviously, the man who planted the vineyard stands for God. In effect, he is Israel's landlord—the property owner who gave the Promised Land to the people of God. In the parable the owner is an absentee landlord; he has been gone for a very long time. He is also a long-suffering landlord. Despite the ill treatment that his servants received when they went to collect the rent, he patiently and mercifully gives them every opportunity to pay what they owe. This is the way God is: even when we fail again and again, he patiently invites our repentance and longs for our obedience.

If God is the landowner, then the vineyard must stand for the people of Israel (or perhaps, more accurately, Israel's place of privilege as the people of God). This is a familiar image from the Old Testament. When Asaph praised God for Israel's experience in the exodus, he said, "You brought a vine out of Egypt; you drove out the nations and planted it" (Ps. 80:8). But Israel was under attack in Asaph's day, so the psalmist said, "Turn again, O God of hosts! Look down from heaven, and see; have regard for this vine, the stock that your right hand planted, and for the son whom you made strong for yourself" (Ps. 80:14–15). We find the same imagery in the prophets. Jeremiah said that God planted Israel like "a choice vine" (Jer. 2:21). Hosea called it a "luxuriant vine" (Hos. 10:1). However, Ezekiel lamented that the vine had become withered and useless (Ezek. 15:1–6; 19:10–14), while Joel said it had been stripped bare by enemy nations (Joel 1:7).

Perhaps the most famous prophecy is the one from Isaiah. It is really a love song, and a lament—"The Song of the Vineyard." The prophet begins by saying, "Let me sing for my beloved my love song concerning his vineyard: My beloved had a vineyard on a very fertile hill" (Isa. 5:1). Isaiah goes on to describe all the hard work the owner had to do to start his vineyard. Yet it all ended in disappointment, because the only fruit it ever produced was wild grapes that were not suitable for wine-making, and in the end the vineyard had to be torn down. In case there is any doubt about what the vineyard represents, in the last stanza Isaiah says, "The vineyard of the Lord of hosts is the house of Israel, and the men of Judah are his pleasant planting" (Isa. 5:7).

The vineyard was a familiar national symbol. Whenever the Israelites encountered this imagery, they knew that it referred to their identity as a nation—much the way Americans identity with the bald eagle or Canadians identify with the maple leaf today. When Jesus started talking about a vineyard, people in Jerusalem knew that he was talking about them and their relationship to God. According to Kent Hughes,

> The vineyard/Israel connection was so much a part of their national consciousness that the very temple in which Jesus was standing sported a richly carved grapevine, seventy cubits high, sculpted around the door that led from the porch to the Holy Place. The branches, tendrils, and leaves were of finest gold. The bunches of grapes hanging upon the golden limbs were costly jewels. Herod first placed the golden vine there, and rich and patriotic Jews would from time to time add to its embellishment. One contributed a new jeweled grape, another a leaf, and still

another a cluster of the same precious materials. This vine had immense sacred meaning in the eyes of the Jews.[1]

Who, then, are the tenants who hold the lease to the owner's vineyard? Or to put the question another way: Who was responsible to care for the people of Israel so that they would bear good fruit for God and produce the wine of sweet obedience? When it is put that way, the answer is obvious: the tenants are the spiritual leaders of Israel. The very priests and scribes and elders who were challenging the authority of Jesus in the temple and trying to destroy him were responsible for the spiritual growth of God's people. God had been away from them for a long time. While he was away, the leaders were supposed to cultivate the people by giving them good spiritual care—feeding them, pruning them, and protecting them. They were supposed to love the people of God the way a winemaker loves his vineyard. This would be for their blessing and God's glory.

Yet the tenants were abusing their authority, and the parable was designed to show this. Several years had passed—enough time for the vines to start producing good grapes. The landowner was ready to drink his share of the profits, which in those days would have been paid in kind. So he sent his servants to collect the latest vintage. But the tenants refused to make the proper payment. Not only did they keep the wine all to themselves, but they abused every last one of the owner's servants.

According to the terms of this allegory, the servants represent the prophets whom God had repeatedly sent to his people (see Jer. 25:4). In the Old Testament, God frequently calls his prophetic messengers "my servants the prophets" (e.g., Zech. 1:6). When he sent Isaiah, Jeremiah, and the rest of his prophets to Israel, it was as if he was sending them out into his vineyard. All through the Old Testament we hear the prophets calling God's people to faith, telling them to bear good fruit, and warning them that if they did not repent, they would perish.

What did these men get for all their troubles? Nothing except rejection, persecution, and abuse, mainly from the tenants of God's vineyard! As God said through the prophet Jeremiah, "I have persistently sent all my servants

---

1. R. Kent Hughes, *Luke: That You May Know the Truth*, 2 vols., Preaching the Word (Wheaton, IL: Crossway, 1998), 2:255.

the prophets to them, day after day. Yet they did not listen to me" (Jer. 7:25–26; cf. 29:19). Most of the prophets were ill-treated, and many of them came to a violent end. Elijah was hated by the queen and had to run for his life (1 Kings 19:1–5). Jeremiah was ridiculed and rejected before being thrown into a pit and left for dead (Jer. 38:1–6). Zechariah was murdered in the precincts of the temple (2 Chron. 24:20–22). John the Baptist was beheaded (Mark 6:14–29). Shortly before his own martyrdom, Stephen summarized it all by saying, "Which of the prophets did not your fathers persecute? And they killed those who announced beforehand the coming of the Righteous One" (Acts 7:52; cf. Neh. 9:26).

Each of the people we meet in the parable teaches us something about living for God. The long-suffering landowner stands for God and teaches us how patient God is in waiting for us to repent. The planted vineyard stands for God's people and teaches us that God wants us to bear good spiritual fruit. The wicked tenants stand for Israel's spiritual leaders and teach us what kind of leadership God loves: leadership that worships God's lordship, honors God's Word, and recognizes that God's people are not there for their own benefit, but for the greater glory of God. The suffering servants represent the prophets, and they teach us to expect hostility to the gospel and persecution for preaching in the name of Christ.

## THE SENDING OF THE BELOVED SON

All of these lessons are valuable to learn, but they are not the heart of the parable. No, the heart of the parable is the sending of the owner's son, and his murder at the hands of evil men. "What shall I do?" the owner said. "I will send my beloved son" (Luke 20:13).

As soon as we hear these words, we know that we are standing on the holy ground at the heart of the universe. The beloved or only beloved son is a precious person in the story of salvation. We first meet him in the story of Abraham, when God called that famous patriarch to make the costliest of all sacrifices. God said to Abraham, "Take your son, your only son, Isaac, whom you love . . . and offer him . . . as a burnt offering" (Gen. 22:2). God was telling Abraham to sacrifice his beloved son.

This was part of God's preparation for the coming of Christ. He too is a beloved son. He is *the* Beloved Son—the only Son of the loving Father. Luke has shown this already. He showed it at the baptism of Jesus, when "a voice came from heaven, 'You are my beloved Son'" (Luke 3:22). Or again, when Jesus went up the mount of transfiguration, "a voice came out of the cloud, saying, 'This is my Son!'" (Luke 9:35).

Do you see what Jesus is doing? He is telling us a story about *himself!* If the parable is about a beloved son, then the parable must be about him, because he is the most beloved of all sons. It is as if Jesus cannot tell a parable about himself as the Son without telling us that he is the *Beloved* Son. Once we see that the parable is about a beloved son, our hearts are drawn both to the Son and to the Father who loves him.

Some skeptical scholars doubt whether Jesus ever knew his own divine identity, just as the scribes and elders of his own day doubted whether he had any divine authority. But here we see that Jesus knew exactly who he was: he was and always will be the Father's beloved Son. Therefore, when he told this parable about the sending of a beloved son, he was bearing witness to the love he shared with the Father from all eternity. From eternity past to eternity future, the Father is always loving and loving the Son. If you want to know for sure who Jesus is, know this: he is the Beloved Son of the Father.

The beloved son in the parable was not simply loved with his father's love, but he was also sent on the father's mission. Out of the love of his loving heart, the father sent his beloved son. "What shall I do?" he asked. Then came the costly answer: "I will send my beloved son; perhaps they will respect him" (Luke 20:13).

This was the last resort. Still hopeful that his tenants would acknowledge his authority and accept their responsibility, the owner sent his only son. Immediately we want to tell him that he is making a huge mistake. Even before we hear the rest of the story, we know that the wicked tenants will *not* respect the man's son any more than they respected his servants. "No!" we want to shout. "Don't send them your beloved son! Don't you know that they will kill him?"

This is exactly what they did, of course: "But when the tenants saw him, they said to themselves, 'This is the heir. Let us kill him, so that the inheritance may be ours.' And they threw him out of the vineyard and killed him" (Luke 20:14–15). After such a long absence, the tenants assumed that the owner must be dead and thus they seized the opportunity to claim the vineyard for themselves. Knowing that the son was the son, they nevertheless refused to acknowledge his rightful claim to the vineyard. Instead, in their foolish wickedness, they took him out and killed him.

This story is much more than a parable; it is really a "prophetic autobiography."[2] The storyteller is telling the story of himself. Jesus knew who he was: he was the last in a long line of prophets, and more than that, he was the Son of God. This is why he had the authority to say the things he said and do the things he did. As it says in the book of Hebrews, "Long ago, at many times and in many ways, God spoke to our fathers by the prophets, but in these last days he has spoken to us by his Son" (Heb. 1:1–2).

Jesus also knew what he was doing. He knew that in sending the Son, the Father was sending him to die. That is why there is such an air of inevitability about the entire story. Jesus knew exactly what would happen to him at the hands of evil men. Already the religious leaders at the temple had rejected him, denying his divine authority and refusing to acknowledge that he came from the Father. Now they were plotting to destroy him, and that very week they would conspire to commit his murder. Having persecuted the prophets, they would slaughter the Beloved Son.

How wicked it all was, and how foolish! God is the owner of all creation. What could possibly be gained by murdering his Beloved Son? People ought to have given him all their worship and all their service. After all, as the Father's Son he had a right to the good spiritual fruit of God's vineyard; it belonged to him.[3] Instead, they "rebelled against God's lawful authority, refused to give Him His rightful dues, rejected the counsel of His prophets, and at length crucified His only-begotten Son."[4] It was a brutal, horrible crime. It was the worst thing that anyone has ever done: the murder of God's infinitely perfect Son.

Nevertheless, this was all part of God's plan. If we were to ask the Father, "Don't you know what they will do to your Beloved Son?" he would answer by saying, "Yes, I know what they will do to my Beloved Son. But don't you know that is why I have sent him into the world?" Both the Father and the

---

2. Hughes, *Luke*, 2:257.

3. David Gooding, *According to Luke: A New Exposition of the Third Gospel* (Grand Rapids: Eerdmans, 1987), 318.

4. J. C. Ryle, *Expository Thoughts on the Gospels, Luke* (1858; reprint Cambridge: James Clarke, 1976), 2:325.

Son knew exactly what would happen. The Father was sending the Son to suffer and to die. This was the main business of his life. Jesus said that the Son of Man must be "lifted up"—lifted up to die on the cross—so that "whoever believes in him may have eternal life. For God so loved the world, that he gave his only Son, that whoever believes in him should not perish but have eternal life" (John 3:15–16).

The question is: Do you believe in Jesus, or not? The Father has sent his Only Beloved Son. If you believe in him, you will be saved forever. He comes to you in love, offering his life for your sins. Yet some people refuse to acknowledge his authority. They prefer to work their own religion, worshiping the God of their own understanding. Or they like to think that God the Owner is dead, and that if somehow they can get rid of Jesus the Son, they can have life all to themselves. This is the choice that everyone has to make: Do you believe in Jesus, or not? "Whoever believes in him is not condemned, but whoever does not believe is condemned already, because he has not believed in the name of the only Son of God" (John 3:18).

## THE END OF THE STORY

What will happen to people who do not believe in the Son of God? What will the consequences be? That is the question that Jesus himself asks at the end of this parable: "What then will the owner of the vineyard do to them?" (Luke 20:15).

Well, what should the owner do? The tenants have murdered his beloved son. What then does justice require? Jesus said, "He will come and destroy those tenants and give the vineyard to others" (Luke 20:16). People do not always like the way that God deals with sinners, but we can hardly argue with him on the basis of justice. These men murdered the owner's beloved son. They no longer deserved to work in his vineyard; they deserved to die.

Remember that this story was really an allegory. The people in the story stand for something in real life. When Jesus said that the vineyard would be taken away and given to others, he was really saying that Israel's priests and scribes—the men who were challenging his authority and planning his murder—would no longer lead the people of God. Spiritual leadership would be transferred to the apostles of the church, as the gospel went out to the Gentiles as well as the Jews. As David Gooding explains: "God's spiritual interests in the earth and the care of people who believed in and served the true God of Israel would pass out of the hands of Judaism's priesthood and eventually to a large extent out of Israel's hands altogether."[5]

The people who were there knew exactly what Jesus was saying, and they could not believe it. Luke tells us that "when they heard this, they said, 'Surely not!'" (Luke 20:16). Surely God would never take the vineyard away from the Jews and give it to the Gentiles. It was completely unthinkable. Remember, these religious leaders had so little spiritual concern for people outside of Israel that they had turned the Court of the Gentiles into a grand bazaar. So perhaps it is not surprising that what made them angry was not the death of the beloved son, but the warning that they would lose their place of spiritual leadership. These men were not concerned with the person and work of Jesus Christ, but only with the importance of their own position in the religious community. This attitude is always deadly in ministry. As soon as we become more concerned about our own reputation than about the honor of Jesus Christ, we no longer deserve our place of spiritual leadership in the church and ought to be replaced.

To confirm what he was saying, Jesus quoted from the Scriptures. The people were all saying "Surely not!" But Jesus "looked directly at them and said, 'What then is this that is written: "The stone that the builders rejected has become the cornerstone"? Everyone who falls on that stone will be broken to pieces, and when it falls on anyone, it will crush him'" (Luke 20:17–20).

This hard saying is one of the most important things that Jesus ever said. The Old Testament quotation he used was essential to his own understanding of his saving work. It comes from Psalm 118—the very psalm that people were singing when Jesus rode into Jerusalem on a donkey. They said, "Blessed is he who comes in the name of the LORD!" (Ps. 118:26; cf. Luke 19:38). The part of the psalm that Jesus quoted came just a few verses earlier: "The stone that the builders rejected has become the cornerstone" (Ps. 118:22).

In its original context, this statement refers to an unusual incident that occurred during the building of Solomon's temple. The great stones for the temple were cut at the quarry and then chiseled into the right shape before

---

5. Gooding, *Luke*, 318.

being transported to Jerusalem, where they were slid into place (see 1 Kings 5:15–18). Apparently one large stone turned out to be the wrong size and shape, so when it arrived at the building site, the workmen had to set it aside. It was the stone that the builders rejected. But to everyone's surprise, that unwanted stone later turned out to be exactly the right size and shape to serve as the cornerstone, or perhaps the capstone—the keystone at the corner that squared the building.[6]

The psalmist used this stone as a metaphor for the nation of Israel. Like the cornerstone, the people of God were rejected by the nations and taken into captivity. But later God rescued them, reestablishing them in Jerusalem, rebuilding the temple, and restoring them to their place of honor. So they praised God by singing, "The stone that the builders rejected has become the cornerstone" (Ps. 118:22).

Jesus knew that the prophecy in this verse was fulfilled in his coming as the Messiah. He himself was the stone that the builders rejected. This is what the religious leaders were doing when they tried to destroy him: they were rejecting the cornerstone of salvation. This is also what the parable was about. The wicked tenants who killed the owner's son were like the builders who rejected the chosen stone: they were acting against the Beloved Son. Thus the words of Psalm 118 were coming true, and Jesus knew it. The rejected stone was about to become the murdered son.

That is not the end of the story, however. The very stone that once was rejected was about to become the cornerstone. Jesus knew the whole prophecy and quoted it in full because it was a promise of the gospel. The Son would be rejected unto death, but he would not be rejected forever; the Father would raise him up again. Thus the stone that was rejected at the cross would become the cornerstone of resurrection life. At the end of the parable that he told about his death, Jesus gave at least a hint that he would come back from the grave.

## THE STUMBLING STONE

This brings us back to the same question that we asked before: Do you believe in Jesus, or not? The Bible says, "Behold, I am laying in Zion a stone,

6. See James Montgomery Boice, *Romans*, 4 vols. (Grand Rapids: Baker, 1993), 3:1146–47.

a cornerstone chosen and precious, and whoever believes in him will not be put to shame" (1 Peter 2:6; cf. Isa. 28:16). Do you believe that Jesus Christ is the cornerstone of salvation? Do you believe that his rejection is your salvation—that he died on the cross for your sins? Do you believe that his resurrection is your life—that he rose again so that you could live forever?

If not, you need to know that you will be crushed under the heavy stone of God's wrath against your sin. Listen again to the warning that Jesus gave: "Everyone who falls on that stone will be broken to pieces, and when it falls on anyone, it will crush him" (Luke 20:18).

Better than anyone else, Jesus knew what would happen to people who reject him. The truth is that many people get tripped up when they encounter Jesus. This image is common in the New Testament: Jesus Christ is the stone that people stumble over (see Luke 2:34; Rom. 9:32; 1 Peter 2:8). It is an image that comes out of the Old Testament. The prophet Isaiah said that the Lord himself would become "a stone of offense and a rock of stumbling" for Israel. "Many shall stumble on it," the prophet said; "they shall fall and be broken" (Isa. 8:14–15). This prophecy referred especially to the Jewish people (see 1 Cor. 1:23), many of whom still think that Jesus is only for Gentiles, that he has little or nothing to do with God's plans for the chosen people of Israel. But this prophecy is also for Gentiles, many of whom refuse to believe that Jesus Christ is the only way to God. The prophet Daniel said that a mighty stone would come and break the godless nations into pieces (Dan. 2:44–45).

What a crushing mistake it is not to believe in Jesus. Jesus said that people who trip over him will be "broken to pieces." This seems to refer to something that happens in this life. If we refuse to accept Jesus as the Beloved Son of God, eventually life falls apart. But something much worse will happen at the final judgment: Jesus Christ will crush us completely. Here is how Norval Geldenhuys explained this verse:

> As a blind man who stumbles and falls over a stone and injures himself against it, so those who through their unbelief and falseness of heart are spiritually blind will find Jesus, as it were, a stumbling-block in their path and so in a spiritual sense they will fall and come to grief. Even in the ordinary course of life this will happen to those who do not believe in Jesus. But whosoever persists in the state of unbelief until the time of grace is expired

will be completely crushed by the judgment of God, carried out by the Son—and be pulverized like one on whom a tremendous rock crashes down.[7]

Jesus said it himself: he is the precious stone that God has chosen to be the cornerstone of the church. But if we trip over him, he will fall on us with crushing force. This is why Jesus was weeping when he rode into Jerusalem. He knew what would happen to people who rejected him as the Only Beloved Son. This is also why he spoke so plainly about the final judgment. Jesus wanted everyone to know that he is the Beloved Son of God, the precious stone of salvation, and also the crushing stone of judgment.

Do not stumble over the stone of salvation, and do not fall under the judgment of God, but believe in his Beloved Son. The God of all grace "is able to keep you from stumbling and to present you blameless before the presence of his glory with great joy." So "to the only God, our Savior, through Jesus Christ our Lord, be glory, majesty, dominion, and authority, before all time and now and forever. Amen" (Jude 24–25).

7. Norval Geldenhuys, *The Gospel of Luke*, New International Commentary on the New Testament (Grand Rapids: Eerdmans, 1951), 499.

# 85

# GOD AND CAESAR

## *Luke 20:19–26*

*He said to them, "Then render to Caesar the things that are Caesar's, and to God the things that are God's." (Luke 20:25)*

*I*f you want to start a good argument, start talking about religion, or politics—either one. But if you want to start a war, then bring your religion into your politics.

Few things seem to cause more difficulty than an unholy alliance between political power and religious faith. This is as true of Christianity as it is of any other religion. Think of the Crusades, or the Inquisition, or apartheid. Or think of the way Christianity was used to defend slavery. Then consider all the trouble we have doing evangelism today because when people hear about Christianity, they immediately associate it with a particular political perspective. In America, the close identification between the evangelical church and conservative politics makes it more difficult for many secular people to give a fair hearing to the gospel. Then when we go abroad, where America is typically regarded as a Christian country, we find that people's attitudes about Christianity are deeply affected by their opinion of U.S. foreign policy—often to the detriment of the missionary work of the gospel.

My point is not to advocate this or that political philosophy, but simply to say that it is hard to get religion and politics right, and that when we get them wrong—as people often do, including Christians—it causes no end of trouble.

## A REAL DILEMMA?

If we want to understand the true relationship between politics and religion, probably the best place to start is with one of the most famous things Jesus ever said: "Render to Caesar the things that are Caesar's, and to God the things that are God's" (Luke 20:25). Even the infamous Jesus Seminar of the 1990s, which tried to cast doubt on almost everything our Lord ever said, agreed that these were the true words of Jesus. Somehow it is not surprising that one of the few sayings they accepted had to do with politics, which many people seem to think is the most important thing in the world!

As always, it is important to understand the context for what Jesus said. It was the last week of his life, and the tension was mounting. The religious leaders in Jerusalem were trying to destroy Jesus, but they could not find a way to do it because people were hanging on his every word (Luke 19:48). First they tried to trap him by asking him if he had a license to preach and perform miracles at the temple, but Jesus gave such a brilliant answer that they were trapped themselves (Luke 20:1–8). Next Jesus told them the story of the owner's son, which made them angrier than ever: "The scribes and the chief priests sought to lay hands on him at that very hour, for they perceived that he had told this parable against them, but they feared the people" (Luke 20:19).

Jesus was prophesying that the religious leaders would put him to death and then lose their position of spiritual authority. When the priests and scribes heard this, they wanted to kill him. It was almost as if they were deliberately trying to fulfill his prophecy, for their murderous intentions proved the truth of what he was saying. The more people listened to Jesus, the more their control was slipping away. The frustrating thing for them was that there was nothing they could do about it! Jesus was much too popular for them to be able to get rid of him. Therefore, they had the most dangerous of all angers—an "impotent rage."[1]

---

1. Norval Geldenhuys, *The Gospel of Luke*, New International Commentary on the New Testament (Grand Rapids: Eerdmans, 1951), 502.

Then one of them had a cunning idea, and one of the best parts about it was that they could get someone else to do their dirty work for them: "So they watched him and sent spies, who pretended to be sincere, that they might catch him in something he said, so as to deliver him up to the authority and jurisdiction of the governor" (Luke 20:20).

Here it is important to remember that the Jewish leaders did not have the authority to execute the death penalty. That right was reserved for the Romans. But maybe there was a way they could get Jesus in trouble with the Roman government. So his enemies seized upon a question that related to public policy. If they could not trap him in religion, maybe they could get him with politics: "So they asked him, 'Teacher, we know that you speak and teach rightly, and show no partiality, but truly teach the way of God. Is it lawful for us to give tribute to Caesar, or not?'" (Luke 20:21–22).

What these men said in setting up their question was all true. Jesus did speak and teach rightly, without showing any partiality. But coming from the lips of such dishonest men, these flattering words were so disgusting they were almost obscene. These pretentious hypocrites were like the wicked man that King David condemned in Psalm 55:21: "His speech was smooth as butter, yet war was in his heart; his words were softer than oil, yet they were drawn swords."

The question itself was designed to discredit Jesus by catching him on the horns of a dilemma. Earlier Jesus had trapped these men by asking whether the baptism of John was from earth or heaven (see Luke 20:4), and now they were trying to beat him at his own game. Was it or was it not lawful to pay tribute to Caesar?

This was an explosive question in those days (we are talking about politics in the Middle East, remember), and the answer one gave was potentially fatal. The tribute was the basic Roman tax imposed on every Jewish citizen—the price one paid for the privilege of living and working in the Roman Empire. The tax was highly unpopular, as most taxes are. This was not just for economic reasons, but also for political and religious reasons, for the Roman tax amounted to a payment that Israelites paid for living on their own land. Thus some zealous Israelites considered the payment of the tribute to be a sin because the Romans were robbing money that rightly belonged to God.[2]

2. See Geldenhuys, *Luke*, 506.

That is why, on occasion, the imposition of the tribute had stirred up violent uprisings in Israel.

If Jesus told people to go ahead and pay the tax, many Jews would consider him a traitor to the cause of his people. Remember, they were expecting the Messiah to liberate them from their oppressors, not keep them under Roman rule. If Jesus told people not to resist the empire, the masses would turn against him, he would lose his popular following, and that would be the end of his influence—or so his enemies hoped.

If Jesus told people *not* to pay the tax, however—as the leaders probably hoped—he would be guilty of subverting the Roman government. Then they would be able to haul him before the governor and accuse him of being an insurrectionist. In fact, this is exactly the strategy they later tried, when they accused Jesus (falsely) of forbidding people to pay tribute to Caesar (see Luke 23:2). If there was one thing the Romans refused to tolerate, it was any kind of rebellion. A man who told people not to pay their taxes would be swiftly arrested and summarily punished.

These men must have thought they finally had Jesus right where they wanted him. He seemed to be caught on the horns of a real dilemma. If he told people to pay their taxes, he was finished as a popular hero; if he told them not to, he was a dead man.

## Q & A

There was one flaw in their reasoning, however, and seeing it will help us understand the answer that Jesus gave. When these crafty men said, "Is it lawful for us to give tribute to Caesar, or not?" they were asking a yes or no question: either the tax was lawful or it wasn't. But this assumed that things belonged either to Caesar or to God, but not in some way to both. In effect, by demanding a simple, categorical answer, these men were insisting on a total separation between religion and politics. Some things are for Caesar and some things are for God. "So tell us, Jesus, do our taxes belong to the government, or do they belong to God instead?"

If these men thought they could trap Jesus with this kind of trick, they were badly mistaken. Luke tells us "he perceived their craftiness" (Luke 20:23)—a word used elsewhere in the New Testament for the diabolical stratagems of Satan (see 2 Cor. 11:3). Jesus said, "Show me a denarius."

Presumably there was a dramatic pause, as someone produced a coin. Then he said, "Whose likeness and inscription does it have?" "Caesar's," they had to admit (Luke 20:24).

Jesus had done it again, countering a question with another question. Obviously the likeness on the coin was Caesar's likeness, and the inscription was Caesar's inscription. It read (in abbreviated form) "Tiberius Caesar, son of the divine Augustus, Augustus."[3] Therefore, the coin was Caesar's coin. As a practical matter, whether they wanted to pay any tribute to Caesar or not, as citizens of his empire they were using the coin of his realm. Their money proved that they were part of the Roman economy, and thus that Caesar had a claim on their economic lives.

Then Jesus gave his dramatic response to their diabolical question: "Render to Caesar the things that are Caesar's, and to God the things that are God's" (Luke 20:25). Once again, his enemies were silenced as he slipped through the horns of their dilemma. People could hardly object to giving Caesar what was rightfully his (not the worship he tried to claim by using a divine title, but the coin of his realm). After all, his face was on the very coins in their pockets! Nor could they object to giving God what belonged to God, because they claimed to be his servants.

By acknowledging both of these duties, Jesus won another victory over his enemies in the ongoing conflict that would lead him to the cross, and they knew it. Luke ends his account by saying, "they were not able in the presence of the people to catch him in what he said, but marveling at his answer they became silent" (Luke 20:26).

## THE THINGS THAT ARE CAESAR'S

The answer Jesus gave is the most important and influential statement that anyone has ever made on the subject of religion and politics: "What is Caesar's belongs to Caesar, and what is God's belongs to God." Yet this still leaves us with two obvious and overarching questions: Which things belong to Caesar, and which things belong to God?

To get the practical benefit of what Jesus said, we need to begin by recognizing that some things really do belong to Caesar. When Jesus tells us to

---

3. R. Kent Hughes, *Luke: That You May Know the Truth*, 2 vols., Preaching the Word (Wheaton, IL: Crossway, 1998), 2:265.

give the government what it deserves, this assumes that the government has legitimate prerogatives. Jesus did not come to overthrow the empire and set up an alternative state, presumably a Christian one. Instead, he acknowledged that even Caesar has his proper place of earthly authority, his appropriate sphere of political influence. Caesar has this authority because it is given to him by God. "Let every person be subject to the governing authorities," the Bible says. "For there is no authority except from God, and those that exist have been instituted by God" (Rom. 13:1). Though not unlimited, the authority of human government is legitimate.

As we acknowledge the divine authority of human government, there are at least four things God wants us to "render unto Caesar." The first is *paying our taxes*. This is the most obvious and immediate application of what Jesus was saying. People were asking whether it was lawful to pay tribute to Caesar. Not only was it lawful, but according to Jesus it was absolutely required: "Render to Caesar the things that are Caesar's." Norval Geldenhuys comments:

> In this reply there is no evasion of the question put to Him but a clear and straightforward declaration that they must pay Caesar tribute and everything due to him as their ruler. Under God's providence the course of history has been so arranged that they have been brought under Roman domination, and through their free use of Caesar's coins they have shown that they acknowledge Caesar as their earthly ruler, and therefore they are under the obligation to pay to Caesar what is due to him.[4]

What makes this so extraordinary is that Jesus was talking about the Roman Empire, which of all governments was cruel in its oppression, even persecuting the people of God. Nevertheless, Jesus wanted his disciples to pay what they owed. The apostle Paul said the same thing, only he said it when Nero was the emperor and things were even worse for the people of God: "Pay to all what is owed to them: taxes to whom taxes are owed, revenue to whom revenue is owed" (Rom. 13:7). We too have a duty to pay taxes to our government, no matter how wisely or unwisely we think some of our money will be spent. Paying the *full* amount of our federal income tax and other taxes is an act of obedience to Jesus Christ.

4. Geldenhuys, *Luke*, 504.

In Philadelphia this includes the special privilege of paying the heavy wage tax imposed on everyone who lives or works in the city, at a rate of more than five percent. Some years ago I discovered to my dismay that this wage tax was due even on money earned out of state. But when I found this out, it was my duty to walk over to the Municipal Building and figure out what I owed in back taxes and penalties. Later, when I discovered that the nine dollars I received for jury duty was taxable income, then that too needed to go on my return. Even taxes can be for the glory of God, if we render them unto Caesar out of obedience to Christ.

The second way we render unto Caesar is by *praying for our leaders.* Jesus may or may not have had this specifically in mind, but it is an important part of the New Testament teaching on politics and religion. Christians are people who pray for God to bless their government.

Praying for the government is an important part of public worship. The apostle Paul urged Timothy "that supplications, prayers, intercessions, and thanksgivings be made for all people, for kings and all who are in high positions." Then he went on to say, "This is good, and it is pleasing in the sight of God our Savior" (1 Tim. 2:1–3). It is also an important part of our private intercession. Pray for the president, asking God to give him wisdom to lead our country. Pray for Congress, asking God to give our senators and representatives integrity in their political office. Pray for the members of the Supreme Court, asking God to make them agents of justice. Pray for the governor and all the other state officials. Pray for local authorities at every level of civic government. As the people of God, the one thing that we alone can do for our country is to pray.

Then we render unto Caesar by *practicing civil obedience.* This is a third thing we owe the government as part of our service to Christ: submission to the law of our land. In the words of the Apology of the Augsburg Confession, "The Gospel does not introduce any new laws about the civil estate, but commands us to obey the existing laws, whether they were formulated by the heathen or by others, and in this obedience to practice love" (Article 16). Of course, there are some exceptions to this. We are not obligated to do anything immoral, or anything that directly conflicts with the revealed will of God. Nor can we ever give up our duty to share the gospel, whatever the government may say. Thus there may be times when, as a matter of conscience, we have to say what Peter and John said to the Sanhedrin: "We must obey God rather than men" (Acts 5:29).

Even under such extraordinary circumstances, however, we must be ready to suffer the penalty of the law with quiet submission. In every other situation we owe Caesar our willing obedience, even when we may not agree with what the government is doing. J. C. Ryle said, "So long as we have liberty to worship God in Christ, according to our conscience, and to serve Him in the way of His commandments, we may safely submit to many requirements of the state, which in our own private opinion we do not thoroughly approve."[5]

The last thing we render unto Caesar is *participation in public life*. We are citizens of an earthly government, and from time to time we will be called to serve our fellow citizens. In a democratic society this includes taking seriously our responsibility to vote, in keeping with biblical principles and our own conscience before God. Some Christians are called to serve God in the military. There are examples of this in the New Testament, like Cornelius, who was a centurion in the Roman army (see Acts 10). Jesus and the apostles did not tell such men to leave the army, but to do their work in a way that brought honor to his name. Other Christians are called to hold public office, and they too should serve with all godliness.

There may also be times when the church has a responsibility to speak—as the church—on public issues. This is an area for boldness, but also for caution. We have a responsibility to bear witness to the biblical truth about poverty, business, education, racism, abortion, marriage, war, the environment, and many other issues that have a moral dimension. As individual Christians, and in private association with other citizens, we also have the freedom to be involved in pursuing political solutions to these problems. Yet as the church it is not our responsibility to control the government (as if politics were the ultimate prize) or even to devise political solutions to social problems. Let Caesar be Caesar, and let the church be the church! Good government has its place in the plan of God, but our primary work as the church is not to gain more political influence in the hope of legislating a Christian society. Rather, we use the spiritual instruments of prayer and the

5. J. C. Ryle, *Expository Thoughts on the Gospels, Luke* (1858; reprint Cambridge: James Clarke, 1976), 2:336.

Word of God, with deeds of mercy, to win people's minds and hearts with the love of Jesus.

Here are some basic practical principles that Christians need to follow in the religion of their politics: Pay your taxes. Pray for your leaders. Practice civil obedience. Participate in public life, according to your particular calling from God.

## THE THINGS THAT ARE GOD'S

If these are some of the things that belong to Caesar, what belongs to God? Moving from the lesser to the infinitely greater, from the emperor in Rome to the King of the universe, Jesus said: "Render to Caesar the things that are Caesar's, and to God the things that are God's" (Luke 20:25).

It takes only a moment to realize that what belongs to God is absolutely everything: "For from him and through him and to him are all things" (Rom. 11:36). This helps us to understand the true relationship between God and Caesar. If everything belongs to God, then this must include Caesar himself.

This was the fatal flaw in the reasoning of the religious leaders. They were trying to make such a distinction between religion and politics that some things belonged to Caesar and other things belonged to God. But the truth is that even the things that belong to Caesar ultimately belong to God. Caesar himself belongs to God, because he is inscribed with God's image (see Gen. 1:27)—almost as if he himself were a coin—and also because God is the one who sets every authority in its place (see Rom. 13:1). Caesar's empire belongs to God, because the kingdoms of this world have become the kingdom of our God, and of his Christ (see Rev. 11:15). Caesar's money belongs to God, even if Caesar's face is on it, because every coin is part of God's economy.

The things we give to Caesar also belong to God. When we "render unto Caesar," what we are really doing is rendering unto God. As we pay our taxes, pray for our leaders, practice civil obedience, and participate in public life, we are doing it all for the glory of God.

This is the heart of the answer that Jesus gave. Rather than separating our political life from our religious life, Jesus claimed that even politics ought to be part of true religion. Notice that the two parts of his famous statement are joined with the word "and," not the word "but." Jesus did not say, "Render unto Caesar, but render unto God," thereby dividing everything into two different categories. On the contrary, he said, "Render unto Caesar, *and* render unto God." This is because rendering unto Caesar is "a subordinate part of the all-embracing obligation to 'render unto God the things which are God's.'"[6] What belongs to Caesar also belongs to God.

Today many secular people take strong objection to this way of thinking. They would prefer to keep religion out of politics altogether. They do not object too much to people practicing their religion, as long as they keep their place. Religion is supposed to be private, not part of public life. Politics is the main thing—the most important thing—and as long as people keep God out of Caesar's business, they can worship any way they like.

But Jesus Christ absolutely refuses to bow at Caesar's throne, which is why biblical Christianity keeps coming into conflict with secular society. We believe that everything is for the glory of God, even politics. As the famous Dutch preacher and politician Abraham Kuyper said, "There is not a square inch in the whole domain of our human existence over which Christ, who is Sovereign over *all*, does not cry: 'Mine!'"[7]

As we have seen, this does *not* mean that Christians are supposed to be in charge of Caesar. This point needs to be emphasized because it is so often misunderstood: God never intended the state to become an extension of the church. There are two different kinds of government in the world. There is an earthly government and there is a spiritual government; there is Caesar and there is the church.

Jesus acknowledged the authority of the state when he said we need to "render unto Caesar." But he said nothing—either here or anywhere else in the New Testament—about Christians taking control of the Roman Empire or claiming any other kind of political authority. This is what many people wanted him to do, but Jesus never did it. In fact, he constantly had to correct this kind of thinking. Far from saying to his disciples, "Listen, if you want to get anything done for the kingdom, you have to get more politically involved," he said, "My kingdom is not of this world" (John 18:36). Nevertheless, Jesus always insisted that Caesar and all the other secular powers

6. Geldenhuys, *Luke*, 505.

7. Abraham Kuyper, "Sphere Sovereignty," in *Abraham Kuyper: A Centennial Reader*, ed. James D. Bratt (Grand Rapids: Eerdmans, 1998), 488.

are under the sovereign authority of almighty God. Therefore, both of the two kinds of government that there are in the world—the earthly and the spiritual—are ultimately under the rule of God.

The Protestant Reformers explained this by talking about "the two kingdoms." One kingdom is the secular government that is conducted by the state. The laws of this government, said Martin Luther, rule our bodies: "Secular government has laws which extend no further than to life and property and to external things and relations on earth." The other kingdom is the spiritual government that is exercised by the church and that rules our souls. "For over the soul," said Luther, "God can and will let no one rule but himself."[8] John Calvin said something similar when he spoke about God's "twofold government" and said that "Christ's spiritual kingdom and the civil jurisdiction are things completely distinct." Therefore, Calvin said, "we do not (as commonly happens) unwisely mingle these two, which have a completely different nature."[9]

What is crucial to understand about this "twofold government" is that *both* the secular kingdom of the state and the spiritual kingdom of the church are under the rule and authority of God, who thus has two instruments of government in the world. In one kingdom God rules by the sword; in the other he rules by the Spirit. One kingdom is for the restraint of evil and the promotion of social order; the other is for the proclamation of the gospel and the spiritual good of the soul. As Christians we belong to both the church and the state, and in both kingdoms we have unique obligations to honor God. Although we believe in the separation of church and state, we do not believe in the separation of *God* and state.

## Everything We Owe

Thus far we have been talking only about government, but of course what Jesus said about God and Caesar has a much wider application. It is not just one of the most important things he said about religion and politics; it is one of the most important things Jesus ever said about anything: give to God what belongs to God.

8. Martin Luther, quoted in Michael Horton, "Defining the Two Kingdoms," *Modern Reformation* 9.5 (Sept./Oct. 2000): 24.

9. John Calvin, quoted in Horton, "Defining," 24.

This includes absolutely everything. Our bodies belong to God. Our eyes, our ears, and our hands are instruments to use in the service of God as we see the needs around us, listen to God's voice, and reach out with the compassion of Christ. Our homes belong to God. They are places that God has set apart for us to rest in his goodness and practice hospitality for people in need. Our time belongs to God. It is the most precious resource we have—the canvas we have for painting his grace. Our work belongs to God; it is service we offer to the Lord of all masters. Our money belongs to God, to be held loosely until we have the next golden opportunity to invest it in the kingdom of God. It all belongs to God!

If we ask what belongs to God, the answer is *everything!* If we ask what right God has to claim all this from us, the answer is that he gave it to us in the first place as the God who made us, takes care of us, and is saving us in Jesus Christ.

To make his point about paying tribute to Caesar, Jesus used a coin that was made in the emperor's image. He could do the same thing with us, because we ourselves are made in the royal image of our King (see Gen. 1:27). The fact that we are created in God's likeness is the proof of his ownership; it shows that we belong to him.

We see an even greater proof in the cross where Jesus died for our sins. The God who demands that we give everything to him has already given everything to us—everything, including his own blood. What will you render to God for the sake of the Savior whose body was rendered for you?

# 86

# THE GOD OF THE LIVING

## *Luke 20:27–40*

*"But that the dead are raised, even Moses showed, in the passage about the bush, where he calls the Lord the God of Abraham and the God of Isaac and the God of Jacob. Now he is not God of the dead, but of the living, for all live to him." (Luke 20:37–38)*

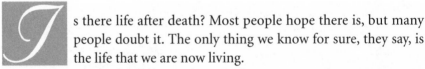s there life after death? Most people hope there is, but many people doubt it. The only thing we know for sure, they say, is the life that we are now living.

According to the worldview of secular humanism and Darwinian evolutionism, our biology is our destiny. When our hearts stop beating, our minds cease to exist, and there is nothing left of us. "Human destiny," writes the philosopher Ernest Nagel, is only "an episode between two oblivions."[1] The same way of thinking is enshrined in a document called the *Humanist Manifesto*, which says: "As far as we know, the total personality is a function of the biological organism transacting in a social and cultural context. There is no credible evidence that life survives the death of the body."[2]

1. Ernest Nagel, "Naturalism Reconsidered," in *Essays in Philosophy*, ed. Houston Peterson (New York: Pocket Library, 1959), 496.
2. *Humanist Manifestos I and II* (Buffalo: Prometheus, 1973), 17.

## One Bride for Seven Brothers

There were some people who said basically the same thing in the time of Christ. They did not talk about biological organisms or social contexts, of course, but they did say that there was no life after death. Some of them even tried to prove it to Jesus: "There came to him some Sadducees, those who deny that there is a resurrection" (Luke 20:27).

The Sadducees were the party of privilege, the ruling elite. Their priests held the majority in the seventy-one-member Sanhedrin, which was the highest court of justice in Jerusalem, and by tradition one of their members held the office of high priest. Most of the Sadducees were wealthy members of the upper class. Norval Geldenhuys calls them "the priestly aristocracy,"[3] while Kent Hughes describes them as "insular, patrician, heartless, philosophical materialists."[4]

The Sadducees disagreed sharply with the Pharisees on most political and religious issues. Whereas the Pharisees wanted to overthrow their Roman oppressors, the Sadducees were more conservative, cooperating with the Romans in order to preserve their political power. In theology, the Pharisees followed the traditions of their forefathers, which included many moral regulations that went beyond the teaching of Scripture. But the Sadducees adopted a more literal interpretation of the law of Moses, accepting only what was written in Scripture, or so they said.

If there was one doctrine that defined the Sadducees, however, it was their denial of eternal life, their rejection of the resurrection. This implies, incidentally, that most Jews in those days *did* believe in life after death: this doctrine distinguished the Sadducees from other Israelites. According to the historian Josephus these men wanted to get rid of "the persistence of the soul, penalties in death's abode, and rewards." In other words, these men denied the doctrines of heaven, hell, and human immortality. "The soul," they said, "perishes along with the body."[5]

---

3. Norval Geldenhuys, *The Gospel of Luke*, New International Commentary on the New Testament (Grand Rapids: Eerdmans, 1951), 513.

4. R. Kent Hughes, *Luke: That You May Know the Truth*, 2 vols., Preaching the Word (Wheaton, IL: Crossway, 1998), 2:273.

5. Josephus, *The Antiquities of the Jews* and *The Wars of the Jews*, as quoted in Hughes, *Luke*, 2:272.

One of the best ways to start an argument in those days was to tell the Sadducees that you believed in the resurrection. There is a notable example in Acts 23, where Paul is on trial before the Sanhedrin. When the apostle realized that some of the members were Sadducees, while others were Pharisees, he shouted, "Brothers, I am a Pharisee, a son of Pharisees. It is with respect to the hope and the resurrection of the dead that I am on trial" (Acts 23:6). In effect, Paul was throwing a theological hand grenade into the courtroom, and it had exactly the result he was hoping for: "And when he had said this, a dissension arose between the Pharisees and the Sadducees, and the assembly was divided. For the Sadducees say that there is no resurrection, nor angel, nor spirit, but the Pharisees acknowledge them all" (Acts 23:7–8).

It hardly seems surprising that the Sadducees denied the resurrection, for they were wealthy men who enjoyed almost all the material comforts that this life has to offer. Or maybe the connection went the other way: because they denied eternal life, these men had nothing better to do than live for the present. In any case, when the moneychangers made their millions in the temple courts, most of the proceeds went to the Sadducees. Like most people who have a lot of money—like most people in our own culture, in fact, and maybe even like us—they were mainly living for today, giving little thought to eternity. This is one of the main spiritual problems with materialism. Who needs eternal life if you can get everything you really want right now?

If there was one man in Israel who threatened the Sadducees' whole way of life, it was Jesus of Nazareth. Earlier that day Jesus had driven their moneychangers right out of the temple (see Luke 19:45). As some of the chief priests of Jerusalem, the Sadducees resented his rising popularity. Like the rest of the men who were trying to "catch him in what he said" (Luke 20:26), they were hoping to find some way of discrediting Jesus, and maybe even getting rid of him once and for all.

So the Sadducees came to Jesus with an elaborate seven-part question that was designed to show the absurdity and impossibility of the very idea of eternal life:

> Teacher, Moses wrote for us that if a man's brother dies, having a wife but no children, the man must take the widow and raise up offspring for his

brother. Now there were seven brothers. The first took a wife, and died without children. And the second and the third took her, and likewise all seven left no children and died. Afterward the woman also died. In the resurrection, therefore, whose wife will the woman be? For the seven had her as wife. (Luke 20:28–33)

This question was actually based on something from the Bible—part of the very law of Moses that the Sadducees said they wanted to defend. According to Deuteronomy,

If brothers dwell together, and one of them dies and has no son, the wife of the dead man shall not be married outside the family to a stranger. Her husband's brother shall go in to her and take her as his wife and perform the duty of a husband's brother to her. And the first son whom she bears shall succeed to the name of his dead brother, that his name may not be blotted out of Israel. (Deut. 25:5–6)

In other words, if a woman was a childless widow, her brother-in-law should marry her for the explicit purpose of producing a son to carry on the family name. Even though we do not follow this law today, one principle behind it is still important: one primary purpose of our sexuality is to procreate. Within the providence of God—who alone is sovereign over life in the womb—we are called to produce children for the glory of God.

In raising their hypothetical question, the Sadducees took this good biblical law to an absurd extreme: one bride for seven brothers. The very absurdity of this situation was an attempt to prove a point. The Sadducees were attempting a *reductio ad absurdum*—an argument that shows how nonsensical something is by taking it to its logical conclusion. In this particular case, they were trying to show how ridiculous the resurrection was by asking Jesus who this woman—so "unlucky" at love—would have for a husband in heaven.

## A Bad Question

It is easy to imagine that as the Sadducees smugly waited for Jesus to answer, they nodded to one another approvingly, proud of themselves for coming up with such a convincing argument for rejecting the resurrection.

Little did they realize how flawed their reasoning was, or what a bad question they were asking.

It was a bad question because it was not really a question at all; the Sadducees were only trying to score a theological point. The question was also highly speculative: What woman would ever marry seven brothers? This is the kind of hypothetical situation that a student asks about in graduate school or some other academic setting, but that never comes up in real life.

It was also a bad question because it used a biblical premise in order to advance an unbiblical conclusion. That people start with a Bible verse does not necessarily mean that they understand what the Bible really says. They can use the Bible and still be unbiblical. In this particular case, the Sadducees were quoting from Deuteronomy, but they were still missing the point—a good example of bad exegesis. Although Luke does not mention this, according to Matthew, Jesus rebuked them by saying, "You are wrong, because you know neither the Scriptures nor the power of God" (Matt. 22:29).

Teachers often say to their students, "Now that's a good question!" In this case, it would have been perfectly appropriate for Jesus to say, "That's *not* a good question." But as bad as the question was, it still needed to be answered because the Sadducees were asking about something that strikes at the heart of the gospel. The word "gospel" simply means "good news," and the gospel is the good news about what Jesus has done to rescue us from our sins. To be specific, the gospel is the cross plus the empty tomb—the crucifixion and the resurrection of Jesus Christ. By dying in our place on the cross, Jesus suffered the punishment that we deserve for our sins. By rising from the dead, Jesus broke the power of death so that we can live forever with God. But the Sadducees denied that there even is a resurrection, thereby eliminating half of the gospel. If there is no resurrection, then there is no good news for sinners. Furthermore, if there is no resurrection, then there is no final judgment, and therefore no need for atonement, which eliminates the need for a gospel at all. This attack on the good news of salvation is such a matter of life and death that Jesus had to respond.

The answer he gave was flatly dismissive: "The sons of this age marry and are given in marriage, but those who are considered worthy to attain to that age and to the resurrection from the dead neither marry nor are given in marriage, for they cannot die anymore, because they are equal to angels and are sons of God, being sons of the resurrection" (Luke 20:34–36).

Jesus began his answer by drawing an important distinction between the present age and the age to come. "The sons of this age" are people who are alive today—anyone who lives from now until the day of judgment. It is characteristic of this present age that people get married. Some people are single, of course, but this is the age when brides and grooms get married. It will be different in the coming age, however, when no one will get married at all. Thus the question that the Sadducees were asking rested on a false assumption. They assumed that if there is a life to come, married people will still be married. This was part of their question's larger assumption, that life after the resurrection is essentially the same as life before the resurrection—the only difference is that it lasts longer. But Jesus said that in some ways our existence then will be very different from our existence now, and one of the differences is that there is no marriage in heaven. Thus the question that the Sadducees were asking will not even arise!

For Christians who are happily married, what Jesus said about marriage comes as something of a disappointment. Many husbands and wives find it hard to imagine that their marriage will not last forever. How are we to understand this, and how can we accept it?

One man consoled himself with the thought that even if he couldn't be married to his wife in heaven, maybe God would at least let them room together! But I find it more helpful to remember that as Christians we are engaged to Jesus Christ, and we can find our full satisfaction only in our marriage relationship with him—truly a match made in heaven. I also find it helpful to remember how little I love my wife now, and how much more I will love her in the coming age. It will be far better for her not to be married to me at all and yet to be perfectly loved.

This truth ought to be especially precious to Christian singles and to anyone who has suffered a broken marriage. Christians tend to put a great deal of emphasis on marriage—maybe too much emphasis. Certainly marriage is a basic relationship of human love, the building block of human society. It is also under attack in our culture, and for that reason in need of special support. But in the scope of eternity, marriage is not the be-all and end-all of human existence. Even under the best of circumstances, marriage is only a temporary institution, and its very transience points us towards an eternal relationship with Jesus Christ. This is one of the main purposes of matrimony. As Paul said, the profound mystery of marriage is not an end in itself, but "refers to Christ and the church" (Eph. 5:32). Among other things, this means that when it comes to the blessings that God has for us in Christ, single people are not at any kind of disadvantage. Even if we do not always understand this now, it will become perfectly clear to us in the coming age.

## THE TRUTH ABOUT THE RESURRECTION

In exposing the false premise of the Sadducees, Jesus was teaching some important truths about life in the resurrection. Jesus was uniquely qualified to do this because he is God the Son, who came down to earth from heaven. Therefore, when he speaks about life after death, and angels, and the coming age, he knows exactly what he is talking about. In his infinite wisdom, there are many things about the life to come that God has decided *not* to tell us. Sometimes we wish that he had told us more; we have questions about heaven that we would love for him to answer. But there are some things that God *has* told us, and anyone who wants to live with God forever needs to know what Jesus said about the resurrection life.

The first truth he taught is the one we have already seen. It is *a truth about matrimony:* there is no marriage in heaven. The second truth is that not everyone will go to heaven, but only those who are "considered worthy" (Luke 20:35). This is *a truth about merit.* The only people who reach the blessings of the resurrection are the people that God considers worthy. (The wicked are also raised to damnation, of course, but that is not the focus of this particular passage.)

This raises an important and obvious question: If I want to go to heaven when I die, and if heaven is only for people who are worthy to be there, then what do I have to do for God to consider me worthy?

Jesus does not answer that question in this passage, but the Greek verb that he uses (*kataxioō*) seems to give us a clue. This word means "counted worthy" or even "made worthy." You see, the worthiness is not something we do, but something done to us; it is not something that comes from inside us, but something that God declares about us and gives to us by his grace. Because of our sin, we are not worthy in ourselves. Nevertheless, God considers, or reckons, or counts us as worthy. We know from the rest of the New Testament that he does this on the basis of the perfect righteousness of Jesus Christ. We are not worthy, but Jesus is, and when we put our faith in Jesus, God considers us to be worthy in his sight. I want to be found in Christ, said the apostle Paul, "not having a righteousness [or worthiness] of my own that comes from the law, but that which comes through faith in Christ, the righteousness [or worthiness] from God that depends on faith" (Phil. 3:9).

The third great truth Jesus teaches about the resurrection is that when God raises us from the dead, we will never die again. This is *a truth about immortality*. As Jesus said, people who are counted worthy of the resurrection "cannot die anymore" (Luke 20:36)—their existence is everlasting.

This also seems to be the main point of the comparison Jesus makes to the angels. When we are raised from the dead, we will be "equal to angels" (Luke 20:36). This does not mean that we will *become* angels. Since the angels are in heaven with God, some people think that when we die and go to heaven we actually become angels ourselves. But that is not what Jesus said; he said that we will be *equal* to angels. Nor does this mean that there is some kind of hierarchy in heaven, and that when we die we get to a higher level. Jesus is not talking about equality the way we talk about it in our culture. He simply means that in certain respects we will be similar to angels. In fact, this is one place where the New International Version may give us a better translation: "they are like the angels" (Luke 20:36 NIV).

So in what way will we be like the angels? There are many possible points of comparison. Angels were made for the glory of God, and so are we. Angels devote their worship to God, and so do we, if we know the living God. Unfallen angels never sin, and neither will we, when we finally reach the glories of heaven. Angels never get married, which is a point of comparison that comes right out of this passage: we will not be married in heaven either. But the main point of comparison here is that the angels are immortal. They will not and they cannot die.

When God raises us from the dead, we too will be immortal. Incidentally, this helps to explain why there is no marriage in heaven. One of the primary purposes of marriage is procreation. From the beginning of the world, God has told us to "be fruitful and multiply and fill the earth" (Gen. 1:28). This is essential to the continuance of the human race: if we do not bear children, then we will die right off the face of the earth. But no one will or can die in eternity. Thus there will be no need for offspring, or even for marriage—this is the logic of the answer that Jesus gave to the question the Sadducees were asking about the resurrection.

Everlasting immortality is essential to the joy of the resurrection life. The joy of our present existence is always muted by the painful reality of death. Even if we try not to think about it, we know that someday we will die—probably someday sooner than we hope. We also know that the people we love will die, if they have not died already. Our mortality inevitably makes this life a tragedy. But there is no sorrow or sadness in heaven, and this is partly because there are no funeral directors there! After the resurrection, no one will ever die again. Eventually even the best things in this life must come to an end, but our happiness in God will be endless. By the power of his resurrection, the glories of the coming age will go on and on forever.

The fourth truth that Jesus teaches us about the resurrection life is that God will raise us up to be his children. This is *a truth about our paternity.* Jesus said that "those who are considered worthy to attain to that age and to the resurrection from the dead . . . are sons of God, being sons of the resurrection" (Luke 20:35–36). There may be another connection to the angels here, because there are one or two places where the Old Testament seems to refer to angels as "sons of God" (see Job 2:1; Ps. 89:6). But there is also a deep truth about our own salvation: we are the sons and the daughters of God, and thus the life of the resurrection is something we share as the family of God.

Jesus calls us the resurrection sons of God. This is the highest status that we can ever be given, and it applies to both men and women. According to ancient property law, only sons could inherit their father's estate. So by calling his daughters "sons," Jesus was assuring the women in his family that as joint heirs of salvation, they will have all the blessings of their Father's house.

The Bible talks about our relationship with our heavenly Father in several different ways. It says that we are God's sons and daughters by regeneration. The Holy Spirit makes us the born-again children of God (see John 3:1–8). It also says we are God's sons and daughters by adoption. In Christ we have received "adoption as sons" (see Gal. 4:5). Here Jesus says we are also God's sons and daughters by resurrection. God will not leave his children in the grave, but raise them up and bring them home to be with him forever. This is what it means for us to be "sons of God, being sons of the resurrection" (Luke 20:36).

## THE PROOF OF THE RESURRECTION

How do we know that all this is really true? How can we be certain that without any merit of our own, but only because God has counted us worthy in Christ, we will be raised up to live forever with our Father in heaven? This is the question that began the whole discussion—the question the Sadducees were asking, and that many people ask today: How can we know the resurrection for sure?

To this point Jesus has simply asserted that the righteous will rise from the dead. His entire answer is based on the assumption of the resurrection. Jesus obviously believed that the dead would rise again, even before he rose from the grave on the first Easter Sunday. But right at the end of his answer, Jesus proved the doctrine of the resurrection by quoting from the Old Testament: "But that the dead are raised, even Moses showed, in the passage about the bush, where he calls the Lord the God of Abraham and the God of Isaac and the God of Jacob. Now he is not God of the dead, but of the living, for all live to him" (Luke 20:37–38).

This was a very persuasive way for Jesus to make his argument. The Sadducees prided themselves on following the Torah—the five books of Moses—and they were convinced that the Torah had nothing to say about the resurrection. But here Jesus was proving the resurrection by quoting the words of Moses himself! This shows how well Jesus knew his Bible, and also how much confidence he had in the truth of what it says.

Nevertheless, there are some people who doubt whether his argument is a very good one. There are even some evangelical scholars who claim that "there is no persuasive connection" between what Moses said and the way that Jesus used it in the Gospels.[6] This forces us to go back to one of the most important passages in the Old Testament to see what God was saying to his people, and what it proves about the resurrection.

---

6. Peter Enns, *Inspiration and Incarnation: Evangelicals and the Problem of the Old Testament* (Grand Rapids: Baker, 2005), 114.

Exodus 3 is the story of the burning bush. It was the time of Israel's slavery in Egypt, and the people of God were crying out for their deliverance. After forty long years in the wilderness, Moses met the living God on a lonely mountainside. God spoke to him out of a fiery bush that burned, but was not consumed. He told Moses to take off his sandals because he was standing on holy ground. Then he called Moses to be his prophet. With this call came God's promise to lead his people out of Egypt and back into the Promised Land, as well as the revelation of his special divine name.

Yet before he said all of this, God identified himself to Moses as the God of the covenant—the God who had made everlasting promises to Abraham, Isaac, and Jacob. The way he said this was significant: "I am the God of your father, the God of Abraham, the God of Isaac, and the God of Jacob" (Exod. 3:6). God spoke to Moses in the present tense. He did not say "I was the God" of these men, but "I *am* the God" of these men. He was telling Moses that he is a living God, and therefore that he is able to save his people.

Jesus rested his proof for the resurrection on this truth, which shows how completely he accepted the full inspiration and authority of the very words of the Bible. Jesus reasoned from the Scriptures—by good and necessary consequence—that when God said, "I am the God of Abraham" and so forth, he was not just saying something about himself, but he was also saying something about Abraham and the rest of them. God's statement is true in its fullest and most complete sense only if these men are still alive today. Centuries after these men died, God was still styling himself as their God, which means that there had to be an Abraham, an Isaac, and a Jacob for him to be the God of! This is true, said Leon Morris, only "if they are alive beyond the grave. The alternative is to think of God as the God of non-existent beings, which is absurd."[7]

But that is not all. How could God even call himself the God of these men unless he kept his promises to them? When he called himself "the God of Abraham, Isaac, and Jacob," God was using the language of the covenant. This is clear from what he said at the end of Exodus 2, when he first responded to the cries of his people: "God remembered his covenant with Abraham, with Isaac, and with Jacob" (Exod. 2:24). These were the men whom God had promised to save forever. God kept many of the gracious

---

7. Leon Morris, *The Gospel According to St. Luke: An Introduction and Commentary*, Tyndale New Testament Commentaries (Grand Rapids: Eerdmans, 1974), 292.

promises that he made to these men during their own lifetimes. But none of these men had full possession of Canaan when they died—the Promised Land. None of them saw offspring like the stars in the sky or the sand in the desert—the promised children. None of them saw the Christ that God said he would give for the nations through the line of Abraham—the promised Savior.

Nevertheless, God said that he was their God, and he could say it without embarrassment or apology because every last one of his promises will come true for these men in the resurrection of the coming age. They will reach the Promised Land of God's glory. They will worship with their children in the eternal city. They will know the crucified and risen Christ. This is all because their God is the covenant God of the resurrection. If he could not raise the dead, he would not be much of a God for them at all, and he could not keep his everlasting covenant. But he is the God of the living, not the dead. He is the God who raises the dead. Therefore Abraham, Isaac, and Jacob are living for him right now, and they will keep on living for him forever.

Everyone who comes to God through faith in Jesus Christ has the same resurrection life. We will be raised from the dead by the power of the living God, so that we can glorify God and enjoy him forever. It all depends on the resurrection, which is essential to the whole relationship that God has with his people. He is not our God unless he is able to raise us from the dead and establish a relationship with us that will last for all eternity.

For the proof for that resurrection, go back to Exodus and read what God said to Moses. Or else go to the empty tomb, where God raised Jesus from the dead. Our God is the God of the living—the God of Abraham, Isaac, and Jacob. He is the God of Moses. He is the God of all the people we love who have gone ahead of us into glory. But most of all he is the God of our Lord Jesus Christ, who on the third day was raised to everlasting life by the resurrection power of God.

87

# David's Son and David's Lord

## *Luke 20:39–44*

*"For David himself says in the Book of Psalms, 'The Lord said
to my Lord, Sit at my right hand, until I make your enemies
your footstool.' David thus calls him Lord, so how is he his son?"*
(Luke 20:42–44)

*I* enjoyed the most privileged of all childhoods. Since my
mother is a voracious reader and my father is a professor
of English literature, I grew up in a house full of books. To
scan the shelves was to learn the names of the world's great authors:
Chaucer, Milton, and Dostoevsky. Then to take the books and read was
to explore new worlds of the mind and heart. But of all the great books
on the family shelves, none held greater promise than a green volume
with a golden title: *Answers to Questions.*[1]

These magical words could almost make a boy believe that the book held
the sum of all knowledge. What questions the book proposed, and what
answers it gave!

---

1. Frederic J. Haskin, *Answers to Questions* (New York: Grosset & Dunlap, 1926).

*Question:* Do fish sleep?
*Answer:* Fish do not sleep. At times they remain quiet in pools and streams.

*Question:* Are pigs naturally dirty farm animals?
*Answer:* Pigs are the cleanest of animals if allowed to be so.

*Question:* Was Clara Barton a lover of music?
*Answer:* On the contrary, Miss Barton is said to have had little if any love for music.

*Question:* Is it true that a person dreaming of falling from a great height will die from shock if he does not awaken before he hits the ground?
*Answer:* Physicians say that such an idea is ridiculous, although this is not susceptible of absolute proof, for if any man has ever died from the shock of landing at the bottom of a dream, he has never had a chance to tell about it.

And so it went. What could be more satisfying to an inquisitive mind than to know the answers to these kinds of questions?

If only we could get the same kind of clarity from God! Most people have some hard questions about life they wish that God would answer. How can I know for sure what is true? Why is this happening to me? What is the meaning of all this suffering? Where will it all end? Even people who know the Bible still have some questions, and people who do not believe in God at all are still looking for the answers.

## ANSWERS TO QUESTIONS

It was the same way in the time of Christ, which is why the Gospels give us so many answers to so many questions. People were always asking Jesus to explain something. In fact, some parts of Luke read like the transcript for a question and answer session. And why not? People always ask their teachers questions, and Jesus was the greatest teacher who ever lived. So people were always coming to him with their questions. Since Luke 20 marks the end of all these questions, it is a good place to review the answers that Jesus gave, as well as the implications of his wisdom for our own relationship to God.

When Jesus forgave a man who was paralyzed, people asked, "Who can forgive sins but God alone?" (Luke 5:21). When he insisted on spending so much time with low-life sinners, people asked him, "Why do you eat and drink with tax collectors?" (Luke 5:30). When he claimed to be the Lord of the Lord's day, they asked him, "Why are you doing what is not lawful to do on the Sabbath?" (Luke 6:2).

People also asked Jesus about the way of salvation—the most important question that anyone can ever ask: "What shall I do to inherit eternal life?" (Luke 10:25; cf. 18:18). When Jesus told them what love it would take to be saved by their own doing, they came back with a follow-up question: "Who is my neighbor?" (Luke 10:29). The questions kept coming: When will the kingdom come? (Luke 17:20). By what authority are you preaching the gospel? (Luke 20:2). Do we have to pay Caesar our taxes, or not? (Luke 20:22).

Many of these questions were asked in malice. Luke tells us plainly that "the scribes and the Pharisees began to press him hard and to provoke him to speak about many things, lying in wait for him, to catch him in something he might say" (Luke 11:53–54). Finally, a group of scholars came to Jesus with a complicated seven-part question about who would be married to whom after the resurrection (Luke 20:28–33). By this point, people had asked him just about every question they could think of.

In each case, Jesus gave an answer that proved his total mastery of theology and his knowledge of the mind of God. He had been doing this ever since he was a boy. On that memorable Passover when Jesus was twelve and stayed behind in Jerusalem, the teachers at the temple "were amazed at his understanding and his answers" (Luke 2:47). Jesus always amazes people with his answers. Just ask Satan. Three times the devil tried to tempt Jesus to claim the crown without suffering the cross, and each time Jesus came back with a devastating answer based on the Word of God.

Jesus was equally devastating when he answered all the questions that his enemies asked. When they asked what right he had to forgive people's sins, he healed a paralyzed man and sent him on his way, fully forgiven (Luke 5:20–25). When they questioned him about breaking the Sabbath, he said, "The Son of Man is lord of the Sabbath" (Luke 6:5). When they asked who counted as a neighbor, he answered with the parable of the good Samaritan—one of the most famous stories ever told.

Jesus had an answer for every question, and with every answer, he was explaining deep truths about God and man, about sin and salvation, about forgiveness and eternal life. Ask Jesus if you have to pay your taxes, and he

comes back with a one-sentence response that governs the whole relationship between religion and politics (see Luke 20:25). Ask him about marriage and the resurrection, and he will open up the mysteries of heaven (see
Luke 20:34–38).

In the end, anyone who was hoping to catch Jesus making a mistake had to
surrender. His intellect was so superior and his answers were so unanswerable that finally "some of the scribes answered, 'Teacher, you have spoken
well.' For they no longer dared to ask him any question" (Luke 20:39–40).
Their defeat was complete, as Jesus claimed total victory over the unbelief
behind all their skeptical questions.

The English poet Richard Crashaw testified to our Lord's triumph in
a poem called "Neither Durst any man from that Day ask him any more
Questions." Crashaw wrote:

'Twas time to hold their peace when they,
Had ne'er another word to say:
Yet is their silence unto thee,
The full sound of thy victory. . . .
To hold their peace is all the ways,
These wretches have to speak thy praise.[2]

In other words, silence really can be golden. When a spiritual skeptic has a personal encounter with Jesus Christ and realizes that Jesus has answers to the
hardest questions anyone can ask, then the skeptic's silence gives glory to God.

The Bible says that one day every mouth will be shut before God (Rom.
3:19). For some people this will not happen until the day of judgment,
when the personal return of Jesus Christ will give a visible and unmistakable answer to anyone who has ever doubted his supreme deity. There will
be nothing that any doubter can say on that great day, and the silence of
every skeptic will give glory to God.

If we are wise, however, we will shut our mouths much sooner and offer
God the silence of a submissive heart. In fact, Martyn Lloyd-Jones goes so
far as to define a Christian as a man whose mouth is shut:

2. Richard Crashaw, "Neither Durst any man from that Day ask him any more Questions," in
*Chapters into Verse: Poetry in English Inspired by the Bible, vol. 2: Gospels to Revelation*, ed. Robert
Atwan and Laurance Wieder (Oxford: Oxford University Press, 1993), 159–60.

> You are not a Christian unless you have been made speechless! How do you
> know whether you are a Christian or not? It is that you "stop talking." The
> trouble with the non-Christian is that he goes on talking. . . . People need to
> have their mouths shut, "stopped." They are for ever talking about God, and
> criticizing God, and pontificating about what God should or should not do,
> and asking "Why does God allow this and that?" You do not begin to be a
> Christian until your mouth is shut, is stopped, and you are speechless and
> have nothing to say.[3]

Jesus always welcomes sincere questions from people who are seeking to
know the truth, and he always gives them answers that will satisfy the soul.
But if we are raising questions only because we want to prove that we are
right and God is wrong, it would be better for us not to say anything at all.

This was the great lesson that Job learned. As he struggled with all his
sufferings, Job had many things he wanted to say to God, and many questions he wanted God to answer. But at the end of his struggle he came face
to face with the power of God the mighty Creator, and by the time God was
through asking Job *his* questions, Job had nothing more to say. However
many questions he had for God, God had even more questions for him—
questions that no merely mortal man could ever answer. When Job finally
realized what he was up against, he put his hand over his mouth (Job 40:4)
and said, "I have uttered what I did not understand. . . . Therefore I despise
myself, and repent in dust and ashes" (Job 42:3, 6). In other words, when
Job was questioning God he did not know what he was talking about. It
would have been better for him to say nothing at all, but simply to sit before
God in silence and awe.

This is what a Christian is: someone whose mouth has been shut—shut
against making any more accusations against God, or any more claims
about his own worthiness, so that Jesus Christ can truly be God.

## What Jesus Asked

The scholars and scribes may have been finished with all their questions for Jesus, but Jesus still had one last question for them. It was

---

3. D. Martyn Lloyd-Jones, *Romans: An Exposition of Chapter 3.20–4.25, Atonement and Justification* (Grand Rapids: Zondervan, 1970), 19.

really more like a riddle, and its answer unlocks the mystery at the heart of the universe.

Remember the context. Jesus was in Jerusalem for the last week of his life, and the religious leaders—who denied that he was the Son of the living God—wanted to know what right he had to preach the kingdom. But Luke's purpose in this Gospel is to help us know salvation for sure by proving to us that Jesus is the Christ. Here is one of Luke's clinching arguments, given in the form of a riddle that we can answer only if we believe that Jesus Christ really is God. Jesus said to the scribes: "How can they say that the Christ is David's son? For David himself says in the Book of Psalms, 'The Lord said to my Lord, Sit at my right hand, until I make your enemies your footstool.' David thus calls him Lord, so how is he his son?" (Luke 20:41–44).

This is absolutely marvelous, especially for anyone who loves a good riddle: God put a riddle in the Old Testament that Jesus used to help us understand the truth that leads to eternal life. The riddle is a real stumper, but if we work hard to understand both the question and the answer, we can learn some of the most important things that anyone can ever know.

Jesus began with something that everyone knew already: the Christ would be David's son. This was common knowledge. "Christ" is simply another word for "Messiah"—the Anointed One, the Savior whom God had always promised to send. David was the greatest of Israel's ancient kings, and the Scriptures prophesied that the Christ would come from his lineage. As God said to David himself, "I will raise up your offspring after you, who shall come from your body, and I will establish his kingdom. . . . And your house and your kingdom . . . shall be established forever" (2 Sam. 7:12, 16). We read the same thing in the prophet Isaiah: "For to us a child is born, to us a son is given . . . on the throne of David and over his kingdom" (Isa. 9:6–7). When the Messiah came, he would belong to the royal bloodline of the house of David.

This was a criterion that Jesus clearly met. He was a direct lineal descendant of King David, and therefore had a right to the messianic title "Son of David" (see Luke 18:38). Luke has shown this several times in his Gospel. When the birth of Jesus was first announced, his earthly father Joseph was identified as a man from "the house of David" (Luke 1:27). The angel Gabriel told Mary that God would give her child "the throne of his father David" (Luke 1:32). Then, when the child was born, Luke told us again that his family "was of the house and lineage of David" (Luke 2:4; cf. 1:69)—a fact confirmed by the genealogy Luke carefully provides in chapter 3.

Nor is Luke the only person who says this. Matthew begins his Gospel by identifying Jesus Christ as "the son of David" (Matt. 1:1), and in Romans Paul says that he "was descended from David according to the flesh" (Rom. 1:3; cf. 9:5). This fact sets up the riddle that Jesus told and is foundational to the answer he gives. Jesus Christ belongs to the most venerable of all kingdoms, the most noble of all houses: he is the Son of David.

## THE WORLD'S GREATEST RIDDLE

So far so good. Everyone knew that the Christ would be David's son. But Jesus proceeds to ask how the Christ could be David's son and at the same time David's Lord?

To see why Jesus posed this riddle, it is necessary to go back to something that David himself once said. Jesus was quoting here from Psalm 110, a psalm of David. Psalm 110 is a messianic psalm—a psalm that makes explicit prophecies about the coming of the Christ. All of the ancient rabbis agreed that David was prophesying about the Christ. Later the Puritan Edward Reynolds would say, "This psalm is one of the fullest and most compendious prophecies of the person and offices of Christ in the whole Old Testament."[4]

David's messianic psalm begins with a dialogue. What is confusing about this two-person conversation is that both participants are called "Lord." David says, "The LORD says to my Lord: 'Sit at my right hand, until I make your enemies your footstool'" (Ps. 110:1). So who are these two "Lords"?

The identity of the first "LORD" is obvious. Most English translations print his title in small capital letters to show that it refers to God himself. David is using the name *Yahweh*—the special divine name that belongs only to God. So the person speaking in this verse is the Lord God Almighty.

But to whom is he speaking? The identity of the second "Lord" is somewhat less obvious, but it is perfectly clear nonetheless. This time David uses a different name for "Lord"—the name *Adonai*. This is a general term that

---

4. Edward Reynolds, quoted in James Montgomery Boice, *Psalms: An Expositional Commentary*, 3 vols. (Grand Rapids: Baker, 1998), 3:893.

can be used for any kind of lord, but here it refers specifically to the Messiah, the Christ, the Anointed One. This is clear from the rest of the psalm, which declares that this "Lord" will rule over the kingdom of God. So David is repeating a dialogue between God Almighty and the coming Christ. He is saying something like this: "The Lord God says to my Lord the Messiah, sit on my throne to rule the universe."

What is puzzling about this is that David regards the Christ as superior to himself, calling him "my Lord." Yet David never called anyone "Lord," except the Lord God himself, and maybe his father, or perhaps Saul, who was king of Israel before him. David certainly did not call anyone "Lord" once he had become the king in his own right. Yet here is a person so great that even David calls him "Lord."

This is puzzling because the Messiah was supposed to be David's son, and in that culture fathers did not call their sons "Lord." This is something that no patriarch would ever do, least of all a man who was a monarch. The son is to honor the father, not the other way around. So when the Messiah came, surely he would pay homage to David as his great father. Yet here David is the one who gives homage, acknowledging the superiority of his son. The Messiah would be David's son, yet David also calls him "Lord."

Furthermore, the second person in Psalm 110—the one whom David calls his Lord—will receive the kingdom. He will sit at the right hand of God until every last one of his enemies is defeated. The right hand of God represents God's own rule and authority. To be exalted is to sit in that awesome place to reign in glory and to share in the royal majesty of God.

Who is this mighty king? Who is this ruler so great that David calls him "Lord"? If the Messiah is David's son, how can he be so superior? Listen again to the question Jesus asked, the riddle that he posed: "How can they say that the Christ is David's son? For David himself says in the Book of Psalms, 'The Lord said to my Lord, Sit at my right hand, until I make your enemies your footstool.' David thus calls him Lord, so how is he his son?" (Luke 10:41–44).

## THE RIDDLE SOLVED

What is the solution to this riddle? Obviously, Jesus was not denying that he was the son of David; he knew that he was. But he was using the

Scripture to prove that he was also *more* than the son of David: Jesus was and is the very Son of God. The Christ was David's Lord because he was and is David's God.

This riddle can be solved only if Jesus is God as well as man—if he is both human and divine. The historical records show that as a man, Jesus of Nazareth was indeed a physical descendant of King David. The Christ was David's son. But the Bible testifies that Jesus is also God, that by the virgin birth he has a divine nature as well as a human nature. As Jesus says himself at the end of Revelation: "I, Jesus, . . . am the root and the descendant of David" (Rev. 22:16). In other words, Jesus Christ is both David's Creator God and his human son.

All of this explains why David called him "Lord." The Son of God was David's Lord the very moment that David said this, because from eternity past he had been ruling with his Father in heaven. His deity made him superior to David—the fact that as God the Son he was very God of very God. James Boice explained it like this: "If David called his natural physical descendant (the Messiah) his Lord, it could only be because the One to come would somehow be greater than David was, and the only way that could happen is if the Messiah were more than a mere man. He would have to be a divine Messiah, that is, God."[5]

Jesus had already given many convincing proofs of his divine power. Every miracle he performed was another proof of his deity. If the leading disciples ever had any doubt about his deity, they simply had to remember what they saw on the mount of transfiguration, when Jesus was revealed in all the splendor of his divine majesty (see Luke 9:29–35). But now Jesus was proving his deity from the Scriptures, clinching his case with a riddle that could be resolved only by the man who was also God.

Some people did not believe this. The scribes and the scholars did not understand that the Messiah had to be God as well as man—that David's son would also be David's Lord. According to Ambrose, "Jesus did not rebuke them because they acknowledged the Son of David but because they do not believe him to be the Son of God." Then he added this practical exhortation: "Let us therefore believe that Christ is God and man."[6]

---

5. Boice, *Psalms*, 3:892.

6. Ambrose, "Exposition of the Gospel of Luke," in *Luke*, ed. Arthur A. Just, Jr., Ancient Christian Commentary on Scripture, NT 3 (Downers Grove, IL: InterVarsity, 2003), 314.

The answer to this riddle unlocks the mystery at the heart of the universe, teaching us some of the most important things that anyone can ever know. It shows us the mystery of the incarnation: Jesus Christ is both human and divine. He has become one of us to save us, but he has done this without abandoning his deity, and therefore he has divine power to save us. When we come to Jesus for salvation, we are coming to the God who has all the authority in the universe.

The riddle of David's Lord also shows us the mystery of the Trinity: there is one God in three persons. How can David say, "The LORD says to my Lord," unless there is more than one person in the Godhead? This conversation is a conundrum that only the reality of the Trinity can resolve. Already in the Old Testament there is a clear indication that although there is only one God, he exists in more than one person. The one and only true God eternally exists in three persons: the Father, the Son, and the Holy Spirit. By quoting Psalm 110, Jesus was pointing to his deity and thereby testifying to his relationship with God the Father as God the Son.

Jesus was also making a prophecy about his eventual exaltation. Psalm 110 is teaching us something about the resurrection and ascension of Jesus Christ. Notice what the Father does for the Son in this passage, what the Lord God does for the Messiah Christ: he exalts him to his royal throne. Jesus knew the promise of David and embraced it as his own eternal destiny. It was the last week of his life, and soon he would be put to death for his people's sins. But the day was coming when he would rise to the throne of the universe and rule in triumph. As the Son of God, our Savior would sit at God's right hand, reigning on his Father's throne with all of his enemies under his feet. As it says in the Apostles' Creed, "He ascended into heaven, and sitteth on the right hand of God, the Father Almighty." Jesus is the Christ. He is the Son of God. He is the divine King who rules over earth and heaven. He is David's son and David's Lord!

What Jesus said about Psalm 110 must have made a deep impression on his disciples, because this is the psalm they quoted more than any other. It shows up more than twenty times in the New Testament. Peter used it on the day of Pentecost, when he preached the gospel of repentance and three thousand people were saved. Peter told them that Jesus had been raised from the dead and exalted to the right hand of God. Then he quoted Psalm 110 as the proof that God had taken the same Jesus who was crucified and made him our Lord and our Christ (see Acts 2:32–36). The apostle Paul used the same psalm to prove that when Jesus raises us from the dead he will destroy all our enemies (see 1 Cor. 15:22–25). The book of Hebrews uses Psalm 110 to show that Jesus is superior to the angels, and therefore that he has supremacy over everything (Heb. 1:13). The apostles celebrated Jesus as David's Christ.

Is this the Jesus that you know? Is this the God that you worship? Does it thrill your soul to know that Jesus Christ, the Son of God, is Lord over all?

What an amazing question Jesus asked, and what an amazing answer he gives—not just to this question, but to all our questions. Jesus *is* the answer. If we believe in him, then the very Son of God is Christ our Lord. This is the answer to the question of all questions, and the riddle of all riddles: Who is Jesus? If we can answer this question, we have the key to unlock all the other mysteries in the universe. All the other answers to our questions will come, as long as we start with Jesus, "who was descended from David according to the flesh and was declared to be the Son of God . . . by his resurrection from the dead, Jesus Christ our Lord" (Rom. 1:3–4).

If you believe the answer to the ancient riddle—that Jesus the Savior is the Son of God—then David's son is not just David's Lord. He is also *your* Lord, and you will be raised with him to eternal life.

# 88

# YOUR TWO CENTS

## *Luke 20:45—21:4*

*Jesus looked up and saw the rich putting their gifts into the offer-
ing box, and he saw a poor widow put in two small copper coins.
And he said, "Truly, I tell you, this poor widow has put in more
than all of them. For they all contributed out of their abundance,
but she out of her poverty put in all she had to live on."*
(Luke 21:1–4)

*P*eople usually think of the biblical Gospels as positive, uplift-
ing books, and so they are. The word "gospel" means "good
news," which is exactly what Luke and the other Gospels
give us: the good news of salvation for sinners. For people who know that
they are in trouble, the Gospels are the best of all books. They offer help to
people who do not know where to turn. They tell the truth to people who
do not have the answers. They provide shelter to people who do not have a
home to call their own. The Gospels do this by giving us Jesus—the living,
dying, rising Savior of the world.

If we read the Gospels carefully, however, we also discover that they are
deeply disturbing. This is partly because Jesus makes so many difficult

demands: "Take up your cross daily and follow me" (see Luke 9:23); "If anyone . . . does not hate . . . his own life, he cannot be my disciple" (Luke 14:26); "Sell all that you have and distribute to the poor" (Luke 18:22). Who is able to do all the things that Jesus tells us to do?

In addition to all the difficult demands that Jesus made in the Gospels, there are also many harsh denunciations, especially the ones he made against the "nice religious people" of his day. Jesus always welcomed sinners who knew they did not deserve anything except to be damned, but he usually made people who thought they had a good spiritual reputation very uncomfortable. His most withering criticism was reserved for churchgoers and other religious insiders. Maybe this explains why Jesus usually preached out of doors and almost never in synagogues. Most churches would not tolerate the kinds of things that Jesus said about religious people. The Gospels are not always comforting; sometimes they are disturbing—especially for people who are satisfied with where they are spiritually.

### BEWARE OF THE SCRIBES!

One of the most disturbing denunciations comes in the last speech Jesus made against the religious leaders of his day. This speech is the culmination of everything Jesus had been saying about their hypocrisy: "In the hearing of all the people he said to his disciples, 'Beware of the scribes, who like to walk around in long robes, and love greetings in the marketplaces and the best seats in the synagogues and the places of honor at feasts, who devour widows' houses and for a pretense make long prayers. They will receive the greater condemnation'" (Luke 20:45–47).

Jesus was speaking directly to his disciples, but this was an open rebuke—a public denunciation of the Bible scholars that everyone respected as the most spiritual men in Israel. Right in front of everyone, Jesus showed what was wrong with their religion, and what is wrong with anyone who tries to impress people by being spiritual.

Jesus mainly criticized these men for their ostentatious lifestyle. With pious pomposity, they paraded around in public wearing fancy attire. Leon Morris says that their long robes "were a sign of distinction and marked the wearers as gentlemen of leisure."[1] These men liked to show how successful they were, with the implication that somehow their financial success proved that God was pleased with the way they lived. Sadly, some prosperity preachers do the same thing today, wearing fancy clothes and driving fine automobiles in order to prove that what they teach will make people rich.

Other scholars claim that Jesus was referring to the tassels that some Israelites wore on the hems of their garments as a way of remembering God's commandments, in keeping with the custom of Moses (see Num. 15:38–39). But this was all for show, and in a way, it revealed exactly what was wrong with their religion. They were concerned with only the outward appearance of obedience, not with having a heart for God. Their piety was really only a cloak for their hypocrisy.

Jesus also criticized these men for their ambitious social climbing. Whenever they were out and about in the marketplace, they loved to be greeted with formal and honorific titles. They wanted people to call them "the most esteemed and learned doctor so-and-so." They expected adulation; indeed, they demanded it. When they went to worship at their local synagogue, they insisted on claiming one of the best seats in the house. When they went to a wedding or some other celebration, they were offended if they did not get a place at the head table (see Luke 14:7–11). These self-important men craved recognition. They wanted everyone to give them the honor they thought they deserved, given their position in life.

This kind of posturing is tempting for all of us, which is why Jesus tells us to beware of the scribes. Some people find their identity in what they wear. If only they had the right clothes, then people would think that they were cool, or that they were in style, or that they were successful in business. Other people find their identity in their social status, in being recognized for who they are. Businesses try to capitalize on this mentality by offering preferred seating, or VIP parking, or platinum service—anything to make their customers feel that they are getting ahead in life.

How deadly these attitudes are in the church, where we still face many temptations to pharisaical pride. We are called to be who we are in Christ—nothing more and nothing less. Instead, we are sometimes tempted to

---

1. Leon Morris, *The Gospel According to St. Luke: An Introduction and Commentary*, Tyndale New Testament Commentaries (Grand Rapids: Eerdmans, 1974), 294.

suggest, even in subtle ways, that we are more spiritual than we really are: more active in service, more faithful in prayer, more knowledgeable in the Scriptures, more concerned about people in need. Even if we do not insist on anyone giving us an honorary title or saving us a good seat in church, we secretly live for the flush of gratification that comes when people praise our ministry. But when our godliness gets overlooked, or when we feel that our service is unappreciated, our resentment begins to burn.

How far this is from the example of Jesus Christ, who did not seek a place for himself, but set aside the glory he deserved to serve us to the very death. What matters to our humble Savior is not what we wear, or what people call us, or where we get to sit, but who we are inside. As the Scripture says, "Man looks on the outward appearance, but the LORD looks on the heart" (1 Sam. 16:7). In the case of the scribes, what the Lord saw inside was not very pretty. His all-seeing eye penetrated their outward religiosity to see their inward insincerity. What does the Lord see in your heart?

In addition to their ostentatious lifestyle and their ambitious social climbing, the scribes were also guilty of pretentious intercession. They tried to enhance their spiritual reputation by offering interminable prayers in public places—in the temple courts and on the city street corners. Most people were very impressed by their prayer life, but Jesus saw it for what it really was: not piety, but hypocrisy.

There is a time and a place for long prayers. No one has ever understood this better than Jesus, who sometimes spent the whole night in prayer. A prayer needs to be as long as it needs to be. Sometimes we have a lot of things to pray about, and sometimes, by the grace of the Holy Spirit, we have a longing to linger in the presence of God, pouring out our praise. But our Father already knows everything about us, so simple prayers can be equally effective. Like little children who know their father's love, we can come right out and tell God our troubles, asking him for what we need. There is no inherent virtue in praying a long prayer.

In fact, when long prayers are offered primarily for the benefit of anyone who might be watching, they are an offense to God. One prominent politician offered this kind of prayer at the Western Wall in Jerusalem. The politician made sure that the cameras were rolling, so that the photos would get back to the Jewish constituency back home. The photograph I saw of the incident was telling. It was shot at a wider angle, showing not only the politician at prayer, but also the crush of photographers trying to capture the moment on film. It was not so much a prayer as it was a publicity stunt. The prayer itself was not important—only the being seen to pray.

These sins all go together—the ostentatious lifestyle, the ambitious social climbing, and the pretentious intercession—and they all add up to deadly hypocrisy. What is disturbing is how often we fall into the same trap by caring more about what people see than about what God sees. Do you really want to be godly, or would you be content to neglect the life of the soul as long as people still thought you were more spiritual than you really are? Beware of the scribes! Do not try to be something in front of other people that is not what you are before God.

## THE GREATER CONDEMNATION

Appearances to the contrary, if we want to see what the scribes were really like, we need only to look at what they were doing to the widows in their community. This is also an excellent way to examine ourselves, because one of the best tests of true spirituality is our practical concern for the poor.

Widows were virtually the most vulnerable members of any ancient society. Typically they had no regular means of financial support, and thus they were dependent on what they already owned, or else on the charity of friends. They had no one to protect them, which is why the Word of God tells us to "plead the widow's cause" (Isa. 1:17) and "visit . . . widows in their affliction" (James 1:27).

As spiritual leaders, the scribes should have been defending widows, but instead they were devouring them. It is hard to know exactly what this means. Maybe it means that they were offering to help widows manage their assets, but then claiming some of the proceeds for themselves. Or maybe the scribes were using their religious influence to persuade some widows to give more money to their ministry than they really could spare. Something similar happens today when unscrupulous evangelists prey on the lonely and the elderly, manipulating them into giving away their children's inheritance.

But however the scribes managed to do it, they greedily used their spiritual influence for personal gain, turning the temple into a den of robbers. This was exactly the opposite of what they were supposed to be doing.

Rather than taking advantage of the weak, they were supposed to be taking care of them. So the scribes were getting ministry backwards. They thought the widows were there for their benefit, rather than the other way around.

This mentality is a temptation for anyone in Christian ministry. We are called to give ourselves to others, the way that Jesus did, not to get something from them. Yet how easy it is for people who need money to do ministry to start thinking primarily in terms of how much people are giving or not giving to their cause. How easy it is as well to start complaining about all the trouble we are having with the people we are called to serve—the students in our class, the members in our small group, the difficult people in our outreach—as if they were there for our benefit! But if we have the love of Jesus, then we will love people for their own sakes, not for what they can give us.

If we are honest, most of us have to admit that we act a lot like the scribes. We do our best to look good on the outside, but so much of it is for show, and we would rather get something than give something any day. What makes this so disturbing is the statement Jesus makes at the end of the chapter: "They will receive the greater condemnation" (Luke 20:47).

These strong words of warning were spoken by the very person who one day will judge the world. Jesus wanted to be sure we knew how badly things will go for many religious people on the day of judgment. It will go badly enough for people who did not want anything to do with God at all, but it will be even worse for people who pretended to be spiritual and worst of all for the spiritual leaders who should have known better. This is a basic principle of divine justice: "Increased responsibility means increased accountability."[2] The more we know about God, the more he expects us to follow him in the truth, and the more he will condemn us for living a lie. "Not many of you should become teachers," the Bible says, because "we who teach will be judged with greater strictness" (James 3:1)—judged in proportion to our hypocrisy.

Luke 20 gives the last of many disturbing denunciations Jesus made against the religious leaders of his day. From this and from many other things that Jesus said, we get the clear impression that he hated hypocrisy as much as any other sin. J. C. Ryle said, "No sin seems to be regarded by

2. R. Kent Hughes, *Luke: That You May Know the Truth*, 2 vols., Preaching the Word (Wheaton, IL: Crossway, 1998), 2:286.

Christ as more sinful than hypocrisy. None certainly drew forth from His lips such frequent, strong, and withering condemnation, during the whole course of His ministry."[3]

Unfortunately, hypocrisy also happens to be one of the sins that religious people are especially prone to commit. In fact, it may be a sin that only someone who is trying to be religious *can* commit. Why is this sin so hateful to God? Because God wants us to be before others what we are before him, and nothing more, and also because when we try to be great ourselves (or at least seem to be great), there is hardly any room left for the greatness of God. Hypocrisy eclipses the glory of God.

This is why, in the end, hypocrisy will lead some people straight to hell. Charles Wesley showed this in a poem about worldly pastors. He began by writing: "They love to be preferred, adored, / Affect the state and style of lord, / And shine magnificently great." Then Wesley alluded to what Jesus said about the scribes: "Greedy the church's goods to seize, / Their wealth they without end increase, / And the poor widow's house devour." But what will become of such men in the end? Wesley's poem closes with these chilling words:

> O what a change they soon shall know,
> When torn away by death, they go
>   Reluctant from their splendid feasts,
> Condemned in hottest flames to dwell,
> And find the spacious courts of hell
>   Paved with the skulls of Christian Priests![4]

Wesley's words may sound harsh, but they were written with merciful intent and they are true to what Jesus said. The hypocrites of the church—especially spiritual leaders who betray their sacred trust to care for the people of God—will fall under the everlasting condemnation of a holy and almighty God. The Bible says that anyone who does not believe in Jesus Christ does not have eternal life and is already under the condemnation of God (see

3. J. C. Ryle, *Expository Thoughts on the Gospels, Luke* (1858; reprint Cambridge: James Clarke, 1976), 2:346.
4. Charles Wesley, "On Worldly Prelates," in *Chapters into Verse: Poetry in English Inspired by the Bible, vol. 2: Gospels to Revelation*, ed. Robert Atwan and Laurance Wieder (Oxford: Oxford University Press, 1993), 160–61.

John 3:18). But on the basis of what Jesus said, some people will be more greatly condemned than others—people who pretended to belong to God but never really did.

The only way to escape this condemnation is to put our genuine faith in Jesus, for there is "now no condemnation for those who are in Christ" (Rom. 8:1). Whatever we are or are not, let us be what we are before God and a watching world. If we are sinners, let us admit that we are sinners, and seek to be saved by grace. If we are not very good Christians, let us admit that we are not very good Christians, and ask God to make us better. In the meantime, let us offer to God only what is genuinely and sincerely true, however weak it is, and however unworthy we are.

## THE WIDOW'S MITES

If anyone seemed weak and unworthy, it was the woman Jesus and his disciples saw putting her two cents into the offering box at the temple. Yet Luke is giving us another one of his brilliant contrasts, like white lace on black velvet.

This widow's piety provides the perfect counterexample to the hypocrisy of the scribes. The scribes wanted to seem religious, but they did not want to make any sacrifices for the kingdom of God. Then along came a poor widow who gave more to God than all of them put together: "Jesus looked up and saw the rich putting their gifts into the offering box, and he saw a poor widow put in two small copper coins. And he said, 'Truly, I tell you, this poor widow has put in more than all of them. For they all contributed out of their abundance, but she out of her poverty put in all she had to live on'" (Luke 21:1–4).

It was the week of Passover, and pilgrims had come to Jerusalem from all over Israel in order to pay their vows to God. In those days there were thirteen collection boxes at the temple, each with a narrow opening at the top.[5] People simply walked up at any time to put their money in the box. While Jesus was there with his disciples, rich people were coming up to give their offerings. Presumably it was obvious they were rich from the way that they dressed, and also because it took them so long to make their

---

5. Morris, *Luke*, 294.

contributions. We get the impression that some of them may have been doing this for show, but it was still appropriate for them to give their money to God—a *lot* of money, given their income. They were doing what they should have done.

Naturally some people were very impressed with how much these rich people were giving. They seemed to be doing more for God than most people. But Jesus was unimpressed. What he noticed instead was a poor old woman who put in two little pennies. The word that Luke uses for these coins *(lepta)* refers to copper currency that was worth only one four hundredth of a shekel.

What the widow gave was hardly big enough to clink as it fell into the treasury. But as far as Jesus was concerned, her contribution was worth more than everything the rich people gave. This is what Jesus meant when he said she "put in more than all of them" (Luke 21:3); he meant more than all of them *combined*. Kent Hughes comments: "Jesus held in his hands the balance scales of eternity. On one side he emptied all the contents of the thirteen trumpets—the shekels, the denarii, the heavy gold and silver. On the other side he placed the two minuscule copper coins. And the massive load of the rich gave way to the eternal weight of the widow's tiny offerings."[6]

Jesus said this because rather than comparing what one person gave to what another person gave, he compared what each person gave to what each person had. The rich people were giving a lot, but then they had a lot to give. As Jesus put it, they were giving "out of their abundance" (Luke 21:4). They had so much money to begin with that even after they had made their contributions, they still had money to spare.

The widow gave everything she had—literally, "all she had to live on" (Luke 21:4). The word that Jesus uses to describe her financial situation *(hysterēmatos)* indicates extreme poverty. The woman had hardly anything to call her own. She was destitute—the poorest of the poor—and when she left the temple that day, she had nothing left to call her own in all the world.

Given her desperate financial straits, it would have been perfectly appropriate for the widow to keep her money. If she believed it was her

6. Hughes, *Luke*, 2:292.

biblical duty to tithe, giving one tenth of her income to God, then she could have rounded her two coins down to zero. Besides, this was all the money she had to live on—her very life was at stake. It certainly would have been appropriate for her to give one penny to God and keep the other penny for herself. At that rate she would have been giving God 50 percent, which is more than most people give! Instead, in a practical act of total devotion, she gave all her pennies to God.

The Bible does not tell us why the woman did this, but I think we know what she believed about God—what she had to believe about God to do this. She had to believe that God was glorious, because she was giving him all her earthly treasure. She had to believe that God was gracious, because she was responding with the kind of costly generosity that only grace compels. She had to believe that God was provident, because once she had nothing left to live on, she would have to depend on him for absolutely everything. To her everlasting credit, here was a woman who offered God unconditional faith, undying gratitude, and unrestrained praise.

## RICH CHRISTIAN, POOR CHRISTIAN

Jesus said, "Where your treasure is, there your heart will be also" (Matt. 6:21). By that standard, when this woman gave her two little coins she was really putting her heart into the box, offering her whole self to God. How different she was from the scribes! They were all about what was on the outside, but she was living for God on the inside, so what came out of her was really there. This is what God wants from us: not just our money, but ourselves, from the inside all the way out.

If it is true that we always put our money where our heart is, then one of the best ways to tell what is inside of us is by what we give to God. However, we have to measure this the way that Jesus does and not the way we usually do: not in comparison to what other people give, but in comparison to our own financial situation. This is one of the basic principles of God's economy. He takes into account how much we have and values what we give in proportion to what we have been given.

How extraordinarily encouraging this is for Christians who are living in poverty! Jesus sees what is in our bank account, he knows what is in our hearts, and he judges accordingly. Even if we have almost nothing, he prizes what we give as highly as a king's ransom. No one should ever think that the small contributions of poor Christians are almost worthless. On the contrary, by grace they are worth as much to God as anything, and they will receive the praise of Jesus Christ. Furthermore, God will use them richly for the work of his kingdom. Just think what God has done with the two little coins that the widow gave—what a wealth of encouragement the church has received from her example of sacrificial giving. God has multiplied her gift by millions and billions!

At the same time, the principle of proportionality ought to be deeply disturbing to Christians who have as much money as most Americans have. Cyril of Alexandria was right when he told his congregation that this story from the Gospel of Luke "may perhaps irritate some among the rich."[7] Indeed, it may well irritate us, because we are some of the richest Christians in the history of the world, with the capacity to give more for the kingdom of God than almost anyone has ever given.

Yet we are giving out of our abundance, and therefore in comparison with the widow we are giving practically nothing. We have so much that even when we give a little it seems like a lot and we are easily satisfied with what we give, as if we have really done something generous for God. But what would it take for us to give as much as the widow gave? It would take most of us months to do it, for one thing, because we have so much property to get rid of. It is good for us to give God whatever we have been giving, but if we are rich, we should not think more highly of our giving than God does. Beware of the scribes! Do not look at your financial giving on the outside, the way the scribes do, but on the inside, the way that God does.

John Calvin summarized what this story means for the rich and the poor by saying:

> The lesson is useful in two ways. The Lord encourages the poor, who appear to lack the means of doing well, not to doubt that they testify to their enthusiasm for Him even with a slender contribution. If they consecrate themselves, their offering which appears mean and trivial will be no less precious than if they had offered all the treasures of Croesus. On the other hand, those who have a richer supply and stand out for their large giving are told that it

---

7. Cyril of Alexandria, "Commentary on Luke," Homily 138, in *Luke*, ed. Arthur A. Just, Jr., Ancient Christian Commentary on Scripture, NT 3 (Downers Grove, IL: InterVarsity, 2003), 316.

is not enough if their generosity far exceeds the commoners and the under-privileged, for with God it rates less for a rich man to give a moderate sum from a large mass, than for a poor man to exhaust himself in paying out something very small.[8]

Bishop Joseph Parker drew the contrast even more sharply: "The gold of affluence which is given because it is not needed, God hurls to the bottom-less pit; but the copper tinged with blood He lifts and kisses into the gold of eternity."[9]

## TREASURE FROM THE HEART

The point of all this is not to set a percentage that every Christian has to give, or even to compare how much we give to what the widow gave in the Gospel. Not every Christian is called to give everything away the way that she did. The point is to have a heart for God and a heart for giving. Missionary statesman Paul Kooistra puts it this way: "The question is not, 'How large is my gift going to be to God's kingdom work?' The real question is, 'How large a place will God have in my life?'"[10]

When your heart is right before God, you will give as much as you can. Doubtless you will give more than you are giving right now—maybe much more—even more than (you think) you can spare.

Giving more is the right thing to do. It is right because we live in a world that desperately needs the mercy of the gospel in word and deed. It is right because through the work of missionaries, evangelists, and church planters our money can change people's lives for eternity. But most of all, it is the right thing to do because of the extravagant grace that God has offered to us in Jesus Christ, who laid down his life for our sins. Given everything that God himself has given to us, we should give ourselves back to him. Sacrificial grace demands sacrificial giving.

When I was a student at Philadelphia's Westminster Theological Seminary, I was always impressed by a framed notice in the lobby of Machen

8. John Calvin, *A Harmony of the Gospels: Matthew, Mark and Luke and the Epistles of James and Jude*, vol. 3, trans. A. W. Morrison (Grand Rapids: Eerdmans, 1975), 72.

9. Joseph Parker, quoted in G. Campbell Morgan, *The Gospel According to Luke* (New York: Revell, 1931), 235.

10. Paul Kooistra, *Faith Promise* (Atlanta: Mission to the World, n.d.), iii.

Hall. The notice read as follows: "Fannie Mulder was called to Glory on October 20, 1987. In a letter from her attorney we learned that she had only the following personal property in her possession when she died, having been on title 19 for the last few years." Then the notice listed the contents of Mulder's apartment. She had some clothes: six robes, two sweaters, thirteen adult diapers, nineteen hospital gowns, one pair of slippers, and five pairs of socks (plus two singles). She also had some personal items: a purse, a mirror, an old thimble, a toothbrush, a comb, some soap, some powder bottles, and a pair of reading glasses. She needed the glasses so she could read her two copies of the Bible, and her Psalter for singing.

In addition to a broken radio, the only other thing Fannie Mulder had in her possession was some money. Do you know how much she had? Not much: only twelve cents—a dime and two pennies. But the lawyer explained that the old woman had drawn up a will because she felt strongly that she should invest whatever she had in the work of the kingdom of God. After the will went through probate, the seminary was the beneficiary of the dime and the two pennies, now gratefully displayed on campus as the lasting testimony of a woman who gave Jesus everything she had.

What legacy are you leaving? The widow in the Gospels had only two cents, but she gave them both to Jesus. Fannie Mulder had a lot more than two cents. She had *twelve* cents, and she gave them all to Jesus too. How much do you have? Whatever you have—whether you are giving out of poverty or abundance—give it all to Jesus.

89

# THE BEGINNING OF THE END

## *Luke 21:5–19*

*"By your endurance you will gain your lives."* (Luke 21:19)

he second temple in Jerusalem was magnificent. With its lofty parapets and grand colonnades, it was one of the most beautiful buildings in the history of the world. According to Josephus,

> The whole of the outer works of the temple was in the highest degree worthy of admiration; for it was completely covered with gold plates, which, when the sun was shining on them, glittered so dazzlingly that they blinded the eyes of the beholders not less than when one gazed at the sun's rays themselves. And on the other sides, where there was no gold, the blocks of marble were of such a pure white that to strangers who had never previously seen them (from a distance) they looked like a mountain of snow.[1]

In those days most Israelites lived in modest houses of mud, brick, or stone. So when they went up to the temple to worship, they were almost overwhelmed with feelings of joy and awe. "We shall be satisfied with the

---

1. Flavius Josephus, *The Wars of the Jews*, as quoted in Norval Geldenhuys, *The Gospel of Luke*, New International Commentary on the New Testament (Grand Rapids: Eerdmans, 1951), 534.

goodness of your house," the people sang, "the holiness of your temple!" (Ps. 65:4). This was the house of their God.

Each year when they went up to Jerusalem, pilgrims would look to see what had been added to the temple. By the time of Christ it had been under construction for almost fifty years (see John 2:20), and from time to time wealthy patrons would add decorative flourishes in gold or precious gems. The conversation Luke describes must have been common: while Jesus was teaching, "some were speaking of the temple, how it was adorned with noble stones and offerings" (Luke 21:5).

## THE FALL OF THE TEMPLE

Rather than joining in the general admiration for the temple's praise-worthy construction, Jesus prophesied that soon the whole building would be torn down: "As for these things that you see, the days will come when there will not be left here one stone upon another that will not be thrown down" (Luke 21:6).

This was an astonishing prophecy—an almost unbelievable prediction of coming cataclysm. Some of the temple's massive marble foundation stones were forty feet long. They weighed more than one hundred tons! But Jesus said they would all fall down. He was right: all the words of his prophecy came true. When the Romans sacked Jerusalem in A.D. 70, they tore down the temple stone by stone.

This catastrophe was an act of divine judgment. God was punishing his people for rejecting his Christ. The destruction of the temple was also a gospel sign of the new salvation that God had provided in Jesus. The ancient system of Jewish religion had come to an end. The old temple sacrifices no longer atoned for sin. Now the only temple that mattered was the temple of Jesus—his own body—which was torn down from the cross and raised again from the grave (see John 2:19–22), giving eternal life to every Jew and every Gentile who trusts in him.

Amazingly, when the disciples heard what Jesus said about the destruction of the temple, they believed that what he said was true. The only thing they wanted to know was when it would all happen. "Teacher," they said, "when will these things be, and what will be the sign when these things are about to take place?" (Luke 21:7). Naturally, the disciples were hoping to get some kind of warning before the great and terrible day when the temple would be destroyed.

When people heard Jesus say the temple would be destroyed, they probably thought he was talking about the final judgment. From their perspective, the destruction of the temple would be the end of the world. So they were thinking about the end times, and the main question they had was not if or how, but when. This is the question people always have about the coming judgment: When will it be the end of the world?

Jesus knew that this question often leads people into unwise and unhealthy speculation, so immediately he clarified what he was saying. His answer addresses *both* the more immediate question of the destruction of the temple and the bigger question of the end of the world. This dual perspective was necessary because what Jesus said about the temple made people think about the final judgment, and Jesus wanted to put both events into their proper perspective. This makes his answer somewhat complex, and to some people confusing, but if we study what Jesus said carefully, his meaning will become clear.

Studying Luke 21 is a little bit like wearing bifocals. The destruction of the temple is near at hand. Many of the prophecies in this chapter deal with specific events that happened before and during the fall of Jerusalem in A.D. 70. Yet the end of the world is always in the background, and we constantly need to keep it in our gaze. The destruction of the temple is a portent of the final judgment; it is the beginning of the end. So Jesus extends the discussion from the destruction of the temple all the way to the end of the world. Looking beyond his first coming to his second coming, he uses the kind of messianic and apocalyptic language that the Old Testament prophets used when they talked about the great and terrible day of the Lord.

Nearly all of the earliest and best commentators of Scripture looked at Luke 21 with this double focus. In fact, this is the way biblical prophecy usually works. There are near fulfillments and far fulfillments. If we look only at the near fulfillments, we miss the big picture. But to understand the far fulfillments at all we also have to look closely at what the prophet was saying to God's people in his own time and place.

Here in Luke 21 the immediate historical context is the time leading up to and including the fall of Jerusalem. Thus the commands of Jesus apply most directly to the disciples who lived through those terrible days. However, the backdrop to that historical act of divine judgment is the judgment that is still to come. Therefore, the exhortations in this passage also apply to us now and in the future as we face various trials and tribulations before the second coming of Jesus Christ.

## DON'T GO CRAZY!

To help us know how to live from now until the end of the world, Jesus gives four practical exhortations that we can list as a series of "don'ts": don't be led astray; don't be afraid; don't miss the opportunity to witness; and don't give up.

Here is the first exhortation, which comes in the form of a warning: do not be led astray by any wild ideas about the end of the world. To be specific, do not let anyone fool you with a false messiah, or with rash predictions about when the end will come. Jesus said, "See that you are not led astray. For many will come in my name, saying, 'I am he!' and, 'The time is at hand!' Do not go after them" (Luke 21:8).

Jesus knew that talking about the end of the world always seems to bring out the crazy in some people. In fact, people seem to make more mistakes in this area of theology than in any other. Sometimes they follow the teaching of a false messiah. In the seventeenth century it was Sabbatai Sevi, whom thousands of European Jews worshiped as the Christ. In the twentieth century it was men like Jim Jones and David Koresh—cult leaders who led their followers to their deaths.

Sometimes the problem is people who try to forecast the future. They develop complex theories about coming events that supposedly are based on biblical prophecy, but in charting out the future they go well beyond what the Scriptures actually teach. Sensational books like Hal Lindsey's *The Late Great Planet Earth* or Tim LaHaye's *Left Behind* series may make for interesting reading, but they contain all kinds of eschatological speculations that leave people with many wrong ideas about theology and the end of the world.

Then there are all the strange ideas people come up with when they try to connect today's political events with specific prophecies in the Bible. Usually this kind of speculation focuses on America's foreign policy towards Israel and the Middle East.

Some people even try to predict when Jesus will come again. There always seems to be some fringe religious group somewhere setting a date for the end of the world. So far they have all been proved wrong, but often they come up with some sort of explanation and set another date. Radio preacher Harold Camping was wrong about 1994, so he said the world would probably end in 2011. To make your own guess, just read "The Rapture Index," a Web site which claims to be "the Dow Jones Industrial Average" for eschatology— "the prophetic speedometer of end-time activity." The Rapture Index goes up or down depending on the price of oil, the climate in Africa, the peace process in the Middle East, and dozens of other variables. Supposedly such events help us know how fast the end is coming.

Jesus knew it would be like this. He knew that people would always be coming up with strange ideas about the end of the world that would lead people away from his gospel, including lots of ideas that misuse Scripture. So rather than making his own prediction, he gave some good pastoral advice, which we have needed ever since: do not be led astray.

## IT'S NOT THE END OF THE WORLD

Jesus also told us not to be afraid. This is important, because when people start thinking about the end times, they often get frightened. It is terrifying to think what will happen at the end of the world, when Jesus comes again and we all appear before God for judgment. Peter said, "The heavens and earth that now exist are stored up for fire, being kept until the day of judgment and destruction of the ungodly" (2 Peter 3:7). He also said, "The day of the Lord will come like a thief, and then the heavens will pass away with a roar, and the heavenly bodies will be burned up and dissolved, and the earth and the works that are done on it will be exposed" (2 Peter 3:10).

When we hear a prophecy like that, it is easy to start panicking about the future. It is also easy to prey upon people's fears and whip them into a frenzy of end-times hysteria. But Jesus tells us not to be afraid of what is going to happen: "And when you hear of wars and tumults, do not be terrified, for these things must first take place, but the end will not be at once" (Luke 21:9).

This is the answer to the specific question that people were asking: "When will these things be, and what will be the sign that these things are about to take place?" (Luke 21:7). Notice that Jesus does not answer the question directly. If God wanted us to know exactly when the end of all things will come, he would have told us. Instead, Jesus prophesied that many terrible things would happen first. It would not all happen all at once. Even the destruction of the temple was not the end of the world.

In the following verses Jesus went on to describe some other signs of the coming judgment: "Nation will rise against nation, and kingdom against kingdom. There will be great earthquakes, and in various places famines and pestilences. And there will be terrors and great signs from heaven" (Luke 21:10–11).

All of these things happened in the years leading up to the destruction of Jerusalem. Nation rose against nation. To be specific, there was a Jewish insurrection against Rome that began in A.D. 66 and finally led to the destruction of Jerusalem. There were great earthquakes, such as the powerful tremor across Phrygia in A.D. 61, or a powerful earthquake at Pompeii two years later. There were famines in various places during the reign of the emperor Claudius, and then again under Nero. There were also cosmic signs in the heavens, like the comet recorded in Josephus.[2]

These were all signs of the coming judgment, and Jerusalem was not destroyed until all of these things had taken place. We find ourselves in a similar situation. We see nation rise against nation. We hear about great earthquakes and other natural disasters. There is famine in various places, and other terrors in many parts of the world. It all has to happen. It is not the end of the world, yet it does remind us of the end of the world, and therefore it can be very frightening.

What fears do you have about the future? Some people worry about the next natural disaster, or the next terrorist strike, or the next financial depression. Others have dark fears about a nuclear attack on American soil, or feel anxious about the scarcity of precious resources like oil or water leading to global war.

Whatever disasters strike, and whatever fears we may have about the future, it is not the end of the world—at least not yet. Jesus speaks to all our anxieties when he says, "Do not be terrified" (Luke 21:9). The main thing that people wanted to know was when the end would come. Jesus spoke to that question by saying that there were many things that had to happen first,

2. These phenomena are documented in Geldenhuys, *Luke*, 531.

but he also addressed an even deeper issue by telling us not to be afraid. People wanted to know the warning signs for the destruction of the temple and the end of the world because they were afraid of what would happen to them. It was not so much the exact timetable they were interested in as it was their own personal safety. Jesus reassured them—not by revealing when the world would end, but by telling them not to be afraid.

The terrors described in these verses first took place in the first century. However, the apocalyptic language used to describe them also applies to our own situation. The kinds of disasters that Jesus prophesied have happened many times over in the history of the world, and they will happen again. Every time they happen, they are signs of the coming judgment that remind us to get ready for the end of the world. So every time they happen, we should remember the words of Jesus: "Do not be afraid."

This practical exhortation is for us as much as it was for the original disciples. Jesus told them not to be afraid because it was not the end of the world. It is not the end of the world for us either, but we have even more reason not to be afraid. We serve a living Savior, who has demonstrated his power over sin and death by rising from the grave. We serve a mighty Savior, who ascended to heaven and is ruling the whole universe for his glory. This Savior has sent the Holy Spirit to be with us in every dark place, at every hour of trouble. Whatever disaster may come, God is with us, and Jesus always says to us: Do not be afraid!

## WHEN OPPORTUNITY KNOCKS

One of the reasons it is so desperately important for us not to be afraid is that trials and tribulations give us an extraordinary opportunity for evangelism. If we are fearless in the face of danger, we will be ready to do what we are told to do in verse 13, and seize the opportunity to tell people about Jesus.

It is easy to be afraid of the future. America gives almost every indication that it is a nation in spiritual decline. We are living in a decadent, arrogant, hyperindividualized, oversexed, ultramaterialistic culture. Whether we will suffer a sudden collapse or go through a long, slow, dispiriting decline remains to be seen. But it seems inevitable that God's judgment will come, as well as growing opposition to the church.

Jesus prophesied the same kinds of difficulties for the people of his generation. He said that Jerusalem would be destroyed. "But before all this," he said, "they will lay their hands on you and persecute you, delivering you up to the synagogues and prisons, and you will be brought before kings and governors for my name's sake" (Luke 21:12). He also said: "You will be delivered up even by parents and brothers and relatives and friends, and some of you they will put to death. You will be hated by all for my name's sake" (Luke 21:16–17).

These prophecies referred specifically to the persecution that the first Christians faced in Israel and across the Mediterranean in the decades between the resurrection of Jesus Christ and the fall of Jerusalem. In verses 8 and 9 Jesus indicated that the destruction of the temple would come before the end of the world; here he makes it clear that something else would happen before the temple was destroyed, namely, the persecution of the church—both by Jews (the religious community) and by Gentiles (the secular state).

What terrible hardships Jesus prophesied: prison, betrayal, hatred, and death! Of course all of these prophecies came true, as Luke documented in the second volume of his writings, which we know today as the book of Acts. When Peter preached in Solomon's portico, he was arrested, imprisoned, and brought before the Sanhedrin for trial (Acts 3:11–4:22)—just as Jesus prophesied. The apostle was released with a warning not to preach again, but he went right on preaching the gospel. Soon he was arrested again, and beaten (Acts 5:17–42). Stephen suffered a much worse fate: he was put to death (Acts 7:54–60). Later James suffered the same fate at the hands of King Herod (Acts 12:1–2).

Then there were all the persecutions of Paul—both the ones he perpetrated before he became a Christian (Acts 8:1–3) and the ones he suffered afterwards for the cause of Christ. Paul was delivered up to the synagogues and prisons (e.g., Acts 16:16–24; 17:1–9); he was brought before kings and governors (e.g., Acts 24–25); he was hated by almost everyone for Jesus' sake (see 1 Cor. 4:13). Eventually, like all the other apostles except for John, he died a violent death.

This privilege of suffering for Jesus' sake was not limited to the apostles. Many ordinary Christians were also persecuted for their faith. Think of all the cruelties that Nero inflicted on the believers in Rome—the burnings

417

and crucifixions they suffered for their Savior, who himself was crucified by the Romans.

The words of Jesus were part of their preparation for all these persecutions. Jesus wanted his disciples to know, in advance, what they would suffer for his sake, so they would be ready to bear witness for him. Every time they were attacked they had a chance to preach the cross and the empty tomb. "This will be your opportunity to bear witness," Jesus said. "Settle it therefore in your minds not to meditate beforehand how to answer, for I will give you a mouth and wisdom, which none of your adversaries will be able to withstand or contradict" (Luke 21:13–15).

All of these words came true as well. As we read through the book of Acts, we never find the apostles at a loss for words. On the contrary, every time they are arrested or imprisoned, they make such a bold declaration of their faith in Jesus Christ that they silence all their accusers. "We must obey God rather than men," Peter and John said to the Sanhedrin (Acts 5:29), and when they were released from custody, "they did not cease teaching and preaching Jesus as the Christ" (Acts 5:42). Stephen kept preaching the gospel right up to his very last breath. The more they persecuted Paul, the bolder he became in his witness for Christ, so that when he arrives in Rome at the end of Acts he is "proclaiming the kingdom of God and teaching about the Lord Jesus Christ with all boldness and without hindrance" (Acts 28:31). In the very moments of their greatest trials, the Holy Spirit was with the apostles and helped them know exactly what to say.

This is what almost always happens when Christians are persecuted: by the grace of God, they bear witness to the crucifixion and resurrection of Jesus Christ, with the result that many people are saved through the cross and the empty tomb. We should not pray for persecutions, which are a great sin against God. But neither should we despair when Christians are under attack, because often that is when the church has its brightest and boldest witness.

Do not be afraid of the enemies of the gospel in all the places of spiritual darkness. The more hatred any society has for Christ, the clearer it becomes what difference it makes to be a Christian. Whether it is under the oppression of communism, or against the evil of Islam, or even in our own godless society, God is always giving us opportunities for witness. The week that I am writing these words, a man in Afghanistan has been on trial for converting to Christianity from Islam. Under the pressure of world opinion, the man was released from prison, but only on the grounds that he was mentally insane. Apparently some people think you would have to be at least a little bit crazy to stand up for Christ in a Muslim society. But the man is not crazy; he is simply a Christian. The opposition he suffers is his opportunity to bear witness, and whether he lives or dies, God will use his testimony to bring other Muslims to faith in Jesus Christ.

The promises that Jesus made about knowing what to say were specifically for the apostles, who were directly inspired by the Holy Spirit (see Mark 13:11) and whose words are recorded in Scripture. When Jesus told them that they did not need to plan their answers in advance, he did not mean that preachers should never prepare their sermons, or that Christians do not need to write out their testimony or memorize a basic outline of the gospel. On the contrary, the Bible talks about "always being prepared to make a defense to anyone who asks you for a reason for the hope that is in you" (1 Peter 3:15).

Nevertheless, what Jesus said in Luke 21 does apply in a general way to every believer, including the promise that the Spirit will help us know what to say. We are in essentially the same situation the first Christians were in. They were waiting for the destruction of the temple. We too are waiting—waiting for judgment. Already we see signs of the coming destruction: wars, earthquakes, and other terrors. There is still time for people to repent of their sin and come to faith in Christ. We will have many perfect opportunities to witness for Jesus, and we do not want to miss any of them.

The more opposition we suffer, the better our opportunities will be, and the Holy Spirit will help us take advantage of them. Even if we do not say exactly the right thing, as the apostles did, the Spirit will take what we say and use it for the glory of God. Often the fact that we are willing to say anything at all for Jesus is more important than what it is that we say. Too many Christians fail to take advantage of the opportunities they have for witness because they are afraid of making a mistake. This is partly a failure of nerve, but it also betrays a failure to trust in the work of the Holy Spirit, who will help us witness for Christ. Do not worry about what to say, but simply give God something that he can use, and he will use it for his glory.

Do not miss your opportunity to bear witness! Every difficult circumstance is an opportunity to tell people about Jesus. In fact, Luke 21:13 is a good verse to memorize and then remember in times of trial. When we are hospitalized with a serious illness, or suffer the grief that comes with a painful loss, or are criticized for thinking and acting like a Christian, the Holy Spirit will remind us of the words of Jesus: "This will be your opportunity to bear witness."

## Don't Give Up!

We are called to keep on witnessing to the very end. Jesus ends the first part of this discourse with a final word of encouragement and exhortation. Having told his disciples not to be led astray, or to be afraid, or to miss their opportunity for witness, he tells them not to give up: "But not a hair of your head will perish. By your endurance you will gain your lives" (Luke 21:18–19).

This raises an immediate and obvious question. In verse 16 Jesus said that some of his followers would be killed (as in fact they were), but here in verses 18 and 19 he says that they will not perish after all. Isn't this a contradiction?

The answer is that in verse 16 Jesus is talking about death in the physical sense, but in verses 18 and 19 he is talking about spiritual life. The word "lives" (in this phrase, "you will gain your lives") could also be translated "souls," and when Jesus talks about the hairs of their heads, he is not speaking literally but metaphorically, using a poetic expression for eternal life. Whatever people did to their earthly bodies, their eternal souls could not be touched: "Although they are to suffer physical pain and death, they can never be plucked from the protecting hand of God—nothing will happen to them outside His will, and He will make all things work together for their highest welfare and their eternal salvation, and at His second advent they will arise with glorified, celestial bodies in which there will be no defect or injury."[3]

Remember, this is the Savior who said that if we lose our lives for him we will save them in the end. Now he has gone ahead of us into glory, and our place in heaven is secure. What courage and confidence this ought to give us as we live for Christ in evil days. We have nothing to fear, because for those who trust in Jesus, even death will be destroyed. If by grace we persevere to the very end, we will be saved forever.

3. Geldenhuys, *Luke*, 527.

The words of Jesus from this farewell prophecy make a dramatic difference in desperate times of danger. A powerful example comes from the preaching ministry of Donald Grey Barnhouse.[4] It was the summer of 1939. While Barnhouse had been preaching in Scotland, his family was vacationing on the coast of France. He was scheduled to be in Belfast, Northern Ireland, by Saturday night, but first he decided to make a quick trip to France so that he could be with his family.

On his way out of Britain Dr. Barnhouse was warned that he might not make it back in time to preach on Sunday. Europe was in turmoil; there were rumors of war, as Hitler threatened to march on Danzig. Barnhouse decided to take his chances, but the official who stamped his passport said, "Don't forget that I warned you."

This proved to be a prescient warning. Just a few days later Hitler invaded Poland and all flights to England were cancelled. Dr. Barnhouse had to make a long, slow journey overland to Paris and then back to the French coast in order to catch a ferry across to England. Everywhere he went there were signs of the coming battle. Church bells were ringing across the countryside—the tocsins of war. Trains were jammed with soldiers mobilizing for war, and some of the towns they passed would be destroyed in the subsequent bombing. Barnhouse made his passage to England late at night, and while he was visiting with the ship's captain the radio reported that the prime minister had issued Germany an ultimatum: unless the Nazis withdrew from Poland, Britain would go to war. It would be the last civilian steamship to cross the English Channel until the war was over.

London was as chaotic as Paris had been. The railway platforms were lined with children being evacuated to the countryside. Many of them were crying—some of the first victims of war. Barnhouse crossed the countryside by train, and then took another night passage, this time to Northern Ireland. By the time he reached Belfast it was three in the morning, and he had only a few hours to get some rest before the morning worship service.

The church was packed, with everyone expecting the declaration of war to be announced at any time. The church's pastor was only too happy for Barnhouse to preach, and kept saying, "Thank God you're here! I pray that God will give you something to say to the lads. This may be the last sermon

4. Donald Grey Barnhouse first told this story in his studies on the "Epistle to the Romans," part 55 (Philadelphia: The Bible Study Hour, 1955), 4–12.

that some of them ever hear." Then, just as Barnhouse was getting ready to step into the pulpit, one of the elders slipped a note to the pastor, who passed it along to Barnhouse. The note said, "No reply from Hitler. The prime minister has declared war."

Barnhouse began by telling the congregation that he had a perfect text for them that morning—a text first spoken by the Lord Jesus Christ as a command to his people: "You will hear of wars and rumors of wars, but see to it that you are not alarmed." He then recounted the alarming experiences he had on his way to Belfast. As he described each terror, he stopped and repeated his text: *Do not be alarmed.* The siren will sound, and soldiers will mobilize: *Do not be alarmed.* Millions of homes will be broken up: *Do not be alarmed.* Children will be torn from their mothers, and their cries will represent the wails that are going up all over the world. But Jesus said, "Do not be alarmed."

As Barnhouse went through this litany of lamentation, piling monstrous grief on agonizing horror, the tension in the church was mounting. Finally, Barnhouse stopped and said, "These words are either the words of a madman or they are the words of God." Then he shook his fist toward heaven, and cried out, "Oh, God, unless Jesus Christ is God, these words are the most horrible that could be spoken to men who have hearts that can weep and bowels that can be gripped by human suffering. Men are dying. *Do not be alarmed?* Children are crying in their misery with no beloved face in sight. *Do not be alarmed?* How can Jesus Christ say such a thing?"

Then Barnhouse gave the answer: Jesus Christ *is* God. He is the Lord of history. He is the God of detailed circumstance. Nothing has ever happened without God knowing it. The sin of man has reduced the world to passion and fury. Men tear at each other's throats. Yet in the midst of the history in which Jesus is Lord, everyone who believes in him will know the power of his resurrection and will learn that no event, however terrible, can ever separate us from the love of God.

This is our hope in all the difficulties of life—the trials and tribulations, the sufferings and the heartbreaks, with all our fears about the future. Jesus says, "Do not be led astray, and do not be afraid, but trust me to the very end." When we have this kind of confidence, we will be bolder in our witness—not as bold as Dr. Barnhouse perhaps, but bold enough to do something useful for the kingdom of God.

422

# 90

# From Jerusalem to the End of the World

## *Luke 21:20–28*

*"Jerusalem will be trampled underfoot by the Gentiles, until the times of the Gentiles are fulfilled. . . . Now when these things begin to take place, straighten up and raise your heads, because your redemption is drawing near." (Luke 21:24b, 28)*

*H*as any city ever endured a more crushing defeat or witnessed more terrible suffering than Jerusalem? The ancient city fell to the Romans in A.D. 70. After long months of siege, during which famine wasted everyone to the bone, Jerusalem was conquered by Titus, the son of the emperor Vespasian. The temple was burned to the ground, and every last man, woman, and child in Jerusalem was either killed or taken captive.

The unspeakable horrors of those dreadful days are recorded by Josephus in *The Wars of the Jews.*[1] Many of the stories that famous historian tells in vivid detail can scarcely be repeated: human sacrifice, cannibalism, crucifixion. By the end, the living envied the dead who were lying unburied in the streets.

1. Flavius Josephus, *The Works of Josephus*, trans. William Whiston (Peabody, MA: Hendrickson, 1987).

As Josephus told this terrible tale, of which he himself was an eyewitness, he offered a lament for the city he loved and lost: "O most wretched city, what misery so great as this didst thou suffer from the Romans, when they came to purify thee from thy intense hatred! For thou couldst be no longer a place fit for God, nor couldst thou longer continue in being, after thou hadst been a sepulcher for the bodies of thine own people, and hadst made the holy house itself a burying-place!" Then the historian became a theologian as he offered this explanation for Jerusalem's devastation. It was because of "the anger of that God who is the author of thy destruction."[2]

## THE FALL OF JERUSALEM

Josephus was right: Jerusalem fell to the Romans because it was under the judgment of almighty God. It all happened just the way that Jesus prophesied. Decades before Titus besieged Jerusalem, Jesus said the city would fall and its temple would be torn to the ground. He did not make this prophecy with joy, but with sorrow, for he knew what terrible suffering it would bring. Listen to the words of his lament:

> But when you see Jerusalem surrounded by armies, then know that its desolation has come near. . . . For these are days of vengeance, to fulfill all that is written. Alas for women who are pregnant and for those who are nursing infants in those days! For there will be great distress upon the earth and wrath against this people. They will fall by the edge of the sword and be led captive among all nations, and Jerusalem will be trampled underfoot by the Gentiles, until the times of the Gentiles are fulfilled. (Luke 21:20, 22–24)

When Jesus spoke about "desolation"—or "the abomination of desolation," as other Gospels have it (e.g., Matt. 24:15; cf. Dan. 11:31)—his listeners immediately would have thought of something that happened centuries earlier, when Antiochus IV Epiphanes desecrated the holy temple of God. In 167 B.C. that infamous Greek king conquered Jerusalem, erected a statue of Zeus in the temple courts, and sacrificed pigs in the Holy of Holies—an outrageous sacrilege that enraged the people of God. Now Jesus was prophesying another desolation. Soon enemy troops would invade the holy city.

---

2. Josephus, *The Wars of the Jews*, 5.1.19, in *The Works of Josephus*, 697.

The standard of the Roman legion would be raised over Jerusalem and the city would be destroyed again.

All of these prophecies came true. Some forty years after Jesus spoke these words, Titus marched on Jerusalem and enemy armies laid siege to the city, surrounding it for almost half a year. By the end of the Roman onslaught, famine had reduced the citizens to such absolute desperation that they were eating the very dust of the ground. What a terrible time it was to be pregnant, or to be the mother of young children, as Jesus knew it would be. Nursing mothers had no milk to give their suckling children. Some babies were left to die, and some were put to death (cf. Deut. 28:56–57).

By the time the walls were broken through and the mighty Romans finally entered Jerusalem, they met with little resistance. The temple was burned to the ground. So many men, women, and children were put to the sword that Josephus claimed that as many as a million Jews were killed, with an additional hundred thousand taken prisoner. The Roman historian Tacitus said it was only half that number, but either way, the loss of life was staggering.[3] After the survivors were led away in chains, scarcely a single Jew was left alive in the entire city. Has any city ever endured a more crushing defeat or witnessed more terrible suffering?

If we ask why all of this happened, the answer is that it was God's judgment against Jerusalem's sin. Jesus indicated this by the words that he used to describe the city's destruction. "These are days of vengeance," he said, "to fulfill all that is written" (Luke 21:22); "There will be . . . wrath against this people" (Luke 21:23). This is the vocabulary of divine judgment. "Vengeance" is the unique prerogative of almighty God, who alone has the right to judge people for their sins. "Wrath" is his holy hatred of sin, with his settled determination to punish it. The fall of Jerusalem was an act of God's justice that fulfilled the ancient law of Moses: "If you will not obey the voice of the LORD your God or be careful to do all his commandments and his statutes . . . then . . . cursed shall you be in the city" (Deut. 29:15–16).

What had Jerusalem done to deserve such a disaster? Jesus preached against many of the city's prevailing sins in the Gospels, but the city's most grievous sin was to reject the Christ by killing him on the cross. There were some believers in Jerusalem, of course, and God gave the people who lived

---

3. Norval Geldenhuys, *The Gospel of Luke*, New International Commentary on the New Testament (Grand Rapids: Eerdmans, 1951), 535–36.

there plenty of time to repent—four decades between the crucifixion of Jesus and the fall of Jerusalem. But by and large the religious community there did not receive Jesus as the Christ.

In the end, the whole old system of temple sacrifice had to be destroyed, while those who defended it perished. Jesus had offered the one and only once-and-for-all sacrifice for all the sins of all his people. Once he died and rose again, the old temple in Jerusalem was no longer the dwelling place of God, and God would not allow it to stand over against the true temple of Christ. It had to be torn down—not by Christians, but by the Romans, who were serving as instruments of divine justice.

This is a reminder of what our own sins deserve. As a matter of justice, we all deserve the wrath and curse of God. At the same time, what happened to Jerusalem is a warning to take seriously what Jesus says about the coming judgment. When it comes to prophecies of destruction, Jesus has a perfect track record. He is the omniscient Son of God, with full foreknowledge of the future. Up until now, all of his words have come true, including his words of judgment on Jerusalem. Therefore, we should believe whatever Jesus says about the coming day of Judgment, and about the pains that sinners will suffer forever, if they die without Christ.

When Charles Spurgeon preached on this passage, he said that the siege of Jerusalem and the destruction of the temple served as "a kind of rehearsal of what is yet to be," as "the uprolling of the curtain on the great drama of the world's doom." To drive this point home, he used a memorable analogy: "That beautiful city was the very crown of the entire earth, because God had dwelt there. It may be compared to the diamond in a ring, the jewel whose setting was the whole world; and when that jewel was destroyed, and God did as it were grind it to powder, it was a warning that the ring itself would, by-and-by, be crushed and consumed."[4]

People scoffed when Jesus said the temple would be torn to the ground, but no one was laughing when it actually happened (except maybe the Romans). So it will be at the final judgment. Most people are inclined to dismiss what the Bible says about the end of the world. They just do not take it seriously. They are like the scoffers the apostle Peter wrote about—

---

4. Charles H. Spurgeon, "Joyful Anticipation of the Second Advent," *Metropolitan Tabernacle Pulpit* (1896; reprint Pasadena, TX: Pilgrim, 1976), 42:601.

people who say, "Where is the promise of his coming?" (2 Peter 3:4). But as Peter went on to say,

> They deliberately overlook this fact, that the heavens existed long ago, and the earth was formed out of water and through water by the word of God, and that by means of these the world that then existed was deluged with water and perished. But by the same word the heavens and earth that now exist are stored up for fire, being kept until the day of judgment and destruction of the ungodly. (2 Peter 3:5–7)

It was by the word of God that the world was first made and later destroyed with a flood. One day, by the word of the very same God, the whole world will be destroyed. Do you believe this? If so, then get ready for that great and terrible day, when every person who has ever lived will stand before God for judgment.

## A Way of Escape

The only safety is for us to believe the words of Jesus—not just his words about judgment, but also his words of saving grace. Everyone who believes the promise of Christ for the forgiveness of sins will be saved from the wrath to come.

There is a good example of a saving promise in the prophecy that Jesus gave about the fall of Jerusalem. In the middle of telling how the city would be destroyed, Jesus also gave these life-saving instructions: "Then let those who are in Judea flee to the mountains, and let those who are inside the city depart, and let not those who are out in the country enter it" (Luke 21:21). Jesus said this so that his own people would know what to do when the time came for judgment. He wanted to protect his disciples from destruction, preserving the church that he had died to save. So he gave them a sign that would spare their lives.

Cities were places of safety and security. Ordinarily, the sensible thing to do in a time of danger was to run from the surrounding countryside to the defense of a city. But Jesus told his disciples to do exactly the opposite. Jerusalem was doomed to destruction, so as soon as they saw the first warning sign of the coming desolation, they were supposed to head for the hills.

This warning saved the early church. Three years before Titus sacked Jerusalem, another Roman general marched against the city. Sometime around the end of A.D. 66 or the beginning of A.D. 67, Cestius Gallus attempted to attack Jerusalem. Happily, the city was able to defend against this attack, and the Romans retreated. Yet the first church in Jerusalem remembered the words of Jesus; when they saw the advance of the Roman legions, they knew their city's desolation was drawing near. According to Eusebius, they recognized this as the signal that Jesus had prophesied, they gathered their belongings, and they fled across the Jordan River to find refuge in the city of Pella.[5] Therefore, nearly all of the Christians who lived in Jerusalem escaped before the city fell. In the providence of God, their lives were spared so that they could carry on with the work of global evangelism. In fact, some of them later returned to Jerusalem with the gospel. This was all because they believed what Jesus said about the day of destruction.

When judgment comes, the people of God always find safety in his promises. This is the way it has been all through history. God told Noah to build an ark so that he would be safe from the great flood. God told Lot to flee from the city of Sodom so that he would be safe from the fire and the brimstone. God told Jeremiah that his life would be spared when Jerusalem was destroyed by the Babylonians. These men were all rescued by the grace of God, whose promises they believed.

This kind of deliverance is not just for people in the Bible, however, but for anyone who trusts in Jesus Christ. To give just one historical example—an example that is indirectly related to Luke 21—when my own Dutch Reformed ancestors escaped religious persecution in Holland and came to this new world, they called their community Pella. Knowing the story of the early church and its escape from Jerusalem, they believed that they too had come to a city of refuge, where they were safe to worship their God. The principle holds true for every believer in Christ: in the dangers of life, whether great or small, our only hope of refuge is found in the promises of our God. To the weak he promises strength; to the troubled he promises peace; to the tempted he promises a way of escape; and to penitent sinners he promises full deliverance from everything our sins deserve.

---

5. Eusebius of Caesarea, *Ecclesiastical History*, 3.5.4, as cited in R. Kent Hughes, *Luke: That You May Know the Truth*, 2 vols., Preaching the Word (Wheaton, IL: Crossway, 1998), 2:301.

There is one exception, however. Once there was a godly man who trusted in all the promises of God, but still suffered the full weight of God's wrath against sin. On the night that he was betrayed, Jesus asked if there was any way that he could avoid the cross where he suffered God's curse against our sin. But there was no other way—no way for us to be saved except through the blood that the sinless Son of God would shed for our sins. Thus, for Jesus, there was no way of escape from the wrath of God. He suffered what we deserved so that we could be safe in him.

Now all God's promises of safety are true for us in Christ. There is a way of escape for us through the cross, where Jesus died for our sins. Whoever believes in him will not perish, but have everlasting life (John 3:16). The righteous person runs to him and is safe (Prov. 18:10). If he is at our right hand, we will not be shaken (Ps. 16:8). Jesus "delivers us from the wrath to come" (1 Thess. 1:10).

## THE COMING OF THE SON OF MAN

All of these promises are true, and they will remain true until the very day when Jesus comes again. As he was making his predictions about the coming desolation, Jesus lifted his gaze from Jerusalem to the end of the world and said:

> And there will be signs in sun and moon and stars, and on the earth distress of nations in perplexity because of the roaring of the sea and the waves, people fainting with fear and with foreboding of what is coming on the world. For the powers of the heavens will be shaken. And then they will see the Son of Man coming in a cloud with power and great glory. (Luke 21:25–27)

Jesus had already said that Jerusalem would be "trampled underfoot by the Gentiles, until the times of the Gentiles are fulfilled" (Luke 21:24). It is hard to be certain exactly what Jesus meant by this. To this day, the Old City of Jerusalem is largely in the hands of Gentiles. Perhaps Jesus was talking specifically about the Romans, who occupied the city for centuries. Or perhaps he was talking about the whole time period between his first and second comings—the gospel age of Gentile evangelism.

In any case, it seems clear from the language he uses that when Jesus starts talking about signs in the heavens and the glorious coming of the Son of Man, he is talking about the end of human history and the beginning of his everlasting kingdom. This is apocalyptic language—language that reveals the end of the world and the life to come. It is the kind of language we find in many of the Old Testament prophets. Joel said there would be "wonders in the heavens and on the earth, blood and fire and columns of smoke. The sun shall be turned to darkness, and the moon to blood, before the great and awesome day of the LORD comes" (Joel 2:30–31). Isaiah said, "the stars of the heavens and their constellations will not give their light; the sun will be dark at its rising, and the moon will not shed its light" (Isa. 13:10). Haggai said that God would "shake the heavens and the earth and the sea and the dry land" (Hag. 2:6). Daniel said the Son of Man would come on the clouds of heaven to gain dominion over all nations and to establish his everlasting kingdom (Dan. 7:13–14). Thus spoke the prophets.

Here it helps to know how apocalyptic literature works. As the prophet speaks to the people of his own day, he looks to the future. He sees a time of judgment coming, a righteous disaster that will strike his own people, if they do not repent. But this disaster is set against the backdrop of the last of all days, when God himself will come to judge the world. Listening to these prophecies of judgment, both near and far, is something like looking at mountains on the far horizon. From a distance, it is hard to distinguish the mountains from the foothills; they all seem to blend together. But once you reach the foothills, it is easy to see that there are higher mountains still to climb. So it is with apocalyptic literature. The prophet sees beyond the foothills of approaching judgment to the far mountains of the last judgment of all.

This perspective helps to explain why the prophets so often sound as if they are talking about the end of the world: it is because they *are* talking about the end of the world. They are looking at the whole mountain range of judgment, viewing the events of their own times in the context of the final judgment.

This analogy also helps us understand what happens in Luke 21. Jesus had already told his disciples not to expect the end of the world to come right away (see Luke 21:8–9). When he prophesied the fall of Jerusalem, he was describing the foothills of divine judgment. The desolation of that great city—as disastrous as it was—was a nearer and smaller destruction than the one that all mankind will see at the end of history. The fall of Jerusalem was a closer sign of the end of the world. Jesus did not simply stop at the foothills, with the fall of Jerusalem; but beginning in verse 25, he also mounted the high and distant peaks to the summit of God's judgment.

How do we know for sure that Jesus was talking about the end of the world? We know this from the way this conversation began, with the disciples asking for a sign as to when the temple would be destroyed (Luke 21:7), and with Jesus telling them that this would not yet be the end (Luke 21:8–9). We also know it because in the parallel account in Mark, Jesus speaks explicitly about heaven and earth passing away (see Mark 13:31–32; cf. Matt. 24:35–36). We know it further because the signs that Jesus describes here in Luke are cosmic cataclysms. Not only do they shake the earth with earthquakes and tsunamis, but they also shake the very heavens with unnatural signs and wonders.

But the main reason we know that Jesus was talking about the end of the world is from the way he describes the coming of the Son of Man "in a cloud with power and great glory" (Luke 21:27). Here Jesus is describing his own second advent, when he will come down to the earth again the same way that he departed the first time: riding on the clouds of glory (see Acts 1:9–10).

Jesus never told us when this would happen. In fact, according to Mark, he did not even know what day it would be (see Mark 13:32). Therefore, we cannot use Luke 21 or any other part of the Bible to draw up a calendar for the second coming. All we know for sure is that when all of the signs have been fulfilled, Jesus will come again.

What a day that great day will be! The Lord Jesus Christ will return visibly; every eye will see his radiant return. He will return universally; every knee will bow before him. He will return majestically, wearing the royal crowns of his eternal kingdom. He will return gloriously; his resurrection body will shine like the sun, with the full brightness of his Father's glory.

## NEARER, MY GOD, TO THEE

Charles Wesley once tried to put the coming glory into song, which may be all that we can do until we see the awesome day. Here is how Wesley's hymn ended:

Yea, amen! Let all adore thee,
High on thine eternal throne;
Savior, take the pow'r and glory,
Claim the kingdom for thine own:
O come quickly, O come quickly;
Alleluia! Come, Lord, come.[6]

Wesley's petition should become the prayer of every believer's soul. Cry out for Jesus to come quickly, especially whenever you see warning signs of the coming judgment.

There are basically two ways to respond when we see signs of God's judgment in our world today, and both responses reveal our true relationship to God. One is to be afraid. This is the way that most people respond, as Jesus said they would. When they witness the fall of a great city, or see terrors in the heavens, or watch the raging sea wipe out entire communities, many people faint with fear. As Jesus prophesied, there is international turmoil—the consternation of the nations. Even for people who say they do not believe in God, the signs of the coming judgment bring a deep sense of foreboding. They are afraid of the future, afraid of death, and afraid of what comes after that. We see this every time there is a disaster like the fall of Jerusalem: some people think it is the end of the world.

This is what we are *supposed* to think. Every terrifying disaster is a portent of the final judgment. Every earthquake and tsunami, every hurricane and tornado, every terrorist attack and military conquest is another foothill in the mountain range of God's justice. But there is also grace. God does not withhold all of his wrath until the very end, but gives the world many merciful warnings in advance of the final day. He does this so that we will run to Jesus and find safety in his cross while there is still time. Trust Jesus to save you in the final judgment, and you will be delivered.

The safety we have in Jesus enables us to respond to each new disaster in faith rather than with fear. If we have the free gift of eternal life, the future does not need to fill us with foreboding—quite the contrary. Jesus said, "Now when these things begin to take place, straighten up and raise your heads, because your redemption is drawing near" (Luke 21:28). Even when

---

6. Charles Wesley, "Lo! He Comes with Clouds Descending," 1758.

it seems like the end of the world, we can stand tall in our faith because we know that God is bringing his saving plan to completion.

Notice what Jesus said: "when these things *begin* to take place." Our hope of redemption begins right now, right away. We do not wait until the end comes, but as soon as we see any sign of the coming judgment—from the fall of Jerusalem right up to the disasters of the present day—we remember that our redemption is near. When terrible things happen, it is always tempting to slump over in discouragement, dismay, and downcast despair. But Jesus lifts us up to stand tall in the hope of our redemption.

Properly speaking, redemption is the procuring of a release through the payment of a price. So in one sense we have already received our redemption. When Jesus offered his infinitely worthy blood for us on the cross, he paid the price to release us once and for all from our bondage to sin and death. But we have not yet received all of the benefits of our redemption, and it is in this sense that our redemption is still drawing near. On the last of all days, when Jesus comes again to judge the world, we will receive every blessing that God has ever had for us. Therefore, said J. C. Ryle,

> However terrible the signs of Christ's second coming may be to the impenitent, they need not strike terror into the heart of the true believer. They ought rather to fill him with joy. They ought to remind him that his complete deliverance from sin, the world, and the devil is close at hand, and that he shall soon bid an eternal farewell to sickness, sorrow, death, and temptation. The very day when the unconverted man shall lose everything, shall be the day when the believer shall enter on his eternal reward.[7]

That day is coming soon, and our spirits should brighten every time we think about its coming. Soon there will be no more death or crying or pain. Soon we will see Jesus himself, in all his beauty. Soon we will receive our own perfect resurrection bodies. Soon we will be reunited with the saints we love, joining the worship of heaven. Soon we will be free from sin—both our own sin and the sins that others sin against us. Soon we will enter the glory that can never end. Our redemption is nearer today than yesterday, nearer at the end of this chapter than at the beginning, nearer this

7. J. C. Ryle, *Expository Thoughts on the Gospels, Luke* (1858; reprint Cambridge: James Clarke, 1976), 2:376.

second than the last. As we wait for that great day, Jesus tells us to stand tall in the promise of his grace, lifting our heads to the coming redemption.

One man who did this in a remarkable way is Daylan Sanders, the founder and director of the Samaritan Children's Home in Batticaloa, Sri Lanka. In an interview televised on CNN, Sanders described what happened to him and to his children the day after Christmas 2004, when a powerful tsunami swept across the Indian Ocean and destroyed hundreds of thousands of lives.

When Sanders saw the waves rushing towards his seaside orphanage, he immediately gathered all twenty-eight of his children into a boat. He said, "It was a thirty-foot wall of sea, bearing down on us like an angry monster. And it was coming at us at such speed I knew there was no place on the ground where we could be safe. So I knew—there was something that told me instantly—we've got to get on top of this wave to stay safe."

The children reached the boat only seconds before the wave hit. "When we got into the boat," Sanders said, "we were eyeball to eyeball with the wave. And immediately a scripture popped into my mind, and from there I got the courage. I just stood up in the small boat, lifted my hands and said, 'I command you in the name of Jesus Christ to stand still.' I thought I was imagining at the time that the massive wall of water stood still, as if something were holding it back, some invisible force or hand."[8]

But Sanders was not imagining things. Strangely, maybe miraculously, the water stopped and swirled past the orphanage, as survivors who climbed to the top of nearby trees later testified. In the roaring of the sea and waves, Daylan Sanders did not faint with fear, but stood up in the courage of his faith and prayed for God to keep his children safe.

When the day of disaster comes, stand tall and lift your head, because Jesus said your redemption is drawing near. He will deliver you from many earthly troubles, and at the end of it all, he has promised to save you forever.

---

8. Daylan Sanders, in an interview with Anderson Cooper on *CNN 360,* Dec. 31, 2004.

# 91

# THE END IS NEAR

## *Luke 21:29–36*

*"But stay awake at all times, praying that you may have strength
to escape all these things that are going to take place, and to stand
before the Son of Man." (Luke 21:36)*

t was the spring of 1953—the season when mountain climbers
pursue the glory of ascending the world's highest mountain-
tops. Three famous expeditions set out that year, trying to con-
quer three of the highest peaks in the Himalayas: the British were climbing Mount Everest, the French were attacking Annapurna, and together the
Germans and the Austrians were making an assault on Nanga Parbat. The
British and the French were both successful, but the third team failed to
reach the summit and was forced to turn back. Except for Hermann Buhl,
that is, for when the team made its decision to leave Nanga Parbat, the brilliant Austrian climber did the unthinkable and continued up the mountain
alone. Over the next forty-one hours he succeeded in reaching the summit
before returning to his companions at the advance camp.

Buhl's conquest of Nanga Parbat remains one of the greatest individual
accomplishments in the history of human adventure—a triumph of the
mind and the will over the suffering of the body. What enabled the man to

ascend such great heights? The translator of the climber's autobiography explained it like this: "Buhl had long decided to be ready when the call came; the whole of his climbing life was, in fact, dedicated to that end. He was ready and able to meet it when it sounded."[1]

"Ready when the call came"—this phrase defines one of the main goals of the Christian life. As followers of Jesus, we are to be ready when the call comes—not just the calling that God has for us to serve him right now, but also the final call he will give on the last of all days. Will you be ready when the call comes?

## THE SIGN OF THE FIG TREE

If Jesus had one overarching purpose for his famous discourse on the fall of Jerusalem and the end of the world, it was to make sure that his disciples would be ready when the call came. The end is near, and whenever we witness any sign of the coming judgment, we should stand tall in the hope of our redemption. Thus Jesus ended Luke 21 by exhorting us to be prepared for the final call. He did this by teaching a *parable* about how near the end is, by making a *promise* about how certain his words are to come true, and by giving *practical advice* about the difference between being ready and not being ready for the end to come.

Jesus introduced this exhortation by telling one of the last and shortest of his many parables: "Look at the fig tree, and all the trees. As soon as they come out in leaf, you see for yourselves and know that the summer is already near. So also, when you see these things taking place, you know that the kingdom of God is near" (Luke 21:29–31). The analogy is a simple one. One of the first harbingers of the approaching summer is the budding of the trees in springtime. In all likelihood, Jesus was passing by a fig tree when he said this, but as he noted, what is true for the fig is true for all trees. No one can stop the change of seasons. Thus the appearance of the early fig blossoms is a sure sign that summertime is near.

According to Jesus, this is a parable about the coming of God's kingdom. Whenever we see the signs of divine judgment that are prophesied in the Bible, we know that the end is near. Many signs are given right here in Luke

---

1. Hugh Merrick, translator of Hermann Buhl, *Nanga Parbat Pilgrimage: The Lonely Challenge*, as quoted by James R. Edwards in *The Edwards Epistle* 14.2 (Summer 2005): n.p.

21, where Jesus prophesied the fall of Jerusalem and the coming of the Son of Man. Jesus told his disciples that nation would rise against nation and that people would suffer from earthquakes, famine, and disease. He said there would be signs in the sky and that the very powers of the heavens would be shaken. Jesus also said that these were all signs of the coming judgment—first for Jerusalem, and finally for the entire world. Similarly, whenever we see disasters in our world today, we know that the kingdom is near, the same way we know that summer is near when we see the first tree blossoms in springtime.

The parable is simple, but what Jesus said next is one of the most difficult verses to interpret anywhere in the Gospels: "Truly, I say to you, this generation will not pass away until all has taken place" (Luke 21:32). The question is: What exactly did Jesus mean by "this generation," and how does it fit in with what he was saying about how near we are to the end of the world?

At first, most people assume that when Jesus says "this generation" he is talking about the people who were alive when he spoke these words and who would die in the coming decades. After all, that is what we usually mean by "generation" today: the people who were born within a decade or two of one another and who generally live and die at the same time in human history.

If that is what Jesus meant by "this generation," then it becomes hard to make sense of the rest of the verse. Most of the people of his generation were dead by the end of the first century. Did Jesus believe that his second coming would happen before his disciples died? Is that what he meant when he said that "all" would "take place" before they "passed away"? We are forced to conclude either that Jesus was completely mistaken or that he was only talking about the fall of Jerusalem in A.D. 70—a judgment many of the people listening to him that day at the temple surely witnessed. But Jesus cannot err; he is the perfect Son of God. Nor was he speaking only about the fall of Jerusalem. As we saw earlier in this chapter of Luke's Gospel, Jesus was looking beyond that time of judgment to the last judgment of all.

Fortunately, there are some other ways to interpret this verse. Sometimes the Greek word for generation (genea) refers to race—a group defined by its ethnicity rather than by the year that it was born. A generation in this sense

437

is everyone who is descended from a common ancestor. This may be the way the term is used earlier in the Gospel, when Jesus talks about charging the blood of all the prophets to "this generation" (Luke 11:50–51; cf. Matt. 11:16; 12:39). If that is the way the term is used here in chapter 21, then Jesus was speaking specifically about the Jews. They are the people who will not pass from this earth until everything in God's plan has taken place. This is certainly one of the great truths of divine providence in human history: although no one has ever suffered greater persecution than the Jews, they have always maintained their ethnic identity—even through long centuries when they had no homeland to call their own. To this day, and to the end of the world, God's purposes for the Jews are coming true, including his plan for many Jews to come to faith in Jesus as their Messiah (see Rom. 11).

"Generation" can also refer to a group of people who are characterized by having the same spiritual condition. In this case, the emphasis falls not on *when* they live, but on *how* they live. For example, the people God destroyed in the great flood were an evil generation (see Gen. 6:11–12; 7:1), and the children of Israel that wandered in the wilderness were a perverse generation (Num. 32:13). The psalmist spoke in a similar way when he prayed that God would "guard us from this generation forever" (Ps. 12:7). So perhaps when Jesus talked about a generation not passing away until everything had taken place, he was talking about people who rejected the Christ and will continue to reject the Christ until the end of time.

Alternatively, and much more positively, Jesus may have been speaking about the chosen people of God—the generation of good disciples who believe the promises of the coming redemption. God will always have his believing people in the world, and they will persevere until everything that Jesus ever promised has taken place, for as the psalmist said, "God is with the generation of the righteous" (Ps. 14:5).

As we consider the various possibilities, it is hard to be entirely certain exactly what Jesus meant by the word "generation." We believe that everything he said was true, so we know he could not have meant that the second coming would happen before his disciples died. We also know this: absolutely everything that Jesus ever said about the end times will take place just the way he said it would. This is what Luke 21:32 is mainly about. Jesus is not trying to give us clues we can use to figure out when the end will come, or who will see it happen. Rather, he is telling us how certain these things are to take place. In the words of I. Howard Marshall, "the emphasis is on the certainty of the End rather than on limiting the date of the end."[2] Even if it is hard to know for sure what "generation" means, what the verse means is unmistakable. As surely as summer follows springtime, the words of Jesus will all come true, from the fall of Jerusalem to the end of the world, when the Son of Man will come with power and everlasting glory.

## THE ABIDING WORD

The parable of the fig tree is confirmed by the promise Jesus made about the truth of his word in verse 33: "Heaven and earth will pass away, but my words will not pass away." This verse takes the main point of verse 32 and extends it. It is not just what Jesus said about the end of the world that will come true, but what he said about anything and everything. Even when this tired old world has passed away, the words of Jesus will still abide.

What Jesus said is a remarkable claim to his deity and authority. Luke 21:33 echoes the words of Isaiah 40:8—a famous verse in which the Old Testament claims its own abiding authority: "The grass withers, the flower fades, but the word of our God will stand forever." It also echoes something Jesus himself said about the Old Testament law of God: "Until heaven and earth pass away, not an iota, not a dot, will pass from the Law until all is accomplished" (Matt. 5:18).

Jesus claimed the same enduring authority for the words that came from his own mouth. His gospel would stand forever. This could only mean that he himself was God, that he had all the authority in the universe, and that he had the almighty power to make sure that what he said would come to pass. Jesus "is not merely the foreteller of the course of history, but is Himself, in unity with the Father and the Spirit, the almighty Disposer thereof."[3] Therefore, whatever may happen on the earth or in the sky—even to the very end of the world—what Jesus said must come true. Charles Spurgeon said it like this:

2. I. Howard Marshall, *The Gospel of Luke*, New International Greek Testament Commentary (Grand Rapids: Eerdmans, 1978), 780.

3. Norval Geldenhuys, *The Gospel of Luke*, New International Commentary on the New Testament (Grand Rapids: Eerdmans, 1951), 539.

> Whatever alteration may come before the last great change, Christ's words shall still stand. . . . And when the greatest alteration of all shall take place, and this present dispensation shall come to an end, and all material things shall be consumed with fire, and be destroyed, yet, even then, there shall remain, above the ashes of the world, and all that is therein, the imperishable revelation of the Lord Jesus Christ.[4]

This promise applies to all the words that Jesus uttered in the Gospels. It applies to all his prophecies, from his predictions about the fall of Jerusalem (which have already come true) to his predictions about the end of the world. It applies to all his commands, such as his two great commandments to love the Lord our God with everything we have and to love our neighbors as ourselves. These commands of Jesus will all stand until the end of time, and then for all eternity. The same is true of all his warnings, like his warning that whoever does not believe in him will fall under the eternal wrath of God and suffer the torments of hell.

But praise God, the promises of Jesus will also stand forever, never to pass away. So do not just heed his warnings and obey his commands, but also trust his promises. Jesus has promised to forgive all our sins through the cross where he died for our salvation. He has promised that whoever comes to him will never be turned away. He has promised to give us everything we truly need. He has promised to be with us in all our troubles, giving us perfect peace and rest through the Holy Spirit. He has promised to heal all the wounds of our bodies and souls. He has promised to prepare a place for us in his Father's house. He has promised that by the power of his resurrection he will raise his children up from the grave when he comes again to take us home.

Jesus Christ made hundreds of promises in the Gospels, and they will all be true until the end of the world, and afterwards. This is the security of our salvation, which is based on the bedrock truth of the living and abiding words of Jesus. As the Scripture says, "all the promises of God find their Yes in him" (2 Cor. 1:20). Therefore, we can build our lives on the promises of Jesus Christ. Here is how Charles Spurgeon applied this principle to his congregation: "Are you very sick and weak, or are you getting very poor?

---

4. Charles H. Spurgeon, "The Perpetuity of the Gospel," in *The Metropolitan Tabernacle Pulpit* (1899; reprint Pasadena, TX: Pilgrim, 1977), 45:397–98.

Well, your health and your property, too, will pass away; but Christ's words will never pass away. Are you dying? Christ's words will never die or pass away; die with them in your heart."[5]

How sad it is that the living and abiding words of Jesus so often are opposed by people who reject the gospel. Whether it is false gospels like the so-called Gospel of Judas or religious hoaxes like *The Da Vinci Code*, someone is always trying to cast doubt on the words of Jesus. But his words will never pass away, which means that eventually anyone who tries to discredit Jesus will be discredited himself. My favorite example comes from Voltaire, the famous French philosopher. Not everyone remembers Voltaire these days, which is ironic, because he predicted that within fifty years people would no longer remember Jesus! It was a rash prediction, because the very year that Voltaire said this, the British Museum paid half a million pounds to purchase an ancient Bible manuscript, while at the same time a book of Voltaire's agnostic writings was selling for only eight pence in the London book stalls.

Move forward fifty years to witness an even greater irony. After Voltaire died, the philosopher's home in Geneva was eventually purchased by the Geneva Bible Society. Fifty years to the day after the philosopher's outrageous prediction, the presses in his very own home were printing thousands of Bibles every day.[6] Every copy included the words of Luke 21:33, written in French: "Le ciel et la terre passeront, mais mes paroles ne passeront point." Which means, as any Frenchman could tell you, "Heaven and earth will pass away, but my words will never pass away."

## Get Ready

If everything Jesus said will come true, this includes everything he ever said about the end of the world. One of the main things he said on this subject is that the end is near. The world has already witnessed the fall of Jerusalem. Nation has risen against nation. There have been earthquakes and tsunamis. People have fainted with fear and foreboding about the future. These are all things that Jesus prophesied, and

5. Spurgeon, "Perpetuity," 45:405.
6. This anecdote is recounted in James Montgomery Boice, *Acts: An Expositional Commentary* (Grand Rapids: Baker, 1997), 221.

like the first fig leaves in springtime, they are warning signs that the end is near.

When the end finally comes, it will affect all of us—every last person who has ever lived. As Jesus said, "It will come upon all who dwell on the face of the whole earth" (Luke 21:35). Obviously, he was not just talking about Jerusalem; he was talking about God judging the entire world, and everyone in it. As the Scripture says, "we will all stand before the judgment seat of God" (Rom. 14:10). One day every single man, woman, and child who has ever lived will appear before God for judgment.

For believers, the day of judgment will be a day of vindication. On the basis of the merits of Jesus Christ, who offered his perfect blood for our sins, we will be declared righteous in the sight of God. As it says in the Westminster Shorter Catechism, "At the resurrection, believers being raised up in glory, shall be openly acknowledged and acquitted in the day of judgment, and made perfectly blessed in the full enjoying of God to all eternity" (A. 38). But for unbelievers, the last of all days will be a day of doom, when God will banish his enemies from the joy of his presence and condemn them to suffer for their sins forever.

This is why we cannot simply drift through life without thinking seriously about the end of the world. The decision we make about Jesus Christ now determines where we will end up for all eternity. This is a matter of spiritual life and death. So every time Jesus talked about the end of the world, he always gave his disciples the same practical advice to get ready for it now, *before* the time comes. Jesus did not give us signs of the coming judgment so we could chart the future, but to exhort us to practice what J. C. Ryle described as "perpetual preparedness."[7] Are you ready for the end of the world?

Some people are not ready at all, and Jesus tells us why: "But watch yourselves lest your hearts be weighed down with dissipation and drunkenness and cares of this life, and that day come upon you suddenly like a trap"(Luke 21:34). Here we are called to serious self-examination. We need to watch out for two of the main things that prevent people from being prepared for the coming judgment: dissipation and distraction.

7. J. C. Ryle, *Expository Thoughts on the Gospels, Luke* (1858; reprint Cambridge: James Clarke, 1976), 2:385.

What the Bible means by "dissipation" is basically what today we would call a hangover: the unpleasant physical effects that inevitably follow the heavy consumption of alcohol. So "dissipation and drunkenness" are not so much two different things as they are two ways of describing the same thing. Some people deal with their fears about the future or the troubles of daily life by getting intoxicated. Rather than finding their comfort in Jesus, they try to make themselves feel better—or else feel nothing at all—by drinking alcohol or using other drugs.

The Bible does not forbid the moderate use of wine. In fact, the Holy Spirit himself tells us that God is the one who causes "wine to gladden the heart of man" (Ps. 104:15). If the wedding at Cana is any indication, Jesus knew the difference between ordinary table wine and a more select vintage. The apostle Paul even recommended a little wine for Timothy, his young protégé in gospel ministry (see 1 Tim. 5:23). But what the Bible sternly forbids is any form of drunkenness. God's command could not be clearer: "Do not get drunk with wine, for that is debauchery" (Eph. 5:18).

If you have been getting drunk—or if people who love you are concerned about how much you are drinking—stop using alcohol immediately. If you find that you can't stop, this proves that you have a problem. Medical attention may be needed to deal with the physical effects, especially if a strong chemical dependency has developed. But at its heart, the abuse of alcohol is a spiritual issue that calls for the repentance of sin. It is a sin not just because of what it does to a person (which is bad enough), or because of what it leads to (which is even worse), but also because of what it keeps a person from doing, namely, serving God in the power of the Holy Spirit.

According to Jesus, one thing that prevents people from getting ready for the day of death or for the end of the world—whichever comes first—is a lifestyle of senseless debauchery. Someone who is going out and getting wasted or drowning his sorrows at home is not ready for the second coming of the Son of Man.

This warning is not limited to drugs and alcohol, however. Drunkenness and dissipation are examples of a broader temptation, which is to fill our lives with so many intoxicating pleasures that we do not have any time left for God: television, computer games, romance novels—the list is endless. Any interest or entertainment that we use to escape from the serious issues of life and death causes the same problem. It keeps us from being ready when the time comes.

The other main thing that prevents people from being prepared is *distraction*. According to Jesus, the "cares of this life" can hinder our spiritual preparedness as much as getting drunk. What he meant by the "cares of this life" was not simply the anxieties that keep us up at night, but all the ordinary duties of daily existence—things like our homes, our jobs, our schoolwork, and our families. Our earthly affairs may be good in themselves, and God certainly calls us to do our daily duty. But these things can also drag us down spiritually, weighing down our hearts the way a heavy textbook strains a child's back on the long walk to school.

Whether we are tempted to dissipation or distraction, we are committing a sin of excess—either excessive drinking or excessive concern with our worldly business. Some people like to break all the rules. Like the younger brother in the story of the prodigal father, who lavished his love on his rebellious son, they run away to spend everything they have on riotous living. Other people like to keep all the rules. Like the older son in the same parable, they work hard in the fields every day. Yet their hearts are just as far from God. It is not so much the bad things that tempt them, but too many of the good things. They are so caught up in what they are doing that they are not looking for their Father's joy.

What is the temptation for you? Are you finding comfort in the drunken pleasures of a fallen world? If so, you are only hurting yourself, and the people you love. But maybe you are driving yourself to distraction with all the things you are doing, including all the things you think you are doing for God. Be careful, or else you will miss Jesus on the last day and come under judgment.

Do not get caught unawares! The day of judgment will come suddenly and almost completely unexpectedly, snapping the world shut like a trap. Even before they realize what is happening, or have time to do anything about it, many people will get caught by the justice of God. Are you ready for the final call?

## Perpetual Preparedness

Earlier I said that some people are not ready for Jesus to return, but some people *are* ready, and Jesus has told us what it takes for us to be ready. It takes faith in him for the forgiveness of our sins through the cross. Do not wait until the last minute, when it will be too late to get right with God. Believe in Jesus now, while there is still time. This is the way to get ready for the end of the world.

Then keep waiting and praying for Jesus to make his return soon. This is the way to stay ready. Jesus said, "But stay awake at all times, praying that you may have strength to escape all these things that are going to take place, and to stand before the Son of Man" (Luke 21:36). With these words, Jesus calls every believer to perpetual preparedness. We are to be constantly at the ready, looking for our Savior's return.

When I think of preparedness, I immediately think of the bomber pilots who used to fly for the Strategic Air Command of the United States Air Force. From the late 1940s until the early 1990s, the Strategic Air Command flew constant missions designed to deter the Russians from making a nuclear attack. When pilots were on flight duty, they always had to stay within a hundred yards of their aircraft, so that they could be airborne with nuclear weapons within moments of any military alert. The flights crews had to be awake at all times. As believers in Christ, we are to be similarly prepared for the coming of Christ, always staying alert, looking for his second coming at any time.

As we wait, we also pray, making the petitions that Jesus himself told us to make. We pray for the God-given strength to pass through all our earthly trials and enter unscathed into the glory that comes after, escaping from the wrath of God. We also pray that when the Son of Man comes, we will still be standing. To "stand before the Son of Man" is an expression that comes from the courtroom and indicates a favorable verdict.[8] Here it serves as a reminder that when we appear before God at the final judgment, we will be qualified to stand in his holy presence by the perfect righteousness of Jesus Christ.

Are you ready for the final call? One man who was always ready was James Montgomery Boice, who preached for more than thirty years from the pulpit of Philadelphia's Tenth Presbyterian Church. Dr. Boice wrote about perpetual preparedness in a hymn he was still working on when he died, getting ready for the last of all days:

8. Marshall, *Luke*, 783.

445

We do not know if Christ will come / when life is rough or steady;
We only know that Jesus said, / "Keep watching, and be ready."

"Keep watching!" For Christ will appear / at night or some bright morning,
Like lightning flashing through the sky / without a moment's warning.

"Be ready!" When the Lord descends / to render final judgment,
When men shall rise to heaven's joy / or suffer dreadful torment.

So watch with care; in grace abound, / get ready soon to greet him,
That when you hear the trumpet's sound / you'll be prepared to meet him.[9]

9. "Keep Watching and Be Ready," in James Montgomery Boice and Paul Steven Jones, *Hymns for a Modern Reformation* (Philadelphia: Tenth Presbyterian Church, 2000), 31.

# 92

# THE PASSOVER PLOT

## *Luke 21:37—22:13*

*Now the Feast of Unleavened Bread drew near, which is called the Passover. And the chief priests and the scribes were seeking how to put him to death, for they feared the people. (Luke 22:1–2)*

Sometime in the late 1970s, an ancient document was stolen from an Egyptian tomb. It was sold to an antiquities dealer and then passed from one dealer to another until scholars finally identified it as a copy of the long-lost Gospel of Judas.

We first read about the Gospel of Judas in the second-century writings of Irenaeus, who said it was rejected by the church because it was not in agreement with the biblical Gospels of Matthew, Mark, Luke, and John. In fact, the Gospel of Judas is not really a gospel at all because it does not tell the good news about the crucifixion and resurrection of Jesus Christ, which is what a gospel is. The story simply ends at the point when Judas handed Jesus over to the Jews. There is no cross or empty tomb in the manuscript, and therefore no forgiveness of sins or hope of eternal life.

Instead, this heretical document is a desperate attempt to make Judas the hero who delivered Jesus from having to live in a physical body by handing him over to be killed. According to the Gospel of Judas, these two men were the best of friends, and Judas betrayed Jesus only because Jesus asked him to do it. Judas and Jesus had many private conversations during the last week of their lives, in which Jesus told Judas many secrets that he never shared with any of the other disciples. This is because Judas was the most important disciple—the only one who really understood Jesus. "Step away from the others," Jesus said to him, "and I shall tell you the mysteries of the kingdom. It is possible for you to reach it."

All of this is utter nonsense, of course—a blatant contradiction of everything the Bible says about both Judas and Jesus. The people promoting this false gospel are trying to rehabilitate Judas by saying that he was never really the villain that Christians say he was; he was just misunderstood. But what these scholars are really doing is betraying Jesus all over again by calling something a gospel that fails to give people any good news.

If we want to know the real good news, we have to go back to what the Bible says. When we do, we discover that the biblical Gospels do not treat Judas as a hero at all, but give a sober, straightforward account of his conspiracy to murder the Son of God. What spiritual lessons can we learn from this conspiracy, and from the counterconspiracy that accomplished our salvation?

## THE CONSPIRACY

It was the middle of the last week of Jesus' life—the most important week in the history of the world. The Messiah had come to Jerusalem, where he had cried for the lost city and cleansed the temple of its spiritual impurity. Luke tells us: "Every day he was teaching in the temple, but at night he went out and lodged on the mount called Olivet. And early in the morning all the people came to him in the temple to hear him" (Luke 21:37–38).

There were crowds of people in the city that week for the Passover festival that celebrated Israel's exodus from Egypt. Quickly the word spread that Jesus was in Jerusalem. He was there to teach people the gospel, and teach people he did, proclaiming the most marvelous truths that anyone had ever heard. When people went to the temple, they heard him defending his true deity and divine authority, speaking in parables, predicting his martyrdom, clarifying the relationship between God and the government, defending the resurrection, and prophesying the fall of Jerusalem and the coming of the

Son of Man (see Luke 20–21). If we are wise, we will do what many people did in Jerusalem and listen to Jesus.

Something else was happening in those days, too, and here dark chords begin to play in the music of Luke's Gospel. So many people were flocking to Jesus that the religious leaders began to worry that things were getting out of hand. They were secretly (and in some cases, not so secretly) opposed to everything that Jesus was saying, so the more popular he became, the more determined they were to stop him.

We have seen people's opposition to Jesus grow throughout the Gospel. The first time he preached at his hometown synagogue in Nazareth, people tried to kill him (see Luke 4:28–29). When Jesus began to get a following, the scribes and the Pharisees criticized the way that his disciples behaved (e.g., Luke 5:33). Soon they were trying to trick him into saying or doing something that would get him into trouble (see Luke 6:7). By the time we get to the end of chapter 11, the religious leaders were "lying in wait for him, to catch him in something he might say" (Luke 11:54).

Their hatred grew to its most furious intensity during the last week of Jesus' life. By then it was not just the party of the Pharisees who wanted to get rid of him; it was the whole leadership of the temple in Jerusalem: the priests, the scribes, and the elders. These men hated Jesus. They hated him for his condemnations of their hypocrisy and for claiming that he was God the Son. They hated seeing him teach at the temple. They hated how much influence he had on people, especially during Passover, when so many people were there to influence. In their hatred they challenged his authority (Luke 20:2), tried to get their hands on him (Luke 20:19), and sent spies to trap him (Luke 20:20). In a word, they were seeking to "destroy" him (Luke 19:47). Maybe this explains why Jesus left the city every day before nightfall: it was too dangerous for him to be in Jerusalem after dark.

The evil intentions of these enemies show that even someone in a God-given place of spiritual leadership is capable of falling into grievous sin. The very men who should have been doing the most to worship Jesus and to spread his gospel were plotting to destroy him. They were supposed to be getting ready for Passover, praising God for delivering his people and preparing to offer a sacrificial lamb for their sins. Instead, they were conspiring to murder the very Son of God.

The problem for these religious leaders, of course, was that Jesus was much too popular for them to do anything to him in public. Their malice against Jesus was constrained only by their cowardice in the face of public opinion. Jerusalem was packed with so many pilgrims for Passover that they could hardly dare to risk an open arrest. Here is how Luke describes their dilemma: "Now the Feast of Unleavened Bread drew near, which is called the Passover. And the chief priests and the scribes were seeking how to put him to death, for they feared the people" (Luke 22:1–2). These wicked men had already decided what they wanted to do. Their mission statement was simple: kill Jesus. The only question was how they could kill him without starting a riot.

Their diabolical dilemma was solved when help suddenly arrived from a source they never expected. He was the most unlikely co-conspirator that anyone could imagine: one of Jesus' own disciples—a man "who was of the number of the twelve" (Luke 22:3). Luke tells us that Judas Iscariot, who had been with Jesus virtually since the beginning of his public ministry, "went away and conferred with the chief priests and officers how he might betray him to them" (Luke 22:4).

To use the proper term for it, this was a *conspiracy*. According to the legal code of the Commonwealth of Pennsylvania, "A person is guilty of conspiracy with another person or persons to commit a crime if, with intent of promoting or facilitating its commission, he agrees with such other person or persons that they or one or more of them will engage in conduct which constitutes such crime."[1] This is exactly what Judas and the chief priests and the officers of the temple police did: they plotted together to commit a crime.

The whole conspiracy was conducted with a view to a kill. Judas would be the betrayer, the spy inside the organization who would spring the trap. As Luke tells us, "he consented and sought an opportunity to betray him to them in the absence of a crowd" (Luke 22:6). This solved the main problem of the chief priests. Judas could give them the inside information they needed to capture Jesus when no one else was around. Then they could do whatever they wanted to do with him.

Just thinking about getting their hands on Jesus made the religious leaders cackle with evil delight. "They were glad," Luke says (Luke 22:5)—simple

1. *Pennsylvania Code* 18 Pa.C.S.A. sec. 903 (a).

words that constitute one of the strongest condemnations we read any-where in Scripture. Here were men who were happy to commit the greatest crime in the history of the world. Their murderous glee came from the heart of darkness.

## THE BETRAYER

Our studies in Luke have shown us some of the reasons why these men hated Jesus, but what motivated Judas? He had been with Jesus from the beginning, and thus he had the extraordinary privilege of knowing the Christ as a personal friend. He had heard everything Jesus had to teach about the kingdom of God and had seen all the miraculous signs that proved the truth of his gospel. But in the end, Judas wickedly decided to betray Jesus at the earliest opportunity. Why did he do it?

The so-called Gospel of Judas claims that Judas really was trying to do Jesus a favor. "You will exceed all of them," Jesus supposedly said to Judas, "for you will sacrifice the man that clothes me." In other words, by getting Jesus killed, Judas would liberate him from his earthly body so that he could become a pure spirit. This way of thinking contradicts everything the Bible says about the body and the soul, but it was common among the Gnostic theologians who tried to corrupt the gospel in the early centuries of the Christian church (which indicates that the Gospel of Judas was written *after* the biblical Gospels). According to the Bible, our bodies are part of God's good creation and they will be glorified in the resurrection. But according to the Gnostics, only the soul is good; the body is evil. So by betraying Jesus unto death, Judas was actually liberating him from his body! This perverse interpretation shows the cruelty of the ancient heresy of Gnosticism: it was even used to justify murder—the crucifixion of Christ.

So if Judas was not trying to do Jesus a favor, what was he trying to do? Maybe he was disappointed with Jesus, as many people were. What most Jews were hoping for in a Messiah was a military leader and political hero who would liberate them from their Roman captivity. They were looking for the earthly king of a worldly kingdom. But by now it was becoming clear that Jesus had no intention of establishing that kind of kingdom right away, especially after his teaching on the fall of Jerusalem and the end of the world. So maybe Judas felt betrayed himself because Jesus had failed to be the kind of Savior Judas wanted him to be. Many people do the same thing today. They have their own ideas about what kind of Savior Jesus ought to be—what kind of physical healing he ought to bring them, or financial prosperity, or personal success—and when he fails to meet their expectations, they turn against him.

The only clue Luke gives us is that Judas had a profit motive. For his part in this conspiracy, the chief priests "agreed to give him money" (Luke 22:5). Matthew tells us that Judas was the one who brought up the whole subject of compensation: "What will you give me if I deliver him over to you?" Judas asked (Matt. 26:15). "They paid him thirty pieces of silver. And from that moment he sought an opportunity to betray him" (Matt. 26:15–16). Later, when Judas felt remorse for what he had done, the first thing he did was to give the money back (Matt. 27:3–5).

All of this fits in with what we learn about Judas earlier in the Gospels. It was Judas, remember, who objected when Mary of Bethany anointed the feet of Jesus with a whole pound of sweet perfume. "Why was this ointment not sold for three hundred denarii and given to the poor?" he complained (John 12:5). John informs us that Judas did not say this "because he cared about the poor, but because he was a thief, and having charge of the moneybag he used to help himself to what was put into it" (John 12:6).

More than anything else, it was the love of money that tempted Judas to his betrayal. Jesus had warned Judas and the other disciples about this when he taught the parable of the rich fool: "Take care, and be on your guard against all covetousness" (Luke 12:15). But Judas failed to heed this warning, to his own destruction. Cyril of Alexandria said it well: "Those who seek to be rich, fall into numerous and unprofitable lusts, which sink people in pitfalls and destruction. The disciple who became a traitor is a clear proof of this, because he perished for the sake of a few miserable coins."[2]

That is all it was: just thirty pieces of silver. To this day, we are still shocked that Judas would perpetrate such a colossal crime for such a paltry sum. But it is often shocking what people will do for money. There is a notable example in the publication of the Gospel of Judas. The Swiss dealer who sold this false gospel to the National Geographic Society for one and a half

---

2. Cyril of Alexandria, "Commentary on Luke," Homily 140, in *Luke*, ed. Arthur A. Just, Jr., Ancient Christian Commentary on Scripture, NT 3 (Downers Grove, IL: InterVarsity, 2003), 327.

million dollars—a woman named Frieda Nussberger-Tchacos—is a known felon who has trafficked in stolen antiquities. In order to avoid doing jail time, she betrayed one of her co-conspirators—a former director of the Getty Museum. The *Los Angeles Times* had this to say about the irony of her situation: "some things don't change—except for inflation. Thirty pieces of silver then, or $1.5 million now: it's still all about money."[3]

Many Christians think of the love of money as one of the lesser sins, but see where it leads. When we refuse to be content with our financial situation—whether we happen to be rich or poor—we open the door to fatal temptation. Once we decide that we want something more than we already have, we start thinking about ways to get it. The more that desire grows, the more tempted we are to get what we want in ways that do not please God or depend on his providence. Are you content with what you have, or has your mind been playing around with ways to get richer? Are there any ways you are compromising your integrity for financial gain? The reason the Bible reveals that Judas had a profit motive is not to stigmatize him, but to show how ordinary his temptation was. Judas did it for the money, which is exactly the reason why a lot of people do a lot of the wrong things they do.

Unfortunately, there is more than a little bit of the betrayer in all of us. Like Judas, we have had the extraordinary spiritual privilege of seeing the person and work of Jesus for ourselves. We have professed our faith in Christ and started to follow him, as Judas did. We have heard the preaching of his gospel, and we know something of his divine power. Yet even a temptation as simple as the love of money might lead us into a deep betrayal of the Lord we say that we worship. Heed this warning:

> The history of Judas, who, although he occupied such a privileged position as one of Jesus' twelve apostles, nevertheless betrayed the Master, serves as a permanent and powerful warning to every member of the church of Christ— there is always the terrible possibility that even among us who apparently live in the closest connection with the Lord there may be those who are inwardly false and are busily engaged in betraying Him.[4]

3. *Los Angeles Times* editorial (April 13, 2006), quoted by Peter Jones in *NewsCWiPP* 26 (April 2006): 1.
4. Norval Geldenhuys, *The Gospel of Luke*, New International Commentary on the New Testament (Grand Rapids: Eerdmans, 1951), 546.

When are we in danger of betraying our Lord? When we spend more time thinking about what we do not have than praising God for what we *do* have. When we want him to do something different for us than what he thinks is best. And when we think we are so strong spiritually that we could never betray him at all.

## THE ULTIMATE CO-CONSPIRATOR

Behind the betrayer there was a darker and more demonic influence. To understand the true nature of the conspiracy that led to the crucifixion, we need to see that it came from the pit of hell. Luke begins his account of the clandestine encounter that Judas had with the chief priests by saying, "Then Satan entered into Judas called Iscariot, who was of the number of the twelve" (Luke 22:3). When he said this, Luke lifted the curtain of concealment to show that there was a supernatural dimension to this conflict. There was a conspirator behind the conspiracy. He was the ultimate co-conspirator: Satan himself—God's ancient enemy, the devil.

What Luke describes must be the most extreme form of demonic possession. Judas Iscariot was not simply possessed by a demon, but by the devil himself, at least during the hours when he conspired against the Son of God, and again later, when he actually went to betray him (see John 13:27). Even if we do not know exactly what kind of control Satan had over Judas, we can agree with J. C. Ryle that this was something "peculiarly awful."[5] Judas was under the evil influence of the archenemy of God.

This was not against the betrayer's will, for Judas had already opened the door for the devil to come in. The Bible promises that if we resist the devil, he will flee from us (James 4:7). Therefore, we should never think—even for a moment—that we are powerless against the schemes of Satan, or that against our will he could do to us what he did to Judas. It is the devil himself who wants us to think that we can do nothing to stop him. What God wants us to believe is his superior power for those who believe, against which the devil cannot stand. As long as we exercise our faith in the victory of Jesus Christ, we are free from the sins and fears that the devil wants to make our

5. J. C. Ryle, *Expository Thoughts on the Gospels, Luke* (1858; reprint Cambridge: James Clarke, 1976), 2:389.

torment. If only Judas had resisted Satan's temptations by trusting in the promises of God, he never would have become the betrayer. Instead, weakened by his own sinful desires, he came under the devil's power.

As happy as the chief priests were when Judas became their co-conspirator, Satan was even happier. Ever since the beginning of human history, he had been sneaking around creation, looking for some opportunity to destroy God's plans for blessing his people.[6] First Satan succeeded at tempting Adam and Eve into sin. But God pronounced a terrible curse against him, announcing that he would be crushed by the woman's son. So the devil did everything he could to prevent that son from ever coming. He tempted Cain to kill his brother Abel, but God preserved his holy line through Seth. The devil tried to turn people against God, and many people did turn against him and were destroyed, but God preserved his holy line through Noah. Satan tempted Abraham to produce his own son, who was not the son of promise, but God preserved his holy line through Isaac.

The people of God ended up in Egypt, where Satan tempted Pharaoh to put all of Israel's sons to death in the Nile. But God saved his people through Moses. The conflict continued—the invisible war between heaven and hell, God and Satan. The children of Israel were taken into captivity, but God preserved a righteous remnant, and eventually the Savior was conceived by the Holy Spirit and born of the virgin Mary. Satan tried to kill him right away, tempting Herod to slaughter all the baby boys in Bethlehem. That diabolical strategy failed as well, and eventually Satan took the fight right to Jesus. Three times he tried to tempt the Son of God into sin. But Jesus resisted the devil in the wilderness, and the devil fled from him.

Since the very moment he first rebelled against God, Satan has been working with all his hateful strength to destroy God's plans for his people. He has been skulking around the shadows of Luke's Gospel. We always knew that we would see him again; it was just a matter of when. After the temptations in the wilderness, the devil departed from Jesus "until an opportune time" (Luke 4:13). From time to time his demons attacked Jesus, and Jesus had cast them out in a show of his superior strength. But now the opportune time had come. Judas the betrayer had joined Satan's conspiracy, and the devil would not stop until he put Jesus to death.

---

6. Satan's long war against the Son of God is documented in Donald Grey Barnhouse, *The Invisible War* (Grand Rapids: Zondervan, 1965).

## THE COUNTERCONSPIRACY

This time Satan's scheme apparently would succeed beyond his wildest expectations. Judas would be the betrayer. The chief priests would arrest Jesus, accuse him, and hand him over to the Romans, who would hang him on a cross. But there was something that Satan didn't know. At the same time he was conspiring against the Son of God, God was operating the counterconspiracy that would crush Satan and bring salvation to all the people of God. This was the real Passover plot: not Satan's wicked scheme to put Jesus to death in Jerusalem during Passover, but the eternal plan of the Father, the Son, and the Holy Spirit to crush Satan through the crucifixion of Jesus Christ.

At the very time that Satan was actively seeking to destroy him, Jesus was still in control. We are reminded of this by the very practical preparations he made to celebrate Passover with his disciples:

> Then came the day of Unleavened Bread, on which the Passover lamb had to be sacrificed. So Jesus sent Peter and John, saying, "Go and prepare the Passover for us, that we may eat it." They said to him, "Where will you have us prepare it?" He said to them, "Behold, when you have entered the city, a man carrying a jar of water will meet you. Follow him into the house that he enters and tell the master of the house, 'The Teacher says to you, Where is the guest room, where I may eat the Passover with my disciples?' And he will show you a large upper room furnished; prepare it there." And they went and found it just as he had told them, and they prepared the Passover. (Luke 22:7–13)

The day of unleavened bread was the day before Passover. It was a day of spiritual and practical preparation, on which God's people swept all the old leaven out of their homes as a symbol of sweeping away sin, and when they slaughtered lambs for the Passover sacrifice. It was the biggest feast of the year, and Jesus sent some of his disciples to do the necessary preparations. It was not just Passover that was being prepared, however, but also the death of Jesus for the salvation of sinners.

Luke gives us these details to show that Jesus was in full control of everything leading up to the crucifixion. Our Savior had determined that he would eat this one last meal with his disciples and institute the sacrament of the Lord's Supper. To that end, his divine providence and sovereign fore-knowledge had arranged a room where they could meet. Possibly the room was prearranged, and the jar of water was a signal (usually carrying such a jar was women's work). Commentators as far back as Cyril of Alexandria have suggested that Jesus may have done this to keep Judas from knowing where they were meeting that night.[7] He did not tell any of his disciples the secret location; he gave Peter and John only the sign they needed to find it. This kept Judas in the dark until Jesus was ready for his betrayal. Soon Judas would betray Jesus, but not yet—not until Jesus knew that the time was right.

Jesus would not offer his life as a sacrifice for our sins until Passover. At the very time when people were celebrating their saving deliverance and offering a lamb as a sacrifice for sin, he would offer himself as the Passover Lamb for the whole world (1 Cor. 5:7). But he would not offer himself on the cross until he kept the feast with his disciples, giving them his body and blood in the bread and wine of the Last Supper. Nor would he let the betrayer betray him until the time for his betrayal had come. This too was part of the plan, in fulfillment of the ancient psalm: "Even my close friend in whom I trusted, who ate my bread, has lifted his heel against me" (Ps. 41:9; cf. Luke 22:21).

It was all part of God's counterconspiracy, and Jesus worked it to per-fection—not just the little details of preparing the feast, but the whole plan of redemption. Jesus knew exactly what he was doing. He knew what Judas wanted to do to him, and what the devil was trying to do, but he also knew what *he* was going to do. His preparations for our salvation were underway. Already Jesus was moving towards the cross. He was as determined as Satan that he would die. On this point both the conspiracy and the countercon-spiracy agreed. They both led straight to the cross.

That is where the conspiracy ended, however: at the cross. When Jesus was crucified, the religious leaders got what they wanted, Judas got what he bargained for, and Satan got what he had been scheming to get since the day God made the world. Only none of them got what they thought they were getting, for at the place where the conspiracy ended, the countercon-spiracy was beginning to bring salvation. Unlike Satan, Jesus knew what his

---

7. Cyril of Alexandria, "Commentary on Luke," Homily 141, 328–29.

death by crucifixion would accomplish. He knew that it would be the death of the devil himself, and the death of sin for everyone who trusts in him, not to mention the death of death for everyone who believes in the cross and the empty tomb.

Which Passover plot do you choose to belong to: Satan's conspiracy or the counterconspiracy of the Son of God? Are you with Jesus or against him? Do you have faith in the cross or do you despise it as something that is unimportant to the kind of life that you want to live? Choose wisely. The conspiracy only leads to death, but the counterconspiracy leads to eternal life after death.

When we believe in Jesus and his counterconspiracy, God works his plan out in our own lives. If he worked his purposes out through the greatest crime in history, he can also work them out in the little things of our own lives, however big they may seem. Admittedly, there are times when it does not seem that way. The Bible says that Satan "prowls around like a roaring lion, seeking someone to devour" (1 Peter 5:8). Sometimes we hear the rumble of the devil's roar, and it terrifies us. We are gripped by the fear of failure, or of financial collapse, or of everything that seems to be going wrong in our family or our church. Sometimes we do not hear the devil at all, but he is stalking us all the same, silently creeping in for the kill. He is tempting us to fall back into the same old pattern of sin, or to find our own way to get what we want out of life, or to use our difficult circumstances as an excuse to be disappointed with God.

Do not be afraid of the devil! Do not let him devour you! Do not give in to his wicked schemes! No matter how much Satan conspires against you, through faith in Jesus Christ you belong to God's counterconspiracy. At this very moment, the same God who planned his victory over Satan—even through the betrayal of Judas—is planning to work everything out in your life, exactly the way it is supposed to be worked out, for your genuine good and God's greater glory. The God who conquered Satan through the cross and raised Jesus from the dead will be your salvation.

# 93

# THE FIRST SUPPER

## *Luke 22:14–20*

*And when the hour came, he reclined at table, and the apostles with him. And he said to them, "I have earnestly desired to eat this Passover with you before I suffer." (Luke 22:14–15)*

t is customary for a condemned man to be given one last request before he is put to death. That convention is observed in America by giving criminals on death row a feast before they are executed. Typically the menu is printed in the newspaper, presumably to satisfy the morbid interest of public curiosity. People want to know: What did the condemned man eat and drink before dying?

We could ask the same question about Jesus Christ, for he too was a condemned man, with one last meal to eat before dying. This was the night on which Jesus was betrayed. Soon he would be condemned and crucified for crimes he did not commit. In just a few short hours he would be arrested and accused, then beaten and abused. He would be dead before nightfall the following day, his lifeless body put in a tomb. This was the last night of our Savior's life on earth, and he had one last meal to share with his disciples.

Christians usually call this farewell feast "the Last Supper." This title makes sense because it was the last time that Jesus would celebrate Passover with his disciples, and the last time he would eat and drink anything with them before he died. But it was also the first time that Jesus celebrated communion with them, the sacred meal also known as the sacrament of the Lord's Supper. So in a sense the Last Supper was also "the First Supper"— the first supper of the new salvation that Jesus gave his disciples by giving them himself. In the words of T. W. Manson, the Lord's Supper "indicates and inaugurates a redemption effected by the death of Christ as a sacrifice."[1]

## THE HEART OF THE HOST

The first thing to understand about this supper is how eagerly Jesus wanted to share it with his disciples. We have already seen the deliberate preparations he made for this meal (see Luke 22:7–13), and how careful he was to make sure that it took place before he was betrayed. But as he sat down to the meal, Jesus opened his heart to his disciples. Luke tells us that "when the hour came, he reclined at table, and the apostles with him. And he said to them, 'I have earnestly desired to eat this Passover with you before I suffer. For I tell you I will not eat it until it is fulfilled in the kingdom of God'" (Luke 22:14–16).

In God's perfect timing, the hour had come for Jesus to sit with his beloved disciples, waiting on them at the meal that signified their salvation (cf. Luke 12:37). With a heart of love, their host told them how much he had been looking forward to being alone with them around the table that night. The words he used for "earnest desire" (*epithymia epethymēsa*) express intense longing. Jesus Christ was a man of perfect passions. We have seen these passions throughout Luke's Gospel: his scornful contempt for religious hypocrisy, his merciful compassion for the lost and broken, his holy jealousy for the true worship of God. Here we see his ardent affection for his disciples. There is no one Jesus would rather have been with on this last night than his closest friends. As he looked into the faces of the men gathered around the table that night, his heart was full because his intense longing to share this meal with them was satisfied.

1. T. W. Manson, *The Gospel of Luke*, Moffatt New Testament Commentary (New York: Harper, 1930), 306–7.

Why did Jesus have this deep desire? It may have been because Passover was such a blessed occasion for the people of God. Passover was a sacramental celebration of God's deliverance—a commemoration of Israel's exodus. Every year the people of God offered a lamb to remember the sacrificial blood that had saved their ancestors on the famous night in Egypt when the angel of death passed over their houses. They ate bitter herbs to remember the bitter years of their slavery to Pharaoh, but they ate them while reclining at table—a symbol of freedom to show that they were no longer slaves. They also ate unleavened bread to symbolize their hasty departure the night they made their exodus from Egypt. The people of God looked forward to doing all of this at Passover. For Jesus and his disciples, the feast brought back some of the happiest memories of childhood: making the annual pilgrimage to Jerusalem, eating roast lamb with their families, and praising God for his salvation.

There is more, however. Jesus was not just longing for Passover, but also anticipating his death on the cross, and it is in this context that he earnestly desired to eat and drink with his disciples. Jesus was specific about this. He said, "I have earnestly desired to eat this Passover with you before I suffer" (Luke 22:15). For many months Jesus had been telling his disciples that he would "suffer many things and be rejected by the elders and chief priests and scribes, and be killed" (see Luke 9:22). Now the conspiracy was under way that would culminate in his crucifixion. But there was something Jesus wanted to do first: before he suffered, he wanted to host the farewell feast for his disciples that would help them understand what he was about to do for their salvation.

Jesus also desired to have this of all Passovers with his disciples because the feast was about to find its fulfillment. Passover was a time to look back and remember how God had saved his people in the past. In the plan of God, however, Passover also looked forward to the full and final salvation that God would provide in the person and work of the Messiah. So Jesus said, "I tell you I will not eat it until it is fulfilled in the kingdom of God" (Luke 22:16).

At first it may sound as if Jesus was telling his disciples that after an undetermined delay, he would sit down and share this meal with them again. If so, then Jesus must have been thinking in terms of his coming glory and referring to the last of all feasts—what the Bible calls "the

461

marriage supper of the Lamb" (Rev. 19:9). Yet Jesus may simply have meant that he would never share Passover with them again. In Hebrew usage, the word "until" does not necessarily imply that something will happen again.[2] To cite just one example, when the Bible says that the prophet Samuel "did not see Saul again until the day of his death" (1 Sam. 15:35), this does not mean that Samuel bumped into Saul the day that he died, but that he never saw him again at all. Similarly, Jesus was telling his disciples that this was their last Passover. Soon that sacrament would find its true fulfillment in the kingdom of the Lord Jesus Christ, and they would never have occasion to celebrate it together again. Instead, the people of God would celebrate the new sacrament of the new covenant in Christ by eating the bread and drinking the wine of the Lord's Supper.

These were some of the reasons why Jesus was so eager to celebrate this Passover with his disciples—the disciples who later that very night would abandon Jesus and deny ever knowing him as the Christ. Johnny Cash once wrote a simple gospel song that captures something of the warm intimacy that the Savior shared with his friends around the table that night. In the song Jesus says to his disciples:

> I can tell by your faces
> That you don't understand
> The awesome things you've felt and seen
> At the touch of my hand.
> But someday you'll understand it,
> When the Father means for you to
> But for now drink the cup and break the bread
> And I'll eat my last supper here with you.

Then comes the refrain:

> Have a little bread, Simon;
> Pass the wine to James my brother.
> Go ahead and eat, fellas,
> And love one another.
> Have a good time, friends,

2. J. C. Ryle, *Expository Thoughts on the Gospels, Luke* (1858; reprint Cambridge: James Clarke, 1976), 2:400.

'Cause tomorrow I must die.
And I'm never going to eat with you again
Till we eat the marriage supper in the sky.[3]

Needless to say, the words "go ahead and eat, fellas" do not appear in any reputable English translation of Luke's Gospel. This phrase is not part of the words of the institution of the Lord's Supper as a sacrament for the Christian church. But it does express the friendly affection Jesus had for his disciples, and the love he felt for them in his heart as they sat down to share their last Passover, which was also the first supper of the kingdom of God. Jesus gave this sacramental meal to his disciples because he loved them.

## THE CUP OF THANKSGIVING

The transition from Passover to the Lord's Supper helps explain why Luke tells us about two cups in this passage, and not just one. Anyone who is familiar with the Christian sacrament of the Lord's Supper knows that there is only one loaf of bread and one cup of communion. In Luke's account of the Last Supper, however, Jesus offers his disciples both a cup of thanksgiving (Luke 22:17) and the cup of the new covenant (Luke 22:20).

Some scholars think that having two cups is a difficulty and have tried to get around it by claiming that the last half of verse 19 and all of verse 20 are not part of the original manuscripts for the Gospel of Luke. They point out that these verses (which are absent from some ancient manuscripts of the New Testament) sound almost exactly like 1 Corinthians 11:24–25, so they may have been "borrowed" from the apostle Paul. Yet the vast majority of the ancient biblical manuscripts include the full text of verses 19 and 20. The reason a few manuscripts differ is probably that some scribe or other tried to resolve the difficulty himself and decided that there should really be only one cup.[4]

Not only do both cups belong here, but they both help us to understand what Jesus was teaching his disciples. In all likelihood, the first cup

3. Johnny Cash, "The Last Supper," sung in a backstage interview with Ken Myers, as recorded in the *Mars Hill Audio Journal* 65.1 (Nov./Dec. 2003): 4.

4. For a full discussion of the textual issues involved, see I. Howard Marshall, *The Gospel of Luke*, New International Greek Testament Commentary (Grand Rapids: Eerdmans, 1978), 799–801.

was not part of the Lord's Supper, but part of the traditional celebration of Passover. Four cups of salvation were raised during the Passover meal— one for each promise of deliverance that God gave to his people through the prophet Moses. This seems to be the context for what Luke tells us in verses 17 and 18: "And he took a cup, and when he had given thanks he said, 'Take this, and divide it among yourselves. For I tell you that from now on I will not drink of the fruit of the vine until the kingdom of God comes'" (Luke 22:17–18). It is not entirely clear which cup this may have been, but whether it was the first cup of the feast or the last, it was part of "this Passover"—the one that Jesus said he wanted to celebrate with his disciples (Luke 22:15).

The first cup that Luke mentions was for thanksgiving. When Jesus raised it for his disciples, he first gave thanks to God. We do not know exactly what Jesus said when he prayed. Presumably, he praised the Father for his mighty works of saving power. But it is enough for us to know that he celebrated this feast with a glad and thankful heart, and that when he gave this thankful cup to his disciples, they drank it together. They were sharing a communal celebration of God's saving power.

Once again, Jesus said that he would not share this cup with them again until kingdom come. Or, to take what he said more literally, he would not drink any wine of any kind. Again, it is hard to be entirely certain what Jesus meant by "until" and what he meant by "the kingdom of God." Many of the early church fathers thought Jesus was talking about the resurrection of his body: his lips would touch no wine until he was raised from the dead. Possibly the word "until" means here what it seems to mean in verse 16, namely, that he will not share this Passover with them again. More likely, Jesus was looking forward to the banquet he has promised to share with us in the coming age. He would not keep a feast of the same kind again until he ate the last of all suppers, on the day when "the grand Consummation has arrived with the final victory over all the evil powers."[5]

What does seem clear is that Jesus connected the sacrament of the Lord's Supper to Passover. "Jesus is interpreting His death in a Passover context,"

5. Norval Geldenhuys, *The Gospel of Luke*, New International Commentary on the New Testament (Grand Rapids: Eerdmans, 1951), 554.

writes Leon Morris, "and making it clear that it has saving significance."[6] The Last Supper is both the last Passover and the first communion. By way of analogy, this meal is like a video sequence in which one image fades away while at the same time a superimposed image is coming into focus. The meal morphs from Passover into communion, from the Last Supper of the old administration to the first supper of the new covenant.

F. W. Krummacher used a different analogy to make the same point, comparing the meal in the upper room to a blossom on a tree that grows into fruit. "Christ has exalted the Mosaic festival of the Passover," Krummacher said, "by changing it into His sacrament."[7] Jesus made this change because it was one of the best ways for his disciples to understand his saving work. Seeing the Lord's Supper in the context of Passover teaches us what Jesus was doing for us on the cross. The apostle Paul made a similar connection when he said, "Christ, our Passover lamb, has been sacrificed. Let us therefore celebrate the festival" (1 Cor. 5:7–8).

## THE BREAD OF REMEMBRANCE

This brings us to the two elements Jesus used to celebrate the First Supper: the bread of remembrance and the cup of the new covenant. We begin the way that Jesus did, with the bread: "And he took bread, and when he had given thanks, he broke it and gave it to them, saying, 'This is my body, which is given for you. Do this in remembrance of me'" (Luke 22:19).

The people of God always ate bread when they celebrated Passover. But here, by the words that instituted the Lord's Supper, Jesus invested the breaking of the bread with new and surprising significance. It is not simply what Jesus did that is important here, but also what he said. The words "do this" indicate that Jesus intended the sacramental acts of breaking the bread (and pouring the cup) to be repeated in the worship of the church. But in order for us to know what it *means* to "do this" in remembrance of Jesus, the physical sign of breaking the bread must be interpreted by the sacramental words of our Savior. They are words it takes only a moment to

6. Leon Morris, *The Gospel According to St. Luke: An Introduction and Commentary*, Tyndale New Testament Commentaries (Grand Rapids: Eerdmans, 1974), 306.

7. F. W. Krummacher, *The Suffering Saviour* (Carlisle, PA: Banner of Truth, 2004), 44.

understand but a lifetime to comprehend, for although they are simple in themselves, they reveal many deep mysteries of the gospel.

What are some of the things we learn from what Jesus said about the bread? We learn that the bread of this sacrament is to be received with thanksgiving, for Jesus gave thanks before he broke it (Luke 22:19). This is why some Christians call communion "the Eucharist," which is simply the Greek word for giving thanks *(eucharisteō)*. The Lord's Supper is a gift of God's grace, and therefore it is to be received with a grateful heart.

We learn further that the sacramental bread "is" the body of Jesus Christ. This immediately raises further questions, because our interpretation of what Jesus meant by saying this depends on what our definition of "is" is. Some Christians believe that Jesus is speaking literally here, and therefore that in some way the physical essence of the bread must be changed or transubstantiated into the very body of Christ. There are many reasons to think that this interpretation is incorrect, including some that are obvious from the immediate context. What sense does it make to say that the bread is identical with the body of Christ when Jesus is right there with his disciples already, in his physical body, breaking bread with them?

The disciples themselves would have been astonished that anyone would even think of taking Jesus literally here. The very idea would have been alien to their whole way of thinking about Jesus or the sacraments. By this time they were well used to their Lord speaking to them in figures of speech. When Jesus said, "I am the door" (John 10:9), they did not start looking for his hinges, and when he said, "I am the bread of life" (John 6:35), they did not assume that his dough was made from scratch! The disciples instinctively recognized that Jesus was not speaking literally at all, but using metaphors to make a spiritual comparison.

Similarly, when Jesus said "This bread is my body," he was not giving his disciples a philosophical theory of the sacraments, but drawing a simple comparison that would help them understand the meaning of his death. He was not describing a physical change, but making a sacramental identification. The union or association between Jesus and the bread is not physical, but spiritual. To say that the bread is his body is to say that it "represents" or "signifies" or "symbolizes" his body. In the words of John Calvin, "the bread is called body because it is symbol of the body."[8]

Undoubtedly one of the reasons Jesus chose bread to serve as this sacramental symbol is that bread is so basic to life itself. We cannot live without our daily bread. So when Jesus tells us to take and eat the bread that signifies his body, he is giving us something we cannot live without—something we need to nourish our souls.

Jesus gives us this life-giving nourishment in the bread of the Lord's Supper. "Give" is just the word to use, because Jesus said, "This is my body, which is given for you." In breaking the bread, Jesus is offering us himself. To be more specific, he is offering us himself in his bodily sacrifice for our sins.

There may be a reminder of this bodily sacrifice in the very fact that the sacramental bread is broken. This action echoes the famous prophecy in Isaiah 53, where it was promised that our Suffering Servant would be "wounded for our transgressions" and "crushed for our iniquities" (Isa. 53:5). Thus the breaking of the bread may serve as a sacramental signification of the bruised servant—a depiction, so to speak, of his sacrifice.

The atoning death of Jesus is even more obviously signified in the words "for you" (Luke 22:19). The New Testament uses this language to indicate that Jesus died on our behalf, that his sacrifice was substitutionary (e.g., Gal. 1:4; 3:13). When Jesus said to his disciples, "This is my body, which is given for you," he was already looking ahead to what he would do for them and for all his disciples on the cross. Jesus was speaking of himself as a saving sacrifice. He would give himself for us, dying in our place to pay the death penalty that we deserve for our sins.

To say that Jesus died "for you" is to say something more than that he died for your benefit; it is to say that he died in your place, suffering the death that you deserved to die. This can be illustrated from something that happened not long after the end of the American Civil War, when a man in farm clothes was seen kneeling at a soldier's grave in Nashville, Tennessee. A sympathetic bystander asked him, "Is that the grave of your son?" "No," the farmer replied, "I have seven children, all of them young, and a wife on my poor farm in Illinois. I was drafted into the Union army, and despite the

8. John Calvin, *Commentary on a Harmony of the Evangelists, Matthew, Mark, and Luke*, 3 vols. (Grand Rapids: Eerdmans, 1956), 3:134.

great hardship it would cause to my family, I was required to serve. But on the morning I was to depart, the man who now lies in this grave—my neighbor's oldest son—came over and offered to take my place in the war." When the farmer stepped away, the bystander could see the words he had written on the gravestone. They simply read, "He died for me."[9] This is the testimony of every believer in Jesus Christ: we have a Savior who offered himself in our place. Whenever we break bread at his table, we say, "He died for me."

The old Scottish Presbyterian John Willison summarized everything we have been saying about the bread in his *Sacramental Catechism*. The catechism asks, "What is the meaning of the words, 'This is My body, broken for you'?" Then it gives this answer: "The meaning is that this broken bread is Christ's body spiritually and sacramentally, or that it signifies and represents His body, and is a visible sign and token of His body's being broken, bruised and crucified; yes, crucified for you, even wounded for your transgressions, and bruised for your iniquities."[10]

We remember all this every time we celebrate the sacrament of the Lord's Supper. Jesus said, "Do this in remembrance of me" (Luke 22:19). So we break the bread in remembrance of Jesus, calling to mind the body that he sacrificed for our sins. We do not sacrifice Jesus all over again, of course. The sacrament is to be celebrated the way that Jesus celebrated it: not on an altar, but at a table. We do not repeat or reenact the sacrifice of Jesus, but we do remember his once-and-for-all death for our sins (see Heb. 7:27). We remember Jesus himself, who even now is blessing us by his grace. We are called to remembrance because "our Savior knows that we have worldly hearts and treacherous memories, and that we stand in need of all these memorials to keep up the lively remembrance of His love."[11]

By faith and by the living presence of the Holy Spirit, we also do something more than remember: we have real spiritual participation in the life of Christ. The apostle Paul taught this by asking, "The cup of blessing that we bless, is it not a participation in the blood of Christ? The bread that we break, is it not a participation in the body of Christ?" (1 Cor. 10:16). Yes, the Lord's Supper is a spiritual participation in the body and blood of Jesus Christ. The sacrament is more than a remembrance. But it is not less. As

---

9. There are many versions of this story, which may be a pious legend.

10. John Willison, *A Sacramental Catechism* (1720; reprint Morgan, PA: Soli Deo Gloria, 2000), 91.

11. Ibid., 97.

often as we do this sacrament, we remember what Jesus did for us in his death and gave to us when he offered his body for our sins.

## THE CUP OF THE NEW COVENANT

It was not just his body that Jesus offered for us, but also his blood, which is signified in the cup of the new covenant: "And likewise the cup after they had eaten, saying, 'This cup that is poured out for you is the new covenant in my blood'" (Luke 22:20).

This is the second cup that Luke has mentioned in his account of the Last Supper. The first cup—the cup of thanksgiving—was probably part of Passover. The second cup—the cup of the new covenant in Christ's blood—is certainly part of the sacrament of the Lord's Supper.

Like the bread, the cup is a symbol that signifies Christ's sacrificial death on the cross. Just as the bread signifies Christ's body, so also the cup signifies his blood. These two words—the "body" and the "blood"—appear together several places in Scripture (e.g., Lev. 17:11–14; Deut. 12:23; Heb. 13:11). When they do, it is always in the context of sacrifice. "The body and the blood" is sacrificial terminology, which makes sense, because it is of the very nature of a sacrifice to separate the blood from the body.[12] When a sacrifice is offered, blood is poured out, which Jesus signified by pouring out the cup for his disciples. Even before he shed his blood on the cross for our sins, he gave us the sacrament that shows this sacrifice.

Jesus said that in pouring out his blood he was establishing a new covenant, the new covenant that was brought into being by his death as a sacrifice. To understand what this means, we need to begin with the old covenant, and the sacrificial blood on which it was based. It is characteristic of the covenants that God has made with his people for salvation that they are made by sacrifice. A covenant is a bond in blood, a solemn commitment that God will keep his saving promise to the very death. This is always indicated by a blood sacrifice.

One of the best places to see this is Exodus 24, a passage in which God makes a covenant with his people through the prophet Moses and speaks specifically about "the blood of the covenant." On the day that covenant

---

12. See Joachim Jeremias, *Eucharistic Words* (London: SCM, 1966), 221–22.

was confirmed, Moses collected the blood of many sacrifices into large basins and threw half of it against the holy altar of sacrifice in the house of God (Exod. 24:6). He took the other half and threw it on the people, saying, "Behold the blood of the covenant that the LORD has made with you" (Exod. 24:8). Making the covenant was a messy, bloody business. It was not signed like a contract, but sealed in blood. This was a sign of God's mercy, for the blood on the altar showed that the people had forgiveness for their sins, while the blood on the people themselves showed that they were included in the covenant of salvation.

That was the old covenant, but now Jesus had come to establish a new covenant. This was the covenant that God promised through the prophet Jeremiah, when he said, "I will make a new covenant with the house of Israel and the house of Judah. . . . I will put my law within them, and I will write it on their hearts. And I will be their God, and they shall be my people. . . . For I will forgive their iniquity, and I will remember their sin no more" (Jer. 31:31–34). Even the old covenant was a covenant of grace, but it was always looking forward to the time when God would fulfill all the promises of salvation. God promised to write his law on our hearts. He promised that he would be our God, and we would be his people. He promised to forgive all our sins forever.

Jesus is the answer to all the old promises of the covenant. This is what Jesus was telling his disciples the night of the First Supper. The new covenant had come! Jesus said, "This cup that is poured out for you is the new covenant." Then he added these staggering words—words that take our breath away, if we understand what they mean: "in my blood" (Luke 22:20). What is new about the new covenant is that it is established by the blood of God. Of all the things that we could say about the newness of the new covenant, this is the place where we must begin: with the fact that the Son of God shed his own blood for our sins—"my blood of the covenant" he calls it in the Gospels of Matthew (26:28) and Mark (14:24).

The old sacrifices were getting God's people ready to understand this amazing reality. The Old Testament is full of blood sacrifices: the sacrifices of Adam, Noah, and all the patriarchs; the sacrifices that were offered at Passover; the sacrifices that Moses made to establish the covenant; the sacrifices at the tabernacle and later at the temple; the sacrifices on the day of atonement—on and on and on it goes, blood after blood after blood. These old covenant sacrifices were offered again and again because they were only animal sacrifices, and therefore in themselves they could not atone for human sin.

Then Jesus came to offer once-and-for-all atonement for sin through the sacrifice of his blood. On the eve of that sacrifice, he announced that he would establish the new covenant with his very own blood—the blood he would shed on the cross for our sins. Understand that God has never asked anyone else to shed any blood to establish the covenant of salvation; he offered the covenant blood himself. This is what Jesus was emphasizing when he instituted the Lord's Supper. "It is *my* blood that will do this thing," he was saying. "It is *my* blood that will establish the covenant. It is *my* blood that will atone for your sins. It is *my* blood that will gain your salvation. All that I ask of you is to believe in the cross where I will give my blood for you, and then by faith you will drink in all the benefits of the sacrifice I have made for you."

## A Sacrament for You

This was the legacy Jesus left for his disciples the night that he was condemned to die. Rather than thinking of what he wanted to have for himself—the way people usually do when they are led to their execution—he was thinking about what he wanted to give of himself. He would give his disciples a meal to remember before making the sacrifice they could never forget.

Do you understand what Jesus has done for your salvation in his death on the cross? Do you understand the bread of remembrance and the cup of the new covenant that Jesus gives in the Lord's Supper? As J. C. Ryle explained, "The two elements of bread and wine were intended to preach Christ crucified as our substitute. They were to be a visible sermon, appealing to the believer's senses, and teaching the old foundation-truth of the Gospel, that Christ's death on the cross is the life of man's soul."[13] This is also the foundation-truth of the Christian life: Christ's death on the cross for the life of your soul.

If you understand this sacrament and the sacrifice that it signifies, then know this as well, and know it for sure: Jesus desires to share his supper

13. Ryle, *Luke*, 2:396.

with you every bit as eagerly as he wanted to share it with his disciples the night of the First Supper. Jesus died for you as much as he died for them, and he loves you as much as he loves them. It is to you that the bread is given and to you that the cup is poured, because it was for you that his body was broken and for you that his blood was shed.

# 94

# TRUE GREATNESS

## *Luke 22:21–30*

*"For who is the greater, one who reclines at table or one who*
*serves? Is it not the one who reclines at table? But I am among you*
*as the one who serves." (Luke 22:27)*

ome arguments never really get settled. They just keep simmer-
ing beneath the surface, waiting for any hot flame to bring them
back to the boiling point.

Such a dispute erupts in the opening scene of *Fiddler on the Roof*, the
famous musical about a Jewish community in Czarist Russia. The drama
begins with Tevya the peasant walking around Anatevka, introducing
the people of his native village. "Among ourselves we always get along
perfectly well," Tevya says. "Of course, there was the time when Itzakh
sold Avram the horse and told him it was only six years old, when it was
really twelve. But now it's all over and everything is peaceful again." Then
Tevya mischievously walks up to one of the men and quietly says, "It was
twelve, you know." "It was six!" Itzakh immediately protests, and as Tevya
walks away, everyone is shouting again. Since the dispute was never really
settled to anyone's satisfaction, one little comment is all it takes to get the
argument going.

Every community has them: ongoing arguments (sometimes over trivial matters) that come up again and again. It happens in families. It happens in churches. It happened with the first disciples, who could never agree about which one of them was the greatest. They even argued about this on the night that Jesus was betrayed.

## THE HAND OF THE BETRAYER

What started the argument again was something Jesus said over dinner. It was the last Passover he shared with his disciples, and the first supper of the new covenant. Jesus was giving the bread of his body and the cup of his blood to his closest friends. Already his thoughts were turning ahead to the cross of his crucifixion. Knowing that he was about to be betrayed, he said, "Behold, the hand of him who betrays me is with me on the table. For the Son of Man goes as it has been determined, but woe to that man by whom he is betrayed!" (Luke 22:21–22).

This statement is remarkable for what it reveals about the sovereignty of God in the plan of salvation. We know already that Judas will betray Jesus, because at the beginning of this chapter Luke took us to the secret room where Judas met with the chief priests and negotiated his price. But we are not the only ones who know this. Jesus also knows it. He knows that an enemy has infiltrated his disciples. One of his closest companions—a man with a place at his holy table—will betray him unto death.

Remarkably, even this was part of God's plan. Jesus said that the Son of Man would die the way that God determined. The whole Gospel of Luke has been moving in this direction. Time and again Jesus has predicted that he will suffer and die and rise again. Ever since he set his face toward Jerusalem and the cross, we have known for sure that he will be crucified. It is all part of God's counterconspiracy—his gracious and eternal plan to save sinners through the death and resurrection of his Son. The cross was not some kind of tragic misfortune. The empty tomb was not a lucky break. It was all in God's perfect and sovereign plan. Even the betrayal was part of God's predetermined purpose! As Peter would say on the day of Pentecost, Jesus was "delivered up according to the definite plan and foreknowledge of God" (Acts 2:23).

Nevertheless, Judas was still responsible for his own free and sinful choice. God's sovereignty does not diminish man's responsibility. This great mystery may be hard for us to understand, but it is easy to see that this is what the Bible teaches. Why did the Son of Man go the way that he went, up the road that led to the cross? According to Jesus, he went that way because it was his Father's will. Calvary was the way that God determined, and even Satan's treachery was part of the plan. We may be tempted to think that this absolves Judas of any responsibility, but Jesus said, "Woe to that man." God would hold Judas fully responsible for choosing to be the betrayer.

We should never use God's sovereignty as an excuse for our iniquity. J. C. Ryle said:

> Though the wickedness of Judas was foreknown, and foreseen, and permitted by God in His infinite wisdom—yet Judas was not the less guilty in God's sight. God's fore-knowledge does not destroy man's responsibility, or justify man in going on still in wickedness, under the excuse that he cannot help sinning. Nothing can happen, in heaven or in earth, without God's knowledge and permission. But sinners are always addressed by God as responsible.[1]

This is why Jesus was so sad about Judas. In pronouncing this woe, Jesus was expressing his distress over what would happen to the man. Alas, his sinful choice would condemn him! For although Judas later regretted what he had done, his remorse was without repentance, and thus he died in despair before going to his damnation (see Matt. 27:3–5). Woe to that man who betrayed the Son of God!

The words of Jesus are a serious warning to anyone who chooses to go against God. Here was a man who was known as a disciple of Jesus Christ, a man whom Jesus called his friend (see Matt. 26:50). Judas saw the miracles that Jesus performed and heard him declare that he was the Christ. He even sat down with Jesus at the Last Supper. But in the end Judas decided not to follow Jesus, and once he made that decision, he had no one to blame but himself.

What decision will you make about Jesus, either for him or against him? What choices will you make about what to worship, what to love,

---

1. J. C. Ryle, *Expository Thoughts on the Gospels, Luke* (1858; reprint Cambridge: James Clarke, 1976), 2:402.

what to look at, what to buy, whom to follow, what language to use, what parties to go to, and whom to embrace as your closest friend? God will hold you fully responsible for the direction you choose in life. Do not fall under the same woe that Jesus pronounced on Judas when he lifted his hand to be the betrayer.

## WHO IS THE GREATEST?

The prophecy that Jesus made about his betrayal instantly caused a commotion among the disciples. Which one of them would be the betrayer, they wondered. Was it really true that a member of their own fellowship would turn out to be a traitor? "And they began to question one another," Luke writes, "which of them it could be who was going to do this" (Luke 22:23).

Luke does not tell us whether any of the disciples suspected that Judas was the guilty party, or whether any other accusations were made. It is easy to imagine that some of them began to defend themselves. "I would never betray Jesus," each man would say, and then he would remind everybody how faithful he had been. "You know, I was the first one that Jesus called," Peter could have said. "Well, you were only a fisherman," Matthew might have replied, the old tax collector. "I left a lot more money on the table when I decided to follow Jesus." "Maybe so," James and John could have rejoined, "but we're the only ones that Jesus calls 'The Sons of Thunder'!" Or maybe the debate started when the disciples took their places for dinner and began jockeying for a position next to Jesus. But however it happened, "a dispute also arose among them, as to which of them was to be regarded as the greatest" (Luke 22:24).

This was not the first time that the disciples had this argument. Luke recorded a similar incident back in chapter 9, when Jesus ended their dispute by taking the nearest child and telling them that the greatest person is the one who is the least (Luke 9:46–48; cf. Matt. 18:1–5). Then there was the time that the mother of James and John asked Jesus to let her sons sit next to him in the kingdom of God. The other ten disciples were indignant because, of course, they were secretly hoping to claim those places for themselves (see Matt. 20:20–24; cf. Mark 10:35–45). Or what about the time Jesus asked them what they had been talking about? The disciples "kept silent, for on the way they had argued with one another about who was the greatest" (Mark 9:34). We get the definite impression that this was a common topic of conversation. Some people like to talk about the weather, or sports, or politics. The disciples liked to talk about which one of them was the greatest. All it took was one little remark to get them going, and all the old arguments came out again.

The whole argument was shockingly inappropriate, especially this time. It was inappropriate because the disciples were not all that great to begin with. In the Gospels we often witness them missing the point, asking dumb questions, and getting in the way of the ministry that Jesus wanted to do. It was also inappropriate because within a matter of hours all of them would abandon Jesus. Even if only one of them actually betrayed him, they all denied him. Yet here they were, trying to figure out which of them was the greatest (!). Furthermore, this was the last night that Jesus would spend with his disciples before going to the cross. This must have filled them with shame every time they remembered it afterwards. The most important events in the history of the world were about to take place, yet instead of focusing on Jesus they wasted their time having a senseless argument.

It was inappropriate, too, because the disciples had just shared holy communion, the sacrament that signified their connection to Christ *and* to one another. This made it a totally inappropriate time to have a divisive debate—like having a huge family argument at Christmas dinner, only worse. It was also inappropriate because Jesus had just warned about his betrayal. It would have been much more appropriate for them to talk about how to stay faithful to Jesus. Yet they quickly moved from worrying about letting Jesus down, as they should have, to speculating about how much credit they deserved for being the great men that they obviously were.

This was a shocking display of self-centered pride, but it was not surprising. When I think of the disciples, I often remember the night we were having family devotions and one of the children suddenly said, "I love the disciples; they're always messing up!" It is true: the disciples *did* mess up, and this is one of the things that we love about them. These men had all the same sinful struggles that we have, and if Jesus had grace for them, we have good reason to hope that he has grace for us.

Like the disciples, we want people to know how great we are. Even if we do not get into many arguments about it, we secretly hope that people will give us the attention we deserve. We want people to know how smart we are, or how athletic, or how musical, or how talented in some other way. At work we want to get ahead of our business competitors. At home we want our brothers and sisters to lose so that we can win. In the church we want people to recognize the value of our ministry. We want them to admire us for how we are teaching the Bible, or raising our children, or giving to Christian work. Our pretensions to greatness are there in the little comments we make to inflate our reputation, in the sudden disappointment we feel when someone else gets ahead, in the sharp criticisms we launch to explode someone else's accomplishments. We find it hard to be happy until we reach the greatness we think we deserve, and even then we will not be happy unless other people know how great we are too.

## A New Kind of Greatness

The problem with us is that we have the wrong definition of greatness. We think the great person is the one who gets ahead of everyone else in life—not a servant, but the master. If that is what we think, then our whole idea of what it means to be great needs to be redefined the way that Jesus redefined it: "The kings of the Gentiles exercise lordship over them, and those in authority over them are called benefactors. But not so with you. Rather, let the greatest among you become as the youngest, and the leader as the one who serves" (Luke 22:25–26).

Here Jesus distinguishes between two completely different definitions of greatness. The Gentiles were people who at that time were outside the people of God. Their definition of greatness represented the way that human beings usually think: the greatest person is the one who has the most power and prestige, which in those days was always the king. As the ruler of his people, the king had all the money and authority that his kingdom had to offer. Everyone else was under him, so he could live for himself. He liked to think of himself as a philanthropist, however, so he wanted people to refer to him as their benefactor.[2] This was a way of identifying himself as the source of all earthly blessing.

2. Leon Morris, *The Gospel According to St. Luke: An Introduction and Commentary*, Tyndale New Testament Commentaries (Grand Rapids: Eerdmans, 1974), 308.

478

This is basically how people still define greatness today: money, power, and prestige. The greatest people in the world are the billionaire businessmen, the movie stars, the professional athletes, and the famous politicians—the powerbrokers, the celebrities, and the superstars. If you want to be great, people have to know who you are. You need to have power over other people's lives, with enough money to satisfy your desires. A clear example comes from Harvard University, where M.B.A. students were assigned to develop a strategic plan entitled "What Do I Hope to Achieve in Life after Graduation?" Their number one priority was wealth; number two was notoriety; and number three was status. Yet none of the students said anything in their strategic plans about serving other people.[3]

Jesus has a totally different definition for true greatness. After giving the world's definition, Jesus said, "Not so with you." The way the world looks at things is not the way that God looks at things. According to him, the greatest person is not the person at the top, but the one who takes a position at the bottom—what Jesus called "the youngest." In those days people gave a great deal of deference to their elders. There were privileges and prerogatives that went with being a man or a woman of a certain age. Younger people stood up when an older person entered a room. They listened carefully to what old folks had to say, on the assumption that wisdom came with experience. Youngsters regarded their elders as their betters.

Here Jesus tells us to take the younger person's place in our daily relationships. Do the difficult job that no one else is willing to do, for no task—however menial—is beneath the dignity of a disciple. Let someone else go first. Offer someone else the biggest piece. Listen to someone else's concerns rather than doing all the talking. Instead of asking other people to do something for you, think of something that you can do for them. Rather than seeking to gain attention, seek out someone who is getting ignored and needs a friend. Follow the command that Paul gave to the Philippians: "In humility count others more significant than yourselves" (Phil. 2:3).

Putting other people first is especially important for anyone in a position of spiritual leadership. People usually think of the leader as someone who has people under him—people to boss around, people who have to do all the hard jobs that he does not want to do. But Jesus said, "Not so with

3. The Harvard M.B.A. survey is quoted by Joni Eareckson Tada in "Sent to Serve," *Wheaton*, (Autumn, 2005): 58.

you." The leader is really the servant, so the more people he leads, the more people he gets to serve. A missionary in Papua New Guinea made a powerful statement of this principle when he translated the New Testament into the language of the Itamul tribesmen. In Itamul society the most important person sits in the middle of the canoe, the second most important person sits in the bow, and the least important person paddles at the stern. Here is how the translation went: "If a person wishes to be a leader, he should not sit in the middle of the canoe. Let him sit at the stern. Let him do everyone's work."[4]

What is your definition of greatness? Do you have the same definition as Jesus, or are you still looking for money, popularity, and the easy life that comes with being in charge? J. C. Ryle said that the true tests of Christian greatness are: "Usefulness in the world and Church—a humble readiness to do anything, and put our hands to any good work—a cheerful willingness to fill any post, however lowly, and discharge any office, however unpleasant, if we can only promote happiness and holiness."[5] We will not pass this test of true greatness by striving for all the earthly things that most people work so hard to gain, but only by giving our lives to others. The greatest disciple is the one who offers the humblest service.

## The Greatest of All

Jesus then proved his point by giving the most perfect example: himself. "For who is greater," Jesus asked, "one who reclines at table or one who serves? Is it not the one who reclines at table? But I am among you as the one who serves" (Luke 22:27). People usually do not respond to rhetorical questions, but in this case Jesus went ahead and gave his own answer. Which is greater: the person sitting down to a feast, or the person waiting on the table hand and foot? The answer, of course, is that the superior person is the one who is lying down and being served.

I saw a memorable example of this in my high school, where the freshman class held an annual fundraiser called "Slave Day." Various freshmen would put themselves up for auction to upperclassmen and then work the next day as slaves for the highest bidder. One enterprising sophomore

---

4. This anecdote is recounted in *Select Words*, Wycliffe Bible Translators, Issue 9 (Nov. 2000): n.p.
5. Ryle, *Luke*, 2:404.

from my French class hired an entourage. The next day he came to class on a litter shouldered by members of the freshman football team. Other slaves carried his books. They were accompanied by several of the best-looking girls in the freshman class, who were fanning their master with palm branches and feeding him grapes by hand. It was an impressive display of teenage greatness.

Now imagine what kind of service the Lord Jesus Christ deserves to receive, for he is the Greatest One of all. He does not come right out and say it in so many words, but that is the obvious, unspoken premise of his argument. In using himself as his example, Jesus assumes his own greatness. This is typical of his humility. He rarely talks about the full extent of his greatness. In the Gospels he does not go on and on about how great he is, although he had every right to do so. Instead, he let the Father and the Holy Spirit testify to his greatness. Nevertheless, Jesus cannot deny who he is, and therefore his divine greatness is the premise of his entire ministry.

To know true greatness, look at Jesus Christ. He is great because of who he is: the Second Person of the Trinity, the only begotten Son of God. Jesus always is, always has been, and always will be very God of very God. He is not merely a man, but has every attribute of deity. Jesus Christ is the Lord God, which means that no one is greater than he is.

Jesus is also great because of what he has done. He has created this great universe; Jesus Christ is the Creator God. Nothing in all the vast galaxies of interstellar space is not the product of his divine mind. Then Jesus lived a great life. Through all the trials and temptations he suffered on earth, he never committed even one little sin. He is the only morally perfect man who ever lived. He also died a great death to gain for us a great salvation. No one has ever done anything greater for the human race than Jesus did when he suffered the death that we deserve for sin and then rose again with the power of eternal life.

Jesus Christ is the Greatest One of all. If you doubt this, just go up to heaven and talk to the angels who have been worshiping him without intermission since the beginning of time, and they will tell you that they have not yet given Jesus even one trillionth of the honor that he deserves. Jesus Christ truly is the Greatest One of all. Because he is so great, he is the one who deserves to be served. He is the infinitely superior person. He is the one who ought to be reclining at the table, with his disciples all serving him. This is the proper order of things, and thus the premise of his example.

But, Jesus said, "I am among you as the one who serves" (Luke 22:27). This turns everything upside down, and opens up for us the true greatness in the heart of God. Earlier Jesus said to his disciples, "Not so with you." Now he is telling them why: "Because it is not so with me." Although I am the Greatest One, I am the one who serves. More literally, I am the one who waits on tables (or, to use the title that the church later adopted, I am the deacon). Jesus had proved this earlier that evening by washing the feet of his disciples. Although Luke does not mention this, the story is told in John 13 and serves as part of the context for what Jesus said to his disciples about service. He truly was among them as the one who serves, for he had washed their feet, and in doing so he had taken the lowest possible place.

Jesus had been serving his disciples since the day they started to follow him—leading them, feeding them, healing them, teaching them, correcting them, training them, and loving them. Soon he would serve them all the way to the death, bearing their sins all the way to the grave. Jesus took his whole life and gave it to his disciples, as he gives it to us. The very Greatest One of all made himself our servant as he did the work of our salvation.

Now Jesus calls us to be like him, to find our true greatness in living for others rather than living for ourselves, forgetting ourselves for the sake of others. As far as Jesus is concerned, the truly great person is the one who serves. The point is not that service will get us to greatness, but that service *is* the greatness. "Jesus is not saying," wrote Leon Morris, "that if His followers wish to rise to great heights in the church they must first prove themselves in a lowly place. He is saying that faithful service in a lowly place is itself true greatness."[6]

To know who the great people are, look for the people who are serving in the lowest places. They will be passing out bulletins at the doorway to the church, or taking care of business at the changing table in the nursery, or sitting down to talk with a needy person who seems only to complain. They will be visiting elderly shut-ins, or teaching a Bible study at the federal prison, or showing hospitality to strangers from a far country. They will be sharing the gospel with street children and prostitutes. They will be

6. Morris, *Luke*, 308.

working as missionaries in places where most people hate the gospel. They will be in all the dark and dirty places where no one else is willing to go. Wherever you find them, they will look like Jesus, with the true greatness of a servant's heart.

## THE PROMISE OF A KINGDOM

One day you will see these great people rejoicing with Jesus in his eternal kingdom. This is the happy promise that Jesus gave to his disciples: "You are those who have stayed with me in my trials, and I assign to you, as my Father assigned to me, a kingdom, that you may eat and drink at my table in my kingdom and sit on thrones judging the twelve tribes of Israel" (Luke 22:28–30).

These words were spoken first to the first disciples and only secondarily to us. The twelve apostles were the ones who stayed with Jesus in his trials. This was an extraordinary thing for Jesus to say, because later that very night, at the time of his greatest trial, all of the disciples would run away from him. Nevertheless, in his mercy Jesus remembered everything the disciples ever did in his name. They suffered the hardships of the open road, traveling homeless. They left behind any regular source of income. They suffered some of the hostility that Jesus endured from all the people who hated his ministry.

The disciples stayed with Jesus in these trials, and none of their faithful service would ever be forgotten. Every service they offered would be remembered *and* rewarded in the kingdom of God. Here Jesus was giving the disciples his last will and testament. "Testament" is just the right word to use, because when Jesus spoke about "assigning" these things to his disciples, he used the biblical verb for making a covenant *(diatithomai)*.[7] These were solemn promises, which Jesus was swearing by oath. He wanted to give his friends what he had received from his Father: an everlasting kingdom.

One day the disciples who were with him that night would sit down with him again at the great banquet, which the Bible uses as a symbol for all the blessings God has for us in his everlasting kingdom. The disciples would also sit down with Jesus on his thrones, ruling the twelve

---

7. Michael Wilcock, *The Message of Luke*, The Bible Speaks Today (Downers Grove, IL: InterVarsity, 1979), 192.

tribes of Israel. This too is symbolic. "The twelve tribes of Israel" is an ancient way of talking about all the people of God, who are now gathered in the church of Jesus Christ. Jesus does not give very many details here, but to "judge" (or to rule) is to have a place of authoritative leadership. The first disciples were promised to receive a place of privilege in the kingdom of God. Indeed, the Bible says that the whole church is built on the foundation of their ministry (Eph. 2:20).

Obviously these promises were mainly for the disciples. Only the twelve apostles were given the authority to rule the people of God. Only their names are written on the foundations of heaven, in the city of the new Jerusalem (Rev. 21:14). But the blessings of the kingdom—the blessings of eating and drinking at God's table—are for all the covenant children of God. Jesus promised a kingdom to us every bit as much as he promised it to his apostles, and he kept his promise by dying on the cross for our sins and rising again.

Now, by the grace of God, true greatness is waiting for us. There is a place for us at God's table—a place for anyone who is sorry for sin and believes in the cross. Jesus Christ, the Greatest One, invites us to come.

When my daughter Karoline was almost two, she was still sitting in a high chair for meals, but starting to believe that she was destined for something greater: soon she would have a place at the family table. If we gave her a chance, she would climb up onto one of the dinner chairs and grab any food within reach. When she managed to get settled, with her chubby little legs dangling off the chair and her chin resting on the edge of the table, she would get a huge grin on her face. "I'm big now," her smile was saying. "I can sit at the table!"

Every believer in Christ will experience this kind of greatness. We will eat and drink at the table of Jesus in the kingdom of God—not because we are such great servants, but because the Greatest One of all served us to the very death.

# 95

# THE SINNER'S SAVIOR

## *Luke 22:31–38*

*"For I tell you that this Scripture must be fulfilled in me: 'And he was numbered with the transgressors.' For what is written about me has its fulfillment." (Luke 22:37)*

*J*esus was in great danger the night that he sat down to celebrate the Last Supper with his disciples. Already Judas Iscariot had made his deadly bargain to betray him. As Jesus said himself, after breaking the bread and passing the cup, "the hand of him who betrays me is with me on the table" (Luke 22:21). Even before the meal was over, Judas slipped away to let the religious leaders know where they could capture Jesus in secret. Armed men were on their way to do Jesus harm. In mortal danger, he would be dead in less than twenty-four hours.

The disciples too were in danger. They were up against the deadliest of all enemies that night: the devil himself. But they did not realize this, which made their situation all the more dangerous. We ourselves are in the same danger until we find safety in the sinner's Savior.

## The Sifting of Satan

Jesus had been in danger since the beginning of this chapter, when Satan "entered into Judas called Iscariot" (Luke 22:3). This was a clear instance of demonic possession, only it was not simply an ordinary demon that entered Judas; it was humanity's oldest enemy—the devil himself. What is perhaps less widely known is that the devil wanted to have control of all twelve of the disciples, and would have done so, if Jesus had allowed him to do it. Jesus turned to his disciples that night and said, "Simon, Simon, behold, Satan demanded to have you, that he might sift you like wheat" (Luke 22:31).

This dramatic statement was designed to get the disciples' full attention. Jesus was speaking specifically to Simon. Usually we call him Peter, because this is the name that Jesus gave to him when he made his famous confession of the Christ (see Matt. 16:16–18). Peter is a great boulder of a name; in contemporary English we would probably call him Rocky. But here Jesus used his given name and called him Simon—a name, perhaps, that would remind him of the frail humanity with which he was born. Jesus also repeated Simon's name for emphasis. He was saying something that Simon Peter desperately needed to hear: Satan was trying to destroy him.

It is not surprising that Satan would go after Peter. After all, he was the leading disciple—the first among equals. Peter was the first disciple that Jesus called, the first to confess him as the Christ, and the first to get out of the boat and walk on water. If Satan could destroy Peter, he could destroy them all. This is what Satan was really after: a chance to destroy all the disciples. When Jesus said, "Satan demanded to have you," he used the plural form of the pronoun "you" *(hymas)*. Rather than saying "you, Peter," he was saying, "you all, disciples." The devil wanted more than Judas and more, even, than Peter; he wanted all the disciples of Christ.

Maybe the devil tried to claim that the disciples were really his to begin with. Satan is the great accuser, the great adversary. In fact, this is what his name means. The Bible calls Satan "the accuser of our brothers" (Rev. 12:10). When it came to the disciples, there were a lot of accusations that he could make. These men were far from perfect. Did they really deserve to be the followers of the Son of God? Would they really remain faithful until the very end? Satan didn't think so, and he demanded to find out. He wanted to sift the disciples like wheat. In other words, he wanted to toss them in the air the way a farmer tosses his grain to separate the wheat from the chaff. Maybe the disciples were solid enough to land back on the ground, but maybe they would get scattered by the harsh wind of persecution. Satan wanted to see if they would get blown away like Judas, in which case they would belong to him forever. But he could not do this without God's permission, so the devil dared Jesus to let him put the disciples to the test.

Satan is never satisfied. He is always greedy for more souls. He wants to have us and possess us. He wants to see us fall into sin and fail. He wants to damn every soul that he can get his hands on. Satan has been greedy like this since the beginning. It explains why he slithered his way into Eden and tempted Eve to eat the forbidden fruit. It explains why he tempted Cain to kill his brother and why he kept the children of Israel enslaved in Egypt. It explains why he went spying all over the world in the days of Job (see Job 1:7). It explains why he came after Jesus in the wilderness. It explains why Peter himself would later write, "Your adversary the devil prowls around like a roaring lion, seeking someone to devour" (1 Peter 5:8). Satan is always ravenous in his appetite for lost sinners.

What Jesus said to Simon Peter, therefore, is also true about us. Satan wants you; he desires you; and he will stop at nothing to have you for himself. His diabolical gluttony is vividly portrayed near the end of C. S. Lewis's book *The Screwtape Letters*. A junior demon named Wormwood has failed to prevent a young man from becoming a Christian. His mentor, an even more infernal demon named Screwtape, is furious about this unhappy development, but at the same time gleeful at the prospect that now he will be allowed to have Wormwood for himself. "I have always desired you," he writes. "I think they will give you to me now; or a bit of you. Love you? Why, yes, As dainty a morsel as ever I grew fat on." The letter is signed, "Your increasingly and ravenously affectionate uncle."[1]

Lewis's literary invention is based on biblical reality: Satan is always looking for someone to consume. His demonic influence is there in the selfish move we make to keep what we have for ourselves rather than giving it away for Jesus. It is there in the ministry conflict that tempts us to quit and go somewhere else. It is there in the sudden impulse to click on the

1. C. S. Lewis, *The Screwtape Letters* (1942; reprint Philadelphia: Fortress, 1979), 130, 133.

link to the pornographic Web site. It is there in the secret resentment we have against someone's spiritual leadership, whether in the home or in the church. It is there in the temptation to give up on a difficult relationship, or in the despair we feel about ever making any progress against the main sin that seems to dominate our heart's daily agenda. Satan and his demons are always lurking in the shadows, desperately hoping that one day we will walk away from Christ completely.

Do you know how much danger you are in? When I hear the warning that Jesus gave to Peter, I sadly think of people who have left the Christian church: the girl who ran away from God as soon as she went off to college; the family that decided they did not even need to be in church, because that is not where God is at work any more; the man who felt so power-less against Satan that he went back to a lifestyle of sexual sin. They are all people that Satan wanted to have, just as he wants to have us. One of the most dangerous things in the world would be to think that we are not in any danger, which is the mistake that Peter made.

## PRIDE GOES BEFORE A FALL

When Jesus told Peter what Satan wanted to have, he also told him that Peter would turn away, at least for a little while. "But I have prayed for you," Jesus said, "that your faith may not fail. And when you have turned again, strengthen your brothers" (Luke 22:32). This time Jesus used the singular form of the pronoun "you" *(sou)*. He prayed for the other disciples too, of course, but this particular petition was for Peter.

The way Jesus prayed assumed that Peter would turn away. Logically speaking, he could turn back only if he first turned away. But Peter would have none of it. He said to Jesus, "Lord, I am ready to go with you both to prison and to death" (Luke 22:33). That's Peter for you: often in error, but never in doubt. Here he was saying that he knew bet-ter than Jesus did. Since he would never go away, he would never need to make a comeback.

Peter's statement sounded bold. After all, this was the first time one of the disciples said that he was ready to walk with Jesus in the way of the cross. Nevertheless, it was still an empty boast. After arguing about which disciple was the greatest, Peter tried to prove it by saying he would go with Jesus all the way to the death. But however much we may admire the man's courage, his overconfidence put him in the way of deadly spiritual danger. Peter's confidence was entirely misplaced. He was confident in himself rather than confident in Christ. So rather than asking God for more strength, he announced that he was already prepared to face any and every danger.

This was the Titanic of all testimonies, and Jesus told Peter that he was headed for disaster: "I tell you, Peter, the rooster will not crow this day, until you deny three times that you know me" (Luke 22:34). This was a shocking prophecy. Peter would deny Jesus almost immediately—that very day. He would deny Jesus repeatedly—not just once or twice, but three times. He would deny Jesus emphatically, protesting that he did not even know the man.

Sadly, the prophecy came true. By the end of this night Peter would weep the bitter tears of his triple denial. He failed because he tried to be strong in his own strength, not knowing his weakness. This is a strong warning for us not to make the same mistake that Peter made. We should never think that we are beyond the reach of any particular sin, or that we can withstand temptation by our own virtue. If we have any confidence in ourselves, instead of having all our confidence in Christ, then we are as likely to fail as Peter was.

One prominent Christian leader was getting ready to speak at a conference when someone asked him how he thought the devil would try to drag him down. "I'm not sure," he said, "but I know one place where he will never get me, and that's in my family life." Sadly, the man later committed adultery and had to leave the gospel ministry. It is in the areas where we think we are strong that we are in the most danger, because we do not perceive the desperate weakness at the heart of the very best things we do for God. "When I am weak, then I am strong," the Scripture says (2 Cor. 12:10). But the opposite is also true, as Peter could testify: when I think I am strong, then I am weak.

## WHY OUR FAITH WILL NOT FAIL

As it turned out, Peter was not ready to go with Jesus to prison and the cross after all. Satan sifted him like wheat, hoping that he would get blown away. Nevertheless, although Peter fell into sin, he did not fall away from the faith. This is because he knew the sinner's Savior, who did two great things to protect him from danger. Jesus prayed for Peter and then he died for Peter, saving him by his intercession and atonement. This is our salvation, too. The devil is always trying to drag us down with our sins, but the Savior of sinners died in our place, and now he lives to pray for our protection.

First, Jesus prayed for Peter, protecting him by the power of his intercession. After warning what Satan would try to do to him, Jesus gave Peter this great promise: "but I have prayed for you that your faith may not fail" (Luke 22:32). The word "but" puts everything that Jesus would do over against everything that Satan would try. Satan was against Peter, *but* Jesus was for him. Satan wanted to destroy Peter, *but* Jesus promised to save him. Satan petitioned to have Peter for himself, *but* Jesus prayed that Peter would hold on to him forever. Peter was saved because he was over on the Savior's side of the sentence. He did not fall away, but returned to Jesus.

It is important to notice what Jesus prayed for. He did not ask any of the things that we probably would have asked. He did not pray that Satan would leave Peter alone. In the providence of God, who works in every situation for the good of his people and the glory of his name, Satan was permitted to make this attack. Jesus did not pray that Peter would never sin. It was God's plan for Peter to see the limits of his own strength, and then out of that painful experience to see how much grace God had for him, so that he would be able to encourage his brothers in their own struggle with sin. Jesus did not pray that Peter would have a rich and easy life, with one spiritual success after another.

Jesus only prayed that Peter's faith would not fail. If Jesus Christ is the all-wise God, and if this is what he prayed for Peter, then it must be the most important thing for us to have. Faith is the very thing Satan was trying to take away from Peter. If Peter were to stop believing, then he would no longer belong to Jesus. This is what Satan always wants to take away from us: the faith in Christ that makes a believer a believer. As Charles Spurgeon once said, "The point of Satan's chief attack on a believer is his faith.... We are engrafted into Christ by faith, and faith is the point of contact between the believing soul and the living Christ. If, therefore, Satan could manage to cut through the graft just there, then he would defeat the Savior's work most completely."[2]

Consider everything that we would lose if our faith were to fail. The Bible says that we are justified by faith (Rom. 3:21–26). Take away faith, therefore, and we cannot be righteous before God. The Bible says that without faith it is impossible to please God (Heb. 11:6). Take away faith, therefore, and nothing we do is accepted by God. The Bible says that faith enables us to extinguish the fiery darts of the evil one (Eph. 6:16). Take away faith, therefore, and the devil will destroy us. The Bible says that the righteous will live by faith (Gal. 3:11). Take away faith, therefore, and you take away life itself, for the believer is nothing without his faith.

On the other hand, if we still have faith, then we live invincible in the power of Christ. The stories of the Bible prove that by faith people "conquered kingdoms, enforced justice, obtained promises, stopped the mouths of lions, quenched the power of fire, escaped the edge of the sword, were made strong out of weakness, became mighty in war, put foreign armies to flight," and "received back their dead by resurrection" (Heb. 11:33–35). This is the faith that Jesus prayed for Peter to have: a faith that saves in any and every situation—even unto death.

This is the prayer that Jesus loves to pray for all his disciples—the Savior's prayer for a sinner's faith not to fail. Jesus is busy praying this way for us right now. The Bible says that Jesus Christ "is at the right hand of God . . . interceding for us" (Rom. 8:34). It says that he "is able to save to the uttermost those who draw near to God through him, since he always lives to make intercession for them" (Heb. 7:25). Jesus Christ is the infinite intercessor; he lives to pray for us.

If only we could see Jesus on his knees and listen to what he is saying to the Father, what courage we would take to live for him through every trouble in life. Jesus is praying for us, that our faith will not fail. He is praying about our chronic pain, that in our physical weakness we will not stop trusting in the goodness of God. He is praying about our troubled marriage, that in our alienation we will not stop trusting in his love. He is praying about our financial situation, that in our urgent concern about paying the bills we will not stop trusting in God to provide. He is praying about

2. Charles Spurgeon, "Christ's Prayer for Peter," *The Metropolitan Tabernacle Pulpit* (Pasadena, TX: Pilgrim, 1977), 45:207.

our secret discouragement, that in our night of dark despair we will not stop trusting him to lead us into the light. He is praying about our wandering into sin, that we will never stop trusting in his forgiveness. Jesus is praying for everything we need.

Surely these prayers will be answered, just the way God answered the prayers that Jesus prayed for Peter. The man's faith did not fail. Although he turned away, he also returned, believing by faith that his sins were forgiven. And because he had faith, he was able to do good works, strengthening his brothers the way that Jesus told him to do.

The same thing will happen in our lives. The Son of God is interceding for us with the Father. How can his petition fail? Jesus prays more wisely, more frequently, and more efficaciously than anyone. He prays more for us than we ever pray for ourselves. Therefore, although we may go through many difficult trials and even fall into wicked sin, as Peter did, we will not be lost, because Jesus has prayed that our faith will not fail. Whatever desperate situation we bring to him, with all of our complaints and objections, the Savior of sinners holds up his hand and says, "but *I* have prayed for you that your faith may not fail" (Luke 22:32).

## Of Moneybags, Knapsacks, and Swords

There was something else that Jesus did for Peter—something even more important than praying for him, and infinitely more costly. But before Jesus told his disciples about this saving work, he also gave them some unexpected instructions: "And he said to them, 'When I sent you out with no moneybag or knapsack or sandals, did you lack anything?' They said, 'Nothing.' He said to them, 'But now let the one who has a moneybag take it, and likewise a knapsack. And let the one who has no sword sell his cloak and buy one'" (Luke 22:35–36).

These instructions are unexpected because they seem to contradict what Jesus told his disciples much earlier, when he sent them out on their first mission. On that occasion, after giving them the power and the authority to heal people and to cast out demons, Jesus said to them, "Take nothing for your journey, no staff, nor bag, nor bread, nor money; and do not have two tunics" (Luke 9:3; cf. 10:4). The disciples took almost nothing with them on that mission trip, but they also lacked nothing. God supplied all of their needs, as they were able to testify. The disciples thus learned that when God's work is done in God's way, it always has God's supply.

Now these men were entering a new missionary situation—one that required a different approach. On their first mission trip they were still in Israel, where the people of God could meet their daily needs. But soon they would be going out into the wider world, where they could not expect people to provide for their ministry. As David Gooding writes, missionaries of the gospel "could no longer expect the nation to meet the costs of their maintenance as on previous occasions; they would have to pay their own expenses and fight their own way with no financial help from the nation or the unconverted."[3]

The time had come, therefore, for the disciples to take a little food and money with them. There is a time and a place to live in total poverty, without any property to call one's own, but there is also a time and a place to work hard and plan ahead. Today the people of God are living in Luke 22, not Luke 9. Every believer is called to live in total dependence on God for every daily need. But this does not mean that every Christian or every missionary should presume on God to meet their needs out of nowhere every day. It is right and good for people in ministry to make provision for their future needs, while at the same time totally trusting in God.

A worthy example of this kind of preparation comes from the Back to Jerusalem missionary movement in China. Before Christian workers are sent out to carry the gospel back along the route of the old Silk Road, they receive intensive practical and spiritual training. This training includes how to reach across cultural and other barriers, how to evangelize specific people groups, how to suffer and die for the Lord, how to witness for the Lord, and how to escape. One leader explains: "We know that sometimes the Lord sends us to prison to witness for him, but we also believe that the devil sometimes wants us imprisoned to stop the ministry God has called us to do. We teach the missionaries special skills such as how to free themselves from handcuffs within 30 seconds and how to jump from second-story windows without injuring themselves."[4] This kind of training may not

---

3. David Gooding, *According to Luke: A New Exposition of the Third Gospel* (Grand Rapids: Eerdmans, 1987), 333–34.

4. Paul Hattaway, Brother Yun, Peter Xu Yongze, and Enoch Wang, *Back to Jerusalem: Three Chinese House Leaders Share Their Vision to Complete the Great Commission* (Carlisle, UK: Piquant, 2003), 83.

be customary in the West, but it is very much in keeping with the instructions Jesus gave his disciples to be prepared for the hard road of missionary service.

What may still be hard to understand is why Jesus told his disciples to go out and buy a sword. Some Christians have assumed that Jesus was speaking literally. Some have even used this verse as a justification for using physical violence to advance the kingdom of God, which is a good reminder why we need good hermeneutics—sound principles for the proper interpretation of Scripture. One of those principles is to let Scripture interpret Scripture, using one clear Bible passage to help us make sense of a passage that is harder to understand.

In this case, all we need to do is read the rest of the chapter. Later that evening, one of the disciples (Peter, as it turns out, to no one's surprise) used his sword to cut off the ear of one of the men who came to arrest Jesus (Luke 22:50; cf. John 18:10). But Jesus said, "No more of this!" (Luke 22:51). No more violence. No more swordsmanship. No more physical force in the name of God. With this rebuke Jesus declared his permanent opposition to any attempt to use the weapons of this world in waging his war (see also 2 Cor. 10:4). But if Jesus was not advocating armed violence, then why did he tell his disciples to buy a sword?

Nearly all the best commentators agree that Jesus was speaking metaphorically. The sword is a symbol of warfare and conflict. Therefore, Jesus was saying that the time of violent danger had come for him and for his disciples, and that in these perilous times they would need to be gospel warriors, prepared for spiritual battle. The old German commentator Adolf Schlatter points out that in time of war, a warrior will give everything he has for the weapon that he needs in order to be able to fight—even the shirt off his back. So too, Schlatter writes, "the disciples require that courage which regards a sword as more necessary than an upper garment and surrenders even its last possession, but cannot give up the struggle."[5] This is the kind of force that Jesus has in mind: not the force of physical violence, but the force of spiritual valor.

This is our calling as well: to contend with all our strength for the cause of Christ—not by seeking worldly power, but by trusting in the power of

---

5. Adolf Schlatter, quoted in Norval Geldenhuys, *The Gospel of Luke*, New International Commentary on the New Testament (Grand Rapids: Eerdmans, 1951), 572.

God's Spirit. Here is how Norval Geldenhuys makes the application: "To be a whole-hearted follower of the Crucified One in a world which is in the power of sin and of the Evil One brings unavoidably for the believer scorn and hate on the part of those who reject God and His Christ. And the only way to remain firm in such a world is to be spiritually equipped with His power and armed with the sword of His Word."[6]

## RECKONED AMONG THE RIGHTEOUS

This is all very useful from the practical point of view, but the most important thing Jesus told his disciples concerned what he was about to do for their salvation. It is not just the intercession of Jesus that saves, but also his atonement—the death that he died for us when he was crucified between two thieves. The disciples' new ministry situation—the one that required the moneybag, the knapsack, and the sword—was connected to the fulfillment of a long-awaited promise. Jesus said: "For I tell you that this Scripture must be fulfilled in me: 'And he was numbered with the transgressors.' For what is written about me has its fulfillment" (Luke 22:37).

Jesus Christ had a clear understanding of his calling and full confidence in the truth of Scripture. He knew that all the old promises of salvation would come true. He also knew that they would be fulfilled in his own person and work. Take, for example, the promises that Isaiah made in the fifty-third chapter of his magnificent prophecy. Isaiah said that the Savior would be despised and rejected, that he would carry his people's sorrows. Isaiah said that the Savior would be wounded for our transgressions and crushed for our iniquities. He said that the Savior would be led like a lamb to the slaughter and then buried in a rich man's tomb. Isaiah said that the Savior would make intercession for sinners, but that before he did, he would be "numbered with the transgressors" (Isa. 53:12). When Jesus read these prophecies, he knew that they were all about him. *He* was the Savior of sinners—the one who would suffer and die for his people's sins.

To help his disciples make the connection, Jesus told them that this Scripture would be fulfilled in his own life and death, as of course it

---

6. Geldenhuys, *Luke*, 571.

was. Jesus was innocent of all charges, yet he was numbered among the transgressors nonetheless. At the end of his legal trials he was unjustly convicted of committing a capital crime, taken to the place of execution, and nailed between two thieves. This is what Jesus came to do—not simply to die, but to die this way, in a death that put him in the place of sinners.

When the Bible says that Jesus was "numbered with the transgressors," it means much more than simply that he was regarded as some kind of criminal. It means that he took all of our sins upon himself and then died, in our place, the death that we deserved to die. The Bible says that "for our sake he made him to be sin who knew no sin, so that in him we might become the righteousness of God" (2 Cor. 5:21). In other words, Jesus Christ was counted as a sinner. In doing his saving work, the Savior of sinners took the guilt of our sin upon himself, and once he did that, he was obligated to pay the death penalty that all our sins deserved.

To give just one pertinent and provocative example, when Jesus died on the cross he was paying the price for Peter's sin. What kind of sinner was Peter? Well, among other things, he was a denier, which meant that when Jesus died for Peter he had to die as a denier. But it was not just for Peter's sins that Jesus died. It was for all the sins of all his people—all our idolatry, adultery, theft, and dishonesty. Whatever kind of sinner we happen to be, Jesus was counted as that kind of sinner on the cross. Jesus was not a sinner, of course, but he was dying in the place of sinners, and therefore God counted him *as* a sinner on the cross. In terms of God's justice, Jesus died as a lying, lazy, thieving sinner. He did this to pay the debt that our sins deserve. Now we can look to the cross and say, "Now there is the Savior of sinners—the one who took my place and died for my sins."

It is doubtful whether the disciples understood this. Later they understood what Jesus was doing for their salvation, of course, but at the time they seem to have missed it entirely. Rather than grasping the spiritual point that Jesus was making, they were still thinking much too literally about those swords and how they were supposed to wield them. So they said, "Look, Lord, here are two swords." But Jesus said, "It is enough" (Luke 22:38). He was not saying that there were enough swords, in all likelihood, but that this was enough of that conversation! The disciples could not yet understand what Jesus was really doing for their salvation, and they would not understand it until Jesus went ahead and did it.

But if we listen to Jesus and look at what he did on the cross, then we can understand his saving work. Jesus was numbered among transgressors like us so that in him we would be counted among the righteous before God. Believe in the saving work of the sinner's Savior. He is praying for you now, that your faith will not fail.

# 96

# THY WILL BE DONE

## *Luke 22:39–46*

*And he withdrew from them about a stone's throw, and knelt
down and prayed, saying, "Father, if you are willing, remove
this cup from me. Nevertheless, not my will, but yours, be done."*
(Luke 22:41–42)

*T*hink of the darkest place you have ever been. Think of the
place of anguish and pain, discouragement and despair. Think
of the place where you were alone in your suffering and all
your worst fears were about to come true. Think of the place where the one
thing you wanted was the one thing God had determined you could not
have. Think of the place where you were trapped and there seemed to be
no way out. Think of the place where you wished to God that you could be
anywhere else in the universe except in the place where you were. Think of
the place where things got so bad that you almost thought you were going
to die, and maybe you almost did.

Jesus went to that dark place, and a place even darker, in the garden
they call Gethsemane. As we follow him through the olive trees to the
secret spot where he met with the Father alone and in anguish, we know
that we are standing on holy ground. To hear the tortured cries that

Jesus uttered that night is to encounter the deepest mysteries of the Son of God and to see how much he suffered for our salvation. In his masterful essay "The Emotional Life of Our Lord," the great Princeton theologian B. B. Warfield wrote:

> In these supreme moments our Lord sounded the ultimate depths of human anguish. . . . The scope of these sufferings was very broad, embracing that whole series of painful emotions which runs from a consternation that is appalled dismay, through a despondency which is almost despair, to a sense of well-nigh complete desolation. In the presence of this mental anguish the physical tortures of the crucifixion retire into the background, and we may well believe that our Lord, though he died on the cross, yet died not of the cross, but of a broken heart, that is to say, of the strain of his mental suffering.[1]

## A PLACE OF LONELY STRUGGLE

Gethsemane was one of our Lord's favorite places to go. Luke tells us that after celebrating the Last Supper, Jesus "came out and went, as was his custom, to the Mount of Olives, and the disciples followed him" (Luke 22:39). This was the secret garden where Jesus loved to go with his disciples. He seems to have gone there every night during the week of his passion, slipping out of Jerusalem before nightfall and hiking up the hillside, getting away from the men who wanted to kill him.

What sweet fellowship Jesus enjoyed there with his disciples: joyful singing, thoughtful discussion, and fervent prayer, with the easy laughter of close friends. Only on this particular night Jesus endured more excruciating suffering than we can imagine. Norval Geldenhuys rightly said, "No man will ever be capable of sounding the depths of what the Savior experienced in Gethsemane when the full reality of His suffering in soul and body penetrated into His immaculate spirit."[2] Yet even if we cannot sound the depths of our Savior's suffering, we can at least believe what the Bible says he endured the night before he went to the cross.

1. Benjamin Breckenridge Warfield, "The Emotional Life of Our Lord," in *The Person and Work of Christ*, ed. Samuel G. Craig (Philadelphia: Presbyterian and Reformed, 1950), 132–33.

2. Norval Geldenhuys, *The Gospel of Luke*, New International Commentary on the New Testament (Grand Rapids: Eerdmans, 1951), 574–75.

As we read Luke's account of this dark night of our Savior's soul, we see that Gethsemane was a lonely place for Jesus. He went to the garden with his disciples (except Judas, of course). When Jesus came to the place where he wanted to pray, he said to them, "Pray that you may not enter into temptation" (Luke 22:40). Then he "withdrew from them about a stone's throw, and knelt down and prayed" (Luke 22:41). Although Jesus was with his disciples, there was a place he needed to go all by himself. Matthew tells us that he kept three disciples closer to him than the others: Peter, James, and John (Matt. 26:36–37). But when it came time for him to pray, he went off by himself to be alone with his Father.

When Jesus returned, he discovered how very alone he was, for the disciples failed to keep their vigil (see Luke 22:45). Already Judas had left to betray him. Soon Peter would deny him and the rest of the disciples would run away. Now, instead of watching and praying as Jesus told them, they were sleeping. Even for the disciples this was a pathetic effort, and it left Jesus alone through the long, dark night. When it came time for our Savior to do the work of our salvation, the disciples did not help him one bit. Jesus alone was called to the cross, and alone he grappled with that calling, for Gethsemane was a lonely place of struggle.

Luke tells us that Jesus was "in an agony" (Luke 22:44). "Agony" *(agōnia)* is a word for the bitter striving of a fierce conflict. It means much more than simply that Jesus went through a strenuous experience of inward pain. It means that there was a fight within his soul. As Jonathan Edwards explained it, the Greek word for agony "implies no common degree of sorrow, but such extreme distress that his nature had a most violent conflict with it, as a man that wrestles with all his might with a strong man."[3]

The source of this intense conflict is revealed in verse 42. Jesus was wrestling with the powers of darkness that were driving him to the cross, but also with the will of the Father who was leading him there. So he said, "Father, if you are willing, remove this cup from me. Nevertheless, not my will, but yours, be done" (Luke 22:42). This was a battle of the wills. There was the will of the Father, which was for the Son to drink the cup. But there was also the will of Jesus, which asked if there might be some other way—any other way—except the way of the cross. Back in the wilderness, where he wrestled

---

3. Jonathan Edwards, "Sermon VI: Christ's Agony," in *The Works of Jonathan Edwards*, 2 vols. (Edinburgh: Banner of Truth, 1979), 2:868.

alone with the devil before he began his earthly ministry, Jesus was tempted to seize the crown without suffering the cross. Now at the end of his earthly ministry he was struggling with the same question: Was there any way out, any alternative to the cross, any easier way to save his people?

Here we are drawn into the deep mysteries of the incarnation. Jesus Christ is both God and man. He is one person with two natures, a divine nature and a human nature, which cannot be divided, but only distinguished. Among other things, the incarnation of the God-man means that Jesus had *both* a human will *and* a divine will. This has been the orthodox teaching of the church at least since the Third Council of Constantinople in A.D. 680. With respect to his divine nature, he had no other will than that of the Father, for the Father and the Son are one. Yet with respect to his human nature, Jesus himself made a clear and careful distinction between his will and the Father's will. If he did the Father's will, this was because he chose to do it, not necessarily because it always came easily or automatically.

In Gethsemane we see the human will of Jesus wrestling with the divine will. Humanly speaking, Jesus did not want to suffer the cross, which was evil in itself and deadly painful. I say "humanly speaking" because we see his true humanity as clearly here as we do anywhere in the Gospels. As a human being, Jesus had the same instinct to preserve his life that anyone has. No one loved life more than he did. How could it be his will, therefore, to suffer the torture of his body and the curse of death? Jesus was averse to death. Everything in his humanity recoiled against it. It was his natural preference to live. So in the agony of his soul he asked the Father for some other way to bring salvation.

## A PLACE OF HARD SUFFERING

In this crucible of spiritual conflict, Jesus suffered more anguish than we will ever know. The Savior we see and hear in the garden is the one described in Hebrews, who "offered up prayers and supplications, with loud cries and tears" (Heb. 5:7). With medical precision, Luke reports that "his sweat became like great drops of blood falling down to the ground" (Luke 22:44). The great bloody drops of sweat falling from the Savior's brow showed that he was at the utmost extremity of human anguish. This may explain why he fell down to pray (Luke 22:41), rather than standing, which was the usual custom. Jesus was at the very limit of his physical and emotional endurance, near the point of complete collapse. Indeed, according to the Gospel of Mark, his soul was "very sorrowful, even to death" (Mark 14:33–34; cf. Matt. 26:38). The horror of the coming cross brought him to the precipice of death, almost killing him in Gethsemane before he ever made it to Calvary. The lonely place of our Savior's struggle was a hard place of suffering.

What caused Jesus such great distress and filled his soul with so much dread? It was the approach of death, to be sure, but it also had to be something more than simply the physical experience of death. After all, other men have also been crucified, and many brave martyrs have faced the prospect of death with less agony and more apparent bravery than Jesus did. Besides, the Jesus we meet everywhere else in Luke seems to be fearless in the face of danger. What made him go through such a trembling night of the soul?

It was because he was facing the humiliating and excruciating suffering that only this death would bring: in dying on the cross, he would suffer for sins. J. C. Ryle asked, "How can we account for the deep agony which Our Lord underwent in the garden? What reason can we assign for the intense suffering, both mental and bodily, which He manifestly endured? There is only one satisfactory answer. It was caused by the burden of a world's imputed sin."[4] Why should sin bring so much suffering? Because sin deserves judgment. When Jesus took our sin upon himself, therefore, he became subject to the punishment that sin deserved, which was the wrath and curse of God—a death "totally exposed to God's abhorrence of sin."[5] His agony, wrote the Puritan Richard Baxter, "was not from the fear of death, but from the deep sense of God's wrath against sin; which He as our sacrifice was to bear; in greater pain than mere dying."[6]

This explains why Jesus used the image of the cup to describe his coming ordeal: "Father, remove this cup from me" (Luke 22:42). The cup was a familiar image from the Old Testament. A person's "cup" was his portion in

---

4. J. C. Ryle, *Expository Thoughts on the Gospels, Luke* (1858; reprint Cambridge: James Clarke, 1976), 2:422.

5. Donald Macleod, *The Person of Christ*, Contours of Christian Theology (Downers Grove, IL: InterVarsity, 1998), 175.

6. Richard Baxter, as quoted in Ryle, *Luke*, 2:427.

life, whatever God had determined to give him. Sometimes this has a positive connotation, as in the Shepherd Psalm: "my cup overflows" (Ps. 23:5). Yet the cup more commonly referred to the judgment of God. "Let him rain coals on the wicked," the psalmist said; "fire and sulfur and a scorching wind shall be the portion of their cup" (Ps. 11:6). Or consider the words of the prophets. When the people of God were suffering for their sins, Isaiah said they had "drunk from the hand of the LORD the cup of his wrath" down to the very dregs (Isa. 51:17). Ezekiel said, "You will be filled with drunkenness and sorrow. A cup of horror and desolation . . . you shall drink it and drain it out" (Ezek. 23:33–34). Similarly, God told Jeremiah to "take from my hand this cup of the wine of wrath, and make the nations . . . drink it" (Jer. 25:15).

This is the cup that Jesus was called to drink on the cross: the bitter brew of the judgment of God. It was not just the immediate prospect of death that made our Savior suffer, but knowing full well what kind of death it would be: a death that would propitiate the wrath of God. In the words of John Calvin, "His horror was not, then, at death *simpliciter*, as a passage out of the world, but because he had before his eyes the dreadful tribunal of God, and the Judge Himself armed with inconceivable vengeance; it was our sins, the burden of which he had assumed, that pressed him down with their enormous mass . . . [and] tormented him grievously with fear and anguish."[7] When we see Jesus kneeling in Gethsemane, we really see how much it would cost him to hang on Calvary, bleeding and dying for the guilt of our sin. When we see the blood on his sweaty brow, it is almost as precious to us as the blood he shed on the cross, because here in the garden we see how much Jesus suffered in choosing to die for our sins—a choice he made over against his own will.

Here is how Norval Geldenhuys summarized the struggle that Jesus suffered alone that night in the garden of Gethsemane:

It is impossible for Him, in His perfect humanity, not to experience a feeling of opposition to the idea of impending humiliation, suffering and death. And all this is made the more intense through his knowledge that He is not only going to suffer and die, but that He will have to undergo this as the

---

7. John Calvin, from his comments on Matthew 26:37 in his *Harmony of the Gospels*, as quoted in Warfield, *Person and Work of Christ*, 129.

expiatory sacrifice for the sin of guilty mankind. The holy and just wrath of God against sin falls on Him in full measure, because He has put Himself unreservedly in the place of guilty mankind. The judgment pronounced on sin is death—spiritual as well as physical. And spiritual death means being utterly forsaken by God. How dreadful, then, must the idea have been to Christ, who had from eternity lived in the most intimate and unbroken communion with His Father, that He would have to endure all this.[8]

We should never imagine that somehow all of this was easier for Jesus because he was the Son of God. No, this was as hard a thing as any man has ever done. It was as a man that Jesus suffered alone in the garden—a man with all of the physical weakness, mental pressure, and emotional anguish that is common to our humanity. He too was tempted. He was tormented and in turmoil. In the agonizing conflict of wrestling with the Father's will, he was weak and in need of God's strength. Jesus suffered all of this, and more. Indeed, Jesus was tempted every which way, yet he never gave in, so the temptation never relented. He was tormented to the very point of death. He was so weak that in mercy "there appeared to him an angel from heaven, strengthening him" (Luke 22:43). He was in such absolute agony that his sweat ran red with blood. Who can ever tell what suffering Jesus endured for our salvation, not just on the cross of Calvary, but also in the Garden of Gethsemane?

In one of his sermons on this passage, Charles Spurgeon said: "Since it would not be possible for any believer, however experienced, to know for himself all that our Lord endured in . . . mental suffering and hellish malice, it is clearly far beyond the preacher's capacity to set it forth to you. Jesus himself must give you access to the wonders of Gethsemane: as for me, I can but invite you to enter the garden."[9] By way of invitation, then, consider a personal experience that seemed to give a little glimpse of what Jesus went through for my salvation. In January 2006 thirteen miners were trapped underground in West Virginia; there had been a collapse down in the Sago mine. In the drama of those desperate days, many people imagined what it would be like to get entombed under rock and dirt.

8. Geldenhuys, *Luke*, 574.
9. Charles H. Spurgeon, "Gethsemane," in *The Metropolitan Tabernacle Pulpit* (Pasadena, TX: Pilgrim, 1969), 9:74.

Watching the rescue efforts reminded me what it felt like to visit underground caves in Central Turkey where Christians had once gone underground to escape persecution. I have never suffered from any acute feelings of claustrophobia. But as I crawled through one long tunnel, I looked ahead and saw someone in front of me get squeezed by a narrow opening. Dozens of people were pressing behind me, and suddenly the man in front of me looked as if he might get stuck. In an instant I felt the dread of getting trapped underground. The feeling of panic lasted only for a moment, because the man in front of me made it through after all, but when I remembered the feeling later, I shuddered. Getting buried underground would be an absolute terror for me.

Then I thought to myself, "But you could do it to save your family, couldn't you? If it were a matter of life and death, and the only way to rescue Lisa and the children was to crawl into some dark hole and get buried alive, you could do it for them, right?" "I'm not sure," I answered. "Maybe not. I don't think so. Oh, God, I hope I never have to find out!"

Then in my inner dialogue I suddenly realized that this is something like what Jesus went through in Gethsemane for me, not just as the Son of God, but also as a man. Jesus felt the terror of the tomb just as much as I would. As far as his human will was concerned, he did not want to die at all. The coming crucifixion filled him with so much dread that it almost killed him. Nevertheless, Jesus was willing to suffer the horror of that dread for my salvation, choosing to drink the bitter cup that my sins deserve.

If I understand Gethsemane at all, it means that Jesus loves me even more than I can imagine. It is not just that he died for me, but that he died this horrible, damnable, God-forsaken death that no one would ever want to die. He died this death because there was no other way for sinners to be saved, no easier road to redemption, no alternative to the cross. Jesus thus volunteered to do what the Father willed, choosing to do the one thing that would bring the most suffering to his body and soul. "The wonder of the love of Christ for his people," writes Donald Macleod, "is not that for their sake he faced death without fear, but that for their sake he faced it, terrified. Terrified by what he knew, and terrified by what he did not know, he took damnation lovingly."[10]

10. Macleod, *Person of Christ*, 175.

This must always be the main lesson we learn whenever we go to the Garden of Gethsemane. Luke does not show us the agony of Jesus to arouse our pity, primarily, or simply to remind us of our Savior's humanity, but to help us see again the love that Jesus has for us in dying for our sins. We will never have to suffer what our Savior suffered in Gethsemane, or at Calvary, for the very reason that everything he suffered there was in our place, on our behalf. The first response we make to Jesus should always be faith in the saving work he did in suffering and dying as our substitute. The lesson of Gethsemane is not that Jesus suffers *with* us, but that he suffered *for* us.

## A Prayer of Full Submission

What else can we learn from listening to our Savior pray in the garden? By following his example we can also learn what we should do in any dark and desperate situation, and of course the main thing for us to do is to pray. This is what Jesus told his disciples to do. That very night they would undergo the most severe of all their trials. So Jesus said to them, "Pray that you may not enter into temptation" (Luke 22:40), which may also mean "testing" or "trial." He said the same thing when he found them asleep from emotional exhaustion: "And when he rose from prayer, he came to the disciples and found them sleeping for sorrow, and he said to them, 'Why are you sleeping? Rise and pray that you may not enter into temptation'" (Luke 22:45–46). Even when their prayer lives were a complete failure, Jesus did not stop telling his disciples to pray.

This is what all the men and women of faith have done when they did not know what to do. When the Lord took what he had given and Job lost everything he had, he blessed the name of the Lord (Job 1:20–21). When Hannah was desolate without children, she prayed to the Lord in her heart (1 Sam. 1:13). When Asaph had to face "the day of trouble," he called on the name of the Lord (Ps. 50:15). When Hezekiah was attacked by enemies, he took their ultimatum to the temple and laid it before the Lord in prayer (2 Kings 19:14–19). Similarly, when Jehoshaphat faced a dire military threat, he prayed, "O Lord . . . we do not know what to do, but our eyes are on you" (2 Chron. 20:6–12). There is no situation we could ever face that is too desperate for prayer. "Is anyone among you suffering?" James asked in the difficult days of the early church. "Let him pray" (James 5:13).

We can take the same principle and apply it to the dark night of every soul. Is anyone ashamed or afraid? Is anyone confused? Is anyone in grief and pain? Is anyone discouraged or desperate? Is anyone striving in lonely agony? Let that person pray. When we do not know what to do, the thing to do is to pray. When there is nowhere else to go, go to God in prayer.

This is not only what Jesus told his disciples to do, but it is also what he did himself. He did not fall asleep the way they did, giving in to the physical and emotional weakness of his body. On the contrary, even in the extremity of his greatest distress he persisted in prayer. In fact, the more agony Jesus was in, the more he prayed. The wording of verse 44 is important: "And being in an agony he prayed more earnestly." Rather than giving up on prayer because he was having so much struggle, Jesus prayed more than ever. The harder things get, the more earnestly we should pray. When we are feeling most afraid of the future, or most discouraged about our work, or most worried about our finances, or most despondent in our grief, or most anxious about our families, or most defeated by the devil, that is just the time when we should be most in prayer.

When we pray, we should pray the way that Jesus prayed, asking our Father for his will to be done. Jesus began this prayer the way he always began, with the name of his Father. The first word out of his mouth was a term of endearment, spoken with reverent affection. The Son was speaking to his Father. This is the way Jesus taught us to begin our prayers as well, by acknowledging the fatherhood of our God (Matt. 6:9).

Then, as he spoke to the Father, Jesus resolved the struggle of his will in favor of his Father's pleasure: "Father, if you are willing, remove this cup from me. Nevertheless, not my will, but yours, be done" (Luke 22:42; cf. John 12:27). This was a prayer of willing submission. Jesus was saying to the Father, "Thy will be done." In one sense he had been doing this throughout his earthly ministry. Jesus did not come to earth to do his own will, but the will of his Father in heaven. This is what his whole life was all about (see John 4:34; 6:38; 8:29). The words he spoke and miracles he performed were in submission to the Father's will. But now he was coming to his ultimate test. This was "the final drama of His voluntary and complete self-surrender to God."[11] Would Jesus do the Father's will, no matter what the cost, and

11. Geldenhuys, *Luke*, 573.

no matter how much he wanted things to be some other way? Praise God! For the sake of our salvation, Jesus submitted to the Father's will. Even in suffering, Jesus was fully committed to doing the work of our salvation, and thus he prayed for God's will to be done in his own life and death. When Jesus did this, his prayers were answered. The Father's will was done, through the cross and the empty tomb, for the glory of Jesus Christ and the everlasting joy of all his children.

Now Jesus empowers us to follow his example in surrendering our own will to the will of God. It is not wrong to tell God what we truly desire, but even the good things we want must always be surrendered to the superior wisdom of his fatherly will. "Thy will be done" is one of the main petitions in the daily prayer that Jesus taught us to pray (see Matt. 6:10). Thus our Lord calls us to pray this way through all the hard situations in life. It is what we pray about our losses and sorrows. It is what we pray for our ministry, in all its sufferings. It is what we pray about our situation in life right now, with all its difficulties and discouragements. It is what we pray about the things in the future we wish that we could control and about everything beyond our power that we would give anything to change. We say, "Father, not my will, but yours, be done" (Luke 22:42).

In your own place of hard suffering and lonely struggle, learn to pray in full submission to the Father. I witnessed an excellent example of this kind of submission in the pulpit of Tenth Presbyterian Church. The example was set by my mentor and friend, the late Dr. James Montgomery Boice, who served his church in Center City Philadelphia for more than thirty years.

On Good Friday in the year 2000 Dr. Boice received the unhappy news that he had an inoperable cancer of the liver. Just two weeks later he stood in front of the congregation he loved for what I knew in my heart would be the last time. In his remarks that morning, as Dr. Boice looked full in the face of death, he followed the example his Savior had set for him in Gethsemane. First he called us all to prayer:

> You have been praying, certainly, and I've been assured of that by many people. A relevant question, I guess, when you pray is, Pray for what? Should you pray for a miracle? Above all, I would say pray for the glory of God. If you think of God glorifying Himself in history and you say, where in all of history has God most glorified Himself? He did it at the cross of Jesus Christ,

and it wasn't by delivering Jesus from the cross, though He could have. Jesus said, "Don't you think I could call down from my Father twelve legions of angels for my defense?" But he didn't do that. And yet that's where God is most glorified.

Then Dr. Boice spoke about submitting to the will of God as we prayed. Never one to miss an opportunity to teach a little doctrine, he said:

> If I were to reflect on what goes on theologically here, there are two things I would stress. One is the sovereignty of God. That's not novel. We have talked about the sovereignty of God here forever. God is in charge. When things like this come into our lives, they are not accidental. It's not as if God somehow forgot what was going on, and something slipped by. God does everything according to His will. We've always said that. But what I've been impressed with mostly is something in addition to that. It's possible, isn't it, to conceive of God as sovereign and yet indifferent—God's in charge, but He doesn't care. But it's not that. God is not only the one who is in charge; God is also good. Everything he does is good. . . . If God does something in your life, would you change it? If you'd change it, you'd make it worse. It wouldn't be as good. So that's the way we want to accept it and move forward, and who knows what God will do?[12]

These wise words from a man facing death are for all those who live for the Christ who suffered for them in Gethsemane and died for them at Calvary. In every difficult circumstance, pray to your Father for the glory of God. Pray in full submission to his good will, accepting his sovereign plan and moving forward. Who knows what God will do?

We know what God will do. Our Father will do what he did when Jesus prayed to him in the garden: he will answer our prayers in a way that brings glory to him and salvation to his suffering people.

12. James Montgomery Boice, as recounted in *The Life of Dr. James Montgomery Boice, 1938–2000* (Philadelphia: Tenth Presbyterian Church, 2001), 45.

97

# THE HOUR OF THE
# POWER OF DARKNESS

## *Luke 22:47–53*

*Then Jesus said to the chief priests and officers of the temple and*
*elders, who had come out against him, "Have you come out as*
*against a robber, with swords and clubs? When I was with you*
*day after day in the temple, you did not lay hands on me. But this*
*is your hour, and the power of darkness." (Luke 22:52–53)*

*T*he English poet Robert Herrick must have been something of
a romantic, because when he asked "What is a kiss?" he gave
this answer: "The sure, sweet cement, glue, and lime of love."[1]
A gentle kiss is the surest, sweetest expression of affection. Consider the soft
kiss a father gives his baby girl at bedtime. Or the first kiss a couple shares
after settling a quarrel. Or the last kiss a mother gives her son before he
leaves home. Consider the kissing embrace of long-lost friends, or a husband and wife in their golden years. The same God who gave us hearts for
love also gave us lips for kissing. In fact, the Greek New Testament verb that
means "to love" *(phileō)* also means "to kiss." To kiss is to love.

1. Robert Herrick, "A Kiss," *Hesperides*, 1648.

Except, that is, when to kiss is to betray. For it happened that on the night Jesus sweated bloody prayers in the Garden of Gethsemane, "while he was still speaking, there came a crowd, and the man called Judas, one of the twelve, was leading them" (Luke 22:47). And Judas "drew near to Jesus to kiss him" (Luke 22:48)—as it were, to love him. Such a kiss was a common greeting in that community, even among men. But it was more than a handshake; it was a gesture of intimate friendship.

Judas gave this greeting for the most evil of all purposes. The kiss was a prearranged signal to identify Jesus as the man to be taken into custody by the temple police. "The one I will kiss is the man," Judas said; "seize him" (Matt. 26:48). When Judas kissed the man (see Mark 14:45), he was betraying him unto death. So Jesus said, with sad reproach, "Judas, would you betray the Son of Man with a kiss?" (Luke 22:48).

## ONE MAN, BETRAYED WITH A KISS

To understand what a bitter betrayal this was, we have to know how much Jesus had done for Judas. Luke reminds us of this when he identifies Judas as "one of the twelve" (Luke 22:47). This is what makes his treachery so utterly despicable: Judas was one of the original twelve apostles—the inner circle of Jesus' closest friends.

Remember all of the things that Jesus had done for Judas, first calling him to be among his disciples and then choosing him to be one of the twelve. Jesus did this after spending a whole night with his Father in prayer (Luke 6:12–13). Judas was named a disciple by the definite will of God and the deliberate choice of Jesus Christ.

Jesus also taught Judas. Judas would have been present for almost all of the teaching that Jesus did throughout the Gospel of Luke. He was there when Jesus said that God's blessing is for the poor, not for people who want to get rich (Luke 6:20, 24). He was there when Jesus said that his disciples should love their enemies (Luke 6:27–36), bear good fruit from a good heart (Luke 6:43–45), and build on the rock of obedience to Christ (Luke 6:46–49). When Jesus told his famous parables, he did not explain them to everyone; but he did explain them to Judas and the other disciples, saying, "To you it has been given to know the secrets of the kingdom of God" (Luke 8:10). Judas heard the parables Jesus taught to warn people against greed (e.g., Luke 12:13–21). He also heard the advice that Jesus gave about counting the cost of discipleship (e.g., Luke 14:26–33).

Not only did Jesus make a major investment in this man's spiritual education, but he also showed him the power of his miracles, including miracles that directly benefited Judas. Presumably Judas Iscariot was out with the other disciples in the boat when Jesus calmed the stormy sea (Luke 8:22–25). Certainly he was there when Jesus fed the five thousand and every apostle gathered a full basket of leftovers (Luke 9:10–17). In his grace, Jesus rescued Judas from danger and provided for his daily needs.

Then Jesus gave Judas the opportunity to serve in ministry. Not only was Judas trusted to serve as treasurer of the common purse, but he also went out with the other apostles "preaching the gospel and healing" in various villages (Luke 9:6). Like the others, Judas was divinely empowered to preach the gospel, heal diseases, and cast out demons (which shows that serving in ministry is no guarantee of salvation!).

During all this time, Jesus was showing Judas again and again that he was the Christ, the Son of the living God. Jesus was giving him the gospel, repeatedly proclaiming his sufferings, death, and resurrection. He even warned Judas not to go astray. Like the rest of the disciples, Judas was taught to pray not to be led into temptation, but delivered from evil (Luke 11:4). He must have been there when Jesus said, "I tell you, everyone who acknowledges me before men, the Son of Man also will acknowledge before the angels of God, but the one who denies me before men will be denied before the angels of God" (Luke 12:8–9). Presumably Judas was also there when Jesus told the parable of the wicked tenants, which ended with the landowner putting his enemies to death for killing his only son (Luke 20:9–18). Jesus gave Judas every possible warning not to become the betrayer.

See how much Jesus had done for Judas! He even washed the man's dirty feet. According to John, this night began with Jesus cleansing the feet of his disciples (see John 13). There was one disciple who refused, but it was not Judas; it was Peter. Then, after Jesus lovingly bathed his betrayer's feet, he shared fellowship with him at the dinner table. Before Judas slipped out into the darkness, Jesus gave him one final warning: "Behold, the hand of him who betrays me is with me on the table. For the Son of Man goes as it has been determined, but woe to that man by whom he is betrayed!" (Luke 22:21).

Even the last words Jesus ever spoke to his betrayer were spoken in love: "Judas, would you betray the Son of Man with a kiss?" (Luke 22:48). Jesus called Judas by his personal name. Matthew tells us that he even called Judas his "friend" that night (Matt. 26:50), and it was as a friend that Jesus called him one last time to repentance. When he asked Judas this question, he was not expressing his own surprise, but trying to startle Judas into the recognition of what he was really doing. "O Judas, Judas! Are you sure you want to go through with this? Don't you see that I am the one and only divine Son of God? Can't you see what you are doing? You are becoming a traitor to the cause of Christ." "Thus to the end Christ seeks to keep him from ruin," writes Alexander Maclaren, "and with meek patience resents not indignity, but with majestic calmness sets before the miserable man the hideousness of his act."[2]

See how much Jesus loved this man, and imagine therefore how bitter it must have been for him to be betrayed. Jesus did more for Judas than any of us has ever done for anyone. If to kiss is to love, then Jesus had been kissing Judas all the way through the Gospel. This was the man who betrayed him: not one of his usual enemies, but someone he had welcomed as a close friend. The Son of Man was betrayed by someone he loved.

In fact, the very manner of this betrayal presumed upon Jesus' affections. Judas knew where to find Jesus only because he was such a close friend. This secret garden was the secluded spot where Jesus loved to meet with his disciples. Judas knew it well because he had been there with Jesus so often (see John 18:2). It was his very friendship that enabled him to arrange this arrest, and the same close friendship that gave him access to greet Jesus with a kiss. Thus the Scriptures were fulfilled: "Even my close friend in whom I trusted, who ate my bread, has lifted his heel against me" (Ps. 41:9); "For it is not an enemy who taunts me . . . but it is you, my equal, my companion, my familiar friend" (Ps. 55:12–13).

Have you ever been betrayed? Have you ever had a close friend turn against you? Jesus knows our pain and understands our suffering, for his betrayal was the bitterest of all. Jesus was the Son of Man—an Old Testament title he used to identify himself as the Messiah, the Christ of God. The unique divine glory of his holy person makes his betrayal an infinitely

---

2. Alexander Maclaren, *Expositions of Holy Scriptures* (Grand Rapids: Baker, 1971), 252.

wicked offense, especially coming from someone to whom he showed so much love. This fact led the famous German preacher F. W. Krummacher to wonder: "Can there be a more appalling or more deeply affecting scene than this treacherous betrayal of his Master?"[3] "Nothing I can say in denunciation of Judas," wrote another commentator, "would begin to approach the realm of words sufficient to denounce the dark and dastardly act."[4]

Jesus suffered this betrayal for us on his way to the cross. In a way, his sufferings would not have been complete without this betrayal. How could Jesus sympathize with us in all our suffering unless he himself had experienced the Judas-kiss of personal betrayal? When you feel betrayed—when you *are* betrayed—tell your heart to Jesus. He understands better than anyone else.

## ARMED RESISTANCE

What is the best way for us to respond when we are betrayed? Usually what we want is some sort of revenge, and immediately we start plotting how to get it. There is something deeply satisfying about seeing people get what we think they deserve.

Some of the great stories in world literature are based on the motif of betrayal and revenge. Consider *The Count of Monte Cristo*, the famous novel by Alexander Dumas in which the young Edmond Dantes is betrayed by three jealous friends and sent to prison. After making his escape and finding his fortune, Dantes systematically takes revenge on each of his hated enemies, driving them into financial ruin, public disgrace, suicide, and insanity. There is something juicy about a story like that, something that appeals to our fallen nature: it satisfies our craving for revenge.

Revenge is exactly what the disciples wanted when they saw Jesus betrayed. They had been praying with Jesus in the garden (or, to be strictly accurate, they had been sleeping in the garden while Jesus was praying). So they must have been startled by the unruly mob coming to make this arrest: "And when those who were around him saw what would follow, they said, 'Lord, shall we strike

3. F. W. Krummacher, *The Suffering Saviour* (1856; reprint Edinburgh: Banner of Truth, 2004), 128.

4. G. Campbell Morgan, as quoted in Norval Geldenhuys, *The Gospel of Luke*, New International Commentary on the New Testament (Grand Rapids: Eerdmans, 1951), 581.

with the sword?' And one of them struck the servant of the high priest and cut off his right ear. But Jesus said, 'No more of this!' And he touched his ear and healed him" (Luke 22:49–51).

We know from the discussion Jesus had with his disciples earlier in the evening that they were carrying two swords (see Luke 22:38). Now the disciples wanted to know whether or not they were supposed to use them. Only one of them did not wait for Jesus to answer. Not surprisingly, Peter was the hasty apostle who lopped off somebody's ear (John 18:10), striking his blow with "poor aim but stout intention."[5] Maybe Peter was still trying to prove that he would never deny the Christ. But in any case, when Jesus was betrayed, the disciples wanted to fight back.

There is a time and a place for the proper use of the sword. In the case of an unprovoked attack by an unlawful aggressor, we have a legitimate right to self-defense. The sword also has a divinely approved authority in the hands of the state, including its lawful use by a legitimate army in the prosecution of a just war.

Yet this was neither the time nor the place for the disciples to engage in any swordplay. To begin with, it was unlawful. However misguided they were, the people who came to arrest Jesus had legal authority under God. Therefore, any armed resistance would make the disciples guilty of resisting an arrest.

Fighting back was also unnecessary. Jesus Christ was the last person who needed anyone to defend him. If he needed help, all he had to do was call on the tens of thousands of angels who are under his Father's command (see Matt. 26:53). Armed resistance was also unsafe. It was certainly unsafe for the servant who got his ear chopped off! But it was even more unsafe for the disciples: Jesus said that those who live by the sword will die by the sword (see Matt. 26:52).

Furthermore, resisting arrest was unwise. The disciples were outmanned, and therefore any resistance would have been futile. But it also would have given the religious leaders exactly the excuse they were looking for. They were about to spend all night desperately trying to find some legal basis for a charge against Jesus. If his disciples fought with their swords, they would be able to justify their own use of arms. They could claim that Jesus was

5. David Gooding, *According to Luke: A New Exposition of the Third Gospel* (Grand Rapids: Eerdmans, 1987), 336.

leading a violent uprising, that his followers were armed and dangerous, and that therefore his forcible arrest was in the interest of public safety.

But the biggest problem with resisting this arrest is that it would undo God's plan for salvation. It was the will of God for Jesus to be betrayed, arrested, tried, convicted, and crucified. Although these things were evil in themselves, they were the pathway Jesus needed to walk for our redemption. Rather than resisting arrest, he was called to submit to the force of these ungodly men, even unto death. Therefore, to strike a blow in his defense is "an action, which, however well meant, is, nevertheless, directed against the very ground and basis of the world's salvation."[6]

All of this helps to explain why Jesus said "No more of this!" and then proceeded to reattach the servant's ear. It was one of the smallest and simplest miracles Jesus ever performed. With clinical precision, Luke tells us that it was the servant's right ear that was cut off, and that Jesus healed the man simply by touching him. "At the very moment of his arrest," writes Kent Hughes, "with blood on the ground and steel in the air," Jesus "reached out to one of his enemies and healed him."[7]

As simple as it was, this miracle was more important than some people realize. It was important because it protected Jesus from the accusation that he was running some sort of terrorist organization; it was a sign instead that he never did anyone any harm. The miracle was important because it showed how utterly opposed Jesus is to wrongful violence. It also ended any attempt to hinder his progress towards the cross where he died for our sins. When Jesus performed this miracle, he was showing his purpose to bring salvation and his willingness to suffer injustice for the glory of God.

At a practical level, the healing of the servant's ear also shows how we should respond when we are mistreated, or even betrayed. We should not seek retaliation and revenge, like the disciples. Instead, we are to follow the example of Jesus in blessing our enemies.

This is an important lesson for the church. Whenever the church has taken up the power of the earthly sword, the results have always been disastrous. As the Anglican bishop J. C. Ryle wisely explained:

6. Krummacher, *Suffering Saviour*, 133.
7. R. Kent Hughes, *Luke: That You May Know the Truth*, 2 vols., Preaching the Word (Wheaton, IL: Crossway, 1998), 2:343.

The sword has a lawful office of its own. It may be used righteously, in the defense of nations against oppression; it may become positively necessary to use it, to prevent confusion, plunder, and rapine upon earth: but the sword is not to be used in the propagation and maintenance of the Gospel. Christianity is not to be enforced by bloodshed, and belief in it extorted by force. Happy would it have been for the Church if this sentence had been more frequently remembered! There are few countries in Christendom where the mistake has not been made of attempting to change men's religious opinions by compulsion, penalties, imprisonment, and death. And with what effect? The pages of history supply an answer. No wars have been so bloody as those which have arisen out of the collision of religious opinions: often, mournfully often, the very men who have been most forward to promote those wars have themselves been slain.[8]

Today there are signs of increasing spiritual conflict everywhere in the world. Some Christians are under hostile attack. In an increasingly secularized America, people of faith often use the language of warfare to describe what is happening in the wider culture. In other countries Christians are actually facing physical forms of persecution. Whatever attack we are under, we must never forget that our real warfare is spiritual warfare and our only weapons are spiritual weapons like prayer and the preaching of the gospel. If only the disciples had prayed the way Jesus taught them to pray, they would have been ready for this midnight assault. But because they did not fight against the principalities and powers of darkness through prayer, they ended up resorting to the use of worthless weapons.

We can also follow the example of Jesus when we suffer our own personal betrayals. Perhaps you have an enemy at work—someone who is trying to make your life miserable. Maybe a close friend has betrayed your trust, or a family member has done you wrong. How easy it is for us to send our swords whistling through the air, not even waiting to hear Jesus tell us not to strike. When we are angry about something, usually our first impulse is to get even. But Jesus gives it to us straight: "No more of this!" No more vengeful thoughts! No more angry words! No more manipulation or retaliation. No more getting even.

8. J. C. Ryle, *Expository Thoughts on the Gospels: St. Matthew* (Cambridge: James Clarke, 1974), 368.

517

Instead, follow the example of Jesus. Bless your enemies and do not curse them. Pray for them and look for ways to serve them. Commit your cause to the Lord, waiting for him to vindicate you when the time is right. Submit and surrender to God's will, even for your suffering. Then people will be able to see what Jesus is like from the way that you treat your enemies. Of course, this is impossible to do apart from the grace of God. But we have a Savior who is able to help us—a Savior who himself was bitterly betrayed, who paid the price for all our own betrayals, and who now lives to save us through all our sufferings.

## This Dark Hour

It is not just *from* our sufferings that God saves us, but *through* our sufferings. As Scripture teaches and experience confirms, it is not always God's will to bring us immediate deliverance. By the power of his grace, God promises that one day our sufferings will be over. But in the meantime, we are often oppressed by the powers of darkness. Nowhere is this more clearly demonstrated than in the sufferings that Jesus endured on the night of his betrayal. "This is your hour," he said to his tormentors, "and the power of darkness" (Luke 22:53).

When Jesus said "the power of darkness," he was referring to Satan and the dark forces of evil. But he was also careful to put those powers in their place. Indeed, Jesus noted how ironic it was for them to arrest him at all. A literary critic would call this "irony of situation," in which what happens is "the opposite of what is expected or appropriate."[9] Jesus pointed out this situational irony when he said "to the chief priests and officers of the temple and elders, who had come out against him, 'Have you come out as against a robber, with swords and clubs? When I was with you day after day in the temple, you did not lay hands on me'" (Luke 22:52–53).

Jesus Christ is the gentlest man who ever lived. As it says in the *Catechism for Young Children*, he is "holy, harmless, and undefiled" (A. 46). Yet a huge arresting party came to take him away, "armed with swords, staves, and spears," as if he were some sort of dangerous criminal.[10] How ironic! Jesus is

9. Leland Ryken, *Words of Delight: A Literary Introduction to the Bible* (Grand Rapids: Baker, 1987), 361.
10. Krummacher, *Suffering Saviour*, 119.

the one man in the history of the world who never took anything that did not belong to him. Yet the chief priests and the temple police deprived him of his liberty—another irony of injustice. These men could have arrested him publicly any day at the temple; instead, in cowardly secret they came in the dead of night. The situation is highly ironic: for a perfectly innocent man to be treated like a guilty criminal is the opposite of what is expected or appropriate.

Here is another irony: Jesus could have destroyed all of these men in a single instant, and none of their weapons would have given them the slightest protection. Their clubs and swords were not only unnecessary; they were also useless. Jesus was so mighty that nothing could have saved them from the power of his revenge.

Nevertheless, it was the will of God for Jesus to be betrayed, arrested, and finally crucified. This was the hour, Jesus said, of the power of darkness (Luke 22:53). This comment is recorded only in Luke, whose account of the arrest is shorter than we find in the other Gospels. Luke wanted to be sure we knew what Jesus said: this was the hour of the power of darkness.

When Jesus said "this is your hour," he was not referring to sixty minutes on the clock, but to the short, definite period of time when evil men would have their way. This was the hour when Judas would give his treacherous kiss and the leaders of Israel would make their unlawful arrest. This was the hour when angry men would call for blood and cruel soldiers would carry out their terrible torture. This was the hour when the Son of Man would suffer unto death.

In other words, this was the hour when Satan would triumph. The devil is the dark lord of spiritual evil, and therefore the hour of darkness must be his hour. The Scripture calls Satan's realm "the domain of darkness" (Col. 1:13). It says that our struggle against evil is a struggle "against the cosmic powers" that rule "this present darkness" (Eph. 6:12). This imagery helps to explain why Judas and his angry mob came at midnight. The cover of darkness was partly to hide their evil deeds, of course, but it was also a sign that they were working in the power of darkness. Luke has told us already that the devil himself had entered into the betrayer (Luke 22:3). Judas was in Satan's grip, and therefore what he did was under the power of darkness. This was the hour of Satan's power. All the forces of his dark realm were arrayed that night against the Son of God, and for a time they triumphed.

At this point it would be encouraging to say that at least Satan's triumph lasted only an hour, whereas the victory of God's Son will last for all eternity. This is true, of course. When Jesus said "this is your hour," he was placing a time limit on the power of darkness. Although Satan seemed to triumph in Gethsemane, at Calvary, and in the dark days when Jesus was buried in the grave, his victory turned to defeat on Easter Sunday. On the third day Jesus rose from the dead, breaking the power of darkness and bringing the light of salvation to everyone who believes in him. The power of darkness had its time, but now that the resurrection power of God has come in Christ, we do not live in Satan's dark hour.

There is deeper encouragement for us in this, however, that even the dark hour that seemed to be under Satan's power was really God's hour. The very fact that Jesus told the forces of darkness which hour was theirs showed that he was Lord of that hour and every hour. Even the dark hour of betrayal was under the greater power of God, and of his Christ. All of the things that seemed at the time like victories for Satan—including Judas and his nefarious kiss—actually fulfilled the prophecies of God. Jesus allowed Satan to have this hour of power only because he knew it would help to accomplish our salvation. By suffering this betrayal and everything else that happened to him on the way to his death, Jesus was paying the price for our sin and purchasing our salvation. Therefore, the hour of Satan's power was at the same time the day of our redemption.

What comfort and courage this gives to us in every dark hour. It is true that our present trials will not last forever. Soon we will enter the eternal light of our salvation. But even this present darkness—whatever it is for us—is under the power of God. If God was at work even during the dark hour of our Lord's betrayal, then whether we can see it or not, we may believe with hope that he is also at work right now in our own dark trials.

God is even at work when we feel betrayed. There is a powerful example of this in the life and death of William Tyndale, the famous Bible translator. Tyndale's burning passion was to put the Greek and Hebrew Scriptures into the English language. For this alleged "crime," as the church considered it, he was forced to flee from his native England and go into hiding in Europe.

Many people know that eventually Tyndale was burned at the stake. What is somewhat less well known is that his capture came as the result of a painful personal betrayal. It was a man Tyndale had trusted and confided in—a man he welcomed to his own dinner table and invited into his secret study, the villainous and perfidious Henry Phillips—who led him down a narrow passageway and into the arms of his enemies. Like Judas, Phillips was paid handsomely for his treachery, and like Judas, he used a prearranged signal to show which man he would betray.[11]

After his arrest, William Tyndale was taken to Vilvorde castle to await his execution. All of his possessions were confiscated, including the precious books he was using to write the Word of God in English. How did Tyndale respond? Did he thirst for revenge, or did he experience the presence of Christ in his own dark trial?

We get a clear answer in Tyndale's last known letter, written humbly to appeal to the local authorities for the return of his warm clothing. "I beg your lordship," he wrote,

> by the Lord Jesus, that if I am to remain here through the winter, you will request the commissary to have the kindness to send me, from the goods of mine which he has, a warmer cap; for I suffer greatly from cold in the head . . . ; a warmer coat also, for this which I have is very thin. . . . My overcoat is worn out; my shirts are also worn out. He has a woolen shirt, if he will be good enough to send it. . . . And I ask to be allowed to have a lamp in the evening; it is indeed wearisome sitting alone in the dark. But most of all I beg and beseech your clemency to be urgent with the commissary, that he will kindly permit me to have the Hebrew Bible, Hebrew grammar, and Hebrew dictionary, that I may pass the time in that study.

These requests reveal how much Tyndale was suffering in the months before he died. But his letter closes with a strong affirmation of faith. "I will be patient," he wrote, "abiding the will of God, to the glory of the grace of my Lord Jesus Christ." When William Tyndale went through his darkest hour, suffering a betrayal that led unto death, he experienced the peace and the comfort of Christ. As a result of his patient suffering and faithful witness, we are told, the jail keeper and his daughter came to faith in Christ, along with other members of their household.[12]

11. The full story of Tyndale's arrest is told by David Daniell in *William Tyndale: A Biography* (New Haven: Yale University Press, 1994), 361–73.

12. The text of Tyndale's letter and an account of his time in prison are found in Daniell, *William Tyndale*, 378–81.

Even the hour that seems to be under the power of darkness is really God's hour, and by faith we will see him use it for his glory. God will comfort us with the presence of his Spirit, give us a peaceful heart that does not seek its own revenge, and help us testify to the grace of our Savior, who was betrayed with a kiss.

# 98

# The Cock-a-Doodle Denial

## *Luke 22:54–62*

*But Peter said, "Man, I do not know what you are talking about."*
*And immediately, while he was still speaking, the rooster crowed.*
*And the Lord turned and looked at Peter. And Peter remembered*
*the saying of the Lord, how he had said to him, "Before the rooster*
*crows today, you will deny me three times." (Luke 22:60–61)*

According to *Black's Law Dictionary*, an arrest is the "taking custody of another for the purpose of holding or detaining him to answer a criminal charge." This is precisely what happened to Jesus on the night that he was betrayed. He was taken into custody for the purpose of answering a criminal charge, as yet unspecified. Luke reports that after Judas gave his fatal kiss and Jesus declared that this was the hour of the power of darkness, "Then they seized him and led him away, bringing him into the high priest's house, and Peter was following at a distance" (Luke 22:54).

The mention of Peter reminds us that there is a loose thread in this story—a dramatic tension that still needs to be resolved. Jesus prophesied that his leading disciple would repudiate the very Christ he once confessed, denying him three times before the first light of morning (Luke 22:34). But

Peter protested that he would follow Jesus all the way to prison, if necessary, and even unto death (Luke 22:33).

Even apart from the words of Jesus, we would have good reason to doubt whether Peter will be able to keep himself from falling. His boast itself gives reason for concern, because pride always goes before a fall. Peter has also neglected his prayers, and there is no telling what sin people will commit once they stop praying for God to deliver them from evil. Peter was trying to follow Christ in his own power, and thus he had put himself in the most vulnerable position anyone ever gets: prayer-less, but full of presumption.

### Once, Twice, Three Times a Sinner

This was Peter's situation as he followed the arresting party down the Mount of Olives, back into the city of Jerusalem, and then into the courtyard of the high priest, where Jesus would undergo the first of several trials. Frank Morison evocatively describes the "small party of men leading a strangely unresisting figure through the darkness, along the rocky defile that skirted the precipitous eastern face of the temple wall, up the historic causeway at the southeastern angle of the city wall to the headquarters of His avowed and inveterate enemies."[1] The night air was chill, someone gathered some wood, "and when they had kindled a fire in the middle of the courtyard and sat down together, Peter sat down among them" (Luke 22:55).

So far, so good. The rest of the disciples had all scattered (see Zech. 13:7; Mark 14:27), but Peter and one other disciple were still with Jesus (presumably it was John, who tells about this in his Gospel; see John 18:15–16). Peter wanted to see what would happen to Jesus (see Matt. 26:58), and he wanted to make good on his boast. Even if the others fell away, he would go to prison with Jesus. He would even die with Jesus. Peter tried to prove it by following Jesus all the way to the high priest.

In fact, "following" is just the word that Luke uses to describe what Peter was doing. This is what a disciple simply is: a follower of Christ. Admittedly, Peter was following "at a distance" (Luke 22:54), but at least he was still following (!), which most of the disciples weren't. The others had already

---

1. Frank Morison, *Who Moved the Stone?* (Grand Rapids: Zondervan, 1958), 15.

gone into hiding, but the bravest of all the disciples was still following Jesus, as a good disciple should. This was one of Peter's best moments, right up there with walking on water (however briefly) and confessing Jesus as the Christ. Peter wanted to go farther than anyone else down the road that Jesus walked to the cross.

Yet all it took was one little challenge from a servant girl for Peter to say that he did not even know Jesus. Within a matter of hours he had denied his Lord—not once, not twice, but three times. From the other Gospels we know that these three denials took place as the evening unfolded, in the give and take of fireside conversation. But here is the tight account that Luke gives, sparing any extraneous details to focus on the denials:

> Then a servant girl, seeing him as he sat in the light and looking closely at him, said, "This man also was with him." But he denied it, saying, "Woman, I do not know him." And a little later someone else saw him and said, "You also are one of them." But Peter said, "Man, I am not." And after an interval of about an hour still another insisted, saying, "Certainly this man also was with him, for he too is a Galilean." But Peter said, "Man, I do not know what you are talking about." (Luke 22:56–60)

How shall we describe this triple denial? Peter denied Jesus *immediately*, without the slightest hesitation. As soon as anyone said he was a follower of Christ, he claimed that he did not know Jesus at all. This, from the man who said he would die for Jesus!

Peter denied Jesus *timidly*. Maybe he could sense that this trial would turn out badly for Jesus. Maybe he was afraid for his own life. Yet the servant girl was hardly a threat to Peter. The consequences for saying that he knew Jesus were merely social, not judicial. He probably did not even know the people accusing him, nor was he likely to see them again. Yet cowardly Peter gave in to the social pressure and said that he did not know Jesus.

Peter also denied Jesus *unconvincingly*. When people took a good look at Peter's face in the firelight, they knew that they had seen him hanging around with Jesus. He had a reputation for being a disciple because he was always with Jesus, and people noticed. Even his accent gave him away. The third man who accused Peter was insistent, and he had the evidence to back it up: "Certainly this man also was with him, for he too is a Galilean" (Luke 22:59). It was not simply the way Peter looked that gave him away, but also the way he talked. Everyone could tell that he was from Galilee, which is where most of the disciples came from.

Then Peter denied Jesus *comprehensively.* It was not just once or twice that he denied Jesus, but three times. It was not just men who heard his denial; it was also women. Furthermore, Peter made this denial in three different ways. First he said that he did not know Jesus (Luke 22:57). Then he explicitly disavowed that he was a disciple. When someone said that he was "one of them," meaning one of the followers of Christ, Peter said that he was not one of them at all (Luke 22:58). The third time he pretended that he did not even know what people were talking about (Luke 22:59–60). Afterwards, he would never be able to say that it had all been some sort of misunderstanding, that he hadn't *really* denied Jesus. No, Peter denied the Christ about as thoroughly as anyone could.

Finally, Peter sinned *grievously:* his sin was a very great sin. Indeed, it was one of the first signs that this hour was under the power of darkness (see Luke 22:53). One of Jesus' own beloved disciples—Peter, whose confession was the rock on which Jesus promised to build his church— denied his Lord. Peter did this after many warnings not to fall away, after celebrating the holy sacrament of the Lord's Supper, and after repeated exhortations to watch and pray. Peter did this against Jesus Christ, the infinitely worthy Son of God. Unless it was confessed and atoned, this triple denial was a damnable sin, for Peter denied the only God who could save him.

Yet at the very moment Peter was making his third denial, his sovereign Lord called him back to his senses: "And immediately, while he was still speaking, the rooster crowed. And the Lord turned and looked at Peter. And Peter remembered the saying of the Lord, how he said to him, 'Before the rooster crows today, you will deny me three times.' And he went out and wept bitterly" (Luke 22:60–62).

## THE TRUE TEST OF DISCIPLESHIP

What can we learn from Peter's cock-a-doodle denial? Consider three important lessons about sin, grace, repentance, and a life of humble obedience to God. The first lesson is this: the true test of discipleship is our witness to the world, and not just the promises we make to God.

Peter was very presumptuous in the promise he made to Jesus: "Lord, I am ready to go with you both to prison and to death" (Luke 22:33). This was not the first time he had said something bold. Kent Hughes remarks that "Peter was always talking. . . . Sometimes he only opened his mouth to change feet, and at other times his words were immortal."[2] Peter was the one who confessed, "You are the Christ, the Son of the living God" (Matt. 16:16). He was the one who said, "Lord, to whom shall we go? You have the words of eternal life" (John 6:68). Then on the night of betrayal, he promised to follow Jesus to the very death.

All of that was in private, however, not in public. It was something Peter said to Jesus when he was safely within the community of faith, but not something he was ready to say in front of the whole world. On the contrary, when Peter was out in the courtyard he had almost nothing to say for himself, and nothing at all to say for Jesus. We find the most verbose of all the disciples strangely at a loss for words. All he can say is that he does not know Jesus.

The true test of discipleship is our witness to the world, and not just the promises we make to God. Does our own discipleship pass this test? People make many promises when they are alone with God—promises about living a better life, spending more time in prayer, or giving more money to charity. But the real test of our discipleship is what we say and do when we are under pressure to take a stand for Christ. What do we say then?

Unless we speak up for what we believe, then we ourselves become the deniers of Christ. I deny Christ when I talk with my friends about being involved at church, but not about what it means to know Jesus. I deny Christ when there is so little that is distinctive about the way I live that people at work or school do not even know that I am a Christian. I deny Christ when I am so afraid about what people think that I shrink back from telling people the biblical truth about controversial issues like abortion, or homosexuality, or the unique claims of Jesus Christ as the world's only Savior. I deny Christ when I say something a Christian shouldn't say or do something a Christian shouldn't do because I want to have fun or to be popular. But if I cannot speak up and say something for Jesus, then what kind of disciple am I anyway?

2. R. Kent Hughes, *Luke: That You May Know the Truth*, 2 vols., Preaching the Word (Wheaton, IL: Crossway, 1998), 2:347.

Peter had an opportunity to take his stand the night that Jesus was betrayed, especially before his third denial. What someone literally said was this: "*In truth* this man also was with him" (Luke 22:59). So what was the truth? Was Peter with Jesus or not? The real test was not what he said when they were alone in the garden, but when he was out talking to people who did not know Jesus.

Peter failed that test. This was partly because he was so proudly confident of his faithful discipleship that he did not even pray for God's help. How vulnerable we are to social pressure when we do not ask God to make us as courageous for Christ as we say we want to be when we are alone with Jesus. J. C. Ryle wisely said,

> The best and highest saint is a poor weak creature, even at his best times. Whether he knows it or not, he carries within him an almost boundless capacity of wickedness, however fair and decent his outward conduct may seem. There is no enormity of sin into which he may not run, if he does not watch and pray, and if the grace of God does not hold him up. When we read the fall of Peter, we only read what might possibly befall any of ourselves. Let us never presume. Let us never indulge in high thoughts about our own strength.[3]

No, let us never presume or think high thoughts about our own godliness. Instead, in our weakness, let us ask Jesus for the grace of a bolder witness, so that we can pass the true test of discipleship.

## Jesus Knows Our Weakness

As often as we sin like Peter, we can draw comfort from a second lesson he learned: Jesus knows our weakness, and even before we fall he has a plan to lift us back up.

We should always see Peter's triple denial in the context of the prophecies that Jesus gave him. Jesus specifically predicted that Peter would deny him: "I tell you, Peter, the rooster will not crow this day, until you deny three times that you know me" (Luke 22:34). Jesus told Peter when he

---

3. J. C. Ryle, *Expository Thoughts on the Gospels, Luke* (1858; reprint Cambridge: James Clarke, 1976), 2:437–38.

would deny him, and how many times, as well as the language he would use to do it. Jesus knew the weakness of Peter's fallen nature, his propensity for falling into sin. He knew this at the very time he was suffering the consequences for that sin and all our sins by going to the cross.

Not only did Jesus know that Peter would fall into sin, but he also knew what he would do to prevent his disciple from falling completely away. Jesus had prayed that Peter's faith would not fail. He had also given him this command: "And when you have turned again, strengthen your brothers" (Luke 22:32). This command presumes that Peter's faith would not fail, but would lead him to repentance. For when Jesus said that Peter would "turn again," he was saying that the man would repent, turning away from his sinful denials to follow Jesus again. This repentance would be so complete that Peter would be restored to a place of leadership in ministry. In fact, it would become his special calling to help other sinners turn back to Jesus and follow him.

Jesus knew all of this *in advance*. He knew Peter's weakness, and even before the man fell into sin he had a plan for his repentance and restoration. This helps to explain the famous "look" that Jesus gave Peter. At the very moment the rooster crowed, "the Lord turned and looked at Peter" (Luke 22:61). Who can begin to describe everything that Jesus communicated to Peter simply by making eye contact? I imagine that Jesus gave him a look of loving compassion and tender mercy. But whatever expression was on his lovely face instantly reminded Peter of what Jesus had said.

How remarkable it is that Jesus was even thinking about Peter at all. His own greatest trial had begun. Over the course of those awful hours Jesus was subjected to various taunts and insults, to say nothing of charges and accusations. "Surrounded by bloodthirsty and insulting enemies," wrote J. C. Ryle, "in the full prospect of horrible outrages, an unjust trial, and a painful death, the Lord Jesus yet found time to think kindly of His poor erring disciple."[4] It reminds me of the way parents with young children will carry on a conversation with another adult in a crowded room, while at the same time trying to keep track of where their children are, and what they are doing. Jesus had been thinking of Peter with similar concern. It was almost as if he had been waiting all night to hear Peter's rooster.

4. Ryle, *Luke*, 2:438.

It is not certain whether Jesus was still inside the high priest's house when this happened—somewhere near the door, perhaps—or whether he was coming out on his way to the next trial, but wherever he was, as soon as Jesus heard the rooster, he turned and looked at Peter. His heart went out to his fallen disciple. At the very moment Peter was sinning, Jesus loved him and called him back to repentance.

Here the wording of verse 61 seems especially significant: "Peter remembered the saying of the Lord," or even "the *word* of the Lord" (Luke 22:61). Jesus looked at Peter to remind him of what he had said. It was not simply what Jesus said about the rooster that Peter needed to remember, but the whole conversation, including what Jesus said about praying for his faith and restoring him through repentance. Jesus knew the man's weakness. Even before he fell into sin, Jesus had a plan for Peter's restoration and gave him the word that would lead to his repentance.

Jesus knows our weakness too, and he has a plan for our salvation. This is why he came into the world in the first place: to die for our sins. This is why he has given us his word: to promise his forgiveness. This is why he has sent us his Spirit: to call us to repentance. One look is all it took for Peter to repent, and now Jesus has sent the Holy Spirit to do the same work in us. If we truly love Jesus, one quiet reminder from the Spirit is all it should take to call us back to repentance.

We do not need to hide our sin. So often we are tempted to think that God will not love us again until we deserve to be loved. But it is right now that Jesus is looking to us in love, even if we have done all we can to deny him. Jesus knows our weakness. He has always known it. Even when we sin he is looking to remind us of his word and call us to saving repentance. Parents sometimes tell their children that God is always watching them, in the hope that this will keep them away from sin. But it is just as important— maybe more important—to know that when we do sin, Jesus is looking at us in love, longing for us to come back to him. There is no need for us to drag ourselves back to repentance when instead we should be running to the love that always looks for our salvation.

This is why Christians have found the story of Peter's denial to give so much hope. On the one hand, it is always heart-rending to see Peter fall into sin. We can feel the lump in our own throats when Jesus gives him that devastating glance, and we can almost taste his salty tears. But at the same time hope rises within us because we know that if there is hope for Peter, who denied Jesus on the very night of his betrayal, then there must be hope for us.

From the beginning, Luke has been "the Gospel of knowing for sure," and this is one of the main things we need to know: there is hope for anyone who comes to Jesus in faith. No matter how much we fall to temptation, Jesus knows our weakness, and in his loving mercy he will lift us up to salvation. C. S. Lewis was right when he said, "Though our feelings come and go, His love for us does not. It is not wearied by our sins, or our indifference; and, therefore, it is quite relentless in its determination that we shall be cured of those sins, at whatever cost to us, at whatever cost to Him."[5]

## AFTER THE TEARS

If ever a man experienced sin's costly cure, it was the apostle Peter. The rest of his story proves the grace of Jesus for fallen sinners and teaches us our third and final lesson: true repentance means more than feeling sorry for sin; it means turning back again and living for Christ. Here Peter is the perfect example, because he turned back almost as quickly as he turned away. "He was like a little child learning to walk," said Charles Spurgeon, "scarcely down before his mother has him up again."[6]

The first thing Peter did after hearing the rooster was to go out and weep bitter tears (see Luke 22:62). Here Luke uses a word *(eklausen)* for intense emotion—the same word someone would use for grieving the dead. Although he does not specify what made these tears so bitter, it is not hard to imagine some of the possibilities. They were tears of disappointment, as Peter recalled his former boast and realized his failure to follow Jesus all the way. They were tears of shame, as Peter remembered his disloyalty and the penetrating look that Jesus gave him. They may also have been tears of sorrow, as he grieved what was happening to Jesus and everything he was about to lose.

Can you relate to Peter's experience? Have you ever gone out to weep the bitter tears of failure, disappointment, shame, loss, or sorrow? If so,

5. C. S. Lewis, *Mere Christianity* (New York: MacMillan, 1952), 118.
6. Charles Spurgeon, "Peter's Restoration," *The Metropolitan Tabernacle Pulpit* (Pasadena, TX: Pilgrim, 1970), 34:398.

then what have you done with those tears? The most important thing about Peter's tears is what happened afterwards. This is always the critical question. Sooner or later most people feel sorry for something they have done, or at least about the consequences of what they have done. But not everyone repents, in the biblical sense of the word. Repentance is more than a feeling; it is a change of direction away from sin and back to God. This is why tears alone do not prove Peter's or anyone else's repentance. What matters more is what we do after our tears are dried away.

Peter's bitter tears show us the difference between repentance and remorse. Remorse is a feeling of regret that may lead to many tears, yet it never makes a lasting difference in anyone's life. Repentance may also lead to many tears, but it does not stop there. It includes the life of obedience we lead *after* we have cried for our sins.

This was the difference between Peter and Judas, who also regretted what he had done. To be sure, there were some important differences between the sins these two men committed. The sin of Judas was more damaging and deliberate, whereas Peter sinned from weakness in a moment of sudden temptation. But the most important difference was that Peter actually repented of his sin, which Judas never did.

Like Peter, Judas soon wished that he had never sinned at all. Matthew tells how that unhappy traitor changed his mind, took back the blood money for his betrayal, and told the chief priests that Jesus was innocent. Feeling hopeless of any mercy from God, Judas went out and committed suicide (Matt. 27:3–5). Judas may well have shed as many tears as Peter shed. He certainly had a guilty conscience for the wrong that he had done. But it was only remorse, never repentance. Rather than praying for God's mercy and then turning back to live for Jesus, Judas died in utter despair. His tragic end illustrates the second part of a contrast Paul drew for the Corinthians: "Godly grief produces a repentance that leads to salvation without regret, whereas worldly grief produces death" (2 Cor. 7:10).

The saving response to sin is repentance, not just remorse. J. C. Ryle said, "Remorse can make a man miserable, like Judas Iscariot, but it can do no more. It does not lead him to God." Repentance, on the other hand, *does* lead a man to God; he is consciously sorry that a sin has been committed against God, yet hoping in faith (this is why Jesus prayed that Peter's *faith* would not fail) that the sin will be forgiven. Therefore, repentance "makes a man's heart soft and his conscience tender, and shows itself in real turning to a Father in heaven. The falls of a graceless professor are falls from which there is no rising again. But the fall of a true saint always ends in deep contrition, self-abasement, and amendment of life."[7]

We should look for all these signs of true repentance in our own response to sin. We certainly see them in Peter. We see his deep contrition and self-abasement in the bitter tears he shed after the rooster crowed his condemnation. Then we see his amendment of life in virtually everything he did afterwards. Jesus prophesied that after Peter sinned, he would turn again (see Luke 22:32)—in other words, he would repent. Peter *did* turn again. He did not isolate himself in his despair, but during the dark days when Jesus was in the grave he went to pray with the other followers of Christ. He was the first disciple to enter the empty tomb (see John 20:6; cf. Luke 24:34), and one of the first to believe in the crucifixion and resurrection of Jesus for his salvation. Peter's faith did not fail, just as Jesus promised (Luke 22:32).

## PETER'S RESTORATION

Soon the very man who denied Jesus was fully restored to his place of ministry. When the risen Christ met his disciples by the Sea of Galilee, Peter reaffirmed his love for Jesus three times—one for each of the three times he had once denied him. In response, Jesus told Peter to care for his church like a good shepherd (see John 21:15–19). From then on Peter was always one of the boldest apostles. One dark night he had been afraid to let even a young slave girl know that he was a Christian. But within a matter of weeks he was preaching the gospel in broad daylight, letting the whole city know that he was a follower of Jesus. Even getting thrown into prison did not deter him. When his enemies tried to silence him, Peter said, "We cannot but speak of what we have seen and heard" (Acts 4:20). He kept witnessing for Christ right up until his own death by crucifixion (see John 21:19).

One could almost say that Peter made good on his promise to follow Jesus to prison and then on to death—not because of his bravado, but because God gave him the gift of repentance. It was true repentance, which is more than feeling sorry for sin; it is turning away from sin and living for

7. Ryle, *Luke*, 2:439.

Christ. Afterwards Peter did what Jesus said that he would do: he turned back to help his brothers and sisters get back on their feet when they fell into sin. "Do not put any confidence in your own spiritual abilities," he would remind them. "Be steadfast in prayer. And when you do fall down, remember that Jesus loves you and will help you back up." Then Peter would testify to the intense joy of being fully restored to God.

What hope Peter's example gives to anyone who has fallen into sin, or failed in the Christian life, or maybe even denied Jesus altogether. A dramatic example comes from the life of the Chinese evangelist Wang Mingdao. Imprisoned in the 1950s for preaching the gospel, Wang was subjected to horrific torture. He denied the faith, and with the promise that he would preach whatever the communist authorities told him to preach, he was released from prison. Yet afterwards he could not bring himself to work against the church. Broken with guilt, he would wander around Beijing muttering, "I am Peter, I am Peter." Eventually Wang Mingdao was re-arrested and sentenced to life in prison. When the authorities approached him again to see if he would collaborate with them against the church, Wang refused outright. While he was languishing in prison, he remembered the precious promise of the prophet Micah: "Do not gloat over me, my enemy! Though I have fallen, I will rise. Though I sit in darkness, the Lord will be my light" (Micah 7:8 NIV). Wang Mingdao proceeded to renounce all his former denials, denouncing them as lies. Though he had fallen, the mercy of Christ enabled him to rise again.[8]

Often the boldest believers are the ones who know they have been the biggest sinners. This must have been one of the reasons God allowed Peter to fall under temptation. Only by knowing his own weakness could he stop boasting in himself and find full strength in the power of God. In his mercy, God often helps us to make the same discovery. He lets us fail in our own strength, so that when we fall we will know how much we need his grace.

Then and only then will we be able to help other sinners find grace. What horrible arrogance would have been a temptation for Peter if he alone had followed Jesus through his trials without falling! But because Peter fell he was able to sympathize as a fellow sinner, wiping away people's bitter tears and telling them about the grace of Jesus. Charles Spurgeon noted

8. This story is recounted in David Aikman, *Jesus in Beijing* (Washington, DC: Regnery, 2003), 55–56.

that there is "a peculiar tenderness, without which one is not qualified to shepherdize Christ's sheep, and to feed his lambs—a tenderness, without which one cannot strengthen his brethren, as Peter was afterwards to do, a tenderness which does not usually come—at any rate, to such a man as Peter, except by his being put into the sieve, and tossed up and down by Satanic temptation."[9]

If you have fallen into serious sin, know that Jesus wants to do the same gracious work in your life. Your sin need not drive you to despair, but can be an opportunity for God to show his grace. The question is: What will you do after all the tears? J. C. Ryle said that "If we fall as Peter fell, we must repent as Peter repented, or else we shall never be saved."[10] But understand as well that Jesus loves you as much as he ever loved Peter. So if you *do* repent the way that Peter repented, you will not only be saved, but have the joy of helping other fallen sinners get up and start following Jesus more boldly than ever.

9. Charles Spurgeon, "Christ's Prayer for Peter," *The Metropolitan Tabernacle Pulpit* (Pasadena, TX: Pilgrim, 1977), 45:207.

10. Ryle, *Luke*, 2:440.

99

# SON OF GOD AND SON OF MAN

## *Luke 22:63–71*

*And they led him away to their council, and they said, "If you are the Christ, tell us." But he said to them, "If I tell you, you will not believe, and if I ask you, you will not answer."* (Luke 22:66b–68)

he Oxford professor and evolutionary scientist Richard Dawkins knows roughly as much about theology as I know about biology. Unfortunately, his relative ignorance did not prevent him from writing *The God Delusion*, a best-selling diatribe against anyone who has faith in God. To believe in any deity, Dawkins writes, is to commit "intellectual high treason." But to believe in the God of the Bible is even worse, for he is "a petty, unjust, unforgiving control-freak; a vindictive, bloodthirsty ethnic cleanser; a misogynistic, homophobic, racist, infanticidal, genocidal, filicidal, pestilential, megalomaniacal, sadomasochistic, capriciously malevolent bully."[1]

These quotations are typical of Dawkins's attitude towards Christianity. Even secular critics have described *The God Delusion* as shoddy, intolerant,

---

1. See Richard Dawkins, *The God Delusion* (New York: Houghton Mifflin, 2006), 31.

amateurish, nasty, grotesquely false, and theologically illiterate.[2] Yet what was perhaps most shocking is that despite all of the positive publicity the book received, there was little if anything new in any of its main arguments. Once again we are told that religion is a hypothesis that cannot meet the demands of scientific investigation, as if science were the only way to know. A man sits in judgment over God, deluded by his own sense of intellectual sovereignty.

## STRICKEN, SMITTEN, AND AFFLICTED

People did the same thing on the night that Jesus was betrayed: they sat in judgment over God. For on that night Jesus went through a series of legal trials—both civil and ecclesiastical—in which he was accused, judged, and ultimately condemned to die.

Generally speaking, there were two main sets of trials: the Jewish and then the Roman. Each trial had several parts, which makes it difficult to keep all the legal proceedings straight, especially since each of the four Gospels includes details that the others omit.

Luke 22 tells the story of the Jewish trials: "When day came, the assembly of the elders of the people gathered together, both chief priests and scribes. And they led him away to their council" (Luke 22:66). By this point Jesus had already been through two trials, or what today we would call "pretrial hearings." First Jesus appeared before Annas, the former high priest, who still exercised a great deal of influence over Jewish affairs. When Annas had finished his preliminary investigation, he had Jesus bound and delivered to Caiaphas, who had become the high priest after him (see John 18:19–24). Caiaphas then conducted his own pretrial hearing, as described in Matthew 26:57–68.

Neither of these legal proceedings had any binding authority, however. According to Jewish law, the high council in Jerusalem could not try a case at night, but only during the daytime. Hence the significance of the opening words in verse 66: "When day came, the assembly . . . gathered." In effect, this was the third part of the Jewish trial, following the hearings before Annas and Caiaphas. It was at those previous trials that the outcome actually had been decided. By the time Jesus appeared before the council,

2. For example, see Terry Eagleton, "Lunging, Flailing, Mispunching," in *London Review of Books* 28.20 (Oct. 19, 2006), available online at http://www.lrb.co.uk/v28/n20/eagl01_.html.

everyone knew what verdict would be pronounced—that is what they had been up all night trying to decide. But to give everything the appearance of legitimacy, the council waited until the first light of day to conduct a formal trial and render the agreed-upon verdict.

This time the whole council was assembled, including both the chief priests and the scribes. It was called the Sanhedrin—a group of seventy elders, plus the high priest. Since it was the highest court of law among the Israelites, it was the last court where Jesus would be tried before being handed over to the Romans, who alone had the power to execute the death penalty.

No one should think for a moment that any of these trials was conducted with a real concern for justice. The same men who insisted on waiting until dawn for the full trial later demanded for Jesus to die. Yet this was also against their regulations, because the same Talmud that required a daytime trial also forbade executing the death penalty on the same day a sentence was handed down.

Then there was all the abuse that Jesus suffered while he was held in custody. Sometime after his nighttime hearings and before his daytime trial, Jesus was tortured. Luke tells us that "the men who were holding Jesus in custody were mocking him as they beat him. They also blindfolded him and kept asking him, 'Prophesy! Who is it that struck you?' And they said many other things against him, blaspheming him" (Luke 22:63–65).

This was an outrageous case of police brutality. The prisoner was totally at the mercy of the temple guards, and when they sensed that he would be condemned, they felt that they could torture him with impunity. The shameful abuse of these cowardly men was partly physical, as they beat Jesus with their fists and other blunt objects. But they also added insult to injury by subjecting Jesus to mental and verbal abuse. Later the Roman soldiers would mock Jesus as king; here the Jewish wardens mocked him as prophet. They had heard that Jesus was a prophet. So in a perverse game of blindman's bluff they blindfolded him and then, as they continued to hit him, challenged him to prophesy who was hitting him. Without warning, they hit him from every side, and with each unexpected blow, came the taunting question: "Tell us, Jesus, who hit you that time?"

For men like these, "religion was always good for a joke, particularly prophets who tried to scare you with warnings about a God who is supposed to be able to see everything you do, and will one day punish sinners."[3] But the men who abused Jesus would never get the last laugh. With divine omniscience, he knew exactly who was hitting him. Indeed, he knew everything that these men had ever done. Unless they repented, their laughter will turn into tears at the final judgment, when Jesus will see that perfect justice is done.

Ironically, the torments Jesus suffered were the fulfillment of prophecy. The very men who mocked Jesus were fulfilling various prophecies about the sufferings of the Christ. Jesus himself prophesied that he would be "mocked and shamefully treated" (Luke 18:32). He also said that these abuses would fulfill the words of the ancient prophets (Luke 18:31), and so they did. For example, the prophet Isaiah foretold that the suffering Christ would be "stricken, smitten . . . and afflicted" (Isa. 53:4). This did not just happen on the cross, but also before that, when Jesus was tied up and tortured.

Never forget that Jesus suffered these things for you. Every wounding blow and every taunting word was an expression of his love for lost sinners. Jesus did more than die for us on the cross; he also suffered for us on his way to the cross. As Isaiah also said, "He was wounded for our transgressions; he was crushed for our iniquities; upon him was the chastisement that brought us peace, and with his stripes we are healed" (Isa. 53:5).

As far as our atonement is concerned—the forgiveness of our sins—it was only necessary for Jesus to die. But in order for Jesus to do the full work of our salvation, it was necessary for him to die in this way: alone, abandoned, and abused. Just as he fulfilled all righteousness, so he fulfilled all suffering, because in order to care for his suffering people, he first had to become our Suffering Servant. Now Jesus is able to sympathize and empathize with us in our sufferings, for he too has suffered shameful cruelty at the hands of sinful men. He knows what it is like to wonder when the next painful blow will strike, or to hear people laughing at him for trusting God. We should never think, therefore, that God does not or cannot understand our pain—even to the point of evil abuse. Jesus endured the worst things that anyone can experience.

3. David Gooding, *According to Luke: A New Exposition of the Third Gospel* (Grand Rapids: Eerdmans, 1987), 338.

Now in grace Jesus comes to help us in our own time of trial. He shows us how to suffer wrong with patience and faithfulness. Kent Hughes describes him standing before his enemies "in regal silence, dripping spittle and blood."[4] Never for one moment did he give in to a victim mentality or the temptation to get revenge. When we are ill-treated, we often ask "Why me?" Or else we want to strike back in anger at the people who are persecuting us. But Jesus patiently endured. "He had undertaken to purchase our redemption by His own humiliation," wrote J. C. Ryle, "and He did not flinch from paying the uttermost farthing of the price."[5]

## JESUS THE CHRIST

It would be an injustice for any innocent man to suffer the abuse that Jesus suffered during the long night before he was crucified. But what this man suffered was an infinite injustice because of who he was. Luke tells us that the men abusing Jesus were "blaspheming him." Luke's word choice here *(blasphēmountes)* is significant because blasphemy is a very particular kind of slander. To blaspheme is to speak against God. As we shall see, blasphemy is the very accusation that the Jewish council later made against Jesus. But by using the word "blasphemy" to describe what these men were doing to Jesus, Luke points us towards his true identity. Who is for God in this situation, and who is really against him? Who is the real blasphemer? Is it Jesus, or the person who opposes Jesus? That is the fundamental question.

In the trial that follows, we see three titles that are used either by or about Jesus. These three titles—Christ, Son of Man, and Son of God—help us to know the true identity of Jesus. Luke has been trying to help us see this throughout his Gospel. He wants us to know who Jesus is, and in knowing Jesus, to know for sure that we have salvation. As we draw closer to the crucifixion, Luke slows down the story to make sure we see who Jesus really is. Jesus would not be killed before making his identity clear.

The first title used for Jesus is *Christ*. The members of the council said to him, "If you are the Christ, tell us" (Luke 22:67). "Christ" is not the last

4. R. Kent Hughes, *Luke: That You May Know the Truth*, 2 vols., Preaching the Word (Wheaton, IL: Crossway, 1998), 2:355.

5. J. C. Ryle, *Expository Thoughts on the Gospels, Luke* (1858; reprint Cambridge: James Clarke, 1976), 2:442.

name of Jesus, but the formal title for a sacred office. It is another word for "Messiah," which simply means "the Anointed One." The Messiah or the Christ is the Savior that God always promised to send.

The title of Christ has kingly overtones, which explains why the council asked this question. Later, when these men brought Jesus before Pilate, they claimed that Jesus had identified himself as "Christ, a king" (Luke 23:2). Everyone knew that the Christ would come from the royal house of David. Many people in Israel thought of this kingship primarily in political terms; they were looking for a Savior to overthrow the Roman Empire. If the council could get Jesus to admit that he was the Messiah, they could claim that Jesus wanted to overthrow the government, and this, in turn, would get him in trouble with Pontius Pilate, the Roman governor. So their question seems to have a malevolent motivation. They are less interested in the ancient promises of God than they are in getting Jesus to claim a kingship that might get him condemned—exactly the kind of situation that the Fifth Amendment to the United States Constitution is supposed to guard against.

The religious leaders tried to get Jesus to incriminate himself by claiming not to know whether he was the Christ. "If you are the Christ," they said. *If* you are the Christ?!? Of course Jesus is the Christ! Luke has been showing us this all the way through his Gospel. Way back at the beginning, when the birth of Jesus was first announced to Mary, the angel Gabriel said, "the Lord God will give to him the throne of his father David" (Luke 1:32). In other words, Jesus would be Israel's anointed king—the Messiah. The Christmas angel said as much to the shepherds out in the fields: "For unto you is born this day in the city of David a Savior, who is Christ the Lord" (Luke 2:11). Later Luke tells us that when the baby Jesus was taken to the temple, a man named Simeon saw "the Lord's Christ" (Luke 2:25–26). Then there is the famous confession of Peter, who declared Jesus to be "the Christ of God" (Luke 9:20). There are no "ifs" about it: Jesus is the Christ.

Nevertheless, the members of the council put the question to Jesus: "If you are the Christ, tell us." If their question had been sincere, Jesus surely would have answered it. Instead, he responded by saying, "If I tell you, you will not believe, and if I ask you, you will not answer" (Luke 22:67–68).

The first part of this answer is easy enough to understand. Jesus knew that even if he told these men that he was the Christ, they would not believe him. He had already performed many wonders for them—the miraculous signs of the Messiah. If they did not believe his works, why would they believe his words? The problem was not that they did not have enough evidence. That is never the problem. God has revealed his wisdom, power, and beauty in everything from the littlest snowflake to the farthest nebula, and the glory of Jesus is revealed on every page of the Gospel. Even Richard Dawkins would get over his atheist delusion if he would only see what is really there. The problem for someone who does not believe that Jesus is the Christ is never a lack of evidence, but always a refusal to accept the evidence given. So Jesus said, "If I tell you, you will not believe" (Luke 22:67).

What may be harder to understand is what he said next: "and if I ask you, you will not answer" (Luke 22:68). What was Jesus thinking about asking these men? Probably the most important question in the world: Do you believe that I am the Christ? Here are some ways to paraphrase what Jesus said: "If I advance any arguments to prove that I am the Messiah," or "If I enquire of you what kind of Messiah is promised in Scripture, and ask you whether the signs of Messiah appear sufficiently in me, you will not give me an honest answer."[6] Here is the question: Is Jesus the Savior whom God promised to send, or not?

Jesus was right: these men never would have given him an honest answer. In fact, they were already in the bad habit of *not* answering him when he asked them a fair question. This happened when Jesus asked them about the baptism of John (Luke 20:4–7), and again when he asked them about David's son and David's Lord (Luke 20:41–44). They would not have answered him this time either. Their minds were already made up. They had decided to take his life, whether he said that he was the Messiah or not.

What answer would you give? As you read the Gospel, Jesus is asking if you believe that he is Christ. Believe the promise of the Christmas angels. Accept the testimony of Peter's confession. Trust the words of the man who was betrayed by Judas, tried by the Sanhedrin, condemned by Pilate, and crucified at Calvary. Believe that Jesus is the Savior whom God promised to send.

## JESUS THE SON OF MAN

There is still more to know about this man. Although Jesus would not tell his tormentors whether he was the Christ, he did tell them one of his

---

6. See Ryle, *Luke*, 2:446.

other titles. "But from now on," he said, "the Son of Man shall be seated at the right hand of the power of God" (Luke 22:69). Jesus the Christ is also *the Son of Man*.

This was far and away Jesus' favorite title for himself. He uses it dozens of times in the Gospels, more frequently than any other expression. To give just one example, when he prophesied his crucifixion and resurrection, he said, "The Son of Man must suffer many things and be rejected by the elders and chief priests and scribes, and be killed, and on the third day be raised" (Luke 9:22). Now Jesus was telling the very men who rejected him that he was, in fact, the Son of Man.

There is a sense in which any person is a "son of man"—the offspring of humanity. However, this title has a special meaning that comes from the Old Testament, where the prophet Daniel saw a vision of the Son of Man coming in heavenly glory and divine judgment:

> I saw in the night visions, and behold, with the clouds of heaven there came one like a son of man, and he came to the Ancient of Days and was presented before him. And to him was given dominion and glory and a kingdom, that all peoples, nations, and languages should serve him; his dominion is an everlasting dominion, which shall not pass away, and his kingdom one that shall not be destroyed. (Dan. 7:13–14)

Although the Son of Man in Daniel's vision is associated with humanity, his glory comes from his deity. For when the prophet saw this "Son of Man," he saw a being of mighty power and awesome splendor, with God-like dominion over the nations. It was a vision of a divine ruler and judge—this was widely recognized by scholars of the Scriptures. At his trial before the Jewish high council, Jesus the Christ claimed that glory for himself. He took the title of the Son of Man, with all its divine connotations, and declared that it belonged to him. It was a term of humanity that pointed toward deity, and therefore it was one of the best expressions he could use to encapsulate his incarnation as the God-man.

Jesus used the title of the Son of Man the same way that Daniel used it: to prophesy the final judgment. The Son of Man will come and sit on the right hand of God, which is the place of divine power and authority. There he will exercise his rule over the universe and his judgment of the nations.

This will happen very soon. "From now on," Jesus said, implying that his elevation to glory had virtually begun. He was absolutely certain of this. Even as he went to the cross, he was totally confident that his Father would raise him from the dead, and rightly so. All of these things were about to happen. In a matter of days Jesus would rise from the grave; in a matter of weeks he would ascend into heaven; and in a matter of years he will come again in glorious judgment to rule the nations.

These prophecies will all come true. The Scripture says that "after making purification for sins," Jesus "sat down at the right hand of the Majesty on high" (Heb. 1:3). It says further that the Son of Man will come again "with power and great glory" (Luke 21:27), and that when he does, he will "judge the living and the dead" (1 Peter 4:5). Jesus will even judge the men who once sat in judgment over him. This makes what he said about the Son of Man highly ironic. At the very time Jesus was being judged, he was also claiming the right to judge!

The time will come, therefore, when everyone who judges Jesus will be judged by him. We do not judge God; he judges us. Many people get this backwards. As they start to investigate religion, they assume that the real question is what they think about Jesus, rather than what Jesus thinks about them. We see this attitude in the explanation one youth leader gave as to why he could not accept orthodox Christian teaching about the sovereignty of God, or his wrath against sin, or the necessity of confessing Jesus Christ as Savior and Lord in order to avoid eternal judgment. "I refuse to believe any of that," he said:

> If those things are true, then God might as well send me to Hell. For better or worse, I simply am not interested in any God but a completely good, entirely loving, and perfectly forgiving One. . . . Such a God may not exist, but I will die seeking such a God, and I will pledge my allegiance to no other possibility because, quite frankly, anything less is not worthy of my worship. Please, don't get me wrong. I am well aware that I don't get to decide who God is. What I do get to decide, however, is to whom I pledge my allegiance. I am a free agent, after all, and I have standards for my God, the first of which is this: I will not worship any God who is not at least as compassionate as I am.[7]

7. Bart Campolo, "The Limits of God's Grace," *The Journal of Student Ministries* (Nov. 15, 2006): 1–4.

What is shocking in these statements is not simply the rejection of cardinal doctrines of the Christian faith, but also the idea that God is the one who has to meet *our* standards. This is the proud posture of our fallen nature: we demand the right to sit in judgment over God. But Jesus claims to be the Son of Man, and if he is the Son of Man, then one day he will sit in judgment over us. Get ready for the day of that judgment. Accept God's perspective on your sin and his way of salvation. Entrust your body and your soul to Jesus, the Son of Man, who is also the Christ.

## JESUS THE SON OF GOD

The religious leaders who conducted this trial understood exactly what Jesus was saying. They knew their Old Testaments, including the prophecies of Daniel. So when Jesus started talking about the Son of Man, they instantly recognized that he was claiming divine power. But to make sure he had said what they thought he had said, they double-checked by asking him, "Are you the Son of God, then?" (Luke 22:70).

There are still some people—including some Bible scholars—who deny that Jesus ever claimed to be God at all. Yet the religious leaders who got Jesus killed knew that this is exactly what he claimed. Indeed, this is one of the reasons they were so angry with him. They were quite sure that he could not be God, and therefore that any claim he made of deity had to be blasphemy, which in those days was a capital offense under Jewish law. Did Jesus really mean what they thought he meant—that he was the divine Son of Man? If so, he deserved to die. So they asked him again if he was the Son of God.

For anyone who has studied Luke, this question is easy to answer. Is Jesus the Son of God? Yes, he is *the Son of God*! Way back at the beginning, when Gabriel first announced his birth to the virgin Mary, the angel said that Jesus would be called "the Son of the Most High" (Luke 1:32). This was confirmed in his baptism, when heaven was opened and the Father said: "You are my beloved Son" (Luke 3:22). It was confirmed again on the mount of transfiguration, when the Father said, "This is my Son" (Luke 9:35). Jesus the Christ is the Son of God as well as the Son of Man.

Jesus declared this at his trial by saying, "You say that I am" (Luke 22:70). This was not an evasion, as it may seem, but an affirmation. To say "You say that I am" was to use a manner of speech that gave assent without necessarily indicating total agreement. It was a way of saying something like this: "I am, as you say, the Son of God."[8] Leon Morris offers the following paraphrase: "I would not put it like that, but since you have, I cannot deny it."[9]

Jesus had a much fuller understanding than anyone else of what it meant for him to be the Son of God. His definition was different from theirs, and therefore he could not agree to their statement without qualification. Is Jesus the Son of God? He is the supreme, unique, divine, and eternal Son of the Father in a way his enemies would never understand. They did not believe that he is the one and only Son of God given for the salvation of sinners. Nevertheless, he could hardly deny the truth of what they were saying. Jesus is the Son of God, and he will be the Son of God, and he has been the Son of God from all eternity. So he said, "You say that I am."

For all practical purposes this was the end of the trial, because when the scribes and priests heard Jesus claim to be the Son of God, they immediately said, "What further testimony do we need? We have heard it ourselves from his own lips" (Luke 22:71). These words were spoken in condemnation by men who had been up all night trying to find a charge against Jesus that would stick in a court of law. Finally they had managed to get him to incriminate himself, for by claiming to be the Son of God, he had spoken blasphemy, or so they thought.

If only these men had answered their own question a different way, they could have been saved. Consider carefully what they said, because when Luke put their words into his Gospel, he was hoping we would catch their irony. Indeed, he was hoping that we would answer this question the right way instead of the wrong way: "What further testimony do we need? We have heard it ourselves from his own lips" (Luke 22:71).

Well, what further testimony *do* we need? We have heard the words of Jesus himself. He claims to be the Savior whom God always promised to send, the divine Judge who will come in glory at the final judgment, the one and only Son of the everlasting Father. With his own lips, Jesus the Christ says that he is both Son of Man and Son of God. What further testimony does anyone need? Believe the testimony he has given, and you will find salvation in the Son of God and the Son of Man, Jesus the Christ.

8. Ryle, *Luke*, 2:444.

9. Leon Morris, *The Gospel According to St. Luke: An Introduction and Commentary*, Tyndale New Testament Commentaries (Grand Rapids: Eerdmans, 1974), 318.

# 100

# THE KING OF THE JEWS

## *Luke 23:1–12*

*And Pilate asked him, "Are you the King of the Jews?" And he answered him, "You have said so." (Luke 23:3)*

uke was careful to place the birth and death of Jesus in their historical context. He wanted his readers to be sure of their salvation, which includes knowing when these things took place. So Luke opens his Gospel by saying, "In the days of Herod, king of Judea" (Luke 1:5). Similarly, his stately account of the first Christmas tells us about a decree that went out from Caesar Augustus, specifically "the first registration when Quirinius was governor of Syria" (Luke 2:2).

The politicians come back with a vengeance at the end of Luke's Gospel, when Jesus appears before Pilate the governor and Herod the tetrarch. This historical fact is highlighted in a famous phrase from the Apostles' Creed: "he suffered under Pontius Pilate." These words remind us that what Jesus endured on his way to the cross is something that really happened.

Skeptics sometimes say that the stories in the Gospels are only make-believe: Jesus never died on the cross, and he certainly never rose from the dead. In fact, some historians used to doubt whether Pontius Pilate ever existed. The only evidence for him was in the Bible, which they would not accept as credible history. Then in 1961 a team of Italian archaeologists discovered the following inscription at Herod's amphitheater in Caesarea: "Pontius Pilate, prefect of Judea, has dedicated to the people of Caesarea a temple in honor of Tiberius."[1] Not only was Pilate a real person, but he was also famous enough to have his name inscribed on a public monument!

## THREE ROMAN TRIALS

Jesus is just as real. In fact, archaeologists have since uncovered the very pavement where he stood the morning of his trial before Pilate. By this point Jesus had already been tried by the Jews, and condemned. Following a couple of contentious pretrial hearings that took place under the cover of night, Jesus appeared before the council of the Sanhedrin at daybreak. Once they were convinced that he had committed the blasphemy of claiming to be the Son of God, they were determined to put him to death (see Mark 14:64). However, the Jews were then under Roman occupation, so they did not have the right to execute a death penalty.

To put Jesus to death, they would need the help of the local Roman authority, a governor by the name of Pontius Pilate. So "the whole company of them arose and brought him before Pilate" (Luke 23:1). This in itself was remarkable. The Sanhedrin was so sharply divided between the Pharisees and the Sadducees that they almost never did anything together. Yet they were so united in their hatred of Jesus that as one man they rose up in a murderous rage and dragged him before the one judge who could put him to death. All they wanted was for someone to ratify the verdict they had already reached, but things would not be so simple. For now began what Kent Hughes has called "the most infamous trial in history, a weird, twisted thing that began before Pilate, the careerist Roman politician, then detoured to the tetrarch Herod, the half-Jew puppet ruler, and finally returned to Pilate where the awful judgment was rendered."[2]

---

1. Quoted in John McRay, *Archaeology and the New Testament* (Grand Rapids: Baker, 1991), 145.

2. R. Kent Hughes, *Luke: That You May Know the Truth*, 2 vols., Preaching the Word (Wheaton, IL: Crossway, 1998), 2:360.

The first complication was that whereas the Jews had tried and convicted Jesus for blasphemy, the Romans did not consider blasphemy a crime at all. Thus they tried to tell Pilate that Jesus was some kind of political subversive, virtually a terrorist. The governor was not persuaded. Yet the council said two things that piqued his interest. One was that Jesus was a king—a claim made in verse 2 and then discussed in verse 3. The other was that Jesus came from Galilee: "When Pilate heard this, he asked whether the man was a Galilean. And when he learned that he belonged to Herod's jurisdiction, he sent him over to Herod, who was himself in Jerusalem at that time" (Luke 23:6–7).

Anyone who has ever tried to get help from any government anywhere in the world will recognize this strategy immediately. Pilate was giving these men the runaround. Give him the slightest chance, and he would avoid taking responsibility by sending people off to see someone else. First he told the Sanhedrin that they needed to deal with Jesus themselves. According to the Gospel of John, "Pilate said to them, 'Take him yourselves and judge him by your own law.'" This would not work, however, because the Jewish leaders wanted Jesus dead, and they could not execute the death penalty. "It is not lawful for us to put anyone to death," they said (John 18:31).

But maybe there was some other way for Pilate to get this case out of his in-box, and when he heard that Jesus was from Galilee, he seized his chance. Under Roman law, a person could either be tried in the place where he was accused or in the province where he came from. Jesus was from Galilee, and it just so happened that the ruler of Galilee was in Jerusalem for Passover. The Galilean ruler was Herod Antipas, the son of Herod the Great, who had been the king when Jesus was born. Antipas was only a tetrarch, but the territory of his jurisdiction included Galilee. So off Jesus went to yet another trial—one Pilate probably hoped would end in death.

Surprisingly Herod was happy to see Jesus coming: "When Herod saw Jesus, he was very glad, for he had long desired to see him, because he had heard about him, and he was hoping to see some sign done by him" (Luke 23:8). Jesus was famous for doing miracles, especially in Galilee. Now, finally, Herod had a chance to see for himself what Jesus could do.

The king was as curious as he was cruel. We know the man's cruelty from his brutal beheading of John the Baptist at the stag party for his birthday (see Matt. 14:1–12), and later from his murder of the apostle James (see

Acts 12:2). Yet we also know that he had at least some interest in spiritual things, even if it was only an idle curiosity. Herod was married to Herodias, the wife of his brother Philip. When John preached against this adulterous match, Herodias insisted on having him thrown into prison. But Herod loved to hear the Baptist preach. As Mark tells us, "Herod feared John, knowing that he was a righteous and holy man, and he kept him safe. When he heard him, he was greatly perplexed, and yet he heard him gladly" (Mark 6:20). Here was a man who heard the gospel and almost wanted to believe it, but never actually did. In fact, this may have been what made him so dangerous: he had dabbled in religion without ever committing his life to Christ, which made him even more resistant to the gospel in the end.

We also sense that Herod sometimes suffered from a troubled conscience. When he started hearing people talk about Jesus, Herod thought he was the ghost of John the Baptist (see Mark 6:16). Why would he make this supposition? Almost certainly because his conscience cried out against him for putting a holy man to death.

Now Herod finally had the opportunity to meet Jesus for himself. Hoping to see some kind of miracle, he wanted to be entertained. So when Jesus refused to perform any tricks, Herod used him for sport. One way or another, he would have his fun. If Jesus would not dazzle him with signs and wonders, then for the sake of his own cruel laughter, Herod would expose him to rude mockery. This is the same attitude many people have today. They want God to entertain them, and they will mock him if he fails to give them the pleasures they want out of life.

Although Herod held Jesus in contempt, he never found him guilty. Surely if he thought that Jesus had committed any crime, Herod (of all people) would not hesitate to have him put to death. Instead, he sent him back to Pontius Pilate: "And Herod and Pilate became friends with each other that very day, for before this they had been at enmity with each other" (Luke 23:12). Here was an unholy alliance. Rather than believing in Jesus and getting reconciled to God, these men were reconciled to one another by mistreating Jesus. Here was a perverse friendship, based on the one thing that unbelievers can always agree on: that they will not put their faith in Jesus Christ. Here too was the fulfillment of an ancient prophecy: "The kings of the earth set themselves, and the rulers take counsel together, against the LORD and against his anointed" (Ps. 2:2).

## THE CLAIM OF KINGSHIP

So, at length, the problem prisoner ended up back before Pontius Pilate. The governor had tried to get rid of Jesus by sending him off to Herod, but now Herod had returned the compliment, so to speak. In effect he was saying, "I don't want to deal with Jesus; you deal with him!"

Jesus is like that: if you try to push him out of your life, hoping you will not have to make a firm decision about him, he keeps coming back. You cannot simply decide to do nothing with Jesus. He claims to be the Son of God and the Savior of the world. If he is, then we should worship him. If he is not, then he is either a liar or a lunatic and we should have nothing to do with him. But the one thing we cannot do is simply leave Jesus alone. If the Bible is right that believing in Jesus is the difference between living forever in heaven and suffering forever in hell, then what we do with him is the most important decision we will ever make. This is why Jesus keeps coming back: he wants us to make the right decision about him.

Here Luke helps us to make that decision by telling us two important truths about Jesus. In his record of the Jewish trial, Luke showed us that Jesus is the Christ, the Son of Man, and the Son of God. Here, in his record of the Roman trial, Luke brings further clarity to the person of Jesus by making a claim of kingship and a claim of innocence: Jesus is both the true King of God's people and a perfectly innocent man.

The subject of kingship was first introduced by the religious leaders who were trying to get Jesus crucified. They accused Jesus of "saying that he himself is Christ, a king" (Luke 23:2). Remember that "Christ" (or "Messiah") is a royal title, signifying kingship. The leaders of the Jews did not believe that Jesus really was the Christ, nor had he admitted that he was the Christ under their interrogation (see Luke 22:67). Yet making this claim was their best chance of getting Jesus into trouble with the law.

The issue here is political subversion. Governments always have a vested interest in defending their right to govern, so if there was one thing Pontius Pilate could not and would not tolerate, it was someone claiming sovereign authority over his territory. Most of the accusations against Jesus were religious, which was of little or no concern to Pilate, who was a politician after all. Yet kingship was a political issue; so he put the question to Jesus: "Are you the King of the Jews?" (Luke 23:3).

Once again, Jesus was faced with a question that was hard to answer. On the one hand, he was not at all the kind of king that Pilate had in mind. He was not seeking the political power to rule a people group or control a geographic territory. If his kingdom had been of this world, he would have been leading an army of soldiers, which he obviously was not (see John 18:36). Pilate did not need to worry: Jesus was not trying to overthrow the Romans—at least not yet.

Nevertheless, even if Jesus did not agree with Pilate's definition of a king, he could not deny that he was Israel's true and rightful king. So he gave the governor this answer: "You have said so" (Luke 23:3). This is similar to what Jesus said when the Sanhedrin asked if he was the Son of God (Luke 22:70). It was an almost reluctant affirmation. Without fully endorsing what Pilate meant, he testified that he was, as the governor said, the King of the Jews.

Later the apostle Paul would say that "in his testimony before Pontius Pilate," Jesus made "the good confession" (1 Tim. 6:13). This was part of his good confession: testifying to his royal kingship. From ancient times, the Jews were God's precious and chosen people. God had promised to give them a king from the house and line of David, a king who would rule forever over Israel and the nations. Jesus was the man born to be that king. This is one of the reasons Luke took the trouble to give us his genealogy back in chapter 3: he wanted to show that Jesus Christ is the son of David. This also explains why wise men from the east brought treasure and spices to Bethlehem. As they said to Herod himself, they were looking for the baby who was "born king of the Jews" (Matt. 2:2). Jesus knew his lineage. So when Pilate asked if he was the King of the Jews, Jesus had to confess that he was.

Some people mocked this claim. Instead of bowing down to swear allegiance, they treated his kingship with royal contempt. We certainly see this in the response of the Romans at the trial before Herod. What happened when Jesus refused to answer the tetrarch's insolent questions, or to put on the show he was hoping to see? Luke tells us that "Herod with his soldiers treated him with contempt and mocked him. Then, arraying him in splendid clothing, he sent him back to Pilate" (Luke 23:11).

Presumably the robes they put on Jesus came from somewhere in Herod's closet—the hand-me-down splendor of a tyrant's wardrobe. Then, once they had dressed him in these clothes, they proceeded to make a royal mockery of his kingly majesty. This was a cruel irony. Jesus should be adored, not abused. He should be treated with reverence, not contempt. Yet just as the temple guards had mocked him earlier as prophet, so now the Roman soldiers mocked him as king.

Many people still mock Jesus today. If they talk about him at all, it is only to use his name as a swear word, to make fun of his followers, or to make jokes about the stories in the Gospels, speaking blasphemy. But these are not the only ways to make a mockery of Jesus. Herod's real sin was that he did not take Jesus seriously, and we are tempted not to take him seriously either. If Jesus really is the King, then anything less than willing obedience and open worship is unworthy of his honor. But sometimes we go an entire day, or a week, or even longer without contemplating his kingly majesty, or going to his throne in prayer, or listening to the royal decrees that are written in his Word.

Kings are not to be ignored; they are to be honored and obeyed. If Jesus truly is our King, then we will show his gentleness in our homes, his patience in our trials, his diligence in our work, his faithfulness in our friendships, and his forgiveness for the people it is hard for us to love. Are you living for the King, or are you mocking him by living as if it hardly matters whether he is the King or not? The claim of kingship is not just a claim that Jesus makes about himself, but a claim that he makes on us.

## THE CLAIM OF INNOCENCE

The second claim Luke makes about Jesus is that he is innocent of all charges. This is important to know because of the manner in which Jesus died. If we knew only that Jesus was crucified, we might get the impression that he was some kind of criminal, when in fact the royal King is also the perfect man. The trial demonstrates this repeatedly by clearing Jesus from accusation after accusation against him.

In his Jewish trial, the accusations against Jesus were primarily religious: in some blasphemous way he had claimed, falsely, to be the Son of God. The accusations in his Roman trial were political. As soon as Pilate gave them a chance to speak, the religious leaders began to accuse Jesus, saying, "We found this man misleading our nation and forbidding us to give tribute to Caesar, and saying that he himself is Christ, a king" (Luke 23:2).

These accusations really amounted to a charge of treason. To mislead the nation was to incite rebellion by starting a revolution. To forbid the giving of tribute was to refuse to pay taxes as an act of civil disobedience. To claim to be a king was to seek the overthrow of Roman rule. No government could ever tolerate this kind of rebellion. Even after Pilate rendered his initial verdict, declaring Jesus not guilty, the religious leaders kept up their attack. In fact, they made their case against him even more intensely than before, applying more pressure on Pilate to get him to do what they wanted: "they were urgent, saying, 'He stirs up the people, teaching throughout all Judea, from Galilee even to this place'" (Luke 23:5). The religious leaders would not let up, but made similar accusations when they went before Herod: "The chief priests and the scribes stood by, vehemently accusing him" (Luke 23:10). These men were relentless in their insistence that as a political revolutionary, Jesus would have to die.

None of these charges seemed very plausible. Since when had Jewish leaders ever been concerned about defending the Roman Empire? That was Pilate's problem, not theirs. As we learn from the other Gospels, Pilate rightly suspected that they were saying this only because they hated Jesus (see Matt. 27:18; Mark 15:10). Nor did it seem very likely that Jesus was a political subversive. Hence Pilate's question in verse 3: "Are you the King of the Jews?" The governor could scarcely believe that this was true. As Leon Morris comments, "What the Jews had said had prepared him to meet a resistance fighter, but one glance at Jesus was enough to show the utter absurdity of such an idea and it wrenched this incredulous question from his lips."[3]

It did not take Pilate long to determine that Jesus could hardly be guilty of any capital crime. Soon he pronounced his verdict to the chief priests and the crowds that by now had gathered: "I find no guilt in this man" (Luke 23:4). Luke does not give us all the details of this trial. He leaves out most of the give and take. But he makes sure we hear the verdict because this is the most important moment in this trial: when Pilate declares Jesus innocent of all charges. Luke wants us to hear this because it helps us to see the whole passion narrative for what it really is: the unjust execution of a perfectly innocent man.

3. Leon Morris, *The Gospel According to St. Luke: An Introduction and Commentary*, Tyndale New Testament Commentaries (Grand Rapids: Eerdmans, 1974), 320.

All of the accusations against Jesus were false. His enemies accused him of misleading the nation. On the contrary, he was leading the nation into the way of truth and life. They said he told people not to pay tribute to Caesar. This was an out-and-out lie, for Jesus had said almost exactly the opposite: people should "render unto Caesar the things that are Caesar's" (Luke 20:25). They accused Jesus of claiming to be the Christ. He *was* the Christ, of course, but in his trial before the Sanhedrin earlier that morning he had refused to say this because they did not understand what kind of king he would be (Luke 22:67). They accused him of stirring people up all over Israel. In a way this was true, but far from stirring up a rebellion, Jesus was actually trying to stir people up to salvation.

So Jesus was innocent of all these charges. Indeed, he was innocent of any charge that anyone could bring against him. He was and is the only perfectly innocent man who ever lived. This was so obvious that even Pontius Pilate managed to recognize it and reach the right verdict, at which point the case should have been closed. Once the judge declares that the accused is not guilty, the trial is over and the prisoner is released immediately—this is the way the legal system is supposed to work. As Michael Wilcock says, "The famous Roman justice system should therefore have dismissed the charges against him, and stopped the whole ghastly affair."[4] But the whole ghastly affair did not stop there. It kept right on going until the King of the Jews was dying, bleeding on the cross in naked innocence.

## HE MADE NO ANSWER

How did Jesus respond to all of this injustice? He mainly responded by not responding. Whenever someone asked him to confess his true identity, he testified that he was the Son of God, or the King of the Jews, or whatever proper title they wanted to give him. But Jesus did not speak one word in his own defense, and to Herod he said nothing at all. Luke tells us that when that wicked king "questioned him at some length," Jesus "made no answer" (Luke 23:9).

Why did Jesus refuse to say anything to defend himself? It may have been because there was nothing else to say. Herod had already had his chance to

4. Michael Wilcock, *The Message of Luke*, The Bible Speaks Today (Downers Grove, IL: Inter-Varsity, 1979), 194.

hear the gospel, but by now he had hardened his heart. By the time that the man closed his conscience and refused to repent, there was nothing left for Jesus or anyone else to say to him. This is a warning to anyone who rejects the free gift of God's grace: eventually the day will come when he will have no more gospel to give you.

Maybe Jesus refused to say anything because he knew that no one would believe him anyway. He said as much to the Sanhedrin earlier that very morning: "If I tell you, you will not believe" (Luke 22:67). What is the point in making a defense when people have already made up their minds?

Maybe Jesus refused to say anything because he was entrusting his cause to the Lord. He knew there was no need to defend himself because his Father would vindicate him at the right time by raising him from the dead. His very refusal to argue his own case was in fact another proof of his perfect innocence. Jesus was heeding the counsel of his father David: "Commit your way to the LORD; trust in him, and he will act. He will bring forth your righteousness as the light, and your justice as the noonday. Be still before the LORD and wait patiently for him; fret not yourself over the one who prospers in his way, over the man who carries out evil devices!" (Ps. 37:5–7).

These were all good reasons for Jesus not to speak in his own defense. His example reminds us not to be so quick to defend ourselves when we are attacked unjustly, but instead to wait patiently for the Lord to defend us. Remember the example Jesus set: "He committed no sin, neither was deceit found in his mouth. When he was reviled, he did not revile in return; when he suffered, he did not threaten, but continued entrusting himself to him who judges justly" (1 Peter 2:22–23).

There is one further reason Jesus refused to speak in his own defense—a reason that goes beyond anything we could ever do. Suffering in silence was part of the work that Jesus was called to do for our salvation. It was the fulfillment of an ancient prophecy, for in his song of the Suffering Servant, the prophet Isaiah made the following promise: "He was oppressed, and he was afflicted, yet he opened not his mouth" (Isa. 53:7). Jesus fulfilled this prophecy by refusing to protest his own innocence, or to strike back at his accusers.

The image Isaiah used to convey the spotless innocence of the afflicted Savior was the pure image of a sacrificial lamb: "Like a lamb that is led to the slaughter, and like a sheep that before its shearers is silent, so he opened not his mouth" (Isa. 53:7). In his quiet submission to the torments of his oppressors, Jesus fulfilled this prophecy and thereby proved that he was the Savior whom God had promised to send.

One missionary to India thought of this prophecy when he witnessed animal sacrifices at a Hindu temple. In one of his letters he described how various animals were dragged to the altar, surrounded by priests, and beheaded with a single blow from a heavy iron knife. Then he saw a little white lamb presented for sacrifice:

> As I watched everything unfolding from my perch atop a large boulder beside the temple, I directed my attention for some time to this poor little lamb and thought I'd never seen anything that looked so pure, so innocent, and so gentle. . . . What made it all the more profound and relevant was the particularly nasty treatment of this same creature. . . . And that's what really got me. It was SO like how it indeed was with our Lord. The MOST pure, and innocent, and gentle, enduring the MOST terrible misuse and mistreatment and death—pushed about, surrounded, roughly handled, and frightfully killed. . . . They hacked its head off and threw its lifeless body on the bloody ground. My God! Is this not powerful? From this can we not grasp even a little of what He undertook—the horrible, frightful anguish He endured Himself for our sakes?[5]

Never forget that the King of the Jews suffered all this in silent majesty, without protest, so that he could do the perfect work of our salvation. Never lose hope that Jesus did this so he would have something to say when we ourselves are put on trial. One day we will all appear before God for judgment. If we have nothing to say then, it will not be because of our perfect innocence, but because there is nothing we can really say in defense of our sinful selves. But *Jesus* will have something to say! Though silent in his own defense, he will not be silent in the defense of anyone who trusts in him. Jesus has promised that one day he will openly acknowledge everyone who openly acknowledges him (Luke 12:8).

Through faith in Christ, when you at last appear before the throne of God, justly accused of all your sin, Jesus will plead the merits of his own royal and innocent righteousness. Having suffered for your sins all the way to the cross, he will speak up and tell his Father not to give you the verdict that you deserve, but the verdict that *he* deserves.

5. Steve Ringeisen, in an e-mail report to Philadelphia's Tenth Presbyterian Church on October 31, 2006.

# 101

# CRUCIFY HIM!

## *Luke 23:13—25*

*Pilate addressed them once more, desiring to release Jesus, but they kept shouting, "Crucify, crucify him!"* (Luke 23:20–21)

ontius Pilate had a serious problem: What was he going to do with Jesus? Jesus had already appeared before the Roman governor once that morning for judgment. After hearing the accusations against him, and after interrogating the prisoner for himself, Pilate declared his judicial verdict: Jesus was not guilty. The problem was that some people still wanted Jesus dead, and thus they would not accept his legal decision. So what was Pilate going to do with this innocent man?

By this point the governor had already made several attempts to resolve his dilemma. First he had tried to say that this was a matter for the local religious leaders to settle in their own courts. But the Jewish leaders had determined that Jesus should die, and only the Romans had the power of the sword. So they brought the case back to Pilate. Next the governor declared that Jesus was innocent, which should have ended the trial. But this was not the verdict that the man's enemies wanted to hear, so they kept calling for his execution. Then Pilate picked up on the fact that Jesus was from Galilee, which meant that he was also under someone else's jurisdiction. So he sent the prisoner off to Herod. But the next thing Pilate knew, Jesus was back, and the problem still was not solved.

As we see Pilate struggle with this dilemma, we are confronted with nearly the same question that confronted him: What will we do with Jesus? As we see Jesus go through these trials in Luke's Gospel, we need to reach a verdict about him in our own minds and hearts. Will we declare his saving innocence or will we try to push him away, as Pilate did? Then there is perhaps the most important question of all: Will we consent to his crucifixion?

## Pilate's Problem

When Jesus appeared before him for the second time, Pilate still had not come up with a solution to his problem. The prisoner was back in his custody, and the crowd of protesters outside his palace was continuing to grow. In desperation, Pilate summarized his findings in the case and suggested a cruel compromise:

> Pilate then called together the chief priests and the rulers and the people, and said to them, "You brought me this man as one who was misleading the people. And after examining him before you, behold, I did not find this man guilty of any of your charges against him. Neither did Herod, for he sent him back to us. Look, nothing deserving death has been done by him. I will therefore punish and release him." (Luke 23:13–16)

This is the first time that "the people" are mentioned, although they will have a crucial role to play before this drama is over. Maybe Pilate was hoping that ordinary people would at least listen to reason; so he invited them to come in and witness the proceedings. As he rehearsed the facts of the case, the governor made yet another public declaration that Jesus was innocent of any and all charges. This was not simply Pilate's personal opinion; it was also the verdict that Herod reached. These two men had almost never agreed about anything, but they agreed about this: Jesus was innocent. He certainly had not done anything to deserve the death penalty. Luke made sure to write this verdict in his Gospel so we would know for sure that Jesus Christ is the Righteous One—the perfectly spotless Lamb of God (see 1 Peter 1:19).

The problem for Pilate was that the enemies of Jesus would never accept this verdict, even though it was the right one. So the governor, who was the most pragmatic of politicians, grasped at a compromise: he would have Jesus punished and then released. This was not unheard of. The Romans sometimes gave their prisoners a good beating before letting them go. This punishment was not as violent as the scourging a man received before being crucified, but it was intended to serve as a painful warning.[1]

Under the circumstances, even a light beating would have been an outrage against every fair principle of justice. No one who loves what is right would ever think of hurting an innocent man. But Pilate loved his own convenience more than doing what his conscience knew was right, so he foolishly tried to bargain with these bloodthirsty men. "Just let me beat Jesus up," he said, "and then let us all agree to leave it at that." Yet even this did not appease the enemies of Jesus. Pilate probably thought he was doing everything he could do to save this prisoner. He seemed to be the only advocate Jesus had! But the angry mob could smell his weakness. The governor seemed as if he might perhaps give in to political pressure, and with every compromise they sensed that they were closer to getting what they really wanted.

Every time Pontius Pilate suggested another way to solve his problem, the crowd shouted him down. It was customary for the governor to release a prisoner at Passover (see Mark 15:6)—a symbol, perhaps, of the exodus from Egypt, when the people of God were released from bondage. Pilate would free whichever prisoner the people demanded. This time he hoped that they would ask for Jesus, and then his problem would be solved. But the people would have none of it. Given the opportunity to reach their own verdict, they did not accept Jesus, but asked for someone else entirely: "But they all cried out together, 'Away with this man, and release to us Barabbas'" (Luke 23:18).

The people who said this were guilty of base hypocrisy, because Barabbas truly was guilty of the very accusations they were bringing against Jesus. David Gooding notes the irony here:

> The situation was beginning to become crazy. Here were priests demanding the execution of Jesus on the ground that he was attempting to overthrow

1. Leon Morris, *The Gospel According to St. Luke: An Introduction and Commentary,* Tyndale New Testament Commentaries (Grand Rapids: Eerdmans, 1974), 322–23.

the political authorities. Yet these very priests would not themselves bow to the political authorities; and what is more, they were calling for the release of a known political activist who in a recent civil disturbance in the city had committed murder.[2]

Once again, Pilate's pitiful strategy had failed. He was still working hard to get Jesus released, but the religious leaders and now also the crowds were refusing. So he appealed to them again: "Pilate addressed them once more, desiring to release Jesus" (Luke 23:20). Yet once more they refused, this time calling for blood. Taking up a death chant, "they kept shouting, 'Crucify, crucify him!'" (Luke 23:21). These people did not want Jesus set free; they wanted him dead. So they called for his crucifixion, which was "not only the most painful, but the most ignominious and disgraceful death, to which a person could be sentenced."[3]

Pilate's problem simply refused to go away, but even at this point the governor was not quite ready to give up. So he went back to one of his earlier arguments—a sure sign that he was running out of answers: "A third time he said to them, 'Why, what evil has he done? I have found in him no guilt deserving death. I will therefore punish and release him'" (Luke 23:22). This was now the third time that Pilate had declared the man innocent (see Luke 23:4, 14)!

Unlike everyone else in the whole situation, Jesus had never done anything evil. But the people still wanted him to die, and there is not much use in arguing with an angry mob. I learned this lesson when I went to City Hall to open the Philadelphia City Council in prayer. There had been a contract dispute, and hundreds of workers from the city unions were packed into the chambers. When the council members walked in to open the session, the angry mob was already in full throat, shouting protest slogans. The noise was deafening, and soon it became apparent that neither invocation nor legislation could take place that day. The same thing happened to Pontius Pilate: "But they were urgent, demanding with loud cries that he should be crucified. And their voices prevailed. So Pilate decided that their demand

---

2. David Gooding, *According to Luke: A New Exposition of the Third Gospel* (Grand Rapids: Eerdmans, 1987), 339.

3. J. C. Ryle, *Expository Thoughts on the Gospels, Luke* (1858; reprint Cambridge: James Clarke, 1976), 2:460.

should be granted" (Luke 23:23–24). Seeing that he was about to have a riot on his hands, the governor finally caved in and agreed to crucify Jesus.

Who was responsible for this grotesque injustice? Luke makes it clear in his sequel to this story—the book of Acts—that the people themselves were responsible. The apostle Peter said as much in the sermons he later preached to the people of Jerusalem. You "crucified and killed" Jesus, Peter said (Acts 2:23); you "delivered [him] over and denied [him] in the presence of Pilate" (Acts 3:13). But the people were not the only ones to blame. Their spiritual leaders were also responsible. Peter said this as well, for when he appeared before the Sanhedrin, he identified Jesus as the man whom they crucified (Acts 4:10) and "killed by hanging him on a tree" (Acts 5:30). It was not just the Jews, however; it was also the Romans— Herod, Pilate, and their soldiers. Michael Wilcock thus concludes: "All are guilty, not only the Jews. Frivolous Herod and feeble Pilate are guilty too, and so is treacherous Judas. And so is Peter. And so are the rest of the disciples. All are sucked into the vortex of Satan's cosmic plan for the destruction of the Son of God."[4]

As we watch Pilate get sucked into this diabolical vortex, we should remember that each one of us is responsible for what we decide to do with Jesus. Here was a man who did everything he could to get Jesus released except actually to release him.[5] Here was a man who thought he was doing what he could for Jesus, but never did the one thing that Jesus most wants from anyone, which is to believe in him. Pontius Pilate recognized that Jesus was an innocent man, yet he refused to receive him as the Savior or worship him as the King. Sadly, he never did solve his problem, but ended up doing the wrong thing with Jesus.

## OUR PROBLEM

What will we decide to do with Jesus? Will we trust him with a Christmas, Good Friday, and Easter faith? Will we believe in the manger, the cross, and the empty tomb? Or will we be like Pontius Pilate, hoping that Jesus will go away and leave us alone so that we can get on with the rest of life?

---

4. Michael Wilcock, *The Message of Luke*, The Bible Speaks Today (Downers Grove, IL: Inter-Varsity, 1979), 196.

5. G. B. Caird makes this point in *The Gospel of St. Luke* (New York: Pelican, 1963), 248.

Pilate is not alone: we all have a decision to make about Jesus. This trial poses a problem for each of us, even if it is not quite the same problem that Pilate faced. To see what the problem is, answer the following questions: What do you hope will happen at the end of this trial? What is your response as you see Jesus dragged from one hearing to the next, hear the false accusations against him, witness his testimony, and watch petty tyrants like Pilate decide what to do with him? Do you find yourself pulling for Jesus to be released or secretly hoping that he will be crucified? When the people began chanting for his crucifixion, would you have tried to quiet them down, or would you have joined them in saying, "Crucify him!"?

On the one hand, anyone on the side of justice must be for Jesus and against his evil accusers. Any impartial observer can see that this man is innocent of all charges, and therefore that he ought to be set free. This is so obvious that our souls cry out for Pilate to do the right thing and release his prisoner. Jesus should not be accused and abused; he should be honored and adored. If only we had the chance, we would plead with Pilate to find the courage of his conscience and deliver Jesus from this horrible miscarriage of justice. If we believe that what Jesus said is true—that as Christ the King he is both the Son of God and the Son of Man—then we must demand his freedom. What we want to shout at the end of this trial, therefore, is "Release him!"

On the other hand, if we really understand what Jesus is doing, we must hope that he will be condemned and crucified, for this is the only way we will ever be saved. It is Christ's death on the cross that atones for our sin and reconciles us to God. But this death came about only because Christ was first condemned in a court of law. So even though we know that he deserves to be set free, we also find ourselves hoping for our own sakes that his trial will end in crucifixion.

This desperate dilemma exposes the problem of our sin. By nature we do not have a right relationship with God, but have gone our own way. Like Peter, we have given in to public pressure and denied our Savior. Like Herod we have loved violence and wrong pleasure. Like Pilate we have followed the path of least resistance, not taking a stand for what is right, no matter what the cost. These are only a few of the many wrong things that we have done—the proud thoughts, the selfish intentions, the angry words, and all the good things we could have done for someone else but never did. We are so caught up in sin that we are on the wrong side of this trial, wishing that Jesus could be cleared of all charges, yet also needing him to be crucified. The trial of Jesus exposes us as the sinners we really are.

Many years ago at Easter I attended a dramatic presentation of the life of Christ. While his trial was unfolding on stage, members of the cast quietly slipped unnoticed into the audience. When the trial reached its climax and Pilate appealed for Jesus to be released, these actors suddenly stood up and started shouting for Jesus to be crucified. "Crucify, crucify him!" they cried. Since they were standing out in the audience, it seemed that we ourselves were part of the crowd that wanted to kill Jesus.

For a moment I almost forgot that this was a drama. My first instinct was to grab the nearest actor and make him sit down and be quiet. I had no intention of being implicated in this injustice. But upon further reflection I realized that I needed Jesus to do what he was about to do, or else be lost forever. God help me: if there is any hope for my sins to be forgiven, it is only through the cross. So I had to join the crowd, not in cruel hatred, but out of desperate necessity—not because I am for injustice, but because I need Christ to go to the cross. "Crucify him," I said in my heart. "Yes, crucify him, if he will be crucified, because I am a sinner who needs a Savior."

## Whose Will Was Done?

The saving work of Jesus is vividly demonstrated by the plea bargain Pilate offered to the angry crowds. Near the end of the trial an exchange took place: while Jesus was punished and crucified, another man was pardoned and released. Luke tells us that Pontius Pilate "released the man who had been thrown into prison for insurrection and murder, for whom they asked, but he delivered Jesus over to their will" (Luke 23:25).

"He delivered Jesus over to their will": These ominous words are full of doom because we know that the will of these people was to crucify Jesus. Jesus only ever wanted to do the will of his Father, but they wanted to have their own way, even to the death of the Son of God. We should never forget, however, that this too was the will of God. There are two wills at work in these world-changing events. One is the will of Satan for our destruction; the other is the will of God for our salvation.

It is strange to say, but at this point in the Gospel, both plans—God's plan and Satan's plan—are working towards the same goal: the death of Jesus by crucifixion. "The two plans converge at Calvary," writes Michael Wilcock. "But the difference between them is all-important, and men must choose on whose side they will be: either beneficiaries of the plan by which God brought Jesus to the cross, or accomplices in the plan by which Satan brought him there."[6] Which side are you on? Are you with God, or against him? Are you part of the devil's plan, or have you crossed over to Jesus?

Understand that these two plans are not equal in strength. Although Satan did not know it yet, his plan was actually part of God's plan. Wilcock goes on to say this: "The most diabolical of all the schemes of Satan was not only countered at every point by a superior plan of God's devising. It was actually woven into that plan, and made to serve its ends."[7] Anyone who doubts this should listen to what Peter preached on the day of Pentecost. He said to the Jews: "you, with the help of wicked men, put him to death by nailing him to the cross." But he also said, "This man was handed over to you by God's set purpose and foreknowledge" (Acts 2:23 NIV).

This strikes just the right balance. Jesus was put to death by real human beings—an unholy alliance of Jews and Gentiles. Ultimately this was Satan's idea, because he was the one who entered Judas before his betrayal (see Luke 22:3). Nevertheless, it was all part of God's preordained plan. Isaiah foretold this in his ancient prophecy: "It was the will of the LORD to crush him" (Isa. 53:10). When the people said "Crucify him!" they were confirming a divine decree, as if God himself were saying "Crucify him!" Long before it was the will of the people for Jesus to die on the cross, it was the will of the Father and the Son for our salvation. That eternal plan does not exonerate these people; they were still guilty before God for the infinite injustice of murdering his Son. But it proves that God knew what he was doing, as he always does. The reason he did not permit Pilate to find a way to save Jesus was that Jesus was there to save us. If God could use the evil plans of wicked men for his own glorious good, will he not also do what is best in our own lives, even if it is still hard for us to see it?

6. Wilcock, *Luke*, 196.
7. Ibid., 197.

## The Wonderful Exchange

The will of God for Jesus was that his death would be our deliverance. There is a dramatic illustration of this gospel truth right in this trial, in the story of Barabbas, whom Luke describes as someone "who had been thrown into prison for an insurrection started in the city and for murder" (Luke 23:19). As a rebel who was in prison for crimes he actually committed, Barabbas was everything that Jesus was not. The apostle Peter noted this contrast when he preached on the day of Pentecost and said, "you denied the Holy and Righteous One, and asked for a murderer to be granted to you" (Acts 3:14). Here is how J. C. Ryle described the difference between these two men: "The one was a sinner against God and man, a malefactor stained with many crimes. The other was the holy, harmless, and undefiled Son of God, in whom there was no fault at all."[8] Even the name Barabbas serves to highlight this contrast, at least in some ironic way, for in Hebrew it means "the son of the father." That name properly belongs to Jesus as the only Son of the Father; if it belongs to Barabbas at all, it must refer to his father the devil (see John 8:44).

The guilty prisoner Barabbas is an apt illustration of our own condition as fallen sinners. According to F. W. Krummacher, "Barabbas does not stand before us merely as an individual. He represents, at the same time, the human race in its present condition—as fallen from God—in a state of rebellion against divine Majesty—bound in the fetters of the curse of the law till the Day of Judgment."[9] Like Barabbas, we are everything that Jesus is not: sinful, selfish, and rebellious against the rule of God. Our guilty sin imprisons us and will not let us go. Even worse, the holy law that we have broken brings us under the judgment of God. Like Barabbas, we are waiting on death row, for the penalty of sin is death, and after that, eternal punishment.

Yet remarkably—almost unbelievably, considering how guilty he was—Barabbas was set free. An exchange took place, in which the innocent man was condemned to die while the guilty man went free. Krummacher invites us to consider the result of Pilate's decision:

> Barabbas and Jesus change places. The murderer's bonds, curse, disgrace, and mortal agony are transferred to the righteous Jesus; while the liberty, inno-

8. Ryle, *Luke*, 2:458.
9. F. W. Krummacher, *The Suffering Saviour* (1856; reprint Edinburgh: Banner of Truth, 2004), 268.

cence, safety, and well-being of the immaculate Nazarene become the lot of the murderer. Barabbas is installed in all the rights and privileges of Jesus Christ; while the latter enters upon all the infamy and horror of the rebel's position. Both mutually inherit each other's situation and what they possess: the delinquent's guilt and cross become the lot of the Just One, and all the civil rights and immunities of the latter are the property of the delinquent.[10]

Here, then, is an illustration of our salvation. The point is not that we have any reason to believe that Barabbas ever came to faith in Jesus Christ. The point rather is that his pardon is a picture of the grace that God has for us in Jesus. Like Barabbas, we were dead in our sins and doomed to die; but an exchange has taken place in which Jesus takes our place so that we can take his. The Innocent One is condemned to die in our place. The true Son of the Father takes upon himself the guilt of all our sin and therefore is condemned to suffer the wrath of God. He does this by dying on the cross. But at the same time his crucifixion is our justification; his condemnation is our pardon; and his bondage is our release. This is the gospel: Jesus dying in our place, as our substitute, suffering the death that we deserved to die.

A vivid example of a life-and-death exchange comes from the end of Charles Dickens's famous novel *A Tale of Two Cities*. Amid the horrors of the French Revolution, during the deadly days of the guillotine, the patriot Charles Darnay is condemned to die. But the Englishman Sidney Carton has a plan to save him. The two men are similar in appearance, and in the hour before the execution Carton suddenly shows up at Darnay's prison cell to exchange clothes . . . and positions. He will go to the guillotine and die in the other man's place.

As he is taken to his public execution, Carton meets an innocent young seamstress who is also condemned to die. She has met Darnay and thus recognizes that Carton must be an imposter, yet instantly she guesses what he is doing. "Are you dying for him?" she wonders. Carton's supremely costly sacrifice reminds her of Jesus and gives her courage to face her own dying hour. Clutching his hand, she says, "I have been able to raise my thoughts to Him who was put to death, that we might have hope and comfort."[11]

10. Krummacher, *Suffering Saviour*, 270–71.
11. Charles Dickens, *A Tale of Two Cities* (New York: Scholastic Book Services, 1962), 442, 465.

The girl was right: to see someone die in someone else's place is to be reminded of the transaction that occurred when Jesus took our place on the cross. This wonderful exchange is beautifully described in the Epistle to Diognetus, a letter from the early church:

> He himself took on Him the burden of our iniquities. He gave His own Son as a ransom for us, the holy One for transgressors, the blameless One for the wicked, the righteous One for the unrighteous, the incorruptible One for the corruptible, the immortal One for them that are mortal. For what other thing was capable of covering our sins than His righteousness? By what other one was it possible that we, the wicked and ungodly, could be justified, than by the only Son of God? O sweet exchange! O unsearchable operation! O benefits surpassing all expectation! That the wickedness of many should be hid in a single righteous One, and that the righteousness of One should justify many transgressors.[12]

Through Jesus we have received a benefit "surpassing all expectation"— just as Barabbas did. Imagine what it must have been like for that prisoner when he heard the good news of his exchange. He was not going to die after all; he was going home free, because Jesus would die instead! For Barabbas this was pure grace. He was still in prison when he heard the happy news. There was nothing he could do to gain his own pardon or grant his own release. He had no way to escape the chains of his bondage. His life was spared only because Jesus died in his place.

The gospel gives us the same good news. It comes to us on death row, in the prison of our fallen nature, from which we have no possibility of escape. There it declares that God has a gracious answer to the problem of our sin. It says that Jesus will die for us, if only we will hold on to him with the hand of faith.

What, then, will you decide to do with Jesus? Will you say, "Away with this man," as Pilate said? If you do, then you will die in your sins. Instead, make the wonderful exchange. Hold on to Jesus. He will save you from the death that your sins deserve and set you free forever.

---

12. Epistle to Diognetus, quoted by Douglas Jones and Douglas Wilson in *Angels in the Architecture: A Protestant Vision for Middle Earth* (Moscow, ID: Canon, 1988), 66.

# 102

# SOMETHING TO CRY ABOUT

## *Luke 23:26–31*

*But turning to them Jesus said, "Daughters of Jerusalem, do*
*not weep for me, but weep for yourselves and for your children."*
(Luke 23:28)

And so, at last, the time came for the Savior to die. The
betrayer had given his fatal kiss. The priests had staged
their midnight trial. The governor had rendered his unjust
verdict. The soldiers had beaten their innocent prisoner. When they were
finished with their bloody work, Jesus took his last, slow steps on the road
to his crucifixion. "And as they led him away," Luke reports, "they seized
one Simon of Cyrene, who was coming in from the country, and laid on
him the cross, to carry it behind Jesus" (Luke 23:26).

### THE CROSS THAT SIMON CARRIED

It was customary in those days for a criminal to carry his own cross—a
final indignity before the fatal event. It seems likely, therefore, that Jesus
was close to the point of total collapse. Why else would the soldiers make

someone else carry his cross, if not for the cruel mercy of making sure that he lived long enough to be crucified?

As we have seen, Jesus was close to death the night before, in the sweaty, bloody teardrops of Gethsemane. That morning he had been scourged with cruel whips and beaten with bloody fists. We know from various ancient sources that such torture often cut to the bone, grotesquely exposing vein and sinew to public view. Here was a man whose appearance was "marred beyond human semblance" (Isa. 52:14)—a man whose life was already bleeding away. As he struggled up Calvary under the weight of his heavy cross, his obvious physical exhaustion must have made the soldiers wonder whether he would die before they had the satisfaction of killing him.

So they seized a passerby and compelled him to carry the cross. He was a man from North Africa—Simon of Cyrene—and since there is little use arguing with soldiers, he did as he was told and carried the cross of Christ. Many preachers have seen this episode as an example for our own Christian discipleship: like Simon, we are called to take up the cross and carry it for Jesus. Just as the world hated our Savior, so it will hate us, and therefore we will have the high privilege to share in his sufferings by bearing the reproach of the enemies of the gospel. Yet perhaps it is better for us to see Simon's carrying the cross as a symbol of our condemnation. We are the ones who deserve to die for sins, not Jesus. As we watch Simon carry the cross up Calvary, therefore, we should see the heavy burden of our own guilty sin. And when we see Jesus nailed to that very cross, we should know that he is dying in our place, for the sins that we deserve to carry.

The whole Gospel of Luke has been leading to this point—the point where we see the cross. Luke is "the Gospel of knowing for sure" (see Luke 1:1–4), and for a long time we have known for sure that Jesus would have to die. Already when the baby Jesus was presented at the temple, Simeon prophesied the piercing of a sword (Luke 2:35). Then, starting in chapter 9, Jesus began to predict his own death. He told his disciples that he would be rejected and killed (Luke 9:22). He spoke with Moses and Elijah about his coming departure (Luke 9:31). He set his face to go up to Jerusalem and the cross (Luke 9:51). He said that he had to go up to Jerusalem because that is the place where prophets always perished (Luke 13:33). He told the twelve that he would be mocked and mistreated and tortured before he was killed

(Luke 18:31–33). He even told a parable about the murder of a father's only beloved son (Luke 20:9–15).

Thus we have long known that Jesus would have to die, and during the course of his legal trials it became increasingly obvious that his enemies would settle for nothing less than execution by crucifixion. But here, finally, Luke shows us the cross. It was the cross that Simon of Cyrene carried up the last and fatal hill—the cross where Jesus was crucified for the salvation of sinners. Luke brings it into focus here to show us Jesus as a man who is about to die.

## DON'T CRY FOR ME, JERUSALEM

The mood of this passage is ineffably somber. How sad it is to see this innocent man—the perfect Son of God, the Beloved Son of the Blessed Father—taking his final footsteps to the cross. The scene is made even more mournful by the intense emotional response of the mourners who went with Jesus up to Calvary that day: "And there followed him a great multitude of the people and of women who were mourning and lamenting for him" (Luke 23:27).

This information is unique to the Gospel of Luke, which is not surprising. Luke took special notice of the relationships that Jesus had with various women. Nor is it surprising that they were weeping audibly. Even to this day, open demonstrations of public grief are common in Israel and the Middle East. We see them any time there is a terrorist bombing: women loudly crying in the streets, wailing with lamentation. In this case, their tears flowed out of sympathy for the Man of Sorrows—out of pity for someone they rightly perceived to be an innocent victim. How sad these women were to see Jesus taken out of the city and cruelly executed.

Some of these women may have been among the disciples. Yet Jesus addresses them simply as "Daughters of Jerusalem" (Luke 23:28). Since most of the women who followed Jesus and supported his ministry came from Galilee rather than Jerusalem (see Luke 23:49), it seems somewhat less likely that many of these mourners had made a personal faith commitment to Jesus. Nevertheless, these kindly women were sympathetic souls. They recognized an injustice when they saw one, and as their tender hearts went out to this innocent man in his painful suffering, their natural and appropriate response was to take up the familiar rituals of a communal lament.

Today lamentation is a forgotten virtue. Yet it is right and good for godly people to mourn the innocent victims of wrongful violence, to weep for children who get gunned down in the streets, and to grieve the loss of life through war and terror. The people of God are called to lament the many losses of a fallen world. When the evangelical statesman Michael Cassidy and his team traveled from his native South Africa to witness the appalling aftermath of the genocide in Rwanda, they found that one of their primary callings was to offer holy lamentation for the dead. Such ministry is exemplified in the biblical prophet Jeremiah, who not only wept for his suffering people (see Lam. 1–5), but also encouraged the daughters of Jerusalem to share his tears (see Jer. 9:20). The women of that holy city did the same thing when Jesus walked his *via dolorosa*—the way of tears winding up to Calvary.

We might well have expected Jesus to thank these women for their sympathies. Instead, to our surprise, Jesus told these women that their pity was misplaced, that they were shedding their tears for the wrong person. Here are the words of his mild rebuke and solemn warning: "But turning to them Jesus said, 'Daughters of Jerusalem, do not weep for me, but weep for yourselves and for your children'" (Luke 23:28).

The women who followed our Savior to the cross thought that *he* was the person to be pitied. After all, Jesus was about to die in excruciating pain. Nevertheless, he did not need anyone's assistance, or even anyone's sympathy. He would do with courage what he was called to do to the very death. He would do it in full reliance on the Holy Spirit, without needing the comfort of anyone's tears.

Rather than weeping for him, therefore, these women should weep for themselves. Their sympathetic tears may not have been sinful, but they were certainly missing the point. According to Spurgeon, Jesus did not rebuke these women "because they were wrong, but because there was something still more necessary to be done than even to weep for him."[1]

If anyone needed to be pitied it was the people of Jerusalem, not the man that they were putting to death. "Do not weep for me," Jesus said, "but weep

1. Charles H. Spurgeon, "Wherefore Should I Weep?" *The Metropolitan Tabernacle Pulpit* (Pasadena, TX: Pilgrim, 1971), 22:592.

for yourselves and for your children" (Luke 23:28). Jesus first spoke these words to the "Daughters of Jerusalem," a phrase that referred to the nation of Israel as a whole. In effect, the women who wept for Jesus represented God's people. So whatever Jesus said to them, he was really saying to the whole city. But he is also saying it to us: "Do not weep for me; weep for yourselves."

This needs to be said, because sometimes people do weep for Jesus. Many paintings of the crucifixion—many statues and icons of the cross—are designed to evoke feelings of pity for Jesus. Similarly, the traditional seven stations of the cross are used to stimulate emotional participation in the sufferings of Christ. This was the theological underpinning of Mel Gibson's blockbuster film *The Passion of the Christ*. Many Christians believe that Good Friday is a day when they should feel sad that Jesus died, and therefore try to get themselves into the right emotional state to grieve his crucifixion. But Jesus does not need our sympathies! He did not need them when he was going to die, and he certainly does not need them now that his sufferings are over. If we weep over the cross, therefore, it should be with sorrow for our sin and gratitude for our salvation, but never with sadness for Jesus. As F. W. Krummacher said, "Tears of sentimentality and pity are nowhere so much out of place as on Calvary. While resigning ourselves to such emotions, we mistake the Lord Jesus—nay, even degrade Him, and as regards ourselves, miss the way of salvation marked out for us by God. Hence the Savior exclaims, once for all, 'Weep not for me!'"[2]

## JUDGMENT ON JERUSALEM

Why does Jesus tell us to weep for ourselves, and not for him? What is the reason for this self-centered lamentation? It is because judgment is coming, and unless we find safety in Jesus, we are in mortal danger of coming under the wrath of God.

The person truly to be pitied is not the Savior who died for sinners, but the sinners who die in their own sins and therefore fall under the judgment of God. This is hard for many people to accept, but Jesus wants us to know enough about God's wrath to seek God's mercy. So after telling the

2. F. W. Krummacher, *The Suffering Saviour* (1856; reprint Edinburgh: Banner of Truth, 2004), 323.

women to weep for themselves instead of for him, he went on to say this: "For behold, the days are coming when they will say, 'Blessed are the barren and the wombs that never bore and the breasts that never nursed!' Then they will begin to say to the mountains, 'Fall on us,' and to the hills, 'Cover us.'" (Luke 23:29–30).

Jesus made this prediction out of pity—pity for the Daughters of Jerusalem and all their children. Even as he went to the suffering cross, Jesus was not concerned about himself, but thinking in love of their salvation. He knew that judgment would soon fall on the holy city. Jerusalem was doomed to be destroyed because the people there rejected the Messiah.

This was at least the seventh time that Jesus had prophesied Jerusalem's destruction.[3] These prophecies all came true in A.D. 70, when the city was sacked by the Romans. Jesus predicted that when that terrible day came, women who were married with children would envy the single and the childless. Typically barrenness was considered a curse, but when judgment came it would be counted a blessing. Better not to have any children at all than to see them suffer famine and the sword, as mothers did in the siege and fall of Jerusalem. The women and children of that city went through such terrible suffering that many of them must have wished to be destroyed. They cried out for the mountains around the city to crush them, and thus to deliver them once and for all from the misery of their distress.

It was out of pity for all this suffering that Jesus pleaded with the Daughters of Jerusalem to pity themselves. Rather than being concerned about what was happening to him, they should be more concerned about what would happen to them and to their children. Then perhaps they would come to him and to his cross for salvation, and on the day of disaster they would escape with their lives. In fact, this is what most Christians did in A.D. 70. Knowing the prophecies of Jesus, the first Christians fled from Jerusalem before the Romans arrived, and then they scattered across the world with the gospel.

To strengthen his warning, Jesus followed his prophecy with this proverb: "For if they do these things when the wood is green, what will happen when it is dry?" (Luke 23:31). Here Jesus is drawing an analogy between his own suf-

---

3. Michael Wilcock, *The Message of Luke*, The Bible Speaks Today (Downers Grove, IL: InterVarsity, 1979), 204. See Luke 11:49–51; 13:6–9; 13:34–35; 19:41–44; 20:16; and especially 21:20–24.

ferings and the subsequent destruction of Jerusalem. As any good Boy Scout can explain, dry wood is more flammable than wood that is still green. A dry, old stick always burns faster and hotter than a living branch torn fresh from the tree. In using this analogy, Jesus compares himself to the green, living tree, and the people of Jerusalem to the old, dry wood. He himself is perfectly innocent, and therefore the last person who ought to be crucified. Nevertheless, he is on his way to the cross; the green wood is about to be thrown into the fire. What then will happen to the people of Jerusalem, who actually deserve to fall under judgment? They will quickly be destroyed.

Here is how J. C. Ryle paraphrased what Jesus said: "If the Romans practice such cruelties on me, who am a green tree, and the very source of life, what will they do one day to your nation, which is like a barren withered trunk, dead in trespasses and sins?"[4] What indeed will the Romans do? More to the point, what will God do? If he did not spare his own innocent Son, how will he spare the sinners who reject him? Leon Morris said it very simply: "If the innocent Jesus suffered thus, what will be the fate of the guilty?"[5]

Jesus knew what their fate would be, and in mercy he told the Daughters of Jerusalem to weep before the coming destruction. The tears he wanted them to cry were not of sadness only, but also of repentance. Jesus was calling people to be concerned enough about their spiritual condition to be sorry for their sin. This is always the way to get ready for the coming judgment: by repenting of sin. The leaders of Jerusalem had already claimed awful responsibility for the blood of Jesus (see Matt. 27:25). Because they rejected him as the Messiah, soon their city would be destroyed. But in mercy Jesus was calling them to repent and be saved. The poet Edwin Cox put the Savior's words into verse:

Weep, O my daughters, but grieve not for me;
Weep for yourselves and your children;
Shed bitter tears of mourning and pray.
O pray *Miserere, nostri Domine.*[6]

4. J. C. Ryle, *Expository Thoughts on the Gospels, Luke* (1858; reprint Cambridge: James Clarke, 1976), 2:466.
5. Leon Morris, *The Gospel According to St. Luke: An Introduction and Commentary*, Tyndale New Testament Commentaries (Grand Rapids: Eerdmans, 1974), 325.
6. Edwin Cox, quoted in R. Kent Hughes, *Luke: That You May Know the Truth*, 2 vols., Preaching the Word (Wheaton, IL: Crossway, 1998), 2:377.

People should pray, in other words, that the Lord would have mercy on their souls. This was infinitely more important than feeling sorry for Jesus. "It is beautiful and good that they should manifest such tenderness and sympathy with Him on His way to the cross," wrote Norval Geldenhuys. But it is "far more urgent that they should weep for themselves and their children: even at this late hour such tears may lead to repentance and avert the approaching doom."[7] As lamentable as it was for Jesus to die, it would be sadder still for people to die in their sins without ever finding forgiveness. For in that case, as far their destiny is concerned, his death would be in vain. How sad it would be for someone to feel sorry for the sufferings of Jesus without ever feeling sorry enough for sin to go to him for the salvation he died to gain.

## THE JUDGMENT TO COME

Will you listen to what Jesus said to the women of Jerusalem and weep for your sin? It is not for his crucifixion that we should weep, but for our transgression. We too are facing the prospect of judgment. What Jesus said was prophetic of the fall of Jerusalem—a national disaster that God used to punish a nation's sin—but it also foreshadows the final judgment that will fall on all nations at the end of the world.

The Bible says that the wrath of God is coming against all unrighteousness. One day Jesus will come again, and on that day every enemy of God will be judged to eternal damnation. Are you ready for that final judgment?

Many people hope that they will never be judged at all. Witness the bumper sticker that reads: "Non-Judgment Day Is Coming."[8] This slogan is a way of making fun of the final judgment and also of insisting that no one should ever be judged for anything. This is not a perspective that the Judge shares, however. According to the Word of God, a day of judgment *is* coming. When it comes, people will say the same thing Jesus said that the women of Jerusalem would say when their city was besieged. People will beg in vain for their own destruction:

7. Norval Geldenhuys, *The Gospel of Luke*, New International Commentary on the New Testament (Grand Rapids: Eerdmans, 1951), 603.
8. As quoted by Dave Shiflett in *Exodus: Why Americans Are Fleeing Liberal Churches for Conservative Christianity* (New York: Sentinel, 2005), 180.

The Savior's sphere of vision evidently extends itself here beyond the terrible days of the destruction of Jerusalem. His words manifestly generalize themselves and point to the judgment of the last day. Those who will then be found rejecting through obstinate unbelief and persevering impenitence, their truest Friend and only Savior will find themselves in a position in which they will prefer annihilation to a continuance of existence. They will call upon the hills to crush them and bury them forever . . . but no outlet of escape will be found.[9]

There is a prophecy about this in the book of Revelation. There we read of terrible calamities in the last days: the earth shaking; the sun going black; the stars falling from the sky; the mountains falling into the sea. Then, according to the Bible's grim prophecy,

> the kings of the earth and the great ones and the generals and the rich and the powerful, and everyone, slave and free, hid themselves in the caves and among the rocks of the mountains, calling to the mountains and rocks, "Fall on us and hide us from the face of him who is seated on the throne, and from the wrath of the Lamb, for the great day of their wrath has come, and who can stand?" (Rev. 6:15–17; cf. 9:6)

There is a close connection between this prophecy from Revelation and what Jesus said to the Daughters of Jerusalem (see Luke 23:30), as well as to a prophecy from the Old Testament (see Hosea 10:8). In each case, people coming under judgment have a death wish for their own destruction. In absolute desperation, they want the mountains to cover them up. Hoping to escape the wrath of God, they dream of annihilation, begging that rocks will fall from the sky and crush them into oblivion. Nevertheless, their pleas are all in vain, for there is no doctrine of annihilation in Scripture. Indeed, the very fact that people in these prophecies beg to be destroyed shows that they are still in torment. Nothing is said about these prayers ever being answered, or about anyone finding salvation outside of Christ.

This is why Jesus tells us to weep for ourselves. He tells us to weep because he believes in the final judgment more than anyone, including the fires of

---

9. Krummacher, *Suffering Saviour*, 326.

hell and eternal damnation. He tells us to weep because he suffered the wrath of God on the cross where he was crucified, and because he loves to show mercy to sinners, if only we will repent. It is for our sake that Jesus says, "Do not weep for me, but weep for yourselves and for your children" (Luke 23:28). This is the greater concern: not what happened to Jesus, but what will happen to us.

Will you listen to Jesus and weep for yourselves and for your children? The Bible everywhere teaches us to believe in the wrath of God. The Old and New Testaments give many examples of divine judgment—people rejecting God, refusing to repent of their sin, and suffering terribly as a result. Every one of these disasters is a prophecy of the coming judgment, a portent of the wrath of God. The same is true of all the disasters in the world today. When disaster strikes, people often feel that it must be the end of the world, and well they should: every tsunami and every terrorist attack should remind us of the great and terrible day of the Lord.

Jesus would have us consider carefully what will happen to us and to our children on that dread day. Rather than trying to give our children heaven on earth, we are to love them and teach them like people who know that judgment is coming. How sad it will be for anyone who dies and goes to that judgment without ever believing in Jesus. For this reason, the best gift that any parent can give to a child is a living example of faith in Jesus Christ. Consider what Jesus suffered on the cross—the wrath that God the Son endured in bearing guilt for sin. Then consider the terrible fate of anyone who never trusts in Jesus to take away sin, and therefore comes under the everlasting judgment of God. It is not annihilation that God has decreed for the unrighteous—the end of existence—but eternal torment. The proverb of the green wood and the dry stick teaches us that God has "judgments preparing for the impenitent and the unbelieving. There is wrath revealed in the Gospel for those who harden themselves in wickedness."[10]

Jesus wants to spare us from that wrath while there is still time. This is why he came into the world and died on the cross. Jesus was suffering the punishment that our sins deserve. He is not looking to get our pity and sympathy, but our repentance and faith. In love he tells us to weep for ourselves and our children, to see the coming judgment, and to say that we

10. Ryle, *Luke*, 2:462.

are sorry for our sins. He calls us to come to the cross and believe that he suffered there for us. When Jesus tells us to weep for ourselves, he is not telling us to feel sorry for ourselves. He is talking about shedding the tears that will lead us to trust in him for salvation and live in hope for the mercy he will show to our children.

The Bible does not say whether Simon of Cyrene ever cried those tears, but it seems likely that he trusted in Jesus and also that he prayed for God to save his children from judgment. Although we do not find this detail in the Gospel of Luke, Mark tells us that Simon was "the father of Alexander and Rufus" (Mark 15:21; cf. Rom. 16:13). There is only one reasonable explanation as to why Mark would think that this little piece of family history was of any interest to the readers of his Gospel: Alexander and Rufus were well-known figures in the early church. They were men like their father, who followed Jesus to the cross and believed in him for salvation.

Simon of Cyrene believed that judgment was coming, and therefore he made sure to get right with God and teach his family the gospel. How privileged he was to carry the cross! How wise he was to listen to Jesus! How joyful he will be on the day of Judgment! And how happy we will be if we are wise enough to follow his example and come to Jesus.

# 103

# A ROYAL PARDON

## *Luke* 23:32–38

*And when they came to the place that is called The Skull, there*
*they crucified him, and the criminals, one on his right and one on*
*his left. And Jesus said, "Father, forgive them, for they know not*
*what they do." (Luke 23:33–34)*

Sometimes a single glimpse is all it takes to know something for sure. My son Josh and I went out cruising the streets of Center City Philadelphia, looking for Josh's little brother Jack. He had gone to the park with some neighbors, and we knew they were walking somewhere in the neighborhood, but in the mile between our house and the park there are dozens of alleys and side streets. We looked down every long street, hoping to catch a glimpse of the one and only Jack Ryken.

Suddenly we saw him through the traffic, blocks away, just before he disappeared behind a building. "There he is!" we shouted, and then we both laughed. I'm not sure we even could have explained how we knew it was Jack. Maybe it was the color of his shirt, or the way he skipped when he walked, but whatever it was, we had both known Jack all his life, and one glimpse was all we needed to know that it was him.

Malcolm Gladwell describes this phenomenon in a book called *Blink: The Power of Thinking without Thinking*. Gladwell's book is about the first few seconds of looking—the decisive glance that knows something in an instant. Our snap judgments are not always correct, of course, and sometimes our first instinct happens to be the wrong instinct. But there are many situations in life where everything comes together and we get the right answer as quick as a blink, in a flash of instantaneous insight.

## The Gospel Blink

There are moments like this in Luke's Gospel, when people instantly know that Jesus is the Christ. Often they are prepared for these moments by their pursuit of spiritual truth, but the recognition itself happens in an instant. The Christmas shepherds went to the manger, and in a blink they knew that the Savior was born (Luke 2:15–17). Old Simeon was waiting for God at the temple, and when he saw a couple bringing their baby boy for purification, he blinked and knew that the child was the light of the world (Luke 2:27–32). John blinked when he baptized Jesus; he saw the dove of the Holy Spirit descend on the Father's beloved Son (Luke 3:21–22). This has happened all the way through the Gospel. Levi blinked when he got up from his tax booth and followed Jesus (Luke 5:27–28). Peter did it when Jesus asked who people thought he was and it came to him all of a sudden that Jesus was the Christ of God (Luke 9:20). Zacchaeus did it too, and when he blinked he almost fell out of a tree (Luke 19:1–10), because salvation was coming to his house.

It happened again and again. Luke is the Gospel of knowing for sure, and every time somebody blinked, Luke hoped that his friend Theophilus would see Jesus (see Luke 1:1–4). Almost every passage in Luke shows something about Jesus that helps confirm that he is the Son of God and the Savior of the world. At each point Luke is hoping that we will blink and see that Jesus is the Savior. Blink when he preaches his first sermon, and you see that he is the Christ who came to bring good news (Luke 4:16–21). Blink when he calms the storm and see that he is the God who rules the wind and the waves (Luke 8:22–25). Blink when he tells the story of the lost sheep and see that he is the Good Shepherd who rescues his lost and chosen flock (Luke 15:1–7). Blink at his triumphal entry into Jerusalem and see that he is the victorious King (Luke 19:36–38). Blink at his trial before the Sanhedrin

581

and see that he is the Son of God and the Son of Man (Luke 22:66–70). It can happen almost anywhere in the Gospel of Luke: the blink that saves your soul by helping you see Jesus.

## Seeing Jesus

But maybe you still do not see it. Maybe you are not altogether certain that Jesus is the true divine Savior that God always promised to send. Maybe you have not yet believed in him as the Christ who has the power to forgive sins and grant everlasting life. Or perhaps you have seen Jesus before, but have not been seeing him very well lately. In any case, here is another opportunity to know Jesus by seeing him on the cross. In telling the story of the crucifixion, Luke provides precise details to identify Jesus and explain his work, including the fulfillment of many ancient prophecies about salvation.

To begin with, Luke shows us the saving Christ by numbering him with transgressors: "Two others, who were criminals, were led away to be put to death with him. And when they came to the place that is called The Skull, there they crucified him, and the criminals, one on his right and one on his left" (Luke 23:32–33). This important detail confirms an ancient prophecy. Isaiah prophesied that when the suffering Christ poured out his soul unto death, he would be "numbered with the transgressors" (Isa. 53:12). In other words, he would be counted a criminal, reckoned by the law to be a lawbreaker.

Of course Jesus was not actually a criminal at all. His innocence was thoroughly demonstrated throughout his legal trials. Nevertheless, he was crucified as a criminal among criminals, put to death between two men who deserved to die. When the soldiers executed him in this way, they unwittingly fulfilled the words of the prophet. What clearer way to number Jesus with transgressors than to hang him in the company of thieves?

This true fact from the crucifixion helps us understand the meaning of the cross. When we see this innocent man dying between two transgressors, we know that although he is not a sinner himself, he nevertheless is dying in the place of sinners. With the blink of faith, we should also see that he is dying in *our* place—that we are among the sinners for whom he died.

Luke also shows us the saving Christ in the very fact that he was crucified. "They crucified him," the Gospel says in verse 33. Luke does not dwell on the horrific suffering this entailed, yet this matter-of-fact expression refers to a form of torture that may be the most agonizing and disgraceful form of public execution ever devised. Death by crucifixion was slow and excruciatingly painful, and it was as physically painful for Jesus as it would have been for anyone. He was nailed to a rough piece of wood with heavy spikes through his hands and feet, and then left to dangle there until he died of "exposure, asphyxia, and the loss of blood."[1]

This too was the fulfillment of an ancient prophecy, for as David said in one of his messianic psalms, "they have pierced my hands and feet" (Ps. 22:16). This means that when Jesus died the painful, shameful death of the cross, he died the way it was prophesied for the Savior to die. He did this for us. According to the prophet, the Savior they pierced was "wounded for our transgressions" (Isa. 53:5).

Blink again, and the Gospel shows us the saving Christ in the way people gambled for his clothing. Luke is faithful to report this detail: "And they cast lots to divide his garments" (Luke 23:34). It has always been an executioner's prerogative to claim the victim's last possessions. In this case, the soldiers decided to throw dice for his clothing—winner take all. This too was prophesied in David's psalm: "they divide my garments among them, and for my clothing they cast lots" (Ps. 22:18).

Look at Jesus on the cross and see a man dying poor and naked, while his enemies play games for the last thing he owned on earth. Blink with the eye of faith and you will also see that he did this for you, dying the way the Savior was supposed to die. Corrie ten Boom writes about this in *The Hiding Place*, her remarkable account of the experiences she and her sister Betsie had in a Nazi concentration camp:

> I had read a thousand times the story of Jesus' arrest—how soldiers had slapped Him, laughed at Him, flogged Him. Now such happenings had faces and voices.
>
> Fridays—the recurrent humiliation of medical inspection.... [We] had to maintain our erect, hands-at-sides position as we filed slowly past a phalanx of grinning guards. How there could have been any pleasure in the sight of these stick-thin legs and hunger-bloated stomachs I could not imagine.... Nor could I see the necessity for the complete undressing....

1. Michael Wilcock, *The Message of Luke*, The Bible Speaks Today (Downers Grove, IL: InterVarsity, 1979), 198.

But it was one of these mornings while we were waiting, shivering in the corridor, that yet another page in the Bible leapt into life for me.

He hung naked on the cross.

I had not known—I had not thought. . . . The paintings, the carved crucifixes showed at the least a scrap of cloth. But this, I suddenly knew, was the respect and reverence of the artist. But oh—at the time itself, on that other Friday morning—there had been no reverence. No more than I saw in the faces around us now.

I leaned toward Betsie, ahead of me in line. Her shoulder blades stood out sharp and thin beneath her blue-mottled skin.

"Betsie, they took *His* clothes too."

Ahead of me I heard a little gasp. "Oh, Corrie. And I never thanked Him."[2]

Have you ever thanked Jesus that when he died for your sins, he died in naked shame? Thank him also for the scorn he suffered from his jeering enemies. Luke shows us this as well, for in his Gospel he says that "people stood by, watching" (Luke 23:35). Presumably they watched the way people watch any spectacle of public suffering. Some were sympathetic, others indifferent, and still others simply curious. But many of them spoke with cruel mockery.

This was true of the priests: "the rulers scoffed at him, saying, 'He saved others; let him save himself, if he is the Christ of God, his Chosen One!'" (Luke 23:35). These men were Israel's religious leaders. They had been abusing Jesus for a night and a day, trying to get him crucified. Now that he was dying on the cross they gave full vent to their fury, mocking Jesus as a helpless Messiah.

Tellingly, and ironically, these men admitted that Jesus had saved others. This was indisputable. Everyone knew that Jesus had performed the many miracles Luke reported in his Gospel. Now they demanded Jesus to come down from the cross, as if they would believe this miracle more than they believed any of the others, and as if the Messiah was even supposed to save himself.

Jesus was also mocked by the soldiers who crucified him. It was not simply the Jews who made fun of him, but also the Gentiles—in effect, the

2. Corrie ten Boom, with John and Elizabeth Sherrill, *The Hiding Place* (Washington Depot, CT: Chosen, 1971), 178–79.

whole human race. Luke says, "The soldiers also mocked him, coming up and offering him sour wine and saying, 'If you are the King of the Jews, save yourself!'" (Luke 23:36–37). These military men did not mock Jesus as a helpless prophet, as the priests did, but as a failed king. Jesus had neither a crown nor a kingdom, only an ignominious death. How then could he be the King?

Yet this too was in fulfillment of the ancient prophecies. David foretold that the Christ would be "scorned by mankind and despised by the people. All who see me mock me; they make mouths at me; they wag their heads; 'He trusts in the LORD; let him deliver him; let him rescue him, for he delights in him'" (Ps. 22:6–8; cf. Isa. 53:3). The priests and the soldiers used similar expressions at the cross, taunting Jesus for his person and work. There was even a prophecy about the sour wine the soldiers offered to Jesus. In one of his other psalms, David wrote: "for my thirst they gave me sour wine to drink" (Ps. 69:21). When we see a crucified man mocked and given bitter wine, we should know that we are seeing the Savior that God promised to send.

In case we are still in any doubt, God even put a billboard on the cross to tell us who Jesus is. There are clues to the Savior's true identity throughout this passage. For example, when he speaks to his Father in verse 34, we should know that he must be the Son. When the priests use titles like "the Christ of God, his Chosen One" (Luke 23:35), they are speaking in unbelief. Nevertheless, they are putting his identity on the agenda, because the titles are true: Jesus is the saving Christ, the Chosen One of God (as the Father said when Jesus was transfigured; see Luke 9:35). When soldiers scornfully call him "the King of the Jews" (Luke 23:36–37), this too is the truth, as anyone can see simply by reading the inscription over his head: "This is the King of the Jews" (Luke 23:38).

There is a story behind this sign. When a criminal was executed, it was customary for the governor to give public notice of his crime. That was problematic in this case because Jesus had committed no crime, and the governor knew it. Pontius Pilate had said it himself: "I have found in him no guilt deserving death" (Luke 23:22). So in the end he decided simply to identify Jesus as "the King of the Jews." By saying this, Pilate was crucifying Jesus for being who he really was. He was also getting back at the Jewish leaders who had given him so much grief over Jesus.[3] They wanted him to kill an innocent man, did they? Well then, he would call the crucified man their king.

When the religious leaders saw the sign, they were apoplectic with rage. Pilate was ruining everything! Somebody needed to climb up the cross and change the sign! Jesus was not the King of the Jews; he only *said* that he was the King of the Jews (John 19:21). Except that Jesus really was the King of the Jews. It said so right on the sign. The title that Pilate meant for mischief and his soldiers used for mockery was the gospel truth: Jesus the Christ is the King of the Jews.

With delicious, saving irony, God himself was the one who had this sign put on the cross, even if it was written in Pilate's handwriting. Nothing is more useful for pointing something out to people than a clear sign. So God has given notice that Jesus Christ is the saving king. The prophet who predicted the fall of Jerusalem (see Luke 23:28–31) and the priest who interceded for his enemies (see Luke 23:34) is also the king of God's people (see Luke 23:37–38).

The handwriting on the cross is a sign that no one should miss because it was put there by the love of God. The sign was there because God loves his Son. Even when Jesus was battered and bruised, dying in the guilt of our sin and therefore forsaken, the Father God declared his kingship, making a royal announcement to the world: "This is the King of the Jews." "Look and see," God was saying with fatherly affection, "my Son is the King!"

The sign was also there because God loves us and wants us to be saved forever. If you are still not sure about Jesus—if you have not yet made up your mind whether he is the Savior or not, or if you have not been seeing him lately for who he really is—look at the sign on the cross and consider his kingship. See who Jesus really is. God put the sign there so that when we see Jesus dying on the cross, we know that he is royalty.

## To Forgive Is Divine

As he tells the true story of the crucifixion, Luke gives us every opportunity to see that Jesus is the saving Christ. The blink of knowing for sure

3. See Norval Geldenhuys, *The Gospel of Luke*, New International Commentary on the New Testament (Grand Rapids: Eerdmans, 1951), 610.

could happen at almost any moment. It could come when we see Jesus crucified and know that he is pierced for our transgressions. It could come when we see him hanging between two robbers and know that he is numbered with transgressors. It could come when we see him stripped and scorned, or when we see the sign heralding his kingship. But maybe we see Jesus most clearly of all in the first of his seven statements from the cross: "Father, forgive them, for they know not what they do" (Luke 23:34).

With these words, King Jesus shows his mercy and declares that he is in the business of forgiving sinners. As the King of the Jews offers his royal pardon, he gives the clearest proof of his divine and saving grace. To err is human, we often say, but to forgive is divine. Here, then, is a divine forgiveness. In crucified love, the Savior announces the forgiveness that he was dying to give.

These words seem to have been spoken at the very time when the soldiers were nailing Jesus to the cross. Kent Hughes writes, "The cosmic trauma had begun. There never had been such pain as physical and spiritual evil now came against Jesus in terrible conjunction. Body and soul recoiled. The initial shock of crucifixion had rendered him paralyzed and quivering. Physical disbelief screamed from severed nerves. And even greater spiritual horror closed in—he would soon become sin."[4] It was just then that Jesus prayed forgiveness for his enemies, just when the nails were piercing and the cross was thrusting into the ground. "As soon as the blood of the Great Sacrifice began to flow," said J. C. Ryle, "the Great High Priest began to intercede."[5]

This fact is remarkable in itself. At the time of his most extreme ordeal, Jesus nevertheless found the courage to pray—not for himself, but for others. Jesus was always at prayer, so this was his instinctive response, as it should also be ours in every discouragement. Spurgeon wrote:

> To cease from prayer is to renounce the consolations which our case requires. Under all distractions of spirit, and overwhelmings of heart, great God, help us still to pray, and never from the mercy-seat may our footsteps be driven by despair. Our blessed Redeemer persevered in prayer even when the cruel iron

4. R. Kent Hughes, *Luke: That You May Know the Truth*, 2 vols., Preaching the Word (Wheaton, IL: Crossway, 1998), 2:378.

5. J. C. Ryle, *Expository Thoughts on the Gospels, Luke* (1858; reprint Cambridge: James Clarke, 1976), 2:467.

rent his tender nerves, and blow after blow of the hammer jarred his whole frame with anguish; and this perseverance may be accounted for by the fact that he was so in the habit of prayer that he could not cease from it; he had acquired a mighty velocity of intercession which forbade him to pause. Those long nights upon the cold mountain side, those many days which had been spent in solitude, those perpetual ejaculations which he was wont to dart up to heaven, all these had formed in him a habit so powerful, that the severest torments could not stay its force. Yet it was more than habit. Our Lord was baptized in the spirit of prayer; he lived in it, it lived in him, it had come to be an element of his nature. . . . I repeat it, let this be our example— never, under any circumstances, however severe the trial, or depressing the difficulty, let us cease from prayer.[6]

There has been a good deal of discussion about the precise extent of this intercession. For whom was Jesus praying? Was his petition limited to the Roman soldiers, or did it also extend to the Jewish priests? When he said "Forgive *them*," was he praying forgiveness only for people who were there when he was crucified, or for everyone whose sins sent him to the grave? Is this forgiveness only for sins committed in ignorance, or is it also for sins committed with full knowledge and willful intent?

At the very least, Jesus was praying for the soldiers who nailed him to the cross. Even though they were only following orders and did not know that they were killing the Son of God (see Acts 3:17; 1 Cor. 2:8), they were guilty nonetheless, and therefore in need of forgiveness for this sin, or else they would be damned. Ignorance does not constitute an extenuating circumstance; not knowing is never an excuse. It is true that these men were ignorant of the enormity of their crime. Yet they still should have known better (especially given the verdict that Pilate had pronounced at his trial; see Luke 23), as we all should know better whenever we sin against God. Jesus had mercy on their relative ignorance and prayed for their sin to be forgiven. This did not necessarily mean that all of their transgressions were completely and immediately forgiven. But it did mean that God would not hold this particular sin against them. The murder of his beloved Son was such a heinous sin that unless they heard the words of Jesus they might

6. Charles H. Spurgeon, "The First Cry from the Cross," *Metropolitan Tabernacle Pulpit* (Pasadena, TX: Pilgrim, n.d.), 15:589–90.

never believe that they could ever find mercy. But Jesus prayed for their forgiveness, and by faith they could be forgiven for this and all their sins.

Notice, however, that Jesus did not specify that his prayer was only for the soldiers, who were not the only people sinning against him. The priests were also there—the religious leaders who had pressed and persecuted Jesus to the cross. Surely they were included in this petition, for they did not know what they were doing much more than the soldiers did, and they too needed the Father's mercy.

So the Savior prayed for the priests as well as the soldiers. But in praying for these Jews and Gentiles, Jesus was showing on the cross how he prays for us all. Even if he were only praying exclusively for the people who actually crucified him, it would still give us hope for our own forgiveness, because here we see the heart of the mercy of God. The Savior's words demonstrated his redemptive purpose in dying on the cross. If Jesus was willing for the Father to forgive the very men who murdered him, then what sinner is beyond the reach of his mercy? Surely anyone who repents will be saved. When his enemies said, "Crucify!" Jesus said, "Forgive," and a man who says that is willing to forgive anyone—even people like us, no matter what we have done, as long as we come to him in faith.

This may explain why Jesus left his prayer so open-ended: he wanted to invite everyone who heard these words to receive his forgiveness. His general petition opened the door for any one of us to apply it to our own particular need of forgiveness. Charles Spurgeon said that he loved this prayer "because of the *indistinctness* of it."[7] In other words, Jesus prayed for "them" without ever saying exactly who "them" included. Therefore, even though this prayer undoubtedly refers specifically to the men who crucified Jesus, it should not be limited to them in its application. When Jesus said "Father, forgive them," he was giving the hope of mercy to every lost sinner who would ever come to him and pray to be forgiven. We too are among the "them" that Jesus prayed for God to forgive. Spurgeon applied this personally when he said, "now into that pronoun 'them' I feel that I can crawl. Can you get in there? Oh, by a humble faith, appropriate the cross of Christ by trusting in it; and get into that big little word 'them'!"[8]

7. Charles H. Spurgeon, "Christ's Plea for Ignorant Sinners," *Metropolitan Tabernacle Pulpit* (Pasadena, TX: Pilgrim, n.d.), 38:318.

8. Ibid., 38:318.

There is room for every sinner in the little word "them," and therefore many people have crawled inside that blessed pronoun to find the forgiveness of their sins. They have heard the prayer of Jesus and dared to hope that God would show them mercy. It started happening that very afternoon, when one of the criminals crucified with Jesus came to faith before he died (see Luke 23:39–43). Could this have been because he heard Jesus ask for his enemies to be forgiven? One of the soldiers also came to faith in Christ—one of the very soldiers Jesus prayed for God to forgive. The Savior's prayer was starting to get answered. In the coming weeks and months many priests would trust in Jesus for their salvation as well. Luke tells us in the book of Acts that "a great many of the priests became obedient to the faith" (Acts 6:7).

God has been answering this prayer ever since, encouraging sinners to believe that we will find mercy in the Father's forgiveness. Furthermore, Jesus has been praying this prayer ever since, interceding for the people he died to save. Even now he is at the right hand of God, praying for our forgiveness. He is praying from the throne the same way that he prayed from the cross. As the Scripture says, he "always lives to make intercession" (Heb. 7:25). Jesus is praying, "Father, forgive."

## He Saved Others

What makes this prayer so powerful? It is powerful because it is prayed to the Father, who is none other than God Almighty, the First Person of the Trinity. It is powerful because it is prayed by the Chosen One, Jesus the Son, the Christ of God. Here, then, is a conversation that takes place within the holy and eternal Trinity. When the Son prays to the Father, how can his prayer not receive its answer? Jesus himself said that the Father *always* hears the Son (see John 11:42). When the Son prays for us to the Father, therefore, our sins surely will be forgiven.

Consider further that this prayer was offered from the cross, so that when he prayed it, Jesus himself was providing the basis for our forgiveness. If the Father needed a just reason to forgive sinners, he only needed to see where Jesus was praying this prayer. He was praying on the cross—the very cross where he was bleeding and dying under the curse of God's wrath, suffering the just penalty that our sins deserve.

Even as he made this petition, his position on the cross was pleading the merits of his blood.

How sadly ironic, therefore, that at that very moment the priests and soldiers were taunting Jesus for not being able to save himself. These men thought that in order for someone to bring salvation, he would have to win a glorious triumph. "What sort of king gets killed?" they thought. "What sort of Christ gets crucified?" If Jesus could not save himself from this ignominious death, they reasoned, how could he save anyone at all?

But of course it was just because he was the Christ that Jesus refused to save himself, and just because he refused to save himself that he is able to save sinners who need forgiveness. The crucifixion that some men scorned was the very death that made his prayer so powerful. It was by *not* saving himself that Jesus saved sinners. His death is for our forgiveness. Rather than thinking of himself and his own sufferings, he was thinking of his enemies, as we know from his prayer. Indeed, this is what the cross is all about: the forgiveness of sins. Jesus showed this in his dying hour by praying, "Father, forgive." Our salvation was gained at the precious cost of his royal blood and by the loving heart of his kingly intercession.

If we believe in the King who died for us on the cross—the King who was counted a criminal, stripped of all his clothing, and mocked by jeering enemies—then we too will receive his royal pardon. We will be forgiven.

Now our lives should demonstrate his mercy, as the gift of our own forgiveness compels us to offer forgiveness to others. Jesus said, "Love your enemies and pray for those who persecute you" (Matt. 5:44). He not only said this, but he also did it by praying his first prayer from the cross: "Father, forgive." Once we receive this forgiveness for ourselves, we pray it for others, including our very worst enemies. Whenever we hear again the first words of Jesus from the cross, we must consider the people that we need to forgive in our family, our church, and the wider community. Is there anyone who has wounded or betrayed you? We are called to pray for our enemies, just as Jesus prayed for his. As Christians, the first calling we have to our enemies is to love them by praying for them. If God is willing, they will be forgiven, not just by us, but also by our Father in heaven.

One man who received forgiveness for himself and prayed it for his enemies was Jacob DeShazer. DeShazer was a crew member on one of the bombers that made the daring Doolittle raid on Japan after the Japanese bombed Pearl Harbor in World War II. His plane was shot down over Japan, and he was imprisoned for more than three years. DeShazer was often tortured and spent most of his time in solitary confinement. He was not a believer, but towards the end of his captivity he was given a Bible and read it cover to cover. Somewhere between his first and his sixth reading, he came to faith in Christ. He repented of his sins and received his royal pardon through the cross.

Not long after the war ended and he was released from his captivity, DeShazer became convinced that he should return to Japan and preach the gospel. He wanted to love his former enemies by sharing with them the message of God's forgiveness. As part of his evangelistic ministry, DeShazer wrote a pamphlet called *I Was a Prisoner of Japan*. A million copies were printed, and as people all over Japan read the pamphlet, many heard the gospel for the very first time.

In the providence of God, one of the men who read DeShazer's pamphlet was Mitsuo Fuchida, who had been the lead pilot in the attack on Pearl Harbor—the very man who gave the infamous order to attack: "Tora! Tora! Tora!" Fuchida saw the pamphlet at a railway station, and at first he was inclined to discard it, but when he noticed that it was written by an American pilot, he decided to read it. Somewhere deep in his heart he was longing for forgiveness, hoping somehow to forgive and be forgiven. After he read DeShazer's pamphlet, Fuchida obtained a Bible and began to read it. The verse that changed his life came from the Gospel of Luke: "Father, forgive them, for they know not what they do" (Luke 23:34). As quick as a blink, Fuchida knew that the Jesus he saw on the cross had mercy for his sins and would give him the grace to forgive his enemies.[9]

See Jesus the way Fuchida did. Listen to his powerful prayer from the cross. Receive the royal pardon he offers, and as quick as a blink, you will be forgiven. Then forgive your own enemies and pray for them to be forgiven.

9. This story is recounted by David Seamands in "The Kamikaze of God," *Christianity Today* (Dec. 3, 2001): 58–60.

# 104

# The "Luckiest" Man Alive

## *Luke 23:39—43*

*And he said, "Jesus, remember me when you come into your king-dom." And he said to him, "Truly, I say to you, today you will be with me in Paradise." (Luke 23:42–43)*

They usually call him "the thief on the cross," which is true as far as it goes.[1] The man *was* a thief, and everyone knew it, includ-ing the man himself. But that is true only at the beginning of the story, not at the end, because by then the man had put his faith in Jesus Christ and was on his way to paradise. It might be better, therefore, to call him "the convert on the cross." Or maybe we should call him "the luckiest man alive," because at the time he was crucified, he was well on his way to hell. But of all the criminals on all the crosses outside all the cities in the entire Roman Empire, the man happened to get crucified next to Jesus, and as a result he had the chance to be saved before he died. How lucky can a man get? So "lucky" that he is still alive today, in the paradise of God.

Then again, the man on the other side of Jesus was almost as lucky. He was crucified next to Jesus too, which gave him one last chance to be saved

---

1. More technically, the term that Luke uses *(lēstēs)* refers to a robber: someone who steals by using force.

before dying. But the man on the other side of the cross never repented, never trusted in Jesus, never prayed the sinner's prayer, and never made it to paradise.

The story of one or the other of these two men is really the story of every sinner. For purposes of comparison and contrast, Luke loved to tell his stories in twos: two women expecting a baby, two old saints waiting for the Messiah, two sisters welcoming Jesus into their home, two men going up to the temple to pray, and so on. Here we see two men at the cross dying two deaths, making two different decisions about Jesus, and meeting two entirely different destinies as a result. Their story compels us to make a choice of our own. Like them, we can see Jesus on the cross, and now we have a decision to make. In fact, this scene is really a dress rehearsal for the final judgment.[2] Will we end up on the right side of Jesus, like the convert on the cross, or on the wrong side of Jesus, like the man who never believed?

## THE RAGE OF A THIEVING SINNER

Luke tells the story of these two men in four parts, starting with the rage of a thieving sinner. We know that the man was guilty of criminal activity because Matthew says as much in his Gospel (see Matt. 27:38). What Luke tells us is that "One of the criminals who were hanged railed at him, saying, 'Are you not the Christ? Save yourself and us!'" (Luke 23:39).

In these few short words we not only get a sense of the man himself, but we also gain clear insight into the sinful condition of our fallen nature. This man is right next to the Savior of the world in his dying hour, but he can respond only with selfish demands and bitter contempt.

People who do not have a saving relationship with God sometimes console themselves with the thought that they will have time for that later (whenever later is). Sometimes they imagine themselves having some sort of deathbed conversion. They will live by their own rules most of their lives, but of course there will always be time for them to come back to God at the very end. Or so they think.

Sometimes this does happen, of course, and the convert on the cross is a famous example. But God is not obliged to give people one last chance

---

2. Richard D. Phillips, *Encounters with Jesus: When Ordinary People Met the Savior* (Phillipsburg, NJ: P&R, 2002), 191.

to repent. Many people die suddenly or unexpectedly. Furthermore, people who do get one last chance to believe in Jesus are just as likely to waste it, which is exactly what this man did. Not even the certainty of his impending death was enough to persuade him to get serious about having a relationship with God. If we are not serious about getting right with God now, we should not expect to get right with him later, either.

Rather than treating Jesus with reverence and repentance, the man on the wrong side of the cross used his dying strength to treat him with sarcasm and contempt. When he heard the priests and soldiers making fun of the man on the cross next to him, he knew that he had not yet hit absolute bottom. Seeing that Jesus was even lower than he was, he raged against him. This is the way people are. If we feel bad about our situation, we take our anger out on someone else, especially someone in a worse situation than we are. No matter how low we go, we look for someone even lower to ridicule.

The angry criminal also demanded Jesus to save him on his own terms. This too is the way of fallen sinners. When we do not get what we want out of life, often our first instinct is to get angry with God and to start telling him what he has to do in order to earn back our allegiance. What this man wanted Jesus to do was to get him down from the cross. He was not interested in having a relationship with Jesus or actually dealing with the eternal consequences of his sin. He wanted salvation only in the very limited sense of escape from immediate death. "For all his pain," writes David Gooding, "there was with him apparently no fear of God, no confession of guilt before God, no expression of repentance, no request even for divine forgiveness."[3]

This is what many people want from God: practical help in temporary emergencies. They want a deity who can work them a few miracles, but not a God who demands their service and obedience. When their circumstances get desperate, they demand for God to intervene, but once the crisis is over they go right back to living for themselves. What kind of relationship are you looking to have with Jesus? Do you want him to be your cosmic "easy button," or do you want to know him in a way that will change your entire life?

3. David Gooding, *According to Luke: A New Exposition of the Third Gospel* (Grand Rapids: Eerdmans, 1987), 344.

The spiritual problem with this impenitent sinner was that he had neither faith nor repentance. Rather than confessing his crimes, he angrily attacked Jesus. Refusing to repent, he kept on sinning. Even though he asked Jesus to deliver him in some sense, he did not believe that Jesus really had the power to save. He did not confess Jesus as the Christ, but questioned whether Jesus was the Christ at all. Here is how David Gooding explains the tragic destiny of this unrepentant sinner:

> He was prepared to believe that Jesus was the Messiah if he would do a miracle and release him from the temporal punishment that was the consequence of his crimes. When Jesus made no attempt to do that he cursed him and his religion as a cheat. But to save people simply from the temporal consequences of their sins without first bringing them to repentance and reconciliation with God, would be no true salvation at all. It would but encourage people to repeat their sins under the impression that any ugly or inconvenient consequences could and would be miraculously removed. . . . No paradise could be built on such an irresponsible attitude to sin.[4]

The truth is that Jesus does have the power to save us. He is able to take us to the everlasting paradise of God. But we must come on his terms, repenting of our sin and trusting in him for salvation, or else he will never receive us at all. Unless we are ready to face up to the serious problem of our sin, we are not ready for the salvation Jesus is ready to give.

## THE REBUKE OF A PENITENT THIEF

There are two convicted felons in this story, and at the beginning of the crucifixion neither one of them was ready to come to Jesus. This is clear from the Gospel of Matthew, which tells us that "the robbers who were crucified with him also reviled him in the same way" (Matt. 27:44). Matthew's use of the plural ("robbers") indicates that *both* men railed against Jesus. So the sinner on the other side of the cross started out just as angry as the man quoted in verse 39, his partner in crime. Both of these hardened criminals ridiculed Jesus: "The men impaled on his right and left hitched them-

4. Gooding, *Luke*, 344.

selves up, gathered in precious air, and exhaled abuse on Jesus in deadly blasphemy."[5]

At that moment, these two men must have seemed like the two most unpromising candidates for salvation in the entire world. Both of them deserved to die on what the Romans called "the unlucky tree." Both of them were adding to their guilt by abusing the Son of God. Yet as unlikely as it was that either of these men would ever make it to heaven, something happened that changed one of their lives forever. We do not know exactly what moved the man from ridicule to repentance, apart from the gracious work of God the Holy Spirit. Maybe it was the gentle patience of Jesus as he suffered ridicule, injustice, and the excruciating pains of the cross. Maybe it was the prayer of forgiveness that Jesus offered for his enemies (see Luke 23:34). But whatever it was, sometime during his dying hour the convert on the cross responded to Jesus with repentance and faith.

We see his repentance in the way he responded to the criminal on the other side of the cross. Here is the rebuke of this penitent thief: "Do you not fear God, since you are under the same sentence of condemnation? And we indeed justly, for we are receiving the due reward of our deeds; but this man has done nothing wrong" (Luke 23:40–41).

John Calvin famously said in the opening words of his *Institutes of the Christian Religion*, "Nearly all the wisdom we possess, that is to say, true and sound wisdom, consists of two parts: the knowledge of God and of ourselves."[6] By that standard, the convert on the cross was in the possession of true wisdom, for he came to know both God and himself.

The man's knowledge of God is evident from his reverence for God. He gave the other criminal a strong rebuke for not showing proper respect. "Do you not fear God?" he said (Luke 23:40). Or, more literally, "Don't you even fear God?" Even if a man does not respect anything else, he should at least fear God, who has the power over life and death, heaven and hell. So the convert on the cross rebuked the angry, unconverted criminal for showing the kind of irreverence that would send him to hell.

---

5. R. Kent Hughes, *Luke: That You May Know the Truth*, 2 vols., Preaching the Word (Wheaton, IL: Crossway, 1998), 2:384.

6. John Calvin, *Institutes of the Christian Religion*, ed. John T. McNeill, trans. Ford Lewis Battles, 2 vols., Library of Christian Classics 20–21 (Philadelphia: Westminster, 1960), 1.1.1.

Not only did the convert on the cross have the proper fear of God, but he also had holy reverence for Jesus. Rather than thinking that somehow he was superior to Jesus, like the man on the other side, he knew that he was inferior. So at the end of verse 41 he says, "this man has done nothing wrong." In saying this, he was not necessarily claiming that Jesus had never sinned. This is true, of course, but the convert on the cross had no way of knowing it. Instead, he was saying something similar to what Pilate had said earlier: "I have found in him no guilt deserving death" (Luke 23:22). Somehow the convert on the cross sensed that this was true. After all, no crime was listed on the sign over his head. Nor did it seem likely that Jesus had done anything to deserve such a degrading death. So the man recognized the righteousness of the Savior's holiness and confessed it as well as he understood it: "this man has done nothing wrong" (Luke 23:41).

What is your testimony about the Jesus you see on the cross? Fear God and honor the King by saying that he is the sinless Savior. Then see yourself and confess that you are not sinless like Jesus, which is why you need a Savior. One of the truest and most important things we need to know about ourselves is the depravity of our sin.

The convert on the cross knew this, which is why he came to Jesus in God-fearing repentance. Out of reverence for God and respect for his authority as the Judge, the man admitted that he was in the wrong. Not only was he upset by what the other robber was saying, but he also confessed his own transgression. We are justly condemned, he said, "for we are receiving the due reward of our deeds" (Luke 23:41). Presumably he was referring specifically to the punishment he was receiving for breaking the law: these men deserved to pay for their crimes. But we sense that something deeper was happening in the man's heart. As he saw himself in comparison to Jesus, he came under the conviction of his sin. This may be the most important lesson the convert on the cross can teach us: not that we can still be saved at the very last minute (which is true to teach, but foolish to depend on), but rather that whenever we come to God we must come knowing that we deserve justice rather than mercy.

What do you deserve from God? See yourself in the criminal on the cross and ask God to have mercy on your soul. The cross next to Christ is for "the praying thief, or those who, penitent as he, still find the Christ beside them on the tree."[7] It is never too late to come to Jesus. However, this story is not primarily about getting saved in the nick of time. It is really about getting saved at all, which always includes repenting for all the things we have done wrong. Donald Barnhouse said:

> This must be the position of anyone who is going to be saved. As long as we cling to our own selves and think that there is even a shred of righteousness in ourselves that could satisfy the demands of a holy God, there is no possibility of salvation for us. But when we recognize that we have sinned . . . then we are in the position of those who may obtain mercy.[8]

If we want to be in a position to receive mercy, we should pray the way that Nicholas Copernicus prayed. When that famous scientist considered this story from the Gospel, he humbly prayed: "I do not ask for the grace that you gave St. Paul; nor can I dare to ask for the grace that you granted to St. Peter; but, the mercy which you did show to the dying robber, that mercy, show to me."[9]

## The Request of a Dying Convert

Genuine repentance is always joined to saving faith. This brings us to the third part of the story, in which we hear the request of a dying convert. Rather than taking something that did not belong to him, the way he usually did, for once the thief asked if he could have something he did not deserve: "And he said, 'Jesus, remember me when you come into your kingdom'" (Luke 23:42).

This is one of the only times in the Gospel of Luke that anyone calls Jesus by his given name. How appropriate it is for the convert on the cross to use it, because Jesus is the name of salvation. Call him "Jesus," the Christmas angel said to Joseph, "for he will save his people from their sins" (Matt. 1:21; cf. Luke 1:31). The name "Jesus" means that God saves, and this is what the

---

7. Miriam LeFevre Crouse, "Upon a Hill," in *The Cross: An Anthology* (Nashville: Thomas Nelson, 2003), 109.

8. Donald Grey Barnhouse, *Exposition of Bible Doctrines Taking the Epistle to the Romans as a Point of Departure*, 10 vols. (Grand Rapids: Eerdmans, 1953), 2:161.

9. Nicholas Copernicus, quoted in Clarence Macartney, *The Making of a Minister* (Great Neck, NY: Channel, 1961), 224.

man was asking: for Jesus to give him the salvation of God. In addition to repenting of his sin, he was making a deliberate request for salvation, trusting Jesus to give him the free gift of eternal life.

It is important to notice that the criminals on both crosses asked Jesus to save them, yet only one of them was saved. What was the difference? Why was only one man saved, while the other man was lost forever? Though their words are different, their requests sound almost the same. One man said "Are you not the Christ? Save yourself and us!" (Luke 23:39), while the other one said, "Jesus, remember me when you come into your kingdom" (Luke 23:42). What was the crucial difference between the prayers of these two sinners?

Even though both of these men asked for some sort of salvation, the attitudes behind their dying requests could hardly have been more different. Consider the differences: one request was made in angry unbelief; the other was offered in humble faith. One thief was not sure whether or not Jesus was the Christ, so he asked him to prove it. The other thief knew Jesus could save him, so he simply asked to be remembered. One man required Jesus to save himself before he saved anyone else. But somehow the other man knew that Jesus had to die first, and only then would he rise to his kingdom. One man was hoping for immediate deliverance from physical suffering, while the other was looking for salvation beyond the grave. He knew in his heart that "while there was no question of his being released from the temporal consequences of his crimes, there was every possibility of his being delivered from the wrath of God and from the eternal penalty of sin."[10]

The second man is an extraordinary example of saving faith. What is truly remarkable is not how late he was saved, but how much faith he had when he finally came to Christ. The convert on the cross believed that Jesus was the king of a coming kingdom. At the time, Jesus was surrounded by scoffers and bleeding a ghastly death. He hardly looked very kingly. In weakness—*in extremis*—he was emptied of all his royal glory. Nevertheless, and although he was crucified, the convert on the cross believed that Christ would have a kingdom. As Spurgeon said, "He saw our Lord in the very extremity of agony and death, and yet he believed in him as the King

10. Gooding, *Luke*, 344.

shortly to come into his kingdom."[11] We do not know how the man knew that Jesus was the King. Maybe the idea came from the sign above his cross, or from the cruel taunts of the crucifying soldiers. Nor is it clear exactly what kind of kingdom he thought Jesus would rule. But wherever the idea came from, the convert on the cross believed in Jesus and wanted to belong to his royal kingdom.

The man also had a "believing expectation" in life after death.[12] Speaking as one crucified man to another, he trusted that this was not the end for Jesus, or for him. He would have immortal life in the world to come. Has any man ever had more faith? What could one dying man possibly do for another? Yet this dying man believed that Jesus could get him into the kingdom of God! As he witnessed the crucifixion, he also had faith in the resurrection, and thus he believed the whole gospel before any of the apostles did.

Do you have as much faith as this crucified man put in the crucified Christ? Here is a man who was fully confident that all he needed for all eternity was for Jesus to remember him. Sometimes people have the idea that it must have been easier for him to believe because, after all, he was there at the crucifixion. Yet it took as much faith for him as it does for anyone—maybe even more. It takes faith to see Jesus crucified and believe that your sins will be forgiven. It takes faith to believe that he has the resurrection power to give you eternal life. It takes faith to rely on his remembrance for your destiny. It takes faith for anyone to pray what that old criminal prayed on the cross: "Jesus, remember me when you come into your kingdom" (Luke 23:42).

## THE REWARD OF A GRACIOUS SAVIOR

Jesus will not forget. Anyone who prays to him in repentance and faith will be saved forever. Jesus said this in the strongest possible terms, as he promised the reward of a gracious Savior: "Truly, I say to you, today you will be with me in Paradise'" (Luke 23:43). "Yes," Jesus was saying, "I will not forget; I will remember you." But he was also giving the convert on the cross far more than he asked or imagined.

11. Charles Haddon Spurgeon, "The Dying Thief in a New Light," in *The Metropolitan Tabernacle Pulpit* (London: Banner of Truth, 1969), 32:54.

12. Norval Geldenhuys, *The Gospel of Luke*, New International Commentary on the New Testament (Grand Rapids: Eerdmans, 1951), 611.

Consider all the blessings contained in this one short statement. Jesus promised to save the man *immediately*. He would not have to wait until tomorrow, but would enter his reward that very day. This helps to answer a question that almost everyone asks: What will happen to me when I die? For the believer in Christ, the answer is that death is the entrance into glory. Our bodies will be laid in the ground, where they will wait for their resurrection on the day of judgment. But our souls immediately enter the presence of God. To be "away from the body," the Bible says, is to be "at home with the Lord" (2 Cor. 5:8).

What hope this promise must have given to the convert on the cross! His simple faith gained him an immediate salvation. He would not have to wait until the end of days to receive his reward. Even if he was the last disciple to follow Jesus, he would be the first one home to glory, because the moment after he took his last breath on earth he would find himself in paradise. This is our hope as well:

> That word "to-day" . . . tells us that the very moment a believer dies, his soul is in happiness and in safe keeping. His full redemption is not yet come. His perfect bliss will not begin before the resurrection morning. But there is no mysterious delay, no season of suspense, no purgatory, between his death and a state of reward. In the day that he breathes his last he goes to Paradise. In the hour that he departs he is with Christ.[13]

Jesus also promised to save this man *eternally*, because paradise is the heaven of God. The word is used elsewhere in Scripture to refer to a place of future blessedness—a home of everlasting rest for the people of God (see 2 Cor. 12:2–4; Rev. 2:7). "Paradise" also refers to the Garden of Eden—humanity's first home. We know from the book of Genesis that the way back to that beautiful garden was closed because of sin. But it is not closed forever, because paradise lost has been regained. By suffering the death penalty for sin, Jesus opened the way back up to God. His cross is the key that opens the gate to heaven—not just for the convert on the cross, but for all the children of God.[14]

13. J. C. Ryle, *Expository Thoughts on the Gospels, Luke* (1858; reprint Cambridge: James Clarke, 1976), 2:473.

14. See Jerome, "On Lazarus and Dives," in *Luke*, ed. Arthur A. Just, Jr., Ancient Christian Commentary on Scripture, NT 3 (Downers Grove, IL: InterVarsity, 2003), 367.

What else did Jesus promise? He promised to save the man *personally*. The convert on the cross asked Jesus, man to man, to save him. This is the only way that any can be saved: by asking Jesus himself for salvation. Jesus responded with these words: "I say to you." He was making a personal transaction, speaking as a friend to a friend. But what is even more personal is the promise of his presence. Heaven is a wonderful place, but what makes paradise to be a paradise is being with Jesus. If he had said only "Today you will be in Paradise," that would almost be enough. But what Jesus actually promised was infinitely better: "Today you will be *with me* in Paradise" (Luke 23:43). In fact, the words at the end of his promise almost seem redundant. What other paradise do we need if we know that we will be with Jesus?

In his "Personal Narrative," the great theologian Jonathan Edwards described a time when he experienced unusual intimacy with Jesus—what he called a "sense of the excellent fullness of Christ." Here is how Edwards recounted the experience:

> Once, as I rode out into the woods for my health; and having lit from my horse in a retired place . . . to walk for divine contemplation and prayer; I had a view, that for me was extraordinary, of the glory of the Son of God; as Mediator between God and man; and his wonderful, great, full, pure and sweet grace and love, and meek and gentle condescension. This grace, that appeared to me so calm and sweet, appeared great above the heavens. The person of Christ appeared ineffably excellent, with an excellency great enough to swallow up all thought and conception. . . . I felt withal an ardency of soul to be, what I know not otherwise how to express, than to be emptied and annihilated; to lie in the dust, and to be full of Christ alone; to love him with a holy and pure love; to trust in him; to live upon him; to serve and follow him, and to be totally wrapt up in the fullness of Christ; and to be perfectly sanctified and made pure, with a divine and heavenly purity.[15]

Apparently Edwards had this experience more than once, because he went on to say, "I have, several other times, had views very much of the same nature, and which have had the same effects." This is how

---

15. Jonathan Edwards, "Personal Narrative," in *Letters and Personal Writings*, ed. George S. Claghorn, *Works of Jonathan Edwards* (New Haven, CT: Yale University Press, 1998), 16:801.

Jonathan Edwards described the joy of being "with Jesus." But if we have never had such an intense spiritual experience, we should not despair. Jonathan Edwards knew Jesus better than most people, and even he had an extraordinary sense of Christ's presence only on rare occasions. But if this has not happened to us yet, one day it will, because Jesus gives us the same promise that he gave to the convert on the cross: "You will be with me in Paradise."

Jesus saved this man immediately, eternally, personally, and also *graciously*—by faith, apart from any works. If ever there was a man whose works could not save him, it was the convert on the cross. His life was almost over. Even if he wanted to do something of his own that would be good enough for God, he couldn't do it, because his hands and his feet were nailed to the cross. He did not even have time to receive any sacraments. The only thing he could do is believe, and believe he did. Having repented of his sin, he trusted Jesus to save him—only Jesus. This is the biblical doctrine of justification by faith alone. As John Chrysostom said (more than a thousand years before the Reformation), "The thief, that was hanged when Christ suffered, did believe only, and the most merciful God justified him."[16] This is the way of salvation for anyone: we can be justified only by grace through faith— faith alone. This faith, it should also be noted, always produces good works, and the thief on the cross is no exception. He used what little time he had left to profess his faith, to rebuke sin, and to speak up for the cause of Christ.

Finally, Jesus saved this man *certainly*, or assuredly. We can always count on anything that Jesus promises anyway, but whenever he begins a sentence with the word "truly," he is making a solemn and unbreakable vow. So here at the end of the Gospel of knowing for sure we meet a man who knew for sure that he would be saved. By the promise of Jesus, the convert on the cross was certain of his salvation.

Do you have the same assurance? Do you know for certain that if you were to die today, you would be with Jesus in paradise? Charles Spurgeon said that Jesus took the convert on the cross with him to paradise "as a specimen of what he meant to do. He seemed to say to all the heavenly powers, 'I bring a

---

16. John Chrysostom, quoted in Ryle, *Luke*, 2:477.

sinner with me; he is a sample of the rest.'"[17] Jesus loves to save sinners. He was busy saving people right up to the end of his life, and he has been doing it ever since. If he was willing to save the thief on the cross, after everything that that man had done, he is willing to save anyone, including you.

## Remember Me

It is sometimes said that there are two kinds of people in the world: people who say there are two kinds of people in the world, and people who don't. Luke clearly fell into the former category. He believed that there are only two kinds of people, not just in this world, but also in the world to come. He shows us these two kinds of people at the cross, one crucified on the left side of Jesus, and the other on the right.

As many preachers have said, that one thief was saved so that no sinner might despair, but only one, so that no sinner might presume. Sometimes, in his mercy and grace, God saves people the way he saved the convert on the cross: right before they die. But why wait until then? The other thief was dying too, but he was never saved:

> Both were equally near to Christ. Both saw and heard all that happened, during the six hours that He hung on the cross. Both were dying men, and suffering acute pain. Both were alike wicked sinners, and needed forgiveness. Yet one died in his sins, as he had lived, hardened, impenitent, and unbelieving. The other repented, believed, cried to Jesus for mercy, and was saved.[18]

This is the choice that every person must make: to repent, to believe, and to pray, or else to die without faith in Jesus and never make it to paradise. Which side of the cross are you on? Here is the prayer that Richard Burnham offered—a prayer for any sinner who wants to be saved:

> Jesus, Thou art the sinner's Friend;
> As such I look to Thee;
> Now, in the fullness of Thy love,
> O Lord, remember me.

17. Charles Haddon Spurgeon, "The Believing Thief," in *The Metropolitan Tabernacle Pulpit* (London: Banner of Truth, 1970), 35:187.

18. Ryle, *Luke*, 2:470.

Remember Thy pure Word of grace,
Remember Calvary's tree,
Remember all Thy dying groans,
And then remember me.

Thou wondrous Advocate with God,
I yield my soul to Thee;
While Thou art pleading on the throne,
Dear Lord, remember me.

And when I close my eyes in death,
And human help shall flee,
Then, then, my dear redeeming God,
O then remember me.[19]

19. Richard Burnham, "Jesus, Thou Art the Sinner's Friend," in *The Cross: An Anthology*, 113–14.

# 105

# THE LIGHT AT THE END
# OF THE CROSS

## *Luke 23:44–49*

*It was now about the sixth hour, and there was darkness over
the whole land until the ninth hour, while the sun's light failed.
And the curtain of the temple was torn in two. Then Jesus, calling out with a loud voice, said, "Father, into your hands I commit my spirit!" And having said this he breathed his last.*
(Luke 23:44–46)

t was the brightest time of day. The sun was striving to reach
its zenith—the high and shining meridian of its daily glory.
Meanwhile the Son of God was making the promise of para-
dise, giving the bright hope of eternal life to a dying thief and to every dying
sinner. Then the darkness descended. "It was now about the sixth hour,"
Luke tells us, "and there was darkness over the whole land until the ninth
hour, while the sun's light failed" (Luke 23:44–45). This was the day that the
sun refused to shine, and so a black curtain fell over the stage of our salvation, shrouding the cross in thick darkness.

This darkness was the first of three crucifixion miracles recorded in the Gospel of Luke: the descent of darkness, the tearing of the veil, and the conversion of the centurion. As we see these three miracles, we also hear the voice of Jesus from the cross, which may not be a miracle, but was an indisputable marvel: the voice of the God-forsaken Son praying in the darkness and trusting the Father he could not see.

## THE DESCENT OF DARKNESS

The miraculous darkness described in the Gospel was a literal darkness with a symbolical meaning. Luke tells us that the whole land was dark for about three hours, from midday to the middle of the afternoon. This claim is repeated by Matthew and Mark (see Matt. 27:45; Mark 15:33). It is also confirmed by other ancient sources. Writing around the year 200, Tertullian confidently informed his Roman readers that this "wonder is related in your own annals and is preserved in your archives to this day."[1] Later both Origen and Eusebius quoted an account from the historian Phlegon, who described an extraordinary darkness that occurred around the time of the crucifixion.[2]

This darkness must have been a miracle—a divine intervention into the ordinary course of nature. It could not have been an ordinary eclipse. For one thing, it lasted for three hours, whereas a full eclipse of the sun lasts for only a few minutes. Furthermore, the crucifixion took place at the time of Passover, which coincides with a full moon. But as any astronomer knows, a full moon is on the wrong side of the earth to cause a solar eclipse. So the darkness that covered the cross for three dread hours on Good Friday had some other cause—a cause that can only be attributed to the sovereign intervention of almighty God.

What was the symbolic meaning of this miraculous sign? The poet Henry Colman asked: "What strange unusual prodigy is here, / The height of day and yet no sun appear, / Nothing but darkness to be seen? What fright / Hath caused the day thus to be turned to night?" Colman thought he knew

1. Tertullian, quoted in James Montgomery Boice, *The Gospel of Matthew* (Grand Rapids: Baker, 2001), 2:623.
2. Norval Geldenhuys, *The Gospel of Luke*, New International Commentary on the New Testament (Grand Rapids: Eerdmans, 1951), 616.

the answer: It was the darkness of death. "God's Son is dead. / No marvel then, the Sun doth hide its head."[3]

Darkness is often used as a symbol of evil. Jesus himself used the word that way on the night that he was betrayed. When the priests and the temple police came to arrest him, he said to those evil men, "this is your hour, and the power of darkness" (Luke 22:53). How appropriate it was, then, for the cruel deed of the crucifixion to be covered with spreading darkness, as if to say that this was the most evil of all crimes.

The darkness was also a sign of sorrow—a symbol of sadness and grief. Listen to the prophecy of Amos: "'And on that day,' declares the Lord GOD, 'I will make the sun go down at noon and darken the earth in broad daylight. . . . I will make it like the mourning for an only son and the end of it like a bitter day'" (Amos 8:9–10). The words of Amos came true the day Jesus was crucified. The sun turned to darkness; the sky began to weep for the death of the Father's only Son. James Boice said it was as if "a veil had been drawn over the unspeakable suffering of God's Son."[4] Or, to quote another commentator, the cross "was draped in the mourning sackcloth of darkness."[5]

The darkening sky was a symbol of evil and sadness, but the Bible also associates darkness with divine judgment. This was a day of judgment, on which the Son of God suffered the wrath of God against human sin. When the ancient prophets spoke about the coming of God's judgment, they always said that it would be a day of signs and dark wonders in the heavens: "A day of wrath is that day, a day of distress and anguish, a day of ruin and devastation, a day of darkness and gloom, a day of clouds and thick darkness" (Zeph. 1:15).

The day Christ was crucified was that kind of day. During his dark hours on the cross, the Son of God was bearing the guilt of our sin. The curse of God was against him. The dark sky showed that he was suffering the hellish curse of God's wrath against human sin. There was a disturbance in creation itself in order to demonstrate what Jesus was doing on the cross: suffering God's judgment against our sin.

3. Henry Colman, "On the Strange Apparitions at Christ's Death," in *Chapters into Verse: Poetry in English Inspired by the Bible*, vol. 2: *Gospels to Revelation*, ed. Robert Atwan and Laurance Wieder (Oxford: Oxford University Press, 1993), 207.

4. Boice, *Matthew*, 2:623.

5. R. Kent Hughes, *Luke: That You May Know the Truth*, 2 vols., Preaching the Word (Wheaton, IL: Crossway, 1998), 2:390.

This was the first crucifixion miracle in the Gospel of Luke: the darkness of damnation. If you believe in this miracle, and understand what it means, then you know that Jesus has suffered the deadly penalty that you deserve for your sins. You are free from the wrath of God.

## THE TEARING OF THE VEIL

The second miracle did not take place at Calvary, where Jesus was crucified, but in the temple, where priests were worshiping God: "And the curtain of the temple was torn in two" (Luke 23:45). Like the curtain of darkness that covered the cross, the tearing of the veil was a literal miracle with a symbolical meaning. Although Luke gives it little more than brief mention, this miracle had monumental significance for the eternal destiny of the people of God because it showed that the way was now open to the presence of God.

The curtain of the temple was a magnificent piece of linen fabric, richly embroidered with red, blue, and purple thread. Its function was to separate the Holy Place from the Most Holy Place, also known as the Holy of Holies. The Holy Place was where the priests performed many of their sacred duties, such as replenishing the oil for the golden lampstand and offering holy incense on the altar of prayer. But the Most Holy Place was strictly off limits. The room behind the curtain was the most sacred space in the world—the place where God had chosen to manifest his holy presence.

Inside the Most Holy Place stood the ark of the covenant. There the mercy seat was sprinkled with the sacrificial blood of the covenant to make atonement for the people of God. The only person who ever went inside the Holy of Holies to meet with God was the high priest of Israel. He went there only once a year, on the day of atonement, and he never went inside without bringing the blood of a pure sacrifice. This was because a sacrifice had to be made for sin before anyone could enter the presence of God. Even when he had the sacrificial blood, the high priest feared for his life when he pulled back the curtain and went inside.

The thick curtain that separated the Holy Place from the Most Holy Place was a form of protection. It formed a barrier between a holy God and his sinful people. It blocked access, as if to say to sinful humanity: "This far, but no farther!"

The temple curtain was torn in two when Christ was crucified. To understand how miraculous this was, it is important to know that the curtain was roughly thirty feet wide and thirty feet high—one hundred square yards of heavy material. It was not a thin sheet of sheer fabric, but the width of a man's hand, almost an inch thick. The curtain was also tightly woven with multiple layers of thread. It must have weighed hundreds if not thousands of pounds. Thus it would have been impossible for any person to tear in two.

Consider further the testimony of Matthew and Mark that this curtain "was torn in two, from top to bottom" (Matt. 27:51; Mark 15:38). Not from bottom to top, notice, but from top to bottom. The only way a human being could have done this was by getting a twenty-five-foot ladder and hacking away at the curtain with a broadsword. But there were always priests in the Holy Place, worshiping the Lord both night and day. Anyone who tried to tear the curtain to the Most Holy Place would have been seized instantly and then summarily executed for perpetrating a sacrilege. No, the ripping of the veil was something that only God could do, and only by his miraculous power.

This miracle must have made a deep impression on the priestly community. In fact, there are references in the Jewish Talmud—dating to around the time of the crucifixion—to strange occurrences at the temple.[6] The priests who actually witnessed the tearing of the veil must have been absolutely terrified. Presumably they were just starting to make their elaborate preparations for the evening sacrifice. Since it was Passover, one of the high holy days, they almost certainly had a heightened sense of spiritual expectancy. Suddenly the holy curtain was ripped in half, and they could see right into the Holy of Holies—the place where God was.

What did this mean? Why did it happen at the very time Christ was crucified? What was the spiritual meaning of this supernatural sign?

It meant that Jesus was offering his body as the last sacrifice his people would ever need for their sins. This was the obvious and dramatic end of the whole Old Testament system of sacrifice. No more lambs needed to be slain for Passover. No more goats needed to be offered on the day of atonement. No more blood needed to be sprinkled on the mercy seat. The Son of God had given himself to be the final sacrifice for sin. As the Scripture

6. Geldenhuys, *Luke*, 616.

says, Jesus "has appeared once for all at the end of the ages to put away sin by the sacrifice of himself" (Heb. 9:26). When Jesus was crucified, the age of animal sacrifice ended forever, and God showed this by tearing the curtain to the Holy of Holies. Although later some of the priests may have tried to sew the temple curtain back together, there was no going back now: God had opened the way to the secret place that could only be entered by the blood of a perfect sacrifice.

This irreversible miracle showed further that the way was open to God forever. Since the time of Moses, the people of God had been denied any direct access to the divine presence. Although God graciously made his presence to dwell at the tabernacle, and then later at the temple, only one person was ever allowed a direct audience with the Almighty, and this was the high priest. Most people never even entered the Holy Place, and even the holy priests never saw the awesome majesty of the living God. But by his death Jesus opened the way to God, and this was symbolized by the tearing of the temple veil.

Now, by faith in Jesus, we have direct access to God. The book of Hebrews says that the old temple curtain closed the way to the holy places of God (see Heb. 9:3, 8). But now Jesus has opened the way back to God. Hebrews uses temple language to say that we have "a hope that enters into the inner place behind the curtain" (Heb. 6:19). Then it declares that "we have confidence to enter the holy places by the blood of Jesus, by the new and living way that he opened for us through the curtain, that is, through his flesh" (Heb. 10:19–20).

We have entrance to the Almighty. What this means in practical terms is that we can go to him with our every need. We should never think that our problems are beneath his notice, or that we have done something so terrible that God will never listen to our prayers again. On the contrary, the Bible says we can "draw near" to God "with a true heart in full assurance of faith" (Heb. 10:22). Jesus has opened the way for us to be close to God.

Do you believe this? Many of the priests believed it. When they went into the Holy Place and saw the holy veil miraculously torn in two, they sensed that God was doing something new. Later, when they heard the good news about the crucifixion and the resurrection of Jesus Christ, they understood that the tearing of the veil was a sign of salvation. Luke tells us the rest of their story in the book of Acts, where we read that "a great many of the priests became obedient to the faith" (Acts 6:7). Anyone who believes in the miracle of the curtain, and understand what it means, will find the way to God, through Jesus, and become obedient to the Christian faith.

## THE CONVERSION OF THE CENTURION

The third miracle in Luke's account of the crucifixion was a miracle of grace: the conversion of the centurion who praised God and proclaimed that Jesus was innocent.

Different people respond to the cross in different ways. This is as true today as it was the day that Jesus was crucified. Many people reacted with grief. Luke tells us that "all the crowds that had assembled for this spectacle, when they saw what had taken place, returned home beating their breasts" (Luke 23:48). The word "spectacle" almost suggests that they had come hoping to be entertained by a bloody display of cruel violence. But if that is why some people came to the cross, they went away in a completely different mood. Watching Jesus suffer in the darkness produced feelings of sorrow and fear. Thus some people went home with heavy hearts, maybe even lamenting the guilt of their sin.

For their part, the disciples were not quite sure what to make of it all. They were sadder than anyone, for they had experienced the unspeakable grief of watching the tortured suffering of someone they loved. But they were also deep in thought, trying to make sense of the crucifixion. Luke says that "all his acquaintances and the women who had followed him from Galilee stood at a distance watching these things" (Luke 23:49). Luke singles out these women for special mention because they were so faithful to Jesus and because they had such an important role to play in his ensuing burial and the story of his resurrection. Like the rest of the disciples, they were watching from a distance, quietly considering the meaning of the cross.

One man was so deeply impressed by what he had seen and heard that he could not keep silent, but wanted to affirm that Jesus was without sin: "Now when the centurion saw what had taken place, he praised God, saying, 'Certainly this man was innocent!'" (Luke 23:47). Truly this was another miracle—not a physical miracle, like the darkness at the cross or the curtain in the temple, but a spiritual miracle in which a sinner's heart was transformed by the supernatural power of God.

According to the spiritual laws of human nature, the sinful heart does not want to praise God. It runs downhill in the other direction—the direction of sin. This was true of the centurion at the cross, who mocked and scourged the Son of God. Whether he had pinned Jesus to the cross, or raised the hammer, or held the nails, he was partly responsible for the greatest crime in the history of the universe. He was one of those "lawless men," as Luke would later describe them, who killed and crucified Jesus (see Acts 2:23). He had a sinful mind that was hostile to God, as we all do, until the Holy Spirit comes into our minds and hearts to take control (see Rom. 8:5–11).

Then a transformation took place. The soldier's cursing was turned to praising, as he started to worship the sinless Son of God. The Bible does not say what brought about this change. Maybe it was the prayer of forgiveness that Jesus offered for his enemies (see Luke 23:34). Perhaps it was the gracious promise of paradise that he made to the thief on the cross (see Luke 23:43). Maybe it was the peaceful way Jesus surrendered his spirit to the Father (see Luke 23:46), or the whole manner of his death by crucifixion. But whatever it was, the man knew that when Jesus died, it was not for anything that he deserved. He was completely innocent.

Some people wonder whether the soldier ever fully repented of his sins and trusted in Jesus for his salvation. It seems safe to assume that he did. Admittedly, the words of his repentance are not recorded in the Gospel. Luke does not specifically say that he asked Jesus for forgiveness, or prayed to receive the free gift of eternal life. It is also true that simply saying that Jesus is innocent is not enough to save anyone. We must believe that he is the Son of God, and our Savior, which we do not know for sure that the centurion ever did.

We need to bear in mind, however, that Luke does not tell us everything the man said. According to Mark, he also said, "Truly this man was the Son of God!" (Mark 15:39). Furthermore, Luke tells us that in addition to saying that Jesus was innocent, he also "praised God" (Luke 23:47). Here is a man, therefore, who stood at the foot of the cross to praise God and to declare that Jesus is the righteous Son of God. This is no small confession! The soldier believed the gospel as well as he could understand it. Later there would be time for him to go deeper in the Christian faith. But as he stood in the dark shadow of the crucifixion, he saw the light at the end of the cross.

This was an absolute miracle: one of the very men who crucified Jesus was one of the first people to trust in him at the cross. In fact, as far as we can tell from the Gospel of Luke, the soldier was the *only* person to praise God at the cross of Christ. Back at the beginning of Luke, Simeon promised that Jesus would be a "light for revelation to the Gentiles" (Luke 2:32). Now the promise was coming true, as it does for everyone who believes. Has the light dawned on you? Can you confess that Jesus is the Son of God, the sinless Savior? Take your place with the converted centurion and praise Jesus on the cross. By the miraculous grace of God, you may know for sure that when he offered up his righteous life it was for you as much as for anyone.

## THE LAST PRAYER OF JESUS CHRIST

What happened to the centurion was the greatest crucifixion miracle in the Gospel of Luke. The descent of darkness showed that Jesus was suffering God's wrath against sin. The tearing of the veil showed that he was opening the way to God. But the conversion of the centurion showed that God can turn his enemies into friends and bring the hardest sinners from darkness into everlasting light.

We should never forget that the Savior who performs this miracle of saving grace went through the darkness to save us. We are reminded of this whenever we listen to the voice of Jesus and hear his last loud prayer from the cross: "Father, into your hands I commit my spirit!" (Luke 23:46). Apparently this is something Jesus said virtually at the same moment the curtain of the temple was torn in two, while the sky was still black with grieving despair. It is something he said with nearly his last breath. These were the dying words of a dying man—a man forsaken by God.

This is what makes his words such a marvel. We know from the Gospels of Matthew and Mark that earlier Jesus had said, "My God, my God, why have you forsaken me?" (Matt. 27:46; Mark 15:34). These words reveal a mystery beyond human thought: as the Son took on himself the guilt of our sin he was forsaken by the Father. Maybe this is why Jesus did not even call him "Father," as he did in every other prayer recorded in the Gospels, but called him "God" instead. As he suffered the wrath our sins deserve, the Son was separated from the intimacy he had known with the Father from all eternity. For the God-forsaken Son, the darkness of the cross meant distance from the Father.

Yet there was light at the end of the cross. In his last prayer before dying, Jesus expressed full confidence in his Father's love. Once again he used the paternal name of the First Person of the Trinity and called him "Father." Jesus did this even before the darkness lifted, which is the marvel of this prayer. Even when he was dying a God-forsaken death, the Son refused to let go of his eternal sonship. The word "Father" was "the sustaining lyric" of his life, and "here at death it expressed his ineffable trust and peace."[7] Jesus trusted that he would not be forsaken forever, and therefore he surrendered himself to the Father's care. As he came to the end of his sin-bearing work on the cross, his sense of the Father's loving presence was restored.

The Savior's sense of being God's Son had been present all through his life and ministry. It was there as a young boy when he was in Jerusalem for Passover and called the temple his "Father's house" (Luke 2:49). It was there at his baptism when the heavens opened and the Father said, "You are my beloved Son" (Luke 3:22). It was there every time he prayed the way he always prayed but no one had ever prayed before, addressing God as "Father." It was there when he prayed in the garden and accepted the cross, saying, "Father . . . not my will, but yours, be done" (Luke 22:42). It was there in his first words from the cross: "Father, forgive" (Luke 23:34). It was there again at the very end of the cross, when he said: "Father, into your hands I commit my spirit!" (Luke 23:46).

Many pious Jews used a similar prayer every night before bedtime.[8] It was their version of the famous prayer for children: "Now I lay me down to sleep, / I pray the Lord my soul to keep; / If I should die before I wake, / I pray the Lord my soul to take." But like almost everything he said on the cross, Jesus took these words straight from Scripture. This is one of the reasons he died so well: he was strengthened and sustained by the Word of God. The Son knew the Scriptures so well that even when he was in the pains of death, he could breathe the words of the Spirit as prayer to the Father.

In this case Jesus was quoting Psalm 31, in which David asked God to save him from his enemies. It was an appropriate psalm for Jesus to use,

---

7. Hughes, *Luke*, 2:393.

8. I. Howard Marshall, *The Gospel of Luke*, New International Greek Testament Commentary (Grand Rapids: Eerdmans, 1978), 876.

because he too was attacked by enemies and wracked with physical pain, just like David. So he uttered David's prayer: "Into your hand I commit my spirit" (Ps. 31:5).

Jesus used this prayer almost word for word, except that he made it more personal by calling God "Father." This is an example for our own intercession. There are times in life when we feel God-forsaken, when we wonder whether God is even there. Jesus knows what this is like because he really *was* forsaken. Nevertheless, he trusted his Father in the darkness, as we should trust him whenever we are feeling desperate. Even when we cannot see the light and prayer seems like nothing more than a cry in the dark, we are called to trust the Father, as Jesus did. By faith we yield everything up to God, surrendering everything we are and have to him for all eternity.

This is not just the way for us to live, but also the way for us to die. When Jesus committed his spirit to the Father, there is a sense in which he was doing something that no other human being can ever do. He was surrendering his body to death by the free exercise of his own will. Remember what Jesus said before: "I lay down my life that I may take it up again. No one takes it from me, but I lay it down of my own accord. I have authority to lay it down, and I have authority to take it up again" (John 10:17–18). Jesus exercised this authority by giving up his spirit (see John 19:30). Notice that his last prayer was uttered "with a loud voice" (Luke 23:46). Jesus was not yet at the feeble extremity of physical existence, but gave his life by the deliberate choice of his sovereign will. It is true that he was crucified by cruel men, in keeping with the will of God (see Acts 2:23, as well as Isa. 53:10). Yet it remains true that Jesus surrendered his body to death in a way that no one else has the authority to do.

Nevertheless, the last prayer that Jesus made before dying is still a good model for our own submission to God, especially at the time of death. In fact, many Christians have used these very words in their dying hour. Stephen used them when he was stoned by the Sanhedrin, except that instead of praying to the Father, he cried out to Jesus himself: "Lord Jesus, receive my spirit" (Acts 7:59). There have been many other examples throughout church history: Polycarp, who was martyred in the days of the early church; Bernard, who preached in the Middle Ages; Martin Luther and Philipp Melanchthon, who led the Protestant Reformation—the list goes on and on. These very words were on the lips of the Czech reformer John Hus when he was burned at the stake.[9]

This is the way for every believer to die well: by entrusting ourselves entirely to God, through faith in Jesus Christ. When Jesus put his spirit into the Father's hands, he was expressing full confidence that death was not the end for him. He believed that there was life beyond the grave; his spirit would survive. Therefore, Jesus rested complete trust in his Father for death and for everything that would come afterwards. From the end of the cross he could see the light of the empty tomb. He knew the Father had always promised to raise his body from the grave, and that this would happen on the third day. In the meantime, he entrusted his soul to the Father. His last words in life were his first words for going home to the Father.[10] So he said, "Father, into your hands I commit my spirit."

This confidence was well placed, as we will see when we get to Luke 24 and look inside the empty tomb. Where is your confidence? Have you made the prayer that Jesus made? Are you able to say what the apostle Paul said: "I know whom I have believed, and am convinced that he is able to guard what I have entrusted to him for that day" (2 Tim. 1:12 NIV). Do you know for sure that you are safe in God's hands, that when you die you will go home to the Father?

We do not need to wait until death to have this confidence. We can submit our spirit to God right now, asking the Father to receive us for the sake of the Son, on the basis of his sacrifice for our sins. Like Jesus, we may entrust our lives to the Father for death and everything that comes afterwards. Then we can keep using the words of his last prayer every night at bedtime, or whenever we are anxious or afraid, or even for the last prayer we make before dying: "Father, into your hands I commit my spirit."

---

9. Charles H. Spurgeon, "The Last Words of Christ on the Cross," in *Majesty in Misery: Select Sermons on the Passion of Christ*, 3 vols. (Edinburgh: Banner of Truth, 2005), 3:285.
10. Spurgeon, "Last Words," 3:272.

# 106

# DEAD AND BURIED

## *Luke 23:50–56*

*Then he took it down and wrapped it in a linen shroud and laid
him in a tomb cut in stone, where no one had ever yet been laid.*
(Luke 23:53)

O ne of the many masterpieces in New York's Frick Collection
is "The Deposition" by Gerard David, who was one of the
leading Flemish artists of the Renaissance. David's painting
dramatically portrays the removal of Christ's body from the cross and
includes all of the central characters in that sad moment from the Gospels. Nicodemus and Joseph of Arimathea are there, wearing the elegant
robes that signify their high office and gently bringing the lifeless body of
their Lord down a ladder from the cross. These noblemen are surrounded
by a group of weeping women, including Mary Magdalene and Mary the
mother of Jesus, who is supported by the arm of John the Evangelist as
she kisses the hand of her son.

The mood of the painting is intensely somber. Gloomy clouds hang over
the cross and the surrounding countryside. Tears glisten on John's cheek.
Mary Magdalene is in a posture of grief as she sadly wipes her eye with the
back of her hand. The ground is dusty and gray, like the ashes to which our

619

mortal bodies will go when they return to dust. There are bones underfoot, including a broken skull—the symbol of death. At the center of all the sadness is the cold and lifeless corpse of the Son of God.

On closer examination, David's painting reveals one detail that seems especially out of place. Looking past Mary Magdalene, the observer spies a windmill on a green hill far in the distance. This is historically inaccurate: there were no windmills near Jerusalem in the time of Christ. Instead, David located the painting somewhere in his own native landscape, where windmills dotted the countryside. He did this to testify to an important truth: the crucifixion is something that actually happened in the same world where we live. For Gerard David this meant the world that includes windmills; for us it is the world of high-speed Internet and high-rise condominiums. But either way, the point is the same: Jesus the Christ really and truly died, and then he was buried, in the world of space and time.

## How Jesus Was Buried

The report Luke gives of this indisputable historical fact is simple and straightforward. After saying his prayers to the Father, Jesus "breathed his last" (Luke 23:46). Death came to him, as it comes to any man, with one final exhalation of the lungs. With one last gasp he surrendered his body unto death and his spirit unto God.

Soon preparations were made for his burial, as Luke describes:

> Now there was a man named Joseph, from the Jewish town of Arimathea. He was a member of the council, a good and righteous man, who had not consented to their decision and action; and he was looking for the kingdom of God. This man went to Pilate and asked for the body of Jesus. Then he took it down and wrapped it in a linen shroud and laid him in a tomb cut in stone, where no one had ever yet been laid. (Luke 23:50–53)

After obtaining the necessary permissions, Joseph of Arimathea drew the nails from the cross, lowered the body of Jesus to the ground, gently wrapped him in clean linen, and laid him in a virgin tomb. This burial is an article of the Christian faith. It is part of the apostolic preaching of the gospel that the Christ who died for our sins was also buried (1 Cor. 15:3–4).

It is also something Christians confess in the words of the Apostles' Creed: he "was crucified, dead, and buried." The significance of this fact is that it confirms the reality of the death of Jesus Christ. There is no question here of him simply swooning on the cross and then recovering in the tomb, as some have tried to argue, however desperately. No, Jesus was actually dead, and therefore needed to be buried.

The death of Jesus was carefully confirmed by the soldiers responsible for his execution. John tells us that the legs of the other victims were broken to hasten their demise, but that this was unnecessary for Jesus because he was dead already (John 19:31–33). Furthermore, when one of the soldiers pierced his side with a spear, blood and water came out (John 19:34). In medical terms, this was "an effusion of blood into the pericardium"—a telltale sign of death.[1]

Still, when Joseph of Arimathea first went to Pontius Pilate to ask for the body, the governor was hesitant. According to Mark, "Pilate was surprised to hear that he should have already died." So before he issued the death certificate, the governor wanted some more information: "And summoning the centurion, he asked him whether he was already dead. And when he learned from the centurion that he was dead, he granted the corpse to Joseph" (Mark 15:44–45). Jesus was buried for the obvious reason that he was really and truly dead.

## THREE GREAT DOCTRINES IN THE DEATH OF JESUS

The death of Jesus has practical and theological significance for our salvation. It is not simply his sufferings on the cross that save us, but the cold reality of his physical death. "This is an essential point," said Charles Spurgeon, "for if Jesus did not die, he has made no atonement for sin. If he died not, then he rose not; and if he rose not, then your faith is vain, ye are yet in your sins."[2]

The death of Jesus is a gospel fact with doctrinal and practical implications. As far as doctrine is concerned, the death of Jesus helps us to know

1. William Stroud, *A Treatise on the Physical Cause of the Death of Christ, and Its Relation to the Principles and Practice of Christianity* (London: Hamilton and Adams, 1847), 74–75.

2. Charles H. Spurgeon, "A Royal Funeral," in *Majesty in Misery: Select Sermons on the Passion of Christ*, 3 vols. (Edinburgh: Banner of Truth, 2005), 3:380.

621

for sure three great doctrines of the Christian faith: the incarnation, the atonement, and the resurrection.

First, the death of Jesus was *the proof of his incarnation.* The doctrine of the incarnation simply teaches that Jesus Christ is both man and God, that he is human as well as divine. His humanity is proven by his death, because in order for Jesus to die, he had to be a real human being of flesh and blood mortality. Luke has shown us the humanity of Jesus all the way through his Gospel, from the manger in Bethlehem to the Garden of Gethsemane. Jesus of Nazareth was a real man with a genuine body and a true human soul. But what clearer or stronger proof of his humanity could there be than the fact that he died?

Death is the lowest common denominator of human experience. Nothing proclaims the frailty of our human condition as powerfully as a corpse. Dust we are, and to the dust we will return. So when Joseph of Arimathea took the body of Jesus down from the cross, he was holding the dust of death. It was a body that had weight to it, that had recently been alive, as anyone could see from the dried blood on its hands, its feet, and its side. Joseph felt cold skin and firm bones as he wrapped the body in pure linen—that is how real it was. It was the human body of the divine Son of God, whose incarnation is proved in the way he came down from the cross.

Second, the death of Jesus is *the payment for our atonement.* It is not the incarnation alone that saves us (God becoming a man), but also the atonement of the incarnate Christ (the God-man dying for our sins).

To understand this, we have to go all the way back to the very beginning, to something God said in the Garden of Eden: if the man ate from the tree of the knowledge of good and evil he would surely die (Gen. 2:17). But of course Adam did eat from the fruit of that forbidden tree, and death has been the unavoidable, inescapable result ever since. According to the justice of God, the wages of sin really is death (Rom. 6:23). But if that is true, then why did *Jesus* die? For if there is one thing we know from his life (especially from his trial), it is that Jesus never committed a single sin. What, then, is the explanation for his death and burial?

The explanation is that Jesus was dying in our place, making payment for our sins. If the wages of sin is death, then Jesus could satisfy the full demand of justice only by dying. In order to secure our salvation, it was not enough for him to live the perfectly righteous life that we could never offer to God. It was not even enough for him to suffer for our sins, languishing on the cross. He had to suffer unto death, and in doing so, to make full atonement for sin.

J. C. Ryle celebrated the death and burial of Jesus by saying: "For ever let us bless God that our great Redeemer's death is a fact beyond all dispute. The centurion who stood by the cross, the friends who took out the nails, and laid the body in the grave, the women who stood by and beheld, the priests who sealed up the grave, the soldiers who guarded the sepulcher, all, all are witnesses that Jesus actually was dead." Then Bishop Ryle went on to explain *why* this is something to celebrate: "The great sacrifice was really offered. The life of the Lamb was actually taken away. The penalty due to sin, has actually been discharged by our Divine Substitute. Sinners believing in Jesus may hope and not be afraid. In themselves they are guilty. But Christ hath died for the ungodly; and their debt is now completely paid."[3]

The death of Jesus was the full payment for sin. This explains why, when the prophets spoke about Jesus and his saving work, they invariably testified to his death. When David sang the song of the suffering Christ, he said, "you lay me in the dust of death" (Ps. 22:15). When Isaiah prophesied about the coming salvation, he said that the Suffering Servant "was cut off out of the land of the living. . . . they made his grave with the wicked and with a rich man in his death" (Isa. 53:8–9). The apostles spoke the same way in the New Testament. "We were reconciled to God by the death of his Son," Paul said to the Romans (Rom. 5:10). Or to the Corinthians: "he died for all" (2 Cor. 5:15). According to Hebrews, it is "through death" that our Savior has delivered us from the power of death and our slavery to sin (Heb. 2:14–15). The apostles and prophets were always saying, "We believe that Jesus died" (1 Thess. 4:14).

When we say we believe that Jesus died, we are saying we believe that he died for us, so that we could be delivered from the wrath of God against our sin. There was a powerful example of this kind of substitution during the 2006 massacre of ten schoolgirls at the West Nickel Mines Amish School in Lancaster, Pennsylvania. When it became apparent what was about to happen that ghastly morning, Marian Fisher turned to her killer and said,

3. J. C. Ryle, *Expository Thoughts on the Gospels, Luke* (1858; reprint Cambridge: James Clarke, 1976), 2:487.

"Shoot me and leave the other ones loose."[4] The girl was only thirteen, but she was ready to die so that others could live. She learned this from Jesus, who gave his life for us, saying, "Crucify me and leave the other ones loose."

Since Jesus died for others, it seems appropriate that he was also buried in someone else's tomb. This true fact from the Gospels made a deep impression on Maximus of Turin, who said, "Let us see why they placed the Savior in someone else's grave instead of his own. They placed him in another person's grave because he died for the salvation of others. . . . Death did not just happen to him, but it benefited us. Why should he . . . have his own grave?"[5] Jesus would not be using it for very long anyway, so why not borrow another man's tomb? Everything he ever did was for others, up to and including his death. It was for us that he died, and for us that he was buried.

Then Jesus rose again, which is a third great doctrine of the Christian faith that his death and burial help us to know for sure. The death of Jesus was not only the proof of his incarnation and the payment for our atonement, but also *the prerequisite for the resurrection.* Jesus had to die before he or anyone else could be raised again.

This is only logical: in order for someone to be raised from the dead, he has to be dead to begin with! There could be no Easter Sunday without Good Friday, no resurrection without the crucifixion, and no empty tomb without the death and the burial of Jesus. Thus what happens in Luke 23 is the prerequisite for what happens in chapter 24.

We need to be careful not to get ahead of ourselves here. In order to experience the full joy of the risen Christ we first have to experience the heavy sorrow of his dark tomb. Yet even as we consider this awful reality, Luke is preparing us for what will happen next. Notice that in the providence of God, Jesus was buried by himself, in an empty tomb (Luke 23:53). This is significant because it meant that his resurrection could be confirmed.[6] In those days it was uncommon for anyone to be buried

---

4. John Hewett, "A Miracle Nobody Noticed," as quoted in Makoto Fujimura, "Operation Homecoming: Epistles of Injury," in his online *Refractions*, vol. 22, http://makotofujimura.blogspot.com/

5. Maximus of Turin, "Sermon 39.3," in *Luke*, ed. Arthur A. Just, Jr., Ancient Christian Commentary on Scripture, NT 3 (Downers Grove, IL: InterVarsity, 2003), 371.

6. David Gooding, *According to Luke: A New Exposition of the Third Gospel* (Grand Rapids: Eerdmans, 1987), 346.

alone. Most tombs contained more than one body. But in this case the body of Jesus was the only body in the grave. Therefore there could be no confusion about which body belonged to him, and therefore no doubt about his coming back to life.

Luke also informs us that "the women who had come with him from Galilee followed and saw the tomb and how his body was laid" (Luke 23:55). This too is significant, because it proves that this was not a case of mistaken identity. The women who came back on the third day knew exactly which tomb to visit, and exactly where the body had been laid. So when they found the tomb totally empty, there was only one reasonable explanation: Jesus had triumphed over death by rising from the grave.

The hope of our own resurrection depends on this gospel fact. The one great question everyone has about life is what will happen at death. This is why the ancient pharaohs built their grandiose pyramids in the desert, and why some people have their bodies stored in ice. They are grasping for some guarantee of life after death. In fact, the only guarantee is the risen Christ. But we can know for sure that Jesus rose again only if we also know that he was actually dead and buried. Once we do know this, we never need to worry again about what will happen when we die. Because Jesus has gone into the grave ahead of us, he can lead us out again and on to eternal life.

## THE COURAGE OF NOBLE MEN

So far we have considered some of the doctrinal implications of the death and burial of Jesus—a gospel fact of the Christian faith that helps us to understand the incarnation, the atonement, and the resurrection of Jesus Christ. But what are some of the practical implications of his death and burial?

One way to answer this question is to consider the courage of the noble men and the compassion of the gentle women who buried Jesus. Luke's simple account of what these people did touches the heart of anyone who loves Jesus and wants to serve him. In his study of this passage, Norval Geldenhuys comments that "The Gospel narrative of Jesus' passion ends on a note of exceptional beauty in the description of His burial. For in it we see how the dead body of the Savior, from the time that it was removed from the rough cross by hands of affection, was cared for by no other hands than those of His faithful followers."[7]

Surprisingly enough, one of those faithful followers was Joseph of Arimathea. This is surprising because up until now this distinguished gentleman had never publicly identified himself with the cause of Christ. In fact, John tells us that Joseph "was a disciple of Jesus, but secretly for fear of the Jews" (John 19:38), meaning his colleagues on the high council of the Jewish community. Luke identifies him not only as a member of the Sanhedrin, but as "a good and righteous man" who "was looking for the kingdom of God," and "who had not consented to their decision and action" (Luke 23:50–51). Joseph of Arimathea was a conscientious objector: he had never agreed that Jesus should be crucified.

Now Joseph had a choice to make—a choice that turned out to be essential to the plan of salvation. Ordinarily the Romans left the bodies of their victims to rot upon their crosses. This was something Joseph decided he would do everything in his power to prevent. In his heart he knew that the disfigured body of Jesus deserved the dignity of a decent burial. So, refusing to let his Lord suffer any further dishonor, Joseph "went to Pilate and asked for the body of Jesus" (Luke 23:52).

This was an audacious request. Private individuals did not go around taking bodies down from crosses—it simply wasn't done (not without permission, at any rate). In fact, Mark tells us that Joseph "took courage" when he went to Pilate (Mark 15:43). It took some courage, because ordinarily no one would want to have anything to do with the corpse from a crucifixion. This was especially true for someone as wealthy as Joseph of Arimathea, who had such a high position that he could get a private audience with the governor. Why would a man like him even think of touching a body on a cross?

Consider how costly this was for Joseph. It would cost him his money—the finest linen and "his own new tomb, which he had cut in the rock" (Matt. 27:60). It would cost him his reputation. By taking Jesus down from the cross and burying him in his own personal tomb, he was deliberately and publicly identifying himself with someone convicted as a criminal. This could very well cost him the career it had taken a lifetime to build.

7. Norval Geldenhuys, *The Gospel of Luke*, New International Commentary on the New Testament (Grand Rapids: Eerdmans, 1951), 618.

How could he go back to his friends in the Sanhedrin, once everyone knew how boldly he had rejected their verdict?

Yet Joseph had the courage of his convictions. The time had come for him to stop being a secret disciple and to start making a public profession of his faith. He understood that even though his faith in Jesus was personal, it could not remain private. Here is how David Gooding explains what Joseph was thinking:

> If . . . Jesus was the Messiah, it was not enough simply to protest that his execution was unjust. Joseph realized that both logic and loyalty demanded that he confess his faith in the truth of Jesus' claim and publicly associate himself with Jesus now in this moment of his profound humiliation, if he wanted to be owned by Christ at his exaltation, whenever and however that exaltation should be brought about.[8]

It was at the cross where Joseph took his stand, confessing Jesus in his death. He had been looking for the kingdom of God, and now he had found it, in the body of the royal Messiah who died for his sins. So with noble courage and gentle affection, Joseph gave honor to his Lord by wrapping his body in a linen shroud and respectfully laying it to rest, thus fulfilling Isaiah's ancient prophecy that the Savior would be buried in a rich man's tomb (see Isa. 53:9).

By burying Jesus, Joseph of Arimathea became an example for every believer to follow. Have you taken your stand with Jesus at the cross? Are you willing to be identified with the Savior who died for you, no matter what the cost? Do you have the courage of your convictions, or is your Christianity more or less a secret?

It is one thing to praise God in church, but another thing to proclaim him out in the community. Do not be so concerned about your reputation that you fail to tell your friends what you really believe. Do not be so ambitious to advance your career that you compromise your commitment to Christ in your art, your schoolwork, or your business. Do not be so jealous to protect everything you have gained in life that you will not give up what you need to give up for the glory of God. Stop being a secret disciple and stand with Jesus at the cross. Indeed, it is always at the cross where

8. Gooding, *Luke*, 347.

Christians stand with Christ, sharing in the offense of his crucifixion and serving him by proclaiming the message of the cross to a world lost in sin.

## THE COMPASSION OF GENTLE WOMEN

If Joseph is an example of noble courage, then the women who watched him bury Jesus are an example of gentle compassion. Here is how Luke begins to tell us their story: "It was the day of Preparation, and the Sabbath was beginning. The women who had come with him from Galilee followed and saw the tomb and how his body was laid. Then they returned and prepared spices and ointments. On the Sabbath they rested according to the commandment" (Luke 23:54–56).

These women had traveled with Jesus from Galilee and had supported him throughout his public ministry (see Mark 15:40–41; Luke 8:1–3). In sharp contrast to the disciples, who by this point had abandoned Jesus completely (see Mark 14:50), they stayed at the cross until the very end. Like Joseph, they wanted to honor Jesus by making sure he received the burial that he deserved. But unlike Joseph, they did not have the power to accomplish their hearts' desire. They had neither the connections to gain custody of his body nor the resources to bury that body in a tomb. So they lingered at the cross, maybe even praying that God would provide a way for them to do one last thing for Jesus.

How amazed they must have been to see Joseph of Arimathea take Jesus down from the cross—someone they never expected, doing something they never expected him to do. Cautiously they followed him to see exactly where he would lay the body of their Lord. Then they went home to prepare the spices and ointments they would need (or so they thought) to complete the embalming process that Joseph had only just begun. The women worked swiftly, finishing their preparations before the approaching Sabbath. Then they rested, keeping the commandment of their God.

Everything these women did commends their godly character. They recognized the dignity of the human body, even at the time of death. They were careful to honor God with a day of worship and rest. If ever there was an exception to the fourth commandment, it would have been on this day (the last Sabbath for the people of God before the coming of the Lord's day with the resurrection) and for this reason (to honor the body of the Son of God). But the closest disciples of Jesus Christ were serious about keeping the Sabbath. In doing so, they were simply following the teaching and example of their Lord, who loved to be in his Father's house every week for worship. This is one of the ways they honored God: by resting on his holy day.

It is hard to find women or men with this kind of character today. Most people in our culture would rather not have anything to do with death at all. They certainly do not have any intention of setting aside one whole day for God. According to *Time* magazine's Nancy Gibbs, "Over time, Sunday has gone from a day we could do only a very few things to the only day we can do just about anything we want. The U.S. is too diverse, our lives too busy, our economy too global and our appetites too vast to lose a whole day that could be spent working or playing or power shopping."[9]

The women who lingered at the cross and followed Joseph to the tomb had stronger character. Though they were grieving with deep sorrow, they were not so overwhelmed by their emotions that they forgot to honor God with holy rest. In their passionate love for Jesus, they were prepared to dignify his death with the honor of a full and proper burial.

I remember a time when there was a death in the family—the death of my sister's only daughter. Our grief was heavy, and there was nothing much that anyone could do. Then I saw a little girl I love as much as anyone in the world busily making something with her hands to give to my sister—a simple gift of sympathy for a grieving mother. With gentle compassion the little girl was busily doing just what needed to be done. I could see then what kind of woman she was becoming. She was like the women who saw Jesus in the tomb and went home to prepare spices. With gentle compassion she would do whatever beautiful, sensible thing she could do for Jesus.

In this world of many sorrows, what will you do for Jesus, who loves you so much that he was crucified, dead, and buried for your salvation? The noble men and gentle women—not to mention the boys and girls—who love Jesus do everything they can to show his love and share his compassion.

---

9. Nancy Gibbs, "And on the Seventh Day We Rested?" *Time* (Aug. 2, 2004): 90.

# 107

# ON THE THIRD DAY

## *Luke 24:1–12*

*"He is not here, but has risen. Remember how he told you, while
he was still in Galilee, that the Son of Man must be delivered into
the hands of sinful men and be crucified and on the third day rise."*
(Luke 24:6–7)

he gospel is the good news about Jesus Christ: his life, his death,
and his resurrection. The gospel promises that if we believe in
Jesus, all our sins will be forgiven and we will live with God
forever. This good news centers on the person and the work of Jesus Christ.
We see this very clearly in the Gospel of Luke, which is all about Jesus from
beginning to end.

Already in the opening verses, Luke announced his intention to give
"certainty concerning the things you have been taught" (Luke 1:4), meaning the things taught about Jesus. He proceeded to report the miraculous
circumstances surrounding the birth of Jesus Christ, who was conceived
by the Holy Spirit and born of the virgin Mary. Then, after a few brief
stories about his childhood—stories that begin to show his saving work
as the divine Son of God—Luke recounted the main events in his earthly
ministry. As we have studied this Gospel, we have heard Jesus preach the

kingdom of God and we have seen him perform many miracles of healing and deliverance. Jesus is the center of everything that happens in the Gospel of Luke: calling disciples, teaching parables, rebuking religious leaders, calming storms, casting out demons, healing diseases, and feeding multitudes. Then, in the last week of his life, Jesus was betrayed, arrested, tried, condemned, and crucified. His living presence dominates every page of Luke's Gospel.

Until we get to chapter 24, that is. Here we find Jesus conspicuous by his absence. It is now the third day since he was crucified, dead, and buried—the day he said that he would rise from the dead. So Christ has risen. Yet in the opening verses of this chapter he is nowhere to be found—at least not in his bodily presence. Why not? If this is the day Jesus rose from the dead, then why don't we see him here, as we do everywhere else in this Gospel? If Luke wants us to know Jesus for sure, then why don't we see him raised from the dead?

## What the Women Found

To understand why Jesus seems to be missing, we need to see what the women found when they went to the empty tomb, what the angel said to them there, and how people responded, whether in faith or unbelief.

We begin with the little group of women who were the last people to leave the cross and the first to arrive at the empty tomb. At the end of chapter 23 these women still had some unfinished business to attend to. They had watched Joseph of Arimathea take the lifeless body of Jesus down from the cross and then lay him in an unused tomb. Taking careful note of where the body was laid, they quickly went home to prepare the spices needed for a full and proper burial. Then they took their Sabbath rest, waiting one holy day before paying their last respects to the teacher they loved.

The women never finished their task, however. They went back to the tomb the following day, which was the first day of the week (and also, as it turned out, the first Lord's day for the resurrection people of God). A surprise was waiting for them: "But on the first day of the week, at early dawn, they went to the tomb, taking the spices they had prepared. And they found the stone rolled away from the tomb, but when they went in they did not find the body of the Lord Jesus" (Luke 24:1–3).

"At early dawn" is a striking expression. When these women set out on their errand of mercy, it was not simply dawn, but *early* dawn—what one scholar translates as "deep earliness,"[1] or what people in the military call BMNT ("Before Morning Nautical Twilight"). This indicates how eager these women were to finish their task. In the providence of God, there had not been time to complete the burial process on the day Jesus was crucified. This was an important part of God's plan because it drew the women back to his tomb. All during the long Sabbath between Good Friday and Easter Sunday they waited to finish their task, and when the time came, they left the house at the earliest possible instant.

The women expected to find the dead body of Jesus. When last they saw him he was as dead as could be, and naturally they assumed that death was the end of his earthly existence. To reparaphrase Mark Antony in Shakespeare's *Julius Caesar*, they had not come to praise their Lord, but to bury him. Thus it never occurred to them that his body would be anywhere except the place where they had seen it laid to rest.

Imagine how shocked they must have been to enter the tomb and find the body missing! For anyone who knows how this story ends—with Jesus triumphing over death through the resurrection of his body—it is hard to appreciate the full extent of their surprise. Kent Hughes reminds us that "As we consider the state of the Galilean women, we must not let our knowledge of the glorious revelation that awaited them dull us to the dark sackcloth covering these women's souls. They were depressed, exhausted, mourning, with no hope whatsoever."[2] When they discovered that the body was gone, this could only add bitter sorrow to their sad distress. It was the shock of their lives—the aftershock that followed the earthquake of the crucifixion. The Jesus who was crucified, dead, and buried had now disappeared.

Luke tells us that "they were perplexed about this" (Luke 24:4). They were at a total loss. It simply did not make any sense to them; they could not explain it. Why did Jesus die the way that he died, suffering the dark reproach of the cross? How could someone so alive end up dead? Where was the body they had seen buried?

1. B. S. Easton, quoted in Norval Geldenhuys, *The Gospel of Luke*, New International Commentary on the New Testament (Grand Rapids: Eerdmans, 1951), 625.
2. R. Kent Hughes, *Luke: That You May Know the Truth*, 2 vols., Preaching the Word (Wheaton, IL: Crossway, 1998), 2:399.

Although the women did not know the answers to these questions, there were hints all around them. Miraculously, the stone had been rolled away from the tomb, leaving the house of death door-less. Even more remarkably, the body was not in the tomb. These were the first intimations of the resurrection, that Jesus has been raised from the dead. For us there is a further hint in the title Luke gives to Jesus in verse 3, where he calls him "Lord." This is one of the specific titles of the risen Christ, for it is by his resurrection that Jesus is declared to be the Lord (see Acts 2:36). Even though Luke has not yet shown us that Jesus is alive, already he is expressing the joy of the resurrection and cannot help but confess that Jesus is Lord.

The women were not ready to say this yet. They were still distressed and perplexed. All they could see was that the body of Jesus was not where they expected it to be. What the women found is that they could not find Jesus.

## What the Angels Said

The women also found some angels at the empty tomb, and their words help us understand why Jesus is missing from this passage: "While they were perplexed about this, behold, two men stood by them in dazzling apparel. And as they were frightened and bowed their faces to the ground, the men said to them, 'Why do you seek the living among the dead? He is not here, but has risen'" (Luke 23:4–6).

Angels are the holy messengers of God. When they appear to human beings (which does not happen often), they are usually robed in radiant splendor. Here they were resplendent in white and shining robes—what Luke calls "dazzling apparel." Understandably, the women were awestruck (as people generally are when they encounter angels), so they bowed down to worship.

Then the angels gave them a mild rebuke, which was phrased in the form of a question: "Why do you seek the living among the dead?" This was the angels' gentle way of saying that the women were operating on the basis of a faulty assumption. They assumed that Jesus was dead, which is why they were at the tomb so early in the morning, carrying the oils and the spices for his embalming. They believed that Jesus was still buried, and therefore they were looking to find him among the dead.

633

They were on the wrong premises because they had the wrong premise! Jesus was no longer dead at all, but alive, and there is no sense looking for someone where he is not to be found. "He is not here," the angels said, "but has risen" (Luke 24:6). Jesus was not dead, but alive, and therefore this was the wrong place to look for him. "He is the Living One," wrote Norval Geldenhuys, "yes, even Life itself, so how can they seek Him among the dead? No bonds of grave or death could keep Him bound, and it is the spontaneous outcome of His whole being as perfect Man and Son of God, that, after He had accomplished full expiation through His suffering and sacrificial death, He arose from the dead in triumph."[3]

When we say that Jesus rose from the dead, we are referring to his bodily resurrection. We are not merely saying that Jesus is alive in our minds, our hearts, or our memories. Nor are we simply saying that his soul is immortal. On the contrary, we are dealing with the objective facts and the physical reality of what happened to a dead man's body. The physical body of Jesus was raised from death to life by the power of God. This was not simply a case of resuscitation: the coming back to life of a mortal body that would die again. Rather, it was a physical resurrection: the raising of Jesus Christ to the immortal splendor of a body that could never die again.

God sent the angels to say: Jesus is alive! He knew that the women would be in the wrong place on the first Easter morning, looking for the living among the dead. So he graciously sent messengers to tell them the good news of the gospel. God often does this: even when we go to the wrong place, he is there ahead of us, pointing us back in the right direction. In this case, the angels were at the tomb to say that although Jesus had been in the grave, he is not in the grave any longer. In the words of one poet: "And all alone, alone, alone / He rose again behind the stone."[4]

How could the women know that this was true? As far as they were concerned, Jesus was still missing. How could they believe in the resurrection of his body unless they could see Jesus with their own eyes? More importantly, how can *we* believe this? Harvard Professor Ernest Wright correctly has said, "In biblical faith everything depends upon whether the central events

3. Geldenhuys, *Luke*, 623.

4. Alice Meynell, "Easter Night," in *Chapters into Verse: Poetry in English Inspired by the Bible*, vol. 2: *Gospels to Revelation*, ed. Robert Atwan and Laurance Wieder (Oxford: Oxford University Press, 1993), 217.

actually occurred or not."[5] If this is true, then how can we know for sure that Jesus really did rise from the dead?

This question was raised in a fresh way by the February 2007 announcement that the caskets of Jesus and other members of his family had been discovered at a burial cave in a Jerusalem suburb.[6] According to James Cameron, who produced a documentary film on the subject, DNA evidence would prove that this was, in fact, the burial cave of the family of Jesus of Nazareth. Two thousand years after the fact, someone was finally claiming to have found the remains of Jesus (which of course the Jewish Sanhedrin would have done anything to produce at the time Christ was crucified, thereby disproving the resurrection and discrediting the apostles!).

What is the best way to respond to such a direct attack on the veracity of the gospel? Some Christians answer by giving evidence for the resurrection.[7] There is a place for this approach in the practice of apologetics, both as a way of confirming the faith and casting doubt on unbelief, if not actually convincing people of the truth of the gospel. The very fact of the empty tomb is evidence that demands a verdict. The body of Jesus was dead, having been crucified. Then it disappeared from the very tomb where it was buried. This was widely known and accepted in the days after Christ was crucified. No one could say that Jesus was still in the grave because the grave was vacant. Furthermore, the body that disappeared was the very body that was crucified. This historical fact—the absence of his body from the empty tomb—joins the crucifixion to the resurrection and helps to confirm that Jesus rose from the dead.[8]

Yet this is not how the angels tried to convince the women at the empty tomb. They did not try to reason on the basis of the physical evidence. Nor did they make a case for Christ by refuting alternative explanations for what happened to the missing body. Instead, the angels simply told these women—and us—to remember what Jesus said: "Remember how he told you, while he was still in Galilee, that the Son of Man must be delivered into the hands of sinful men and be crucified and on the third

---

5. G. Ernest Wright, *God Who Acts* (SCM Press, 1952), 38.

6. As first reported by Tim McGirk, "Tales from the Crypt," *Time/CNN*, Feb. 23, 2007.

7. See, for example, Frank Morison, *Who Moved the Stone?* (1930; reprint Grand Rapids: Zondervan, 1958), or, more recently, Lee Strobel, *The Case for Christ* (Grand Rapids: Zondervan, 1998), 191–257.

8. Paul Beasley-Murray, *The Message of the Resurrection*, The Bible Speaks Today (Downers Grove, IL: InterVarsity, 2000), 65.

day rise" (Luke 24:6–7). We are to believe in the resurrection on the basis of what Jesus said. The empty tomb is not self-explanatory. There is a word that explains the deed, and this word is the gospel message that Jesus not only died, but also rose again with a glorious and everlasting body that would never die again.

The angels told the women to remember the prophecies Jesus made of his death, burial, and resurrection. Immediately after Peter confessed that he was the Christ of God, Jesus said, "The Son of Man must suffer many things and be rejected by the elders and chief priests and scribes, and be killed, and on the third day be raised" (Luke 9:22; cf. 9:44). We find the same thing in chapter 18: "For he will be delivered over to the Gentiles and . . . after flogging him, they will kill him, and on the third day he will rise" (Luke 18:32–33; cf. 17:25). Everything happened just the way that Jesus said. The words of his prophecies all came true. He was crucified, dead, and buried.

Now it was the third day—the day Jesus promised to rise from the grave. Indeed, this was the day when he *must* rise from the grave, for the earlier promises of the gospel expressed a divine compulsion. Therefore, when the women saw the empty tomb, they should have known that Jesus was alive from the dead. The reason they were perplexed was that they did not yet believe what Jesus said. This is often the case: unless and until we believe in the Word of God, life is all too perplexing. But when we do believe, everything starts to fall into place.

This explains why Jesus is "missing" from this passage. The risen Christ does not make a personal, physical appearance until later in the chapter. The other Gospels all show Jesus appearing to Mary Magdalene and others in the garden.[9] Luke first shows us the empty tomb and only later shows us the risen Christ. He does this to repeat and therefore to emphasize the gospel prophecy that Jesus would rise from the dead on the third day. So although Jesus may not be in this passage, his word certainly is.

*This is how we know for sure:* by believing the gospel promise that Jesus died and rose again. We have not yet seen Jesus in his resurrection body, any more than the women saw him when they went into the empty tomb.

---

9. Some scholars have attacked the historical reliability of the Gospels on the basis of apparent discrepancies between the resurrection narratives. For a biblical defense and summary of possible harmonizations, see Geldenhuys, *Luke*, 626–28.

But we *have* heard the gospel word, which should be enough for us, as it should have been enough for them. Remember what Jesus said: he would be crucified to atone for our sins and raised to give us eternal life. If we believe this, God will forgive our sins, raise our body from the grave, and give us everlasting joy.

## HOW THE DISCIPLES RESPONDED

How did people respond to this saving message of the gospel? We have seen what the women found (and failed to find) at the empty tomb. We have also heard what the angels said. How should we respond to their message of the cross and the empty tomb?

The women responded in faith: "And they remembered his words, and returning from the tomb they told all these things to the eleven and to all the rest. Now it was Mary Magdalene and Joanna and Mary the mother of James and the other women with them who told these things to the apostles" (Luke 24:8–10).

These godly women had followed Jesus almost from the beginning. They had supported him throughout his earthly ministry. They had heard his teaching, and therefore could remember what he said. As soon as they remembered his words, they were no longer perplexed. They understood why the tomb was empty: Jesus was not among the dead, but among the living. He had risen from the grave!

This was the best of all possible news. It meant that they would see Jesus again. It meant that God had won the total victory over sin and death. It meant that when they died, they would live again with God. Such news was too good to keep to themselves. Immediately they went and found the eleven remaining disciples and all the other followers of Christ. They testified to what they had seen and heard, and thus they became, as Augustine said, "the first preachers of the resurrection."[10]

This is the way to respond to the resurrection, by remembering what Jesus said, believing what Jesus did, and then telling other people about it. We are called to be showers and tellers of the resurrection. Another word for this is evangelism. We do not seek to compel anyone to become a Christian by

---

10. Augustine, quoted in J. C. Ryle, *Expository Thoughts on the Gospels, Luke* (1858; reprint Cambridge: James Clarke, 1976), 2:497.

force, but we do announce the saving message that Jesus died and rose again, and that simply by believing in him anyone may have eternal life.

But we do need to make this announcement! It is only by gospel words that anyone ever comes to faith in Jesus Christ. In a little booklet called *A Shy Person's Guide to the Practice of Evangelism*, Steven Bonsey writes, "Let's pretend that you are someone who might be willing, in theory, at some point, possibly, to consider maybe doing something that, while not 'evangelism'-type evangelism, still could be in some way construed as a sort of sharing of hope. Kind of."[11] Obviously, Bonsey is having a little fun at the expense of those of us who are timid in our evangelism. But even if we do not always feel comfortable talking to other people about Jesus, we should follow the example of the women at the empty tomb. Using simple words, they told their friends about Jesus and the resurrection.

At first the apostles did not believe a word of it. They did not respond in faith, but in unbelief, for the words of the women "seemed to them an idle tale, and they did not believe them" (Luke 24:11). What the women said about the empty tomb and about Jesus rising from the dead sounded like unintelligible nonsense. In fact, the Greek word for "idle tale" *(lēros)* "is applied in medicinal language to the wild talk of the sick in delirium."[12] The disciples thought that the women were out of their minds—that their emotional response to the death of Jesus had overpowered their reason. They simply did not believe that Jesus had risen from the dead.

The same thing still happens today. Many people think that the Bible is a fairy tale. They do not believe that Jesus was crucified to pay for the guilt of our sins, and they certainly do not believe that he came back to life. They are like the people Jesus described in the story of the rich man and Lazarus, who would not even believe in God if they saw someone rise from the dead (see Luke 16:31).

How encouraging it is to see that the disciples of Jesus were just as skeptical. At first they did not believe in the resurrection either, but later they came through their doubts to give a strong testimony of faith in Jesus Christ. In fact, they became so committed to Christ that they kept preaching his gospel even when they were persecuted, most of them unto death.

11. Steven C. Bonsey, *A Shy Person's Guide to the Practice of Evangelism* (published by the Episcopal Church's Diocese of Massachusetts).

12. A. Plummer, quoted in Geldenhuys, *Luke*, 626.

This gives us reason to hope that many of the people we love and pray for will come to Christ. Like the disciples, they may still come through their unbelief and into faith in Jesus Christ. This also encourages us in our doubts. If we are not yet sure that Jesus rose from the dead, we can still hope that God will grant us the gift of faith so that we may believe in Jesus and be saved.

Anyone who doubts the resurrection would be wise to follow the example of Peter. When the rest of the disciples could not believe what the women were saying, Peter went to check things out for himself. He "rose and ran to the tomb; stooping and looking in, he saw the linen cloths by themselves; and he went home marveling at what had happened" (Luke 24:12).

Running ahead like this was typical of Peter. He was a man of action, who sometimes said things and did things somewhat impulsively. But running to the tomb was the right thing to do. When Peter heard the first news of the resurrection, he wanted to investigate for himself. Was it really true? Did Jesus rise from the dead? Is there solid hope of a bodily resurrection for everyone who believes in him? Is there any chance, Peter must have wondered, that someone who denied the Christ might still be forgiven?

When Peter saw the empty tomb (or the almost empty tomb: Luke tells us that the linen cloths were lying there), he still wasn't sure. The word "marveling" *(thaumazōn)* expresses astonishment and amazement without indicating whether Peter understood the full implications of what he was seeing. Maybe he was still thinking things through. But he would not stop thinking things through until he was sure he understood what God wanted him to know about Jesus.

## A Word That Demands Faith

Have you carefully considered the claims of Christ? Have you honestly investigated the empty tomb, as Peter did, to find out whether Jesus rose from the dead? Sadly, some people refuse to take the trouble. J. B. Phillips lamented:

> Over the years I have had hundreds of conversations with people, many of them of higher intellectual caliber than my own, who quite obviously had no idea of what Christianity is really about. I was in no case trying to catch

639

them out; I was simply and gently trying to find out what they knew about the New Testament. My conclusion was that they knew virtually nothing. This I find pathetic and somewhat horrifying. It means that the most important Event in human history is politely and quietly by-passed. For it is not as though the evidence had been examined and found unconvincing: it had simply never been examined.[13]

Will you examine the evidence? In his Gospel, Luke has written an orderly, reliable, eyewitness historical account of the life and death and resurrection of Jesus Christ. His report challenges us to reach our own decision as to whether Jesus is among the living or the dead.

There are many good reasons to believe that Jesus is alive. There is the evidence of history, starting with the empty tomb itself. Where did Jesus' body go if it did not rise from the grave and ascend to heaven? There is also the existence of the church. How did the first Christians recover from their despair over the death of Jesus so quickly and change the world in so many ways if not by the power of the risen Christ? Then there is the worship of the church on Sunday. Why did Christians ever begin worshiping on the first day of the week, if not because this is the day that Jesus rose from the dead?

Consider as well the testimony of the people we meet in the Gospels. There is the witness of the women, who were the first to see the empty tomb, and also the testimony of the apostles, who did not believe at first, but later took the gospel of Jesus all over the world. There is also the proclamation of Peter, who stood up a few weeks later to preach that God raised the crucified Christ, "loosing the pangs of death, because it was not possible for him to be held by it" (Acts 2:24). Beyond all this, we have the witness of the rest of the New Testament, that Jesus "was raised" (Rom. 8:34), that he "was raised on the third day" (1 Cor. 15:4), that he was "raised from the dead, the firstfruits of those who have fallen asleep" (1 Cor. 15:20). Therefore, we are "born again to a living hope through the resurrection of Jesus Christ from the dead" (1 Peter 1:3).

But even if you do not find any of this evidence fully persuasive, will you at least believe the true words of Jesus Christ, who is a faithful prophet and the divine Son of God? Jesus said that he would be crucified, dead, and

13. J. B. Phillips, quoted in Beasley-Murray, *Message of the Resurrection*, 67.

buried, and that on the third day he would rise again. Do you believe his words, or not?

Some people think it would be easier to believe in Jesus if they could go back and see the empty tomb for themselves. But the men and the women who did see the empty tomb struggled with spiritual doubt as much as anyone. They did not believe at first, but only came to believe later on. When they believed, it was because they believed the same words of Jesus that we have been given. At first they did not see the risen Christ, any more than we have seen them. But they remembered his words—the same words that Luke put in his Gospel so that we would know Jesus for sure.

It all comes back to the gospel words of Jesus. The risen Christ may not be in this passage, but his testimony is, and therefore we have as much reason to believe as anyone.

According to the word of the gospel, Jesus is not among the dead, but among the living. He was crucified for the forgiveness of all our sins. His sacrifice has been accepted by God and now he has risen from the grave. Death is not the end for us, but by faith we have the free gift of eternal life. Now the resurrection body of the Lord Jesus Christ is at the right hand of God the Father in heaven, shining in glory and ruling the universe. One day soon he will raise us up to be with him forever, to the glory of God.

# 108

# ON THE GOSPEL ROAD

## *Luke 24:13–27*

*That very day two of them were going to a village named
Emmaus, about seven miles from Jerusalem. . . . And beginning
with Moses and all the Prophets, he interpreted to them in all the
Scriptures the things concerning himself.* (Luke 24:13, 27)

f you could travel back in time to witness any event in biblical
history, which event would you choose? Some people would
go back to the creation of the world to see the first ray of light
shoot across the blackness of space and hear the morning stars sing for
joy. Some would go back to the great flood, so they could see Noah and
all his animals safe in the ark, while the rains fell from the darkening sky.
Some would go back to the exodus, when Moses and the children of Israel
walked through the sea on dry land. Some would go back to Joshua and
the battle of Jericho, where the walls came tumbling down. Some would
go back to the time of David, who slew Goliath, or Solomon, who built
the golden temple.

Then there all the famous events from the life of Christ that people wish
they could see: the shepherds at the manger, the baptism in the Jordan, the
healing of the lame and the blind, the feeding of the five thousand, Jesus

walking on water, or his glorious transfiguration on the mountain. Perhaps you would choose to see your Savior weeping in the garden before dying on the cross. But I would choose to travel the gospel road from Jerusalem to Emmaus, walking with two disciples on an Easter afternoon and listening to Jesus explain how everything in the whole Bible is all about him.

## THE MYSTERIOUS STRANGER

This amazing story is told only in the Gospel of Luke. It adds to what we already know about the resurrection by giving us another eyewitness account of people who actually saw the risen Christ. They walked with him; they talked with him; they even had supper with him.

This encounter with Jesus took place towards the end of Resurrection Sunday. We know from verse 13 that it was still "that very day"—the first day of the week, when the women went to the empty tomb. From verse 29 we know that by the end of this conversation it was almost evening. On this Easter afternoon "two of them were going to a village named Emmaus, about seven miles from Jerusalem, and they were talking with each other about all these things that had happened" (Luke 24:13–14).

Considering everything that had happened over the last few days, the conversation between these traveling companions must have been animated. Many people have wondered who these two disciples were. Obviously they were close friends who had been to Jerusalem for Passover and were heading home to spend the night. We know from verse 18 that one of them was named Cleopas. Is this the same man as the Clopas mentioned in John 19:25, or is it someone else? If it is the same man, then his wife was named Mary, and she may well have been his unnamed companion on this journey. But whether they were husband and wife or simply two close friends, Cleopas and the other member in this couple were walking down the road to Emmaus and talking about everything that had happened to Jesus.

There was a good deal to discuss, from the triumphal entry to the empty tomb, and they were probably taking their time doing it. We know from the words used to describe them later in the chapter that they were disappointed, sad, and bewildered. Indeed, they were grieving, because their beloved Jesus had died and was now missing. As they made their slow, sorrowful way to

Emmaus, a stranger overtook them on the road: "While they were talking and discussing together, Jesus himself drew near and went with them. But their eyes were kept from recognizing him" (Luke 24:15–16).

Cleopas and his companion were sure they knew where this man was coming from, because in verse 18 they infer that he had just left Jerusalem. What they did not know was who the man was. This is very mysterious. If they knew Jesus well enough to love him, they must have known what he looked like. Yet they did not or could not recognize who he was—a common occurrence in the resurrection appearances of Jesus Christ. This confirms that Jesus was a real human being, even after his resurrection from the dead, but it still leaves us struggling to understand why people failed to recognize him.

What prevented these disciples from seeing Jesus? Perhaps it was their unbelief, for as we shall see, they did not yet have faith in the resurrection. Maybe they failed to recognize Jesus because they never expected to see him again. Or maybe they were too weighed down with grief to lift their heads and take a good look at him.

Alternatively, Cleopas and his friend may have been prevented from seeing Jesus by a direct act of God. Mark tells us that Jesus "appeared in another form" to a pair of disciples who were "walking into the country" (Mark 16:12). Luke simply says that "their eyes were kept from recognizing him" (Luke 24:16), which implies some sort of divine hindrance. Jesus was traveling incognito because this was the gracious will and saving purpose of God. If the disciples could not see Jesus, it was because God would not let them see Jesus, at least not yet. This is a story of delayed recognition, therefore, and for that very reason it can help us see Jesus for ourselves. It is not simply the physical sight of Jesus that brings the assurance of salvation, but believing in Jesus by seeing him in the gospel, whether or not we have ever walked with him on the road to Emmaus.

As Jesus fell into stride beside the two disciples, he asked a common question: "What are you folks talking about?" Or, to say it the way Jesus said it, feigning ignorance, "What is this conversation that you are holding with each other as you walk?" (Luke 24:17). Obviously Cleopas and his friend were having a serious conversation about spiritual things, and like a good evangelist, Jesus wanted to engage them in a way that would give him a chance to share the gospel.

The answer the disciples gave indicates their spiritual condition: "And they stood still, looking sad" (Luke 24:17). The disciples were downcast and dispirited, still grieving the loss of their beloved teacher. But they were not too sad to be surprised that the third traveler did not know what they were talking about. As far as they were concerned, he had interrupted their conversation to ask what seemed to be a rather stupid question. With irritated astonishment, Cleopas said, "Are you the only visitor to Jerusalem who does not know the things that have happened there in these days?" (Luke 24:18).

This comment indicates that everybody knew what had happened to Jesus. Jerusalem was abuzz with the news of his crucifixion, and maybe also by now with the news of his reported resurrection. Everyone was talking about Jesus . . . except, that is, the mysterious stranger who interrupted them on the road to Emmaus and who apparently was more out of touch than anyone else in the whole city.

The question in verse 18 creates another one of the situational ironies that Luke uses to such dramatic effect in his Gospel. In truth, *Cleopas* was the one who did not know what was happening in Jerusalem! Jesus knew it all, better than anyone, for it had happened to him! He alone could explain what had transpired during his Jewish and Roman trials. He alone could testify what it was like to be mocked and tortured and to die in disgrace. He alone had felt the thorny crown upon his brow and the steely nail through his hands and feet. He alone could describe the inside of the dark tomb at the first light of the resurrection.

Instead of being the only person who did *not* know what was happening, Jesus was the only person who did! But rather than acting like a know-it-all, he took the time to help these disciples see their salvation. "What things?" he said in verse 19, inviting them to tell him what they understood. This is good evangelism: asking people questions that help clarify where they are in relationship to Jesus.

Jesus must have asked this question with a twinkle in his eye and kindness in his heart. David Gooding points out how loving it was for Jesus, "having journeyed from Galilee and entered Jerusalem as King, to travel back with two of his disciples down the road of their disillusionment," and then to listen to all of their doubts.[1] Jesus will show us the same kindness.

---

1. David Gooding, *According to Luke: A New Exposition of the Third Gospel* (Grand Rapids: Eerdmans, 1987), 351.

He will overtake us along life's road, falling in stride with our sorrow and confusion. Then he will ask what we know about him, hoping that we will listen to the gospel and see him as our Savior.

## THE GOSPEL ACCORDING TO CLEOPAS

Cleopas and his companion were out on the road between Jerusalem and Emmaus, standing somewhere between faith and unbelief. When the mysterious stranger asked them what they were talking about, and what things had been happening in Jerusalem, all of their thoughts and feelings came pouring out. Incidentally, this shows that Jesus is good company. He is the friendly kind of man that people instinctively trust, and with whom they will share the secrets of their souls.

After Jesus asked his question, both disciples started talking at once, in what turns out to be one of the longest speeches in Luke's Gospel. What they told their new traveling companion was that they were talking about things:

> Concerning Jesus of Nazareth, a man who was a prophet mighty in deed and word before God and all the people, and how our chief priests and rulers delivered him up to be condemned to death, and crucified him. But we had hoped that he was the one to redeem Israel. Yes, and besides all this, it is now the third day since these things happened. Moreover, some women of our company amazed us. They were at the tomb early in the morning, and when they did not find his body, they came back saying that they had even seen a vision of angels, who said that he was alive. Some of those who were with us went to the tomb and found it just as the women had said, but him they did not see. (Luke 24:19–25)

Michael Wilcock calls this speech "the Gospel according to Cleopas."[2] It includes almost all of the basic facts one would find in the Gospel according to Anyone. Yet something still seems to be missing. In fact, one commentator says it reads like "an unfinished creed."[3] Can you tell what is missing?

2. Michael Wilcock, *The Message of Luke*, The Bible Speaks Today (Downers Grove, IL: Inter-Varsity, 1979), 208.
3. Raymond A. Blacketer, "Word and Sacrament on the Road to Emmaus: Homiletical Reflections on Luke 24:13–35," *Calvin Theological Journal* 38 (2003): 324.

Cleopas started with the life of Jesus—his earthly ministry (Luke 24:19). He said that Jesus was a man—a real flesh and blood human being. He also said that Jesus was a mighty prophet; literally, Cleopas called him "the prophet-man." Like the prophets of old, Jesus had worked mighty miracles and spoken timely truths that came from the mind of God. This verse is a fair summary of everything in the Gospel of Luke from the baptism of Jesus in the Jordan River to his arrest in the Garden of Gethsemane. Generally speaking, chapters 4 to 9 mainly show us the miracles of Jesus (his mighty deeds), whereas chapters 10 to 21 give us his teaching (his mighty words). This was the earthly ministry of Jesus Christ, as witnessed by God and man.

Next the two disciples told about the tragic death of Jesus (Luke 24:20). Rather than blaming the whole thing on the Romans, they rightly said that it was the chief priests and the rulers of Israel who set him up to die. As a result of such animosity, Jesus the mighty prophet was condemned and crucified. This broke the travelers' hearts, because they had hoped that Jesus would redeem his people Israel. More than anything else, this is why they were so disheartened. They were at the place—and maybe you have been to a place like this in your own life—where all their expectations were dashed and all their hopes disappointed. These disciples said they were looking for a redeemer. They had hoped that Jesus would purchase their salvation—not by dying on the cross, but by delivering them from the Romans. In their lament we sense their love for Jesus; they hoped that he would be "the one."

Then, without pausing for breath, Cleopas and his companion told the stranger they met on the road about the extraordinary things which had happened that very day. They specified that this was now "the third day" since Jesus was crucified (Luke 24:21). This phrase is a signal of the resurrection, reminiscent of the prophecy that on the third day Jesus would rise again. But for the Emmaus disciples it seems to have meant that the situation was beyond any earthly hope. They were not thinking in terms of a resurrection at all, so when the third day came, they thought Jesus was as dead as he could be.

Amazingly, some people were saying that Jesus was alive again. As they walked on down the dusty road, the disciples quickly recounted the events of the first Easter: what the women found and did not find when

647

they went early to the empty tomb; what the angels said about the missing body; what another party of disciples (presumably Peter and John; see Luke 24:34, John 20:3–8) saw and did not see when they went to investigate. It had been quite a day! There were many things to think about and talk about, but they ended it all by saying that they did not see Jesus. Notice the last words in the Gospel according to Cleopas: "him they did not see" (Luke 24:24).

At this point the two disciples were not entirely sure whether the empty tomb was good news or bad news. Initially the mystery of the missing body was a source of dismay. Where could it be? Maybe someone had stolen it, adding insult to injury. It was all very upsetting and perplexing. But then there were rumors that maybe Jesus was alive. They were not sure whom to believe or what to make of it all. They had basically all the facts they needed about the cross and the empty tomb, including the witness of the apostles, but in their confusion it did not yet add up to a gospel. It was like hearing the punch line without getting the joke. The reason they did not get it was that they had not yet seen Jesus—not with the faith of knowing him as the risen Christ.

So the Gospel according to Cleopas really was not a gospel after all. The word "gospel" means "good news," but there is no good news unless Jesus has risen from the grave. As Michael Ramsey has said, "The Gospel without the Resurrection is not merely a Gospel without its final chapter; it is not a gospel at all."[4] This explains why Cleopas and his friend were still so sad. They did not know for sure that Jesus was alive. If they did not know the truth of the resurrection, they could not know that their sins were forgiven through the cross or that the empty tomb was God's guarantee of eternal life.

This is true for all of us: there is no good news unless Jesus rose from the dead. The gospel is the crucifixion plus the resurrection, which equals forgiveness for our sins and everlasting joy in the presence of God. If Jesus did not rise from the dead, then everything that is wrong with this world will never be made right. It is only when we see Jesus as our crucified Savior and our risen Lord that we know how he will satisfy every genuine need and every deep longing of our souls.

---

4. Michael Ramsey, quoted in Paul Beasley-Murray, *The Message of the Resurrection*, The Bible Speaks Today (Downers Grove, IL: InterVarsity, 2000), 17.

## THE GOSPEL ACCORDING TO THE OLD TESTAMENT

Cleopas and his companion were not quite there yet; they still could not see Jesus. What makes this so deliciously ironic is that they were looking straight at him! The irony of their words at the end of verse 24 is intense. At the same time these disciples sadly lamented that their friends did not see Jesus, they themselves were looking him right in the face. Yet they did not see him either. So Jesus "said to them: 'O foolish ones, and slow of heart to believe all that the prophets have spoken! Was it not necessary that the Christ should suffer these things and enter into his glory?' And beginning with Moses and all the Prophets, he interpreted to them in all the Scriptures the things concerning himself" (Luke 24:25–27).

The word "foolish" is obviously intended to be a rebuke, but scholars disagree about how forceful it is. Some think it simply means that the disciples were slow on the uptake, whereas others see it as a sharper criticism. Maybe a good parallel in contemporary English usage is the word "clueless." "O clueless ones," Jesus was saying—not unkindly, but accurately. Cleopas and his companion should have known better. The Savior was staring them straight in the face, but their minds and hearts would not let them believe it! Although there were many things that they *did* believe about Jesus, as we have seen, they were slow to believe everything they needed to believe for their salvation. They did not believe "all that the prophets had spoken" (Luke 24:25). To be specific, they did not have room in their theology for a suffering and rising Messiah.

The disciples did not yet understand that far from proving that he was *not* the Messiah, the sufferings of the cross proved that he was. So Jesus proceeded to preach them the Gospel according to the Old Testament. What any preacher would give to hear *that* sermon, when the Word of God Incarnate explained the Word of God written! The preaching Jesus did was biblical: it was based on the law and the prophets. His preaching was thorough: he wanted his friends to know everything the prophets had spoken. His preaching was Christ-centered, for he was preaching about himself. It was also gospel-centered, including both the crucifixion and the resurrection: Jesus proclaimed the agonies of the cross and the glories of the empty tomb. His preaching was persuasive: Jesus argued for the absolute necessity of doing his saving work the way that he did it—it was necessary for the

Christ to suffer and then to be glorified. There has never been a better evangelistic sermon than the one the risen Christ preached to his disciples on the first Easter Sunday, somewhere on the gospel road between Jerusalem and Emmaus.

We do not know exactly what Jesus said on this occasion. If we needed to know, then undoubtedly God would have told us. But the fact is that we really do not need to know, because we still have the same Old Testament that Jesus used as the text for his sermon (not to mention all the New Testament sermons of the apostles that are clearly based on the Old Testament, just the way that Jesus taught them to preach). Here Jesus gives us the golden key to unlock the meaning of the Hebrew Scriptures: they are all about him. Every part of the Old Testament finds its meaning and purpose in relationship to the person and work of Jesus Christ. The Scripture says that it is only in Jesus that all things hold together (Col. 1:17), and this is true of the Old Testament. We cannot fully and properly understand anything from Moses to Malachi unless we see its connection to the whole gospel, including both the cross and the empty tomb.

What do the Scriptures say about the sufferings of the Christ? The way to begin is the way Jesus began: with the writings of Moses. If we turn to Genesis, the Scripture says that the seed of the woman—a man of flesh and blood—will be bruised by the devil before crushing the devil's head (Gen. 3:15). If we turn to Exodus, the Scripture says that the people of God are delivered from death through the offering of a Passover lamb (Exod. 12:13). If we turn to Leviticus, the Scripture says that atonement can be made only through the offering of sacrificial blood (Lev. 16:14–16). If we turn to Numbers, the Scripture lifts up the sign of the bronze serpent, and everyone who sees it is delivered from death (Num. 21:9). If we turn to Deuteronomy, we discover that cursed, covenant-breaking sinners may find grace at the blood-sprinkled altar of God (Deut. 27:1–26).

All of these truths find their fulfillment in the saving work of Jesus Christ. He is the son of the woman who was bruised on the cross before crushing Satan's head. He is the Lamb who offered his blood for our sins (John 1:36) and was lifted up for our salvation (John 3:14–15). He is the covenant-maker who was cursed for all our covenant breaking and who sprinkled his redeeming blood on the altar of the cross (Gal. 3:13).

650

So much for Moses. Consider also the prophets. If we turn to Isaiah, the Scripture says that the Savior will be wounded for our iniquities and pierced for our transgressions (Isa. 53:5). If we turn to Jeremiah, the Scripture says that he will be mocked and abused (Jer. 20:7–10). If we turn to Zechariah, the Scripture says that he will make atonement for the whole land in a single day (Zech. 3:9). These prophecies also find their fulfillment in the sufferings and death of Jesus Christ, who was wounded, pierced, and abused in offering himself as an atoning sacrifice for our sins.

Even this is only the beginning, for after Jesus began with Moses and the prophets he went on to the rest of the Old Testament Scriptures. What do they say about the sufferings of the Christ? To give only one example, Psalm 22 says that he will die a God-forsaken death—a dry and thirsty death, surrounded by enemies who pierce his hands and feet and then gamble for his clothes.

This is only the first half of the gospel: the sufferings of the crucifixion. Jesus also told his disciples that it was necessary for the Christ to "enter into his glory." Therefore, he also preached to them about the resurrection, proving the empty tomb from Moses and the prophets. We see the risen Christ in the faith of Abraham, who believed that God would raise his son from the dead (see Gen. 22 and Heb. 11:17–19). We see the risen Christ in the sign of Jonah, who spent three days in the belly of the great fish, just as Jesus spent three days in the darkness of the tomb (Matt. 12:39). We see him in Daniel's prophecy of the Son of Man rising on the clouds of heaven and coming in glory (Dan. 7:13–14). Jesus did not have to stop there. If he preached the resurrection from the rest of the Old Testament, he could preach it from Psalm 16, where the holy one is not abandoned to the grave but joyfully enters the presence of God, and also from Psalm 110, where he reigns in glory at the right hand of God.

Even this was only the beginning. Jesus continued his Bible exposition by using all the principles of his Christ-centered, gospel-driven interpretation (his "hermeneutic," for this word has its origins in the term that Luke uses for "interpreted") to explain what was said "in all the Scriptures . . . concerning himself" (Luke 24:27). Jesus is not just here or there in this prediction or that prophecy: he is everywhere in the Old Testament. He is the ark of the covenant and the blood on the mercy seat. He is the light on the golden lampstand and the bread of life. He is the prophet who preaches like Moses, the priest who prays like Aaron, and the king after David's heart. We follow his method of interpretation when we see Jesus in the redemption of Ruth by Boaz, the selfless sacrifice of Samson, the kingship of Josiah, the miracles of Elijah, and all the other types and signs and figures of the Old Testament.

What more shall I say? I could preach from the Scriptures every day for the rest of my life and not begin to exhaust everything that is said about Jesus in the Old Testament. On every page his coming is prophesied, his life is prefigured, his sufferings are personified, or his resurrection life is promised. The Old Testament has one central theme, and that theme is Christ.

To say this another way, the Old Testament is not simply background material for the New Testament, but it contains the very message of the gospel. It is so full of Christ that Jesus could prove the good news from any page. He knew that the cross and the empty tomb were the logical deduction, the necessary consequence of everything the Spirit taught from Genesis to Malachi. Rather than pointing to his resurrection body first of all, Jesus pointed to the Scriptures that pointed to himself. As Dinsdale Young has written, "I should have imagined that the Risen Lord would be independent of the Bible. But no! He cleaves to it with all the old affection. He came up from the grave and hastened to the Holy Book."[5] Jesus did this because he knew that he would not be able to walk down every road to give every believer the gospel in living person. But he also knew that by the Holy Spirit his word had the power to make every road a gospel road wherever Christ is preached.

Praise God that we have the same word to preach that Jesus preached. This word was enough for Jesus—only Moses and the prophets, the Gospel according to the Old Testament. It was enough for the apostles, too, for Philip (see Acts 8:35) and Peter (Acts 10:43; 1 Peter 1:11) and Paul (Acts 26:22–23). Jesus said it should have been enough for Cleopas and his companion. Is the word enough for you?

Earlier in Luke, Jesus warned that unless people believe the message of Moses and the Prophets, they will never believe in the resurrection (Luke 16:31; cf. John 5:39–40). This, then, is how we know Jesus for sure: by believing everything spoken in the Word that proclaims his gospel. Have you met this Jesus before on some gospel road, or is he only now overtaking you? Let him fall into stride and walk beside you like a friend. Listen to his words. See who he is. Believe him as your Savior and your God.

5. Dinsdale T. Young, "Three Phases of the Risen Christ," in Wilber M. Smith, *Great Sermons on the Resurrection of Christ* (Natick, MA: W. A. Wilde, 1964), 90.

# 109

# SEEING JESUS IN WORD
# AND SACRAMENT

## *Luke 24:28–35*

*When he was at table with them, he took the bread and blessed
and broke it and gave it to them. And their eyes were opened,
and they recognized him. And he vanished from their sight.*
(Luke 24:30–31)

*T*he famous Renaissance artist Michelangelo Merisi—usually
known as Caravaggio—produced two different paintings
called the *Supper at Emmaus* (1601, 1606). The second of the
two masterpieces is a dramatic study in light and shadow. A man is seated
at a table with two friends. There is bread on the white tablecloth in front
of him. His eyes are closed in prayer, and while one of his hands rests on
the table, the other is raised to bless the bread that he is about to break.

Anyone who knows the Gospel of Luke recognizes instantly that the man
praying is Jesus. We know this from the title of the painting, which indicates
that the men with Jesus at the table are the disciples who traveled from
Jerusalem to Emmaus on the afternoon of the first Easter and begged Jesus
to stay for dinner. We also know that this is Jesus from the light that falls

on his face and illuminates the rest of the scene. We know it as well from the lamb that a woman is bringing to the table—a symbol of his sacrificial death. Everything in the painting helps us to see Jesus.

The disciples are seeing Jesus too, and what is perhaps most striking about *Supper at Emmaus* is their reaction. In his former painting of the same subject, Caravaggio had portrayed the men with exaggerated gestures. One disciple has his arms spread out in worship, or perhaps amazement; the other is gripping the arms of his chair and getting ready to jump out of his seat. Both men are astonished to see Jesus.

By contrast, the later painting is more subdued, more intimate, and if possible, even more intense. The disciple on the left—who has his back to the viewer—is leaning forward, hanging on Jesus' every word. The disciple on the right is gripping the edges of the table with both hands. He too is leaning forward, gazing at Jesus with an expression of burning intensity. His right hand is forward, touching or almost touching the hand of Jesus. Everything in life is coming together for these men as they see Jesus in the breaking of the bread.

## STAY A LITTLE BIT LONGER

What a day it had already been for these two disciples. It had started with grief for a crucified man and strange reports about his empty tomb. When the two friends left Jerusalem and headed for home, they were heavy with sorrow and struggling to understand what had happened to Jesus, the man they thought would be their Messiah.

Then Jesus himself overtook them on the road, although their eyes were kept from recognizing him (Luke 24:16). The mysterious traveler challenged them to make room in their theology for a crucified Messiah rising from the grave. He did this by giving them a comprehensive survey of the Old Testament: "And beginning with Moses and all the Prophets, he interpreted to them in all the Scriptures the things concerning himself" (Luke 24:27). It was the most dynamic, life-changing Bible teaching the two disciples had ever heard. In fact, when they talked about it later, they said they felt their hearts were burning as they heard this man preach the gospel.

What the man had to say was so compelling that the disciples could not get enough of it: "So they drew near to the village to which they were going.

He acted as if he were going farther, but they urged him strongly, saying, 'Stay with us, for it is toward evening and the day is now far spent.' So he went in to stay with them" (Luke 24:28–29).

This situation is familiar from everyday life. A visitor is getting ready to go, but someone says, "Please don't go yet; stay a little bit longer." "No," the visitor says, "I really must be going." Back and forth it goes, but sometimes it is possible to persuade the person to stay, which is what happened in this instance.

We are not exactly sure where Jesus was going. When the Bible says he "acted as if he were going farther," this does not mean that he was only pretending. Jesus had other places to go and other people to see. Soon he would return to his Father, but in the meantime he was pressing on with his saving work. Yet the disciples wanted him to stay, even if they were not entirely sure why. They pointed out that it was getting late, and that soon it would be unsafe to travel. So they urged the man to stay with them at least for the night. They insisted that he come home with them, and they would not take "no" for an answer. They would not let him go until he blessed them with his presence (cf. Gen. 32:26).

How glad Jesus must have been to be entertained at the home of his disciples! He was not afraid of the dark or of any danger on the road, but he always loves to be loved by his disciples. When Jesus first came into the world, people would not even make room for him at the inn (see Luke 2:7). But now that he was getting ready to leave the world altogether, people were welcoming him into their homes and their hearts.

How glad the disciples must have been when Jesus said that he would stay. Now they could offer him the gift of their hospitality and go deeper into the Word, hearing more of what the man had to say from the Scriptures. How glad they must have been afterwards, when they realized whom they had welcomed into their home! As Norval Geldenhuys points out, "If they had not invited Him He would have passed on, and they would have forfeited the inexpressible privilege of discovering that it was their risen Lord who had been with them and had instructed them."[1]

The example of the Emmaus disciples teaches us the value of Christian hospitality—a neglected virtue in these post-Christian times. In America, at

1. Norval Geldenhuys, *The Gospel of Luke*, New International Commentary on the New Testament (Grand Rapids: Eerdmans, 1951), 634.

least, most people love their privacy more than they love to welcome people into their homes. To our own detriment, this is not a culture of dropping by for a visit and staying longer. But the people of God are called to practice hospitality. We see this in the example of Abraham, who entertained angels (Gen. 18:1–8). We also see it in the example of Gideon, who insisted on preparing a meal for the angel of the Lord (Judg. 6:18; cf. 13:15). In the New Testament, Christians often are exhorted to practice hospitality (e.g., Heb. 13:2; 1 Peter 4:9), welcoming one another as Christ has welcomed us (Rom. 15:7). So welcome strangers from out of town and overseas. Invite people over for dinner. Ask travelers to stay with you overnight. Show hospitality to missionaries and other people who have a special calling to proclaim the gospel. Hospitality is one of the regular duties and high joys of the Christian life.

The most important hospitality of all is to open the home of your heart and ask Jesus to come in. If Jesus happened to overtake you on the road, would you invite him to stay? Are you drawn to him the way these disciples were drawn to him? Feel his joy. Listen to his teaching. Experience more of his life-giving life. For if ever there is someone you should invite to stay a little longer, it is Jesus, whom Charles Spurgeon aptly described as "a guest worth pressing."[2] The disciples felt a kind of urgency about getting Jesus to stay with them. For reasons that perhaps they could not fully explain, they sensed how valuable it would be for them to spend more time with him. Unlike the Emmaus disciples, we *do* know who Jesus is. Therefore, we should feel even more urgency about the time that we spend with Jesus, wanting to hear more of what he says about his cross and the empty tomb and yearning to know him better than we know him now. Even though we cannot enjoy the physical presence of Jesus the way that those disciples did, we can experience his presence by the power of the Holy Spirit.

It is easy to think that inviting Jesus was the natural thing to do and that we would have done the same thing the disciples did, begging him to stay. It seems so obvious: given the chance, *of course* we would ask Jesus over for dinner! But is that really the decision we are making (metaphorically speaking) every day—the decision to stay with Jesus and to ask him to stay with us? Do you linger with him longer in prayer, listening to more of what

2. Charles H. Spurgeon, "The Blessed Guest Detained," *The Metropolitan Tabernacle Pulpit* (London: Banner of Truth, 1971), 28:225.

he wants to say to you in his Word? Or are you always rushing off to do the next thing?

Jesus loves it when we invite him to stay. "If anyone hears my voice and opens the door," he said, "I will come in to him and eat with him, and he with me" (Rev. 3:20). Jesus wants to have a deeper relationship with us—the kind of relationship we have when we sit so close to someone at the table that our hands are touching. He is always willing to say more to us from his Word. He never shuts the Bible and says, "That's enough for today; I don't have anything more to teach you." He is always willing to hear more from us in prayer. Jesus never leaves a Bible study before the prayer time, and he never walks out of the closet before we are finished praying.

Through the ministry of the Word and prayer, we have the same extraordinary privilege the first disciples had: the privilege to be with Jesus. He will stay with us for as long as we are willing to be with him. Will you invite Jesus into your life this morning or evening, this week, and forever?

## THE BREAKING OF THE BREAD

At first the Emmaus disciples did not realize that the man they invited to dinner was Jesus. This is characteristic of the resurrection stories. Jesus was traveling incognito. People saw him, but they did not recognize him. In this case, the disciples were actually prevented from recognizing Jesus (Luke 24:16), we assume by God himself.

Yet this is a recognition story, and eventually both disciples realized that they were seeing Jesus, as all the disciples did. Here is how it happened: "When he was at table with them, he took the bread and blessed and broke it and gave it to them. And their eyes were opened, and they recognized him. And he vanished from their sight" (Luke 24:30–31).

It is unusual for someone to vanish from sight, but there is something else unusual here as well. Ordinarily the host would be the one to offer prayer and break bread. But in this case the guest became the host as Jesus took the role of the head of the household. This unusual occurrence shows that Jesus commands our respect. As the Emmaus disciples heard Jesus teach, they recognized his superior wisdom and perfect godliness. Thus it was natural for them to defer to him by giving him the honor of breaking their bread. Right in their own home, they acknowledged Jesus as the one who should be at the head of their table.

As we witness this domestic scene, we see an important spiritual principle in action: namely, that in all things Christ should be preeminent (see Col. 1:18). Jesus Christ should be the Lord of every believer's dinner table, every believer's bedroom and living room, every believer's classroom and place of business. At every place in life, ask Jesus to take the lead and to give you his blessing.

The meal that Jesus blessed at this table should remind us of some other meals he shared with his disciples in the Gospels. We often observe him sitting down to eat with people. In fact, we could almost describe the life of Christ as a series of social engagements, punctuated by various sermons and miracles. But two meals have an especially close connection with the meal he shared with his disciples in Emmaus.

One of those meals was the feeding of the five thousand, as recorded in Luke 9. Jesus had been teaching all day and people were hungry. The disciples thought he should send them away to get something to eat. Instead, Jesus took what was on hand: "And taking the five loaves and the two fish, he looked up to heaven and said a blessing over them. Then he broke the loaves and gave them to the disciples to set before the crowd" (Luke 9:16). Luke uses almost identical words to describe what Jesus did at Emmaus, without the miraculous multiplication. Jesus took the bread; then he blessed it, broke it, and gave it to his disciples.

We should also connect this meal with the Last Supper. This point has been hotly disputed by Bible scholars. Some have argued that the dinner at Emmaus was in fact a reenactment of the Lord's Supper. Jesus was "breaking the bread" in the technical sense of that expression: he was celebrating the sacrament of the Lord's Supper. For example, Augustine said that "no one should doubt that his being recognized in the breaking of bread is the sacrament, which brings us together in recognizing him."[3]

Other scholars have pointed out that Jesus did not celebrate the sacrament in any proper or formal way. Craig Blomberg compares Luke 24:30 with Luke 22:19 and observes that two different tenses of the verb for

---

3. Augustine, "Letter 149," in *Luke*, ed. Arthur A. Just, Jr., Ancient Christian Commentary on Scripture, NT 3 (Downers Grove, IL: InterVarsity, 2003), 382.

breaking are used.[4] There is also a verbal difference between thanking God for the bread, as Jesus does in Luke 22:17, and blessing the bread as he does in Luke 24:30.[5] If Luke wanted to show that both meals celebrated the same sacrament, then why didn't he highlight this by using the same vocabulary? Notice as well that no wine is mentioned on the table, only bread; but the sacrament of the Lord's Supper always includes both the bread and the cup. Nor does Jesus repeat the words of the institution of the Lord's Supper to consecrate the bread, an omission which would be highly irregular if he intended to use the bread for any sacramental purpose. Then there is the simple fact that as far as we know, the Emmaus disciples were not present for the Last Supper (although they may have heard about it). Can we really expect them to draw a connection with something they had never experienced?

It seems clear, therefore, that the supper at Emmaus was not the Lord's Supper, properly speaking. However, there are enough similarities to make it equally clear that Luke wants to remind us of that sacrament. The supper Jesus shared with the Emmaus disciples reminds us of various meals, including the feeding of the five thousand and the banquet he has promised to share with us in his Father's kingdom (see Luke 22:16; Rev. 19:9). But it is also an echo from the upper room where he broke bread with his disciples as a sign of the body he would offer on the cross.

Notice when the disciples knew that it was Jesus: in the breaking of the bread (Luke 24:30–31, 35). Prior to this they were kept from recognizing this mysterious stranger (see Luke 24:16), but now they knew who he was. Maybe there was something characteristic about the way Jesus blessed the bread that the disciples instantly recognized—a familiar gesture or inflection in his voice.[6] Possibly when he took the bread they saw the nail prints in his hands. Or perhaps their ability to identify Jesus came simply by the power of God. Verse 31 uses the passive voice ("their eyes were opened"), which indicates that the disciples did not open their eyes for themselves and may in fact imply that the Holy Spirit did the opening for them.

4. Craig L. Blomberg, *Contagious Holiness: Jesus' Meals with Sinners*, New Studies in Biblical Theology (Downers Grove, IL: InterVarsity, 2005), 158.

5. Raymond A. Blacketer, "Word and Sacrament on the Road to Emmaus: Homiletical Reflections on Luke 24:13–35," *Calvin Theological Journal* 38 (2003): 323.

6. David Gooding describes the action of Jesus as "an inimitable gesture of self-revelation" in *According to Luke: A New Exposition of the Third Gospel* (Grand Rapids: Eerdmans, 1987), 353.

Luke wants us to notice that this moment of recognition coincided with the breaking of bread. At the feeding of the five thousand Jesus promised his disciples that he would offer his body as bread for the life of the world (John 6:51). At the Last Supper he gave them bread to remember the body he was preparing to offer for their salvation (Luke 22:19). Then the next day he actually gave his body, offering it for crucifixion—the sacrifice that would pay for their sins. When the Emmaus disciples saw the very same Jesus break bread, they knew it was him. As Augustine explained it, "something had come upon their eyes which was suffered to remain until the breaking of the bread, in reference to a well-known mystery, so that only then was the different form in Him made visible to them, and they did not recognize Him, as is shown by Luke's narrative, until the breaking of the bread took place."[7] Everything came together for them with the simple action of breaking the bread. Now they knew for sure that it had to be Jesus.

They also knew this: Jesus was no longer dead, but alive. The friend at their table had been walking and talking with them. He was blessing them with his presence—his living, physical presence. This convinced them of the reality of the resurrection. What the women said about the empty tomb had to be true, because they had seen Jesus with their very own eyes. He was risen indeed!

## BACK TO JERUSALEM

No sooner did the disciples recognize Jesus than he completely vanished, disappearing as suddenly as he had appeared. This gives us a clue that the resurrection body has supernatural properties. The body of Jesus, said J. C. Ryle, was "in some wonderful way different from the common body of man. It was a real material body, and true flesh and blood. But it was a body capable of moving, appearing, and disappearing after a manner that we cannot explain."[8]

Even if we cannot fully explain the resurrection, we can still believe it and tell other people about it. The body that dies can live again, through faith in

7. Augustine, *Harmony of the Gospels*, 3.25.72, in *Nicene and Post-Nicene Fathers*, First Series, ed. Philip Schaff (1888; reprint Peabody, MA: Hendrickson, 1994), 6:217.
8. J.C. Ryle, *Expository Thoughts on the Gospels, Luke* (1858; reprint Cambridge: James Clarke, 1976), 2:508.

Jesus, and by the power of his resurrection—this is the great good news that the Emmaus disciples simply had to share. They did not waste a moment, but leaving their dinner on the table, they went back out on the road: "And they rose that same hour and returned to Jerusalem" (Luke 24:33).

Earlier that day the two disciples had traveled down the same road in the opposite direction. The two journeys could not have been more different. When they left Jerusalem, they were sad and dejected as they mourned the apparently tragic death of Jesus. But they went back to Jerusalem rejoicing. The first time they traveled down that road the news they shared was distressing and confusing. But now they had good news to share—a gospel of such great joy it was impossible for them to keep it to themselves. They had become evangelists for the risen Christ. What a difference it made for them to see Jesus!

What a difference they found in the other disciples when they arrived back in Jerusalem: "And they found the eleven and those who were with them gathered together, saying, 'The Lord has risen indeed, and has appeared to Simon!'" (Luke 24:33–34; cf. John 20:19–23). As soon as the Emmaus disciples walked in the door, the disciples started bombarding them with good news of their own. Reports of the resurrection had been coming in all day, and the disciples were trying to understand what it all meant.

Perhaps most significantly, they said that Jesus had appeared to Simon Peter. The personal encounter Peter had with the risen Christ is not recorded anywhere else in the Gospels, although the apostle Paul alludes to it in 1 Corinthians 15:5. We do not know what Jesus said to Peter, but of all the disciples, it was Peter who had denied Jesus most blatantly, and who had therefore the most reason to be anxious about seeing him again. But Jesus came to Peter in loving mercy, and now almost all the disciples were starting to believe that he was alive from the dead.

The disciples who had just walked back from Emmaus added more fuel to the fire of their faith, for they had seen Jesus too: "Then they told what had happened on the road, and how he was known to them in the breaking of the bread" (Luke 24:35).

## TWO WAYS TO SEE JESUS

It is hard not to envy these disciples. They were there for the first Easter. Therefore, they were the first to hear the good news of the resurrection and the first to see the risen Christ. In fact, they did not know it yet, but Jesus himself was just about to walk through the door (or maybe through the wall!). Don't you wish that you could see what they saw and rejoice the way that they rejoiced?

Actually, you can. As Luke tells us this true story from the Gospel, he wants us to know that we can see Jesus as clearly as these disciples saw him, and in virtually the same way. As we review what happened to the Emmaus disciples, we should notice that they saw Jesus in two different ways, and that they are both ways that we can see Jesus too.

First, these two friends saw Jesus in the Word. This is what "happened on the road" (Luke 24:35), as Jesus "interpreted to them in all the Scriptures the things concerning himself" (Luke 24:27). When Jesus went through the Old Testament with them, preaching the cross and the empty tomb, the disciples were seeing the person and the work of the Christ. Afterwards, they said to one another, "Did not our hearts burn within us while he talked to us on the road, while he opened to us the Scriptures?" (Luke 24:32). Even after the miraculous, supernatural disappearance of Christ, what captivated the Emmaus disciples was the ministry of God's Word. The disciples did not fully understand what was happening to them at the time, but God was burning the gospel into their hearts so that they could see Jesus in all the Scriptures. This experience was so intense that later they said it was like being on fire. We can almost imagine them glowing as they walked back to Jerusalem in the dark: two flaming disciples sparking down the Emmaus road.

The fire of that first Easter is rekindled anytime that anyone sees Jesus in the Scriptures. It leaps into flame whenever people see Jesus for the first time and trust him for salvation. It happened to the brilliant French philosopher Blaise Pascal, and when it did, the best word he could use to describe it was "FIRE."[9] John Wesley gave a similar description of his famous conversion to faith in Jesus Christ at a prayer meeting in London. As Wesley heard about the change God works in the heart through faith in Christ, he said, "I felt my heart strangely warmed. I felt I did trust in Christ, Christ alone, for salvation; and an assurance was given me that

---

9. Blaise Pascal, quoted in Donald W. McCullough, *The Trivialization of God* (Colorado Springs: NavPress, 1995), 77.

He had taken away my sins, even mine, and saved me from the law of sin and death."[10]

Have you experienced the fire of the Holy Spirit? Your heart will be strangely warmed when you trust in Jesus. It will be warmed again every time you open the Bible and see—really see—the love and the grace that God has for you in Jesus. It happens when you read and study the Bible. In fact, it happens to me almost every week as I prepare to preach the gospel: I see something new about Jesus, or something old about him in a new way, and a flame is kindled in my cold heart. It often happens to people when they hear Bible-based, gospel-centered preaching: as someone opens the Word for people the way that Jesus opened it for his disciples, the Holy Spirit sets their hearts on fire. Anyone who has the Word of God can see Jesus as clearly as the Emmaus disciples saw him, and then burn with the fire of the same gospel.

We also see Jesus in the breaking of the bread, which is the second way these disciples saw him. Jesus was "known to them in the breaking of the bread" (Luke 24:35). Remember that the bread he broke was not the sacrament of the Lord's Supper. Nevertheless, their experience undoubtedly would have reminded many disciples of what happened in the upper room. It is easy to imagine that when the Emmaus disciples said they saw Jesus in the breaking of the bread, some of the eleven disciples exchanged knowing glances, remembering how *they* had seen Jesus in the breaking of the bread.

This is one of the ways that we know Jesus too: in "the breaking of the bread." Luke used this phrase to remind us of the Lord's Supper. What he says, therefore, has enduring significance for the church. The Word is not the only place we see Jesus; we also see him in the sacrament. When Jesus is present spiritually in our celebration of the Lord's Supper, we too experience the reality that he is risen from the dead.

Understand that the Jesus we see in the sacrament is the same Jesus we see in the Word, only we see him in a different way. In fact, one of the best ways to understand the sacrament is to think of it as a visible word. The Lord's Supper testifies to the same sacrificial death that we read about in the gospel—the death that Jesus died on the cross when he offered his body

10. The story of Wesley's conversion is recounted in Michael Wilcock, *The Message of Luke*, The Bible Speaks Today (Downers Grove, IL: InterVarsity, 1979), 210.

and his blood for our sins. But the Lord's Supper gives us a visible sign to go with that gospel word—the sign of the bread and the cup. As we eat this bread and drink this cup, we see Jesus in the sacrament.

The confessional reading used for evening communion services at Philadelphia's Tenth Presbyterian Church proclaims, "the supper presents to our physical senses what God declares to us in his Word." The sacrament does not offer us a grace that is any different from the grace we receive by believing what the Bible says about the death and resurrection of Jesus Christ. What the sacrament does is to give us the same grace in a different way—a way that helps us to see Jesus. When we participate in this sacrament, we remember the only Savior whose body was broken and blood was shed for our sins.

Have you seen Jesus in the preaching of the Word? Can you see Jesus in the breaking of the bread? If not, then ask God to open your eyes, for this is a prayer he loves to answer (see Ps. 146:8; Acts 9:18; Eph. 1:18). Then again, maybe you have seen Jesus before, but are having trouble seeing him lately. Sometimes the trials of life and our own unrepentant sin make it hard for us to see Jesus. If that is the case, the place we will see him again is in the Word and the sacrament, not in some other place.

Do not miss the opportunity to see Jesus. Imagine what the Emmaus disciples would have missed if they had let Jesus go on his way instead of asking him to stay. They would have regretted it for the rest of their lives. "I can't believe we didn't invite Jesus to say with us that night," they would have said. "What *were* we thinking?"

Ask Jesus to stay. He loves for us to see him in the preaching of his gospel and in the breaking of his bread. Ask the Holy Spirit to help you see Jesus in word and sacrament. Ask Jesus to stay with you forever.

# 110

# DISBELIEVING FOR JOY

## *Luke 24:36–43*

*And when he had said this, he showed them his hands and his feet. And while they still disbelieved for joy and were marveling, he said to them, "Have you anything here to eat?"*
(Luke 24:40–41)

Some people believe in the resurrection of the body, but many people do not. Christians are the ones who believe (or so they say). The physical resurrection of the human body after death is a basic tenet of the Christian faith. The ancient ecumenical creeds clearly state that Jesus rose again on the third day. The Nicene Creed ends by saying, "We look for the resurrection of the dead and the life of the world to come." "We believe," it says in the Apostles' Creed, "in the resurrection of the body." Yet most people do not believe this. In fact, according to a 2006 survey by Ohio University, only one out of three Americans believe that after they die, their bodies will rise again.

People have many reasons for not believing in the resurrection of the dead. Some people do not believe in life after death at all. The only thing we can know for certain, they say, is the life we are now living. Any future existence is a miracle that goes beyond anything we have seen or could ever prove. Other people believe in life after death, but think that the life to come is merely a spiritual existence. There is no resurrection of the body, they say, but only a soul that returns to God. Then there all the people who hope that their bodies will be raised from the dead yet find this very hard to believe. A dead body is so lifeless, especially after it has turned to dust, that its resurrection seems impossible.

It certainly seemed impossible to the first disciples, who found it hard to believe in the bodily resurrection of Jesus Christ. Mark tells us both that they "would not" and that they "did not" believe (Mark 16:11, 13). Luke adds the unusual reason they had for not believing: they "disbelieved for joy" (Luke 24:41).

## THE END OF EASTER

The disciples experienced this joyful disbelief at the end of the most extraordinary day in human history. The day had begun at the first light of dawn, when a little group of women went to the garden tomb with spices for burial. There they saw angels, who announced the stunning news that Jesus was risen. For the rest of the morning there was a good deal of running back and forth, as various disciples checked and rechecked the empty tomb, trying to confirm whether it was really true that Jesus was alive.

Soon people started spreading reports that they had seen the risen Christ. But this was so hard to believe that people who had not seen Jesus for themselves were not sure what to make of it. The main example in Luke is Cleopas, who left Jerusalem that afternoon with a friend, heading for Emmaus. The two of them had heard what the women said about the empty tomb, but they were still grieving the death of Jesus. Their conflicting emotions were such a struggle between hope and despair that they could not quite bring themselves to believe that Jesus was alive. Then Jesus himself overtook them on the road out of the city. He walked with them, and talked with them, and preached them the Gospel according to the Old Testament. Finally, when he broke bread with them around the dinner table, they realized that it was really Jesus.

Immediately they went back to Jerusalem to tell the other disciples. This part of the story is essential in completing the pattern we observe in all of the stories from the first Easter. As eyewitnesses of the resurrection, the disciples moved from being bewildered, to getting rebuked for their unbelief, to receiving instruction about the gospel plan of God, to sharing the good news that Jesus Christ had risen from the grave.[1] Cleopas and his companion shared this joyful news with the eleven remaining disciples and with other followers of Jesus. There the disciples made a statement that has become famous all over the world as a greeting for Easter Sunday: "The Lord has risen indeed!" (Luke 24:34).

Suddenly Jesus appeared, in the flesh: "As they were talking about these things, Jesus himself stood among them, and said to them, 'Peace to you!'" (Luke 24:36). The sudden appearance of the living Jesus was the final, confirming, and convincing proof of his bodily resurrection. The Venerable Bede pointed out that this was a fulfillment of one of the promises Jesus made before his passion.[2] Wherever "two or three are gathered in my name," he said, "there am I among them" (Matt. 18:20). Jesus *was* among them, and now they knew for sure that he was alive from the dead.

Jesus was among his disciples with as much loving grace as ever. This is evident from the gift he offered—the gift of peace. Some commentators have seen this as little more than a polite or friendly greeting. It is true that the giving of peace is a conventional greeting in the Middle East. To this day, Arabs greet one another with the word "salaam," while Jews say "shalom"—the Hebrew word for peace. When the risen Christ says "Peace to you!" however, he is doing something more than simply saying "Hello!" He is giving the very peace of God. As J. C. Ryle once said, "I am quite unable to regard this expression as being nothing more than the ordinary salutation of courtesy. It seems to me to be full of deep and comfortable truth."[3]

"Peace" was the first word that Jesus spoke to his disciples after his resurrection. He mainly said it to let them know that they did not need to be afraid, as we shall see. But the peace of Jesus is a deep and comfortable truth for everyone.

1. This pattern is described by R. Kent Hughes in *Luke: That You May Know the Truth*, Preaching the Word (Wheaton, IL: Crossway, 1998), 2:401.
2. The Venerable Bede, "Homilies on the Gospels," 11.9, in *Luke*, ed. Arthur A. Just, Jr., Ancient Christian Commentary on Scripture, NT 3 (Downers Grove, IL: InterVarsity, 2003), 384.
3. J. C. Ryle, *Expository Thoughts on the Gospels*, *Luke* (1858; reprint Cambridge: James Clarke, 1976), 2:513.

For the disciples, the word "peace" meant that the man in their midst really was Jesus. By now they would have recognized the familiar tone of his voice. They might also have remembered that he had offered them peace before. "Peace I leave with you," Jesus said before his passion; "my peace I give to you" (John 14:27).

Now Jesus was giving them peace again, only this time he was doing it from the other side of the grave, and everything really was right with the world. There was peace for Jesus, because all his earthly sufferings were over. There was peace for his disciples too. They had peace from their sorrow and grief, because Jesus was not dead after all. They also had peace with God, because all their sins were forgiven through the cross where Jesus died. At the beginning of Luke's Gospel, Zechariah the priest prophesied that Jesus would "guide our feet into the way of peace" (Luke 1:79), and the Christmas angels promised that he would bring peace on earth (Luke 2:14). Now Jesus was preaching the peace that would give all of his disciples fellowship with God the Father (Eph. 2:17–18).

At the same time, these men and women had peace with Jesus himself. What makes this so surprising is that only days before they had completely abandoned him at the time of his greatest trial. In cowardly fear, the disciples broke all of their promises to stay with him to the very end. Therefore, as amazing as it is that Jesus rose from the dead, it is equally extraordinary that he went back to his disciples afterwards, and that when he did, he went in peace. Jesus would have been fully justified to rebuke his disciples for their desertion. "You know, I'm really disappointed with you guys," he might have said. "You really let me down back there in the Garden of Gethsemane. I can't say I remember seeing very many of you at Calvary either. Where were you guys when I needed you?" In fact, Jesus would have been fully justified in choosing a completely new set of disciples. Instead, Jesus came to them as a peacemaker.

He comes to us the same way. Even after we have fallen away, or broken our promises, or turned our backs on him, Jesus comes to us in peace. He does not wait for us to get our lives together first, or to settle all our doubts, or to come crawling back to him, begging for one more chance. No, Jesus comes to the sinners and the doubters with his arms open wide, offering peace. Patrick Miller Kirkland took this promise and turned it into a prayer that is part of the Easter hymn "Jesus, Lord, Redeemer":

In the upper chamber, where the ten in fear
Gathered sad and troubled, there you did appear.
So, O Lord, this evening, bid our sorrows cease;
Breathing on us, Savior, say, "I give you peace."

This is every believer's prayer for every troubled time in life. It is a prayer for anyone who is grieving a painful loss or anxious about the future. It is a prayer for anyone in the grip of a powerful temptation. It is a prayer for anyone who is lost in life and looking for the answer, for anyone who feels rejected, for those who cannot fix what is broken in the hearts of the people they love. In every troubled sorrow, the living Jesus comes and says, "Peace to you!"

## No Ghost Story

Sometimes it is hard for us to rest in the peace that really is ours in Jesus. Even after Jesus said "peace," the disciples were still troubled. It was the end of Easter Sunday, but they still had trouble believing in the resurrection. According to Luke, when they first saw Jesus, "they were startled and frightened and thought they saw a spirit" (Luke 24:37).

The word "startled" probably is not strong enough to convey what the disciples were feeling. They were more than startled; they were terrified. Even though they had heard that Jesus was alive, they hardly expected to meet him in person. Imagine how surprising it would be if Jesus suddenly showed up in *your* living room! Some of the disciples were starting to believe in the resurrection, but it is one thing to believe in the risen Christ and something else to experience the actuality of it. This is hardly an everyday occurrence—risen Lords suddenly appearing out of nowhere!

Imagine the commotion in that room and the looks on the disciples' faces when they saw Jesus. Michael Wilcock describes them as "believing and unbelieving, startled and joyful and afraid all at once."[4] They must have been scared half to death—as frightened as we would be if someone jumped out from behind a corner and said, "Boo!"

4. Michael Wilcock, *The Message of Luke*, The Bible Speaks Today (Downers Grove, IL: Inter-Varsity, 1979), 211.

"Boo" is just the word for it, because at first the disciples thought they were seeing a ghost. This is understandable—a "natural reaction to the supernatural."[5] It was as hard for the disciples to believe in the bodily resurrection as it is for anyone. They could not believe it, or at least they only half-believed it. Therefore, their first thought was that they were only seeing a spirit—not a risen Savior of flesh and blood, but "some kind of insubstantial apparition. Spirits were considered to be less than real people. Existing in a shadowy world, they were viewed as but empty shells of their previous selves."[6] Many people still think the same thing today. They believe in life after death, but the kind of afterlife they imagine is neither solid nor substantial. It is more like the shadowy ghost that floats away from a character in a cartoon show. The spirits of the dead are disembodied. Maybe they can see and hear, but they cannot touch or feel.

This is part of a deeper tendency for people to think that physical existence is inferior to spiritual existence; the body is something inherently evil that the soul is trying to escape. Even many Christians still think of heaven as something immaterial. Rather than believing that our bodies will have a home in the new heavens and the new earth, they envision heaven as an eternal resting place for disembodied souls.

The gospel is not a ghost story, however. Our mortal bodies will be raised again. Even for all our physical weakness and suffering, which come as a result of living in a fallen world, our bodies have the blessing of God. This is why we should show respect for them, even in weakness and death. One highway patrolman described the aftermath of a horrific bus accident on a busy highway. He said the first order of business was to rescue the living, many of whom were still trapped in their vehicles. After that, he said, it was time to give the dead the dignity of a decent burial.

Caring for someone's body, even after death, is sound theology. God is not in the business of discarding bodies; he is in the business of resurrecting them. The body that is buried will rise again. Though our physical bodies will return to the dust when we die, by faith we will rise to be redeemed—

5. Leon Morris, *The Gospel According to St. Luke: An Introduction and Commentary*, Tyndale New Testament Commentaries (Grand Rapids: Eerdmans, 1974), 341.

6. Paul Beasley-Murray, *The Message of the Resurrection*, The Bible Speaks Today (Downers Grove, IL: InterVarsity, 2000), 77.

body and soul—in the resurrection. This is what we mean when we say that we believe in the resurrection of the body.

## TOUCH ME, AND SEE

Jesus proved this gospel truth to his disciples by appearing to them in the full reality of his resurrection body. The body that rose from the garden tomb was a marvelous, mysterious body with extraordinary abilities. It could suddenly appear, as it appeared to these disciples. It could also disappear, the way it disappeared from Cleopas at the dinner table (see Luke 24:31). Apparently Jesus could transport himself from place to place. He could even pass through locked doors, as he did on more than one occasion (see John 20:19, 26).

These supernatural abilities may help to explain what Paul means when he describes the resurrection body as a powerful, imperishable, and spiritual body (1 Cor. 15:42–44). It *is* a body, yet it is also a *spiritual* body—a body that transcends the ordinary limitations of time and space. In the words of Norval Geldenhuys, Jesus appeared "in a glorified, celestial body that was not bound by limitations of an ordinary earthly body."[7] As another commentator explains:

> The resurrection of Jesus was not his transformation into an immaterial body, but his acquisition of a "spiritual body" which could materialize or dematerialize at will. When, on occasion, Jesus chose to appear to various persons in material form, this was just as really the "spiritual body" of Jesus as when he was not visible. . . . In his risen state Jesus transcended the normal laws of physical existence. He was no longer bound by material or spatial limitations.[8]

This is something we can believe only by faith, however, and something the disciples could hardly accept without fear. They did not yet understand what a resurrection body could do. Nor did they fully believe that Jesus was alive from the dead. So their hearts were troubled, as our hearts always are

7. Norval Geldenhuys, *The Gospel of Luke*, New International Commentary on the New Testament (Grand Rapids: Eerdmans, 1951), 640.

8. M. J. Harris, *From Grave to Glory: Resurrection in the New Testament* (Grand Rapids: Zondervan, 1990), 142–43.

until we believe. So Jesus said to them, "Why are you troubled, and why do doubts arise in your hearts?" (Luke 24:38).

If the disciples had thought about these words for a moment, they might have realized that this was the same Jesus they had always known. Once again he was gently rebuking their unbelief, the way he always did (e.g., Luke 8:25). As Charles Spurgeon pointed out, "Our Lord had never been unwisely silent as to their faults. He had never passed over their errors with that false and indulgent affection which gratifies its own ease by tolerating sin; but he had pointed out their faults with the fidelity of true love; and now that he thus admonished them, they ought to have perceived that it was none other than he."[9]

Jesus was also identifying what was happening in their hearts, the way he always knew. The disciples were troubled; their emotions were stirred up; all kinds of doubts were coming to mind. In their internal dialogue, they were thinking that what they were seeing could be this or might be that. So Jesus lovingly challenged them to consider what was keeping them from believing in his resurrection.

This is a good question for anyone to consider. Do you believe in the bodily resurrection of Jesus Christ? To take this a step farther, do you believe in the resurrection of your own body? If not, why not? What is causing you to doubt what Luke says about the empty tomb, or what Jesus says about the resurrection and the life? Our doubts will be dispelled only by listening and looking to Jesus, who is the perfect cure for troubled hearts.

What Jesus showed his disciples was the physical evidence for the reality of his resurrection. "See my hands and my feet," he said. "It is I myself. Touch me, and see. For a spirit does not have flesh and bones as you see that I have" (Luke 24:39). The disciples had heard Jesus speak, so they already had sensory evidence from their sense of sound. Now he lovingly invited them to feel his hands and feet, using their sense of touch. Indeed, the word that Jesus used *(psēlaphēsate)* means more than simply to touch; it means to grasp or handle. The very body of Jesus had been raised from the dead. When the disciples clasped his hands, therefore, they could feel his knucklebones. Maybe they could even feel the blood coursing through

---

9. Charles H. Spurgeon, "The First Appearance of the Risen Lord to the Eleven," *The Metropolitan Tabernacle Pulpit* (London: Banner of Truth, 1969), 33:219.

his veins with every beat of his loving heart. The apostle John testified to these and other physical realities when he described the gospel as something "which we have heard, which we have seen with our eyes, which we looked upon and have touched with our hands, concerning the word of life" (1 John 1:1).

We ourselves have only *heard* the word of life. We have not seen Jesus with our eyes, or touched him with our hands. But we have the reliable testimony of people who did. They are the eyewitnesses of the risen Christ, the men and women who touched Jesus with their own hands. Their word gives us strong testimony because it comes from multiple witnesses: men and women who saw Jesus on various occasions—not just on Easter Sunday, but also afterwards—and in various places, from Jerusalem to Galilee. It is strong testimony because the people who gave it had ample opportunity to examine the evidence firsthand, and thus to verify that they were really in the physical presence of Jesus. Their testimony is strong because they saw Jesus when they were together, not just when they were alone and in private, and thus they could corroborate mutually what they each had seen and touched.

Their testimony is also strong because the disciples were skeptical at first, and only later came to a faith they were willing to die for. It took some convincing for these people to believe in the resurrection of the body. Their trust in the risen Christ was not wishful thinking, but a reasoned response to solid evidence—what Luke later described as "many proofs" given over the course of many days (Acts 1:3).

These men and women came to believe that Jesus Christ had risen from the dead. The person who stood before them and said "it is I myself" was the same Jesus they had always known. This was clear from the way he spoke to them, giving them peace and challenging their unbelief. But it was even more obvious from what he did next, for "when he had said this, he showed them his hands and his feet" (Luke 24:40). These appendages were the proof of his passion, for they plainly displayed the marks of his crucifixion. The wounds from the nails that pierced his hands and feet were no longer bleeding; they were healed and glorified. Yet they were still visible, so when the disciples saw them, they knew for sure that it was Jesus himself. The same Jesus who died on the cross for their sins was standing before them, in the flesh.

The wound-marks will remain on the resurrection body of Jesus Christ as a permanent reminder of everything he has done for our salvation. His hands and feet show the Father that he has paid the full price for sin. At the same time, they show us that our sins are fully forgiven. In fact, the glorified wounds of Jesus show us the whole gospel. The marks on his body bear witness to the cross where he died. But his hands and his feet belong to the same resurrection body that came out of the empty tomb. These are the two great facts of the gospel: Jesus died, and then in the same body he rose again. These two great facts give us the good news of our salvation: by the cross our sins are forgiven, and by the empty tomb we have the free gift of resurrection life.

To give his disciples one final proof, Jesus asked, "Have you anything here to eat?" (Luke 23:41). This time the disciples actually had some fish: "They gave him a piece of broiled fish, and he took it and ate before them" (Luke 24:42–43). Nothing is more basic to the physical reality of the human body than eating food. Once they had seen Jesus eat fish (and honey, some ancient manuscripts add), the disciples would never say again that they had only seen a ghost. Jesus did not merely *seem* to have a body; he actually had one—a body that could enjoy the pleasures of eating and drinking, even if it might not actually need food to survive. This meal was Luke's final proof for the gospel fact of the bodily resurrection of Jesus Christ.

The apostle Peter later referred to this meal when he preached the good news. We have been chosen as witnesses, Peter said, "who ate and drank with him after he rose from the dead" (Acts 10:41). The poet Ezra Pound once imagined how Peter might have described the resurrection of Jesus. Here are the words that Pound put into the mouth of that salty sailor:

A master of men was the Goodly Friend,
A mate of the wind and sea,
If they think they have slain our Goodly Friend
They are fools eternally.

I have seen him eat of the honey-comb
Since they nailed him to the tree.[10]

---

10. Adapted from Ezra Pound, "Ballad of the Goodly Fere," in *Chapters into Verse: Poetry in English Inspired by the Bible*, vol. 2: *Gospels to Revelation*, ed. Robert Atwan and Laurance Wieder (Oxford: Oxford University Press, 1993), 231.

## Too Good to Be True

Are you as certain as Peter was that Jesus rose from the dead? Some people believe in the resurrection of the body, and some people do not. What do you believe?

Luke uses a curious expression to indicate what the disciples believed. He says that they "still disbelieved for joy and were marveling" (Luke 24:41). "Marveling" is a word for wonderment and amazement. The disciples were witnessing the most extraordinary thing they had ever seen—that anyone had ever seen. It was the marvel of all marvels: the living and immortal body of someone who was dead and buried before he came alive in a body that would never die again.

It seemed too good to be true, which is why the disciples were still in disbelief: they were disbelieving *for joy*. They were not refusing to believe in the resurrection of the body because they rejected God's Word, or because they would not accept the evidence that Jesus provided, but simply because it was such joyful good news that they could hardly believe it. Their joy almost overwhelmed their faith.

Luke says that the disciples "disbelieved," and sometimes people talk the same way today. They say, "I can't believe it!" They really *do* believe it, but it is such good news that they almost can't. "I can't believe I passed that test," they say, or "I can't believe we won that game!" The disciples felt the same way. They were starting to understand that Jesus really had risen from the grave, but this was such unbelievably good news that they could hardly believe it. Here is how Augustine described their emotions: "While they were still flustered for joy, they were rejoicing and doubting at the same time. They were seeing and touching, and scarcely believing."[11]

What joy it brings to believe in the resurrection of the body, even if we can hardly believe it. Now there is a principle of death at work in the entire universe. Things are falling apart. Everywhere we look, we see signs of death and decay. Whether the universe is cooling down, or planet earth is heating up, the reality is that eventually everything will be destroyed. But by the power of the resurrection, the creation will be restored again. God will undo all that death has done. There will be a new heaven and a new earth. Physical matter will be redeemed (see Rom. 8:21).

11. Augustine, "Sermon 229J.3," in *Luke*, ed. Just, 386.

The hope of the coming resurrection brings true joy to physical suffering! Whatever pains we experience in our earthly bodies—whatever weakness, disability, or disease—God will make everything perfect when we rise again. There will be no more sadness or pain, only perfect health and joy.

This hope brings special joy at the time of death. Sooner or later we will say good-bye to the people we love the most in the whole world. We will lay their bodies in the dust, or else we ourselves will go down to the grave. But through faith in Jesus, and by the power of his resurrection, we will rise again. We will see the glory on the other side, and we will rise with Jesus on the final day. Do not disbelieve in the resurrection of the body, but believe it . . . for joy!

# 111

# THE EASTER SERMON
# OF JESUS CHRIST

## *Luke 24:44–48*

*Then he opened their minds to understand the Scriptures, and
said to them, "Thus it is written, that the Christ should suffer and
on the third day rise from the dead, and that repentance and forgiveness of sins should be proclaimed in his name to all nations,
beginning from Jerusalem." (Luke 24:45–47)*

ASTER was over. The women had made their early journey to
find the empty tomb. Peter had raced to see the grave clothes.
Cleopas and his companion had walked to Emmaus with Jesus,
as it turned out, and then back to Jerusalem with their hearts on fire. Jesus
himself had suddenly appeared among his disciples, showing them his
hands and feet. It was the day of resurrection—the first of all Easters—and
it filled the disciples with so much joy they could hardly believe it.

Now it was time for Jesus to do what he loved to do as much as anything
in the world: preach the gospel of his saving grace (see Luke 4:43). Maybe
Jesus did this on the same night that he appeared to his disciples. What
seems more likely, though, is that there is a gap in Luke 24 between verse 43

677

and verse 44, between Easter evening and all the teaching Jesus did in the following weeks. Luke 24 almost gives the impression that Jesus went back to heaven the same day he rose from the dead. But he was with his disciples for forty days between his resurrection and his ascension, as Luke said himself in Acts 1:3. So presumably the end of chapter 24 is a summary of what he taught during those weeks—one long sermon to explain Easter Sunday, everything that led up to it, and everything that would follow.

When Jesus says "while I was still with you" in verse 44, he is hinting that he is about to leave his disciples. But before he goes, he has something supremely important to do, and that is to prepare them to reach the world. The destiny of humanity depended on their faithful witness, so at the end of Luke's Gospel, Jesus briefed them on their mission to the world.[1]

## A BIBLICAL SERMON

Only Luke records the Easter sermon of Jesus Christ, in which he preached the gospel of his own resurrection and its implications for the world. It was a biblical, Christ-centered, evangelistic, missionary sermon.

To begin with, Jesus preached a biblical sermon, in which he proclaimed the gospel promise from the Old Testament. Jesus wanted to give his disciples a complete course in biblical interpretation. He said to them, "These are my words that I spoke to you while I was still with you, that everything written about me in the Law of Moses and the Prophets and the Psalms must be fulfilled" (Luke 24:44).

One time-honored principle for public speaking is to start by telling people what you are going to tell them, then tell them, and finally tell them what you told them. Jesus followed that principle here. Back in Nazareth he had begun his public ministry by preaching the good news of the kingdom from the prophet Isaiah. He kept preaching that gospel message throughout his earthly ministry. Now, in his last sermon, Jesus wanted to tell his disciples again what he had told them before. When he said "these are my words," he was referring to everything he had taught his disciples.

This time they were finally ready to hear what he had to say. Jesus had always told them that he would die and rise again, but the disciples had

1. David Gooding, *According to Luke: A New Exposition of the Third Gospel* (Grand Rapids: Eerdmans, 1987), 355.

never really understood what he was talking about. Things were different now, though, because they were in the very presence of the crucified and risen Christ. So they were ready to understand the gospel and its implications for the world, as well as their own call to gospel ministry. "Don't you see," Jesus could say to them now, "*this* is what I was talking about. What I did on the cross and through the empty tomb was the outworking of everything I have ever taught you."

What Jesus taught came right out of the Bible, which is where his sermon begins: with the Scriptures of the Old Testament. In briefing his disciples on their mission to the world, Jesus does not begin with their personal spiritual experience. He does not even begin with the physical reality of his own resurrection. Rather, he begins the same place that we should always begin everything in life: with the Word of God. As Kent Hughes comments, Jesus "did not want them to rest their belief in his resurrection on their personal experience alone. He was not interested in their becoming an esoteric coterie, an elite group with a special knowledge of Christ. Resting their faith on a miracle was not sufficient. He wanted them to ground their experience of his resurrection on the massive testimony and perspective of Scripture."[2] Thus the Easter sermon of Jesus Christ is a biblical sermon.

The way Jesus refers to the Bible here is by calling it the Law of Moses, the Prophets, and the Psalms. This is the way many Jews referred to the three traditional parts of the Hebrew Scriptures. For them, the Law was the first five books of the Bible: Genesis, Exodus, Leviticus, Numbers, and Deuteronomy. The Prophets included the Major and Minor Prophets, and also the historical books, like Samuel and Chronicles. The Psalms referred not only to Israel's hymnbook, but also to other writings in the wisdom literature, like Proverbs and Ecclesiastes. Thus talking about "the Law of Moses and the Prophets and the Psalms" was really a shorthand way of referring to the whole Old Testament.

Jesus based his life and ministry on everything those writings said about his saving work. In fact, Jesus said that everything in the Bible was about him. What an audacious claim to make! What right did Jesus have to say that everything in the Bible is all about him? Who does he think he is anyway? Jesus knows who he is: the Son of God and the Savior of the world,

---

2. R. Kent Hughes, *Luke: That You May Know the Truth*, 2 vols., Preaching the Word (Wheaton, IL: Crossway, 1998), 2:415.

and therefore the fulfillment of every promise that God has ever made to his people. Jesus Christ is the key to understanding the Old Testament. To know the Old Testament truly is to know Jesus, and to know Jesus, one has to know the Old Testament.

Jesus used every part of the Old Testament in his own ministry. He taught his disciples many things that were written about him in Moses, the Prophets, and the Psalms. Jesus used the Law of Moses right at the beginning of the Gospel, when he was tempted in the wilderness and answered the devil by quoting directly from Deuteronomy (Luke 4:1–11; cf. Deut. 6:13, 16; 8:3). Jesus also used the Prophets, starting with his very first sermon (Luke 4:17–21; cf. Isa. 61:1–2) and including many specific fulfillments of their prophecies. For example, when Jesus rode into Jerusalem on Palm Sunday, he was fulfilling Zechariah's prophecy of a king coming "humble and mounted on a donkey" (Zech. 9:9). Then Jesus often taught from the Psalms. He did it the very week that he was crucified, using Psalm 110 to prove that the Christ is both David's son and David's Lord (see Luke 20:41–44).

Jesus taught this way because he knew that all these Scriptures had to come true. Everything written about him "*must* be fulfilled" (Luke 24:44), he said, and the word "must" expressed a divine necessity. The life of Jesus was governed by the prophecies and promises of the Word of God. In order for God to fulfill his plan—and in order for us to be saved—Jesus had to come into the world the way he came, live the way he lived, die the way he died, and rise again the way he rose again. It all had to happen the way the Bible said it would happen, the way it was promised in the Scriptures. To show this, Jesus preached a biblical sermon at the end of Easter.

## A CHRIST-CENTERED SERMON

Jesus also preached a Christ-centered sermon, as any biblical sermon ought to be. The main thing that Jesus had taught his disciples—from the Old Testament—was the crucifixion and the resurrection of the Christ. In other words, he preached the gospel, because these are the two basic facts of the gospel: the dying and the rising of the Savior whom God promised. In his Easter sermon, Jesus preached that same gospel again: "Then he opened their minds to understand the Scriptures, and said to them, 'Thus it is written, that the Christ should suffer and on the third day rise from the dead'" (Luke 24:45–46). The gospel promise that was given in the Old Testament—the promise of the Christ—finds its fulfillment in Jesus and his saving work.

These were all things that Jesus had told his disciples before. He said: "The Son of Man must suffer many things . . . and be killed, and on the third day be raised" (Luke 9:22). He said: "See, we are going up to Jerusalem, and everything that is written about the Son of Man by the prophets will be accomplished. . . . After flogging him, they will kill him, and on the third day he will rise" (Luke 18:31, 33). But even though Jesus said these things, the disciples did not understand them. When he said the Son of Man would be delivered over to death, "they did not understand this saying, and it was concealed from them, so that they might not perceive it" (Luke 9:45). Similarly, when he prophesied his death and his resurrection on the third day, "they understood none of these things. This saying was hidden from them, and they did not grasp what was said" (Luke 18:34). The minds of the disciples were closed to the gospel.

We should not be surprised, therefore, when people have trouble understanding the gospel or believing in Jesus today. It did not seem all that important to the disciples at first either. They really did not understand what Jesus was talking about.

Then Jesus actually did what he always said that he would do: he offered his body for suffering unto death, and then on the third day he rose again. At that point one might think that the disciples would believe the gospel. Yet they *still* did not understand! When Jesus appeared to them after his resurrection, they thought they were seeing a ghost (Luke 24:37), not a living Savior. Somehow they were still missing something.

What made the difference for these disciples? How did they ever start trusting in the cross and believing in the empty tomb? Luke tells us that Jesus "opened their minds to understand the Scriptures" (Luke 24:45; cf. 24:32). What these men needed—what everyone needs—is the mind-opening work of God. Christianity is rational, but understanding the gospel is not merely intellectual. It takes a work of God for anyone to know Jesus in a saving way. The Bible says that "the natural person does not accept the things of the Spirit of God, for they are folly to him, and he is not able to understand them because they are spiritually discerned"

(1 Cor. 2:14). It does not matter how smart we are; we will never understand the message of God's salvation unless and until God enables us to understand it. This is what Jesus did for his disciples, and what he will do for anyone who sincerely asks him for understanding: he will open our minds to see his salvation.

Knowing Jesus is the work of God the Holy Spirit—a work he does when the Bible is preached in a Christ-centered way. Notice that when his disciples had trouble understanding what he was saying from the Scriptures, Jesus did not decide to try some other method. He did not say, "The Bible must be too hard for them to understand; I need to find some other way to communicate." On the contrary, Jesus knew that God does his saving work by the Word. So he went back to the same Scriptures he had always preached, and preached them again. Here is an example for our own evangelism, in which we should always trust the Word to do the real work of our witness.

Jesus preached Christ from Moses, the Prophets, and the Psalms. Maybe he turned to Exodus 12 and talked about the Passover, and how an offering of blood saved people from death. Or maybe he quoted Leviticus 16 and preached about the sacrifice that was sprinkled on the mercy seat to atone for all his people's sins. Then he might have turned to one of the prophets, like Isaiah, who said that the Savior would be stricken, smitten, and afflicted, that he would be wounded for our transgressions and crushed for our iniquities (see Isa. 53). Or perhaps Jesus preached Psalm 22—the song he quoted from the cross when he was dying a God-forsaken death. But wherever he turned in the Scriptures, Jesus preached the sufferings and death of the Christ.

That is not all he preached, however. Jesus also preached the resurrection of the Christ. Maybe he preached it from the story of Moses and the burning bush, where God styled himself as the God of Abraham, Isaac, and Jacob—the God of the living, and not the dead (Exod. 3:1–6; cf. Luke 20:37–38). Or maybe he preached the resurrection from the prophet Jonah, who came back on the third day (see Jonah 1:17), or from Hosea, who said, "on the third day he will raise us up, that we may live before him" (Hos. 6:2). Jesus also preached the resurrection from passages like Psalm 16, where the Christ said, "You will not abandon me to the grave" (Ps. 16:10 NIV; cf. Acts 2:25–32).

When Jesus preached his Easter sermon, he preached Christ crucified and Christ risen, Christ suffering and dying and rising again. He preached Christ from all the Scriptures, opening minds to understand the basic facts of his saving gospel. Jesus did what was prophesied, and then he preached what he had done—his saving work in human history. This is the basic message of the whole Bible: Jesus the Christ suffered and died and rose again.

## AN EVANGELISTIC SERMON

If we believe the gospel, as promised in the Scriptures and accomplished by the Christ, then we must repent of our sin. This too was part of the Easter preaching of Jesus Christ. His biblical, Christ-centered sermon was also an evangelistic sermon—a sermon that called people to respond by repenting and receiving forgiveness for their sins. Jesus thus ended his ministry the same way he began it: by preaching repentance (see Matt. 4:17).

The biblical gospel is more than a set of facts. We need to know that Jesus died and rose again, of course, but we also need to understand what those facts mean and respond to them in a saving and believing way. This too was promised in the Scriptures. The same Old Testament that promised the sufferings and the resurrection of the Christ, also promised repentance and forgiveness. "Thus it is written," Jesus said, "that repentance and forgiveness of sins should be proclaimed in his name" (Luke 24:47).

This could be proved from almost any page in the Bible. It is not just this text or that text which proclaims repentance and the forgiveness of sins; it is the whole message of the Old Testament. Ever since Adam and Eve committed the first sin, God has been calling his people to repentance. The biblical prophets were forever telling the people of God to turn away from sin. "Let the wicked forsake his way," they said, "and the unrighteous man his thoughts" (Isa. 55:7). The very best men and women of God show us how to repent by their example. "Have mercy on me, O God," said King David. "Against you, you only, have I sinned" (Ps. 51:1, 4).

God did have mercy—not only on David, but on every penitent sinner. This too is the message of the Old Testament: God freely offers forgiveness to anyone who is truly sorry for sin. "As far as the east is from the west," David testified, "so far does he remove our transgressions from us"

(Ps. 103:12). The prophet who told the wicked man to forsake his way also said, "let him return to the LORD, that he may have compassion on him, and to our God, for he will abundantly pardon" (Isa. 55:7). "Whoever conceals his transgressions will not prosper," the Scripture says, "but he who confesses and forsakes them will obtain mercy" (Prov. 28:13).

Now repentance and forgiveness are to be preached in the name of Jesus, or on the name of Jesus—on the basis of what he has done on the cross and through the empty tomb. This is how we know that the ancient promise is true, that by the saving grace of gospel repentance, all our sins will be forgiven. We are sure of this because Jesus went to the cross for us, and said, "Father, forgive them" (Luke 23:34). We are forgiven "through the merit and the mediation of Christ."[3] We know that his sacrifice has been accepted because God raised him from the dead. It is not only the crucifixion that guarantees our forgiveness, but also the resurrection.

The way for us to respond is to repent and believe, and then we too will be forgiven. Here is how a little old verse for children describes what it means for us to repent:

> Repentance is to leave
>   The things we loved before,
> And to show that we in earnest grieve
>   By doing so no more.

Leaving the things we loved before takes courage, and also humility—the humility to admit that God cannot accept us just the way we are, but that we need to be forgiven. A good illustration of penitent humility comes from the ancient traditions of the Luo tribe in Tanzania. When a tribe member commits a serious crime, he has violated the community covenant and is banished from his village for life. He will go somewhere else, maybe for decades. But when he grows old, he will ask if he can return to his fathers and come home to die in his own village. There is only one way for the sinner to return, only one way to undo the evil that he has done: a sacred ritual of atonement. A low opening is made in the village wall, opposite the entrance. Then a lamb is sacrificed, and as the man confesses his crime,

---

3. J. C. Ryle, *Expository Thoughts on the Gospels, Luke* (1858; reprint Cambridge: James Clarke, 1976), 2:522.

its blood is sprinkled on him for cleansing. This takes place outside the walls of the village. But once the sacrifice has been made and the blood has been sprinkled, the man is allowed to come inside, stooping low to enter in humility before being welcomed into his father's house.[4]

So it is for anyone who wants to enter the family of God. We must bow in humility. We must confess the wrong that we have done. We must believe in the power of the sacrificial blood that Jesus sprinkled on the cross. Then we will be fully forgiven and warmly welcomed into the Father's house.

## A Missionary Sermon

This message of repentance and forgiveness is for everyone in the whole world, which is why Jesus ended his biblical, Christ-centered, evangelistic sermon by turning it into a missionary sermon. First we believe the gospel for ourselves, confessing our own sin and trusting Jesus with our own faith. Next we proclaim that gospel message to others. So Jesus told his disciples that repentance and forgiveness should be preached in his name "to all nations, beginning from Jerusalem" (Luke 24:47). Then he said, "You are witnesses of these things" (Luke 24:48). Like all the resurrection stories in Luke, this one ends with witness (see Luke 24:9–10, 33–35).

Thus the Easter sermon of Jesus Christ is a missionary sermon for the world. This had been God's plan from the beginning. He was never the God of the Jews only; he had always had a heart for the world. This too was "written in the Scriptures." The same Old Testament that said the Christ would suffer and rise again, and that promised repentance and forgiveness, also said that this saving gospel would be preached throughout the world. It would start in Jerusalem, of course, because that is where Jesus died and rose again, and also because that is what the Scripture promised (see Isa. 2:3; Joel 3:16). But the gospel would go from Jerusalem to the nations.

We see this missionary promise in every part of the Old Testament. We see it in the Law of Moses, which promised that God would bless all nations through the son of Abraham (see Gen. 12:2–3; 17:1–7; cf. Gal. 3:16, 29). We see it in the Prophets, who said, "I will make you as a light for the nations, that my salvation may reach to the end of the earth" (Isa. 49:6). We see it

---

4. This story is told by Bishop Kisare in Joel B. Green and Mark D. Baker, *Recovering the Scandal of the Cross* (Downers Grove, IL: InterVarsity, 2000), 188–89.

perhaps most clearly in the Psalms. Psalm 22, the same psalm that prophesied that Christ would suffer a God-forsaken death, also made this promise: "All the ends of the earth shall remember and turn to the Lord, and all the families of the nations shall worship before you" (Ps. 22:27). We find the same global promise in many of the praise psalms: "The Lord has made known his salvation; he has revealed his righteousness in the sight of the nations" (Ps. 98:2; cf. 96:3; 97:6; 100:1).

So it was written. The Old Testament promises of God included the missionary age of the church. If anyone understood the global reach of the gospel it was Luke. Since the beginning of this book, he has been preparing us to see that salvation is for all nations. He announced that Jesus came to bring peace on earth (Luke 2:14), that his salvation would be for all peoples (Luke 2:31), that it would be a light for the Gentiles (Luke 2:32). Luke quoted Old Testament stories about Gentiles coming to faith, like Naaman the Syrian, or the widow of Zarephath (Luke 4:25–27). He also told us stories about Gentiles coming to Jesus, like the Roman centurion with the dying servant (Luke 7:1–9).

Now the time had come for all the ancient promises to be fulfilled. Just as it was promised that the Christ would suffer and rise again, so it was promised that forgiveness would be preached to all nations. As far as the plan of God and the fulfillment of Scripture are concerned, the missionary work of the church is as necessary and as important as the cross itself, and as the empty tomb. The Bible thus teaches three great redemptive acts in history: the cross, the resurrection, and the missionary work of the church. The ancient promises to the nations must be fulfilled. As Spurgeon said, "there was a divine necessity that Christ should die, and an equally imperative *must* that he should arise again from the dead; but there is an equally absolute necessity that Jesus should be preached to every creature under heaven."[5] Therefore Jesus sent his apostles out on their mission to the world, which was really *his* mission to the world. This is why Jesus had invested so much of himself in these men, to the point of death. His plan all along was for these apostles to go global with the gospel. As eyewitnesses of the resurrection, they would preach repentance and forgiveness to all nations, through the crucified and risen Christ.

5. Charles H. Spurgeon, "Beginning at Jerusalem," *The Metropolitan Tabernacle Pulpit* (London: Banner of Truth, 1971), 29:375.

This is exactly what the apostles did: they shared Christ everywhere. Their story is told in the book of Acts, which is volume two of Luke's collected writings—the sequel to his Gospel. In Acts we read that starting from Jerusalem the apostles went out into the world with the gospel. Again and again we are told that they were witnesses for Jesus (e.g., Acts 1:8; 2:32; 5:32), as Jesus said they would be.

The apostles witnessed the same way that Jesus preached. Their sermons were biblical. They did not preach merely on the basis of their personal experience (which they sometimes did and could do better than anyone). Instead, they also (and primarily) preached from the Old Testament (e.g., Acts 2:17–28; 13:26–41). Their sermons were Christ-centered; the apostles were always preaching the crucifixion and the resurrection of Jesus Christ. "You crucified him," they said, "but God raised him up" (see Acts 2:23–24, 32; cf. 17:2–3). Their sermons were evangelistic. They said, "Repent . . . in the name of Jesus Christ for the forgiveness of your sins" (see Acts 2:38). They preached this way to Gentiles as well as to Jews, for Jesus had told them to preach to all nations (see Acts 13:47–48; 17:30). Although it is true that we do not have the full text of Jesus' Easter sermon in the Gospel of Luke, there is a sense in which the notes from that sermon are scattered throughout the New Testament, for it is the same message that the apostles always preached.

Today we continue to carry out that mission by multiplying gospel ministry to the world. Through the work of the church, and through the faithful ministry of Christian missionaries, repentance and forgiveness are proclaimed everywhere in the name of Jesus. Every time someone preaches a biblical sermon that gives people the gospel and calls them to repent for the forgiveness of their sins, the Easter sermon of Jesus Christ is preached all over again—his global, universal, missionary gospel.

We too are called to be witnesses. We are not eyewitnesses, of course, because we have not seen the risen Christ the way the apostles saw him. But we are witnesses nonetheless. We have heard the Easter sermon of Jesus Christ. We know the gospel message of the cross and the empty tomb. We believe God's promise of the forgiveness of sins. So now we are the ones who carry the message of the apostles wherever we go in the world. Paul Beasley-Murray said, "The task of every disciple—and not just of every preacher—is to interpret the significance of the life, death and resurrection of Jesus for others, and in doing so to spell out the gospel offer of forgiveness and the gospel demand for repentance."[6]

When we think of the nations, we should not think only of people who live far away. The "nations" includes all the people who are outside the family of God, who do not yet believe that Jesus died for them on the cross, or that their sins can be forgiven. In fact, some of the people who are farthest away from God are the people who are closest to us. Who will be their witness?

After almost a decade of going to the same barber, I finally had the perfect chance to share the gospel. My friend's mother-in-law had died the week before, and he had been deeply affected by something strange that happened in her final days. The woman had pancreatic cancer and against every medical expectation she had lingered *in extremis* for weeks. The barber knew why: she was not ready to die, so she kept herself alive by sheer force of will. For days she lay on her hospital bed, seemingly unresponsive. Then suddenly she sat up with a loud cry, turned her head, and moved her arm wildly. Everyone in the room was shocked. They were also deeply troubled, for to some of them it seemed that she was fending off a demon—a demon that was trying to capture her soul.

My barber wanted to know what I thought about what had happened (because I was a "priest," he said, I was the person to ask). I told him that the passage from this life to the next is a great mystery, and that I did not have any opinion about what had happened to his mother-in-law. But I told him that I did know how to be ready to die and go to heaven:

"By trying to be a good person, right?" the barber said.

"No," I said, "I'm sure that none of us can really be good enough for God. All we need to do is believe in Jesus."

"But what does that mean?" he wanted to know—the kind of question that sometimes we have to wait a decade before we get a chance to answer.

"It means believing that Jesus died on the cross," I said, "and believing that he rose again from the dead." Immediately the barber said that he believed all of that. Then I said, "And it means telling God that you are sorry for your sins, and asking him to forgive you for Jesus' sake."

---

6. Paul Beasley-Murray, *The Message of the Resurrection*, The Bible Speaks Today (Downers Grove, IL: InterVarsity, 2000), 82.

My friend did not say whether he was ready to repent or not; the conversation moved on, as it often does when we start talking about sin. But without repentance no one will ever see the kingdom of God. It is not enough simply to believe the basic facts of the gospel—that Jesus died and rose again. We also need to apply those facts to ourselves by saying, "Dear God, I am sorry that I am such a sinner. Please forgive me for Jesus' sake."

Anyone who repents and believes in Jesus' name will be forgiven. This is the promise of God, as it was made in the Old Testament Scriptures, preached in the Easter sermon of Jesus Christ, and given to all people everywhere—every one of us.

# 112

# HE ASCENDED INTO HEAVEN

## Luke 24:49–53

*Then he led them out as far as Bethany, and lifting up his hands*
*he blessed them. While he blessed them, he parted from them and*
*was carried up into heaven.* (Luke 24:50–51)

Good writers know how to finish as well as they start. T. S. Eliot's famous poem "East Coker," from *The Four Quartets*, begins and ends with a beautifully matched, perfectly balanced pair of poetic lines. "In my beginning is my end," the poem starts—a line that expresses the frail mortality of human existence. The poem closes with the same line in mirror image: "In my end is my beginning." These words give a pleasing sense of closure and capture the meaning of the poem as a whole.

This is typical of a great work of literature: the beginning and the end are constructed to fit together harmoniously. The conclusion brings things full circle, reminding us where things began while at the same time showing how much progress has been made. There is a sense of completion, but also a sense of movement, and usually the future is full of promise.

Most of the books in the Bible end as well as they begin, and the Gospel of Luke is no exception. Luke may have had a journalist's love for facts, but he also had a poet's love for style. His Gospel thus ends where it began: at the temple in Jerusalem—the place where people went to meet with God. Back at the beginning, Zechariah the priest was in the Holy Place, offering incense on the altar of prayer (Luke 1:5–23). Here at the end we are back at the temple again; only now there is a large crowd of worshipers joyfully praising God for Jesus Christ. The salvation that was only anticipated at the beginning has fully come.

Another way to see how the beginning and the ending of Luke fit together is by comparing the coming of Christ to what might be called the "going" of Christ. Luke begins with the stories of the first Christmas—the coming of the Son of God. But he ends his Gospel with the story of the ascension, with Jesus Christ rising and returning to heaven. Here is how David Gooding describes the movement of the book:

> Luke's inspired presentation of Christ is arranged in two great movements: first the "Coming" of the Lord from heaven to earth; and then his "Going" from earth to heaven. . . . Appropriately, the climax of the "Going" shows the man, Jesus, rejected and crucified on earth, but now risen and ascending, being received up into glory. The "Coming" and the "Going": between them they sum up Luke's message of salvation. The pre-existent and eternal Son of God came to our world and became a man like us so that he might secure for us here in this world forgiveness, wholeness, peace with God and the certainty that God's will shall eventually be done on earth even as it is done in heaven. But there is more. By his "Going" he has taken humanity to the pinnacle of the universe. . . . All who trust him will one day be brought to share his glory in that exalted realm, and to reign with him at his return.[1]

## THE ASCENSION

The "Going" of Christ reaches its dramatic climax at the end of Luke's Gospel. In the days and weeks following his resurrection, Jesus had been appearing to his disciples, and then disappearing, only to reappear again—"now you see him, now you don't." But he had promised that according to the Scriptures, it was necessary for Jesus to "enter into his glory" (Luke 24:26). A resurrection without an ascension would be unthinkable; according to the plan of God, there needed to be a suitable exaltation of the Christ.

1. David Gooding, *According to Luke: A New Exposition of the Third Gospel* (Grand Rapids: Eerdmans, 1987), 9.

So the Gospel ends with an "indescribably august event, the ascension of the King."[2]

Luke simply tells us that Jesus "led them out as far as Bethany, and lifting up his hands he blessed them. While he blessed them, he parted from them and was carried up into heaven" (Luke 24:50–51). Theologians call this "the ascension," by which they mean the glorious elevation of Jesus Christ—his visible departure from earth and triumphant return to heaven, from which he will return on the last of all days to judge the world.[3]

Luke describes this miraculous event more fully in his other best-seller, the book of Acts. From that book we know that Jesus was with his disciples for forty days, preaching the kingdom of God and giving many proofs of his resurrection (Acts 1:3). At the end of that extended spiritual and theological seminar, Jesus took his disciples to one of their favorite retreats, on the slopes of the Mount of Olives (Acts 1:12). They were near Bethany, which was the home of Mary, Martha, and Lazarus. While they were there, Jesus ascended into heaven.

This important historical event is a wonderful truth that all Christians confess, but most people rarely contemplate. What does it mean that Jesus ascended into heaven? Is this merely something that we say when we recite the Apostles' Creed, or is it something we understand with our minds, believe in our hearts, and celebrate with our praise? Do we understand that even the joys of Easter Sunday are surpassed by the glories of the ascension?

When Jesus was "carried up into heaven" (Luke 24:51), or "taken up into heaven," as it says elsewhere (see Mark 16:19; Acts 1:11; 1 Tim. 3:16), he was removed from the presence of his disciples. This was not like the other sudden disappearances Jesus made after the resurrection. This time he did not simply vanish (see Luke 24:31), but ascended into heaven, rising from their sight on a glorious and mysterious cloud (see Acts 1:9). This marvelous cloud represented the presence of God and gave the ascension an air of

---

2. Gooding, *Luke*, 356.

3. Some scholars have questioned whether Luke really is describing the ascension here after all. Instead, they see everything in Luke 24 as something that happened on Easter Sunday. When Jesus departed from his disciples at Bethany, they say, it was not a final return to heaven, but simply a temporary removal from the presence of his disciples, which was later followed by the ascension proper, as described in Acts 1. Yet there is no specific indication of time in Luke 24:50–53, and the wording in these verses corresponds closely with the vocabulary Luke uses in Acts 1 to describe the way Jesus returned to heaven, which means that we are well justified in connecting these verses with the ascension.

finality. Here then is "the consummation of Christ's earthly work," writes Leon Morris, "the indication to His followers that His mission is accomplished, His work among them come to a decisive end."[4]

When he "ascended far above all the heavens" (Eph. 4:10), the Son of God returned to the place he left behind when he became a man (see John 17:5). He was restored to the glories of heaven and the worship of the heavenly angels. In leaving the world, he was going to the Father (see John 16:10, 28; 20:17), and when he returned to the presence of God, he took his exalted place at the Father's right hand (see Acts 2:33; 7:56; Col. 3:1; Heb. 1:3; 10:12). This expression symbolically indicates his supreme dominion and authority over heaven and earth. The right hand of any ancient monarch was a place of exalted honor and royal government. Thus for Jesus to sit down at the right hand of the Father was to exercise equal and absolute rule over the entire universe. The risen Christ is the eternal King. He has "gone into heaven," wrote the apostle Peter, "and is at the right hand of God, with angels, authorities, and powers having been subjected to him" (1 Peter 3:22; cf. Ps. 110:1; 1 Cor. 15:27; Eph. 1:20–22; Phil. 2:9–11).

Understand that Jesus exercises this supreme authority as the God-man. He has never discarded the human nature that he assumed in his incarnation, but has ascended into heaven in bodily form. We have faith in the *ascension* of the body as much as we have faith in the resurrection of the body. The same Christ who was born and suffered in the body also ascended in the body. We believe in the bodily ascension of the crucified, risen, and glorified Christ.

This means that humanity itself has now been elevated to the most exalted place of highest possible authority. "The divine descended," wrote Francis Turretin, "but the human ascended."[5] Comprehend this staggering thought: because of the bodily ascension of Jesus Christ, the dust of earth now sits on the throne of heaven.

By way of comparison, consider how awe-inspiring it is to touch a meteorite—a solid mass of metal or stone that has hurtled to the earth from some far place in outer space. A meteorite is an object from another world.

---

4. Leon Morris, *The Gospel According to St. Luke: An Introduction and Commentary*, Tyndale New Testament Commentaries (Grand Rapids: Eerdmans, 1974), 344.

5. Francis Turretin, *Institutes of Elenctic Theology*, 3 vols., trans. George Musgrave Giger, ed. James T. Dennison, Jr. (Phillipsburg, NJ: P&R, 1994), 2:368.

But now consider how infinitely marvelous it is that the physical body of Jesus Christ, in all the humanity of our own flesh and blood, has taken up eternal residence in the heights of heaven. As Clement of Alexandria once said, "he was carried up into heaven so that he might share the Father's throne even with the flesh that was united to him."[6]

One day we will see this for ourselves. The worthy Scottish theologian Thomas Boston said that when the people of God reach heaven, they will

> see Jesus Christ, God and man, with their bodily eyes, as He will never lay aside the human nature. They will behold that glorious blessed body, which is personally united to the divine nature, and exalted above principalities and powers and every name that is named. There we shall see, with our eyes, that very body which was born of Mary at Bethlehem, and crucified at Jerusalem between two thieves: the blessed head that was crowned with thorns; the face that was spit upon; the hands and feet that were nailed to the cross; all shining with inconceivable glory.[7]

## A PARTING GIFT

In the meantime, Jesus has given us two precious blessings—the blessings he gave his disciples when he ascended into heaven: a parting gift and a farewell benediction. These are both things that people often give their friends when they say good-bye, especially if they will be gone for a very long time, perhaps never to see them again. What a joy it is to receive a keepsake from a friend, and to hear someone say, "God bless you, my friend"—a benediction that places us under God's care. These are the same blessings Jesus gave to his disciples: a parting gift and a farewell benediction.

The gift Jesus promised to give is the best of all gifts. "And behold," he said to his disciples, "I am sending the promise of my Father upon you. But stay in the city until you are clothed with power from on high" (Luke 24:49). What Jesus meant by the "promise" of his Father was the Third Person of the Trinity—the Holy Spirit himself. With this parting gift, Jesus gave his disciples the very power of God.

6. Clement of Alexandria, "Commentary on Luke," in *Luke*, ed. Arthur A. Just, Jr., Ancient Christian Commentary on Scripture, NT 3 (Downers Grove, IL: InterVarsity, 2003), 392.
7. Thomas Boston, *Human Nature in Its Fourfold State* (Edinburgh: Banner of Truth, 1989), 452–53.

The word "promise" is the perfect word to use in this regard because God had long promised to send his people the Holy Spirit. In fact, the sending of the Spirit is one of the things Jesus said was written in the Scriptures (see Luke 24:46). The same Bible passage which said that the Christ would die and rise again (Luke 24:46), and which promised the preaching of repentance and forgiveness to all nations (Luke 24:47), also said that God would pour out the Holy Spirit on his people.

There was a time, for example, when God took the Spirit from Moses and gave it to his seventy elders. When this happened, Moses said he wished that God would pour his Spirit out on all his people (see Num. 11:29). This is exactly what the prophets promised. Isaiah prophesied that the Spirit would be "poured upon us from on high" (Isa. 32:15)—upon all the offspring of Jacob (Isa. 44:3). Ezekiel said that God would put his Spirit in people's hearts (Ezek. 36:27). Joel said that in the last days God would pour his Spirit on all his people: men and women, young and old (Joel 2:28–29; cf. Ezek. 39:29). Jesus promised the same thing when he said that the Father would send the Spirit in the name of the Son (John 14:16–17, 26). The gift of the Holy Spirit is the promise of God—a gift that would come only if and when Jesus returned to the Father (see John 16:7).

The gift of the Spirit is absolutely essential and totally necessary for any effective ministry. Jesus was sending the apostles out to be his witnesses to the world. As they preached repentance and forgiveness through the cross and the empty tomb, they would be utterly dependent on the work of the Holy Spirit. How could they ever fulfill their calling to reach the world for Christ in their own strength? Without the Spirit, not even the preaching of the gospel would have any effect on people, because faith in Jesus and repentance for sin are gifts of the Holy Spirit. No one ever comes to faith in Christ without his regenerating work. But praise God! Jesus has sent us the Spirit he promised to send. He knew that we could never make it on our own; we need the power of God for ministry and for missions. We have that power by the presence and the work of the Holy Spirit. Our gospel does not come to people in words alone, "but also in power and in the Holy Spirit" (1 Thess. 1:5).

The gospel does this because Jesus fulfilled his promise, sending the Spirit on the day of Pentecost. With flames of fire and the rushing of a mighty wind, the Holy Spirit was poured out on the church (see Acts 2:1–4,

33). The Spirit has been with us ever since, clothing us with "power from on high," just as Jesus promised. Now, by the gifts and graces of the Holy Spirit, even our own feeble efforts to share the gospel can bring people salvation. We should never be discouraged, but believe that whatever we do for Jesus may yet succeed by the Holy Spirit, who is the power of God.

One of the reasons this parting gift is so essential is that the missionary work of the gospel is so dangerous. Jesus told the apostles that they would be his witnesses (Luke 24:48). Strangely enough, the biblical word for "witness" (*martys*) ended up becoming the same word for "martyr." This is almost certainly because almost all the first witnesses to the crucifixion and resurrection of Jesus Christ were killed for preaching the gospel. In the age of the apostles, witness was virtually synonymous with martyrdom. To this day, many Christians are persecuted for their faith in many places around the world. But we do not face this persecution alone: we have received the promise of God and therefore we always have the strengthening presence of the Holy Spirit.

This necessary gift happens to be the best legacy that Jesus could possibly leave us, because it is the gift of God himself. Like the Father and the Son, the Spirit himself is divine. This makes Luke 24:49 one of the most strongly trinitarian verses in the entire Bible. It is spoken by God the Son with reference to both the Father and the Spirit. Jesus is telling us that the gift of the Spirit is sent from the Father and the Son. To receive this parting gift, therefore, is to receive the gift of God himself.

What greater gift could God possibly give us than the gift of himself, in the person and the work of his Spirit? To have the Spirit is to know the truth of God's Word, because the Spirit who inspired the Word also opens our minds and hearts to understand it. To have the Spirit is to know forgiveness, because the Spirit convicts the conscience and leads us to repent of our sin. To have the Spirit is to have eternal life, because the Spirit convinces us of the truth of the gospel and enables us to believe in Jesus Christ. Finally, to have the Spirit is to have God's comfort in every trial we suffer, because when Jesus said that he would be with us always (see Matt. 28:20), he was talking about the abiding presence of the Holy Spirit, who is the comforting Helper of God (see John 14:16).

When he gives us the Spirit, Jesus is giving us himself, in all his saving grace. To receive the gift of the Holy Spirit, all we need to do is ask: God has promised to give his Spirit to anyone who asks in faith (see Luke 11:13). Thank God for this best of all gifts—the one gift that brings us all the blessings of God. Without the Spirit we would never believe the Bible. Without the Spirit we would never confess our sins. Without the Spirit we would never know Jesus for sure or receive eternal life. Thank God for the gift of his Spirit!

Some of the sweetest hymns praise God for the gift of the Holy Spirit. The German hymn writer Paul Gerhardt invoked the presence of the Spirit when he wrote:

> Holy Ghost, dispel our sadness, pierce the clouds of sinful night;
> Come, O source of sweetest gladness, breathe your life and spread your light.
> From that height which knows no measure, as a gracious show'r descend;
> Bringing down the richest treasure man can wish or God can send.
> Come, O best of all donations God can give or we implore;
> Having your sweet consolations we need wish for nothing more.[8]

Similarly, the Canadian hymn writer Margaret Clarkson praised Jesus for the best of all gifts:

> For your gift of God the Spirit, pow'r to make our lives anew,
> Pledge of life and hope of glory, Savior, we would worship you.
> Crowning gift of resurrection sent from your ascended throne,
> Fullness of the very Godhead, come to make your life our own.[9]

## A FAREWELL BENEDICTION

With the parting gift of the Holy Spirit came a second blessing, as Jesus gave his disciples a farewell benediction. "Lifting up his hands he blessed them," and "While he blessed them, he parted from them and was carried up into heaven" (Luke 24:50). This is the perfect way for Luke to end his Gospel. It matches the way Luke began, with a priestly blessing for the people of God (Luke 1:68–69). It also enables the Gospel to end the same way a worship service ends: with a benediction. In other words, Luke ends with

---

8. Paul Gerhardt, "Holy Ghost, Dispel Our Sadness," 1648.
9. Margaret Clarkson, "For Your Gift of God the Spirit," Hope Publishing Company, 1987.

a verbal expression of the blessing of God, imparted with the gesture of a raised hand or outstretched arms.

The pronouncing of a benediction is an ancient and honorable tradition. When Aaron was ordained to serve as the first high priest of Israel, he "lifted up his hands toward the people and blessed them . . . and the glory of the LORD appeared to all the people" (Lev. 9:22–23). This became the tradition for all of Israel's priests. The famous words of their traditional benediction are still used in the church today: "The LORD bless you and keep you; the LORD make his face to shine upon you and be gracious to you; the LORD lift up his countenance upon you and give you peace" (Num. 6:24–26).

When Jesus blessed his apostles, he was serving as the final priest for the people of God.[10] As a priest he had offered himself as the sacrifice for their sins on the cross. Now as their priest he also pronounced their benediction. Indeed, Jesus had *become* their benediction, for when he blessed his disciples, he blessed them with lifted hands that still bore the prints of the nails that crucified him and which therefore proclaimed his undying love for sinners. As Charles Wesley wrote in "Hail the Day That Sees Him Rise," his beautiful hymn on the ascension: "See, he lifts his hands above! / See, he shows the prints of love! / Hark! His gracious lips bestow / blessings on his church below."

The priestly blessing of Jesus Christ gives the assurance that our sins are forgiven. In the Old Testament, the blessing of the high priest followed the sacrifice of atonement and served to reassure God's people of the forgiveness of their sins. So too the benediction of Jesus Christ follows his atoning work and helps us to know for sure that we are accepted by God. Here is how the Puritan Thomas Goodwin summarized the meaning of Christ's farewell benediction: "I have been dead, and in dying made a curse for you; now that curse I have fully removed, and my Father hath acquitted me and you for it; and now I can be bold to bless you, and pronounce all your sins forgiven, and your persons justified."[11]

The blessing Jesus gave his disciples was the best of all blessings, for our Lord does not pronounce a benediction without also giving a blessing. As

10. See Kelly M. Kapic, "Receiving Christ's Priestly Benediction: A Biblical, Historical, and Theological Exploration of Luke 24:50–53," *Westminster Theological Journal* 67 (2005): 247–60.

11. Thomas Goodwin, *The Works of Thomas Goodwin*, ed. John C. Miller, 12 vols. (1651; reprint Edinburgh: James Nichol, 1861–66), 4:46.

he ascended into heaven, Jesus kept blessing and blessing the apostles, giving them love and grace and mercy. He was blessing them on their way, for soon they would go out into the world as witnesses to the gospel. As they went, they would have both the gift of the Spirit and the blessing of Christ—the promise of his presence. What strength this gave them in ministry, what comfort in suffering, and what hope for the future: they had received the blessing of the risen and ascended Son of God. Here was the fulfillment of the ancient psalm: "May God be gracious to us and bless us and make his face to shine upon us, that your way may be known on earth, your saving power among all nations" (Ps. 67:1–2).

We too are under the blessing of Jesus. This is the meaning of the benediction at the end of any proper worship service. In his book on corporate worship in the evangelical church, Robert Rayburn writes: "No worshipers should ever be sent forth to serve in their own strength. They must ever be dismissed in the name of the Lord with the assurance of the power and presence of the Triune God to accompany them always."[12]

The same Son who sent us the Spirit of the Father is blessing us today. We receive his benediction at the end of our worship. Whenever a minister pronounces the benediction, God's blessing is repeated. It is as if Jesus himself is lifting his hands over us—nail-prints and all—to bless us with his grace. He is giving us strength for ministry, comfort in suffering, and hope for the future. He is calling us to serve as a blessing to the nations. Jesus blesses us and blesses us again, placing all our lives and all our service under his holy benediction.

## Implications of the Ascension

These are the two precious blessings Jesus bestowed on his disciples at the time of his ascension: the parting gift of the promised Spirit and his own farewell benediction as the Son of God. The gift and the blessing are closely related, for they both signify the ongoing presence of Christ with his church. However, this is only the beginning of all that could be said about the implications of the ascension. Although most people rarely meditate on what it means that Jesus ascended into heaven, the reality of

12. Robert Rayburn, *O Come, Let Us Worship* (Grand Rapids: Baker, 1980), 217.

his ascension is full of holy comfort and joyful strength for daily Christian living.

What does it mean to believe that Jesus ascended into heaven? "It means," wrote Zacharias Ursinus,

> that he did truly, and not merely in show, ascend into heaven, and is now there, and will be called upon at the right hand of God, until he shall come from thence to judge the world. And that he has ascended for my sake and thy sake, and now appears in the presence of God, makes intercession for us, sends us the Holy Spirit, and will at length take us to himself, that we may be with him where he is, and reign with him in glory.[13]

The ascension of Jesus Christ means the forgiveness of our sins. Now that he has ascended into heaven, Jesus is our advocate at the throne of God's justice, pleading that the eternal Judge will have mercy on our sins. As our defense attorney, so to speak, he raises his wounded hands in the courts of heaven as the proof that the price of our guilt is fully paid (see Heb. 9:24).

At the same time, the ascension means the answer to our prayers. The Bible says that Jesus "is able to save to the uttermost those who draw near to God through him, since he always lives to make intercession for them" (Heb. 7:25; cf. Rom. 8:34). But this saving intercession depends on the fact of the ascension. It is because Jesus ascended into heaven that he is able to present our requests before the throne of God's grace. Sadly, today there are thousands of people who e-mail their prayer requests to Jerusalem every day, paying for their petitions to be broadcast at the Western Wall or at other holy sites in Israel.[14] Apparently the people who support this multimillion dollar business believe that God answers prayer only at the site of Israel's ancient temple. But this is unnecessary: the risen and ascended Son answers our prayers everywhere by the omnipresence of the Holy Spirit.

The ascension of Jesus Christ also guarantees the effectiveness of our evangelism and the ultimate triumph of the gospel around the world, for in ascending to heaven, Jesus sent us the Spirit—the descent of the dove. Now,

---

13. Zacharias Ursinus, *The Commentary of Dr. Zacharias Ursinus on the Heidelberg Catechism*, trans. G. W. Willard (1852; reprint Phillipsburg, NJ: P&R, n.d.), 253.

14. Christopher Rhoads, "Web Site to Holy Site: Israeli Firm Broadcasts Prayers for a Fee," *Wall Street Journal*, Jan. 25, 2007, B1.

by the Spirit, people all over the world are turning away from their sins to worship the ascended Son of God.

The ascension means that Jesus is closer to us than ever. This is one of the great mysteries of the work of the Holy Spirit. Jesus told his disciples that actually it would be advantageous for them if he left and returned to heaven, because then the Holy Spirit would come (John 16:7) and enable them to do even greater works than he had done (John 14:12)! In his resurrection body, the person of Jesus could not be present in all places at all times. Rather, it is by the Holy Spirit that he is with us always (see Matt. 28:20). Yet the Spirit could not come to us unless he was sent by the Father and the Son, and he would not be sent until the Son returned to the Father. So rather than keeping us farther away from Jesus, the ascension actually brings him closer to us. His bodily absence means his spiritual omnipresence.

Then the ascension is the promise of our own exaltation to the presence of God. Without the ascension, there could be no second coming, and without the second coming, no return to heaven for the people of God. When Jesus ascended into heaven, the angels told the apostles that he would come back to earth the same way that he departed (Acts 1:11): with heavenly clouds of glory. When he returns at his second coming, Jesus will take us up to heaven with him, in our own resurrection bodies. His ascension is our ascension, just as his resurrection is our resurrection. As it says in the famous Easter hymn of Charles Wesley: "Soar we now where Christ has led, foll'wing our exalted Head; made like him, like him we rise; ours the cross, the grave, the skies." Or consider the welcoming words of the poet John Donne, who invites us to "Salute the last and everlasting day. . . . Behold the Highest, parting hence away. . . . First he, and he first enters the way."[15] Jesus is the first to ascend, but only the first, for Hebrews says that Jesus has entered heaven "as a forerunner on our behalf" (Heb. 6:20).

## A Benediction of Our Own

Whenever the truth of our own ascension into heaven has captured people's minds and hearts, they have always responded with the highest praise.

---

15. John Donne, "Ascension," in *Chapters into Verse: Poetry in English Inspired by the Bible*, vol. 2: *Gospels to Revelation*, ed. Robert Atwan and Laurance Wieder (Oxford: Oxford University Press, 1993), 231–32.

In his sermon on this great doctrine, Leo the Great celebrated the joy of following Christ into glory: "Our human nature, united with the divinity of the Son, was on the throne of his glory. The ascension of Christ is our elevation. . . . Let us exult, dearly beloved, with worthy joy and be glad with a holy thanksgiving. Today we not only are established as possessors of paradise, but we have even penetrated the heights of the heavens in Christ."[16]

Maybe this is why the disciples worshiped with such great joy in the days and weeks following the ascension. The first time Jesus told them how soon he would be leaving them, they were filled with sorrow (see John 16:6). Everything we know about these weak men and their needy dependence on Jesus leads us to expect them to be distraught by his departure. Yet when he ascended into heaven, "they worshiped him and returned to Jerusalem with great joy, and were continually in the temple blessing God" (Luke 24:52–53).

Luke chooses his words very carefully. The word he uses for worship in verse 52 *(proskyneō)* is frequently used for the worship of God. Here it shows that the disciples knew who Jesus was. Having witnessed his ascension to divine glory, they knew for sure that he was the Christ, the divine Son of God, and that therefore he was worthy of all their worship. Then the word Luke uses for "blessing" in verse 53 is the same verb he used back in verse 51 *(eulogeō)*. There is a reciprocal relationship here—a divine call and a human response. First Jesus blessed the disciples, and then the disciples blessed Jesus. Not that Jesus could ever be any more blessed than he already is, of course. Yet this is the appropriate way for us to adore his majesty: by blessing him for blessing us. The disciples pronounced a benediction of their own by glorifying Jesus as their crucified, risen, and ascended Lord.

The disciples worshiped Jesus early and they worshiped him often. For a while they lingered on the Mount of Olives, but soon they did what Jesus told them to do and went back to Jerusalem. There, as they waited for the gift of the Spirit, they joyfully kept worshiping day after day, not only in private homes, but also at the temple (see Acts 1:10–14). They were worshiping Jesus all the time, with "ineradicable joy, irresistible longing to glorify God, and deep gratitude."[17]

16. Leo the Great, "Sermon 73.3–4," in *Luke*, ed. Arthur A. Just, Jr., Ancient Christian Commentary on Scripture, NT 3 (Downers Grove, IL: InterVarsity, 2003), 393.

17. Norval Geldenhuys, *The Gospel of Luke*, New International Commentary on the New Testament (Grand Rapids: Eerdmans, 1951), 646.

Anyone who knows the same Jesus they knew will have the same joy, the same longing, and the same gratitude. Do you know this Jesus—the one Luke wrote about in his Gospel?

Anyone who does not know him needs to know him for sure. Anyone who does know Jesus ought to worship him. Worship Jesus for his miraculous virgin birth—a birth celebrated by angels and welcomed by shepherds. Worship Jesus for his perfect obedience to the Father, even when he was tempted in the wilderness by the devil. Worship Jesus for the powerful miracles that cured the sick, healed the disabled, fed the hungry, and raised the dead. Worship him for the wisdom of his teaching—for all of his amazing parables and dramatic demands for discipleship. Worship him for the love he showed in seeking all the lost and lonely people we meet in Luke's Gospel—sinners just like us, in all of their spiritual need.

Worship Jesus most of all for his saving work: his courageous sufferings, his atoning death, his triumphant resurrection, and last of all, his glorious ascension. After we have seen Jesus rising to heaven and returning to the Father, there is nothing more for us to say, except "Glory to God in the highest, and praise to Jesus the exalted Son!"

# INDEX OF SCRIPTURE

# INDEX OF SUBJECTS AND NAMES

investment, in kingdom of God, **2:**319–20, 325

Irenaeus, **2:**447

Isaac, **1:**136, **2:**48, 354, 384–85

Isaiah, **1:**117–18, 168–69, 174, 331, 357, **2:**352, 495, 556, 651

Islam, **1:**349, 515

Israel

faithlessness of, **1:**485

gracious invitation to, **2:**80

grumbling in wilderness, **2:**114

rejection of Jesus, **2:**357–59

twelve tribes of, **2:**483–84

as vineyard, **2:**351–52

Jackson, Andrew, **1:**115

Jacob, **1:**141–42, 149, **2:**48, 384–85

Jairus, daughter of, **1:**322, 407, 413–17

James, **1:**381, 499–501, **2:**417, 549

at transfiguration, **1:**470–71, 477, 479, 483, 489

James, Carolyn Custis, **1:**555n5

Jehoshaphat, **2:**506

Jeremiah, **1:**38, 446, 637, **2:**58, 353–54, 428, 572, 651

Jericho road, **1:**542

Jerome, **2:**273

Jerusalem, **1:**12, 107, 109, 497, **2:**350

as center of worship, **2:**57

destruction in A.D. 70, **2:**341–42, 411–12, 415, 423–32, 437, 573–76

Jesus' lament for, **2:**52, 58–62

Jesus' love for, **2:**340–42

journey toward, **1:**496–98, 507–8

Jesus (name), **1:**56, 89

Jesus Christ

anointed with Holy Spirit, **1:**451

answers to questions, **2:**387–90

ascension of, **1:**466, 498, **2:**691–94, 699–701

authority of, **1:**312, 320, **2:**346–49, 439, 693

baptism by fire, **1:**695–97, 704

baptism of, **1:**133–38, 476, 567, **2:**355

as Beloved Son, **2:**354–57, 361, 571

birth of, **1:**69–76, 79

childhood of, **1:**101–13, 448, **2:**388

on children, **1:**485, 489, **2:**270–71

compassion of, **1:**219, 319, 341, 434, 501, **2:**17–18, 23, 58–61

conception by Holy Spirit, **1:**35–36

crucifixion of, **1:**451–54, 696, **2:**561—64, 573, 591

death and resurrection of, **1:**52, 372, 443, 474, 487–88, 498, 588, 611–12, **2:**236

death of, **1:**473, 478, 637, **2:**56–57, 92, 289–91, 461, 505, 563, 620–21

deity of, **1:**36, 80, 106, 224, 390–91, 394, 439, 445, 533–34, **2:**229n8, 275

dependance on Holy Spirit, **1:**165–66

divine and human will of, **2:**501

as divisive, **1:**697–700

earthly family of, **1:**375–76, 378

as elder brother, **2:**167

exaltation of, **1:**472, **2:**74, 237, 395, 691

as example, **1:**113, 386–87, **2:**400

forsaken on the cross, **2:**252–53, 616–17

as fulfillment of Old Testament, **2:**189–91, 678–81

glory of, **1:**82, **2:**333–35

greatness of, **2:**481–82

healing of, **1:**193–96, 218–26, 233–34, 316, 409–10, **2:**66, 297

humanity of, **1:**72–75, 104–6, 143, 148–50, 156, 245, 386, 410–11, **2:**339–40, 501, 622, 693–94

741